The Foundations of Remembering

The Foundations of Remembering

Essays in Honor of Henry L. Roediger, III

Edited by
James S. Nairne

Psychology Press
Taylor & Francis Group

NEW YORK AND HOVE

Published in 2007
by Psychology Press
270 Madison Avenue
New York, NY 10016
www.psypress.com

Published in Great Britain
by Psychology Press
27 Church Road
Hove, East Sussex BN3 2FA
www.psypress.com

Psychology Press is an imprint of the Taylor & Francis Group, an informa business

Typeset by RefineCatch Limited, Bungay, Suffolk, UK
Printed and bound in the USA by Edwards Brothers, Inc. on acid-free paper
Cover design by Anú Design
Cover image: René Magritte, Belgian, 1898–1967, *Time Transfixed*, 1938, oil on canvas,
147 × 98.7 cm, Joseph Winterbotham Collection, 1970.426, The Art Institute of Chicago.
Photography © The Art Institute of Chicago

10 9 8 7 6 5 4 3 2 1

Library of Congress Cataloging in Publication Data

The foundations of remembering : essays in honor of Henry L. Roediger III / edited by
James S. Nairne.
    p. cm.
    Includes bibliographical references and index.
    ISBN-13: 978-1-84169-446-7 (hardback : alk. paper) 1. Memory—Congresses.
2. Memory—History—Congresses. I. Roediger, Henry L. II. Nairne, James S.

BF371.F65 2006
153.1′2—dc22

                    2006024735

ISBN: 978-1-84169-446-7 (hbk)

Contents

Contributors

Pictured (left to right): **Front row:** Elizabeth Bjork, Alice Healy, Kathleen McDermott, Roddy Roediger, Elizabeth Loftus, Suparna Rajaram, Randi Martin. **Second row:** Aimée Surprenant, Elizabeth Marsh. **Third row:** James Neely, Stephen Schmidt, Robert Bjork, John Wixted, Larry Jacoby. **Fourth row:** David Balota, Robert L. Greene, Richard Shiffrin, Mark McDaniel, Richard Schweickert. **Fifth row:** Randall Engle, Daniel Schacter, Fergus Craik, James Nairne, Ian Neath. (Not pictured: Endel Tulving.)

David A. Balota
Department of Psychology
Washington University in St. Louis
St. Louis, MO, USA

Kelly Biegler
Department of Psychology
Rice University
Houston, TX, USA

Tamra J. Bireta
Department of Psychology
The College of New Jersey
Ewing, NJ, USA

Elizabeth L. Bjork
Department of Psychology
University of California, Los Angeles
Los Angeles, CA, USA

Robert A. Bjork
Department of Psychology
University of California, Los Angeles
Los Angeles, CA, USA

Gordon D. A. Brown
Department of Psychology
University of Warwick
Warwick, UK

Larry Cahill
Department of Neurobiology and
  Behavior
University of California, Irvine
Irvine, CA, USA

Bethany J. Caughey
Department of Psychology
University of California, Los Angeles
Los Angeles, CA, USA

Fergus I. M. Craik
Rotman Research Institute
Toronto, ON, Canada

Amy H. Criss
Department of Psychology
Carnegie Mellon University
Pittsburgh, PA, USA

Thomas F. Cunningham
Department of Psychology
St. Lawrence University
Canton, NY, USA

Janet M. Duchek
Department of Psychology
Washington University in St. Louis
St. Louis, MO, USA

Gilles O. Einstein
Department of Psychology
Furman University
Greenville, SC, USA

Randall W. Engle
Department of Psychology
Georgia Institute of Technology
Atlanta, GA, USA

Lisa A. Farley
Department of Psychological
  Sciences
Purdue University
West Lafayette, IN, USA

Lisa K. Fazio
Psychology and Neuroscience
Duke University
Durham, NC, USA

David A. Gallo
Department of Psychology
University of Chicago
Chicago, IL, USA

Robert L. Greene
Department of Psychology
Case Western Reserve University
Cleveland, OH, USA

Alice F. Healy
Department of Psychology
University of Colorado
Boulder, CO, USA

Larry L. Jacoby
Department of Psychology
Washington University in St. Louis
St. Louis, MO, USA

Elizabeth A. Kensinger
Department of Psychology
Harvard University
Cambridge, MA, USA

Krystal A. Klein
Department of Psychological and
    Brain Sciences
Indiana University
Bloomington, IN, USA

James A. Kole
Department of Psychology
University of Colorado
Boulder, CO, USA

Elizabeth F. Loftus
Department of Psychology and
    Social Behavior
University of California, Irvine
Irvine, CA, USA

Jessica M. Logan
Department of Psychology
Washington University in St. Louis
St. Louis, MO, USA

Elizabeth J. Marsh
Psychology and Neuroscience
Duke University
Durham, NC, USA

Randi C. Martin
Department of Psychology
Rice University
Houston, TX, USA

Mark A. McDaniel
Department of Psychology
Washington University in St. Louis
St. Louis, MO, USA

Kathleen B. McDermott
Department of Psychology
Washington University in St. Louis
St. Louis, MO, USA

James S. Nairne
Department of Psychological
    Sciences
Purdue University
West Lafayette, IN, USA

Ian Neath
Psychology Department
Memorial University
St. Johns, NL, Canada

James H. Neely
Department of Psychology
University at Albany,
    State University of
    New York
New York, USA

Suparna Rajaram
Department of Psychology
State University of New York at
    Stony Brook
Stony Brook, NY, USA

Matthew G. Rhodes
Department of Psychology
Colorado State University
Fort Collins, CO, USA

Daniel L. Schacter
Department of Psychology
Harvard University
Cambridge, MA, USA

Stephen R. Schmidt
Department of Psychology
Middle Tennessee
    State University
Murfreesboro, TN, USA

Richard Schweickert
Department of Psychological
    Sciences
Purdue University
West Lafayette, IN, USA

Kathleen M. Shea
Department of Psychology
University of Colorado
Boulder, CO, USA

Richard M. Shiffrin
Department of Psychological and
    Brain Sciences
Indiana University
Bloomington, IN, USA

Aimée M. Surprenant
Psychology Department
Memorial University of
    Newfoundland
St. John's, NL, Canada

Chi-Shing Tse
Department of Psychology
University of Albany,
    State University of New York
Albany, NY, USA

Endel Tulving
Rotman Research Institute
Toronto, ON, Canada

Department of Psychology
University of Toronto
Toronto, ON, Canada

Department of Psychology
Washington University in St. Louis
St. Louis, MO, USA

Nicholas B. Turk-Browne
Department of Psychology
Yale University
New Haven, CT, USA

Nash Unsworth
Department of Psychology
Georgia Institute of Technology
Atlanta, GA, USA

John T. Wixted
Department of Psychology
University of California at San Diego
La Jolla, CA, USA

Preface

In May, 2004, Purdue University awarded Henry L. Roediger, III an honorary doctor of letters in recognition of his many accomplishments in research and service to the field of psychology. In connection with this award, the Department of Psychological Sciences at Purdue decided to organize a conference, populated by top memory scholars, as a fitting capstone. Although not technically a Festschrift—"I'm too young for that," Roediger exclaimed—the conference was dedicated to honoring Roddy and celebrating his career. The conference, affectionately labeled "RoddyFest," was held Easter weekend, March 24–27, 2005.

Speakers were given a simple charge: choose your own topic, but try to place your work in historical context. Roediger is fascinated by the intellectual lineage of ideas, so addressing historical "foundations" seemed appropriate. The chapters contained in this volume help to establish the foundations of remembering, circa the first decade of the 21st century, as perceived by some of the leading memory researchers in the world. Not surprisingly, each of the chapters touches on Roediger's work as well, largely because his work has helped to define and clarify the topics of interest to the memory field.

The unofficial theme of the conference was the classic Frank Capra movie *It's a Wonderful Life*. The film tells the story of a man, played by Jimmy Stewart, who is allowed a glimpse of what the world would have been like had he never been born. It is a measure of one man's impact, which, as it turned out, far surpassed his awareness and imagination. So, too, has Roddy impacted on the lives of many, including most at the conference, through his mentorship, support, and outstanding contributions in scholarship. Roddy's "reach" has been profound, in ways that I doubt he has ever imagined.

The conference would not have been possible without the support of Purdue University, particularly Dean Toby Parcel of the College of Liberal Arts, Associate Dean Howard Zelaznik (who originated the idea for the conference), and Department Head Howard Weiss. Julie Smith and Erica Wilson played an important role making the conference itself run smoothly. Additional financial support was generously provided by Psychology Press and the American Psychological Society.

James S. Nairne, PhD
Purdue University

1

Roddy Roediger's Memory

JAMES S. NAIRNE

*F*ortunately, unlike memory proper, we can search through Roddy Roediger's memory. With a corpus exceeding 175 publications, the ever-expanding Roediger repository is accessible and open to all. If one chooses to rummage about, turning over things under which, or within which, or alongside of which manuscripts lie, empirical, methodological, and theoretical insight soon comes into view. An exhaustive review is beyond my reach, but I intend in this opening chapter to touch on the highlights, place the work in historical context, and to characterize the "Roedigerian" style.

Temporally, Roediger's research divides itself neatly into three decade-long periods spent investigating: (1) the mnemonic consequences of recall (particularly its self-limiting properties), (2) retrieval in the absence of conscious intent (implicit memory), and (3) the conditions that foster retrieval errors (i.e., false memory). There is a fourth period, currently in progress, focusing on the educational implications of testing. The common denominator throughout is retrieval. Sample randomly from the Roediger repository and you are certain to find work investigating the characteristics and consequences of retrieval; it is the lens through which his work, both empirical and theoretical, needs to be viewed.

PERIOD ONE: RETRIEVAL AND ITS CONSEQUENCES

Roddy Roediger entered graduate school at Yale in 1969, 2 years after the publication of Neisser's influential *Cognitive Psychology* (1967). The cognitive revolution was ascending, but memory researchers, by and large, remained committed to the verbal learning tradition. As its name implies, verbal *learning* is concerned largely with acquisition, either acquisition rates (e.g., transfer) or acquisition consequences (e.g., interference). The modern notion of a retrieval experiment—holding encoding conditions constant while manipulating the conditions of testing—was virtually unknown, having made only isolated appearances on the empirical landscape (e.g., Luh, 1922; Tulving & Pearlstone, 1966).

Retrieval neglect seems mystifying to the modern memory researcher, but it is understandable in its context. Scholars of the 1960's recognized the distinction between learning and performance; they assumed that responses compete at the point of test, that the availability of a response can change systematically with time (e.g., Briggs, 1954), and that changing stimulus conditions exert powerful effects on performance (McGeoch, 1942; Yum, 1931). Such phenomena were well established empirically and used frequently as tools to explain troublesome findings (see Postman, 1961). But to learning mavens they were tangential, not germane, to the topic of main interest. With an acquisition focus, understandably, researchers sought fixed testing environments that could adequately assess what had been learned.

For Roddy Roediger, however—then and now—accessibility, not acquisition, has occupied center stage. As he noted in 1974, "One of the primary problems in the study of memory is the discovery of why so little of available, stored information can be actively retrieved" (p. 261). In free recall, for example, one typically finds variability across output opportunities. Subjects often recall items on a second test that they failed to recall initially, even in the absence of an interpolated learning trial. An appropriate retrieval cue, such as a pertinent category label, also can dramatically affect both the quality and quantity of what is recalled (Tulving & Pearlstone, 1966). From an acquisition (or storage) perspective such findings may be troubling, or at least a methodological nuisance, but to Roediger they seemed paramount. Accessibility, not availability, forms the *sine qua non* of the study of memory.

Roediger recognized early on that there are two ways to attack the accessibility problem. First, you can study the effectiveness of retrieval cues, a path blazed by one of his mentors, Endel Tulving (e.g., Tulving & Thomson, 1973).[1] (This path led to the development of the encoding specificity principle, a passive version of the more active transfer-appropriate processing that Roediger was to champion a decade later.) Second, the focus can be placed on the retrieval process itself: How does retrieval, or at least the products of retrieval, change the accessibility of other, yet-to-be-retrieved, information? Students of memory have long assumed that recall can be self-propagating. Once recalled, an item can serve as a retrieval cue, triggering the recall of additional information. But in a sweeping review of the literature published in 1974, Roediger argued convincingly that retrieval had inhibitory, or self-limiting, properties as well.

Retrieval, he reasoned, seems to have a curious design flaw: Recalling an item increases its accessibility—it "primes" the item—which then biases, or calibrates, the search process. The act of recall "strengthens the representation of an item in memory, which means that on future attempts to retrieve additional items, the ones already recalled will be retrieved again to the exclusion of new items" (p. 262). The priming part, of course, helps to explain the advantages of repeated testing (Bjork, 1975; Roediger & Karpicke, 2006), and ultimately the importance of transfer appropriate testing (Roediger, Weldon, & Challis, 1989), but it tends to induce forgetting of other relevant target information as a side effect. Sampling with replacement clutters up the search process, making it difficult to recover additional items (see also, Brown, 1968; McGill, 1963; Shiffrin, 1970). Roediger wondered about the evolutionary significance of such a process, concluding that "it seems maladaptive for the very act of recall to produce forgetting of information that needs to be recalled later" (p. 268).

The Empirical Domain

The self-limiting properties of recall, he argued, can be clearly seen in three empirical contexts. First, it is apparent in the temporal course of recall. If you track recall over time, it shows a negatively-accelerated form (Bousfield & Sedgewick, 1944). "In attempting recall of a specified set of items without regard to their order, Ss typically emit items very rapidly at first and show a decreased responding with time" (Roediger, 1974, p. 261). This characteristic pattern occurs for both episodic and semantic recall (e.g., recalling instances from categories) and cannot be explained by appealing simply to fatigue or to temporal variations in item "strength." It is consistent, however, with the assumption that the search for new items is slowed by the resampling of already recalled, and thereby primed, list items.

Second, under controlled testing environments, such as cued recall, performance declines regularly as a function of the position of the item in the testing sequence. Testing early items impairs performance on later items, a phenomenon known generally as output interference (Tulving & Arbuckle, 1963). Although initially controversial—output interference was thought to result only from primary memory loss—later research established it as a potent factor in many retrieval contexts, especially recall (see Roediger & Schmidt, 1980). Again, the act of recall primes representations, biasing the search process and thereby hindering the accessibility of yet-to-be-recalled items.

Third, if subjects are supplied with some list items as retrieval cues after list presentation—so-called part-list cueing—recall of the remaining "critical" items can suffer compared to recall under noncued conditions. This vexing empirical phenomenon, first demonstrated by Slamecka (1968), runs counter to the claim that recall is self-propagating. To the extent that interitem dependencies are formed during list acquisition, list cues should facilitate, not impair, subsequent recall. On the other hand, if the memory traces for the cued items are primed by the cueing process, thereby biasing the search process away from the noncued items, then part-list cueing can be seen as yet another example of retrieval-based inhibition or interference (see Rundus, 1973).

Throughout the 1970s, much of Roediger's research focused on the idea that items, once retrieved, block the accessibility of otherwise available information in memory. Portions of this research are reviewed elsewhere in this volume (see especially Bjork et al. chapter 2) but his main empirical concerns were twofold: (1) mapping out the conditions under which experimenter-provided cues help and hinder performance, and (2) understanding the role that retrieval dynamics, particularly the time course of free recall, play in mnemonic phenomena (particularly hypermnesia). I briefly review this research in the following two sections.

Part-List Cueing

The phenomenon of part-list cueing puzzled Roediger as a graduate student, for good reason. After all, as a protégé of Endel Tulving, he had been imprinted on the idea of cue-driven remembering. Tulving and Pearlstone (1966) had shown that the presentation of category labels at test substantially improves recall of a categorized list. Yet, given Slamecka's (1968) findings, wouldn't we expect these category labels to block rather than cue subsequent recall? For that matter, why is elaboration such an effective mnemonic strategy? Internally generating associates to target words, we typically argue, increases the constellation of potential retrieval cues. But why don't these elaborations, presumably primed by the generation process, block recall of the target words in a manner akin to part-list cueing?

Roediger (1973) offered a simple solution in his dissertation. He suggested that retrieval cues, produced internally or externally, facilitate recall if and only if they provide access to relevant "higher order units." Memory traces are not stored haphazardly, he argued, but rather in organized domains or bundles—e.g., as elements of List 1, the category *furniture*, or as some other subjective unit. To recover a particular target requires first accessing the relevant bundle, from among many potentially searchable bundles, and then recovering its content. Pertinent category labels improve recall because they direct the search to relevant bundles. However, "when more retrieval cues than are needed to produce access to higher-order units are provided (for example, other instances from the higher-order unit) recall of items from the higher-order unit will be impaired" (p. 645).

He provided evidence for this two-factor theory of cueing in a clever twist on the Tulving and Pearlstone (1966) paradigm. Following the presentation of a categorized list, subjects were provided with the appropriate category labels accompanied, or not, by additional within-category instances. The category labels, he reasoned, should provide access to relevant higher-order units, aiding recall, but additional category instances, those not needed to access the category, will block recall of its remaining members. This is exactly what Roediger found and, moreover, the within-category impairment grew with the number of cued instances. He later showed that similar things operate at the category level: Presenting some of the category labels from a categorized list improves recall of words from the cued categories (relative to free recall), but impairs recall of the other categories on the list. Importantly, this category-based part-list cueing effect was specific to the recall of categories and failed to affect recall of words within a category, once accessed (cf. Roediger, 1978, p. 61).

Roediger viewed his results as broadly consistent with several contemporary search models, especially a hierarchical model proposed by Rundus (1973; see also, Estes, 1972; Shiffrin, 1970), and with classical interference theory as well. The first factor of the famous two-factor theory of interference (McGeoch, 1942) is response competition, wherein the stronger of two associated responses to a single cue effectively blocks the weaker one; in Roediger's case, primed instances, strengthened by virtue of their presentation as retrieval cues, effectively block recovery of noncued instances (that is, those associated to the same higher-order unit) because of biased sampling. The mechanisms may be somewhat different—e.g., biased sampling is not necessarily cue-based—but both appealed ultimately to the notion of response competition (see Roediger, 1974; Roediger & Neely, 1982).

Retrieval Dynamics

As noted above, the self-limiting character of recall can also be seen by tracking its temporal course. Subjects continue to recall items successfully over an extended period of time, quite long in fact, although successes arrive at a slower rate. Recall of later items is delayed, presumably, because early recalls clutter up the search process (i.e., there is response competition from primed traces). Search models of this type make specific predictions. For example, mean recall latency—the average amount of time that it takes to recall an item—is expected to increase with the size of the search set or space (see Wixted & Rohrer, 1994); similarly, because it takes longer, on average, to recall an item, it should take longer to reach asymptotic recall levels when the sample set is large.

Roediger recognized that retrieval dynamics of this sort have implications for a variety of mnemonic phenomena. For example, if subjects effectively "recall" experimenter-provided cues, subjecting the remaining critical items to output interference, then it should take longer for subjects to recall the critical items compared to uncued controls (either because the subjects "check" sampled items against the cues, or continually sample the cues themselves). Indeed, Roediger, Stellon, and Tulving (1977) found that when cues were present subjects took longer to reach asymptotic levels of performance; final asymptotic levels were lower as well, suggesting that subjects either give up recalling items that are potentially accessible (i.e., they employ a stopping rule) or some other factor inhibits or blocks the accessibility of the uncued items.

From a purely practical level, the observation that subjects approach asymptotic recall levels at different rates, depending on the size of the search set, suggests that important mnemonic differences can be masked when short recall intervals are used. In an elegant analysis, Roediger used this observation to help explain why hypermnesia—the increase in recall performance that is sometimes seen across successive tests—varies across materials and type of encoding task. Lists containing pictures, for example, typically show more hypermnesia than lists of words. Although it might be tempting to conclude that hypermnesia therefore depends on some form of imaginal encoding (Erdelyi & Becker, 1974), Roediger, Payne, Gillespie, and Lean (1982) showed how a much simpler account, based solely on retrieval dynamics, could explain the data (see also Roediger, 1982).

Imagine that an initial recall test of 7 min is employed after subjects study lists containing either pictures or words. A second test is then given, without any intervening study trial, and net improvements in performance are noted (hypermnesia). Because pictures ultimately produce higher levels of recall than words, perhaps because imaginal processing leads to more net target encodings, the approach rate to asymptote will be lower for pictures than for words. This means that after the first 7-min test, more picture targets should be available for sampling on a successive test—hence, more hypermnesia will potentially be observed for pictures than for words. In this sense recall level, because of the inverse relationship between recall asymptote and the rate of approaching that asymptote, can be used to "predict" the extent of hypermnesia. Roediger and his colleagues brought the recall-level hypothesis under experimental control by manipulating type of encoding (e.g., shallow or deep) and showing that hypermnesia varied directly with final recall level (for a review, see Roediger & Challis, 1989).

Roediger et al.'s (1982) recall-level hypothesis is not meant to be a complete account of hypermnesia. Hypermnesia ultimately depends on a trade-off between the forgetting that occurs between successive tests (intertest forgetting) and the amount of new information that is recovered (reminiscence),[2] but the original insight about retrieval dynamics remains important. Understanding how retrieval unfolds over time provides a window into the recovery process; and, depending on the length of the recall interval employed, it can be easy to underestimate, or fail to detect, potentially accessible mnemonic information. Researchers today still tend to employ relatively short recall intervals, but the time course of recall is now a popular weapon in the arsenal of the memory researcher. Roediger's pioneering efforts in this area helped make this happen (see Wixted & Rohrer, 1994).

Summarizing Period One

Over the first decade and a half of his career, Roediger established his signature as a researcher: Start with a simple idea, consider its empirical implications, and stick close to the data. In choosing to focus on the determinants of accessibility, in particular how retrieval potentially blocks access, his laboratory established a variety of empirical benchmarks, ones that continue to provide grist for the mill of the memory modeler. He was one of the first scholars to recognize the importance of retrieval-based (output) interference and its potential relevance to a host of mnemonic phenomena, including the tip-of-the-tongue state (Roediger, 1974) and even Einstellung (set) effects in problem solving (Roediger & Neely, 1982). In this sense, of course, he was prescient because the field has now moved sharply in his direction; the study of retrieval-induced "inhibition," for example, now rages (e.g., see Anderson, 2003; Bjork et al., chapter 2, this volume).

It is worth remembering as well that the Roediger lab toiled away on problems of accessibility during the "golden age" of encoding, the ascendancy of the levels of processing framework (Craik & Lockhart, 1972). This may have put Roediger somewhat out of the loop, in terms of initial impact, but it helped him develop a perspective that would serve him, and the field, extremely well in the future. For example, his focus on retrieval, specifically on how recall affects accessibility, colored his approach to the study of implicit memory and to the general memory systems debate, as discussed in the next section.

PERIOD TWO: RETENTION IN THE ABSENCE OF AWARENESS

In the 1980s, memory researchers began to embrace alternative assessment techniques, particularly ones designed to measure retention in the absence of conscious awareness. Traditional *explicit* memory tests, ones that direct the subject to consciously recollect the contents of a prior episode (e.g., the items from a just-presented list), were contrasted with *implicit* tests, those meant to detect mnemonic residue when the subject is not actively trying to remember. Popular examples of implicit tests included word stem or fragment completion, perceptual identification, category generation, and, at least nominally, the famous Ebbinghaus savings method (see Roediger, 1990).

Implicit tests attracted attention for two primary reasons: First, comparisons between implicit and explicit tests revealed tantalizing empirical dissociations, which occur when independent variables show differing, even opposite, effects on selected dependent variables. Generating an item usually produces a significant mnemonic advantage over reading on an explicit test, such as recall or recognition, but reading can yield the superior performance on an implicit test (Jacoby & Dallas, 1981). Second, the performance patterns found on implicit tests resembled those found for amnesic patients; for example, amnesic patients perform well below normal control subjects on traditional explicit tests of memory, but performance is often equivalent when implicit tests are employed (Warrington & Weiskrantz, 1970). This suggested that implicit tests tap a different form of retention—perhaps even a different memory system—than explicit tests, one that is preserved for many amnesic patients (e.g., Schacter, 1987; Squire, 1987; Tulving, 1983).

The Value of Dissociations

Like the rest of the field, Roediger found these empirical dissociations intriguing. What is it about completing word fragments in an implicit domain, for example, that preserves the effects of experience in a way that an explicit test does not (see Tulving, Schacter, & Stark, 1982)? For someone immersed in the problem of accessibility, any test-based pattern of dissociation is apt to perk interest. But he was skeptical about their diagnostic value, especially as metrics for identifying memory systems. To Roediger, empirical dissociations need to be attacked functionally, as patterns of data generated by idiosyncratic tests. He doesn't deny that distinct memory systems exist—quite the opposite, he believes they must on logical grounds—his major beef is with the wild and woolly use of empirical dissociations to draw inferences about hypothetical systems. True identification of systems should be left to direct investigations of the brain, an enterprise that he endorses wholeheartedly (e.g., Roediger, Marsh, & Lee, 2002).

Here's the problem: Empirical dissociations are the norm, not the exception (Kolers & Roediger, 1984). Consequently, without converging operations (preferably neural-based), rampant use of dissociations as a diagnostic metric will lead to proliferating—even nonsensical—memory systems. Functional dissociations are common across recognition and recall (e.g., after manipulating word frequency), yet few, if any, scholars would appeal to separate memory systems to handle such effects. Similarly, it is relatively easy to demonstrate empirical dissociations within acknowledged systems, such as episodic memory or priming in semantic memory (Roediger, Buckner, & McDermott, 1999). Within a completely implicit domain, for instance, generating words from conceptual cues can either benefit or impair performance compared to reading depending on the nature of the implicit test (Blaxton, 1989).

From a Roedigerian perspective, of course, the issue is one of accessibility: How do explicit and implicit tests, and the retrieval processes they engender, differentially tap the remnants of prior experience? The major lesson from Period One was that priming, or increased accessibility, biases or calibrates the search process. More generally, experience tunes or sharpens cognitive processes, regardless of whether the experience arises from encoding or the act of retrieval. Performance on a test will reflect this tuning, leading to either facilitation (priming) or impairment (inhibition) depending on the circumstance. To understand a dissociation, then, requires one to start from the back-end, by studying the nature of the test.

Transfer-Appropriate Procedures

Unfortunately, comparing performance across retention tests is a dangerous business, fraught with potential confoundings (much like comparing across items raises the specter of item selection concerns). Retention tests are not single entities, tapping single processes, but instead represent more or less complex concatenations of component processes (Roediger, Gallo, & Geraci, 2002). This makes unraveling empirical patterns (such as those produced by implicit and explicit tests) difficult because changing a single component out of many can produce a dissociation.

In the case of implicit versus explicit tests, the critical component is assumed to be retrieval intentionality—does the task require one to access a particular prior episode intentionally? But building on ideas proposed initially by Jacoby (1983), Roediger and his colleagues shifted the locus away from intentionality toward a set of more tractable candidates. Most implicit memory tests, it turns out, tap primarily perceptual (or data-driven) processes—that is, processes that rely on perceptual data, or data fragments, to drive stimulus identification. Explicit tests, on the other hand, tend to be conceptually-based, relying on meaning, elaboration, and inferences based on context. Depending on the specific processes that are tuned by encoding, data-driven or conceptually-driven, one can then expect either implicit or explicit tests to benefit, but probably not both (Roediger & Blaxton, 1987; Roediger & Weldon, 1987).

Consider the classic case of reading versus generating. As noted above, generating an item usually produces a significant advantage over reading on an explicit test, such as recall or recognition, but reading yields the superior performance on some implicit tests, such as perceptual identification. Generating is clearly a conceptually-driven encoding task—no target-specific "data" are actually presented—whereas reading an isolated word out of context maximizes data-driven operations. Each encoding task calibrates the settings of particular component processes, which then transfer, appropriately or not, to the component processes engendered by the test. Accordingly, one finds a generation advantage for conceptually-driven tests and a read advantage for data-driven tests.

This explanatory framework, which Roediger calls *transfer-appropriate procedures or processing* (Kolers & Roediger, 1984; Morris, Bransford, & Franks, 1977), generates testable predictions. For example, it should be possible to create implicit tests that tap conceptual processing and thereby mimic retention patterns that are characteristic of explicit tests. Category exemplar generation is one obvious candidate, and generate rather than read advantages have been detected in this task (Srinivas & Roediger, 1990). It should also be possible to produce dissociations within a class of purely implicit tests by manipulating the conditions of encoding. The picture superiority effect—the mnemonic advantage that pictures hold over words on most explicit tests—reverses on an implicit (data-driven) word fragment completion test, but reappears on a implicit picture fragment naming test (Weldon & Roediger, 1987). Again, what matters is not retrieval intentionality, but the fit between the processing components primed by encoding and the processing components required by the retention test.

Over the course of a decade, Roediger and his team produced a stream of elegant studies showcasing the value of the transfer-appropriate procedures approach, especially as applied to the interpretation of implicit memory tests. Many of these studies have become standards in the field and have accumulated hundreds of citations (e.g., Roediger, 1990; Roediger & McDermott, 1993). Yet, perhaps ironically, Roediger remains a staunch critic of implicit memory *per se*, a term he worries adds little to our understanding of retention. The fact that experience changes, or primes, behavior in the absence of conscious awareness is important, but it encompasses "much of the experimental study of behavior" (Roediger, 2003, p. 13). Various structures in the body show lasting effects of experience, such as the immune system or even the female reproductive system (Roediger, 1993), but is it sensible to characterize somatic-based "priming" as memory proper? In this sense the concept of implicit memory, defined simply in terms of priming without awareness, points to everything and thereby points to nothing (cf. Roediger, 2003).

Despite these reservations, Roediger is a strong advocate for broadening how we think about remembering and, without question, the implicit memory "boom" has greatly increased the size of the retention test toolkit. Moreover, even though the presence or absence of conscious recollection may be but one of many processing components separating explicit from implicit tests, the role of consciousness in remembering is certainly a worthy topic of investigation (Tulving, 1985). In fact, the Roediger lab has played a pivotal role in developing appropriate methodologies to study the role of phenomenological experience in remembering (e.g., Rajaram, 1993, which is based on a dissertation conducted under Roediger's direction). Perhaps most importantly to Roediger, though, the study of implicit memory places the focus of attention where it should be, on how the characteristics of the retrieval environment enhance or constrain accessibility.

Summarizing Period Two

On the surface, the study of part-set cueing, retrieval blocking, hypermnesia, and implicit memory seem vastly different. But from a Roedigerian perspective, of course, each is simply a manifestation of how retrieval environments afford accessibility. The second stage of Roediger's career, focusing largely on implicit memory, is the point at which the majority of memory researchers caught up with his perspective. Although the natural tendency of some, once again, was to think in terms of acquisition, via the postulation of unique memory systems, Roediger's elegant and influential case for transfer-appropriate procedures (or processing) provided the field with a telling, and highly influential, alternative.

PERIOD THREE: REMEMBERING FALSELY

By any metric, Roediger entered the 1990s as one of the most influential memory psychologists of his time. But like many accomplished scholars, he remains fascinated by the intellectual lineage of ideas; he refuses to relinquish the past, and often relies on it as a source of ideas, both theoretical and empirical. A case in point is the mnemonic effect of repeated testing, a phenomenon that has interested Roediger throughout his career. As discussed earlier, net improvements are sometimes found across repeated tests in free recall (hypermnesia), even in the absence of an intervening study trial, and subjects often recall items on the second test that they failed to recall initially (reminiscence).

These basic effects were noted nearly a century ago by Ballard (1913), but they contrast sharply with the findings of Ebbinghaus (1885/1964) and Bartlett (1932) who showed that memory worsens with delay in predictable ways. In Bartlett's case, of course, college students were asked to recall the Indian folktale *The War of the Ghosts* repeatedly over time—performance not only got worse, but the students reconstructed the story in false, but now-famous schematic, fashion. How do we account for the fact that repeated testing leads to increases in performance in one case and decreases in another? This is exactly the kind of historical paradox that interests Roediger and he invested considerable energy in attempting to reconcile the two data patterns (for the solution, see Wheeler & Roediger, 1992; also see Bergman & Roediger, 1999, for a replication of Bartlett's, 1932, study).

More pertinent to the third period of Roediger's career, however, is a study reported by James Deese in 1959. Deese was interested in using the associative structure of word lists to generate predictions about recall, including so-called errors of commission—that is, instances in which subjects intrude nonlist items into their recall protocol. Extralist intrusions are usually quite rare in free recall, but Deese discovered that he could rig word lists to improve recall and/or to increase the probability of intrusions. The critical determinant of an intrusion, not surprisingly, was the likelihood that it would be generated as an associate to the individual words in the list. For example, if subjects are given *thread, pin, sewing, point, pricked, thimble,* and *sharp* in a list, there is a good chance that the nonpresented word *needle* will be generated as an associate and produced as an incorrect intrusion in subsequent recall. In fact, Deese discovered that intrusion rates for critical nonpresented items exceeded 40% for some lists.

Deese's (1959) study was given some attention when it first appeared, but its impact languished in the ensuing decades. Its replication and extension by Roediger and McDermott (1995) needs no introduction and, of course, an entire industry of Deese–Roediger–McDermott (DRM) studies subsequently emerged (see chapter 18 for a personal account of how the DRM research originated). In addition to replicating Deese, Roediger and McDermott extended the paradigm to recognition memory, yielding remarkably high false alarm rates for the critical distractors, and applied Tulving's remember–know procedure to assess subjects' phenomenological experiences during false recognition. Not only do subjects falsely recognize critical distractors at a high rate, they claim to "remember" the experience.

Why all the fuss? From an associative framework, the Deese findings are understandable, even comforting, but the high intrusion rates are perplexing. Again, intrusions in free recall are typically rare because, it has long been assumed, we possess excellent response selector mechanisms that enable us to discriminate list from nonlist items (Underwood & Schulz, 1960). When we engage in elaboration, drawing connections between to-be-remembered information and other things in memory, we rarely, if ever, intrude the "elaborations." What then is it about DRM lists that leads to such spectacular breakdowns in our response selector mechanisms? Besides introducing the DRM paradigm to modern memory researchers, the Roediger team has worked hard to develop an adequate explanatory account of the phenomenon.

Activation/Monitoring

If we put on our Roedigerian thinking cap, the logical focus shifts to retrieval. Perhaps, for example, veridical recall of DRM lists primes related but nonpresented items leading to intrusions in the recall protocol. The fact that false recalls tend to occur relatively late during output is certainly consistent with such an account (Roediger & McDermott, 1995). During recognition as well, presentation of related list items is apt to occur prior to the critical distractor thereby priming the distractor and leading to false recognition. However, subsequent research has failed to provide much support for a simple retrieval account. In recognition and cued-recall, little, if any, evidence for test-induced priming has been found (Dodd, Sheard, & MacLeod, 2006; Marsh, McDermott, & Roediger, 2004; although see Coane & McBride, 2006). Moreover, warning people about the likelihood of false recall or recognition prior to list presentation reduces the effect somewhat (McDermott & Roediger, 1998), but warnings just prior to retrieval produce little effect (Gallo, Roediger, & McDermott, 2001).

In response to the data, Roediger and his colleagues offered an activation/ monitoring account that combines a focus on associative activation with selective monitoring at retrieval, as in Johnson's source monitoring framework (e.g., Johnson, Hashtroudi, & Lindsay, 1993). During list presentation, activation spreads along associative lines priming related, but not necessarily presented, items; the fact that false memory is predicted well by measuring backward associative strength—the extent to which the falsely remembered item is produced by list items in a free association task (Deese, 1959; Roediger, Watson, McDermott, & Gallo, 2001)—dovetails nicely with this proposal. At test, primed items are recalled, but accuracy depends on the ability of the subject to discriminate between items activated by list presentation as opposed to other, presumably internal, means. In the case of the critical (nonpresented) item, the activation induced by the list of strongly related items is sufficient to trick the subject into thinking it occurred. Note this account assigns important roles to both encoding (activation induced by associative connections) and retrieval (failure to discriminate the source of the activation).

In addition to the data already discussed, the activation/monitoring account is supported by experiments showing that false recall rises and falls with list presentation rates; very short presentation times reduce the effect, presumably because less activation is available to "spread" to the critical item (McDermott & Watson, 2001; Seamon, Luo, & Gallo, 1998). In addition, if list-specific distinctive information is given about studied items, such as presenting them in pictorial format, false memories are reduced somewhat because the subject is better equipped to discriminate actual occurrence information (e.g., Schacter, Israel, & Racine, 1999). Similar reductions in false memory occur with multiple study–test opportunities—again, any manipulation that enhances the subject's ability to discriminate what did and did not actually occur, over and above the presence of activation, moderates the extent of false recognition (Watson, McDermott, & Balota, 2004).

Some issues remain unresolved. For example, relying on "activation" as the main diagnostic dimension is troubling because the concept is poorly specified. False memories induced by DRM-like procedures have been observed after long delays (e.g., weeks), far longer than the typical span of semantic activation (cf. McDermott & Watson, 2001). Moreover, it is still not clear exactly why DRM lists, as opposed to more typical list constructions, break down our usually efficient response selector mechanisms. It is unlikely to be the extent of priming *per se*—e.g., list items prime the related distractor above some critical threshold—because subjects are quite capable of excluding strongly activated associates from a recall protocol (e.g., the byproducts of elaborative processing). The key may lie in some kind of conscious marking of the source of the activation, but no one knows for sure.

Summarizing Period Three

Chapter constraints prevent me from discussing the full impact of the DRM movement, or the viability of competing accounts (e.g., Reyna & Brainerd, 1995; Whittlesea, Masson, & Hughes, 2005). Suffice to say, though, the impact has been substantial: The Roediger and McDermott (1995) article has amassed nearly 600 citations in its relatively short lifetime (as of July 2006) and the original Deese (1959) study, which was cited approximately 40 times between 1959 and 1995, has now accumulated over 400 citations.

One should note as well that Roediger's interest is not really in DRM lists *per se*, but rather in developing simple procedures for investigating illusory recollections. The DRM paradigm has received the brunt of the attention, but the Roediger lab has explored other procedures as well. For example, Goff and Roediger (1998) showed how imagining that an action has been performed (such as breaking a toothpick) can lead subjects to believe later that they actually performed it (see also Loftus and Cahill, chapter 23, this volume). Roediger, Meade, and Bergman (2001) showed how erroneous reports from confederates can produce false memories through a kind of social contagion. The third "period," like the previous two, is really about delineating the determinants of accessibility, although the emphasis shifted from "true" to "false" items. From the perspective of the memory system, of course, the problem is the same—how do the conditions of encoding and the requirements of test conspire to produce an appropriate response?

CONCLUSIONS

In this chapter I have attempted to retrieve some of Roddy Roediger's memory. It has been a selective sampling, with some notable omissions, but common themes do abound. Perhaps most important, as noted throughout, is Roediger's proclivity to interpret the mnemonic landscape through the lens of retrieval—a decision, by the way, he believes is firmly grounded in principled logic. If you think about it, virtually every experience leads to some kind of experiential residue in our brains. Each stored experience affords the opportunity for memory, like light affords the opportunity for visual perception, but what matters is the process that selects and converts these experiences into conscious experience. "Experiences that are encoded and stored but never retrieved are like reflected light that is never perceived—the information is available but of no use" (Roediger, 2000, pp. 57–58). To a Roedigerian, retrieval is the key to understanding memory.

In terms of specific contributions, I have tried to show how each research period has played an important role in establishing empirical benchmarks and in shaping theoretical perspectives. In some cases the field has lagged behind a bit—e.g., the study of retrieval-induced blocking—but in others Roediger's contributions have been recognized promptly and profoundly (e.g., implicit memory and DRM). Of course, besides his scholarly contributions, which have been the exclusive focus of this chapter, Roediger is well known in other ways as well—as a journal editor, department chair, office holder (e.g., APS President), mentor, and general prognosticator. But his contributions to the science of memory are pervasive and likely to last the longest. The chapters in this volume all touch on Roediger's influence, both personal and intellectual, and stand as a fitting testament to his impact.

NOTES

1.   Roediger had two primary mentors in graduate school, Endel Tulving and Robert G. Crowder. Crowder was Roediger's graduate advisor at Yale and an enormous

influence on the development of the Roedigerian functional style of investigative analysis. Roediger has written elsewhere about Crowder's influence, both personal and professional, on his work (see Roediger & Stadler, 2001). It was Crowder, for example, who first introduced Roediger to the mysteries and allure of the part-list cueing phenomenon.

2. For a fuller discussion, the reader is referred to a dissertation by David Payne, which was conducted under Roediger's direction (e.g., Payne, 1987).

REFERENCES

Anderson, M. C. (2003). Rethinking interference theory: Executive control and the mechanisms of forgetting. *Journal of Memory and Language, 49*, 415–445.

Ballard, P. B. (1913). Oblivescence and reminiscence. *British Journal of Psychology Monograph Supplements, 1*, No. 2.

Bartlett, F. C. (1932). *Remembering: A study in experimental and social psychology.* Cambridge, UK: Cambridge University Press.

Bergman, E., & Roediger, H. L., III. (1999). Can Bartlett's repeated reproduction experiments be replicated? *Memory and Cognition, 27*, 937–947.

Bjork, R. A. (1975). Retrieval as a memory modifier: An interpretation of negative recency and related phenomena. In R. L. Solso (Ed.), *Information processing and cognition: The Loyola symposium* (pp. 123–144). Hillsdale, NJ: Lawrence Erlbaum Associates, Inc.

Blaxton, T. A. (1989). Investigating dissociations among memory measures: Support for a transfer appropriate processing framework. *Journal of Experimental Psychology: Learning, Memory, and Cognition, 15*, 657–668.

Bousfield, W. A., & Sedgewick, C. H. W. (1944). An analysis of sequences of restricted associative responses. *Journal of General Psychology, 30*, 149–165.

Briggs, G. E. (1954). Acquisition, extinction, and recovery functions in retroactive inhibition. *Journal of Experimental Psychology, 47*, 285–293.

Brown, J. (1968). Reciprocal facilitation and impairment in free recall. *Psychonomic Science, 10*, 41–42.

Coane, J. H., & McBride, D. M. (2006). The role of test structure in creating false memories. *Memory and Cognition, 34*, 1026–1036.

Craik, F. I. M., & Lockhart, R. S. (1972). Levels of processing: A framework for memory research. *Journal of Verbal Learning and Verbal Behavior, 11*, 671–684.

Deese, J. (1959). On the prediction of occurrence of particular verbal intrusions in free recall. *Journal of Experimental Psychology, 58*, 17–22.

Dodd, M. D., Sheard, E. D., & MacLeod, C. M. (2006). Re-exposure to studied items at test does not influence false recognition. *Memory, 14*, 115–126.

Ebbinghaus, E. (1964). *Memory: A contribution to experimental psychology.* New York: Dover. (Original work published 1885)

Erdelyi, M. H., & Becker, J. (1974). Hypermnesia for pictures: Incremental memory for pictures but not words in multiple recall trials. *Cognitive Psychology, 6*, 159–171.

Estes, W. K. (1972). An associative basis for coding and organization in memory. In A. W. Melton & E. Martin (Eds.), *Coding processes in human memory* (pp. 161–190). New York: Halsted Press.

Gallo, D. A., Roediger, H. L., III, & McDermott, K. B. (2001). Associative false recognition occurs without strategic criterion shifts. *Psychonomic Bulletin and Review, 8*, 579–586.

Goff, L. M., & Roediger, H. L., III. (1998). Imagination inflation for action events: Repeated imaginings lead to illusory recollections. *Memory and Cognition, 26*, 20–33.

Jacoby, L. L. (1983). Remembering the data: Analyzing interactive processes in reading. *Journal of Verbal Learning and Verbal Behavior, 22*, 485–508.

Jacoby, L. L., & Dallas, M. (1981). On the relationship between autobiographical memory and perceptual learning. *Journal of Experimental Psychology: General, 110*, 306–340.

Johnson, M. K., Hashtroudi, S., & Lindsay, D. S. (1993). Source monitoring. *Psychological Bulletin, 114*, 3–28.

Kolers, P. A., & Roediger, H. L., III. (1984). Procedures of mind. *Journal of Verbal Learning and Verbal Behavior, 23*, 425–449.

Luh, C. W. (1922). The conditions of retention. *Psychological Monographs, 31* (3, Whole No. 142).

Marsh, E. J., McDermott, K. B., & Roediger, H. L., III. (2004). Does test-induced priming play a role in the creation of false memories? *Memory, 12*, 44–55.

McDermott, K. B., & Roediger, H. L., III. (1998). Attempting to avoid illusory memories: Robust false recognition of associates persists under conditions of explicit warnings and immediate testing. *Journal of Memory and Language, 39*, 508–520.

McDermott, K. B., & Watson, J. M. (2001). The rise and fall of false recall: The impact of presentation duration. *Journal of Memory and Language, 45*, 160–176.

McGeoch, J. A. (1942). *The psychology of human learning.* New York: Longmans, Green.

McGill, W. J. (1963). Stochastic latency mechanisms. In R. D. Luce, R. R. Bush, & E. Galanter (Eds.), *Handbook of mathematical psychology* (pp. 309–360). New York: Wiley.

Morris, C. D., Bransford, J. D., & Franks, J. J. (1977). Levels of processing versus transfer appropriate processing. *Journal of Verbal Learning and Verbal Behavior, 16*, 519–533.

Neisser, U. (1967). *Cognitive psychology.* New York: Appleton-Century-Crofts.

Payne, D. G. (1987). Hypermnesia and reminiscence in recall: An historical and empirical review. *Psychological Bulletin, 101*, 5–27.

Postman, L. (1961). The present status of interference theory. In C. N. Cofer (Ed.), *Verbal learning and verbal behavior* (pp. 152–179). New York: McGraw-Hill.

Rajaram, S. (1993). Remembering and knowing: Two means of access to the personal past. *Memory and Cognition, 21*, 89–102.

Reyna, V. F., & Brainerd, C. J. (1995). Fuzzy-trace theory: An interim synthesis. *Learning and Individual Differences, 7*, 1–75.

Roediger, H. L., III. (1973). Inhibition in recall from cueing with recall targets. *Journal of Verbal Learning and Verbal Behavior, 12*, 644–657.

Roediger, H. L., III. (1974). Inhibiting effects of recall. *Memory and Cognition, 2*, 261–269.

Roediger, H. L., III. (1978). Recall as a self-limiting process. *Memory and Cognition, 6*, 54–63.

Roediger, H. L., III. (1982). Rejoinder to Erdelyi. *Journal of Verbal Learning and Verbal Behavior, 21*, 662–665.

Roediger, H. L., III. (1990). Implicit memory: Retention without remembering. *The American Psychologist, 45*, 1043–1056.

Roediger, H. L., III. (1993). Learning and memory: Progress and challenge. In D. E. Meyer & S. Kornblum (Eds.), *Attention and performance XIV: Synergies in experimental psychology, artificial intelligence, and cognitive neuroscience* (pp. 509–528). Cambridge, MA: MIT Press.

Roediger, H. L., III. (2000). Why retrieval is the key process to understanding human memory. In E. Tulving (Ed.), *Memory, consciousness and the brain: The Tallinn conference* (pp. 52–75). Philadelphia: Psychology Press.

Roediger, H. L., III. (2003). Reconsidering implicit memory. In J. S. Bowers & C. Marsolek (Eds.), *Rethinking implicit memory* (pp. 3–18). Oxford, UK: Oxford University Press.

Roediger, H. L., III., & Blaxton, T. A. (1987). Effects of varying modality, surface features and retention interval on priming in word fragment completion. *Memory and Cognition, 15,* 379–388.

Roediger, H. L., III., Buckner, R. L., & McDermott, K. B. (1999). Components of processing. In J. K. Foster & M. Jelicic (Eds.), *Memory: System, process, or function?* (pp. 31–65). Oxford, UK: Oxford University Press.

Roediger, H. L., III., & Challis, B. H. (1989). Hypermnesia: Increased recall with repeated tests. In C. Izawa (Ed.), *Current issues in cognitive processes: The Tulane Floweree symposium on Cognition* (pp. 175–199). Hillsdale, NJ: Lawrence Erlbaum Associates, Inc.

Roediger, H. L., III., Gallo, D. A., & Geraci, L. (2002). Processing approaches to cognition: The impetus from the levels-of-processing framework. *Memory, 10,* 319–332.

Roediger, H. L., III., & Karpicke, J. D. (2006). Test-enhanced learning: Taking memory tests improves long-term retention. *Psychological Science, 17,* 249–255.

Roediger, H. L., III., Marsh, E. J., & Lee, S. C. (2002). Varieties of memory. In D. L. Medin & H. Pashler (Eds.), *Stevens' handbook of experimental psychology: Vol. 2. Memory and cognitive processes* (3rd ed., pp. 1–41). New York: John Wiley.

Roediger, H. L., III., & McDermott, K. B. (1993). Implicit memory in normal human subjects. In F. Boller & J. Grafman (Eds.), *Handbook of neuropsychology* (Vol. 8, pp. 63–131). Amsterdam: Elsevier.

Roediger, H. L., III., & McDermott, K. B. (1995). Creating false memories: Remembering words not presented in lists. *Journal of Experimental Psychology: Learning, Memory, and Cognition, 21,* 803–814.

Roediger, H. L., III., Meade, M. L., & Bergman, E. (2001). Social contagion of memory. *Psychonomic Bulletin and Review, 8,* 365–371.

Roediger, H. L., III., & Neely, J. H. (1982). Retrieval blocks in episodic and semantic memory. *Canadian Journal of Psychology, 36,* 213–242.

Roediger, H. L., III., Payne, D., Gillespie, G. L., & Lean, D. S. (1982). Hypermnesia as determined by the level of recall. *Journal of Verbal Learning and Verbal Behavior, 21,* 635–655.

Roediger, H. L., III., & Schmidt, S. R. (1980). Output interference in the recall of categorized and paired associate lists. *Journal of Experimental Psychology: Human Learning and Memory, 6,* 91–105.

Roediger, H. L., III., & Stadler, M. A. (2001). Robert G. Crowder and his intellectual heritage. In H. L. Roediger, III., J. S. Nairne, I. Neath, & A. Surprenant (Eds.), *The nature of remembering: Essays in honor of Robert G. Crowder* (pp. 3–16). Washington, DC: American Psychological Association.

Roediger, H. L., III., Stellon, C., & Tulving, E. (1977). Inhibition from part-list cues and rate of recall. *Journal of Experimental Psychology: Human Learning and Memory, 3,* 174–188.

Roediger, H. L., III., Watson, J. M., McDermott, K. B., & Gallo, D. A. (2001). Factors that determine false recall: A multiple regression analysis. *Psychonomic Bulletin and Review, 8,* 385–407.

Roediger, H. L., III., & Weldon, M. S. (1987). Reversing the picture superiority effect. In M. A. McDaniel & M. Pressley (Eds.), *Imagery and related mnemonic processes: Theories, individual differences, and applications* (pp. 151–174). New York: Springer-Verlag.

Roediger, H. L., III., Weldon, M. S., & Challis, B. H. (1989). Explaining dissociations between implicit and explicit measures of retention: A processing account. In H. L. Roediger, III, & F. I. M. Craik (Eds.), *Varieties of memory and consciousness: Essays in honour of Endel Tulving* (pp. 3–41). Hillsdale, NJ: Lawrence Erlbaum Associates, Inc.

Rundus, D. (1973). Negative effects of using list items as recall cues. *Journal of Verbal Learning and Verbal Behavior, 12*, 43–50.

Schacter, D. L. (1987). Implicit memory: History and current status. *Journal of Experimental Psychology: Learning, Memory, and Cognition, 13*, 501–518.

Schacter, D. L., Israel, L., & Racine, C. (1999). Suppressing false recognition in younger and older adults: The distinctiveness heuristic. *Journal of Memory and Language, 40*, 1–24.

Seamon, J. G., Luo, C. R., & Gallo, D. A. (1998). Creating false memories of words with or without recognition of list items: Evidence for nonconscious processes. *Psychological Science, 9*, 20–26.

Shiffrin, R. M. (1970). Memory search. In D. A. Norman (Ed.), *Models of human memory* (pp. 375–447). New York: Academic Press.

Slamecka, N. J. (1968). An examination of trace storage in free recall. *Journal of Experimental Psychology, 76*, 504–513.

Squire, L. R. (1987). *Memory and brain*. New York: Oxford University Press.

Srinivas, K., & Roediger, H. L., III. (1990). Classifying implicit memory tests: Category association and anagram solution. *Journal of Memory and Language, 29*, 389–412.

Tulving, E. (1983). *Elements of episodic memory*. New York: Oxford University Press.

Tulving, E. (1985). How many memory systems are there? *The American Psychologist, 40*, 385–398.

Tulving, E., & Arbuckle, T. Y. (1963). Sources of intratrial interference in paired-associate learning. *Journal of Verbal Learning and Verbal Behavior, 1*, 321–334.

Tulving, E., & Pearlstone, Z. (1966). Availability versus accessibility of information in memory for words. *Journal of Verbal Learning and Verbal Behavior, 5*, 381–391.

Tulving, E., Schacter, D. L., & Stark, H. A. (1982). Priming effects in word fragment completion are independent of recognition memory. *Journal of Experimental Psychology: Learning, Memory, and Cognition, 8*, 336–342.

Tulving, E., & Thomson, D. M. (1973). Encoding specificity and retrieval processes in episodic memory. *Psychological Review, 80*, 352–373.

Underwood, B. J., & Schulz, R. W. (1960). *Meaningfulness and verbal learning*. Chicago: Lippincott.

Warrington, E. K., & Weiskrantz, L. (1970). Amnesic syndrome: Consolidation or retrieval? *Nature, 228*, 629–630.

Watson, J. M., McDermott, K. B., & Balota, D. A. (2004). Attempting to avoid false memories in the Deese/Roediger-McDermott paradigm: Assessing the combined influence of practice and warnings in young and old adults. *Memory and Cognition, 32*, 135–141.

Weldon, M. S., & Roediger, H. L., III. (1987). Altering retrieval demands reverses the picture superiority effect. *Memory and Cognition, 15*, 269–280.

Wheeler, M. A., & Roediger, H. L. (1992). Disparate effects of repeated testing: Reconciling Ballard's (1913) and Bartlett's (1932) results. *Psychological Science*, *3*, 240–245.

Whittlesea, B. W. A., Masson, M. E. J., & Hughes, A. D. (2005). False memory following rapidly presented lists: The element of surprise. *Psychological Research*, *69*, 420–430.

Wixted, J. T., & Rohrer, D. (1994). Analyzing the dynamics of free recall: An integrative review of the empirical literature. *Psychonomic Bulletin and Review*, *1*, 89–106.

Yum, K. S. (1931). Transfer as a function of changed conditions at recall. *Journal of Experimental Psychology*, *14*, 68–82.

2

Retrieval as a Self-Limiting Process: Part II

ROBERT A. BJORK, ELIZABETH L. BJORK, and BETHANY J. CAUGHEY

Across much of the history of systematic research on human memory, three stages critical to the memory process have been postulated: trace formation, trace storage, and trace utilization or retrieval (see, e.g., Melton, 1963). It was not, however, until Tulving and Pearlstone's (1966) seminal study that the fundamental importance of retrieval processes in human memory—and the need to distinguish the conditions affecting storage from those affecting retrieval—became clear. By providing cues to participants during the recall of items from categorized lists, Tulving and Pearlstone were able to demonstrate that what is stored or available in memory cannot be indexed in a precise or reliable way by what is recallable or accessible at a given point in time.

Prior to the Tulving and Pearlstone (1966) study, a typical paradigm used by researchers to investigate both storage and retrieval processes was to ask participants to recall all the items they could following the presentation of different types of lists, and it was simply assumed that what was recalled reflected what information had been successfully stored and, furthermore, how that information was organized in memory. Items on a list that are semantically related tend to be recalled together, for example, even if they are presented at disparate positions in the list, which was taken as evidence that interitem associations formed at the time of storage then guided the retrieval process at the time of recall. In other words, the retrieval process underlying recall was thought to be self-propagating: The recall of one item triggers the recall of a next, associated item, which triggers the recall of yet another item, and so forth. Such a self-propagating property was—and still is, to a large extent—intrinsic to associative and organizational theories of the recall process.

In J. R. Anderson's (1972) model of recall, for example, it was assumed that to-be-learned items, such as a list of randomly presented words, are associated with each other at the time of study and that a participant's later recall of the list is guided and sustained by such interitem associations. In other words, the items recalled first serve as cues for items to be recalled later. As Roediger (1978) pointed out, this self-propagating nature of recall—that is, the act of recall itself providing the cues that guide additional recall—was originally proposed by Aristotle and "the intervening 2,000 years have done little to damage the idea" (p. 54).

During about the same period, however—that is, the late 1960s and early 1970s—the results of other studies demonstrated that the act of recall could also function to *limit* further recall. One such example is the research of Slamecka (1968, 1969) demonstrating inhibition owing to part-list cueing. If, following the presentation of a list of words to be remembered, some items from the list are given as cues for the remaining items in the list, the recall of the remaining items is not enhanced, but, rather, is impaired. The fact that inhibition owing to part-list cueing has been referred to as an "enigma for memory researchers" (Nickerson, 1984) reflects not just that it has proved difficult to understand from a detailed process standpoint, but also that it is highly counterintuitive, given that the self-propagating nature of recall seems so compelling.

A second example of the self-limiting property of recall comes from research on the recall of categorized lists. If, following the presentation of a list consisting of multiple exemplars of a number of categories, participants are then cued with category names to aid their recall of members of a given category, recall of such category members decreases with the output position of the provided category cue. That is, the later in the recall test that a given category name is presented as a cue, the fewer members of that category are recalled, a demonstration of "output interference" (e.g., Smith, 1971; Smith, D'Agostino, & Reid, 1970).

ROEDIGER'S ROLE: RETRIEVAL AS A SELF-LIMITING PROCESS

Henry L. Roediger, III, inspired by such effects, became one of the first researchers to champion the notion that the act of recall can function to attenuate further recall. He embarked on a program of research during the 1970s and early 80s that revealed the robustness of such negative effects, which he frequently referred to as *recall interference* (e.g., Roediger & Schmidt, 1980). In what follows, we briefly review Roediger's body of work, focusing on the studies that examined the recall of categorized lists—studies that led Roediger to conceptualize recall as a self-limiting process and to argue for hierarchical theories of memory structure (e.g., Estes, 1972; Mandler, 1967; Rundus, 1973) versus interitem associative theories of memory, such as Anderson's (1972) model. We then discuss a new type of recall interference—the more recently discovered phenomenon of *retrieval-induced forgetting*—and we conclude with a speculation that a suppression mechanism that has been put forward to explain retrieval-induced forgetting (e.g., Anderson, Bjork, & Bjork, 1994; Anderson & Spellman, 1995) might also, when elaborated, account for earlier retrieval-interference effects as well.

Positive and Negative Consequences of Retrieval Cues

Beginning with his work as a graduate student in Robert Crowder's laboratory at Yale University, Roediger carried out numerous studies demonstrating that retrieval is a "self-limiting process" (1978). From a theoretical standpoint, he struggled with why retrieval had both positive and negative consequences, depending on the particular paradigm and procedure employed in a given experiment. Research carried out by Endel Tulving and his collaborators and by Norman Slamecka and his collaborators, as summarized below, was particularly influential from that standpoint.

As demonstrated by Tulving and his colleagues (e.g., Tulving & Osler, 1968; Tulving & Pearlstone, 1966), the amount of information that can be recalled from memory depends critically on the nature of the retrieval cues provided at the time of recall. After presentation of a blocked categorized list, for example, participants cued with category names recall significantly more items from the list than do participants simply asked to free recall as many items as they can remember from the list. As argued by Tulving and Pearlstone, such results indicate both that more information is stored and available in memory than can be accessed on a typical free recall test and that the presentation of words in a categorized list apparently determines both the way that they are then organized in memory and later retrieved from memory.

If, as indicated by these results, the items presented in a list to be memorized are stored in such a dependent manner (e.g., in terms of direct associative bonds among the items), then it should be possible to reveal such dependence by presenting some of the items from the list as retrieval cues to aid participants' recall of the remainder of the items in the list. Reasoning in just this way, Slamecka (1968, 1969) conducted a series of studies presenting subsets of items from the presented list as retrieval cues for the rest of the list. To his great surprise, providing some list items not only did not facilitate recall of the remaining words, they appeared instead—over a wide variation of the proportion of list items presented as cues—to have a slight but consistently *negative* effect on the recall of the remaining items. Even when using categorized lists, as in the Tulving and Pearlstone study (1966), Slamecka found presentation of items as retrieval cues to impair, rather than facilitate, recall of the remaining items. The following quotation summarizes Slamecka's reaction to his own findings.

> In the face of our compelling preconceived expectations, we were annoyingly disappointed to find that the experiment failed to show any advantage for the cued group, and worse, that it revealed a small but significant inhibitory effect in that condition. . . . [Six experiments later], I had no choice but to conclude that the classical theoretical portrayal of memory traces as being joined by direct associative links was wrong.
>
> (Slamecka, 1984, p. 96)

Interpreting the Effects of Retrieval Cues

Given these apparently inconsistent effects of providing retrieval cues—that is, the facilitative effects found by Tulving and Pearlstone (1966) versus the deleterious effects found by Slamecka (1968, 1969), Roediger (1973, 1974) argued that a major challenge to the understanding of memory was to determine the conditions under which the provision of retrieval cues benefit versus impair recall and, further, to provide a compelling theoretical explanation to account for these differing effects of retrieval cues. As a step toward this latter goal, Roediger (1973, 1974) proposed a two-factor explanation for when retrieval cues would be beneficial and when they would be detrimental. Basically, he argued that the effects are positive when cues enable access to more higher-order units (e.g., the names of categories) than can be recalled by a participant unaided by such cues, and the effects are negative when more retrieval cues than are needed to access higher-order units are provided (e.g., additional instances from the category).

The reasoning behind Roediger's proposed second factor was that the impairment resulting from the presentation of list cues on recall of the remaining list items could be an instance of output interference—the deleterious effects of earlier recall upon later recall, as first systematically studied by Tulving and Arbuckle (1963). Although Tulving and Arbuckle, on the basis of their work with short paired-associate lists, argued that the phenomenon of output interference was limited to recall of only very recently presented material—that is, recall of items from primary memory—subsequent research with longer lists and delayed recall tests demonstrated that output interference occurred in recall from secondary/long-term memory as well (e.g., Dong, 1972; Smith 1971; Smith et al., 1970). If, as Roediger (1973) proposed, the presentation of cues to participants could be assumed to simulate their own uncued retrieval of those items, then the presentation of these cues should have the same effect as the participants having retrieved these items early in their own recall output; namely, they would impair the recall of later items.

To test the adequacy of this second factor for predicting when providing retrieval cues would impair additional recall, Roediger (1973) performed an experiment in which—following the presentation of fairly long and blocked categorized lists—participants were given either category names as retrieval cues or, in some cases, category names plus a varying number of instances from the categories. Roediger found impaired recall of additional category instances when both category names and instances were provided as retrieval cues, versus when only category names were provided as retrieval cues, with the detrimental effect increasing as the number of instances given as cues increased—a pattern that was consistent with Roediger's two-factor hypothesis as to when retrieval cues would and would not be beneficial.

Additionally, owing to the construction of his categorized list, Roediger (1973) was able to rule out a plausible alternative explanation of these findings involving guessing. By showing that the detrimental effect persisted even when the remaining number of items available for recall was held constant, he was able to demonstrate that the increasingly detrimental effect on recall as the number of provided cues increased did not stem from the fact that as the number of cues increase the number of yet-to-be-recalled items typically decrease, making participants—in principle, at least—more likely to output a correct response by guessing when fewer cues are presented.

Roediger's (1973) study thus went a long way toward resolving what had appeared to be contradictory findings regarding the effects of retrieval cues on recall. When retrieval cues increased access to higher-order units, they increased participant's recall, consistent with the findings of Tulving and Pearlstone (1966) and Tulving and Osler (1968). When category instances were also provided as cues, however, recall of additional items was impaired, with the impairment increasing as the number of instances provided as cues increased, consistent with the part-list cueing effects observed by Slamecka (1968, 1969).

Roediger (1973), like Slamecka (1968, 1969) before him, concluded that his findings were inconsistent with interitem associative theories of memory. He argued instead for hierarchical theories of memory and, in particular, that a model proposed by Rundus (1973) to account for output interference effects in recall could be generalized to account for the observed negative effects of providing retrieval cues as well. Rundus's model, which provided a kind of framework for Roediger's research on recall as a self-limiting process (e.g., Roediger, 1973, 1978; Roediger & Schmidt, 1980; Roediger, Stellon, & Tulving, 1977), is described in the next section.

Rundus's (1973) Model of Recall

The Rundus (1973) model of recall, which builds upon Shiffrin's (1970) model of memory search, was proposed to account for the retrieval process underlying recall and, in particular, to account for the occurrence of output-interference effects in recall. In his model, Rundus assumed that during the presentation of a list of items to be learned, the learner (or participant) attempts to organize the list in some way, and whatever ideas or units the participant uses for such organization then become the higher-order retrieval cues (Tulving, 1966) for the subset of list items organized under them. In the case of a categorized list (e.g., one containing instances of fruits, flowers, birds, etc.), the names of the categories are assumed to serve as these higher-order organizing units. The nature of the hierarchical organizational structure that would result from the presentation of a list, based on the Rundus model, is illustrated in Figure 2.1.

As indicated in Figure 2.1, the words (W) presented in the list are grouped into subsets according to their association with the higher-order retrieval cues (RQ), which in the case of a categorized list would be the names of the categories, and the strength of association between a given higher-order retrieval cue, say RQ_i, and an item under it, say W_j, is denoted as A_{ij}. These higher-order RQs are to be thought of as control elements (Estes, 1972) in the sense that they control the recallability of the words under them. Further, the RQs themselves are assumed to be associated with a contextual cue (denoted as "List" in Figure 2.1) specifying the particular list under consideration. In other words, the association of all the RQs to this contextual cue would indicate that the categories all occurred in that particular

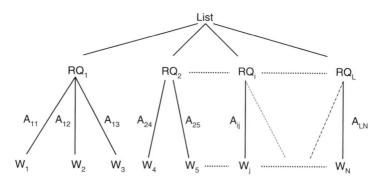

FIGURE 2.1   Organization in memory of items (W) and retrieval cues (RQ) after presentation of a list as proposed by the Rundus model of recall (based on Rundus, 1973).

list. It is also assumed that the strength of association between the various RQs and the list control element, as well as that between a given RQ and the items in its subset, will not be equal, perhaps owing to different amounts of covert rehearsal during list presentation or owing to pre-experimentally established associations in the case of categorized lists.

Three rules assumed in the model determine how the process of recall unfolds. First, the likelihood that a given RQ is retrieved when the participant is asked to recall the list is determined by a ratio rule. Specifically, the likelihood of a given RQ being retrieved is equal to the ratio of the strength of that RQ's association to the "List" cue to the sum of the strengths of association of all RQs to the "List" cue. After retrieval of one of the RQs, the participant attempts to retrieve the items subsumed under that retrieval cue, and the probability of recalling a particular item is determined by the same ratio rule (i.e., the strength of association of that item to that particular RQ divided by the sum of strengths of association of all items to that RQ). If the retrieved item has not been recalled yet, the participant outputs that item and then returns to the same RQ to continue the recall process. If the item had been output previously, that fact would be noted before returning to the RQ, but, critically, it is assumed that the retrieval process involves sampling with replacement, such that previously retrieved words or categories remain available for future recall attempts. Thus, according to this second rule—sampling with replacement—RQs and items (e.g., category names and instances, respectively) may be re-retrieved. Also of critical importance to the model's ability to account for output interference is the assumption that the act of recalling a unit (either the name of a category or an instance) increases the strength of its association to its higher-order control element.

Finally, the model incorporates a stopping rule. According to this rule, attempts to retrieve items associated to a given RQ (e.g., instances within a given category) will continue until a series of k consecutive retrievals produces no new items, at which point the participant abandons further use of that RQ, returns to the context "List" cue to retrieve another RQ, and begins retrieving items organized under that RQ. The participant is assumed to continue in this manner until a series of m

consecutively retrieved RQs produces no new items for recall. Thus, in the model, the parameter k determines when the participant decides that continuing to search for new items under the current RQ is unlikely to be productive and, consequently, samples another RQ; and the parameter m determines when the participant decides that further sampling of RQs is unlikely to produce any new items for recall and, consequently, stops the recall process for that list altogether.

Given these assumptions, the Rundus (1973) model can account for both output interference and part-list cueing effects. Output interference is predicted because recall of an item strengthens the association between that item and its RQ, making it more likely to be retrieved again owing to the ratio rule and, at the same time, making it less likely that some other item associated with the same RQ will be retrieved. Additionally, recall of an item increases the likelihood that a participant will stop searching for additional items under that RQ and will go on to sample a new RQ owing to the stopping rule. That is, as more items are retrieved from the same RQ, the probability increases that the criterion number k of no new items retrieved is reached, causing the participant to abandon further retrieval attempts from that RQ. The negative consequences of part-list cueing can be explained in terms of the model by assuming that—when participants are given a subset of the list just studied as cues for recall of the remaining items—it is actually the presented items that tend to be retrieved first with these retrievals acting to block access to the other items from the list.

Tests of Rundus's Model

Over the next 10 years or so, against a theoretical background that pitted hierarchical models against horizontal-associative models, Roediger and colleagues continued to investigate the self-limiting nature of recall via empirical studies on the dynamics of output interference and inhibition owing to part-list cueing. In one particularly important study, Roediger et al. (1977)—by increasing the time available to participants to recall and then measuring the rate of recall—were able to demonstrate that the detrimental effect of cues is not overcome by allowing participants to spend a longer time attempting to recall. Additionally, by comparing the performance of participants who were allowed to output the list items presented as cues as well as any remaining items in the list (i.e., target items) with the performance of participants who were only allowed to output the target items, Roediger et al. were able to rule out the notion that the negative effects of part-list cues might arise from the necessity for participants to check each retrieved item against the set of provided cues. Although relieving participants of this extra checking task by allowing them to output cues as well as target items did increase their recall of target items when compared to the condition where they were not allowed to recall cues, it did not eliminate the negative effects of part-list cueing relative to free recall.

In another series of experiments, Roediger (1978) also obtained retrieval-interference effects consistent with hierarchical associative theories of recall. When he provided participants with some but not all category names as cues, recall for cued categories was facilitated while recall of noncued categories was impaired relative to free recall (Experiment 1) and the impaired recall of noncued categories increased as the number of cued categories from the list increased (Experiment 2). In a third experiment, in which recall of noncued categories was delayed by various types of interpolated activities, he was able to rule out that the impaired recall of noncued categories relative to free recall was attributable to nonspecific effects of the prior recall of cued categories—analogous, perhaps to the way that any interpolated task, such as counting backwards by threes, might impair recall.

On the basis of these and other findings, Roediger (1978) argued that the assumptions of Rundus's (1973) model allow for *both* the self-propagating and self-limiting characteristics of recall. Recall of items within the cued categories is aided, relative to free recall, by providing the participant with the RQs or control elements under which those items were hierarchically or vertically associated. Because, however, the RQs or control elements for the cued categories are strengthened by such recall, access to the noncued RQs or control elements is decreased, owing to both the ratio rule for determining probability of retrieval and the assumption that sampling is with replacement. Furthermore, consistent with the assumptions of the Rundus model, the consequence of presenting cues for some categories but not others is to impair the recall of the noncued categories, not the items within the categories. Finally, the detrimental effect of providing *both* category names and instances is explained by the Rundus model in the same manner as part-list cueing effects are explained—namely, by assuming that the presentation of the additional instances has the same effects as does covert recall of those items by the participant and, thus, represents an instance of output interference. In terms of the Rundus model, the instances presented as cues are strengthened, making them more likely to be retrieved again owing to the sampling-with-replacement rule and thereby to block retrieval of any additional items from that category.

In summary, although some of the results obtained by Roediger and others (see, in particular, Roediger & Schmidt, 1980; Roediger et al., 1977; and Watkins, 1975) could not be explained—at least not efficiently, by Rundus's model—the bulk of Roediger's findings from his many cueing experiments proved consistent with the model. To this day, in fact, Rundus's (1973) model—at the conceptual level, if not at the detailed mathematical-model level—remains the dominant explanation of output interference and inhibition owing to part-list cueing.

We turn now to a discussion of the retrieval-practice paradigm and to retrieval-induced forgetting, which constitutes a more recent type of evidence that retrieval is a self-limiting process.

RETRIEVAL-INDUCED FORGETTING

Retrieval-induced forgetting (RIF), first reported by Anderson et al. (1994), refers to the negative impact on the recall of some items associated to a given cue or configuration of cues when other items associated with that cue are repeatedly retrieved. The practiced items become more recallable than they would have been without such practice, which is hardly surprising, and the unpracticed items become less recallable than corresponding unpracticed items from unpracticed categories—which *is* surprising.

The retrieval-practice paradigm, as implemented by Anderson et al. (1994), has its roots in research on test effects—or, said differently, on "retrieval as a memory modifier" (Bjork, 1975), another research domain in which Henry Roediger has been, and continues to be, heavily involved. The specific procedure used by Anderson et al. was developed as a means of assessing the effects of increasing the retrieval strength of some items on the retrieval strength of related items—and, more specifically, to test some predictions of a "new theory of disuse" proposed by Bjork and Bjork (1992) in a chapter honoring one of the greatest theorists in the history of research on human memory, William K. Estes. The theory, designed to account for a number of "important peculiarities" of human memory, consists of a set of assumptions as to how study and retrieval events impact two presumed dimensions of an item's representation in memory—its "storage strength" and its "retrieval strength"—as a function of that item's current levels of those strengths.

The key assumptions of the theory for present purposes, as summarized by Bjork (2001), are the following.

- Memory representations are double indexed in memory—by their current "retrieval strength" (how accessible or active they are) and their "storage strength" (how well learned or interassociated they are with other memory representations). Storage strength is assumed to accumulate as a consequence of study or practice and, once accumulated, is permanent. Retrieval strength, however, which completely determines the probability of being able to access a given stored representation, is volatile. It is assumed to increase as a consequence of study or practice, but to decrease as a consequence of study or practice of competing responses or behaviors. The theory is a "new" theory of disuse because, in contrast to Thorndike's (1914) original "law of disuse," it is access to learned representations (retrieval strength) that is lost over a period of disuse, not the representation *per se* (storage strength).
- In distinguishing between storage strength and retrieval strength, the theory resurrects a distinction that was common among learning theorists of an earlier era. The distinction is essentially the same, for example, as Hull's (1943) distinction between *habit strength* and *momentary excitatory potential*, or Estes's (1955) distinction between *habit strength* and *response strength*. The distinction also corresponds, in a general way, to the time-honored distinction between learning and performance, a distinction necessitated by a wide range of findings from research on both humans and animals: What we observe is *performance*; what we are often trying to infer is *learning*. Storage strength and retrieval strength also correspond, roughly, to Tulving's distinction between the *availability* and *accessibility* of memory representations (see, e.g., Tulving & Pearlstone, 1966).

- What *is* new about the theory are the assumptions governing how the current storage and retrieval strengths of a representation influence (a) the increments in the storage strength of that representation that result from study or practice; and (b) the increments and decrements, respectively, in the retrieval strength of that representation that result from study or practice of that representation or competing representations. The assumptions of special pertinence to the issues of the present chapter are the following:

  (1) Storage strength serves to enhance the gain and retard the loss of retrieval strength. That is, access to representations in memory, as indexed by retrieval strength, is lost more slowly with disuse—and regained more rapidly given study or practice—the higher that representation's current storage strength.

  (2) The higher the current retrieval strength of a representation, the smaller the increments in both storage strength and retrieval strength that result from study or practice of that representation. Thus, somewhat surprisingly, the more accessible a representation, the smaller the increment in storage strength (learning) that results from additional study or practice of that representation. Put differently, conditions that result in forgetting (loss of retrieval strength) also create opportunities for additional learning (i.e., increments in storage strength).

From the foregoing assumptions, retrieval as a self-limiting process emerges in an intrinsic way—because retrieving some item associated to a given cue not only increases that item's retrieval strength, but also decreases the retrieval strength of other items associated with that cue. The theory also makes the counterintuitive prediction that items high in retrieval strength—other things being equal—will be the most susceptible to retrieval-induced forgetting.

The RIF Paradigm and Basic Findings

As implemented by Anderson et al. (1994), the RIF paradigm includes four distinct phases: a study phase, a directed retrieval-practice phase, a distractor phase, and a final test phase. In the study phase, participants are given a list of materials categorized in some way and the retrieval-practice phase involves directed retrieval of some members of some of the categories. In Anderson et al.'s initial experiments, participants were presented with six members of each of eight categories (e.g., *Fruit Orange*; *Weapon Rifle*), with the pairs presented one pair at a time and intermixed by category. The retrieval-practice phase consisted of repeated recall of half the members of half the categories, triggered by cues such as *Fruit–Or_____*. To increase the effectiveness of such retrieval practice, each practiced pair was given three such tests separated by expanding intervals (cf. Landauer & Bjork, 1978). Finally, after a retention interval (20 minutes) filled with a distracting activity, participants were asked to try to recall all of the members of all of the categories. Depending on the experiment, the final test consisted of either category-cued free recall or—as a means of controlling the order of output of the members of a given category—cued recall consisting of prompts such as *Fruit B_____*, *Fruit O_____* for the six members of a given category.

Of central interest in the RIF paradigm are the levels of recall of three different types of items: (a) practiced exemplars from practiced categories (e.g., *Orange*), called *Rp+* items; (b) unpracticed exemplars from practiced categories (e.g., *Banana*), called *Rp–* items); and (c) unpracticed exemplars from unpracticed categories (e.g., *Rifle*), called *Nrp* or baseline items. The typical pattern of findings is that the recall of Rp+ items exceeds the recall of the Nrp or baseline items, consistent with a long history of research on test effects (e.g., Allen, Mahler, & Estes, 1969; Bjork, 1975; Landauer & Bjork, 1978; Roediger & Karpicke, 2006; Whitten & Bjork, 1977), and, of considerably more interest, however, that the recall of the Rp– items is *impaired* relative to the recall of the Nrp or baseline items. Such retrieval-induced forgetting of Rp– items is surprising because one might expect such items also to profit from the retrieval-practice phase, owing to dynamics such as covert rehearsal or spreading activation of the type intrinsic to horizontal interitem associative models of memory.

The pattern of results observed by Anderson et al. (1994) has now been replicated many times, not only with category-exemplar pairs, but also with a wide range of other materials, including newly-learned visuospatial materials (Ciranni & Shimmamura, 1999); visual scenes and event narratives in eye-witness memory (e.g., Saunders & MacLeod, 2002; Shaw, Bjork, & Handal, 1995); examination materials (Macrae & MacLeod, 1999), autobiographical memories (Barnier, Hung, & Conway, 2004); and stereotypical and/or valenced attributes of hypothetical individuals (Dunn & Spellman, 2003; Storm, Bjork, & Bjork, 2005).

Interpreting Retrieval-Induced Forgetting

In principle, RIF could also reflect blocking and sampling-with-replacement dynamics of the type favored by Roediger and others—in the context of the Rundus (1973) model—as an explanation of output interference—and, more generally, retrieval as a self-limiting process. That is, it could be the case that when participants try to recall all the members of a practiced category, the Rp+ items come readily and repeatedly to mind, blocking access to the Rp– items and impairing their recall.

For several reasons, however, Anderson et al. (1994) argued that they could reject blocking-type explanations of RIF. One such reason is that RIF was still obtained when the order of recall of items from a given category was controlled. That is, even when Rp– items were the first to-be-recalled items from a given practiced category (in response to prompts such as *Fruit–B_____*), their recall was impaired relative to corresponding Nrp items. A second reason is that Anderson et al. found that it was the strong exemplars of a given category, such as *Orange* or *Banana*, that were most susceptible to RIF; whereas, the recall of weak exemplars, such as *Guava* and *Papaya*, was not impaired by the practice of other exemplars. Such a finding is consistent with the predictions of Bjork and Bjork's (1992) new theory of disuse, but is inconsistent with blocking as instantiated by ratio-rule mechanisms, which predicts the opposite pattern (for a more detailed version of that argument, see Anderson et al., 1994, Appendix A, p. 1085).

As an alternative explanation of RIF, Anderson et al. (1994) argued for an inhibition/suppression mechanism. The basic idea is that responding to a retrieval-practice prompt such as *Fruit–Or*_____ requires not only selecting *Orange*, but also suppressing other exemplars of the *Fruit* category. The fact that it is the strong exemplars of a given category that are most susceptible to RIF is consistent with such a mechanism—because such exemplars are the most likely to come to mind in response to *Fruit* and, hence, are the most frequent targets of suppression. Recently, in research on the possible role of RIF in impression formation, Storm, Bjork, and Bjork (2005) have also found that it is the more recallable attributes of a given hypothetical person, positive or negative, that are most susceptible to RIF. Once again, the argument is that such attributes are the ones that have to be selected against most often, leading to their suppression. It needs to be stressed, however, that this suppression is assumed to occur automatically and without conscious attention; that is, as some information is retrieved, other competing information is selected against and thereby suppressed, with its suppression occurring rather like a by-product of the selection process.

In a second study, Anderson, Bjork, and Bjork (2000) found that the direction of retrieval practice also mattered with respect to whether RIF was obtained, and mattered in a fashion consistent with such a suppression mechanism. When practice was prompted in the standard direction, recalling *Orange* in response to *Fruit–Or*_____, RIF was obtained; when practice was prompted in the other direction—that is, recalling *Fruit* in response to *Fr*_____–*Orange*—there was no RIF of unpracticed members of the *Fruit* category. Such a result is consistent with a suppression mechanism because it is only retrieval practice in the standard direction that requires the selection of *Orange* and the suppression of other studied fruits.

The fact that the direction of retrieval practice mattered not only supports the suppression idea, but also—in combination with the fact that the strengthening effects of retrieval practice did not depend on direction—argues against a blocking mechanism. That is, Anderson et al. (2000) found that the subsequent recall of Rp+ items profited to the same degree, relative to Nrp items, whether retrieval practice was in the *Fr*_____–*Orange* direction or in the *Fruit–Or*_____ direction. Given that finding, the blocking of access to Rp– items by Rp+ items should also be commensurate in the two conditions, according to any unelaborated implementation of the blocking idea.

Additional Support for an Inhibitory Account of Retrieval-Induced Forgetting

Two other findings strongly implicate inhibitory processes in RIF. The first derives from the independent-probe technique introduced by Anderson and Spellman (1995). This technique was devised to test whether Rp– items are inhibited in the strong sense of the word—that is, whether access to those items would be impaired in general, not just in response to a category cue under which those items were studied in phase one of the experiment. Anderson and Spellman reasoned that if competing responses are truly suppressed during the retrieval attempt for a designated target, then these inhibited items should be more difficult to retrieve, not only from the studied retrieval cue, but also from other appropriate cues as well. Consistent with that conjecture, practice retrieving some exemplars of a studied category (e.g., *Red Blood*) impaired the later recall of unpracticed exemplars in that category (e.g., *Red Radish*) even when recall on the final test was cued by a novel category cue, such as *Food*—a cue that was not used in the retrieval practice phase.

A critical aspect of this finding is that the recall of the unpracticed exemplars in response to the unpracticed cue was impaired even though that cue was unrelated to the items strengthened during retrieval practice. The unpracticed cue, therefore, provides a measure of the accessibility of these related, unpracticed items that is independent of associative interference from the practiced targets. Using this same cue-independent technique but with very different materials—multidimensional geometric stimuli that could be categorized in terms of their location, shape, and color—Ciranni and Shimmamura (1999) also found evidenced supporting the inhibitory account of retrieval-induced forgetting. (See, however, Perfect et al., 2004, for a criticism of the logic behind the cue-independent technique.)

Finally, some newer findings also provide strong support for an inhibitory account. Storm, Bjork, Bjork, and Nestojko (2005) tested inhibitory versus noninhibitory accounts of RIF by introducing an interesting retrieval-practice condition—namely, one in which some cues, such as *Metals–Mu_____*, posed an impossible retrieval task for the participants. That is, no studied member of the *Metals* category started with *Mu*, nor does any metal—at least among those known to the typical undergraduate—begin with those letters. Participants in Storm, Bjork et al.'s experiment, after having studied a typical Anderson et al. (1994) list of category-exemplar pairs, then received practice for half of the categories on the studied list. For half of these practiced categories, the retrieval practice involved retrieving new exemplars from that category, but ones that had not been presented in the studied list (e.g., *Fruit Or_____*). For the other half of the practiced categories, the retrieval practice was impossible (e.g., *Metals Mu_____*).

As expected, consistent with the findings of research by Bauml (2002), retrieving extralist members of a given category (the possible condition) resulted in RIF. Of more interest and greater theoretical importance, the impossible condition also produced RIF. Such a finding is especially difficult to explain via a noninhibitory account, such as blocking, because no member of the earlier-studied category is retrieved and strengthened in the impossible condition.

As Storm, Bjork et al. (2005) emphasize, it has often been assumed that retrieval practice must be successful in order for retrieval-induced forgetting to occur, but an inhibitory account does not require any such assumption. If, as is assumed in the inhibitory account, potentially interfering and competing information is suppressed in order to facilitate retrieval of target information, this process should occur whether the retrieval attempt succeeds or not. Indeed, aspects of Storm, Bjork et al.'s results suggest that the arguably more difficult impossible retrieval practice may have more RIF, consistent with the idea that a search for an impossible target might entail suppression of more competing responses than would the retrieval search for a possible target, which can be expected to cease as soon as a given desired target is retrieved.

Adaptive Consequences of the Retrieval Inhibition Assumed to Underlie RIF

As observed in the RIF paradigm, when information is retrieved from memory, it becomes more recallable than it would be otherwise, while other information associated with the same cue or configuration of cues becomes less recallable. As discussed earlier, these positive and negative effects of retrieval both illustrate the role of retrieval as a memory modifier (Bjork, 1994) and support the new theory of disuse (Bjork & Bjork, 1992) in which it is assumed that retrieval of an item associated to a given cue not only increases that item's retrieval strength but decreases the retrieval strength of other items associated with the same cue. We see these positive and negative effects of retrieval as being both adaptive and essential to an efficiently functioning memory system: Access to information likely to be needed again in the future is increased, while interference from competing information is reduced. Moreover, because it is the retrieval strength of the unpracticed information that is assumed to be inhibited or suppressed while its storage strength in memory remains unchanged—although retrieval access to such information may be temporarily impaired—should our circumstances change and we need to regain access to such information in the future, we can become fluent in its use again more quickly than were we to have to learn it anew from scratch. (For a more detailed discussion of the adaptive consequences of the retrieval inhibition or suppression assumed to underlie retrieval-induced forgetting—as well as some potentially negative consequences—the reader is referred to Bjork, Bjork, & MacLeod, 2006).

RESOLVING PART 1 AND PART 2: SOME SPECULATIONS

In the foregoing section, we argued that RIF is attributable to a selection/suppression mechanism and that RIF phenomena cannot be explained by blocking mechanisms of the type that emerged, 30 years or so ago, as the dominant explanation of phenomena such as output interference and the effects of part-list cueing. In this final section we consider the other side of the coin: What role might selection coupled with suppression play in output interference and part-list cueing, if any?

On the Possibility of Overlapping and Interacting Processes

As a kind of preamble to our speculations, it is important to emphasize that the various theoretical mechanisms that have been proposed to account for recall as a self-propagating or self-limiting process tend not to be mutually exclusive. Selection, suppression, spreading activation, blocking, sampling with replacement, associative chaining, covert mediation or rehearsal, and metacognitive processes, such as stopping rules, may all be involved, often in parallel, especially across the range of materials and procedures that have been used in laboratory studies.

Even in the case of research on RIF, the involvement of processes other than selection and suppression are clearly indicated. One such indication is the tendency for items weakly associated to a given cue to profit, rather than suffer, from retrieval practice on other items associated with that cue, which suggests that spreading activation, as well as selection and suppression, may be involved in the RIF paradigm. Another indication is the tendency for RIF to shift toward retrieval-induced facilitation as studied materials become more linked or integrated. Anderson and McCulloch (1999), for example, report multiple results on "integration as a boundary condition for retrieval-induced forgetting"—results that suggest that processes such as associative chaining during study and mediation during recall can result in unpracticed items being helped, not hindered, by retrieval practice on other items. Recently, and consistent with Anderson and McCulloch's findings, Chan, McDermott, and Roediger (in press) have found clear evidence of retrieval-induced facilitation when strong linkages exist between Rp+ and Rp− items. After having participants study an article on the biological characteristics and living habits of the toucan bird, Chan et al. structured the retrieval-practice phase so that the questions asked in that session (e.g., "Where do toucan birds sleep at night?") bore a relationship to other, unasked, questions (e.g., "What other bird species is the toucan related to?"). From the article it was clear that toucans are not themselves able to make holes in trees, but that they often sleep in holes made by woodpeckers, to which they are related. Given that linkage, final recall of the Rp− question, as well as the Rp+ question, was facilitated for these participants compared to that of control participants who only read the article and were not asked any questions about it prior to the final recall test.

Selection and Suppression in Output Interference

Extending the selection-plus-suppression idea to output-interference effects in free recall requires, first of all, the mostly uncontroversial assumption that all studied items are associated with a common list node or episodic context. The second necessary assumption is that recalling a given item from the list or study episode requires selecting that item from among all the items in that list or episode, which also seems uncontroversial. The final, and crucial, assumption is that the process of selection requires that competing items—that is, other list items that might be recalled—be suppressed. As free recall proceeds, then, the repeated suppression of yet-to-be-recalled items makes those items harder and harder to access and the recall process gradually grinds to a halt. When categorized lists are studied and recall is cued by category names the corresponding argument seems straightforward—and much the same as that advanced by Anderson et al. (1994) to explain the RIF observed with categorized materials: Each retrieval of a member of the category requires suppressing others and, gradually, makes the remaining members of the category hard to access.

Specifying the possible contributions of selection-plus-suppression to part-list cueing effects seems much less straightforward. To begin with, for example, RIF-type effects have not generally been found when opportunities to restudy some of the items presented earlier replace actual retrieval of those items during the retrieval-practice phase of the RIF paradigm (see, e.g., Anderson et al., 2000; Bauml, 2002; Ciranni & Shimamura, 1999). The restudied items benefit from additional study, but apparently not at a cost to the Rp− items. In terms of the selection-plus-suppression account of RIF, this lack of a cost to the Rp– items arises because such items do not compete for retrieval—and thus do not have to be selected against—when Rp+ items are re-presented as intact items for study as opposed to being retrieved.

In contrast, the typical part-list cueing procedure differs in possibly important ways from the RIF paradigm, particularly at the time of the final test, and these differences may provide opportunities—as outlined below—for selection-plus-suppression dynamics to play a role in the production of part-list cueing effects. (For a detailed comparison of procedural differences between the RIF, part-list cueing, and retroactive-interference paradigms, see Anderson & Bjork, 1994; Anderson et al., 1994.) Typically, the effects of part-list cueing have been examined in the context of free recall, with participants told either to recall all list items, including the items presented as cues, or to recall only the remaining list items (i.e., targets), excluding the cue items. Given that the cue items have been re-presented, it seems safe to assume that they are the items most available for recall. In the case where they, too, are to be recalled, they tend to be recalled first, in which case their selection could be accompanied by suppression of the yet-to-be-recalled target items. When the cue items are not to be recalled, the argument becomes more complicated and other factors may well come into play, such as retrieval-strategy disruption (see Basden & Basden, 1995; Nickerson, 1984). The editing burden entailed by the instructions not to recall the strongest items (i.e., the items presented as cues) may, however, lead to a covert cycle of such items being recalled, but not written down, which then may introduce suppression dynamics such as those we have hypothesized may play a role in output interference. What can be said with some confidence is that inhibition owing to part-list cueing is not only highly unintuitive from a layperson's standpoint, but also an "enigma for memory researchers" (Nickerson, 1984)—in part, no doubt—because it is a product of multiple interacting dynamics.

CONCLUDING COMMENT

Our coverage of the earlier era of research on "recall as a self-limiting process" (Roediger, 1978) in the context of the current era of research on "retrieval-induced forgetting" (Anderson et al., 1994) illustrates that fundamental issues in memory research tend to reappear, clothed, often, in different paradigms. Our chapter also illustrates, as do the other chapters in the present volume, that—from his student days to the present—Henry (Roddy) Roediger, III has been a mover and a shaker in virtually every successful effort our field has made to understand the complex, unintuitive, and multifaceted dynamics of human memory.

REFERENCES

Allen, G. A., Mahler, W. A., & Estes, W. K. (1969). Effects of recall tests on long-term retention of paired associates. *Journal of Verbal Learning and Verbal Behavior, 8*, 463–470.

Anderson, J. R. (1972). FRAN: A simulation model of free recall. In G. H. Bower (Ed.), *The psychology of learning and motivation* (Vol. 5, pp. 315–379). New York: Academic Press.

Anderson, M. C., Bjork, E. L., & Bjork, R. A. (2000). Retrieval-induced forgetting: Evidence for a recall-specific mechanism. *Psychonomic Bulletin and Review, 7,* 522–530.

Anderson, M. C., & Bjork, R. A. (1994). Mechanisms of inhibition in long-term memory: A new taxonomy. In D. Dagenbach & T. Carr (Eds.), *Inhibitory processes in attention, memory, and language* (pp. 265–325). New York: Academic Press.

Anderson, M. C., Bjork, R. A., & Bjork, E. L. (1994). Remembering can cause forgetting: Retrieval dynamics in long-term memory. *Journal of Experimental Psychology: Learning, Memory, and Cognition, 20,* 1063–1087.

Anderson, M. C., & McCulloch, K. C. (1999). Integration as a general boundary condition on retrieval-induced forgetting. *Journal of Experimental Psychology: Learning, Memory, and Cognition, 25,* 608–629.

Anderson, M. C., & Spellman, B. A. (1995). On the status of inhibitory mechanisms in cognition: Memory retrieval as a model case. *Psychological Review, 102,* 68–100.

Barnier, A. J., Hung, L., & Conway, M. A. (2004). Retrieval-induced forgetting of emotional and unemotional autobiographical memories. *Cognition and Emotion, 18,* 457–477.

Basden, D. R., & Basden, B. H. (1995). Part-list cueing: A retrieval strategy disruption interpretation. *Journal of Experimental Psychology: Learning, Memory, and Cognition, 21,* 1656–1669.

Bauml, K.-H. (2002). Semantic generation can cause episodic forgetting. *Psychological Science, 13,* 356–360.

Bjork, E. L., Bjork, R. A., & MacLeod, M. D. (2006). Types and consequences of forgetting: Intended and unintended. In L.-G. Nilsson & N. Ohta (Eds.), *Memory and society: Psychological perspectives* (pp. 134–158). Psychology Press: Hove, UK.

Bjork, R. A. (1975). Retrieval as a memory modifier: An interpretation of negative recency and related phenomenon. In R. L. Solso (Ed.), *Information processing and cognition: The Loyola Symposium* (pp. 123–144). New York: Wiley

Bjork, R. A. (1994). Memory and metamemory considerations in the training of human beings. In J. Metcalfe & A. Shimamura (Eds.), *Metacognition: Knowing about knowing* (pp. 185–205). Cambridge, MA: MIT Press.

Bjork, R. A. (2001). Recency and recovery in human memory. In H. L. Roediger, J. S. Nairne, I. Neath, & A. M. Suprenant (Eds.), *The nature of remembering: Essays in honor of Robert G. Crowder* (pp. 211–232). Washington, DC: American Psychological Association Press.

Bjork, R. A., & Bjork, E. L. (1992). A new theory of disuse and an old theory of stimulus fluctuation. In A. Healy, S. Kosslyn, & R. Shiffrin (Eds.), *From learning processes to cognitive processes: Essays in honor of William K. Estes* (Vol. 2, pp. 35–67). Hillsdale, NJ: Lawrence Erlbaum Associates, Inc.

Chan, J. C. K., McDermott, K. B., & Roediger, H. L. (in press). Retrieval-induced facilitation: Initially nontested material can benefit from prior testing of related material. *Journal of Experimental Psychology: General.*

Ciranni, M. A., & Shimamura, A. P. (1999). Retrieval-induced forgetting in episodic memory. *Journal of Experimental Psychology: Learning, Memory, and Cognition, 25,* 1403–1414.

Dong, T. (1972). Cued partial recall of categorized words. *Journal of Experimental Psychology, 93,* 123–129.

Dunn, E. W., & Spellman, B. A. (2003). Forgetting by remembering: Stereotype inhibition through rehearsal of alternative aspects of identity. *Journal of Experimental Social Psychology, 39,* 420–433.

Estes, W. K. (1955). Statistical theory of distributional phenomena in learning. *Psychological Review, 62,* 369–377.

Estes, W. W. (1972). An associative basis for coding and organization in memory. In A. W. Melton & E. Martin (Eds.), *Coding processes in human memory* (pp. 161–190). Washington, DC: Winston.

Hull, C. L. (1943). *The principles of behavior.* New York: Appleton-Century-Crofts.

Landauer, T. K., & Bjork, R. A. (1978). Optimum rehearsal patterns and name learning. In M. M. Gruneberg, P. E. Morris, & R. N. Skykes (Eds.), *Practical aspects of memory* (pp. 625–632). London: Academic Press.

Macrae, C. N., & MacLeod, M. D. (1999). On recollection lost: When practice makes imperfect. *Journal of Personality and Social Psychology, 77,* 463–473.

Mandler, G. (1967). Organization and memory. In K. W. Spence & J. T. Spence (Eds.), *The psychology of learning and motivation* (pp. 327–372). New York: Academic Press.

Melton, A. W. (1963). Implications of short-term memory for a general theory of memory. *Journal of Verbal Learning and Verbal Behavior, 2,* 1–21.

Nickerson, R. S. (1984). Retrieval inhibition from part-set cueing: A persisting enigma in memory research. *Memory and Cognition, 12,* 531–552.

Perfect, T. J., Stark, L., Tree, J. J., Moulin, C. J. A., Ahmed, L., & Hutter, R. (2004). Transfer appropriate forgetting: The cue-dependent nature of retrieval-induced forgetting. *Journal of Memory and Language, 51,* 399–417.

Roediger, H. L. (1973). Inhibition in recall from cueing with recall targets. *Journal of Verbal Learning and Verbal Behavior, 12,* 644–657.

Roediger, H. L. (1974). Inhibiting effects of recall. *Memory and Cognition, 2,* 261–269.

Roediger, H. L. (1978). Recall as a self-limiting process. *Memory and Cognition, 6,* 54–63.

Roediger, H. L., & Karpicke, J. D. (2006). Test-enhanced learning: Taking memory tests improves long-term retention. *Psychological Science, 17,* 249–255.

Roediger, H. L., & Schmidt, S. R. (1980). Output interference in the recall of categorized and paired-associate lists. *Journal of Experimental Psychology: Human Learning and Memory, 6,* 91–105.

Roediger, H. L., Stellon, C. C., & Tulving, E. (1977). Inhibition from part-list cues and rate of recall. *Journal of Experimental Psychology: Human Learning and Memory, 3,* 174–188.

Rundus, D. (1973). Negative effects of using list items as recall cues. *Journal of Verbal Learning and Verbal Behavior, 12,* 43–50.

Saunders, J., & MacLeod, M. D. (2002). New evidence on the suggestibility of memory: The role of retrieval-induced forgetting in misinformation effects. *Journal of Experimental Psychology: Applied, 8,* 127–142.

Shaw, J. S., III, Bjork, R. A., & Handal, A. (1995). Retrieval-induced forgetting in an eyewitness-memory paradigm. *Psychonomic Bulletin and Review, 2,* 249–253.

Shiffrin, R. M. (1970). Memory search. In D. A. Norman (Ed.), *Models of memory* (pp. 375–447). New York: Academic Press.

Slamecka, N. J. (1968). An examination of trace storage in free recall. *Journal of Experimental Psychology, 76,* 504–513.

Slamecka, N. J. (1969). Testing for associative storage in multitrial free recall. *Journal of Experimental Psychology, 81,* 557–560.

Slamecka, N. J. (1984). Commentary on "An examination of trace storage in free recall." *Citation Classics, 25,* 96. (Original work published in *Journal of Experimental Psychology, 76,* 504–513).

Smith, A. D. (1971). Output interference and organized recall from long-term memory. *Journal of Verbal Learning and Verbal Behavior, 10*, 400–408.

Smith, A. D., D'Agostino, P. R., & Reid, L. S. (1970). Output interference in long-term memory. *Canadian Journal of Psychology, 24*, 85–89.

Storm, B. C., Bjork, E. L., & Bjork, R. A. (2005). Social metacognitive judgments: The role of retrieval-induced forgetting in person memory and impressions. *Journal of Memory and Language, 52*, 535–550.

Storm, B. C., Bjork, E. L., Bjork, R. A., & Nestojka, J. F. (in press). Is retrieval success a necessary condition for retrieval-induced forgetting? *Psychonomic Bulletin and Review*.

Thorndike, E. L. (1914). *The psychology of learning*. New York: Teachers College.

Tulving, E. (1966). Subjective organization and the effects of repetition in multitrial free recall learning. *Journal of Verbal Learning and Verbal Behavior, 5*, 193–197.

Tulving, E., & Arbuckle, T. Y. (1963). Sources of intratrial interference in immediate recall of paired associates. *Journal of Verbal Learning and Verbal Behavior, 1*, 321–334.

Tulving, E., & Osler, S. (1968). Effectiveness of retrieval cues in memory for words. *Journal of Experimental Psychology, 77*, 593–601.

Tulving, E., & Pearlstone, Z. (1966). Availability versus accessibility of information in memory for words. *Journal of Verbal Learning and Verbal Behavior, 5*, 381–391.

Watkins, M. J. (1975). Inhibition in recall with extralist "cues." *Journal of Verbal Learning and Verbal Behavior, 14*, 294–303.

Whitten, W. B., & Bjork, R. A. (1977) Learning from tests: The effects of spacing. *Journal of Verbal Learning and Verbal Behavior, 16*, 465–478.

3

Are There 256 Different Kinds of Memory?

ENDEL TULVING

A n academic Festschrift, as every reader of this volume knows, is a book honoring a respected scholar or scientist. It is usually published to celebrate an important landmark in the honoree's life. In our case the honored academic is Henry L. (Roddy) Roediger, III, a brilliant cognitive psychologist, mentor and teacher, friend and colleague. And the landmark, as far as I know, was the discovery in 2004 by Roddy's colleagues at Purdue, primarily Jim Nairne, that they had had the good fortune of having had a truly remarkable colleague in their very midst when Roddy was a faculty member there. The discovery resulted in Roddy's being nominated for and awarded an honorary doctor's degree by Purdue, followed by a scientific conference to celebrate his achievements, and now this volume to record it for posterity.

Wikipedia, the source of infinite knowledge and wisdom in our day and age, offering an explication of the term, declares that "A Festschrift can be anything from a slim volume to a work in several volumes. It often includes important contributions to scholarship of science." Please note that the operative word in this pithy definition is "often." Often means "not always." An appropriate elaborative emendation of Wikipedia's definition would say that a Festschrift frequently enough also serves as a convenient place in which those who are invited to contribute find a permanent resting place for their otherwise unpublishable or at least difficult to publish papers.

My contribution to Roddy's Festschrift, I suspect, belongs in this latter category. Having spent a lifetime watching journal editors, referees, reviewers, and all kinds of other experts, I am reasonably certain that I could not have gotten the present piece into a respectable journal. It has few strengths and many faults; it does not follow the standard procedures; above all it is not clear what the point of the paper is. Therefore, I am deeply grateful to Roddy for having done well enough in his career to have earned himself a Festschrift. And I very much appreciate that Jim Nairne who organized the conference and is editing the present volume invited me to be a part of it. It allows me to publish this paper, which otherwise would probably not have seen the light of day.

I do feel a bit embarrassed for pulling what some might regard as a stunt on my esteemed friend and colleague. I know full well that Roddy deserves better than having his (first) Festschrift serve as a dumping ground for others' failed ambitions. But he knows that science is a risky business, and every now and then you run into a bum deal or situation. My minor excuse is that some people very close to Roddy encouraged me to publish this paper and that Roddy himself suggested the title. Perhaps even more relevant is the fact that the topic of the paper is not totally unrelated to Roddy's own interests. This fact should please Jim Nairne in his role as editor of the Festschrift. When he issued instructions to the writers as to their precise mission, he made it exceedingly plain that their papers had to have a clear bearing on Roddy's own contributions to our science. The same fact also kept me from committing a sin to which Festschrift writers frequently fall prey and which an astute observer of the ways of scholars and scientists has put succinctly as follows: "All too often, the festschrift consists of a disparate and uneven collection of papers on a range of subjects that . . . only vaguely intersect with the interests of the individual whose work is being honored by the volume" (David Nunan, Cambridge Journals Online, doi: 10.1017/S0272263199223078).

My paper does intersect with Roddy's interests. Indeed, it could be thought of as a commentary on, or at least a footnote to, a long important dissertation (chapter) that Roddy and two of his pupils wrote for the venerable *Stevens' Handbook of Experimental Psychology* (Roediger, Marsh, & Lee, 2002) on "Kinds of Memory."[1] Before writing that chapter on varieties of memory, Roddy had already achieved critical fame as an expert on a particular kind of "kinds of memory" known as "memory systems." He discovered not only the now widely acclaimed "female reproductive system" (Roediger, 1993, see also 2003) but also the smallest human memory system known to science, namely the "red fruit memory" system (Roediger, 1990.)

Thus, the topic of "kinds of memory" has an established position among Roddy's widespread interests. Even if it is not one of his truly great scholarly passions—it cannot compete with cueing inhibition, or implicit memory, or false memory, or testing effects (see Nairne, chapter 1, this volume)—Roddy's connection with the problem area is clear, and I am safe to proceed with my story.

The thumbnail sketch of the story I tell in this paper is as follows: In the old days, there was only one kind of memory. To study memory meant to study that one kind. Then things changed, and among other changes there appeared on the scene different kinds of memory. Although Roddy, in his formative years, had misgivings about multiplicity of memory of any kind, like other good scientists he reconsidered, relented, and reformed. As frequently happens with religious and ideological converts, Roddy also went too far in his tolerance of newfangled ideas, and on his own, voluntarily, without any external pressure, although with the help of two young people, wrote that aforementioned long paper entitled "Kinds of Memory" (Roediger et al., 2002). The paper was thorough, thoughtful, and scholarly, and, as the title suggests, it explicitly admitted to there being in existence many different kinds of memory. So far so good. But the otherwise great paper was marred by an error. My contribution to Roddy's Festschrift is to proffer a correction of that error.

ONE LEARNING, ONE MEMORY

Everybody knows (well, all wise people like our honoree Roddy know) that life was simpler in the old days. It was simpler in science, too. There were fewer problems, fewer uncertainties, and fewer ideas. Scientists' ignorance was remarkably limited. As late as 1977, everything that scientists did not know could be presented in two thin volumes, judging by available evidence (Duncan & Smith, 1977). It was not even unknown for a thinker to declare that all important problems in science were solved.

Life was similarly simpler in the field of the psychology of memory. The field was established by Ebbinghaus' (1885) ground-breaking magnum opus entitled "On Memory," although by our current standards there was actually rather little memory in it. Instead, the book described many experiments on what later came to be called verbal learning. As time went by, verbal learning became very popular in North America. It also greatly simplified the life of anyone interested in memory, because it offered few challenges and required little original thought.

In the field of verbal learning, there was only one kind of learning ("verbal learning"). It was studied only in the laboratory (named the "verbal learning laboratory"). Its study relied on one basic method ("list learning"). Subjects' performance was judged by either "trials to criterion" or "proportion correct." The data were interpreted (when it was deemed necessary to interpret them, which was not always the case) in terms of a single concept ("association") that had only a single property ("strength"). Most people of Roddy's age or older know all about these "old days," and younger ones can find out more about them by reading history (e.g., Bower, 2000; Cofer, 1979).[2] A telling sign of the overarching power of verbal learning was the fact that memory was not talked about. In what at the time was the psychology student's bible of retention and use of knowledge and skills acquired through learning, "Psychology of Human Learning" by McGeoch and Irion (1952), the term "memory" occurred only in the expression "memory span." It looked as if memory as such did not exist in the psychologists' world.

Eventually, as everybody knows, the verbal learning movement was freed from its self-imposed fetters by cognitively oriented psychologists. Memory was welcomed back from its exile and allowed a place at the center of the stage of cognitive psychology. But as frequently happens in revolutions, some old bad habits were retained by the revolutionaries. In the case of the reborn memory one such bad habit was to think that there was only one kind of memory. Thus, instead of being ruled by one learning (mainstream) psychological thinking was ruled by one memory.

In this unitary-memory attitude students of memory took their cue from their once banished forebears. Ebbinghaus' (1885), in his otherwise innovative work, had not displayed any awareness of different kinds of memory. At the beginning of his magnum opus he did talk about different ways in which memory manifests itself, but memory itself was undivided. Memory was memory. Richard Semon (1904), an unappreciated giant of the memory world of the time, had many profoundly insightful ideas about memory that went beyond Ebbinghaus' work, but he was in excellent agreement with Ebbinghaus in the matter of the concept of memory. Memory was memory. (For a fascinating story of Semon's life and work on memory see Schacter, 2001). Nor was there any hint offered about different kinds of memory in Frederic Bartlett's (1932) classic book "Remembering," which in many other ways represented the polar opposite of Ebbinghaus. Just about the only hint about different "kinds" of memory was found in William James's "Principles of Psychology" (James, 1890), but few psychologists knew about it.

MORE THAN ONE?

The world has changed greatly over the last century. The science of memory is no exception: It too has seen many changes including those having to do with the very concept of memory and, accordingly, the scope and the nature of memory research. Among other things, memory has split into numerous fragments.

When psychologists of the younger generation, who rebelled against the behaviorist ways of their elders, embraced mind as their new love, and began to celebrate the event loudly, memory was invited to the party, too. Actually, memory was let in through the back door, as it were. Some of the young revolutionaries discovered William James (1890). They adopted his views of psychology as a science of the mind (Miller, 1962) and took seriously his distinction between two kinds of memory, one "primary" and the other "secondary" (Waugh & Norman, 1965). Aided and abetted by innovative experimental work by John Brown in England (1958) and Lloyd and Peggy Peterson in the US (Peterson & Peterson, 1959), and against the noble but eventually ineffectual rearguard action by traditionalists (Keppel & Underwood, 1962), this younger generation cleanly separated "short-term" memory from "long-term" memory. This action was the beginning of memory's fate like that of Humpty Dumpty: what started as a nice round whole became many pieces. The pieces have come to have many names, but collectively, and at the most general level of classification, we can refer to them as "kinds of memory." The term "memory" itself has become just an umbrella term covering all the different kinds, and one-time dreams of psychologists of coming up with a comprehensive "theory of memory" have become as irrelevant as psychological theories about umbrellas.

By the time that Roediger and his two collaborators (Roediger et al., 2002) took stock of the situation regarding "kinds of memory," there was so much relevant material that they had a real ball. Their approach was thorough and scholarly. They first surveyed the grounds and reasons for distinguishing types of memory. They discussed many different kinds of distinctions that had found their way into the psychologists' vocabulary. They presented their own veritable collection of kinds or types of memory: declarative, procedural, explicit, implicit, conscious, unconscious, voluntary, involuntary, retrospective, prospective, code-specific, sensory, iconic, echoic, working, long-term, episodic, autobiographical, semantic, as well as some others. Their conclusion was thoughtfully wise: "[T]he single term memory does not do justice to the underlying concepts it represents."

HOW MANY?

The Roediger et al. (2002) paper, admirable in many ways, had a flaw (all right, because it is a Festschrift, let us call it a minor flaw). The flaw is not easy to find. Therefore it makes a suitable test to amuse the reader of this piece who has stuck it out to this point. So, try it.

Here are the first three sentences of the Roediger et al. (2002) paper:

> Memory is a single term, but refers to a multitude of human capacities. There are many different kinds of memory. Philosophers have analyzed memory for 2,000 years; psychologists have studied the topic experimentally for 115 years; and neuroscientists have examined the neural bases of memory for the past 70 years.

The flaw is contained in this text. Where? Do you see it? I give you a hint: The flaw is hidden between (sic!) the second and the third sentences. See it? Not yet? I give you another hint: It is something that is missing there. What is it? If you got it, congratulations! If not, here is a final chance to redeem yourself: The missing thing, the flaw, is the information that is provided in the present paper, as well as in the heading of this section of the paper. Got it now? Good! But do not get too cocky—you were mightily primed.

So, the missing part, the flaw (sorry, the minor flaw), is the answer to the implicit question of "how many?" After Roddy and his co-authors noted that, "There are many different kinds of memory," they should have told the reader how many. Readers of papers of the kind that we are talking about like data, and they like quantitative data. The mention of merely "many different kinds" leaves many a reader deeply disappointed. Roddy and his friends should have known it, and should have taken steps not to bring such disappointment into the hearts of their readers. That is why I call it a flaw in the paper.

Well, as it happens, I have been searching for varieties of memory for some time now. It is, at least was, a sort of a hobby of mine. Whenever I come across yet another "kind of memory," I enter its name into my master list creatively labeled "kinds of memory." I kept adding name after name of kind of memory, the list kept growing and growing, and I was running out of space in my computer. I then decided to declare the list closed. Life is too short for everything one is tempted to do, hobbies included. A happy consequence of this decision was that I am now in the position to share with Roddy, his colleagues, and indeed the rest of the curious world the answer to that question of "How many?" The missing number, believe it or not, is 256! In the remainder of this paper, I name all 256, and then tackle the question that most readers are likely to ask: "Big deal! So what?" In answering that question I offer some practical suggestions as to how the list of 256 kinds of memory can be put to good scientific, educational, recreational, and perhaps even to commercial use.

WHAT ARE THEY?

The 256 kinds of memory are duly listed in the Appendix of this paper. (If you do not believe that there are 256 entries in the Appendix, feel free to count them.)

How did the items in the list get in? After all, the term "kind of memory" is vague, fuzzy, polysemous, impressionistic, and not precisely definable. This fact created a certain difficulty for me in my undertaking of producing a definite inventory of currently existing kinds of memory. But the problem was not insurmountable. We psychologists are resourceful when it comes to solving fuzzy problems, because most problems in our field are fuzzy. They are best treated flexibly and with imagination.

In the present instance I relied on an old crafty device called "operational definition." Younger readers who have grown up in the happy-go-lucky, currently fashionable world of "exploratory science," may not be familiar with operational definitions, although they should be, even if it is true that operational definitions have acquired a somewhat unsavory repute (Green, 1992). Briefly, an operational definition describes concrete operations that an impartial observer of nature—yes, they did believe in the existence of impartial observers in the old days—performs to create or construct the to-be-defined entity. The construction, that is the description of how you "got there," defines what it is that you wanted to define. A famous operational definition of intelligence is, "Intelligence is what tests test." (This is inspired by a famous paper by one of my own professors—Boring, 1923.) The ultimate perfection here would be not what intelligence tests test, but what an intelligence test tests, and there are these versions of the definition in existence, too. You cannot get much craftier than that! And it does simplify life.

The great advantage of operational definitions is that no one can argue with you when you use them. At least they are not allowed to, according to theory. Operational definitions are totally objective, and scientists are supposed to love objectivity. If someone does disagree with your operational definition, you simply turn off your hearing aid.

After this preamble, I trust, you are ready for the precise operational definition of "kind of memory." Here it is: A kind of memory is the noun "memory" preceded by an appropriate adjectival modifier. For example, event memory, iconic memory, olfactory memory, recognition memory, short-term, and verbal memory are examples of "kinds" of memory. (As the astute reader observes, some of the memory qualifiers here are not adjectives but nouns, and some indeed are rather extended phrases. Grammarians would frown on such practice, of course, but scientists are practical people and as such they usually do not get terribly excited about how grammarians treat their beloved subject matter.)

Note that because of my clever use of the given operational definition you cannot argue about an entry's presence in the list. That is, you cannot ask whether an entry X in the Appendix refers to a true, real, or valid kind of memory, or whether it rightly belongs there. It is true, real, and valid by virtue of its presence in the list. With operational definitions you cannot lose!

To remind the reader: The way the different kinds of memory found their way into the list was simple. Every time I saw a kind, as defined, in a scholarly article or book, and remembered the project, and had an implement handy to make a note of it, and did not lose the note, the kind ended up as a member of the list. Anyone who wishes to replicate the study can either use the same method, or an improved one. At any rate, we now have the list of 256 names of kinds of memory and can try to figure out what to do with it.

WHAT CAN WE DO WITH 256 KINDS OF MEMORY?

At this point in the proceedings the inevitable "so what?" question would undoubtedly crop up. So there is this list of 256 kinds of memory. So what? What is the list good for? What can you do with it? Who would want to bother about it in any form or fashion? Is it more than an idle exercise, a trivial sort of amusement?

The easiest question here is the one about what it is good for. I have already answered that question—the list was, still is, good for me in that it gave me something to publish in Roddy's Festschrift. Without it there would have been the Festschrift, but I would not have been in it. That would have been sad.

As to the other skeptical queries, I know that some of you would simply want to, and will, ignore the list altogether. This happens all the time in a developing science such as ours in which new ideas and findings crop up that practitioners do not like, and there are many reasons for that. (How many? I can think of four, but they are outside the purview of this paper.) Anyhow, it is reasonable to expect that ignoring the list in the Appendix would be the preferred action by many if not most people who ever become aware of its existence.

Then there are those who will not quite ignore the list but will wonder whether they should take it seriously. Can anyone be serious when he talks about 256 kinds of memory, or is he just kidding others to see how they react? Is someone going to write, some time, somewhere, something like, "scientists have now discovered 256 kinds of memory"? Or is someone going to say, "psychological science of memory is running amuck; witness the silly claim of . . ."?

For those who are still reading this epistle at this point, and are still wondering what is going to happen next, I do have some concrete suggestions on how one might use the list for scientific, educational, recreational, and perhaps even commercial purposes. The items below serve only as examples, the actual possibilities are many more, limited only by your imagination. Again, however, it is up to you to decide whether you want to take them seriously or not.

Possible scientific uses include:

(1) Examining the list for errors of omission or commission. If you find any, email or phone Roddy and let him know. He can start a new list. This one is closed, as I mentioned, but there is no law against a new, better list.

(2) Determining the scientific relevance of the number 256. How important do you think is this figure? If someone argued with you and maintained that the true number is 283, or 251, or 200, or 135, or whatever, how would

you react? This is your problem, esteemed reader, because the list in the Appendix is closed, finished, done. But if someone asked me, I would say that although I would not argue about the figure 256, I like it. I like it very much, because it is such a nice number. Besides, in the binary number system it would be recorded as 100,000,000, and that is even nicer. Nevertheless it is probably wise not to take 256 too literally. It does not carry the same connotation as would expressions such as "256 shopping days left to Christmas" or "256 dollars that IRS thinks you owe them." You cannot go far wrong if you think of the figure 256 as just a convenient placeholder symbol for something like the expression "many more than anyone who has not spent hours in deep thought about, and scoured all sorts of believable and unbelievable sources, is likely to come up with when asked about the number of kinds of memory." In this sense, although on a somewhat more modest scale, "256" is not unlike "google," which, as we know now, means something like a "rather large number, much larger than anyone could have imagined." Anyhow, in my opinion, 256 does not hold much promise as a source of a kind of hot scientific controversy that many of our friends and colleagues live for.

(3) Figuring out whether there is a way of organizing the data in the Appendix more meaningfully than I have done (listing the items alphabetically). Again, I will leave the problem to you, but I myself think the answer, indeed the question itself, is uninteresting because the answer is, "Of course it can, in a very large number of ways, and this is why the outcome is no more revealing or useful than any particular order of a well-shuffled deck of 52 playing cards." But, if you think otherwise, go ahead and prove the proposition wrong.

(4) As a final example, consider the question of what *kinds* of kinds of memory are those listed in the Appendix. They make a motley collection. Could we say that some of them are more important or fundamental or crucial or central, or whatever, for the "Science of Memory," and on what criteria (Roediger, Dudai, & Fitzpatrick, in press)? Although this problem, like all others here are not for me but for the readers and future generations of memorists to solve, let me give you a hint about one possible method of classifying memories in the Appendix, one that would please Roddy. As many of you know, and as Jim Nairne reminds us again in (chapter 1, this volume), Roddy and his colleagues have intensively studied, and made important contributions to the exploration of "false memory," a "hot" issue in contemporary memory research (Roediger & McDermott, 1995, 2000). The essence of the phenomenon is that normal, healthy, intelligent learners who are exposed to a list of common words are highly likely to consciously recollect having seen or heard words in the study list that in fact were not presented in that list. If you are a memory expert, I invite you to scan the entries in the Appendix, and decide what kinds of memory could be false, or in what kinds of memory one might expect to find that "false memory" can or could be demonstrated. If you decide that "false memory" is associated with some but not all kinds of memory, would you still say that false

memory is an interesting phenomenon of "memory," or an interesting property of "memory"? And if it is not phenomenon of "memory," what is it a phenomenon of?

Educational uses of the list in the Appendix include: (i) Testing those students' specific interests who come to you and tell you that they are thinking of "getting into memory." You can show them the list and ask which of the 256 kinds of memory did they have in mind for study, or which subset of the total. (ii) Testing those students' strength of motivation who come to you and tell you that they are thinking of "specializing in memory." You can show them the list and ask them whether they really are willing to spend the time necessary to become familiar with the 256 different kinds of memory, as at least some people would expect them to do if they were to become specialists in memory. The exact form of the prospective memorist's response, together with their reaction time, would allow you to help make an informed career decision for them.

Recreational uses of the list include various games, to be played in parlour or pubs, when a group of experts is present:

(1) In the list of 256 "kinds," you ask the experts, how many are names of "memory systems"? When they point to declarative memory, episodic memory, working memory, and some other legitimate entry, you pat them on the back. But when they make false claims, you cluck your tongue. For instance—taking a random example—when they claim that "implicit memory" in the list refers to a memory system, you know that they are not as knowledgeable as they think they are, and you inform them of the fact. If they protest, you inform them that they are not supposed to argue with authorities and ask them to phone or email Dan Schacter and ask him.

(2) In the list, how many kinds of memory are dead? Yes, dead. There are dead kinds of memory, and your experts' job is to spot them. This game, when played after the systems game, is also a test of priming, because primeable experts ought to be able to tell you that "implicit memory" is not only the right answer to the question of "which items in the list" are *not* systems, but also the right answer to the question about dead kinds. If you are confused, phone or email Dan Willingham, and he will tell you what I have in mind when I talk about dead kinds of memory. But, are there other dead kinds in the list? If your players have obvious difficulty, you are permitted to give them a hint: There is indeed another "kind" that was officially pronounced dead, and whose obituary was published by Roddy Roediger's PhD dissertation supervisor at Yale.

(3) If you find an expert who passes both the systems and dead memories tests satisfactorily, you allow them to proceed to the real acid test: Can they find an item in the list of 256 that is not only a kind of memory (which all are, of course, by definition) but that is also science. A science? Are you kidding, they ask. No, you tell them, you are not, and you have proof.[3]

(4) For the lesser experts among the readers (those who can solve easy but not difficult Sudoku puzzles, say) another fun game can be suggested: What is

the biggest matryoshka you can make out of the different kinds of memory in the Appendix? As most readers know, matryoshka refers to a set of Russian dolls in which one fits inside the other. When they make the dolls out of wood, the world's record number of embedded matryoshkas is over 70. Now, as it happens, there exist in this world also "memory matryoshkas," virtual arrangements in which one kind of memory is embedded within another. The fact is not widely advertised—it might make another good PhD final exam question—but it is true. These are expressed in statements that, when carefully analyzed, assert that "memory is in memory is in memory." Memory matryoshkas of size 2 are easy to find the Appendix: For instance, iconic memory is embedded within sensory memory, and semantic memory is embedded within declarative memory. Now, can you find matryoshkas of size 3? Size 4? (If you find a matryoshka of size 4, please do send it to Roddy Roediger with your good wishes.)

(5) Once you identify ("discover"?) one or more memory matryoshkas in the list, you will be in a position to think great thoughts about your subject matter, which you possibly could not have done without the discovery. You can ask and try to answer the question: Does the fact that we can have one (kind of) memory within another (kind of) memory that is within another (kind of) memory make memory a truly unique biological capacity? Or should we just try to clean up the terminological mess? How many other behavioral or cognitive processes do you know that include themselves? How about one kind of running that is embedded in another kind? One kind of breathing embedded in another kind? One kind of color vision embedded in another?[4]

Finally, to conclude the paper, I am happy to tell the patient reader that the rules for commercial use of the copyrighted information in the Appendix are being worked out. The results will be made available, for a hefty fee, on the Internet. The proceeds will go toward the establishment of the "Club of 256."

ACKNOWLEDGMENT

My current research is supported by an endowment by Anne and Max Tanenbaum in support of research in cognitive neuroscience.

NOTES

1.   Roddy tells me the story of how he had agreed to write the chapter on one condition: The title of the chapter should be "Varieties of Memory" rather than "Kinds of Memory". The responsible parties agreed to the condition. So Roddy submitted the paper under the "varieties" title. The title was approved by the copy editor and went through various proof stages intact. In final page proofs it still read as "varieties." However, when the book appeared in print, Roddy witnessed a miracle: The title had again turned into "Kinds of Memory." How do these kinds or varieties of miracles

happen? I do not know. The experts' ways, like those of other powers in our world, are unfathomable.

2. I am simplifying matters a bit, of course. Also, I am talking about the mainstream practices and received wisdom. An alert student of history of science may be able to find exceptions to the caricature I have presented, but the exceptions were rare.

3. I regret that I cannot provide the proof here publicly, for educational reasons. But those readers of this paper who try this fun game and who cannot find the name of a science in the Appendix, can phone or email Roddy Roediger for the answer. Roddy knows. In case Roddy has forgotten, the answer is: Brainerd, C. J., & Reyna, V. F. (2005). *The science of false memory.* New York: Oxford University Press.

4. A parenthetical note, and another practical suggestion to readers who think that talking about "memory matryoshkas" in a Festschrift is unbecoming, or worse. Take the previous paragraph, the one about memory matryoshkas, and rewrite it in loftier, scientific language. You might try invoking the concept of class-inclusion hierarchies; even better, try to tackle the matryoshka problem as an instance of ontological conjunction of N-dimensional mereological and mereotopical relations. Anyhow, try it out, it might be fun.

REFERENCES

Bartlett, F. C. (1932). *Remembering.* Cambridge, UK: Cambridge University Press.

Boring, E. G. (1923, June 6). Intelligence as the tests test it. *New Republic,* 35–37.

Bower, G. H. (2000). A brief history of memory research. In E. Tulving & F. I. M. Craik (Eds.), *The Oxford handbook of memory* (pp. 3–32). New York: Oxford University Press.

Brown, J. (1958). Some tests of the decay theory of immediate memory. *Quarterly Journal of Experimental Psychology, 10,* 12–21.

Cofer, C. N. (1979). Human learning and memory. In E. Hearst (Ed.), *The first century of experimental psychology* (pp. 323–370). Hillsdale, NJ: Lawrence Erlbaum Associates, Inc.

Duncan, R., & Smith, M. W. (1977). *Encyclopedia of ignorance.* Oxford, UK: Pergamon Press.

Ebbinghaus, H. (1885). *Über das Gedächtnis.* Leipzig, Germany: Duncker & Humblot.

Green, C. D. (1992). Of immortal mythological beasts—Operationism in psychology. *Theory and Psychology, 2,* 291–320.

James, W. (1890). *Principles of psychology.* Cambridge, MA: Harvard University Press.

Keppel, G., & Underwood, B. J. (1962). Proactive inhibition in short-term retention of single items. *Journal of Verbal Learning and Verbal Behavior, 1,* 153–161.

McGeoch, J. A., & Irion, A. L. (1952). *The psychology of human learning.* New York: Longmans, Green.

Miller, G. A. (1962). *Psychology: The science of mental life.* Harmondsworth, UK: Penguin Books.

Peterson, L. R., & Peterson, M. J. (1959). Short-term retention of individual verbal items. *Journal of Experimental Psychology, 58,* 193–198.

Roediger, H. L., III. (1990). Implicit memory: A commentary. *Bulletin of the Psychonomic Society, 28,* 373–380.

Roediger, H. L., III. (1993). Learning and memory: Progress and challenge. In D. E. Meyer & S. Kornblum (Eds.), *Attention and performance XIV: Synergies in experimental psychology, artificial intelligence, and cognitive neuroscience* (pp. 509–528). Cambridge, MA: MIT Press.

Roediger, H. L., III. (2003). Reconsidering implicit memory. In J. S. Bowers & C. J. Marsolek (Eds.), *Rethinking implicit memory* (pp. 3–18). Oxford, UK: Oxford University Press.

Roediger, H. L., Dudai, Y., & Fitzpatrick, S. (in press). *Science of memory: Concepts*. London: Oxford University Press.

Roediger, H. L., III, Marsh, E. J., & Lee, S. C. (2002). Kinds of memory. In D. L. Medin & H. Pashler (Eds.), *Stevens' handbook of experimental psychology: Vol. 2. Memory and cognitive processes* (3rd ed. pp. 1–41). New York: John Wiley.

Roediger, H. L., & McDermott, K. B. (1995). Creating false memories: Remembering words not presented in lists. *Journal of Experimental Psychology: Learning, Memory, and Cognition, 21*, 803–814.

Roediger, H. L., & McDermott, K. B. (2000). Tricks of memory. *Current Directions in Psychological Science, 9*, 123–127.

Schacter, D. L. (2001). *Forgotten ideas, neglected pioneers: Richard Semon and the story of memory*. Philadelphia: Psychology Press.

Semon, R. (1904). *Die Mneme*. Leipzig, Germany: W. Engelmann

Waugh, N. C., & Norman, D. A. (1965). Primary memory. *Psychological Review, 72*, 89–104.

APPENDIX: ALPHABETICAL LISTING OF KINDS OF MEMORY

(In most cases only the term modifying "memory" is printed.)

abnormal
abstract
accessible
acoustic
acquisition
active
active cultural
affective
age-related
age-related relational
allocentric
allocentric spatial
animal memory
anterograde
archival cultural
arousal-mediated
articulated
associative
auditory
autobiographical
bodily
brain-stem
cache memory
categorical

cellular
cerebellar
chemical
childhood
cognitive
collective
color memory
concrete
configural
conscious
constructive
context
context-dependent
cortical
cultural
declarative
diencephalic
direct
discovered
disembodied
distinct
distributed
dream memory
dynamic

early
echoic
elementary
emotional
enhanced
episodic
episodic-like
ERP (event-related potentials)
evaluative
event memory
everyday
experiential
expert
explicit
external
eyewitness
facial
fact memory
factual
false
fear-dependent
fear memory
first

flashbulb
forgotten
frontal
future
general
general political
generic
genetic
genuine
gist memory
global
habit
hippocampally-mediated
historical
human
iconic
illusive
illusory
immediate
immunological
impaired
implicit
implicit conceptual
improved
inaccessible
inaccurate
independent
indirect
individual autobiographical
infant memory
intentional
involuntary
involuntary conscious
item-based
item memory
labile
latent
later
lexical
life
list
literal
locale memory
long-term
long-term familiarity
material-specific
mechanical
medial temporal lobe
melodic
meta-memory

mobile memory
modal memory
mood-dependent
motor
muscular
musical
narrative
natural
network
neural
neuronal
new memory
nonconscious
nondeclarative
nonhippocampally
    dependent
normal
object-in-place
object–object association
object-recognition
object–reward association
object working
odor memory
older memory
olfactory
ordinary
organized
original
particular political
Pavlovian
Pavlovian fear
perceptual
perceptually-rich
permanent
personal
personal episodic
personal semantic
phonetic
phonological
place memory
political
potential
practiced
prefrontal
primary
primate
primitive
prior
procedural
prose

prospective
public autobiographical
raw
reactivated
re-embodied
real-world
recall memory
recent
recognition
recollective
reconstructive
recovered
reference
reflective
relational
remote
repisodic
representational
representative
retrieved
retrograde
retrospective
reviewed
right memory
rote
scratch-pad
screen
secondary
self-defining
self memory
semantic
semi-permanent
sense memory
sensitive
sensory
sentence
shape memory
short-term
single
skilled
sleep memory
social
socialized
source
spatial
spatial working
specific
standard
state-dependent
stimulus–response habit

stored
subcortical
subsequent
superior
synaptic
tacit
target memory
temporal
temporal context
test memory
time memory
topographical
traceless

traditional
transactive
trauma
traumatic
trial-unique object
   recognition
true
typical
unaware
unconscious
uncontaminated
unimpaired
unintentional

unitary
unwanted
verbal
verbatim
veridical
visual
visual spatial
voice
waking
well-practiced
working

4

Foxes, Hedgehogs, and Mirror Effects: The Role of General Principles in Memory Research

ROBERT L. GREENE

"*T*he fox knows many things, but the hedgehog knows one big thing." This famous observation (attributed by Berlin, 1953, to a line in fragments of writing believed to be by the ancient Greek poet Archilochus) captures the idea that there are two separate ways of dealing with knowledge. One can be a hedgehog and capture a realm of facts with a single generalization, although inevitably this will lead to the loss of information. Alternatively, one can be a foxlike master of details, although this involves the risk that the big picture may not truly be captured. In any field of research, there is inevitably a need for both foxes and hedgehogs.

Memory research is no exception. Looking at the field of verbal learning from the unreliable perspective of the 21st century, it seems that the early history of this topic was a golden age for hedgehogs. Indeed, much of memory research seems to have been driven by the handful of principles embodied by interference theory (for a review, see Crowder, 1976). More generally in psychology, the research program of the Behaviorist era can be viewed as an ambitious attempt to discover general principles of learning that can apply to different types of information and different species.

Perhaps as a response to the perceived failure of the Behaviorist program and the limitations that became obvious in interference theory, many theorists became skeptical about the wisdom of seeking general principles at all. For example, Baddeley (1978) claimed that "the most fruitful way to extend our understanding of human memory is not to search for broader generalizations and 'principles', but is rather to develop ways of separating out and analyzing more deeply the complex underlying processes" (p. 150). Mandler (1979) called for researchers in memory to "abandon the promised land of simple principles and return to the complexities of the human mind" (p. 305). Tulving (1985) argued for a foxlike approach to memory because "no profound generalizations can be made about memory as a whole, but general statements about particular kinds of memory are perfectly possible" (p. 385).

If the point of these statements is to point out that no memory principles have been found that do not have exceptions, then there is no way to argue against them. However, it seems as if the establishment of principles has been an important path to progress in memory research. Establishing a principle has been an invaluable way to make sense out of a large body of literature. Indeed, some of the most important contributions made by general principles have been those times when they spurred investigations into how they fail.

Interference theory presents a clear case of this. At least since the time of McGeoch (1942), verbal-learning researchers operated under the assumption that a complete understanding of interference would be equivalent to an adequate understanding of memory. To be fair to McGeoch, it should be noted that he actually had a multifactor theory of forgetting; however, his emphasis on interference, and particularly retroactive interference, was his most visible contribution (Crowder, 2003). The development of the basic principles of proactive and retroactive interference was a tremendous accomplishment, well earning Crowder's (1976) praise as "the most comprehensive theoretical system in the field of human learning and memory" (p. 217). The fruitfulness of this system is evident in the repackaging of this approach in newer concepts such as the *fan effect* (Anderson, 1974), *cue overload* (Watkins & Watkins, 1975), and *retrieval-induced forgetting* (Anderson, Bjork, & Bjork, 1994). However invaluable the concept of interference has been, cases where interference has failed to occur have been very influential in the development of memory theory. Release from proactive inhibition (Wickens, Born, & Allen, 1963) and the reverse-interference effect in free recall (Burns, 1989; Thapar, 1996) are particularly important examples.

An example of the changes that may occur in the popularity of a memory principle over time is found in the literature on spaced (or distributed) practice effects. Ebbinghaus (1885/1964, p. 89) noted an advantage for spaced practice and speculated that "*with any considerable number of repetitions* a suitable distribution of them over a space of time is decidedly more advantageous than the massing of them at a single time" (emphasis in original). McGeoch (1942, p. 119) noted, "The generalization that some form of positive distribution yields faster learning than does massed practice holds over so wide a range of conditions that it stands as one of our most general conclusions." Later research on distributed-practice effects was less encouraging, and Underwood (1961), in his review of the literature, emphasized the fact that a distributed-practice advantage was often small or nonexistent. Bugelski (1962) soon found empirical support for the importance of total time spent studying material, no matter how that time is distributed. Cooper and Pantle (1967) carried out an impressive review of the literature and found overwhelming support for a total-time principle. However, the empirical tide turned again, as the method of choice soon became the manipulation of spacing of individual items on a free-recall list (Melton, 1967). A massive literature on spacing effects and distributed practice (see Greene, 2003a, for a review) has established beyond question that the way in which study time is temporally distributed can be critical. The total-time law served its historical purpose by directing researchers' attention at spacing of repetitions and has dropped out of contemporary memory theory. This lesson that distribution of study matters may have been too well-learned. Although the total-time law may have been forgotten, the literature that inspired it still exists, and our historical amnesia about that law has not advanced memory theory. There are many circumstances in which distribution of study has little or no effect, and only total time spent studying matters. Theories of spacing effects that do not offer explanations of situations where only total time matters must be considered inadequate on their face.

The most famous memory principle of all is that of levels of processing (Craik & Lockhart, 1972), rightly argued to have been "cognitive psychology's most successful theory of learning and memory" in recent times (Roediger, 1993, p. 511). This principle was capable of explaining a huge set of empirical findings with a set of simple, easily understood assumptions. However, as Roediger (1993) noted, one reason for its success was undoubtedly that it was (in part) false and could be easily disproven. Indeed, demonstrations of the importance of retrieval conditions (Fisher & Craik, 1977; Morris, Bransford, & Franks, 1977) lent support to principles such as encoding specificity and transfer-appropriate processing. These latter principles have been among the most useful of current ideas in memory theory but are not necessarily without exception.

A principle does not have to be ambitious to be useful. Sometimes, principles can make a contribution by explaining a single, troublesome phenomenon. One such case rises in the literature on hypermnesia, the finding that net recall can increase across several successive recall tests administered on a single list (Erdelyi & Becker, 1974). Arguably, the most puzzling aspect of hypermnesia was that it could be easily found with some materials (e.g., pictures) but not others (e.g., abstract words). Roediger, Payne, Gillespie, and Lean (1982) accounted for this puzzling state of affairs by a recall-level hypothesis: The amount of hypermnesia that could be expected for a particular set of materials depends upon recall levels, with higher recall leading to greater hypermnesia. Although later research indicated that this principle has its limitations (Payne, 1986), it successfully reduced a puzzle about this phenomenon to a functional observation about recall curves.

THE MIRROR EFFECT

Principles or regularities continue to be proposed by theorists. Recognition memory is particularly fertile ground for such principles, as this procedure has been arguably the task most often addressed by formal theories (Ratcliff & McKoon, 2000). Recognition is typically viewed from the perspective of signal detection. This perspective involves the assumption that items in memory can be ordered on a single dimension, sometimes called strength or familiarity. Probability of a positive recognition decision increases as a function of familiarity, which can be viewed in psychophysical terms (Tussing & Greene, 2001). Global-matching models (e.g., Gillund & Shiffrin, 1984; Hintzman, 1988; Murdock, 1982), in which familiarity is determined by the total similarity of a test stimulus to the recent contents of memory, are particularly prominent examples of this approach.

According to this viewpoint, old test stimuli are more likely to receive a positive response than new test stimuli because they are more familiar. How should one treat stimulus differences from this perspective? For example, low-frequency words receive more hits than high-frequency words. The obvious way to explain this finding is to assume that low-frequency words appear more familiar than high-frequency words (perhaps because their more distinctive orthography attracts attention). However, any approach assuming that low-frequency words inherently appear more familiar than high-frequency words on a test would predict that low-frequency new items should receive more false alarms than high-frequency new items. In fact, as a review of the literature by Glanzer and Adams (1985) showed, false-alarm rates were the mirror (i.e., reverse) image of hit rates: Whereas low-frequency items receive more positive responses than high-frequency items when the stimuli are old, high-frequency items receive more positive responses than low-frequency items when the stimuli are new. Glanzer and Adams referred to this pattern as the mirror effect. They later saw this mirror relationship between hit rates and false alarms as one of the "regularities of recognition memory"—that is, one of the empirical principles that should guide theorizing about recognition (Glanzer, Adams, Iverson, & Kim, 1993).

Table 4.1 presents typical mirror-effect data from an unpublished experiment that I carried out. Participants received a 60-item list presented one at a time at a 2 s rate. Half of the items were high-frequency words (frequencies of 100–150 occurrences per million; Thorndike & Lorge, 1944), and the others were low-frequency words (frequencies of 1–5 occurrences per million words). Immediately after presentation of the study list, participants received a self-paced yes/no recognition test. The first column of Table 4.1 presents hit rates and shows the expected pattern of more positive responses to low-frequency words than to high-frequency words. The second column presents false alarms and shows a reversal of conditions, with low-frequency words having a lower rate of false alarms than high-frequency words. The fact that the ordering of conditions in false-alarm rates is the mirror image of the ordering of hit rates is what makes this an example of the mirror effect.

One can find situations, through a manipulation of the instructions given either at encoding or test, where word frequency does not lead to a mirror effect in recognition (e.g., Greene, 1996; Joordens & Hockley, 2000). Still, the generality of the mirror effect when word frequency is manipulated is well-established. Glanzer and Adams (1985) also reviewed evidence that concreteness can lead to a mirror effect, with concrete words receiving more hits and fewer false alarms than

TABLE 4.1 Proportion of Positive Responses in Recognition as a Function of Word Frequency

	Item status	
	Old (hits)	**New (false alarms)**
Low frequency	.84	.08
High frequency	.71	.22

abstract words; however, this pattern was more inconsistent, possibly because concreteness has only a weak and inconsistent effect on recognition.

The mirror effect is a simple pattern, but it seems rather difficult for familiarity theories, such as the global-matching models, to explain. Why should one class of stimuli seem less familiar than another class when both are old but more familiar when both are new? This awkwardness is why the mirror effect is one of the phenomena "that are at the heart of testing and evaluating the models" of recognition memory (Ratcliff & McKoon, 2000, p. 575). Theorists have adopted several different strategies here. One possible strategy is to assume that recognition responses are based on familiarity but that weak new items gain disproportionately in strength when they are presented in a list so that they become exceptionally strong when old. Murdock (2003) suggested this leapfrog effect as a general tendency in recognition. Alternatively, some theorists have seen the mirror effect as requiring a change in the response–decision stage in recognition. For example, by assuming the use of likelihood ratios in recognition so that subjects essentially ask themselves "How likely is it that this stimulus is old given this familiarity level and this type of stimulus?", one can come up with a mirror pattern (Glanzer et al., 1993; McClelland & Chappell, 1999; Shiffrin & Steyvers, 1997). Approaches like these are only reasonable if it is the case that the mirror pattern is indeed a general principle of recognition memory.

EXCEPTIONS TO THE MIRROR PATTERN

Not all occurrences of the mirror-effect pattern, where a condition with higher hit rates will have lower false-alarm rates, are theoretically important. This mirror pattern may be found in between-subject or between-list manipulations of experimental conditions, such as retention interval. This does not present a problem for any reasonable theory of memory because this pattern can be easily explained by assuming that participants use different response criteria in different conditions. If two lists differ markedly in strength and participants use different criteria for the lists, one list can have more hits and fewer false alarms than the other (Stretch & Wixted, 1998). However, the mirror effect is more difficult to explain when different stimulus classes are compared on a single list. Participants sometimes seem quite unaware of differences between stimuli (Greene & Thapar, 1994; Wixted, 1992) and appear reluctant to shift response criteria back and forth on a single list even when strength differences are obvious (Morrell, Gaitan, & Wixted, 2002; Stretch & Wixted, 1998). Thus, a simple criteria-shift explanation appears implausible for this type of situation.

However, it is not at all clear that the mirror effect is commonly found in within-list manipulations of stimulus class, outside of word frequency. If the mirror effect is the exception, not the norm, the argument for trying to explain it in terms of general principles of recognition (be they leapfrogging or reliance on likelihood ratios) would seem to be more strained.

A mirror effect would be found when two stimulus classes differ in recognition accuracy and when the class with higher accuracy has both more hits and fewer false alarms than the other. One way in which the mirror principle can be violated is if two conditions differ in accuracy but one class has both more hits and more false alarms than the other condition. Maddox and Estes (1997) called this arrangement of data a concordant pattern. A review of the literature suggests that concordant patterns are far from rare and that the mirror effect has quite limited generality.

The Revelation Effect

Watkins and Peynircioglu (1990) reported a series of experiments on a phenomenon that they happened upon serendipitously. Participants saw a list of eight-letter words. They were then given a recognition test. On this test, some words were presented normally. However, some were presented in an "unfolding" format, so that subjects might first see two letters of the test word, then three, then four, until the entire word is presented; in this condition, no response could be given until the complete word was shown so that the objective stimulus at the time of test was identical in the two testing formats. Participants gave more positive responses when tested in this unfolding condition than when test stimuli were presented normally. This effect was present in both hits and false alarms. Watkins and Peynircioglu referred to this pattern as the *revelation effect* because it seemed that test stimuli that were revealed to the subject were more likely to elicit positive responses than stimuli that were presented normally. Watkins and Peynircioglu explored several different methods of revelation (such as letter unscrambling or rotation) and found similar effects.

Table 4.2 presents an unpublished replication that I have carried out in my lab. Participants received an 80-word list presented one at a time at a 2 s rate. Immediately after presentation of the list, they were given a self-paced yes/no recognition test on 160 words. Half of the test words (the control condition) were presented normally. The other test words (the revelation condition) required unscrambling; that is, they were initially presented as anagrams that had to be solved before a recognition judgment could be made. As is obvious in Table 4.2, both hits and false alarms were more common in the revelation condition than in the control condition, with the difference between conditions being greater in false-alarm rates than in hit rates.

It turns out that the term *revelation effect* is somewhat misleading because gradual revelation of the test stimulus is not truly needed at all. Westerman and Greene (1996) showed that a similar pattern would be obtained even when the

TABLE 4.2   Proportion of Positive Responses in Recognition as a Function of Revelation

	Item status	
	Old (hits)	New (false alarms)
Revelation	.70	.45
Control	.59	.28

items that were revealed did not match the items that were recognized. We used anagram-solution as our revelation task. People would receive a study list of words normally. On the subsequent recognition test, some items would be shown normally. Other test items would be preceded by revelation of a different word. For example, a participant may have to solve the anagram DNRPOIAR to reveal the word RAINDROP. Immediately afterward, a different word (e.g., VINEYARD) was shown, and the participant would have to make a recognition decision on it. Both hit and false-alarm rates were higher in this revelation condition than in the control condition. This finding seems perplexing because it appears so irrational. Why should having solved an anagram for RAINDROP make you more likely to believe that VINEYARD was on the study list? Subsequent experiments showed that many different experimental tasks, when presented immediately prior to a recognition response, can elicit a revelation effect (Westerman & Greene, 1998). Indeed, even presenting test stimuli in pairs can significantly increase hits and false alarms (Greene & Klein, 2004).

For the revelation effect to constitute a violation of the mirror pattern, it must be the case that hits and false alarms are concordant when a difference in accuracy is found. The concordant pattern is regularly found. The difference in accuracy is statistically significant less often because it is usually smaller in magnitude than the difference in rates of positive responses. Still, the typical result is that revelation increases false alarms more than it increases hits, leading to a numerical decrease in accuracy. Although this decrease is not significant in every study, it becomes clear in a quantitative review of the literature (Hicks & Marsh, 1998).

The meaning and interpretation of the revelation effect are still controversial issues. One interpretation is that the revelation effect can be viewed as a sort of cognitive leakage, where activation caused by the revelation task is attributed to the recognition test item, which then appears particularly familiar (Greene & Klein, 2004; Westerman & Greene, 1996, 1998). However, some have argued that the revelation effect is a complex phenomenon requiring multiple explanations for the different designs in which it may be found (Verde & Rotello, 2004). Still, for our purposes, the most important point is that this is an easily-replicated pattern where the mirror effect is clearly violated.

Pre-Exposure Effects

Presumably, the most straightforward way to manipulate the familiarity of a stimulus is to repeat it. A common way of executing this manipulation has been called the three-phase design by Maddox and Estes (1997). In a prototypical version of this design, the first phase is a pre-exposure phase, in which participants are given a set of stimuli. In a second phase, participants receive a study list that contains some of the pre-exposed items, as well as other items that had not been shown earlier. In the third phase, a memory test on the study list is administered.

The results of experiments using this design are fairly consistent. Pre-exposure leads to a marked reduction in recognition accuracy. That is, on a recognition test requiring discrimination between stimuli either presented or, or absent from, the study list given in the second phase, accuracy is lower for items that had been pre-exposed (e.g., Chalmers & Humphreys, 1998; Dobbins, Kroll, Yonelinas, & Liu, 1998; Greene, 1999; Maddox & Estes, 1997; Tulving & Kroll, 1995). For our purposes, the central focus of concern is on the relationship between hits and false alarms. The most common pattern is for pre-exposure to increase both hits and false alarms, with the effect being greater on false alarms than on hits. This disparate effect on hits and false alarms accounts for the accuracy difference that is observed. That is, a concordant pattern, not a mirror pattern, is typically observed.

If familiarity is viewed in psychophysical terms (Tussing & Greene, 2001), this pattern is entirely reasonable. Pre-exposure presumably can make a stimulus appear more familiar. However, presentation on a study list will have a less obvious effect on a stimulus that is already strong (as a result of pre-exposure) than on a weaker stimulus, so that pre-exposure will have a greater effect on false alarms than on hits. Still, this concordant pattern is evidence that the mirror pattern is far from constituting a general law of recognition functioning.

Pseudoword Effect

It might be argued that generalizations about the mirror pattern were never intended to apply to experimental manipulations but only to stimulus differences. However, even when looking at recognition performance on different stimulus classes, a mirror pattern is not always found. The best documented such case would involve comparisons of words with pseudowords (pronounceable nonwords). (An equivalent comparison would be between common words and extremely rare words that can be presumed to be unknown by the participants; these extremely rare words can be assumed to be like pseudowords.) The standard finding is that, although recognition accuracy is greater for words than for pseudowords, participants give more positive responses to pseudowords than to words (e.g., Greene, 2003b; Hintzman & Curran, 1997; Hockley & Niewiadomski, 2001; Whittlesea & Williams, 2000, 2001; Wixted, 1992). The difference between pseudowords and words is greater for false alarms than for hits, leading to the accuracy advantage for words.

One class of explanation for the pseudoword effect (i.e., greater hits and false alarms to pseudowords than to words) could be termed overcompensation accounts. According to this sort of account, participants know that pseudowords are not as memorable as words. When they are tested for recognition, participants try to compensate for this memorability difference by using a much lower response criterion for pseudowords than for words (Hockley & Niewiadomski, 2001; Stretch & Wixted, 1998). Alternatively, participants may compensate by rescaling the familiarity values of the pseudowords (Hintzman & Curran, 1997). These accounts assume that participants go overboard in this compensation process, and this overcompensation leads to a response bias in favor of pseudowords. However, this sort of overcompensation appears unlikely. Although it is reasonable that people may make mistakes when trying to set response criteria, it is not clear why they should systematically make mistakes in the same direction (i.e., overcompensation). Moreover, there are empirical findings that are inconsistent with this account. A bias in favor of pseudowords can be found in forced-choice recognition, where no response criteria may be needed (Greene, 2003b; Wixted, 1992). Moreover, the pseudoword effect can still be found even when there is no memorability advantage for words and therefore no need for compensation at all (Greene, 2003b).

The explanation that I favor is that pseudowords are truly more familiar than words (Greene, 2003b). Familiarity is assumed to be determined by the similarity of a stimulus to the study list. All words contain semantic features that make each of them distinctive and unique. These distinctive semantic features may make them less similar to other items on the study list, reducing their overall familiarity. In contrast, pseudowords have much less semantic content. Their similarity to the study list would be based largely on their physical features that overlap greatly between items. Indeed, similarity ratings suggested that pseudowords are viewed as more similar to each other than are words.

Whatever the cause of the pseudoword effect, it is clear that this constitutes a case where the mirror pattern can be violated with a stimulus comparison. Ironically, the prototypical case of the mirror effect involved comparing high-frequency with low-frequency words. However, if extremely low-frequency words are used instead, the mirror pattern is violated.

Similarity and Associative Recognition

The studies reviewed so far have involved recognition of words. However, it has been common also to test recognition of pairings. In this associative-recognition task, participants study lists of word pairs. At the time of test, they again receive pairs. All of the words in the test pairs had been presented on the study list. However, some pairs on the test are rearranged (that is, combining words that had not been paired on the study list) while others are intact. The participants are told to give positive responses to intact pairs and negative responses to rearranged pairs.

When dealing with memory for pairs, similarity is an obvious variable to examine, insofar as theorists dating back at least to Aristotle have noted that similarity influences the formation of associations. In our lab, we studied associative recognition for pairs composed either of similar (or related) words, such as INFANT–BABY or unrelated words (Greene & Tussing, 2001). Our central finding was that similarity impaired accuracy. That is, both hits and false alarms were more common to related pairs than to unrelated pairs. This effect was greater on false alarms than on hits, leading to a decrement in accuracy for related pairs. The causes of this pattern are somewhat obscure. However, the explanation that we favored emphasized the assumption that related words presumably occurred together often in pre-experimental contexts. These pre-experimental occurrences can increase the familiarity of a pair of related words.

Affect and Recognition Memory

Although the original Glanzer and Adams (1985) paper has been justly hailed as establishing an important regularity of recognition memory, that study actually noted that exceptions to the pattern already existed in the literature. In subsequent years, these exceptions have received little notice. One such exception that was mentioned by Glanzer and Adams had been published by Ortony, Turner, and Antos (1983), who investigated the role of affect in recognition memory for sentences. They compared recognition for positive sentences, such as "The warm blanket covered the new puppy," and negative sentences, such as "The dangerous landslide scattered the rotten garbage." They found that participants gave more positive responses to positive sentences than to negative sentences. In our laboratory, we have successfully replicated this pattern, finding both a small (but statistically significant) effect on accuracy and a larger effect on positive response rates, with participants making more hits and false alarms to positive sentences than to negative sentences. Thus, the limitations on the mirror effect as a regularity of recognition memory should have been clear even at the time of the first paper on the topic.

CONCLUSION

The discovery of the mirror effect by Glanzer and Adams (1985) was an important contribution to the literature on recognition memory. It led to much more sophisticated view of the role of word frequency in recognition, demonstrated the importance of the relationship between hits and false alarms, and encouraged consideration of complex decision processes in recognition. However, like all memory principles, the mirror effect is useful only as long as its exceptions are also kept in mind. As is obvious from the above review, many stimulus comparisons can lead to a concordant pattern, rather than a mirror pattern.

One impulse among memory theorists has been to deal with the mirror effect by altering our assumptions about the nature of recognition memory (e.g., McClelland & Chappell, 1999; Murdock, 2003; Shiffrin & Steyvers, 1997). However, none of these approaches even attempts to offer an explanation of when mirror effects will not be found. If it turns out that few stimulus comparisons lead to mirror effects, then it may be more useful to explain the mirror effect not in terms of broad conceptions of recognition but rather as a result of the properties of the stimuli used in experiments that find mirror effects. For example, some theorists now attribute the mirror effect in word-frequency experiments to greater recollection of low-frequency targets than high-frequency targets and greater familiarity of high-frequency lures than low-frequency lures (Joordens & Hockley, 2000; Reder et al., 2000). Such accounts can successfully explain the presence of mirror effects in word-frequency experiments without necessarily predicting that they must always be found in all stimulus comparisons. However, it should be noted that no theory has attempted to offer even a post hoc explanation of when mirror patterns will and will not occur. Theories capable of making a priori predictions to new stimulus domains seem to be even further away in the future.

In recent years, recognition memory has been arguably the central focus for those interested in developing formal models of memory. The mirror effect has become one of the central principles that must be explained by such models.

However, no theory currently exists that even attempts to explain both the mirror effect and its exceptions. A successful account of recognition memory will require us to be both hedgehogs, ever in search of general principles, and foxes, never forgetting the particular exceptions.

Long ago, Berlin (1953) noted that many of the world's great figures in fields such as literature, philosophy, and science can be classified as either foxes or hedgehogs. However, a field clearly benefits from both approaches. To take an example from the field of memory, I think that few would deny that we have benefited both from the presentation of broad principles, such as levels of processing and transfer-specific processing, and from the demonstrations of exceptions to these principles. In practice, the most fascinating accomplishments in the psychology of memory have been those that enabled us to see remembering in new ways. We will always benefit from being reminded of the elegant simplicity and beautiful complexity of human memory.

REFERENCES

Anderson, J. R. (1974). Retrieval of prepositional information from long-term memory. *Cognitive Psychology, 6,* 451–474.

Anderson, M. C., Bjork, R. A., & Bjork, E. L. (1994). Remembering can cause forgetting: Retrieval dynamics in long-term memory. *Journal of Experimental Psychology: Learning, Memory, and Cognition, 20,* 1063–1087.

Baddeley, A. D. (1978). The trouble with levels: A reexamination of Craik and Lockhart's framework for memory research. *Psychological Review, 85,* 139–152.

Berlin, I. (1953). *The hedgehog and the fox: An essay on Tolstoy's theory of history.* New York: Simon & Schuster.

Bugelski, B. R. (1962). Presentation time, total time, and mediation is paired associate learning. *Journal of Experimental Psychology, 63,* 409–412.

Burns, D. J. (1989). Proactive interference: An individual item versus relational processing account. *Journal of Memory and Language, 28,* 345–359.

Chalmers, K. A., & Humphreys, M. S. (1998). Role of generalized and episode specific memories in the word frequency effect in recognition. *Journal of Experimental Psychology: Learning, Memory, and Cognition, 24,* 610–632.

Cooper, E. H., & Pantle, A. J. (1967). The total-time hypothesis in verbal learning. *Psychological Bulletin, 68,* 221–234.

Craik, F. I. M., & Lockhart, R. S. (1972). Levels of processing: A framework for memory research. *Journal of Verbal Learning and Verbal Behavior, 11,* 671–684.

Crowder, R. G. (1976). *Principles of learning and memory.* Hillsdale, NJ: Lawrence Erlbaum Associates, Inc.

Crowder, R. G. (2003). McGeoch, John A. (1897–1942). In J. H. Byrne (Ed.), *Learning and memory* (2nd ed., pp. 362–364). New York: Macmillan.

Dobbins, I. G., Kroll, N. E. A., Yonelinas, A. P., & Liu, Q. (1998). Distinctiveness in recognition and free recall: The role of recollection in the rejection of the familiar. *Journal of Memory and Language, 38,* 381–400.

Ebbinghaus, H. E. (1964). *Memory: A contribution to experimental psychology.* New York: Dover. (Original work published 1885)

Erdelyi, M. H., & Becker, J. (1974). Hypermnesia for pictures: Incremental memory for pictures but not for words in multiple recall trials. *Cognitive Psychology, 6,* 159–171.

Fisher, R. P., & Craik, F. I. M. (1977). Interactions between encoding and retrieval operations in cued recall. *Journal of Experimental Psychology: Human Learning and Memory, 3,* 701–711.

Gillund, G., & Shiffrin, R. M. (1984). A retrieval model for both recognition and recall. *Psychological Review, 91,* 1–65.

Glanzer, M., & Adams, J. K. (1985). The mirror effect in recognition memory. *Memory and Cognition, 13,* 8–20.

Glanzer, M., Adams, J. K., Iverson, G. J., & Kim, K. (1993). The regularities of recognition memory. *Psychological Review, 100,* 546–567.

Greene, R. L. (1996). Mirror effect in order and associative information: The role of response strategies. *Journal of Experimental Psychology: Learning, Memory, and Cognition, 22,* 687–695.

Greene, R. L. (1999). The role of familiarity in recognition. *Psychonomic Bulletin and Review, 6,* 309–312.

Greene, R. L. (2003a). Distributed practice effects. In J. H. Byrne (Ed.), *Learning and memory* (2nd ed., pp. 115–118). New York: Macmillan.

Greene, R. L. (2003b). Recognition memory for pseudowords. *Journal of Memory and Language, 50,* 259–267.

Greene, R. L., & Klein, A. A. (2004). Does recognition of single words predict recognition of two? *American Journal of Psychology, 117,* 215–227.

Greene, R. L., & Thapar, A. (1994). Mirror effect in frequency discrimination. *Journal of Experimental Psychology: Learning, Memory, and Cognition, 20,* 946–952.

Greene, R. L., & Tussing, A. A. (2001). Similarity and associative recognition. *Journal of Memory and Language,* 573–584.

Hicks, J. L., & Marsh, R. L. (1998). A decrement-to-familiarity interpretation of the revelation effect from forced-choice tests of recognition memory. *Journal of Experimental Psychology: Learning, Memory, and Cognition, 24,* 1105–1120.

Hintzman, D. L. (1988). Judgments of frequency and recognition memory in a multiple-trace memory model. *Psychological Review, 95,* 528–551.

Hintzman, D. L., & Curran, T. (1997). Comparing retrieval dynamics in recognition memory and lexical decision. *Journal of Experimental Psychology: General, 126,* 228–247.

Hockley, W. E., & Niewiadomski, M. W. (2001). Interrupting recognition memory: Tests of a criterion-change account of the revelation effect. *Memory and Cognition, 22,* 713–722.

Joordens, S., & Hockley, W. E. (2000). Recollection and familiarity through the looking glass: When old does not mirror new. *Journal of Experimental Psychology: Learning, Memory, and Cognition, 26,* 1534–1555.

Maddox, W. T., & Estes, W. K. (1997). Direct and indirect stimulus-frequency effects in recognition. *Journal of Experimental Psychology: Learning, Memory, and Cognition, 23,* 539–559.

Mandler, G. (1979). Organization and repetition: Organizational principles with special reference to rote learning. In L. G. Nilsson (Ed.), *Perspectives on memory research: Essays in honor of Uppsala University's 500th anniversary* (pp. 293–327). Hillsdale, NJ: Lawrence Erlbaum Associates, Inc.

McClelland, J. L., & Chappell, M. (1999). Familiarity breeds differentiation: A Bayesian approach to the effects of experience in recognition memory. *Psychological Review, 105,* 724–760.

McGeoch, J. A. (1942). *The psychology of human learning*. New York: Longmans, Green.

Melton, A. W. (1967). Repetition and retrieval from memory. *Science, 158*, 532.

Morrell, H. E. R., Gaitan, S., & Wixted, J. T. (2002). On the nature of the decision axis in signal-detection-based models of recognition memory. *Journal of Experimental Psychology: Learning, Memory, and Cognition, 28*, 1095–1110.

Morris, C. D., Bransford, J. D., & Franks, J. J. (1977). Levels of processing versus transfer appropriate processing. *Journal of Verbal Learning and Verbal Behavior, 16*, 519–533.

Murdock, B. B. (1982). A theory for the storage and retrieval of item and associative information. *Psychological Review, 89*, 609–626.

Murdock, B. B. (2003). The mirror effect and the spacing effect. *Psychonomic Bulletin and Review, 10*, 570–588.

Ortony, A., Turner, T. J., & Antos, S. J. (1983). A puzzle about affect and recognition memory. *Journal of Experimental Psychology: Learning, Memory, and Cognition, 9*, 725–729.

Payne, D. G. (1986). Hypermnesia for pictures and words: Testing the recall level hypothesis. *Journal of Experimental Psychology: Learning, Memory, and Cognition, 12*, 16–29.

Ratcliff, R., & McKoon, G. (2000). Memory models. In E. Tulving & F. I. M. Craik (Eds.), *The Oxford handbook of memory* (pp. 571–581). New York: Oxford University Press.

Reder, L. M., Nhouyvanisvong, A., Schunn, C. D., Ayers, M. S., Angstadt, P., & Hiraki, K. (2000). A mechanistic account of the mirror effect for word frequency: A computational model of remember–know judgments in a continuous recognition paradigm. *Journal of Experimental Psychology: Learning, Memory, and Cognition, 26*, 294–320.

Roediger, H. L. (1993). Learning and memory: Progress and challenges. In D. E. Meyer & S. Kornblum (Eds.), *Attention and performance XIV: Synergies in experimental psychology, artificial intelligence, and cognitive neuroscience* (pp. 509–528). Cambridge, MA: MIT Press.

Roediger, H. L., Payne, D. G., Gillespie, G. L., & Lean, D. S. (1982). Hypermnesia as determined by level of recall. *Journal of Verbal Learning and Verbal Behavior, 21*, 635–655.

Shiffrin, R. M., & Steyvers, M. (1997). A model for recognition memory: REM: Remembering effectively from memory. *Psychonomic Bulletin and Review, 4*, 145–160.

Stretch, V., & Wixted, J. T. (1998). On the difference between strength-based and frequency-based mirror effects in recognition memory. *Journal of Experimental Psychology: Learning, Memory, and Cognition, 24*, 1379–1396.

Thapar, A. (1996). Reverse-interference effect in free recall. *Journal of Experimental Psychology: Learning, Memory, and Cognition, 22*, 430–437.

Thorndike, E. L., & Lorge, I. (1944). *The teacher's word book of 30,000 words*. New York: Columbia University Press.

Tulving, E. (1985). How many memory systems are there? *The American Psychologist, 40*, 385–398.

Tulving, E., & Kroll, N. (1995). Novelty assessment in the brain and long-term memory encoding. *Psychonomic Bulletin and Review, 2*, 387–390.

Tussing, A. A., & Greene, R. L. (2001). Effects of familiarity level and repetition on recognition accuracy. *American Journal of Psychology, 114*, 31–41.

Underwood, B. J. (1961). Ten years of massed practice on distributed practice. *Psychological Review, 68*, 229–247.

Verde, M. F., & Rotello C. M. (2004). ROC curves show that the revelation effect is not a single phenomenon. *Psychonomic Bulletin and Review*, *11*, 560–566.

Watkins, M. J., & Peynircioglu, Z. F. (1990). The revelation effect: When disguising test items induces recognition. *Journal of Experimental Psychology: Learning, Memory, and Cognition*, *16*, 1012–1020.

Watkins, O. C., & Watkins, M. J. (1975). Build-up of proactive interference as a cue-overload effect. *Journal of Experimental Psychology: Human Learning and Memory*, *1*, 442–452.

Westerman, D. L., & Greene, R. L. (1996). On the generality of the revelation effect. *Journal of Experimental Psychology: Learning, Memory, and Cognition*, *22*, 1147–1153.

Westerman, D. L., & Greene, R. L. (1998). The revelation that the revelation effect is not due to revelation. *Journal of Experimental Psychology: Learning, Memory, and Cognition*, *24*, 377–386.

Whittlesea, B. W. A., & Williams, L. D. (2000). The source of feelings of familiarity: The discrepancy-attribution hypothesis. *Journal of Experimental Psychology: Learning, Memory, and Cognition*, *26*, 547–565.

Whittlesea, B. W. A., & Williams, L. D. (2001). The discrepancy-attribution hypothesis: I. The heuristic basis for feelings of familiarity. *Journal of Experimental Psychology: Learning, Memory, and Cognition*, *27*, 3–13.

Wickens, D. D., Born, D. G., & Allen, C. K. (1963). Proactive inhibition and item similarity in short-term memory. *Journal of Verbal Learning and Verbal Behavior*, *2*, 440–445.

Wixted, J. T. (1992). Subjective memorability and the mirror effect. *Journal of Experimental Psychology: Learning, Memory, and Cognition*, *18*, 681–690.

5

Signal-Detection Theory and the Neuroscience of Recognition Memory

JOHN T. WIXTED

I used my opportunity at the conference in honor of Henry Roediger to weigh in on an issue that is dear to my heart but not to his, namely, the validity and utility of the signal-detection theory of recognition memory. This venerable theory has been applied to problems from virtually every domain of experimental psychology. With regard to recognition memory, the idealized version of signal-detection theory involves two equal-variance Gaussian distributions (one representing targets and the other representing lures) and one decision criterion. Any test item that generates a memory strength exceeding the criterion is declared to be Old, otherwise it is declared to be New (as illustrated in the upper panel of Figure 5.1). Although the idealized equal-variance detection model is often used to illustrate signal-detection theory, much evidence suggests that a quantitatively more accurate version of the theory is an unequal-variance model in which the standard deviation of the target distribution somewhat exceeds that of the lure distribution (Egan, 1958, 1975; Ratcliff, Shue, & Gronlund, 1992), as illustrated in the lower panel of Figure 5.1.

I have long been aware of the fact that signal-detection theory has no place in any of Roediger's research, nor does it have a place in the research of his esteemed mentors, such as Endel Tulving. The theory has, however, been used against them. Santa and Lamwers (1974), for example, took issue with Tulving's interpretation of "recognition failure of recallable words" (Tulving & Thomson, 1973) based on signal-detection theory considerations. In fact, they claimed that this famous phenomenon, which has been taken by many to refute the generate-recognize theory of free recall, actually proved nothing because recognition failure might simply reflect the attractiveness of the lures (not the absence of memory for the targets). More recently, Miller and Wolford (1999) argued that the apparent false memories that are produced by the widely used Deese-Roediger-McDermott (DRM) procedure are not false memories at all. Instead, they argued, a signal-detection

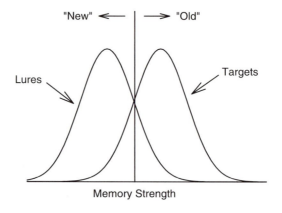

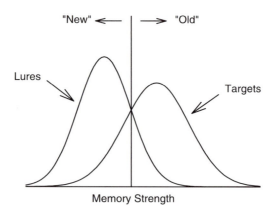

FIGURE 5.1   Equal-variance (upper panel) and unequal-variance (lower panel) signal-detection models of recognition memory.

analysis reveals that those false alarms reflect nothing more than a bias to declare critical lures as being Old.

In the DRM procedure, subjects study a list of words that are all related to a critical item (like *sleep*) that is not presented on the list. When that critical item is presented as a lure on the subsequent recognition test, the false alarm rate is usually very high. Whereas the false alarm rate to typical lures might be .30, the false alarm rate to critical lures is often closer to .70 (about the same as the hit rate to the targets that appeared on the list). Miller and Wolford (1999) asked what the hit rate to the critical item might be if it appeared on the list. As it turned out, the hit rate to the critical item was quite high—in the vicinity of .90, which was much higher than the hit rate associated with the other items that appeared on the list. The authors correctly noted that the high hit and false alarm rates associated with critical items, when run through the computational machinery of signal detection theory, suggest that the difference between normal items (which have lower hit and false alarm rates) and critical items is a matter of bias, not discriminability.

They then made the unfortunately easy mistake of concluding that their analysis therefore showed that the high false alarm rate to critical lures reflected a change in bias, not the presence of false memory. This gave me an opportunity to do something that had not been done before: provide a signal-detection defense of Roddy Roediger's work (Wixted & Stretch, 2000). The story is somewhat detailed; in a nutshell, we showed that precisely the same result (namely, a high false alarm rate *and* a high hit rate) is also predicted by the most basic signal-detection interpretation of the idea that the DRM really does create false memories. As such, the interesting new result reported by Miller and Wolford (1999)—namely, a high hit rate to critical items—far from being dispositive, was actually beside the point.

WHY CARE ABOUT SIGNAL-DETECTION THEORY?

Roediger has worked mostly on problems that do not easily lend themselves to signal-detection theory analyses, and so he has not used the theory in his own work. My own interest stems from a revelation I had years ago as a newly minted PhD with strong ties to operant psychology. When I branched out into human recognition memory, I was appalled to encounter a theory that made unreasonably detailed assumptions about memory strength (e.g., memory was distributed according to Gaussian distributions) and that seemed capable of explaining everything (and, so, explained nothing). My strong inclination was to avoid all of the intricate theoretical baggage associated with signal-detection theory and to instead approach the study of memory, including recognition memory, atheoretically. As a start, I vowed to avoid d' (a measure that seemed too bound to untestable theoretical assumptions) and to stick with an atheoretical measure whenever I wished to quantify recognition memory performance. I would, for example, use percent correct as my measure, or hits minus false alarms, perhaps.

But then I had a revelation, which came from reading Green and Swets (1966) and Macmillan and Creelman (1991). Those books point out something that I initially seriously doubted, namely, that there is no such thing as an atheoretical measure when it comes to quantifying recognition memory performance. As it turns out, the choice is between a measure that lays its assumptions out on the table (e.g., d' of signal-detection theory) versus a measure that hides its assumptions from view (e.g., percent correct), assumptions that, when finally exposed to the light of day, turn out to be preposterous.

Even if its implicit underlying assumptions were not preposterous, taking the "percent correct" approach (or the "hits minus false alarms" approach) removes from consideration any analysis of the Receiver Operating Characteristic (ROC). The reason it does is that ROC data invariably show those measures to be empirically problematic. For example, the hit rate (H) is the proportion of targets that correctly receive an "Old" decision, and the false alarm rate (FA) is the proportion of lures that incorrectly receive an "Old" decision. If there are an equal number of targets and lures on the recognition test, then the proportion correct (p) is given by:

$$p = [H + (1 - FA)]/2$$

Imagine that H = .8 and FA = .3, so p = .75 (i.e., 75% correct). If, before the recognition test, the subject had been asked to respond in a conservative manner (e.g., "only say Old if you are fairly sure the item appeared on the list") both the hit rate and false alarm rate would have been lower. Despite the lower hit and false alarm rates, p should remain the same because changing bias after the list is encoded should not change memory (and p is intended to be a measure of memory). Thus, for example, if instructions to respond in a conservative manner reduced H to .60 and FA to .10, p would still equal .75, in which case our assessment of the state of the participant's memory would remain unaltered (which is as it should be).

If p remained constant across *all* levels of bias, then the relationship between H and FA would be given by solving the above equation for H, which yields:

$$H = FA + (2p - 1)$$

That is, the relationship would be a straight line (of the form $y = mx + b$) with a slope (m) of 1 and an intercept (b) of $2p - 1$. As described in more detail in the next section, the ROC is nothing more than a plot of H versus FA over different levels of bias, and ROCs are almost never linear. The fact that ROCs are curvilinear is another way of saying that p varies as a function of bias instead of remaining constant, as it should. Thus, percent correct is not a valid measure of memory, and the fact that this is known (though not as widely as it should be) illustrates part of the value of ROC analysis.

THE BASICS OF ROC ANALYSIS

How is an ROC actually constructed? Whereas a typical recognition test yields only a single pair of hit and false alarm rates for a given condition (from which basic performance measures like percent correct or d' can be computed), multiple pairs of hit and false alarm rates can be obtained by asking subjects to provide confidence ratings for their recognition decisions. A pair of hit and false alarm rates can be computed for each level of confidence, and those values can be plotted against each other to construct an ROC. For example, imagine that participants respond to the test items using a confidence scale ranging from 1 (definitely new) to 6 (definitely old). Using a scale like this, one simultaneously obtains the old/new decision and the confidence rating in a single response. Ratings of 1 through 3 mean new (with varying degrees of confidence), whereas ratings of 4 through 6 mean old (again, with varying degrees of confidence). One could, of course, ask for the old/new decision first, followed by a confidence rating on a 1–3 scale (unsure to sure), which is a two-step procedure, but the one-step procedure is simpler, and whatever small differences that might exist between them are unlikely to be theoretically significant. As such, the one-step procedure is commonly used.

Whether the one-step or the two-step procedure is used, five pairs of hit and false alarm rates can be computed from the obtained confidence ratings. Using the one-step procedure, for example, the first hit and false alarm rate pair would consist of the proportion of targets and the proportion of lures that received a confidence rating of 6; the second pair would consist of the proportion of targets and the proportion of lures that received a confidence rating of 5 or 6, and so on down to the fifth pair, which would consist of the proportion of targets and the proportion of lures that received a confidence rating of 2 or more (confidence ratings of 1 are not included in an ROC analysis because 100% of the targets and 100% of the lures received a confidence rating of 1 or more). With these five pairs in hand, one can plot the hit rate versus the false alarm rate, and that is the ROC.

Note that one could construct an ROC using other methods that are less convenient than the one outlined above. For example, one could run five separate biasing conditions to obtain the five pairs of hit and false alarm rates. In each condition, subjects would study a list of words and would then be given biasing instructions before the start of the recognition test. In one condition, for example, they would be instructed not to declare an item to be Old unless they were sure that it was. This conservative condition would likely yield hit and false alarm rates much like the hit and false alarm rates that would have been obtained had subjects simply provided confidence ratings on a standard recognition memory test (i.e., by computing the hit and false alarm rates using only decisions associated with a 6 on a 6-point confidence scale). In another biasing condition, subjects might be instructed not to declare an item to be New unless they were sure that it was. Again, this liberal condition would likely yield hit and false alarm rates much like the hit and false alarm rates that would have been obtained had subjects provided confidence ratings on a standard recognition memory test (i.e., by computing the hit and false alarm rates using all decisions except those associated with a 1 on a 6-point confidence scale). The confidence-based ROC is simpler to obtain because one need not run separate biasing conditions, but either method would work.

The question of interest is what theoretically relevant information the ROC provides. If percent correct were a reasonable dependent measure, the five points of the ROC would trace out a linear path. Signal-detection theory, by contrast, predicts that the ROC will be curvilinear. A curvilinear ROC that is consistent with the predictions of signal-detection theory is illustrated in the upper panel of Figure 5.2. Although signal-detection theory predicts a curvilinear ROC when the hit rate is plotted against the false alarm rate, it predicts a linear ROC when the hit and false alarm rates are converted to z-scores (yielding a z-ROC, as shown in the lower panel of Figure 5.2). According to the signal-detection model, the slope of the z-ROC line provides an estimate of the ratio of the standard deviation of the lure distribution to the standard deviation of the target distribution (s_{Lure}/s_{Target}). If an equal-variance model applies (as in the upper panel of Figure 5.1), then the curvilinear ROC should be symmetrical about the diagonal and the slope of the linear z-ROC should be 1.0. But if the standard deviation of the target distribution exceeds that of the lure distribution (as in the lower panel of Figure 5.1), then the curvilinear ROC should be asymmetrical and the slope of the linear z-ROC should be less than 1.0. Previous meta-analyses of confidence-based ROC data generally

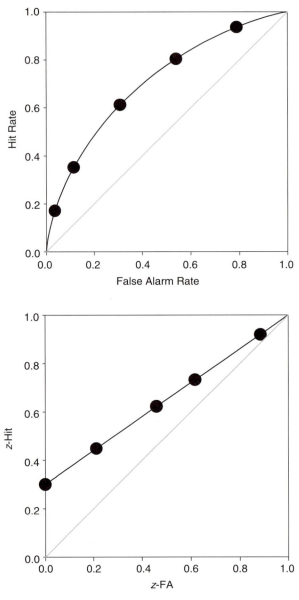

FIGURE 5.2   Idealized ROC data predicted by the signal-detection model (upper panel). The lower panel shows the corresponding ROC data in z-space.

show that curvilinear ROCs are asymmetrical and z-ROCs are well-characterized by a straight line with a slope that is, on average, approximately 0.80 (Glanzer, Kim, Hilford, & Adams, 1999; Ratcliff et al., 1992). Thus, according to the signal detection account, the standard deviation of the target distribution is typically about 1.25 (i.e., 1/0.80) times that of the lure distribution. Findings like these explain why the UVS model shown in the lower panel of Figure 5.1 is regarded by many as the standard model of decision making on a recognition memory task.

ROC ANALYSIS IN COGNITIVE NEUROSCIENCE

The shape of an ROC has been a matter of great interest to the field of cognitive neuroscience in recent years, not because of a newfound appreciation of signal-detection theory but because a newer dual-process theory—one that differs from the standard signal-detection model—suggests that ROC analysis sheds light on the neural correlates of the component processes of recognition memory. A great deal of evidence suggests that recognition memory is supported by two processes, namely, recollection and familiarity (Atkinson & Juola, 1973, 1974; Hintzman & Curran, 1994; Jacoby, 1991; Jacoby & Dallas, 1981; Mandler, 1980). Recollection is a relatively slow process that consists of retrieving specific details associated with the prior presentation of an item, whereas familiarity is a relatively fast process that allows one to appreciate the fact that the item was previously encountered even though no contextual detail can be retrieved.

A model proposed by Yonelinas (1994) was the first dual-process model that could also provide a good description of curvilinear ROCs. According to this account, item recognition is based on recollection whenever recollective strength exceeds a high threshold, otherwise it is based on familiarity. The familiarity process is characterized by an equal-variance signal-detection model (as illustrated in the upper panel of Figure 5.1), but the frequent occurrence of recollection changes the shape of what would otherwise be a symmetric curvilinear ROC with a z-ROC slope of 1.0. Thus, the fact that the slope of the z-ROC for item recognition is typically less than 1.0 is explained not by assuming an unequal-variance detection model but instead by assuming that some responses are based on threshold recollection, whereas others are based on an equal-variance detection model. Yonelinas (1999a) suggested that this high-threshold signal-detection (HTS) model fits ROC data as well as the standard unequal-variance signal-detection (UVS) model. A further advantage of the HTS model is that it yields quantitative estimates of recollection and familiarity when it is fit to ROC data, and its estimates have been shown to approximately correspond to estimates of recollection and familiarity provided by the remember/know procedure (Yonelinas, 2002).

Yonelinas, Kroll, Dobbins, Lazzara, and Knight (1998; Yonelinas et al., 2002) reported that patients with damage thought to be restricted to the hippocampus produced symmetrical ROCs with a z-ROC slope of 1.0 (not less than 1.0, as is usually the case). This is the pattern that, according to the HTS model, occurs when responding is based solely on the familiarity process. Thus, these findings were interpreted to mean that the hippocampus is exclusively involved in the recollection process (not the familiarity process). Recently, Fortin, Wright, and Eichenbaum (2004) conducted an odor recognition study using rats in which ROCs were generated using a reinforcement biasing manipulation. Their results were quite consistent with the HTS model and with the idea that the hippocampus selectively subserves the recollection process. Control rats produced a typical asymmetrical curvilinear ROC when recognition was tested following a 30-min interval, which, in terms of the HTS model, means that responding was based on both recollection and familiarity. By contrast, rats with hippocampal lesions tested under the same conditions exhibited weaker memory and produced a symmetrical curvilinear ROC (one that would have a z-ROC slope of about 1.0). This pattern matches the pattern observed in human amnesics (Yonelinas et al., 1998, 2002) and, according to the HTS model, suggests that responding by the hippocampal rats was based solely on the familiarity process. Fortin et al. (2004) also weakened the memories of control rats by introducing a long (70 min) retention interval, which resulted in a low level of recognition performance that was comparable to that of the hippocampal rats. Even so, the ROC produced following a long retention interval was not symmetrical but was instead so asymmetrical that it was essentially linear (note that this is a linear ROC, not a linear z-ROC). According to the dual-process/detection model, a linear ROC occurs when responding is exclusively based on the all-or-none recollection process. Fortin et al. interpreted their data to mean that familiarity faded rapidly to zero as the retention interval increased (whereas recollection was more durable).

These are remarkable results not only because they provide strong support for the idea that the hippocampus selectively subserves recollection but also because they support the dual-process HTS model and, therefore, contradict the UVS model (a model that has withstood decades of scrutiny). The HTS model can predict a linear ROC by assuming that responding is based exclusively on all-or-none recollection, but the UVS model always predicts a curvilinear ROC.

AN ROC ANALYSIS OF RECOGNITION AND FAMILIARITY IN HIPPOCAMPAL PATIENTS

A natural question to ask is whether the results observed in rats would also be observed in humans. For example, in normal human controls, would the ROC really become linear with increasing retention interval even though nearly five decades of research has not yielded a single linear ROC in humans tested with old/ new recognition? That seemed highly unlikely, but in light of the results reported by Fortin et al. (2004), it also seemed worth testing. Thus, Wais, Wixted, Hopkins, and Squire (2006) investigated this issue.

In addition, we wanted to know how patients with hippocampal lesions might perform. In particular, why do amnesic patients yield a symmetric curvilinear ROC (instead of the usual asymmetric ROC that is explained by the unequal-variance signal-detection model)? In some ways, this outcome may not be surprising at all. Control subjects—who have stronger memories—yield data that are consistent with the unequal-variance detection model, whereas amnesics—who have weaker memories—yield data that are consistent with the equal-variance detection model. Unlike a linear ROC, which contradicts the detection model, the fact that the ROC is more symmetrical when memory is weaker is to be expected in light of prior evidence showing that as memory strength weakens, the difference in variance between the target and lure distributions decreases

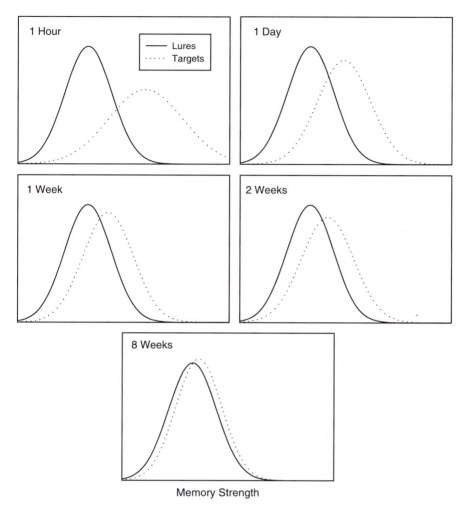

FIGURE 5.3   Illustration of how the target and lure distributions become more similar (i.e., their means and standard deviations become more similar) as the retention interval increases.

(Glanzer et al., 1999). This basic idea is illustrated in Figure 5.3. If the target and lure distributions become more similar as the retention increases (i.e., if their means and standard deviations become more similar), then the ROC should become more symmetrical. And because amnesics have weaker memories than controls, it stands to reason that they should exhibit a more symmetric ROC for that reason alone. However, in the Fortin et al. (2004) study, as memory weakened in the control rats, this expected result did not materialize. Instead, as memory weakened with increasing retention interval, the ROC became linear instead of remaining curvilinear and becoming more symmetric (as the model in Figure 5.3 would predict).

A linear ROC in an old/new recognition procedure—which is what the control rats exhibited following a long retention interval—is an unprecedented finding despite more than 40 years of ROC analysis, and the question arises as to whether that result might be specific to the experimental procedure that Fortin et al. (2004) used. Would the same result be observed using standard recognition memory procedures in humans? We investigated this issue by analyzing the shape of the ROC over a wide range of strength conditions in which young adults were randomly assigned to one of five retention interval conditions (1 hour, 1 day, 1 week, 2 weeks, and 8 weeks). The study lists consisted of 50 words, and the old/new recognition test involved those 50 targets randomly intermixed with 50 lures.

The recognition performance of the young adults decayed as expected over time (Figure 5.4), and the ROCs at each retention interval were clearly curvilinear (Figure 5.5). Even at the longest retention interval, where the ROC must become more linear as it approaches the negative diagonal, the data were much better described by a symmetric curvilinear model than by a linear recollection model. In addition, the ROC was typically asymmetric at the 1 hour retention interval (slope = 0.63) and became ever more symmetric as the overall level of performance decreased. At the longest retention interval, the slope of 1.03 was not significantly different from 1.0. These retention interval results are consistent with the signal detection model depicted in Figure 5.3 and are consistent with Glanzer et al. (1999) reported for a variety of other strength manipulations (e.g., study time, list

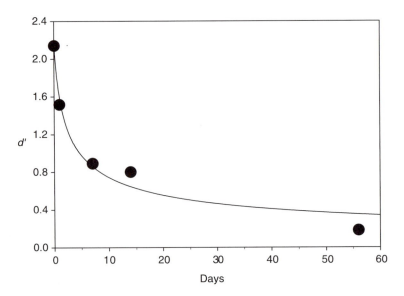

FIGURE 5.4   Recognition memory performance of young adults tested with 50-item lists at five different retention intervals (1 hour, 1 day, 1 week, 2 weeks, 8 weeks). The data were taken from Wais et al. (2006), and the solid curve represents the least squares fit of a three-parameter power function that typically provides a good description of forgetting data (Wixted, 2004).

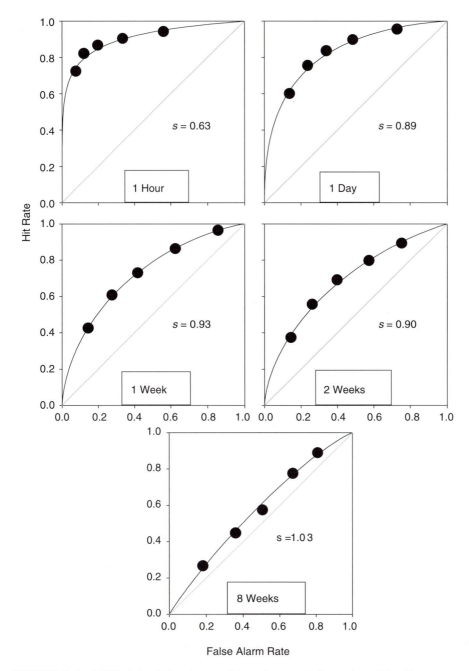

FIGURE 5.5 ROC data (hit rate vs. false alarm rate) produced by the young adults at each retention interval in Wais et al. (2006). The smooth curves represent the best fits from the standard signal-detection model, and the slope (s) values represents one of the parameters that is estimated when performing those fits.

length, word frequency). But they are inconsistent with the results observed in rats (Fortin et al., 2004). It is not clear why rats yielded such an unusual ROC, but the point is that the same result is not observed in humans.

The fact that our young adults yielded an increasingly symmetric ROC as memory strength weakened is consistent with the idea that memory-impaired patients tend to exhibit symmetrical ROCs because they have weak memories (not because their hippocampal lesions have selectively destroyed the recollection process). If this way of thinking is correct, then if memory in the amnesic patients were somehow strengthened (e.g., by extra study time or by using shorter study lists), then they, too, should exhibit an asymmetry. To investigate this issue, we tested six amnesic patients with damage restricted to the hippocampus and eight age-matched elderly controls, all of whom were tested following a 3-minute retention interval. For both groups, the study lists consisted of 50 words. As might be expected, the memory performance of the patients was much worse than that of the controls. We then tested the hippocampal patients again using shorter, 10-item lists, which brought their recognition memory performance to a level closer to that of the elderly controls in the 50-item condition. Were the patients' ROCs as asymmetric as that of the controls once memory strength was equated? This was the critical test.

As shown in the upper panel of Figure 5.6, the ROC produced by the elderly controls following a 3-minute retention interval was also asymmetric, which is to say that the slope (0.83) was less than 1.0. The ROC produced by the hippocampal patients tested under the same conditions, shown in the middle panel of Figure 5.6, was characterized by a slope value of 1.14, which was not significantly different from 1.0 ($p > .15$). The slopes of these two ROCs (patients vs. elderly controls tested with 50-item lists) were significantly different from each other. Thus, these findings are consistent with prior results in that memory-impaired patients do not have a slope less than 1.0 (it was actually somewhat greater than 1.0), whereas control subjects do. This could either mean that the hippocampal patients lack the capacity for recollection and so respond solely on the basis of familiarity (as Fortin et al., 2004, might argue) or, more simply, that the slope decreases as memory strength increases (and the controls have greater memory strength).

When the hippocampal patients were tested using shorter lists, thereby increasing their memory performance to a level near that of the elderly controls, their ROC was as asymmetric as that of the elderly controls as well (lower panel of Figure 5.6). That is, the slope of the z-ROC (0.83) was less than 1.0. Note that the pattern observed for the hippocampal patients is the same one seen in the young adults: As memory strength increases, the ROC becomes more asymmetric. This should not happen if (a) the asymmetry is a reflection of recollection, and (b) the hippocampus subserves the recollection process. Instead, the results suggest that the processes that determine the shape of the ROC are the same in hippocampal patients and controls. What differs is the overall strength of memory. For a given amount of study, amnesic patients will encode less than controls (though the same processes will underlie memory in both cases).

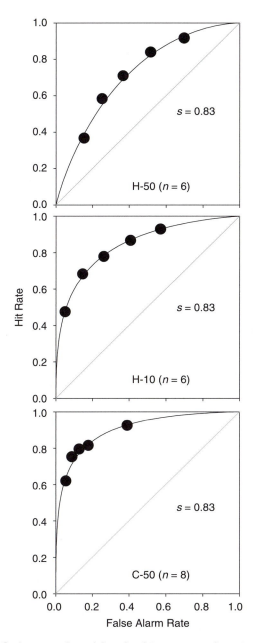

FIGURE 5.6   ROC data produced by the hippocampal patients in the 50-item condition (top panel) and the 10-item condition (middle panel) and by the controls in the 50-item condition (bottom panel) in Wais et al. (2006).

DUAL-PROCESS THEORY AND
SIGNAL-DETECTION THEORY

In the study by Wais et al. (2006), each group ROC was fit by the two-parameter dual-process HTS model and by the two-parameter UVS model using maximum likelihood estimation. In each case, the chi-square goodness-of-fit statistic was lower (indicating a better fit) for the UVS model than for the dual-process HTS model. This was true in all five young adult conditions and in all three of the conditions involving the patients and matched controls. These tests were performed on group ROC data, but the same outcome has been observed in three other studies, all of which compared the fits of the two models at the level of the individual subject (Healy, Light, & Chung, 2005; Heathcote, 2003; Rotello, Macmillan, Hicks, & Hautus, in press). In each case, the signal-detection model far outperformed the dual-process HTS model.

All in all, the results suggest that the standard unequal-variance detection model still provides the only viable account of ROC data. As shown in Figure 5.1, though, the UVS model involves a single decision axis that is simply labeled "memory strength." Does that mean that the results contradict dual-process models in general, not just the dual process HTS model? Not at all. A common misconception is that the unidimensional memory strength axis in signal-detection theory necessarily implies a single process (i.e., one strength dimension = one process). However, this is not the case. Kelley and Wixted (2001), Rotello, Macmillan, and Reeder (2004) and Wixted and Stretch (2004), argued that the memory strength variable in question consists of a combination of recollection and familiarity. This account differs from all other dual process theories, in that it assumes that memory itself is not process pure. That is, instead of individual memory decisions being based *either* on recollection *or* on familiarity, this account assumes that they are typically based on a combination of the two.

In fact, as argued by Wixted and Stretch (2004), such a modification seems sensible in light of the graded nature of the recollection process. If recollection were an all-or-none variable (as the HTS model assumes), then it would make sense to base a recognition decision solely on recollection whenever it occurred (without any regard for familiarity) and to resort to familiarity as a backup whenever recollection was completely absent. But the logic changes the moment one accepts the possibility that recollection is a graded phenomenon. Why would a decision be based exclusively on recollection if only some information about the word is recollected? And why would a decision be based solely on familiarity if partial recollection for that item happens to be available as well? If both recollection and familiarity are continuous variables, combining them into a single memory signal would make more sense than responding based on either one alone. That simple assumption is not only sensible, it also serves to immediately reconcile what might be called the twin peaks of recognition memory, namely, signal-detection theory and dual-process theory. These two theories have remained intact for more than 30 years, yet they have never been reconciled. The only assumption that has kept them apart is the assumption that individual recognition decisions are based either on recollection or on familiarity. But that either/or assumption is not supported by any compelling empirical findings. It is an assumption that was made at the outset and has never been challenged or even seriously investigated. The moment one drops the either/or assumption (as one should if recollection is a graded process), the twin peaks of recognition memory—signal-detection theory and dual-process theory—become reconcilable.

REFERENCES

Atkinson, R. C., & Juola, J. F. (1973). Factors influencing the speed and accuracy of word recognition. In S. Kornblum (Ed.), *Attention and performance IV* (pp. 583–612), New York: Academic Press.

Atkinson, R. C., & Juola, J. F. (1974). Search and decision processes in recognition memory. In D. H. Krantz, R. C. Atkinson, & P. Suppes (Eds.), *Contemporary developments in mathematical psychology* (pp. 243–290). San Francisco: Freeman.

Egan, J. P. (1958). *Recognition memory and the operating characteristic* (Tech. Note AFCRC-TN-58-51). Bloomington, IN: Indiana University, Hearing and Communication Laboratory.

Egan, J. P. (1975). *Signal detection theory and ROC analysis*. Academic Press: New York.

Fortin, N. J., Wright, S. P., & Eichenbaum, H. (2004). Recollection-like memory retrieval in rats is dependent on the hippocampus. *Nature, 431*, 188–191.

Glanzer, M., Kim, K., Hilford, A., & Adams, J. K. (1999). Slope of the receiver-operating characteristic in recognition memory. *Journal of Experimental Psychology: Learning, Memory, and Cognition, 25*, 500–513.

Green, D. M., & Swets, J. A. (1966). *Signal detection theory and psychophysics*. New York: Wiley.

Healy, M. R., Light, L. L, & Chung, C. (2005). Dual-process models of associative recognition in young and older adults: Evidence from receiver operating characteristics. *Journal of Experimental Psychology: Learning, Memory, and Cognition, 31*, 768–788.

Heathcote, A. (2003). Item recognition memory and the ROC. *Journal of Experimental Psychology: Learning, Memory, and Cognition, 29*, 1210–1230.

Hintzman, D. L., & Curran, T. (1994). Retrieval dynamics of recognition and frequency judgments: Evidence for separate processes of familiarity and recall. *Journal of Memory and Language, 33*, 1–18.

Jacoby, L. L. (1991). A process dissociation framework: Separating automatic from intentional uses of memory. *Journal of Memory and Language, 30*, 513–541.

Jacoby, L. L., & Dallas, M. (1981). On the relationship between autobiographical memory and perceptual learning. *Journal of Experimental Psychology: General, 3*, 306–340.

Kelley, R., & Wixted, J. T. (2001). On the nature of associative information in recognition memory. *Journal of Experimental Psychology: Learning, Memory, and Cognition, 27*, 701–722.

Macmillan, N. A., & Creelman, C. D. (2001). *Detection theory: A user's guide*. Mahwah, NJ: Lawrence Erlbaum Associates, Inc.

Mandler, G. (1980). Recognizing: The judgment of previous occurrence. *Psychological Review, 87*, 252–271.

Miller, M. B., & Wolford, G. L. (1999). Theoretical commentary: The role of criterion shift in false memory. *Psychological Review, 106*, 398–405.

Ratcliff, R., Sheu, C. F., & Gronlund, S. D. (1992). Testing global memory models using ROC curves. *Psychological Review, 99*, 518–535.

Rotello, C. M., Macmillan, N. A., Hicks, J. L., & Hautus, M. (in press). Interpreting the effects of response bias on remember–know judgments using signal-detection and threshold models. *Memory and Cognition*.

Rotello, C. M., Macmillan, N. A., & Reeder, J. A. (2004). Sum-difference theory of remembering and knowing: A two-dimensional signal detection model. *Psychological Review, 111*, 588–616.

Santa, J. L., & Lamwers, L. L. (1974). Encoding specificity: Fact or artifact? *Journal of Verbal Learning and Verbal Behavior, 13*, 412–423.

Tulving, E., & Thomson, D. M. (1973). Encoding specificity and retrieval processes in episodic memory. *Psychological Review, 80*, 352–373.

Wais, P. E., Wixted, J. T., Hopkins, R. O., & Squire, L. R. (2006). The hippocampus supports both the recollection and the familiarity components of recognition memory. *Neuron, 49*, 459–468.

Wixted, J. T. (2004). On common ground: Jost's (1987) law of forgetting and Ribot's (1881) law of retrograde amnesia. *Psychological Review, 111*, 864–879.

Wixted, J. T., & Stretch, V. (2000). The case against a criterion-shift account of false memory. *Psychological Review, 107*, 368–376.

Wixted, J. T., & Stretch, V. (2004). In defense of the signal detection interpretation of remember/know judgments. *Psychonomic Bulletin and Review, 11*, 616–641.

Yonelinas, A. P. (1994). Receiver-operating characteristics in recognition memory: Evidence for a dual-process model. *Journal of Experimental Psychology: Learning, Memory, and Cognition, 20*, 1341–1354.

Yonelinas, A. P. (1999). Recognition memory ROCs and the dual-process Signal Detection Model: Comment on Glanzer, Kim, Hilford, and Adams (1999). *Journal of Experimental Psychology: Learning, Memory, and Cognition, 25*, 514–521.

Yonelinas, A. P. (2002). The nature of recollection and familiarity: A review of 30 years of research. *Journal of Memory and Language, 46*, 441–517.

Yonelinas, A. P., Kroll, N. E. A., Dobbins, I. G., Lazzara, M., & Knight, R. T. (1998). Recollection and familiarity deficits in amnesia: Convergence of remember/know, process dissociation, and receiver operating characteristic data. *Neuropsychology, 12*, 1–17.

Yonelinas, A. P., Kroll, N. E., Quamme, J. R., Lazzara, M. M., Sauve, M. J., Widaman, K. F., & Knight, R. T. (2002). Effects of extensive temporal lobe damage or mild hypoxia on recollection and familiarity. *Nature Neuroscience, 5*, 1236–1241.

6

Is Expanded Retrieval Practice a Superior Form of Spaced Retrieval? A Critical Review of the Extant Literature

DAVID A. BALOTA, JANET M. DUCHEK, and JESSICA M. LOGAN

*C*onsider the following scenario: You are in the age range of most of the contributors to this volume and are at a neighborhood party. You are introduced to a person named Mark Finglestein. What would be the best procedure to learn this person's name so you are not embarrassed in future chance encounters in the neighborhood? One procedure would be to simply rehearse the name over and over again via massed practice. Of course, as students of learning and memory, we all know that this procedure is doomed to failure. Another procedure would be to space one's retrieval such that after every minute or so one attempts to retrieve the name Mark Finglestein. Because of the well-known benefits of spaced practice, this procedure is much more likely to succeed. A third procedure would be to gradually expand the intervals between the retrieval attempts. For example, you may first retrieve the name after 15 seconds, then 45 seconds, and then 2 minutes. This procedure takes advantage of the benefits of spacing but also maintains relatively high levels of retrieval success. There is evidence suggesting that this procedure may indeed be better than the simple spaced retrieval. In fact, the benefits of expanded retrieval have been at the center of considerable work in both educational and clinical settings.

The present chapter reviews the evidence concerning the benefits of expanded retrieval over equal interval conditions. We will first provide some historical background on the spacing effect, since expanded retrieval may be considered a special case of spacing. We will then critically evaluate the evidence concerning expanded and equal interval retrieval practice. We will conclude with a discussion of some potential limits of expanded retrieval, theoretical implications, and possible avenues for future research.

THE SPACING EFFECT

The spacing effect is one of the most ubiquitous findings in learning and memory. Performance on a variety of tasks is better when the repetition of the to-be-learned information is distributed as opposed to massed during acquisition. This observation was first formalized in Jost's law, which states that "if two associations are of equal strength but of different age, a new repetition has a greater value for the older one" (McGeogh, 1943). Spacing effects occur across domains (e.g., learning perceptual motor tasks vs. learning lists of words), across species (e.g., rats, pigeons, and humans), across age groups and individuals with different memory impairments, and across retention intervals of seconds to months (see Cepeda, Pashler, Vul, Wixted, & Rohrer, 2006; Crowder, 1976; Dempster, 1996, for reviews). In this light, it is interesting that spacing effects have not received much attention in Cognitive Psychology textbooks. In fact, in our sampling of seven such textbooks, only one had a section dedicated to this topic, while virtually all cognitive textbooks discussed mnemonic techniques such as the pegword or method of loci. Given the power and simplicity of implementing spaced practice, we clearly hope this changes in the future.

As a sidebar, we felt it was particularly fitting to discuss the spacing effect as part of a book honoring the contributions of Roddy Roediger. Roddy's mentor, Robert Crowder (1976) devoted considerable discussion (over 40 pages) of his classic book, *The Principles of Learning and Memory*, to the effects of spacing on learning and memory. Moreover, Arthur Melton, Roddy's academic grandfather, wrote a definitive piece on this topic in 1970. As noted in Melton's paper, spacing effects, like many things, can be traced back to observations by William James (Roddy's great-great-great grandfather) concerning the benefits of alternating swimming in the summer and skating in the winter. In addition to his academic lineage, spacing effects are also quite consistent with Roddy's functionalist approach in his work and the importance of making a connection between practical implications and basic experimental research. Recently, Roddy has been exploring the application of cognitive principles to educational practice, and has already made important contributions in this domain (see, for example, Roediger & Karpicke, 2006). Expanded retrieval and the spacing effect have been at the center of considerable work in educational settings, and Roddy has been exploring this issue in a number of recent projects (e.g., Karpicke & Roediger, 2005).

SPACING EFFECTS, POSSIBLE LIMITATIONS, AND THE APPEAL OF EXPANDED RETRIEVAL

Although spaced presentation is clearly beneficial in most situations, as with everything, there are some limitations. For example, there is evidence of a spacing by retention interval interaction. Specifically, massed items are actually better retained after a short retention interval, whereas spaced items are better retained after a long retention interval. This observation was first obtained by Peterson,

Wampler, Kirkpatrick, and Saltzman (1963), and was replicated by Glenberg (1977) and Balota, Duchek, and Paullin (1989).

There are numerous theoretical accounts of the spacing effect (see Cepeda et al., 2006, for a review); however, the spacing by retention interval interaction would appear to be most consistent with an encoding variability account. Because of the relevance of this theoretical framework to our discussion of the benefits of expanded retrieval in a later section, we will briefly describe the encoding variability account of the spacing by retention interval interaction. According to encoding variability theory, performance on a memory test is dependent upon the overlap between the contextual information available at the time of test and the contextual information available during encoding. During massed study, there is relatively little time for contextual elements to fluctuate between presentations and so this condition produces the highest performance in an immediate memory test, when the test context strongly overlaps with the same contextual information encoded during both of the massed presentations. In contrast, when there is spacing between the items, there is time for fluctuation to take place between the presentations during study, and hence there is an increased likelihood of having multiple unique contexts encoded. Because a delayed test will also allow fluctuation of context, it is better to have multiple unique contexts encoded, as in the spaced presentation format, as opposed to a single well-encoded context, as in the massed presentation format.

Because of evidence regarding a contextual encoding deficit in older adults (see Burke & Light, 1981; Duchek, 1984), Balota et al. (1989) investigated the spacing by retention interval interaction in young and older adults, and found that both groups produced clear evidence of the interaction, with older adults being overall lower. More importantly, as suggested in Crowder (1976), Balota et al. fit their data to Estes' (1955) stimulus sampling model (a precursor of encoding variability theory), which was developed to account for aspects of extinction and spontaneous recovery, among other findings, in the animal learning domain. Interestingly, when animals are placed in an environment at varying times after extinction of a response, the response appears to spontaneously recover, even though it had been extinguished earlier. The results of this simple modeling endeavor indicated that older adults were different from younger adults in two parameter values. Specifically, older adults were less likely to store contextual elements in memory and elements also fluctuated between available and unavailable states across time at a slower rate in older adults than younger adults. As shown in Figure 6.1, changes in these two parameters of the Estes' model nicely fit the Balota et al. data (also see Spieler & Balota, 1996, for an extension to an implicit memory task). Thus, the spacing by retention interval interaction nicely extends to individuals with different levels of memory competence, and converges on a particular theoretical account of the spacing effect that emphasizes contextual drift (encoding variability) across time.

The spacing by retention interval interaction indicates that there are limitations to the spacing effect. This tradeoff between lag (the amount of spacing between two events) and retention interval has led some researchers (e.g., Greene, 1992) to speculate that the ratio between spacing and retention interval is the

Balota, Duchek, & Paullin (1989)

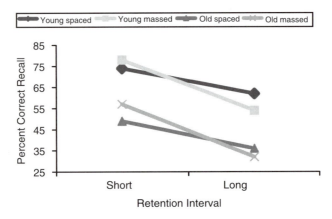

Estes' (1955) Stimulus Sampling Model

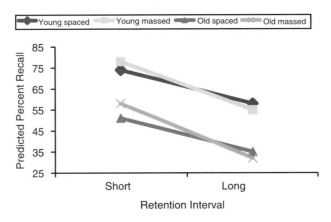

Changes in Two Parameters

Fluctuation (Young = .76; Old = .54)

Prob. of Storage (Young = .50; Old = .30)

FIGURE 6.1   Percent correct recall as a function of group and retention interval from Balota et al. (1989), along with the predictions from Estes' (1955) stimulus fluctuation model.

critical variable. Although there is some tradeoff between retention interval and spacing, there are probably some limits even here. For example, if one considers a spaced interval of 1 year between two repetitions, one may not expect much benefit even at a very long retention interval, since the initial trace may have either decayed or been completely overwhelmed by interfering material. Of course, this leads us to an important question. Are there ways to maintain the strength of the initial encoding so as to minimize the disruptive effects at long lags? Enter expanded retrieval practice. The goal in this procedure is to gradually increase the lag between retrieval events, thereby maintaining relatively high levels of retrieval success at long lags.

In an often-cited chapter, Landauer and Bjork (1978) were the first to carefully explore expanded retrieval in two well-controlled experiments. In their first experiment, subjects were presented a deck of cards that included fictitious first and second names of individuals during the acquisition phase. For present purposes, we will focus on the trials in which subjects were first presented both the first and second names intact followed at varying schedules of receiving cards with only the first name of the study pair as a retrieval cue for the second name. For example, in an expanded retrieval schedule, subjects may receive the first name as a retrieval cue at 1, 4, and 10 intervening cards versus an equal interval condition of 5, 5, and 5 intervening cards. A massed condition (study of the name followed by three immediate tests) was used to obtain a baseline estimate of the influence of simple repetition without spacing. The results of a later cued recall test yielded a large benefit for both the expanded and equal interval condition over the massed condition. More importantly, there was a small, but significant effect (approximately a 5% benefit, based on interpolation from their Figure 2) of the expanded condition over the equal interval condition in the final cued recall test.

The Landauer and Bjork (1978) results have been quite influential and would appear to naturally maximize the benefits of spacing. They originally suggested that the benefit of expanded retrieval involves insuring successful retrieval at longer and longer intervals, thereby increasing the difficulty of retrieval, while still yielding success. One could also view these benefits within an encoding variability framework described above. Specifically, with the passage of time and intervening information, there is an increased likelihood of greater fluctuation of context, and hence a greater likelihood of distinct encodings. The notion here is that in a long-term retention test, stimuli that have more distinct encodings, afforded by the longest interval in the expanded condition, would produce a greater benefit compared to stimuli with less distinct encodings due to shorter retention intervals.

Both of the above accounts emphasize the additional benefit beyond successful retrieval in the expanded condition compared to the equal interval condition. In particular, the reason there is an advantage in the expanded condition is that the participants are indeed retrieving items in the face of a longer retention interval during the final retrieval attempt in the expanded compared to the equal interval condition. Importantly, Landauer and Bjork (1978) provided retrieval success data during initial list presentation to directly examine this. Based on interpolation from their Figure 1, Table 6.1 displays performance of an expanded condition compared to an equal interval condition estimated from Landauer and Bjork's first experiment. As shown, there is an initial benefit of expanded retrieval that actually decreases across subsequent retrieval attempts. Hence, the benefit of expanded over equal interval is larger during the acquisition phase than in final

TABLE 6.1   Interpolated Results from Landauer and Bjork (1978)

	Retrieval attempt			Final recall
	1	2	3	
Expanded	.61	.55	.50	.45
Equal interval	.42	.42	.43	.40

recall. This is somewhat counterintuitive because one might expect an advantage of expanding over equal interval schedules above and beyond the retrieval success advantage produced during the acquisition phase. Specifically, at the last retrieval event, the retrieved items have persisted in the face of a longer retention interval and more intervening information in the expanded than in the equal interval condition. On the other hand, the "expanded retrieval effect" may be due to the fact that the first retrieval success occurs soon after study, permitting greater retrieval success in the expanding relative to the equal interval condition, as opposed to greater retrieval efficiency at the longest delays. Of course, this could ultimately overestimate the benefits of expansion. We will return to this possibility later.

The Landauer and Bjork (1978) results are clearly provocative, and the benefits of expanded retrieval have been explored in both educational and clinical settings. Below we will provide a review of the influence of expanded retrieval in these areas. It will become clear that although expanded retrieval is clearly a useful memory aid, there has been relatively little controlled work, akin to Landauer and Bjork's, that attempts to isolate the influence of expansion over comparable equal spaced conditions. Given the potential importance of this procedure, this is surprising.

Before turning to the review of the literature, we believe that it is noteworthy to identify the conditions that are important to make strong inferences regarding the specific role of expanding retrieval, many of which were available in Landauer and Bjork's seminal study. For example, it is important to include at least three levels of spacing: an expanded condition (e.g., 1, 4, 10), an equal interval condition that matches the average spacing of the expanded condition (e.g., 5, 5, 5), and a massed condition (e.g., 0, 0, 0). With these three levels, one can both measure the influence of expansion with spacing equated (e.g., 1, 4, 10 vs. 5, 5, 5), and also the benefits of spaced (1, 4, 10 and 5, 5, 5) over massed practice (e.g., 0, 0, 0) to insure one obtains a clear spacing effect. In addition, it is useful to measure retrieval success during the initial acquisition phase to obtain an estimate of the original level of learning. As we shall discuss below, it is preferable to include two different delays for the final memory test, because it appears that one can obtain different effects depending upon the delay. Of course, this has some resemblance to the spacing by retention interval interaction. Finally, it would also be useful to include a study alone condition with the same spacing and testing conditions to measure the specific influence of retrieval during study. Unfortunately, as noted, these conditions have rarely been available in the same study to isolate the specific benefits of expanded retrieval.

EXPANDED RETRIEVAL PRACTICE IN EDUCATIONAL SETTINGS

The additional benefit of expanded retrieval over equal interval spacing obviously has important implications for educational settings. Although Landauer and Bjork's (1978) work sparked considerable interest in applying expanded retrieval to educational settings, Roddy informed us of relevant work nearly 40 years before Landauer and Bjork's study. Specifically, Spitzer (1939) incorporated a form of expanded retrieval in a study designed to assess the ability of sixth graders to learn science facts. Impressively, Spitzer tested over 3600 students in Iowa—the entire sixth-grade population of 91 elementary schools at the time. The students read two articles, one on peanuts and the other on bamboo, and were given a 25-item multiple choice test to assess their knowledge (such as "To which family of plants does bamboo belong?"). Spitzer tested a total of nine groups, manipulating both the timing of the test (administered immediately or after various delays) and the number of identical tests students received (one to three). Spitzer did not incorporate massed or equal interval retrieval conditions, but he had at least two groups that were tested on an expanding schedule of retrieval, in which the intervals between tests were separated by the passage of time (in days) rather than by intervening to-be-learned information. For example, in one of the groups, the first test was given immediately, the second test was given seven days after the first test, and the third test was given 63 days after the second test. Thus, in essence, this group was tested on a 0-7-63 day expanding retrieval schedule. Spitzer compared performance of the expanded retrieval group to a group given a single test 63 days after reading the original article. On the first (immediate) test, the expanded retrieval group correctly answered 53% of the questions. After 63 days and two previous tests, their score was still an impressive 43%. The single test group correctly answered only 25% of the original items after 63 days, giving the expanded retrieval group an 18% retention advantage. This is quite impressive, given that this large benefit remained after a 63-day retention interval. Similar beneficial effects were found in a group tested on a 0-1-21 day expanded retrieval schedule compared to a group given a single test after 21 days. Of course, this study does not decouple the effects of testing from spacing or expansion, but the results do clearly indicate considerable learning and retention using the expanded repeated testing procedure. Spitzer concluded that ". . . examinations are *learning devices* and should not be considered only as tools for measuring achievement of pupils" (p. 656, italics added), and we are sure Roddy would agree (see Roediger & Karpicke, 2006).

Since Spitzer (1939), there was very little work published on expanded retrieval using educationally-relevant materials for 45 years until Rea and Modigliani (1985) tested the effectiveness of expanded retrieval in a third-grade classroom setting. In separate conditions, students were given new multiplication problems or spelling words to learn. The problem or word was presented audio-visually once and then tested on either a massed retrieval schedule of 0-0-0-0 or an expanding schedule of 0-1-2-4, in which the intervals involved being tested on old items or learning new items. After each test trial for a given item, the item was re-presented in its entirety so students received feedback on what they were learning. Performance during the learning phase was at 100% for both spelling words and multiplication facts. On an immediate final retention test, Rea and Modigliani found a performance advantage for all items—math and spelling—practiced on an expanding schedule compared to the massed retrieval schedule. They suggested, as have others, that spacing combined with the high success rate inherent in the expanded retrieval schedule produced better retention than massed retrieval practice. However, as in Spitzer's study, Rea and Modigliani did not test an appropriate equal interval spacing condition. Hence, their finding that expanded retrieval is superior to massed retrieval in third graders could simply reflect the superiority of spaced versus massed rehearsal—in other words, the spacing effect.

More recently, Cull (2000) compared expanded retrieval to equal interval spaced retrieval in a series of four experiments designed to mimic typical teaching or study strategies encountered by students. He examined the role of testing versus simply restudying the material, feedback, and various retention intervals on final test performance. Paired associates (an uncommon word paired with a common word, such as *bairn–print*) were presented in a manner similar to the flash-card techniques students often use to learn vocabulary words. The intervals between retrieval attempts of to-be-learned information ranged from minutes in some experiments to days in others. Interestingly, across four experiments, Cull did not find any evidence of an advantage of an expanded condition over a uniform spaced condition (i.e., no significant expanded retrieval effect), although both conditions consistently produced large advantages over massed presentations. He concluded that distributed testing of any kind, expanded or equal interval, can be an effective learning aid for teachers to provide for their students.

Karpicke (2004) investigated the effectiveness of using expanded retrieval to learn material commonly encountered by students—prose passages. Participants were given 7 minutes to read an encyclopedia article and practice free recalling the article on an expanding or equal interval schedule. An important feature of Karpicke's study was that he matched the timing of the first recall attempt in the acquisition phase in the expanded and equal interval conditions. As noted, in most expanded retrieval studies, the first practice for the expanded items comes sooner than practice for the equal interval items. Hence, in Karpicke's study, the first recall attempt for both equal and expanded conditions was either immediate (given just after reading the article) or delayed (given after 7 minutes of a distractor task). He tested a total of four recall schedules in the acquisition phase: 0-2-4, 0-2-2, 2-2-4, 2-2-2. The final free recall test was given 1 week later. In both the immediate and delayed practice conditions, Karpicke found no difference in memory performance when expanded and equal interval schedules were matched on the timing of the first retrieval attempt. This was true in the acquisition phase as well as the final free recall test. However, one might compare the 0-2-4 condition to the 2-2-2 conditions to investigate the expanded retrieval effect.

Interestingly, Karpicke (2004) did find an advantage for the expanded condition in both the acquisition phase as well as the final free recall test, similar to

Landauer and Bjork (1978). Because there was no delay in the first retrieval event in the immediate retrieval conditions in this study, and the 0-2-4 and 0-2-2 produced equivalent and better performance than the 2-2-2 and the 2-2-4, Karpicke points out that it is difficult to isolate the influence of expansion from the immediacy of the first recall event. In this light, it would have been useful to have 0-1-2-3 and 0-2-2-2 conditions for comparison. In any case, Karpicke's findings support the notion that any expanded retrieval effect at a final test is strongly linked to greater retrieval success for the expanded condition compared to the equal interval condition during the first acquisition phase. When these two conditions were matched in performance during the acquisition phase, the expanded retrieval effect did not emerge.

Researchers have also attempted to extend the utility of expanded retrieval to other "real world" settings such as in our original example of learning the name Mark Finglestein (remember Mark?) at a neighborhood party. Morris and Fritz (2000; see also Morris & Fritz, 2002; Morris, Fritz, & Buck, 2004) modified the expanded retrieval technique to create a "name game" to help individuals learn the names of members in their group. In the name game, an individual introduces herself, while a group leader writes their name on a board and then erases it once the other group members had read it. A second individual then repeats the first person's name aloud and introduces himself to the group. The third individual then repeats the names of the first and second individuals (in that order) and adds her name, etc. This technique of repeating previous names (starting with the first person's name) then adding a new name to the group is followed until all group members are introduced. Thus, the interval between hearing a given name progressively expands as each new person is introduced. In the Morris and Fritz (2000) study, participants were given a final recall test on the names after 30 minutes and again after 2 weeks and 11 months. Performance in the name game condition was compared to a condition in which individuals were simply paired with another group member and then asked to introduce their partners aloud to the group. In two experiments, participants recalled significantly more full names from the name game condition than the partner condition, even after 11 months. This condition also produced superior performance compared to when the group leader simply read the previous names back after each new introduction without ever asking individuals to retrieve the names. In a follow-up study, Morris and Fritz (2002) found that a reversed version of the name game, in which names were recalled in reverse chronological order, produced better performance than the original version used in the previous study. They noted that the reversed name game more closely mimics the technique originally employed by Landauer and Bjork (1978), and it was more effective than the original name game because there was less chance of forgetting a new name when the delay between learning and retrieval was reduced. Although the name game clearly does work, there is again no comparable equal interval condition to examine if the schedule is the critical dimension or the spacing.

The studies reviewed above specifically cited a desire to apply the expanded retrieval technique to nonlaboratory settings and explored its applications to a variety of learning situations (science and multiplication facts, spelling words, and first and last names). The studies found an advantage for expanded retrieval compared to information that is simply repeated or reread (Cull, 2000; Morris & Fritz, 2000, 2002), tested only once (Spitzer, 1939), or tested on a massed retrieval schedule (Cull, 2000; Rea & Modigliani, 1985). In addition, Karpicke (2004) presents intriguing evidence that provides support for the utility of expansion for text materials, but overall his results primarily show the importance of the immediacy of a first testing session. Only Cull (2000) directly compared the utility of expanded retrieval to other schedules of spaced retrieval and this study did not obtain any benefits of expanded retrieval over an equal interval schedule. In a later section, we will further discuss the Cull study and other studies that have attempted to decouple the influence of spacing from expansion in more traditional laboratory settings.

EXPANDED RETRIEVAL PRACTICE IN COGNITIVELY IMPAIRED POPULATIONS

Another area where expanded retrieval has been viewed as having considerable potential is as a cognitive rehabilitation technique for various memory-impaired populations. This area has been very active. The specific appeal of expanded retrieval is that the benefits of expanded retrieval are relatively automatic and nonstrategic, as opposed to teaching memory impaired individuals mnemonic techniques such as the pegword method or method of loci, which demand considerable strategic/attentional control processes.

Schacter, Rich, and Stampp (1985) utilized the expanded retrieval procedure to improve memory performance in four patients with cognitive impairment due to a variety of etiologies. In this study, subjects first studied faces and associated characteristics (i.e., names, hometowns, occupations, hobbies) and then utilizing the face cue, engaged in retrieval practice for the associated characteristics at expanded time intervals. Initially subjects were given a verbal prompt to engage in retrieval practice and over time the verbal prompt was removed to see if subjects would engage in expanded retrieval practice on their own. The results indicated that memory performance for the associated characteristics improved after expanded retrieval practice relative to baseline performance as measured prior to the introduction of the expanded retrieval strategy. Importantly, two out of the four subjects were relatively successful in spontaneously using expanded retrieval practice without prompts. Thus, Schacter et al. concluded that expanded retrieval practice might be a particularly effective strategy for memory enhancement in cognitively impaired populations.

The vast majority of the work employing the use of expanded retrieval in clinical populations has been conducted by Camp and his colleagues, with individuals in various stages of Alzheimer's disease (AD; for a review, see Camp, Bird, & Cherry, 2000). Given that memory loss is the hallmark symptom of Alzheimer's disease, targeting this population with such a behavioral intervention could prove quite beneficial to both patients and caregivers. In an effort to apply Landauer and Bjork's (1978) expanded retrieval practice to the AD population, Camp and colleagues adopted a clinical protocol for teaching AD patients new information using spaced retrieval practice (Camp, 1989; Camp & McKitrick, 1992). In this procedure, subjects are first given one piece of information to remember (e.g., the name of a staff person) and are then tested for immediate recall. If this immediate recall attempt is successful, then the next retrieval attempt is queried after 5 s, and then expanded to 10 s, 20 s, 40 s, 60 s. After successful retention of the item for 60 s, intervals are increased by 30 s (90 s, 120 s, etc.). If a person does not successfully retrieve the information, he/she is given the correct response, asked to immediately repeat the correct response, and then is tested at the last successful interval. Expanded retrieval attempts are again initiated from that point forward on successful retrieval events.

As Camp, Foss, Stevens, and O'Hanlon (1996) describe, there are some key features of this spaced retrieval strategy that promote success in memory-impaired patients. First, the expansion of retrieval attempts occurs over time, not over intervening to-be-remembered items. Thus, the time intervals are typically filled with social conversation or other non-related activities. As Camp and Mattern (1999) argue, the expanded retrieval training can be efficiently used within a therapy session wherein the intervening time intervals can be used for other therapeutic activities. Second, this technique is analogous to a shaping procedure wherein an association is formed between a stimulus (i.e., the retrieval query) and a single response (i.e., the name). Because the learning occurs very gradually over time, the initial retrieval attempts are likely to be successful, even for individuals in the moderate stages of AD. Third, the expanded retrieval strategy incorporates the neurorehabilitation technique of errorless learning (Wilson, Baddeley, Evans, & Shiel, 1994). Wilson and colleagues have argued that memory-impaired populations show better long-term retention for information when they are not allowed to make errors during training (Baddeley & Wilson, 1994; Wilson & Evans, 1996). The notion is that explicit memory is necessary for error recognition and elimination during learning. When the explicit system is deficient, then errors may be implicitly incorporated into the learning and thus each repetition of an erroneous response may serve to further strengthen that incorrect response, thereby hindering the retention of the correct information. Thus, the expanded retrieval procedure used by Camp and colleagues requires that when there is a failure of retrieval, the correct response be given immediately and repeated by the subject. Finally, the implementation of the expanded retrieval strategy requires little cognitive effort and/or resources on the part of the learner. Camp and colleagues have argued that expanded retrieval training makes use of implicit memory, which is relatively spared even in the later stages of AD (e.g., Balota & Ferraro, 1996; Camp et al., 2000; Faust, Balota, & Spieler, 2001). Thus, it is ideally suited for memory-impaired patients.

Indeed there have been numerous reports in the literature of the successful use of expanded retrieval practice in teaching new information to individuals in the relatively advanced stages of AD. Specifically, Camp and colleagues have used this technique to teach AD individuals various types of information, such as names of common objects (e.g., McKitrick & Camp, 1993), face-name associations (e.g., Camp & Schaller, 1989), object-location associations (e.g., Camp & Stevens, 1990), and even prospectively remembering to perform a task (e.g., McKitrick, Camp, & Black, 1992). Moreover, long-term retention of information has been demonstrated over several days in some cases (e.g., Camp et al., 1996). For example, in the latter study, Camp et al. employed an expanding retrieval strategy to train 23 individuals with mild to moderate AD to refer to a daily calendar as a cue to remember to perform various personal activities (e.g., take medication). Following a baseline phase to determine whether subjects would spontaneously use the calendar, spaced retrieval training was implemented by repeatedly asking the subject the question, "How are you going to remember what to do each day?" at expanding time intervals. The results indicated that 20/23 subjects did learn the strategy (i.e., to look at the calendar) and retained it over a 1-week period.

There have been numerous other studies utilizing this protocol of expanded retrieval practice to induce memory-impaired patients to learn clinically relevant behaviors. For example, this technique has been employed to teach a demented client with dysphagia (i.e., a swallowing disorder) to use a compensatory strategy of alternating bites of food with sips of liquid to prevent aspiration (Brush & Camp, 1998a). Expanded retrieval training has been applied to attaining goals during speech therapy sessions (Brush & Camp, 1998b) with demonstrated retention over a 4-week period in demented clients. Patients with dementia associated with Parkinson's disease have successfully learned new motor tasks (Hayden & Camp, 1995) and patients with dementia associated with HIV have been trained in the use of external aids (Lee & Camp, 2001) with expanded retrieval practice. Likewise, a client with AD was able to learn the names of 11 members of his social group with a combined intervention of errorless learning and expanded retrieval (Clare et al., 2000). There has even been a case report of an individual in the early stages of AD who trained himself to spontaneously use expanded retrieval practice to remember new information (Riley, 1992). Thus, the benefits of expanded retrieval have been widely documented in the literature across various targeted behaviors and clinical populations.

What is somewhat surprising in reviewing all of these studies is that there has been no attempt to systematically compare expanded retrieval practice with other schedules of spaced retrieval practice, such as equal interval spacing or even massed spacing of retrieval practice. In most of these studies, performance after expanded retrieval practice is simply compared relative to baseline performance (e.g., Camp et al., 1996; Cherry, Simmons, & Camp, 1999). More recently, Bourgeois et al. (2003) compared expanded retrieval training with a modified cued hierarchy training in teaching demented individuals to use various external memory aids. The modified cued hierarchy training is initiated in a similar way as the expanded retrieval training in that patients are first given the target information (e.g., when you want to know what activity to perform today—look at your activity list) and then immediately queried for that information. If patients cannot immediately give the correct response or give an incorrect response, they are given a hierarchy of cues in the following order until the correct response is given: semantic ("Something to look at"), phonemic (the first syllable of "activity list"), visual (point to list), tactile (touch list), imitation ("I look at my activity list"). No cues are given in the expanded retrieval training. The results indicated that both strategies improved usage of external aids, but the expanded retrieval strategy was more effective. Of course, the latter study simply indicates that spaced retrieval practice leads to better retention than providing a hierarchy of cues. It did not address the question of which specific pattern of spacing leads to the greatest benefit in long-term retention.

This issue of isolating which component of expanded retrieval is critical with a clinical sample was more systematically addressed in a recent study by Hochhalter, Overmier, Gasper, Bakke, and Holub (2005). Individuals with AD were presented pill names (Exp. 1; $n = 10$) under five different schedules of retrieval practice: massed, uniform distributed (i.e., equal interval), spaced/expanded adjusted based on performance (similar to the Camp protocol), expanded without adjustment, and random. The results indicated that only 6/10 individuals showed long-term retention for at least one pill name and there was no difference in the number of "learners" across the different schedules of retrieval practice. Thus the spaced/expanded retrieval condition did not show a benefit relative to any of the other schedules of practice. If anything, more subjects showed long-term retention in the random condition ($n = 5$) than the spaced/expanded condition ($n = 3$) and also had fewer errors during training.

The Hochhalter et al. (2005) study is clearly informative, but the relatively small number of subjects and more variable applied therapeutic setting makes it difficult to draw any firm conclusions. However, as described below, Balota, Duchek, Sergent-Marshall, and Roediger (2005) provide a study comparing equal interval and expanded practice in a laboratory context with a large set of healthy young, older adults, and individuals with early stage Alzheimer's disease and come to a very similar conclusion as the Hochhalter et al. study regarding comparisons of equal interval and expanded retrieval.

It is interesting to note that in their initial study described above, Schacter et al. (1985) acknowledged that it was unclear whether it was the actual expanding pattern of retrieval that led to the performance benefit in their study or whether it was merely due to the simple repetition of retrieval attempts. They argued that to some extent the latter question is not really clinically important given that expanded retrieval practice does indeed work for memory-impaired patients. Clearly, one would agree with this statement on an individual patient basis, where the goal of treatment is to enhance memory for important personal information. It is clear from the literature that having memory-impaired individuals engage in an expanded retrieval strategy does improve memory performance under a variety of situations, at least relative to baseline (no treatment) performance (Camp et al., 2000). Furthermore, one can see how the gradual expansion of recall attempts with the initial accompanying retrieval success would be relatively easy to implement in a clinical setting or in a home setting by caregivers (McKitrick & Camp, 1993). However, from a theoretical perspective, it is also critical to examine the properties of the most effective spacing of retrieval practice to enhance long-term retention. This research could also provide evidence for designing the best intervention strategies for memory-impaired individuals.

RE-EXAMINATION OF THE EVIDENCE FOR THE BENEFITS OF EXPANDED RETRIEVAL OVER EQUAL SPACED RETRIEVAL: BACK TO THE LABORATORY

As reviewed in the previous two sections, there is clear evidence that expanded retrieval practice has considerable potential in both educational and applied settings. The question that we will now turn to is an examination of how much of this evidence is specific to "expanded" retrieval. This of course depends on what is the appropriate baseline. As in Landauer and Bjork's (1978) original paper, we believe the appropriate baseline to be a comparably matched equal interval schedule. In this way, one can directly investigate if there is an additional benefit of expansion over mere spacing. For these studies, we are forced to return to the laboratory where more control of critical variables is available.

In one of the most comprehensive studies in this area, Cull, Shaughnessy, and Zechmeister (1996) explored the benefits of expanded retrieval over uniform spacing in a series of five experiments. They compared the expanded schedule of 1-5-9, with the equal interval schedule of 5-5-5, and included a 0-0-0 massed presentation condition, as a baseline to measure the benefit of spacing on a later final recall test. As shown in Table 6.2, the results generally support the benefit of expanded retrieval over equal interval conditions. Experiments 1 and 4 produced reliable expanded retrieval benefits compared to an equal interval condition, whereas the results from Experiments 2 and 3 were in the same direction, but did not reach significance. Experiment 5 produced near ceiling effects in both spaced conditions. Somewhat surprisingly, the comparison of the equal interval condition to the massed condition did not consistently produce spacing effects. A test for the spacing effect was not directly provided for Experiments 1 and 2, and in Experiments 3 and 4, these two conditions produced identical performance. Only, their fifth experiment provided strong evidence for a spacing effect, but this experiment did not provide evidence for an expanded retrieval effect, because of ceiling problems.

Cull (2000, Exp. 1) provided a direct follow-up study to the initial Cull et al.

TABLE 6.2   Results from Cull et al. (1996), and Cull (2000) Studies

Experiment	Presentation schedule		
	1-5-9	5-5-5	0-0-0
Cull et al. (1996)			
1. Test only	.33	.23	.17
2. Test only	.27	.18	.11
3. Test only	.34	.28	.28
4. Test only	.72	.59	.59
5. Test–study	.91	.91	.62
Cull (2000, Exp. 1)			
Test only	.38	.34	.18
Study only	.27	.29	.14
Test–study	.48	.49	.19

(1996) study. He included the same three spacing schedules used in the earlier Cull et al. study, along with three different types of study. In essence, his first experiment included three different experiments, as these conditions were between participant manipulations. In the study-only condition, the cue and response item of a paired associate were both presented on each repetition for 8 s. In the test-only condition, the cue for retrieval was presented on each occasion for 8 s. In the study–test condition, the cue was presented for 6 s for retrieval, followed by the response item for 2 s. As shown in Table 6.2, Cull did not obtain an advantage for the expanded over the equal interval condition in any of these conditions. As noted earlier, Cull also explored more educationally relevant manipulations in three additional experiments. None of these experiments afforded any benefit of expanded retrieval over a comparable equal interval condition.

Carpenter and DeLosh (2005, Exp. 2) have recently investigated face-name learning under massed, expanded (1-3-5), and equal interval (3-3-3) conditions. This study also involved study and study and test procedures during the acquisition phase. Carpenter and DeLosh found a large effect of spacing, but no evidence of a benefit of expanded over equal interval practice. In fact, Carpenter and DeLosh reported a reliable benefit of the equal interval condition over the expanded retrieval condition. Although Carpenter and DeLosh did report a reliable (20%) benefit of expanded retrieval during the acquisition phase, they did not break this down by each retrieval event to determine the size of the difference at the last retrieval event in the expanded condition.

In addition to studies with healthy young adults, there have been two recent studies that have explored the benefits of expanded retrieval with healthy older adults and early stage individuals with Alzheimer's disease. Balota et al. (2005) compared a massed presentation condition (0-0-0-0-0-0) with an equal interval (0-0-3-3-3) and an expanded retrieval schedule (0-0-1-3-5). Because this study included healthy young adults, older adults, and individuals with Alzheimer's disease, who have quite a wide range of memory ability, Balota et al. had subjects engage in two massed retrieval attempts before each of the three schedules to insure all groups were off the floor in their final recall performance. The results of performance during the acquisition phase are shown in Figure 6.2. Here one can see that the expanded retrieval condition indeed produced a benefit over the equal interval condition that persisted until the last retrieval event for all groups of participants. Hence, because performance on the last retrieval event reflects longer maintenance of the memory in the 0-0-1-3-5 condition than the 0-0-3-3-3 condition, one would expect a benefit to persist in the final cued recall tests. This was not what the results indicated. Specifically, as shown in Figure 6.3, all three groups produced large spacing effects in a final cued recall test; however, there was no evidence of a reliable difference between the expanded and equal interval conditions for any of the groups. Moreover, the lack of a difference in final recall between the expanded and equal interval condition was replicated in two subsequent experiments, in which corrective feedback was given to participants. Hence, the Balota et al. results converge nicely with the recent Cull (2000) and Carpenter and DeLosh (2005) studies and extends this pattern to both healthy older adults and individuals with early stage Alzheimer's disease.

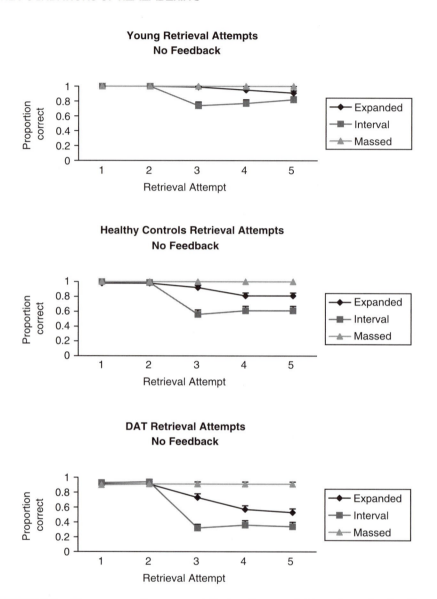

FIGURE 6.2   Mean proportion correct during the acquisition phase for the Young (top panel), Old (middle panel) and DAT (bottom panel) individuals, as a function of spacing, and retrieval attempt from Balota et al. (2005, Exp. 1).

Of course, one might be concerned that both the Balota et al. (2005) and Carpenter and DeLosh (2005) studies used the 3-3-3 and 1-3-5 comparison. Logan (2004) conducted a comprehensive study that compared three schedules of retrieval practice in healthy young and older adults, i.e., 0-0-0 versus 1-2-3 versus 2-2-2; 0-0-0 versus 1-3-5 versus 3-3-3; 0-0-0 versus 1-3-8 versus 4-4-4. An important additional contribution of the Logan study is that she also included both an

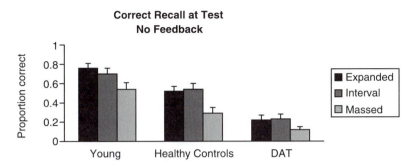

FIGURE 6.3   Mean final cued recall performance as a function of group and spacing schedule from Balota et al. (2005, Exp. 1).

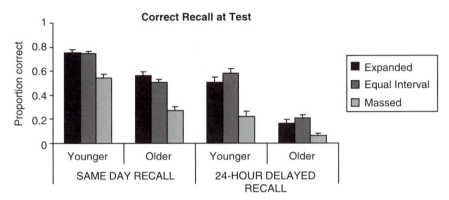

FIGURE 6.4   Mean final cued recall performance as a function of group, spacing schedule, and retention interval from Logan (2004).

immediate and a delayed retention interval. The retrieval schedule did not modulate the difference between expanded and equal spaced retrieval and so we will collapse across these schedules here. As shown in Figure 6.4, Logan obtained benefits of expanded retrieval over equal interval during the acquisition phase for both the young and the older adults. This acquisition advantage was retained on an immediate final cued recall test, at least in older adults. However, after a 24 hour delay between acquisition and final test, the advantage for items practiced on an expanding schedule compared to an equal interval schedule was lost in both age groups. In fact, memory was significantly worse for expanded items compared to equal interval items in younger adults. Thus, the findings from Logan imply that when an expanded retrieval advantage is found, it may be short-lived, compared to comparable equal interval spacing.

The Logan results are particularly intriguing in light of a recent study by Karpicke and Roediger (2005). These investigators compared massed (0-0-0), equal interval (5-5-5), and expanded (1-5-9) retrieval conditions for paired associates (vocabulary GRE practice items, such as *sobriquet–nickname*) in both an immediate 10 minute delayed, and 48 hour delayed cued recall test. The results indicated that again both spaced schedules produced better performance than the massed schedule at both retention intervals. More importantly, there was evidence of a benefit of the expanded condition over the equal interval condition in the immediate test, but the equal interval condition produced a clear benefit in the delayed recall test. This later pattern was replicated in a second study in which feedback was provided after each testing event, although the immediate test performance was limited by ceiling problems. Hence, the short-term gains of expanded over equal interval retrieval found in both the Logan (2004) and Karpicke and Roediger (2005) studies were either eliminated or turned into long-term losses in a delayed testing condition.

THEORETICAL IMPLICATIONS

The results of the current review lead us to conclude that, as expected, spaced practice produces considerable benefits in learning compared to massed practice; however, the additional benefits of expanded practice over equal interval practice have not been well substantiated in recent research. We find the lack of a benefit of expanded retrieval quite intriguing, because the acquisition phase data (when measured) clearly indicate that participants are at higher levels of retrieval success over a longer retention interval in the expanded condition than in the equal interval condition. For example, at the last retrieval event during the acquisition phase of the Balota et al. (2005) study, subjects correctly retrieved 16% more items in the expanded retrieval condition than in the equal interval condition, even though at this last retrieval event, the expanded retention interval was five items, and the equal interval was three items. Clearly, one would expect such a benefit to either persist or increase during a final recall test. However, there was no benefit in the final cued recall performance of expansion. Moreover, the results from Logan (2004) and Karpicke and Roediger (2005) indicate that one can either eliminate or actually reverse any acquisition benefit of expanded over equal interval retrieval when tested at a 1 or 2 day retention interval.

Why might the benefits of expanded retrieval over equal interval retrieval observed during the acquisition phase be lost in a later cued recall test? One simple possibility is that long-term retention is simply a function of the average amount of spacing. Since this is equated in the equal interval and expanded condition, there is, on average, no effect. A more intriguing possibility is that there are counteracting influences, as a function of retention interval. Specifically, it is indeed beneficial to maintain high levels of retrieval success during acquisition, but there is a potential cost of maintaining these high levels, i.e., a loss of one of the spaced intervals. Consider for example, the 1-3-5 schedule compared to the 3-3-3 schedule. The initial retrieval event during acquisition in the expanded condition occurs after only one intervening item. In some sense, one could argue that the 3-3-3 condition involves *three* functional spaced events during acquisition, whereas, the 1-3-5 condition only involves *two* spaced events during acquisition.

As noted earlier, one theoretical account of the spacing effect is encoding variability theory, which nicely handles the intriguing spacing by retention interval interaction described above. This framework may also be relevant to the expanded versus equal interval spacing results. Specifically, although expanded retrieval does indeed produce higher performance during the acquisition phase, this benefit may be lost at longer delays, precisely as any benefit of massed spacing is relatively short lived. The notion is that the equal interval condition will on average involve three distinct encoding events, whereas, as noted above, the expanded condition on average will involve two distinct encoding events. Because long-term retention is a reflection of the context at retrieval matching one of the encoding events, the equal interval condition may produce a benefit in long-term retention, since this condition affords an additional unique encoding of context. Interestingly, as noted above, there is already evidence by Logan (2004) and Karpicke and Roediger (2005) that initial benefits of expansion during a short retention interval turn into losses a day or two later. Thus, although there is the benefit of expansion in maintaining high levels of performance at increasing delays during acquisition, the long-term consequence of expansion may produce a decreased amount of contextual variability, because of the relatively immediate presentation of the first test. Of course, we know that maintaining high levels of retrieval success during acquisition is not the only variable that is critical to memory performance, since massed study produces the highest level of perform-ance during acquisition but the lowest level of performance during a long-term retention test. Clearly, further work is needed to better understand the balance between spacing and retention interval in more complex expanded and equal interval schedules.

PRACTICAL IMPLICATIONS

Although the review of recent empirical work has questioned the benefits of expanded retrieval over equal spaced retrieval, there are two reasons that may support the use of expanded retrieval in more applied settings. First, as Camp and colleagues have nicely demonstrated, this procedure is relatively easy to imple-ment in a clinical setting. That is, gradually increasing retrieval intervals, while maintaining success, benefits from feedback driven performance, i.e., providing positive feedback at increasing retention intervals because of retrieval success. Alternatively, a priori picking the best spaced retrieval practice schedule may be relatively difficult to accomplish, especially for someone who is having global cognitive impairments. Second, and more importantly, maintaining high levels of retrieval success during acquisition in the face of increasing retention intervals is likely to be reinforcing for the user. Of course, such reinforcement should ulti-mately increase the likelihood that individuals will use such a schedule in the future, and so this is a natural way of nurturing the use of spaced practice. Thus, although there may be reasons to question the long-term benefits of expanded over equal interval schedules, there may also be practical reasons to use the expanded retrieval schedule to implement simple spaced acquisition.

FUTURE RESEARCH

Clearly, there is much work to do to better understand the influence of study schedules on long-term retention. Comparing different acquisition schedules is a natural avenue to pursue. Most studies have only used three retrieval attempts, and the extension to a greater number of retrieval attempts would be likely to reflect the sequence of events in more applied settings, such as in the Camp et al. studies. Consider, for example, the possibility of comparing an expanded schedule of 1-2-3-4-5-6-7 with a retrieval schedule of 4-4-4-4-4-4-4. Without feedback provided, we would expect that in this case the expanded schedule may produce a benefit over the equal interval schedule, but this is an open empirical question. Likewise, in addition to exploring different schedules, the influence of feedback and the possibility of restudying nonretrieved information are both aspects of acquisition that typically occur outside the laboratory. With feedback, one might expect the equal interval condition to possibly produce better performance in the above example. Finally, as Logan (2004) and Karpicke and Roediger (2005) have nicely demonstrated, retention interval is critical. In general, what appears to be a benefit of expanded retrieval during acquisition can be quickly lost and even reversed at longer retention intervals. In this light, we are reminded of Bjork's (1999) arguments regarding the importance of desirable difficulties during acquisition, and the counterintuitive observation that variables that produce benefits immediately on tests sometimes produce losses in long-term retention. Although there will clearly be constraints on when expansion will and will not produce benefits over equal interval schedules, the present review makes clear that the power of spacing is paramount in learning and memory.

ACKNOWLEDGMENTS

Portions of this research were supported by NIA PO1 AGO3991 and P50 AGO5681. Thanks are extended to Roddy and Jim Nairne for helpful comments on an earlier version of this manuscript.

REFERENCES

Baddeley, A. D., & Wilson, B. A. (1994). When implicit learning fails: Amnesia and the problem of error elimination. *Neuropsychologia, 32,* 53–68.

Balota, D. A., Duchek, J. M., & Paullin, R. (1989). Age-related differences in the impact of spacing, lag and retention interval. *Psychology and Aging, 4,* 3–9.

Balota, D. A., Duchek, J. M., Sergent-Marshall, S. D., Roediger, H. L., III. (2005). Does expanded retrieval produce benefits over equal interval spacing? Explorations of spacing effects in healthy aging and early stage Alzheimer's disease. *Psychology and Aging, 21,* 19–31.

Balota, D. A., & Ferraro, F. R. (1996). Lexical, sublexical, and implicit memory processes in healthy young, healthy older adults, and in individuals with dementia of the Alzheimer's type. *Neuropsychology, 10,* 82–95.

Bjork, R. A. (1999). Assessing our own competence: Heuristics and illusions. In D. Gopher & A. Koriat (Eds.), *Attention and performance XVII: Cognitive regulation of performance: Interaction of theory and application* (pp. 435–459). Cambridge, MA: MIT Press.

Bourgeois, M. S., Camp, C., Rose, M., White, B., Malone, M., Carr, J., & Rovine, M. (2003). A comparison of training strategies to enhance use of external aids by persons with dementia. *Journal of Communication Disorders, 36,* 361–378.

Brush, J. A., & Camp, C. J. (1998a). Using spaced retrieval to treat dysphagia on a long-term care resident with dementia. *The Clinical Gerontologist, 19*(2), 96–99.

Brush, J. A., & Camp, C. J. (1998b). Using spaced retrieval as an intervention during speech-language therapy. *The Clinical Gerontologist, 19,* 51–64.

Burke, D. M., & Light, L. L. (1981). Memory and aging: The role of retrieval processes. *Psychological Bulletin, 90,* 513–546.

Camp, C. J. (1989). Facilitation of new learning in Alzheimer's disease. In G. C. Gilmore, P. J. Whitehouse, & M. L. Wykle (Eds.), *Memory, aging, and dementia* (pp. 212–225). New York: Springer.

Camp, C. J., Bird, M. J., & Cherry, K. E. (2000). Retrieval strategies as a rehabilitation aid for cognitive loss in pathological aging. In R. D. Hill, L. Backman, A. Neely Stigsdotter (Eds.), *Cognitive rehabilitation in old age* (pp. 224–248). Oxford, UK: Oxford University Press.

Camp, C. J., Foss, J. W., Stevens, A. B., & O'Hanlon, A. M. (1996). Improving prospective memory task performance in persons with Alzheimer's disease. In M. Bandimonte, G. O. Einstein, & M. A. McDaniel (Eds.), *Prospective memory: Theory and applications* (pp. 351–367). Mahwah, NJ: USum Associates.

Camp, C. J., & Mattern, J. M. (1999). Innovations in managing Alzheimer's disease. In D. E. Biegel & A. Blum (Eds.), *Innovations in practice and service delivery across the lifespan* (pp. 276–293). New York: Oxford University Press.

Camp, C. J., & McKitrick, L. A. (1992). Memory interventions in Alzheimer's-type dementia populations: Methodological and theoretical issues. In R. L. West & J. D. Sinnott (Eds.), *Everyday memory and aging: Current research and methodology* (pp. 152–172). New York: Springer-Verlag.

Camp, C. J., & Schaller, J. R. (1989). Epilogue: Spaced-retrieval memory training in an adult day care center. *Educational Gerontology, 15,* 81–88.

Camp, C. J., & Stevens, A. B. (1990). Spaced-retrieval: A memory intervention for dementia of the Alzheimer's type. *The Clinical Gerontologist, 10*(1), 58–61.

Carpenter, S. K., & DeLosh, E. L. (2005). Application of the testing and spacing effects to name learning. *Applied Cognitive Psychology, 19,* 619–636.

Cepeda, N. J., Pashler, H., Vul, E., Wixted, J. T., & Rohrer, D. (2006). Distributed practice in verbal recall tasks: A review and quantitative synthesis. *Psychological Bulletin, 132,* 354–380.

Cherry, K. E., Simmons, S. S., & Camp, C. J. (1999). Spaced retrieval enhances memory in older adults with probable Alzheimer's disease. *Journal of Clinical Geropsychology, 5*(3), 159–175.

Clare, L., Wilson, B. A., Carter, G., Breen, K., Gosses, A., & Hodges, J. R. (2000). Intervening with everyday memory problems in dementia of Alzheimer type: An errorless learning approach. *Journal of Clinical and Experimental Neuropsychology, 22,* 132–146.

Crowder, R. G. (1976). *The principles of learning and memory.* Oxford, UK. Lawrence Erlbaum Associates Ltd.

Cull, W. L. (2000). Untangling the benefits of multiple study opportunities and repeated testing for cued recall. *Applied Cognitive Psychology, 14,* 215–235.

Cull, W. L., Shaughnessy, J. J., & Zechmeister, E. B. (1996). Expanding understanding of the expanding-pattern-of-retrieval mnemonic: Toward confidence in applicability. *Journal of Experimental Psychology: Applied, 2*(24), 365–378.

Dempster, F. N. (1996). Distributing and managing the conditions of encoding and practice. In E. L. Bjork & R. A. Bjork (Eds.), *Handbook of perception and cognition: Memory* (pp. 317–344). San Diego, CA: Academic Press.

Duchek, J. M. (1984). Encoding and retrieval differences between young and old: The impact of attentional capacity usage. *Developmental Psychology, 20*(6), 1173–1180.

Estes, W. K. (1955). Statistical theory of distributional phenomena in learning. *Psychological Review, 62,* 369–377.

Faust, M. E., Balota, D. A., & Spieler, D. H. (2001). Building episodic connections: Changes in episodic priming with age and dementia. *Neuropsychology, 15,* 626–637.

Glenberg, A. M. (1977). Influences of retrieval processes on the spacing effect in free recall. *Journal of Experimental Psychology: Human Learning and Memory, 3*(3), 282–294.

Greene, R. L. (1992). Repetition paradigms. In R. L. Greene (Ed.), *Human memory: Paradigms and paradoxes* (pp. 132–152). Hillsdale, NJ: Lawrence Erlbaum Associates, Inc.

Hayden, C. M., & Camp, C. J. (1995). Spaced-retrieval: A memory intervention for dementia in Parkinson's disease. *The Clinical Gerontologist, 16*(3), 80–82.

Hochhalter, A. K., Overmier, J. B., Gasper, S. M., Bakke, B. L., & Holub, R. J. (2005). A comparison of spaced retrieval to other schedules of practice for people with dementia. *Experimental Aging Research, 31,* 101–118.

Karpicke, J. D. (2004). *Test-enhanced learning: The effects of repeated tests and the spacing of tests on long-term retention.* Unpublished Masters thesis, Washington University, St. Louis, MO.

Karpicke, J. D., & Roediger, H. L., III. (2005). *Does expanding retrieval work?* Poster presented at the Midwestern Psychological Association conference, Chicago.

Landauer, T. K., & Bjork, R. A. (1978). Optimum rehearsal patterns and name learning. In M. Gruneberg, P. E. Morris, & R. N. Sykes (Eds.), *Practical aspects of memory* (pp. 625–632). London: Academic Press.

Lee, M. M., & Camp, C. J. (2001). Spaced-retrieval: A memory intervention for HIV+ older adults. *The Clinical Gerontologist, 22*(3/4), 131–135.

Logan, J. M. (2004). *Spaced and expanded retrieval effects in younger and older adults.* Unpublished doctoral dissertation, Washington University, St. Louis, MO.

McGeogh, J. A. (1943). *The psychology of human learning.* New York: Longmans Green.

McKitrick, L. A., & Camp, C. J. (1993). Relearning the names of things: The spaced-retrieval intervention implemented by a caregiver. *The Clinical Gerontologist, 14,* 60–62.

McKitrick, L. A., Camp, C. J., & Black, F. W. (1992). Prospective memory intervention in Alzheimer's disease. *Journal of Gerontology: Psychological Sciences, 47,* 337–343.

Melton, A. W. (1970). The situation with respect to the spacing of repetitions and memory. *Journal of Verbal Learning and Verbal Behavior, 9,* 596–606.

Morris, P. E., & Fritz, C. O. (2000). The name game: Using retrieval practice to improve the learning of names. *Journal of Experimental Psychology: Applied, 6,* 124–129.

Morris, P. E., & Fritz, C. O. (2002). The improved name game: Better use of expanding retrieval practice. *Memory, 10,* 259–266.

Morris, P. E., Fritz, C. O., & Buck, S. (2004). The name game: Acceptability, bonus information and group size. *Applied Cognitive Psychology, 18,* 89–104.

Peterson, L. R., Wampler, R., Kirkpatrick, M., & Saltzman, D. (1963). Effect of spacing presentations on retention of a paired associate over short intervals. *Journal of Experimental Psychology, 66*(2), 206–209.

Rea, C. P., & Modigliani, V. (1985). The effect of expanded versus massed practice on the retention of multiplication facts and spelling lists. *Human Learning: Journal of Practical Research and Applications, 4*(1), 11–18.

Riley, K. P. (1992). Bridging the gap between researchers and clinicians: Methodological perspectives and choices. In R. L. West & J. D. Sinnott (Eds.), *Everyday memory and aging: Current research and methodology* (pp. 182–189). New York: Springer-Verlag.

Roediger, H. L., III, & Karpicke, J. D. (2006). Test-enhanced learning: Taking memory tests improves long term memory. *Psychological Science, 17*, 249–255.

Schacter, D. L., Rich, S. A., & Stampp, M. S. (1985). Remediation of memory disorders: Experimental evaluation of the spaced-retrieval technique. *Journal of Clinical and Experimental Neuropsychology, 7*, 70–96.

Spieler, D. H., & Balota, D. A. (1996). Characteristics of associative learning in younger and older adults: Evidence from an episodic priming paradigm. *Psychology and Aging, 11*, 607–620.

Spitzer, H. F. (1939). Studies in retention. *Journal of Educational Psychology, 30*, 641–657.

Wilson, B. A., Baddeley, A., Evans, J., & Shiel, A. (1994). Errorless learning in the rehabilitation of memory impaired people. *Neuropsychological Rehabilitation, 4*, 307–326.

Wilson, B. A., & Evans, J. J. (1996). Error-free learning in the rehabilitation of people with memory impairments. *Journal of Head Trauma Rehabilitation, 11*, 54–64.

7

A Brief History of Memory and Aging

AIMÉE M. SURPRENANT, TAMRA J. BIRETA, and LISA A. FARLEY

*I*n addition to his empirical work, Roddy Roediger has written tutorials, commentaries, encyclopedia articles, summaries of entire areas, textbooks, practical guides to research, career guides, and guides to professional development. Throughout all of his work there is a clear sensitivity to history. He has written and given talks on the works of Ebbinghaus, Bartlett, Ballard, Deese, Nipher, and others, and, through his many editorships, he has supported the efforts of others in this direction. Even though he is no longer the editor, *Psychonomic Bulletin and Review*, a journal Roddy reinvented, is known to welcome submissions exploring the history of experimental psychology. If that were not enough, in recent years Roddy's research program has added a new facet, exploring age-related differences in memory, particularly as it concerns false memory. Thus, it seemed appropriate to combine those interests and delve into the history of memory and aging at the conference in his honor.

The purpose of this chapter, therefore, is to summarize the history of beliefs and research that serves as the foundation of current work on memory and aging. Although there have been in-depth articles on the history of life-span developmental psychology (Baltes, 1983), histories and surveys of the psychology of aging (Birren, 1961a, 1961b; Birren & Schroots, 2001; Granick, 1950; Pressey, Janney, & Kuhlen, 1939), and comprehensive considerations of the history of memory (e.g., Burnham, 1888; Murray, 1976; Yates, 1966), there is no published look into the history of *aging* and *memory* specifically. Our review begins by briefly mentioning some of the ideas on aging and memory in the ancient (primarily western) world and then jumps to European philosophy/early science in the late 1700s/early 1800s. After devoting some time to the early part of the 20th century, we wind up in the post Second World War era. Along the way we will point out the similarities and differences in the questions and controversies that were important then with current conceptions of memory and aging. This account will, of necessity, be extremely selective.

THE ANCIENT WORLD

Many ancient religions acknowledged the fundamental importance of memory (and learning) by making a deity in charge of that faculty. For example, the ancient Egyptians had Thoth (*circa* 3000 BCE), the scribe, who was said to have invented the sacred writing of hieroglyphics (Bleeker, 1973). This gift of writing was not entirely appreciated as a memory aid: Socrates told a fable in which the King of Egypt spurned Thoth's gift of writing, suggesting that,

> this discovery of yours will create forgetfulness in the learners' souls, because they will not use their memories; they will trust to the external written characters and not remember of themselves. And so the specific which you have discovered is an aid not to memory, but to reminiscence.
>
> (Hermann & Chaffin, 1988, p. 38)

Living to old age in ancient Egyptian society was considered a gift from the gods, and elders were revered for their wisdom and often consulted in times of need.[1] Extant writings on tombs and other monuments make reference to the many top officials in the ancient Egyptian government who were in their 60s and 70s, demonstrating that they had retained their intellectual faculties, including memory (Janssen & Janssen, 1996). Many of the Kings and Pharaohs were said to have lived over 100 years.

Similarly, the ancient Greeks had Mnemosyne (*circa* 1000 BCE), a Titaness who was the goddess of memory and the mother of the Muses (muse means one who remembers). From her name we take the words "memory," "mnemonic," and "mnemonist" (Puhvel, 2000). Mnemosyne was considered to be one of the most powerful goddesses of her time. This is not surprising because, at least as the Greeks saw it, it is the capacity for conscious memory that that distinguishes humans from all other animals. Memory is the faculty that allows us to reason, to predict, and to anticipate outcomes, and is thus the foundation upon which civilization rests. Out of Mnemosyne come the Muses, her daughters, all of whom have a science or an art to protect. Thus, metaphorically, the sciences and the arts arise from memory. Mnemosyne is also attributed with the power to call things to memory and to remembrance (mneme). The distinction between memory storage and recollection or reminiscence is one that has gained a lot of interest in recent times (e.g., Tulving, 1999, 2000) but it seems rather commonplace in the ancient world (see also Aristotle, below).

There is not much in the written record in this era on what happens to memory when people grow old (or what Mnemosyne does to people). However, gauging by mythological tales and Greek literature (Richardson, 1969), the ancient Greeks did not seem to hold old age in a very positive light. The gods were distinguished from humans by not "suffering" from old age. In one myth, Eos, a goddess, successfully cajoled Zeus into granting her lover Tithonus immortal life. However, she made the critical error of neglecting to ask for eternal youth. As her lover aged, he became increasingly feeble and unbalanced, eventually driving Eos to desperation with his constant babbling. As a last resort, she turned him into a grasshopper. This myth explains why grasshoppers chirp incessantly—like demented old men.

In contrast to the pessimistic view of aging seen in Greek mythology, eastern traditions, similar to those of ancient Egypt, have endowed old age with wisdom and have respected the knowledge and memories of their elders. For example, Confucius (551–479 BCE) is almost always portrayed as an old man with a tremendous memory. In the Analects of Confucius he discusses memory with an acolyte:

> The Master said, "Ci [Zi-gong], do you think I learned by being widely read and well retained?" Answered: "Yes. Is this not so?" [The Master] said, "No. I learned by threading everything together into a unified whole."
> (Confucius, 1999, Book 15, Part 3, p. 183)

In the above quote Confucius explains that he uses previously-existing knowledge to bind meaningful information together in order to remember it. This is perhaps the first written description of how structure and organization can aid memory. Contrary to Socrates' dismissal of the art of writing, Confucius felt that it was a very useful memory aid: "The palest ink is better than the best memory."

Moving forward in time we come to Aristotle (384–322 BCE), who is a favorite of memory researchers because he wrote a treatise specifically on the topic, *De Memoria et Reminiscentia* (*On Memory and Reminiscence*). According to Aristotle, perception stamps an impression on memory like a seal into hot wax. Although the impression remains over time, it eventually becomes fuzzy and cracked at the edges as the wax changes with heat and cold. If the wax is young and motile or old and frayed the initial impressions are less distinct, leading to memory failures. Or, as Aristotle put it, "Hence both very young and very old persons are defective in memory; they are in a state of flux, the former because of their growth, the latter, owing to their decay" (Herrmann & Chaffin, 1988, p. 65).

Essentially, Aristotle's view is an encoding deficit hypothesis for both very young and very old individuals: The information does not make a firm impression on their minds and thus is not well-remembered. This idea of encoding deficits accompanying aging is at least part of many modern theories of memory and aging (Simon, 1979). Aristotle's view also might also be mapped on to some of the generalized slowing (e.g., Birren, 1956; Salthouse, 1985a) or common cause (e.g., Baltes & Lindenberger, 1997) theories of aging and cognition.

Next in our survey of the ancient world comes the Roman senator and consul (the highest Roman office) Marcus Tullius Cicero (106–143 BCE) who wrote a treatise specifically *On Old Age* (*De Senectute*). He spoke in the voice of Cato the Elder in the year 150 BCE when Cato was 84 years old. The essay consists of a series of answers by Cato to questions posed by two younger men about the nature of old age. Cato supports a fatalistic standpoint on aging, saying it is inevitable and arguing that to rebel against it is to rebel against Nature. However, he also has an optimistic view, suggesting that those reasonable men who keep themselves active and part of society can actually contribute more than young men: "Old men retain their intellects well enough, if only they keep their minds active and fully employed."

In the same essay, Cato also says:

> Nor, in point of fact, have I ever heard of any old man forgetting where he had hidden his money. They remember everything that interests them: when to answer to their bail, business appointments, who owes them money, and to whom they owe it.

This, then, is a statement of a disuse theory of memory and aging—use it or lose it. Cicero, through Cato, also suggests that things that are important to older adults are remembered and they may deliberately choose to feign senility when it suits them.

From the ancient world, then, we have an encoding deficit theory, perhaps a common cause or generalized slowing theory and a disuse theory of memory and aging.

100–1700 CE

We then enter a long period of very little attention given to memory and aging. There was a lot of interest in aging, why we age and how we might avoid aging including the search for the fountain of youth as well as anti-aging elixirs. In addition, there was a lot of interest in memory, how it works, and how external mnemonics might be used to aid memory. However, there seems to have been little written on the intersection of age and memory. Even so, we can make some inferences about how some famous thinkers might describe memory and aging from their writings on other topics.

Galen (131–201 CE), a physician, believed that as we age the fuel of the body begins to dry up and the body becomes more and more cold. Thus, logically, all faculties would tend to decline. According to Galen, nature does everything for the best; old age is not contrary to nature and so old age is not a disease. Because all bodily functions, including intellectual functioning, are tied to the heat given off by the body, Galen would be likely to support a common cause view of aging and cognition.

Whereas Galen attributed aging to part of a natural process, Augustine (354–430 CE) attributed aging to original sin and felt it was God's will and not to be tampered with. Accordingly, any decline in abilities as a function of age would be assumed to be predestined.

Roger Bacon (1214–1292) and other alchemists, on the other hand, were always searching for the medicine that would cure diseases and prolong life. "Old age," he wrote, "is the home of forgetfulness." In 1250 he wrote a treatise on the retardation of old age, *The Cure of Old Age and Preservation of Youth* (*De Retardatione Accidentum Senectutis cum Aliis Opusculus de Rebus Medicinalibus*). As a consequence, it is easy to imagine that Bacon would suppose that mental decline as a function of age is not inevitable and that a magic pill or elixir could be found to reverse the ravages of time.

Renaissance memory theorists tended to focus on mnemonics and did not specifically worry about memory and aging (see Yates, 1966, for a review). Even towards the end of the renaissance, focus was still on memory and not on memory and aging. For example, Francis Bacon (1561–1626) is often credited with emphasizing empirical discoveries rather than metaphysical speculation. He suggested that successful memory retrieval consists of prenotion (in modern terms, narrowing the search set) and emblem (concreteness). He also articulated an early form of depth of processing (Craik & Lockhart, 1972): "things which are waited for and raise the attention dwell longer in the memory than what flies quickly by" (Herrmann & Chaffin, 1988, p. 166). Bacon did not specifically address memory and aging.

EUROPEAN PHILOSOPHY/EARLY SCIENCE

The systematic study of memory and aging, as with most of psychology, has its roots in European philosophy. However, it comes from a lifespan development, rather than associationist or empiricist, tradition.

One of the earliest developmental psychologists/philosophers was Johann Nicolas Tetens (1736–1807). Tetens was a professor of physics and metaphysics as well as philosophy and mathematics in Bitzow and Kiel in Germany. He is described as a founding father of developmental psychology and as an early empirical psychologist who had a "firm determination to rely on nothing other than immediate observation as such or evident reason confirmed by compatible observations" (Müller-Brettel & Dixon, 1990). Tetens posited three fundamental issues in aging (from Baltes, 1983):

(1) Does the performance decrement as observed in older persons necessarily index decline or can it be seen instead as evidence for further development (change, not deficit, theory)?
(2) To what degree is the performance a function of nonuse (a disuse theory)?
(3) Is aging due to regression or the reverse of development?

Tetens suggested that memory decrements in elderly persons could be seen as adaptive. In his view, sensations and ideas are modified by the mind and reproduced internally. This reproduced form is put inside the soul and "enveloped" with other ideas leaving a trace corresponding to it (a trace theory of memory). According to Tetens, a major problem in memory performance of older people is not one of storing the memory trace but one of retrieval, that of reaching the "enveloped" memory material or making it conscious. The ideas are not forgotten, they are just enveloped by other ideas. This seems to be one of the first mentions of a retrieval deficit hypothesis as a cause of memory deficits as a function of age.

The Galton Laboratory was founded at University College London ("the godless institution of Gower Street") in 1904, as a center for research in human genetics. Its director, Sir Francis Galton (1812–1911) was one of many Victorian natural philosopher/scientists who had wide-ranging interests including geography, meteorology, experimental psychology, eugenics, and more. He is considered to be one of the founders of differential psychology, invented fingerprint identification, and was a pioneer of statistical correlation and regression. In 1885 he created what he called an "Anthropometric Laboratory" whose purpose was "For the Measurement in Various Ways of Human Form and Faculty." Today, visitors to the Galton Laboratory, housed at University College, London, can see photos of his laboratory, copies of the advertisement for his laboratory, subject data sheets, and the apparatuses that were used. Over the course of many years the laboratory collected observations on over 9000 individuals ranging in age from young children to the very aged. The Galton laboratory measured such things as head size, height, response time to sound and sight. Due to the massive amount of data collected, a great deal of it was not analyzed until much later (if at all).

In 1923 Koga and Morant published a new analysis of some of Galton's data on simple response times to visual and auditory stimuli as a function of age. Figure 7.1 shows the data for response time to sound along with a cubic function that Koga and Morant fit to the data. Although we only display the auditory data here, the curves for both audition and vision were quite similar: There was a dramatic decrease in simple response times from early childhood to adulthood and a much more gentle increase from early adulthood to old age. In addition, both visual and auditory acuity declined as a function of age.

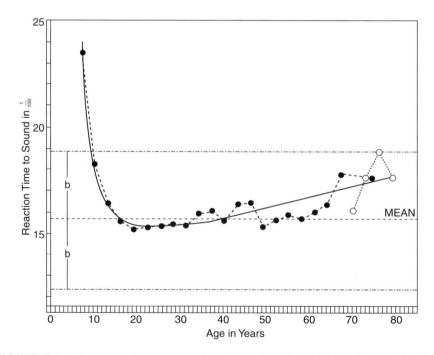

FIGURE 7.1   Response time to sound as a function of age. The points are the data and the continuous curve is a cubic function fit to the data. From Koga and Morant (1923).

However, the data show that, although sensory acuity does decline as a function of age, and response time increases as a function of age, the correlation between auditory and visual reaction times was much larger than that between auditory acuity and auditory reaction time or between visual acuity and visual reaction time. In other words, time to respond to a stimulus is mainly due to central, rather than peripheral, factors. Koga and Morant suggested that, "reaction times are a function of mental rather than sensory effectiveness and must be taken as a measure rather of mental briskness than sensory fitness" (p. 372). This, then, is a generalized slowing theory of aging (Salthouse, 1985b). These observations, collected more than a century ago with what today would seem to be very crude techniques, have stood the test of time and have been replicated using multiple response and sensory modalities (Birren & Botwinick, 1955; Birren & Fisher, 1995; Johnson et al., 1985; see also Salthouse, 1985a, for a review).

At about the same time that the Galton Laboratory was being created, Alois Alzheimer (1864–1915), a German neurologist and psychiatrist, presented the first pathological findings of presenile dementia at a psychiatrist's conference in 1906. Alzheimer published the same findings in 1907 in the article "A Characteristic Disease of the Cerebral Cortex." The article (1907/1987) introduces Auguste D, a 51-year-old wife of an office clerk, who had become a patient of Alzheimer's 5 years prior to exhibiting symptoms similar to senile dementia. Along with delusions and hallucinations, Auguste suffered from severe memory impairments: Although she could correctly identify many items shown to her, she could not recall the items shortly after their presentation (Maurer, Volk, & Gerbaldo, 2000).

In postmortem analyses, Alzheimer identified fibroid plaques that were typical of advanced senile dementia. In addition, Alzheimer also found evidence of dense fibroid tangles, which "indicated the site where once the neurons had been located" (1907/1987, p. 2). This led Alzheimer to believe he was encountering a "peculiar, little-known disease process" (p. 3) that was unique from senile dementia. Also, due to the relatively young age at which the disease seemed to begin, Emil Kraepelin, a colleague of Alzheimer who is credited with naming the disease "Alzheimer's disease," later classified the disease as "a more or less age-independent unique disease process" (1910/1987, p. 77). Thus, although most people think of Alzheimer's disease as a disease of old age, it in fact is not necessarily related to age, as Alzheimer himself noted. However, the observation that memory capabilities were directly tied to brain functioning was an important one in the history of memory.

Even as late as 1906 when James Rowland Angell (1869–1949) published the third edition of his well-received textbook *Psychology: An Introductory Study of the Structure and Function of Human Consciousness*, there was little in the way of experimental data on memory and aging. However, like the ancients, these early psychologists acknowledged certain patterns of memory impairment associated with increasing age:

> Memory of proper names is among the earliest of the losses and the more concrete are our ideas the earlier do we lose the memory of the words for them. It is a familiar fact too that old people are much more forgetful of recent

occurrences than of those which happened further back in the past. This is no doubt attributable to the loss of normal receptivity by the brain. It retains fairly well impressions made upon it at an earlier period, but it cannot now take on new ones.

(Angell, 1906, pp. 234–235)

Thus, Angell, like Aristotle, espoused an encoding/storage deficit of memory and aging. However he also proposed a temporal gradient with older memories being more robust than newer memories. Like others writing in this area at the time, the section of the text on aging and memory is long on supposition and extremely short on experimental data.

EXPERIMENTAL INVESTIGATIONS OF AGING AND MEMORY

Even though there had been sporadic investigations of cognitive aging up until this point, "research on the psychological aspects of aging did not begin seriously until the work of Walter Miles and associates about 1930" (Birren, 1959, p. 3). Miles directed the Stanford Later Maturity Study (Miles, 1931, 1933, 1967), which collected a variety of measurements on 863 individuals ranging in age from 6 to 95. In his 1931 paper Miles developed a unique theory of what changes as we age:

It is well known that cortical function is economical of energy and that motor function is spendthrift. A possible theory then for the slower and more difficult action in the old is that neural conservation mechanisms are built up or become more potent, with increasing lifetime. A particular decrement according to this theory would not be chiefly chargeable to a defect in the mechanism but to a positive check on it—a neural governor device protective of the mechanism. The weight of years may be in large part neural inhibition-interference to action. This is perhaps the core, or the basic behavior element, in the caution and proverbial good judgment of the old. Decrement appears more in feeling than it exists in fact.

(p. 633)

This "neural governing device" essentially prevents the brain from short-circuiting. As far as we can tell, no one has followed up on this curious theory.

Another example of early investigations of cognitive aging comes from Jones and Conrad (1933), who looked at the rate at which intelligence grows during childhood and declines during older adulthood. They used a test battery, which included memory measures such as digit-symbol substitution, that was used for assessing soldiers during "the World War." Jones and Conrad attempted to test all the individuals in particular New England communities between the ages of 10 and 60, thus completing a true population study. Their recruitment methods were somewhat sneaky and unlikely to be approved by ethics boards today:

The procedure involved a shrewd appeal to Yankee thrift and fair play. A free moving picture show was offered in a community hall. Then, during an intermission, the audience was asked to take the test . . . Individuals who did not attend the free movie were visited in their homes, and, if possible, were wheedled into taking the test there.

(Pressey et al., 1939, p. 164)

A total of 1191 individuals were tested. The data are reproduced in Figure 7.2. As is evident from the figure, there is a rapid increase in intelligence scores in early childhood to adulthood and then a gradual decline from a peak of about 20–30 years old. This figure looks remarkably like the inverse of the response time curves reported by Koga and Morant (1923; see Figure 7.1). Like contemporary lifespan researchers, Jones and Conrad (1933) and others studying intelligence in the field at the time (e.g., Shakow, Dolkart, & Goldman, 1938; Wechsler, 1944; Willoughby, 1929) considered issues such as cohort effects, physical health, etc., as difficulties in interpreting such cross-sectional data as a real reduction in intelligence.

Although these early psychometric investigations included memory tasks among a battery of other cognitive tasks, one of the first large-scale studies on aging and *memory* specifically was conducted by Gilbert (1941). The report was published in the *Journal of Abnormal and Social Psychology*, presumably because there was no more appropriate venue. The paper is unexpected in that it reads like a contemporary article.[2] The behaviorist language that characterizes much of the early verbal learning literature is absent and the methods for each test are almost all identical to ones still in use today.

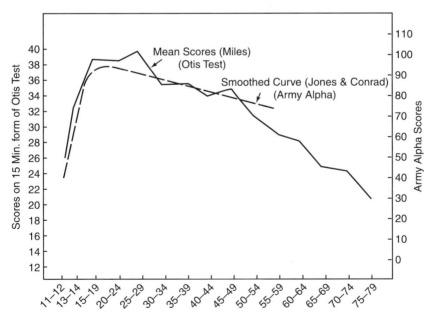

FIGURE 7.2 Growth and decline of intelligence from 10 to 80 (from Jones & Conrad, 1933; Miles, 1933). As with Galton's data, these observations are readily replicable using modern intelligence tests (see Salthouse, 1985a, for a review).

Gilbert (1941) tested 174 individuals between the ages of 60 and 69 years old and the same number of individuals between the ages of 20 and 29 years. Each individual was exactly matched with another individual in the other age group in terms of his or her score on a vocabulary test. They were then given eleven separate memory tests ranging from digit span to retention of a paragraph of text over a delay interval. Her data are plotted in Figure 7.3.

Gilbert's (1941) tasks included three measures of span (visual, auditory, and backward span); immediate sentence repetition and immediate and delayed paragraph memory tasks (from the Stanford-Binet battery); and immediate, delayed paired associates, and a Turkish-English vocabulary test (from the Revised Babcock Test of Mental Efficiency). The Knox cubes test (Knox, 1914), is similar to Corsi blocks task except that there are only four cubes placed in a single row. The experimenter uses a small cube to tap on one of the four larger cubes in patterns of increasing complexity. The subject is asked to recreate each sequence. Although there were significant differences between the groups in all of the conditions, the more complex the task, the larger the difference. Gilbert then compared the "brightest older persons" in the sample to the total 20-year-old group and found that this select group was actually superior to the younger group on many of the tasks, but even so fell below the younger group on those tasks requiring the formation and retention of new associations.

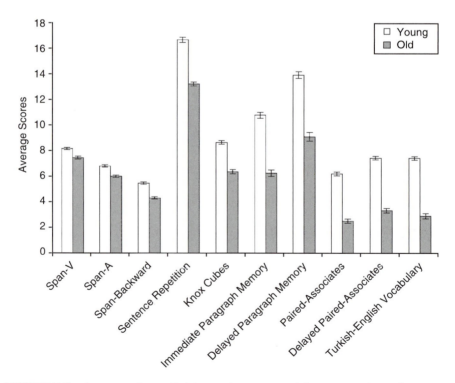

FIGURE 7.3 A comparison of older and younger adults on a variety of memory tests ($N = 348$). From Gilbert (1941).

Gilbert concluded that "[t]he greatest obstacle is in the formation of entirely new associations, particularly if these may interfere in any way with previously formed associations, as in paired associates (both immediate recall and retention) and in the retention of Turkish-English vocabulary" (1941, p. 85). These data have been replicated many times and this conclusion is a direct precursor to the associative deficit hypothesis supported by Naveh-Benjamin and colleagues (e.g., Naveh-Benjamin, 2000; Naveh-Benjamin, Hussain, Guez, & Bar-On, 2003).

Along with the increase in experimental data on memory and aging came an increase in physiological investigations on the same topic. In 1942 Donald O. Hebb noticed that the tests that are not impaired by late brain injury (i.e., tests of vocabulary and information) appear to remain intact with advancing age. Hebb suggested two types of intelligence: "(A) the development of direct intellectual power, by neural maturation, and (B) the establishment of routine modes of response to common problems, or of perceptual and conceptual modifications leading to qualitative modifications of behavior" (p. 289). Intellectual power is what is often being tested in intelligence tests. This power "which is generally thought to reach its peak earliest, perhaps between the ages of 12 to 15 years, is the kind which is also apt to be sensitive to the effect of brain injury after this period, and sensitive as well to the changes of senescence" (p. 289). However, intelligence does not involve only (A), but also (B), and should thus "continue to rise to the point at which declining intellectual power offset the increase of intellectual products" (p. 290). This is clearly a distinction between crystallized and fluid intelligence from a physiological point of view.

It is sometimes instructive to look at contemporary textbooks to as an indication of the prominent theories in any time period. One of the most well-known textbooks of the time was written by McGeoch (1942) and had a chapter on learning as a function of chronological age, sex, and test intelligence. In the section on age, McGeoch says:

> Age, in the sense of the length of time lived by an individual, cannot itself be a determiner of learning. Time, in and of itself, does nothing, but is scientifically important not only as an index of other variables which are correlated with it or, in more figurative terms, because it is the bearer of other conditions. When we use age as an independent experimental variable, we retard it as a useful symbol for the complex conditions which age brings with it.
>
> (p. 207)

This lesson is one that has been well-taken by future researchers in the area and is why most of the results are couched in terms of "age-related" differences between older and younger adults. (As an aside it is interesting to note that in the 1952 revision of the textbook, published after McGeoch's death, the chapter is retitled "Individual differences and learning," placed at the end of the book, and says little about age-related differences.)

In the chapter McGeoch (1942) discusses methodological issues such as advantages and disadvantages of cross-sectional and longitudinal designs and cohort effects. From the theoretical side, he mainly focuses on a maturation–

degeneration hypothesis (aging is the un-doing of development) and a hypothesis of changing conditions of learning (transfer, motivation, and personality traits). McGeoch suggests that older adults will show decreased learning rates in conditions that require a reorganization of older learned behaviors. Thus, the bulk of the difference between older and younger adults has to do with increasing negative transfer as a function of more and more experience. Again, chronological age or time, *per se*, is not the causal factor in age-related differences in memory; it is what occurs during that time.

In 1946 Alan Welford, along with Frederick Bartlett, founded the Nuffield Unit for Research into Problems of Ageing at Cambridge and became one of the founding fathers of aging research in Great Britain. Alan Welford is best known for his book *Ageing and Human Skill* (1958) in which he challenged the use of reductionist methods in studying aging and, instead, suggested that a better strategy would involve "taking complex, continuous performances and making analyses to reveal their essential 'key' features" (p. 2). Fittingly, this suggestion foreshadows the "components of processing" approach described by Roediger, Buckner, and McDermott (1999). Welford also emphasized the whole organism and the need to take genetics, environment, and accumulated skills into account when developing theories of aging and cognition. In addition, Welford stressed the idea that not only do older adults perform more slowly on many complex tasks, they also can and will carry them out in qualitatively different ways. Thus, we should look at the pattern of data as well as overall level of performance in making inferences about differences between older and younger adults.

In addition to the impact Welford had on the field of human factors, he also discussed the importance of the limited capacity short-term store and noted that individual differences in problem solving are mainly caused by short-term or working memory limitations. He realized that older individuals tend to exhibit a greater deficit the more complex a task becomes. In today's parlance, we would say that performance of older adults is more affected by working memory tasks that require active reorganization of materials than short-term memory tasks that merely require a passive retention of information. This was a prescient idea and, indeed, as Rabbitt (1997) put it, "In all but the coinage of their indispensable phrase 'working memory', Alan [Welford] seems to have anticipated Baddeley and Hitch (1974) by nearly 30 years" (p. 977).

The Nuffield Institute and others of its kind spurred a great deal of research in aging, and in 1959, James E. Birren edited one of the first compendia of the literature on the psychology of aging in his edited volume, *Handbook of Aging and the Individual*. The volume covers the entire field from the biological bases of aging to social and personality theories of aging and includes chapters on age and learning, experimental studies, theories of learning and aging; intelligence and problem solving.

In one of the chapters in the *Handbook*, entitled "Theories of Learning and Aging", Harry Kay provides a comprehensive review of the literature up until that point. He breaks down the stages that make up learning into "its traditional three R's—registration, retention, and recall" (p. 615). The theories he reviews mainly spring from a behaviorist tradition, although Kay is careful to give credit to the influences of the biological and physical sciences as well as mathematics on the field. He delves deeply into Hullian theory as it pertains to aging and touches briefly on plasticity and Hebbian learning. The relatively new "cybernetics and communication theory" and "information theory" are also given a brief consideration.

Kay identifies five theoretical constructs employed in studies on aging: maturation degeneration, transfer, retroactive and proactive inhibition, and the influences of early experiences, all of which are, to one extent or another, constructs that are still used today. Finally he considers some of the difficulties in conducting studies on aging and learning including inter- and intraindividual variability, task complexity, motivation, and the difficulties in comparing different types of tasks. In conclusion Kay notes: "This chapter has been concerned with the interaction between learning theory and aging phenomena. Such interaction is more a pious hope for the future than a matter of recordable history" (1959, p. 649). In the years that followed, there has been an explosion of research on memory and aging, more than fulfilling Kay's wishes.

SUMMARY AND CONCLUSIONS

From the ancients we have theories of disuse, encoding deficit, and generalized slowing as explanations of age-related decline. Tetens added a change in processing idea as well as aging being the reverse of development. The psychometricians generally seemed to prefer a generalized intellectual decline, with Hebb adding physiological basis for the difference between crystallized and fluid intelligence. Gilbert suggested an associative deficit, while learning theorists discussed interference (or inhibition) as possible causes of age-related differences in memory functioning.

Current theories of differences in memory as a function of age include disuse, episodic decay (Tulving, 1983), slowed speed of processing/generalized decline (Baltes & Lindenberger, 1997; Salthouse, 1985b; 1996; Verhaegen & Salthouse, 1997), inhibition deficit (Hasher & Zacks, 1988; Hasher, Zacks & May, 1999), encoding/storage deficit (Craik & Byrd, 1982; Rabinowitz, Craik, & Ackerman, 1982), binding/associative deficit hypothesis (Naveh-Benjamin, 2000; Naveh-Benjamin et al., 2003), and reduced resources and/or lack of environmental support (Craik, 1983, 1986; Craik, Anderson, Kerr, & Li, 1995). All of these views have clear historical precedents.

Theories that did not stand the test of time include Miles' "neural governor" and Cicero's idea that older adults feign senility when it serves their purposes. In addition, the disuse theory is not terribly popular for very good reasons (Salthouse, 1991). However, one could say that the majority of modern theories are represented, in one form or another, in the early writings and theorizing about memory and aging.

Although the bulk of the research on memory and aging is primarily found after 1960, its beginnings can be found in early philosophy and science. Many elements of contemporary ideas about aging and memory have similarity with ancient beliefs. In the early history of scientific psychology emphasis was placed on either experimental methods involving nonhuman animals, young adults, or children. Histories of cognitive psychology and developmental psychology generally do not include much consideration of age or adult development past late adolescence. However, in the past decades there has been a strong resurgence in interest in memory, and the literature is increasing exponentially. A knowledge of and appreciation for the early literature will surely be of use to any investigator hoping to make useful contributions.

ACKNOWLEDGMENT

Preparation of this chapter was sponsored by National Institute on Aging Grant AG021071 awarded to Aimée M. Surprenant.

NOTES

1. Much like many people consult Roddy.
2. At least up until the last paragraph in which Gilbert suggests that it is important to keep mentally active and cautions those older adults "who in later years tend either to cease reading entirely or to read trashy literature they would have scorned in their younger days" (1941, p. 86).

REFERENCES

Alzheimer, A. (1987). A characteristic disease of the cerebral cortex. In K. Bick, L. Amaducci, & G. Pepeu (Eds.), *The early story of Alzheimer's disease: Translation of the historical papers by Alois Alzheimer, Oskar Fischer, Francesco Bonfiglio, Emil Kraepelin, and Gaetano Perusini* (pp. 1–3). New York: Raven Press. (Original work published 1907)

Angell, J. R. (1906). *Psychology: An introductory study of the structure and function of human conscious* (3rd Ed.). New York: Henry Holt & Company.

Baltes, P. B. (1983). Life-span developmental psychology: Observations on history and theory revisited. In R. M. Lerner (Ed.), *Developmental psychology: Historical and philosophical perspectives* (pp. 79–111). Hillsdale, NJ: Lawrence Erlbaum Associates, Inc.

Baltes, P. B., & Lindenberger, U. (1997). Emergence of a powerful connection between sensory and cognitive functions across the adult life span: A new window to the study of cognitive aging? *Psychology and Aging, 12,* 12–21.

Birren, J. E. (1956). The significance of age changes in speed of perception and psychomotor response. In J. E. Anderson (Ed.), *Psychological aspects of aging* (pp. 97–104). Washington, DC: American Psychological Association.

Birren, J. E. (1959). *Handbook of aging and the individual.* Oxford, UK: Oxford University Press.

Birren, J. E. (1961a). A brief history of the psychology of aging, Part I. *The Gerontologist, 1,* 69–77.

Birren, J. E. (1961b). A brief history of the psychology of aging, Part II. *The Gerontologist, 1,* 127–134.

Birren, J. E., & Botwinick, J. (1955). Age differences in finger, jaw, and foot reaction time in auditory stimuli. *Journal of Gerontology, 10,* 429–432.

Birren, J. E., & Fisher, L. M. (1995). Aging and speed of behavior—possible consequences for psychological functioning. *Annual Review of Psychology, 46,* 329–353.

Birren, J. E., & Schroots, J. J. F. (2001). The history of geropsychology. In J. E. Birren & K. W. Schaie (Eds.), *Handbook of the psychology of aging* (pp. 3–28). San Diego, CA: Academic Press.

Bleeker, C. J. (1973). *Hathor and Thoth: Two key figures from the ancient Egyptian religion.* Leiden, The Netherlands: E. J. Brill.

Confucius. (1999). *The analects of Confucius. A new-millennium translation* (D. H. Li, Trans.). Bethesda, MD: Premier.

Craik, F. I. M. (1983). On the transfer of information from temporary to permanent memory. *Philosophical Transactions of the Royal Society of London, B302,* 341–359.

Craik, F. I. M. (1986). A functional account of age differences in memory. In F. Klix & H. Hagendorf (Eds.), *Human memory and cognitive capabilities, mechanisms and performances* (pp. 409–422). Amsterdam: North-Holland/Elsevier.

Craik, F. I. M., Anderson, N. D., Kerr, S. A., & Li, K. Z. (1995). Memory changes in normal aging. In A. D. Baddeley, B. A. Wilson, & F. N. Watts (Eds.), *Handbook of memory disorders* (pp. 221–241). New York: Wiley.

Craik, F. I. M., & Byrd, M. (1982). Aging and cognitive deficits: The role of attentional resources. In F. I. M. Craik & S. E. Trehub (Eds.), *Aging and cognitive processes* (pp. 191–211). New York: Plenum Press.

Craik, F. I. M., & Lockhart, R. S. (1972). Levels of processing: A framework for memory research. *Journal of Verbal Learning and Verbal Behavior, 11,* 671–684.

Gilbert, J. C. (1941). Memory loss in senescence. *Journal of Abnormal and Social Psychology, 36,* 73–86.

Granick, S. (1950). Studies in the psychology of senility—a survey. *Journal of Gerontology, 5,* 44–58.

Hasher, L., & Zacks, R. T. (1988). Working memory, comprehension, and aging: A review and a new view. In G. H. Bower (Ed.), *Advances in research and theory: Vol. 22. The psychology of learning and motivation* (pp. 193–225). San Diego, CA: Academic Press.

Hasher, L., Zacks, R. T., & May, C. P. (1999). Inhibitory control, circadian arousal, and age. In D. Gopher & A. Koriat (Eds.), *Attention and performance XVII: Cognitive regulation of performance: Interaction of theory and application* (pp. 653–675). Cambridge, MA: MIT Press.

Hebb, D. O. (1942). The effect of early and late brain injury upon test scores, and the nature of normal adult intelligence. *Proceedings of the American Philosophic Society, 85,* 275–292.

Herrmann, D. J., & Chaffin, R. (Eds.). (1988). *Memory in historical perspective: The literature before Ebbinghaus.* New York: Springer-Verlag.

Janssen, R. M., & Janssen, J. J. (1996). *Getting old in ancient Egypt.* London: Rubicon Press.

Johnson, R. C., McClearn, G. E., Yuen, S., Nagoshi, C. T., Ahern, F. M., & Cole, R. E. (1985). Galton's data a century later. *The American Psychologist, 8,* 875–892.

Jones, H. E., & Conrad, H. S. (1933). The growth and decline of intelligence: A study of a homogeneous group between ages of 10 and 60. *Genetic Psychology Monographs, 13,* 223–298.

Kay, H. (1959). Theories of learning and aging. In J. E. Birren (Ed.), *Handbook of aging and the individual* (pp. 614–654). Oxford, UK: University of Chicago Press.

Knox, H. A. (1914). A scale, based on the work at Ellis Island, for estimating mental defect. *Journal of the American Medical Association*, 10, 741–747.

Koga, Y., & Morant, G. M. (1923). On the degree of association between reaction times in the case of different senses. *Biometrika*, 15, 346–372.

Kraepelin, E. (1987) Senile and pre-senile dementias. In K. Bick, L. Amaducci, & G. Pepeu (Eds.), *The early story of Alzheimer's disease: Translation of the historical papers by Alois Alzheimer, Oskar Fischer, Francesco Bonfiglio, Emil Kraepelin, and Gaetano Perusini* (pp. 32–81). New York: Raven Press. (Original work published 1910)

Maurer, K., Volk, S., & Gerbaldo, H. (2000). The history of Alois Alzheimer's first case. In P. J. Whitehouse, K. Maurer, & J. F. Ballenger (Eds.), *Concepts of Alzheimer disease: Biological, clinical, and cultural perspectives* (pp. 5–29). Baltimore: Johns Hopkins University Press.

McGeoch, J. A. (1942). *The psychology of human learning*. New York: Longmans, Green.

McGeoch, J. A., & Irion, A. L. (1952). *The psychology of human learning*. New York: Longmans, Green.

Miles, W. R. (1931). Measures of certain human abilities throughout the lifespan. *Proceedings of the National Academy of Sciences of the United States of America*, 17, 627–633.

Miles, W. R. (1933). Age and human ability. *Psychological Review*, 44, 99–123.

Miles, W. R. (1967). Walter R. Miles. In E. G. Boring & G. Lindzey (Eds.), *A history of psychology in autobiography* (Vol. V, pp. 221–252). New York: Appleton Century Crofts.

Müller-Brettel, M., & Dixon, R. A. (1990). Johann Nicolas Tetens: A forgotten father of developmental psychology? *International Journal of Behavioral Development*, 13, 215–230.

Murray, D. J. (1976). Research on memory in the nineteenth century. *Canadian Journal of Psychology*, 30, 201–220.

Naveh-Benjamin, M. (2000). Adult age differences in memory performance: Tests of an associative deficit hypothesis. *Journal of Experimental Psychology: Learning, Memory, and Cognition*, 26, 1170–1187.

Naveh-Benjamin, M., Hussain, Z., Guez, J., & Bar-On, M. (2003). Adult age differences in episodic memory: Further support for an associative-deficit hypothesis. *Journal of Experimental Psychology: Learning, Memory, and Cognition*, 29, 826–837.

Pressey, S. L., Janney, J. E., & Kuhlen, R. G. (1939). *Life: A psychological survey*. New York: Harper & Brothers Publishers.

Puhvel, J. (2000). Memory, shmemory, lest we forget Mnemosyne: The vocabulary of memory and mindfulness in antiquity. In E. Tulving (Ed.), *Memory, consciousness, and the brain: The Tallinn conference* (pp. 3–6). Philadelphia: Psychology Press.

Rabbitt, P. (1997). Ageing and human skill: A 40th anniversary. *Ergonomics*, 40, 962–981.

Rabinowitz, J. C., Craik, F. I. M., & Ackerman, B. P. (1982). A processing resource account of age differences in recall. *Canadian Journal of Psychology*, 36, 325–344.

Richardson, B. E. (1969). *Old age among the ancient Greeks: The Greek portrayal of old age in literature, art, and inscriptions*. New York: Greenwood Press.

Roediger, H. L., Buckner, R. L., & McDermott, K. B. (1999). Components of processing. In J. K. Foster & M. Jelicic (Eds.), *Memory: Systems, process, or function?* (pp. 31–65). Oxford, UK: Oxford University Press.

Salthouse, T. A. (1985a). *A theory of cognitive aging*. Amsterdam: North-Holland.

Salthouse, T. A. (1985b). Speed of behavior and its implications for cognition. In J. E. Birren & K. W. Schaie (Eds.), *Handbook of the psychology of aging* (2nd ed., pp. 400–426). New York: Van Nostrand Reinhold.

Salthouse, T. A. (1991). *Theoretical perspectives on cognitive aging.* Hillsdale, NJ: Lawrence Erlbaum Associates, Inc.

Salthouse, T. A. (1996). The processing speed theory of adult age differences in cognition. *Psychological Review, 103,* 403–428.

Shakow, D., Dolkart, M. B., & Goldman, R. (1938). The effect of age on the Stanford Binet vocabulary score of adults. *Journal of Educational Psychology, 29,* 241–256.

Simon, E. (1979). Depth and elaboration of processing in relation to age. *Journal of Experimental Psychology: Human Learning and Memory, 5,* 115–124.

Tulving, E. (1983). *Elements of episodic memory.* New York: Oxford University Press.

Tulving, E. (1999). On the uniqueness of episodic memory. In L.-G. Nilsson & H. J. Markowitsch (Eds.), *Cognitive neuroscience of memory* (pp. 11–42). Ashland, OH: Hogrefe & Huber Publishers.

Tulving, E. (Ed.). (2000). *Memory, consciousness, and the brain: The Tallinn conference.* Philadelphia: Psychology Press.

Verhaeghen, P., & Salthouse, T. A. (1997). Meta-analyses of age-cognition relations in adulthood: Estimates of linear and nonlinear age effects and structural models. *Psychological Bulletin, 122,* 231–249.

Wechsler, D. (1944). *The measurement of adult intelligence.* Baltimore: Williams & Wilkins.

Welford, A. T. (1958). *Ageing and human skill.* Oxford, UK: Oxford University Press.

Willoughby, R. R. (1929). Incidental learning. *Journal of Educational Psychology, 20,* 671–682.

Yates, F. A. (1966). *The art of memory.* London: Routledge & Kegan Paul.

8

Making Distinctiveness Models of Memory Distinct

IAN NEATH and GORDON D. A. BROWN

*R*oddy is well known for many different contributions to experimental psychology in general and to the study of memory in particular. Although not usually thought of as a modeler, he is well known for his SPAM ("Sponge Associative Memory") model. Given the distinctive nature of that model, we thought a history of distinctiveness models of memory, in which we describe, compare, and contrast different formulations of distinctiveness, would be an appropriate contribution to this volume in his honor.

Many theories of memory utilize the principle of distinctiveness, i.e., the idea that the difficulty in correctly recalling or identifying an item depends primarily on the degree to which it "stands out" from other items in the set. The basic idea is not new, of course. Burnham (1888), for example, traces the concept back to Aristotle; Calkins (1894) reports early experimental work on distinctiveness; and Koffka (1935) includes a detailed theoretical discussion (see also Köhler, 1929). One charge often leveled at theories based on distinctiveness is that they rarely provide a precise definition of what it means for an item to be distinct (cf. Hunt, 1995). Such a position overlooks the many distinctiveness theories that have been quantified and therefore mathematically define "distinctiveness".

We first review the major distinctiveness models that have been proposed, dividing them into three classes: Global Distinctiveness models, Local Distinctiveness models, and Temporal-Ratio models. We show that global distinctiveness models have an inherent fatal flaw, whereas Temporal-Ratio models are limited in scope. We then describe SIMPLE (Brown, Neath, & Chater, 2002; Neath & Brown, 2006), a recent local distinctiveness model, and analyze the formal relations among the models. Finally, we show how SIMPLE can be seen as a generalization of Temporal-Ratio models, such that it becomes a local distinctiveness model that includes some Temporal-Ratio models as a special case.

GLOBAL DISTINCTIVENESS MODELS

The hallmark of a global distinctiveness model is that it proposes that the distinctiveness of an item is given by the degree to which it differs from all the other items. Murdock's (1960) influential formulation provided the foundation for many subsequent accounts, but it shared some similarities with Helson's (1947) adaptation-level theory. In particular, both emphasized that all stimuli can affect a particular item in a group and both proposed unifying links between results from disparate paradigms.

Murdock's (1960) global distinctiveness model[1] was designed to provide a unifying account of the ubiquitous serial position functions observed in both absolute identification and serial learning paradigms. In a typical absolute identification experiment, subjects are exposed to a set of stimuli that vary systematically along only one dimension (e.g., nine tones of different frequencies, or seven lines of different lengths). A label, often a digit, is associated with each stimulus. The task is simply to produce the correct label in response to the presentation of an item from the set. In the case of serial learning, the sole dimension is ordinal position and the subject's task is to recall all of the items.

Murdock's model begins with the assumption that the value of each item (i.e., its length in millimeters, or its ordinal position) undergoes a logarithmic transformation, resulting in a Log Energy (LE) value. The total distinctiveness, TD, of item i in a set of n items is calculated by summing the difference between the LE value of the item and the LE value of all the other items, as shown in Equation 8.1.

$$TD_i = \sum_{j=1}^{n} |LE_i - LE_j| \qquad\qquad 8.1$$

The relative percent distinctiveness of an item, D%, for item i in a set of n items is the item's total distinctiveness divided by the sum of total distinctiveness of all the items, as shown in Equation 8.2. Note that there are no free parameters.

$$D\%_i = 100 \times \frac{TD_i}{\sum_{j=1}^{n} TD_j} \qquad\qquad 8.2$$

Table 8.1 shows an example calculation for the case of 5 pure tones that vary only in frequency. The values were picked to produce log energy values that differed by 0.05. The D% scale predicts the percentage of correct responses that will be given to each of the stimuli. It therefore makes predictions about relative performance rather than absolute performance.

When applied to serial learning, Murdock (1960, p. 24) assumed that "distinctiveness is a function of the ordinal position in the series" so the only change necessary is to use the ordinal position of the to-be-remembered item instead of the physical value. This produces the characteristic bow-shaped serial position

TABLE 8.1   Example Calculation of D% in Murdock's (1960) Global Distinctiveness Model for Five Pure Tones that Vary Only in Frequency; the Values were Picked to Produce Log Energy Values that Differed by 0.05

Frequency (Hz)	Log energy	TD	D%
316.23	2.50	0.500	25.0%
354.81	2.55	0.350	17.5%
398.10	2.60	0.300	15.0%
446.68	2.65	0.350	17.5%
501.18	2.70	0.500	25.0%

curve because end items have a greater summed distance and thus greater relative distinctiveness than middle items.

The D% scale has several interesting properties. First, D% will be the same regardless of whether one uses a natural log or log base 10 to transform raw stimulus energy values, and using a power function rather than a log transform (e.g., Stevens, 1957) does not markedly alter the performance of the model (except by skewing the serial position curve), although it does add a parameter. Second, D% does not change if either (1) all stimulus values are multiplied by some constant greater than zero or (2) all stimulus values are raised to some power greater than zero. Third, it is mathematically impossible to create a set of three or more stimuli in which all stimuli have the same D% value. Fourth, it is a mathematical requirement that the middle item (or middle items for lists with an even number of stimuli) must always be the least distinctive.

Many other global distinctiveness models have been based on Murdock's (1960) formulation. For example, Rips (1975) adopted a multidimensional generalization to account for aspects of inductive reasoning, but preserved the global characteristics of the model. Johnson (1991) proposed a distinctiveness model of associative learning in which the strength of a remote association is determined by the distinctiveness of a given position code. Nairne, Neath, Serra, and Byun (1997) also proposed a global distinctiveness model that, like Murdock's, used position as the distinctiveness-determining dimension. However, rather than using ordinal position as the underlying dimension along which items are represented (values that remain unchanged over time), they invoked perturbation theory (e.g., Estes, 1972; Nairne, 1991) to describe how memories of position become fuzzy and uncertain.

Neath (1993) proposed using a temporal dimension when modeling recognition and recall rather than one based on ordinal position. The "temporal distance" of an item is the time that elapses between the item's presentation and recall of the item. Distinctiveness is calculated the same way as in Murdock's (1960) model except that the values are based on the log-transformed temporal distance of items rather than on ordinal position. This approach has the advantage of being able to predict different levels of performance for an item at serial position 2, for example, when the temporal presentation schedule of the list varies. Of most interest is the ability to account for the decrease in recency and increase in primacy as the retention interval increased (cf. Knoedler, Hellwig, & Neath, 1999).

Global distinctiveness models, such as those described above, make a clear prediction: The middle item must always be the *least* distinct because it item is always the least distant from the other items (Bower, 1971; Murdock, 1960). Consider two sets of 9 rods used in an absolute identification experiment (Neath, Brown, McCormack, Chater, & Freeman, 2006, Exp. 2). In the uniform condition, the shortest rod is 60 mm long and each successive rod is 19.49% longer; thus, the middle rod is 104.94 mm and the longest rod is 183.50 mm.[2] In the isolate condition, each rod is only 12% longer than the preceding item, with the exception of the fifth rod, which is 36% longer than the fourth rod and 36% shorter than the sixth. However, the shortest rod is still 60 mm, the middle rod is still 104.94, and the longest rod is still 183.50 mm. Subjects are shown each rod and are asked to identify it (i.e., respond that it is Rod 2 or Rod 7).

The upper left panel of Figure 8.1 shows the results of the experiment: Identification of the middle item in the isolate condition was excellent, roughly equivalent to identification of the end items in the uniform list. The upper right panel shows the predictions of Murdock's (1960) global distinctiveness model: The model clearly predicts the data for the uniform condition accurately, but equally clearly fails to predict the data for the isolate condition. The reason is that within the model, a middle item such as Rod 5 must always be the least distinct.

LOCAL DISTINCTIVENESS MODELS

Global distinctiveness models contrast sharply with local distinctiveness models, according to which it is mainly the similarity to nearby items in psychological space that determines the distinctiveness of that item. Although not framed as such, Bower's (1971) stimulus generalization model can be seen as a local distinctiveness model because the generalization gradient causes near items to become more important to subsequent performance than distant items.

The stimulus generalization model, like Murdock's (1960) model, builds on ideas from Helson's (1947, 1964) adaptation-level theory. Each stimulus is compared to the adaptation level, AL, which is the geometric mean of the set of items. For a set of items that are equally spaced on a log scale and presented equally often, the AL will correspond to the middle item. The effective stimulus or code, C_i, for physical stimulus S_i, is simply the difference between the log of the physical stimulus and the AL, also on a log scale:

$$C_i = \log S_i - \log AL \qquad\qquad 8.3$$

In a typical absolute identification experiment, the subject is told whether each response is correct or incorrect. In terms of the model, being told that a response is correct is viewed as reinforcing, and thus the feedback strengthens the association between the response, R_i, and the stimulus, S_i. However, the response R_i also generalizes to other stimuli according to their closeness to S_i. The strength of the

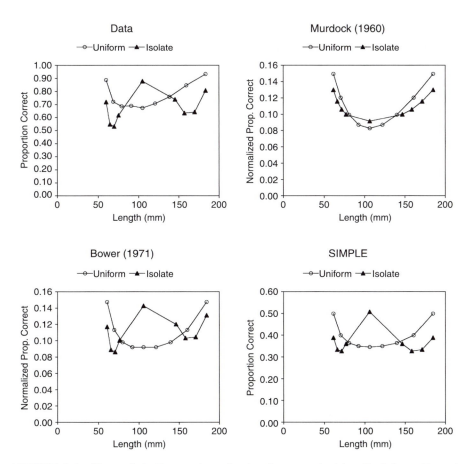

FIGURE 8.1 Upper left: Proportion of stimuli correctly identified from Experiment 2 of Neath, I., Brown, G. D. A., McCormack, T., Chater, N., & Freeman, R. (2006). Distinctiveness models of memory and absolute identification: Evidence for local, not global, effects. *Quarterly Journal of Experimental Psychology*, *59*, 121–135. Reprinted by kind permission of the Experimental Psychology Society. Upper right: Predictions from Murdock's (1960) distinctiveness model. Lower left: Predictions from Bower's (1971) stimulus generalization model with *h* set to 0.24. Lower right: Predictions from SIMPLE with *c* set to 5.

association (or habit strength, $_xH_i$) between response R_i to a given stimulus, S_x, is given by:

$$_xH_i = h[1 - 1/h|C_i - C_x|] \qquad 8.4$$

if $|C_i - C_x| = h$ and is 0 otherwise. The number of free parameters in the model depends on whether the height of the generalization gradient, h, is also used to express the slope, $1/h$, and also whether the limit is expressed as h.

Table 8.2 shows an example calculation using the same five tones used to illustrate the calculation of Murdock's (1960) model in Table 8.1. The geometric mean of the frequencies corresponds to the middle stimulus, so that is the *AL*, and

TABLE 8.2   Example Calculation Using Bower's (1971) Stimulus Generalization Model for Five Pure Tones that Vary Only in Frequency When h is 0.15 and the Slope is $1/h$

Frequency (Hz)	Stimulus	Effective code	R1	R2	R3	R4	R5	Response ratio	Response prob.	Relative PD
316.23	2.50	−0.10	0.15	0.10	0.05	0.00	0.00	0.15:0.30	0.50	0.24
354.81	2.55	−0.05	0.10	0.15	0.10	0.05	0.00	0.15:0.40	0.38	0.18
398.10	2.60	0.00	0.05	0.10	0.15	0.10	0.05	0.15:0.45	0.33	0.16
446.68	2.65	0.05	0.00	0.05	0.10	0.15	0.10	0.15:0.40	0.38	0.18
501.18	2.70	0.01	0.00	0.00	0.05	0.10	0.15	0.15:0.30	0.50	0.24

the effective codes are calculated as differences between each item and the AL. Habit strength (as defined in Equation 8.4) determines the number of responses, and then a response ratio is calculated for each stimulus. The relative percentage distinctiveness, PD, is the proportion of correct responses that stimulus produced (e.g., 0.50 for Stimulus 1) divided by the sum of all response probabilities (e.g., 0.50 + 0.38 + 0.33 + 0.38 + 0.50). The parameter h is set to 0.15, and the PD is comparable to D% predicted by Murdock's model.

Not only does the model correctly predict performance in the uniform condition of the rods experiment mentioned above, it also correctly predicts performance in the isolate condition (see lower left panel of Figure 8.1). With h set to 0.24 (and slope $1/h$), the normalized proportion identified accounted for the data from both conditions extremely well. The reason is that the generalization gradient makes the model local, rather than global: In the isolate condition, items are further away from the middle item and so occur further along the gradient.

One obvious difference between the two models is that because Murdock's (1960) global distinctiveness model has no free parameters, it makes unambiguous, a priori predictions. In contrast, Bower's (1971) stimulus generalization model has more flexibility. For example, if one has slope = 1/height, then as the height approaches 0 and also as the height approaches a sufficiently large number, the model predicts the same performance for each item: The relative PD for each item approaches 0.20 in both cases.

Although there are many other local distinctiveness models, most are better classed as temporal-ratio models because they rely on some form of ratio of temporal values (e.g., Baddeley, 1976; Baddeley & Hitch, 1993; Bjork & Whitten, 1974; Crowder, 1976; Glenberg, Bradley, Kraus, and Renzaglia, 1983; Glenberg & Swanson, 1986; Hitch, Rejman, & Turner, 1980; Neath & Crowder, 1990; Tan & Ward, 2000). The models propose a variety of different ways in which temporal distance ratios combine to determine memory performance, but they all contrast with the global distinctiveness models described above in that they typically assume (either explicitly or implicitly) that the immediate temporal neighbors of an item will be more important than will temporally distant neighbors in determining the distinctiveness, and hence recallability, of an item. Indeed we will argue that temporal-ratio models are too local.

TEMPORAL-RATIO MODELS

In 1935, Koffka developed a theory of recency effects founded on the premise that the memory process is dynamic. Koffka assumed that as events are perceived, their traces are laid down by a continuously moving process. The result, which he called the trace column, is not unlike a tape recording where "time becomes spatialized" (p. 446). The traces in the column are assumed to be subject to the same spatial grouping principles that determine visual phenomena: The most recent items, temporally, would be the most distinct just as in visual perception the closest items, spatially, would be the most distinct.

More recently, Bjork and Whitten (1974, p. 189) suggested that the recency effect observed in free recall might be "specified by an empirical law of sorts based on the ratio of the temporal separation of successive to-be-remembered items (or sets of items) to the temporal delay from those items to the point of recall." Crowder (1976, p. 462) used the analogy of a series of telephone poles to illustrate Bjork and Whitten's ratio-like mechanism:

> The items in a memory list, being presented at a constant rate, pass by with the same regularity as do telephone poles when one is on a moving train. The crucial assumption is that just as each telephone pole in the receding distance becomes less and less distinctive from its neighbors, likewise each item in the memory list becomes less distinctive from the other list items as the presentation episode recedes into the past. Therefore, retrieval probability is being assumed to depend on discriminability of traces from each other.

We focus on three specific instantiations of this idea.

Baddeley (1976) proposed a ratio-like rule from an analysis of data from the Brown–Peterson paradigm. In this paradigm, subjects typically see three consonants to remember, are then distracted for a certain period of time, and are then asked to recall the trigram. They then receive a second trial, and so on. Turvey, Brick, and Osborn (1970) had three groups of subjects who received four trials in a Brown–Peterson procedure. One group had 10 s of distractor activity, a second group had 15 s of distractor activity, and a third group had 20 s of distractor activity.[3] On the fifth trial, however, all groups had 15 s of distractor activity. Despite the fact that the time between presentation and recall was identical in the three groups on the fifth trial, recall performance was *not* equivalent.

According to Baddeley's (1976) account, what primarily determines recall is the ability of the subject to distinguish the current item (the trigram on the fifth trial in the above example) from the preceding item (the trigram on the fourth trial).[4] The larger the ratio of the time between the presentation of the fourth item and recall of the fifth item and presentation of the fifth item and recall of the fifth item, the better the recall of the fifth item. This is schematically shown in Table 8.3. What is important is that recall depends upon the *relative* duration of the distractor activity rather than the absolute duration. The ratio for group 20 is higher than that for the other groups. In other words, the fifth item is more distinct

TABLE 8.3   Three Conditions from Turvey et al. (1970) Showing How Baddeley's (1976) Temporal Ratio Idea Predicts Different Levels of Recall Even Though the Absolute Amount of Time between Presentation (P5) and Test (R5) in all Three Groups is Identical

Group	0	5	10	Time 15	20	25	30	35	P4–R5	P5–R5	Ratio
10	P4		P5			R5			25 s	15 s	1.67:1
15	P4			P5			R5		30 s	15 s	2.00:1
20	P4				P5			R5	35 s	15 s	2.33:1

Presentations P1–P3 are not shown, and recall of the fourth trial (R4) is omitted for ease of exposition. Note: This is an adaptation of Table 6.5 from Neath and Surprenant (2003) and is reproduced by permission.

because it is more separated in time from a competitor (the fourth item) than in the other conditions.

A second influential temporal-ratio model was proposed by Glenberg et al. (1983), and can be thought of as a quantification of Bjork and Whitten's (1974) suggestion. Glenberg and colleagues focused on the recency effect observed in free recall, defining recency as the slope of the least-squares line for the final three positions. The ratio rule predicts the slope as a function of the interitem presentation interval, IPI, and the retention interval, RI:

$$Slope = \log\left(\frac{IPI}{RI}\right) \qquad 8.5$$

Glenberg et al. reanalyzed data from an earlier set of studies (Glenberg et al., 1980) and found this description fit well data from IPIs ranging from 4 to 36 s and RIs ranging from 12 to 72 s. They also reported data showing the ratio rule quite accurately accounted for data with either a 1 day or 7 day IPI and a 1 day or 14 days RI. Nairne et al. (1997) also provide data consistent with this rule.

The third account is in essence an expansion of Glenberg's ratio rule. Neath and Crowder (1990) suggested that according to the ratio rule, it should be possible to devise a presentation schedule (spacing of items along the temporal dimension) that results in a flat serial position curve.[5] One way of doing this is to have successively smaller intervals between items so that the duration of the IPI decreases through the list. Recall of item i, R_i, is proportional to the ratio of the duration separating item i from item $i-1$ and the duration separating item i to the time of recall (which includes the retention interval). Thus, if IPI_i represents the temporal duration separating item i from the previous item and RI is the duration of the retention interval,

$$R_i \propto \frac{IPI_i}{\sum_{j=i+1}^{n} IPI_j + RI} \qquad 8.6$$

Neath and Crowder did not completely succeed in constructing a list that resulted in equivalent recall of all items, but their data, especially the visual condition in Experiment 3, are remarkably close to a horizontal line.

One problem with all of these temporal-ratio models is, we suggest, that they are too local. In the Baddeley (1976) account, which is focused on last-item recall, no items other than the immediately preceding ones are critically important in determining whether an item will be remembered or identified. The ratio rule is also limited, as it includes only two temporal intervals; even the extended ratio rule cannot make predictions about the first item in the list. Models such as these have difficulty in accounting for primacy effects and for interference from nonimmediate neighbors in a to-be-remembered list.

SIMPLE

Brown et al. (2002; see also Neath & Brown, 2006) describe a local distinctiveness model of memory that is related to many of the models discussed above. SIMPLE (Scale Invariant Memory, Perception, and Learning) has as its focus any situation in which an item must be discriminated from other items along one or more psychological dimensions. It is essentially a simplified exemplar model (e.g., Nosofsky, 1986) with the addition of a temporal dimension.

When an item is presented in an absolute identification experiment, the subject is assumed to compare a log-transformed representation of the test item's magnitude (e.g., the item's weight, brightness, or time of presentation) to representations of other test items. The similarity, $\eta_{i,j}$, between two log-transformed memory representations, M_i and M_j, is given by Equation 8.7:

$$\eta_{i,j} = e^{-c|M_i - M_j|} \qquad 8.7$$

As in many other models, it is assumed that similarity falls off as a decreasing function of the separation between any two representations on the internal scale (Shepard, 1987). The main free parameter in SIMPLE is c and is what instantiates the locality assumption. Higher values of c correspond to greater distinctiveness of memory traces, i.e., less influence of more distant items.

The probability of producing the response associated with item i, R_i, when given the cue for stimulus j, C_j, is given by Equation 8.8, in which n is the number of items in the set:

$$P(R_i \mid C_j) = \frac{\eta_{i,j}}{\sum_{k=1}^{n} \eta_{j,k}} \qquad 8.8$$

This one-parameter version of SIMPLE can account for the pattern of results observed in the absolute identification data that Murdock's (1960) global model could not. With c set 5, the predictions of the model are shown in the lower right panel of Figure 8.1.[6] SIMPLE is able to fit the data because an item's distinctiveness is determined mainly by its near neighbors and only to a lesser extent by its more distant neighbors.

SIMPLE has also been applied to a number of standard memory paradigms (Brown et al., 2002; Neath & Brown, 2006). In these cases it is assumed that items are typically represented in memory in terms of their positions along a logarithmically transformed temporal distance dimension. It is also easy to extend SIMPLE to situations in which items are represented along multiple dimensions by using an attentional parameter, W, to weight each dimension (see Nosofsky, 1992). For example, consider a task that uses both a position dimension and a list dimension. Each dimension would be weighted, but the weights used must sum to 1.0, i.e., $W_P + W_L = 1.0$. In this case, the similarity between i and j's locations will be given by:

$$\eta_{i,j} = e^{-c(W_P|P_i - P_j| + W_L|L_i - L_j|)}$$

8.9

where P_i and L_i are the values of item i in memory on the position and list dimensions respectively. Multidimensional scaling can be used to determine the underlying psychological space (Nosofsky, 1992).

RELATIONS AMONG THE MODELS

In this section, we compare SIMPLE to the other distinctiveness models. We first illustrate the differences between SIMPLE and the other models in terms of which other items in a set contribute to the distinctiveness of a given item. We then re-cast SIMPLE in terms of ratios, to facilitate comparison with temporal-ratio models, and finally we consider the relation between SIMPLE and both extreme local distinctiveness models and global distinctiveness models.

Determinants of Distinctiveness

One way in which the models vary is in terms of the items that contribute to the relative distinctiveness of a given item. Consider the case of recalling item C from presented list A B C D E, as shown in Figure 8.2. The list items are shown in terms of their distance from the point of recall. According to most distinctiveness models, the discriminability of C will depend partly on C's distance from the point of recall—call this D_c (and, generally, let the distance of item X be D_x). A global distinctiveness model (e.g., Murdock, 1960; Neath, 1993) would state that the distances between the items in logarithmically transformed space—$|\log(D_a) - \log(D_c)|$, $|\log(D_b) - \log(D_c)|$, $|\log(D_d) - \log(D_c)|$, and $|\log(D_e) - \log(D_c)|$—will sum to determine the "total" distinctiveness of C, and that the discriminability of C will depend on C's distinctiveness relative to the summed distinctiveness of all items.

The notion of distinctiveness incorporated in SIMPLE is very different from that in the global models. SIMPLE emphasizes the local neighborhoods of items: The influence of one memory trace on the retrievability of another reduces as the psychological distance between them increases. Interference from psychologically distant neighbors is normally negligible. In terms of Figure 8.2, $|\log(D_b) - \log(D_c)|$

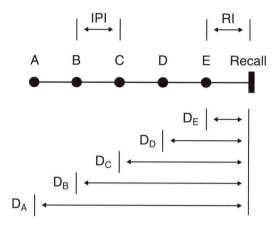

FIGURE 8.2   Illustration to elucidate differences between the various distinctiveness models of memory discussed (see text for details).

and $|\log(D_d) - \log(D_c)|$ are more important in determining the probability of recalling item C than are $|\log(D_a) - \log(D_c)|$ and $|\log(D_e) - \log(D_c)|$. In what we have termed global distinctiveness models, the dimensional values of all items in memory, no matter how distant, enter into the calculation of the distinctiveness of each item. This can lead to problems in delineating the set of "relevant" items for the distinctiveness determination; some cutoff must be imposed if each item is not to be compared with every other item in the whole of memory (for example, there may be an implicit assumption of a separate "list memory" that defines the search set). The local distinctiveness approaches offers the intuitively more appealing suggestion that psychologically distant items are effectively irrelevant and can be ignored in the calculation of distinctiveness.

A more local temporal discrimination model such as that of Baddeley (1976) assumes that D_c and D_b are all that matter, i.e., that it is C's discriminability relative to that of B that is important (see Baddeley, Ecob, & Scott, 1970, cited in Baddeley, 1976; Hitch et al., 1980, cited in Baddeley & Hitch, 1993). This is an extreme local distinctiveness model, a kind of nearest-neighbor model, as it implies that only the preceding item's distance is relevant.[7] Other similar "ratio rule" models of memory (e.g., Bjork & Whitten, 1974; Crowder, 1976) state that the ratio between the interitem spacing, e.g., $|D_b - D_c|$, and the retention interval D_c, will determine recall probability (see Equation 8.6). This normally amounts to the implicit claim that one or both of an item's immediate neighbors are relevant in determining discriminability. The two types of ratio rule are very similar, both stating that recall probability will increase linearly with the ratio of interitem spacing to retention interval. These accounts therefore both differ from that given by SIMPLE, which allows a contribution, albeit diminished, from more distant neighbors.

The final class of "ratio rule" models focus on predicting the size of recency effects as a joint function of interpresentation interval and retention interval (e.g., Glenberg et al., 1983). These models state that the size of the recency effect (measured as a slope of the last three list items) will depend on the ratio of the interitem presentation interval (IPI), the duration between any two items, to the retention interval (RI), the duration between the final item and the test, as shown in Equation 8.5. Although this recency-predicting ratio rule is clearly similar in spirit to the others reviewed above, it is not formally equivalent.

SIMPLE and Ratios

Many of the distinctiveness models have, at the core, the idea that distinctiveness is often well described as a ratio. SIMPLE can be easily reframed in terms of ratios to facilitate comparison with the temporal-ratio models. Because the memory representation of an item, M_x, is simply a log transform of stimulus magnitude S_x, $M_x = \log(S_x)$, we can rewrite Equation 8.7 as

$$\eta_{i,j} = e^{-c|\log(S_i) - \log(S_j)|} \qquad 8.10$$

or more simply

$$\eta_{i,j} = e^{-c|\log(S_i/S_j)|} \qquad 8.11$$

We use the fact that $|\log(S_i/S_j)| = \log(S_i/S_j)$ if $S_i \geq S_j$, and $|\log(S_i/S_j)| = \log(S_j/S_i)$ if $S_i < S_j$, to obtain

$$\eta_{i,j} = (S_j/S_i)^c \qquad 8.12$$

if $S_i \geq S_j$, and

$$\eta_{i,j} = (S_i/S_j)^c \qquad 8.13$$

if $S_i < S_j$. The interpretation of this is straightforward. Given values of S_i and S_j, say 5 and 15, the similarity between them is the smaller value divided by the larger (here 5/15 = 1/3). If the values are separated by a large ratio (e.g., 1 and 10) the similarity will be small (0.1); conversely if they are identical, their similarity will be maximal, at 1, equal to their ratio.

Let us define a function $Ratio(x, y)$, which divides the smaller of x and y by the larger. Then we can write:

$$\eta_{i,j} = Ratio(S_i, S_j)^c \qquad 8.14$$

Substituting into equation 8.8, we obtain:

$$P(R_i \mid C_j) = \frac{Ratio(S_i, S_j)^c}{\displaystyle\sum_{k=1}^{n} Ratio(S_j, S_k)^c} \qquad 8.15$$

Thus, the response probabilities can be expressed purely in terms of the ratios (raised to the power c) of stimulus energy values. When memory is being modeled, and the S_i values are temporal distances from the point of retrieval, the resulting emphasis on ratios of temporal distances brings out the close relationship of SIMPLE to the temporal ratio models.

To the extent that the assumptions of SIMPLE are correct, earlier ratio rule models represent an oversimplification in two respects: first, in assuming that only ratios of temporal distances to the target items' immediate neighbors are relevant and, second, in not allowing for the additional parameter implied by SIMPLE's c parameter (which has the effect of raising temporal distance ratios to the power c). Both of these allow SIMPLE to explain the primacy effects that occur when rehearsal is prevented or controlled, while temporal-ratio rule models typically have difficulty in explaining this primacy.

A Local to Global Continuum

A final comparison concerns the relation between SIMPLE and both the most local and the most global models. Baddeley's ratio model is the "most local" of the models considered here. The SIMPLE model is related to this model in that the same temporal distance ratios are used to determine item retrievability, albeit in a different way. Consider the case in which there are just two items, separated by an interpresentation interval, IPI, and followed by a retention interval, RI. Then, from the point of retrieval, the temporal distances of the two items will be IPI+RI (for the first item) and RI (for the second item). Baddeley's model predicts that the relative ease of retrieving the second presented item (i.e., the one located RI in the past) compared to an interference-free initial recall will be given by the ratio (RI + IPI)/RI. Call this *TDR* (for temporal discriminability ratio). When c is set to 1.0, SIMPLE predicts that the probability of retrieving the second item will be proportional to $1/(1 + 1/TDR)$. Thus, under the simplifying assumptions above (e.g., two items, an exponential similarity-distance function) the models use the same ratios to predict memory performance; the difference is that the Baddeley model bounds recall probability estimates by predicting performance as a proportion of the level of interference-free performance, whereas SIMPLE uses a squashing function. As noted above, however, SIMPLE also differs from the Baddeley model in modifying the temporal distance ratio with the c parameter and in its assumption that multiple pairwise similarities will conspire to determine retrieval probability.

Finally we note that the contrast between local and global distinctiveness can be viewed as a continuum. Equation 8.7 did not show a parameter, q, that can be set to 1.0 for an exponential function relating similarity to distance and 2.0 for a Gaussian function relating similarity to distance:

$$\eta_{i,j} = e^{-c|M_i - M_j|^q} \qquad 8.16$$

In SIMPLE, the shape of the function relating similarity to distance will combine with the c parameter to determine the relative influence of (and interference from) distant as opposed to local neighbors. For example, if the similarity-distance function is Gaussian then similarity (and hence interference) between close neighbors will be relatively great for constant c, and interference between distant neighbors will be relatively low, compared with behavior when an exponential distance function is used. The relative amount of interference from psychologically near and far neighbors (i.e., the degree of emphasis on local rather than global neighborhoods) will vary smoothly as a function of the value of q while it is positive (c held constant). When the exponent becomes negative then the "similarity" becomes "dissimilarity" and (equivalently) the measure becomes greater for psychologically more distant items than for near items. The measure then becomes very similar to the value calculated for each item in the Murdock–Neath model, similar to a point where it would be difficult to distinguish the measures empirically: for example, the correlation between $\log(n)$ and

$$e^{-c(n^{-0.5})}\qquad\qquad 8.17$$

is 0.996 for values of n between 1 and 100 when $c = 2.56$.

Thus, in SIMPLE there can be a continuum from localness to globalness. In the extreme of globalness, when distance and "similarity" become positively rather than negatively correlated, SIMPLE and the Murdock–Neath model begin to converge (in terms of psychological interpretation rather than formal equivalence).

SUMMARY

SIMPLE can be viewed as an extension of Murdock's (1960) distinctiveness theory that accommodates time-based and local neighborhood effects. It thus solves a fundamental problem with global models in which the middle item must always be the least distinct. It can also be seen as a generalization of early temporal ratio models of memory (e.g., Baddeley, 1976; Bjork & Whitten, 1974; Crowder, 1976; Glenberg et al., 1983; Koffka, 1935) in which the basic ratio idea is applicable to more than just recency items or immediately adjacent items. Moreover, because of the ratio, SIMPLE emphasizes that it is relative rather than absolute time that critically affects memory performance.

ACKNOWLEDGMENT

This research was supported, in part, by supported by ESRC Grant RES 000 231038 to the second author.

NOTES

1. Implementations of many of the models discussed in this chapter are available at http://memory.psych.mun.ca
2. The weights of the rods were identical, despite the difference in length.
3. There were actually five conditions, but we ignore the shortest and longest distractor conditions for simplicity.
4. This description of Baddeley's (1976) original proposal is simplified but nonetheless accurately reflects the essentials of his original account.
5. Note that the goal of Neath and Crowder is impossible according to global distinctiveness models.
6. Neath et al. (2006) show how a more complex version of SIMPLE that includes additional assumptions is able to produce a better quantitative fit.

7. The statement that only the previous item's distance is relevant is not explicit in the account, but is implicit in the calculation of memory performance; see, for example, Baddeley (1976).

REFERENCES

Baddeley, A. D. (1976). *The psychology of memory*. New York: Basic Books.

Baddeley, A. D., Ecob., J. R., & Scott, D. (1970, November). *Retroactive interference effects in short-term memory*. Paper presented at the annual meeting of the Psychonomic Society, San Antonio, TX.

Baddeley, A. D., & Hitch, G. J. (1993). The recency effect: Implicit learning with explicit retrieval? *Memory and Cognition, 21*, 164–155.

Bjork, R. A., & Whitten, W. B. (1974). Recency-sensitive retrieval processes in long-term free recall. *Cognitive Psychology, 6*, 173–189.

Bower, G. H. (1971). Adaptation-level coding of stimuli and serial position effects. In M. H. Appley (Ed.), *Adaptation-level theory* (pp. 175–201). New York: Academic Press.

Brown, G. D. A., Neath, I., & Chater, N. (2002). *A ratio model of scale-invariant memory and identification*. Unpublished manuscript.

Burnham, W. H. (1888). Memory, historically and experimentally considered. *American Journal of Psychology, 2*, 39–90, 255–270, 431–464, 566–622.

Calkins, M. W. (1894). Association. *Psychological Review, 1*, 476–483.

Crowder, R. G. (1976). *Principles of learning and memory*. Hillsdale, NJ: Lawrence Erlbaum Associates, Inc.

Estes, W. K. (1972). An associative basis for coding and organization in memory. In A. W. Melton & E. Martin (Eds.), *Coding processes in human memory* (pp. 161–190). Washington, DC: Winston.

Glenberg, A. M., Bradley, M. M., Kraus, T. A., & Renzaglia, G. J. (1983). Studies of the long-term recency effect: Support for a contextually guided retrieval hypothesis. *Journal of Experimental Psychology: Learning, Memory, and Cognition, 9*, 231–255.

Glenberg, A. M., Bradley, M. M., Stevenson, J. A., Kraus, T. A., Tkachuk, M. J., Gretz, A. L., et al. (1980). A two-process account of long-term serial position effects. *Journal of Experimental Psychology: Human Learning and Memory, 6*, 355–369.

Glenberg, A. M., & Swanson, N. (1986). A temporal distinctiveness theory of recency and modality effects. *Journal of Experimental Psychology: Learning, Memory, and Cognition, 12*, 3–24.

Helson, H. (1947). Adaptation-level as a frame of reference for prediction of psychophysical data. *American Journal of Psychology, 60*, 1–29.

Helson, H. (1964). *Adaptation-level theory: An experimental and systematic approach to behavior*. New York: Harper.

Hitch, G. J., Rejman, M. H., & Turner, N. C. (1980, July). *A new perspective on the recency effect*. Paper presented at the meeting of the Experimental Psychology Society, Cambridge, UK.

Hunt, R. R. (1995). The subtlety of distinctiveness: What von Restorff really did. *Psychonomic Bulletin and Review, 2*, 105–112.

Johnson, G. J. (1991). A Distinctiveness model of serial learning. *Psychological Review, 98*, 204–217.

Knoedler, A. J., Hellwig, K. A., & Neath, I. (1999). The shift from recency to primacy with increasing delay. *Journal of Experimental Psychology: Learning, Memory, and Cognition, 25*, 474–487.

Koffka, K. (1935). *Principles of Gestalt psychology*. London: Routledge & Kegan Paul.

Köhler, W. (1929). *Gestalt psychology*. New York: Liveright.

Murdock, B. B., Jr. (1960). The distinctiveness of stimuli. *Psychological Review*, 67, 16–31.

Nairne, J. S. (1991). Positional uncertainty in long-term memory. *Memory and Cognition*, 19, 332–340.

Nairne, J. S., Neath, I., Serra, M., & Byun, E. (1997). Positional distinctiveness and the ratio rule in free recall. *Journal of Memory and Language*, 37, 155–166.

Neath, I. (1993). Distinctiveness and serial position effects in recognition and sentence processing. *Memory and Cognition*, 21, 689–698.

Neath, I., & Brown, G. D. A. (2006). SIMPLE: Further applications of a local distinctiveness model of memory. In B. H. Ross (Ed.), *The psychology of learning and motivation* (Vol. 46, pp. 201–243). San Diego, CA: Academic Press.

Neath, I., Brown, G. D. A., McCormack, T., Chater, N., & Freeman, R. (2006). Distinctiveness models of memory and absolute identification: Evidence for local, not global, effects. *Quarterly Journal of Experimental Psychology*, 59, 121–135.

Neath, I., & Crowder, R. G. (1990). Schedules of presentation and distinctiveness in human memory. *Journal of Experimental Psychology: Learning, Memory, and Cognition*, 16, 316–327.

Neath, I., & Surprenant, A. M. (2003). *Human memory: An introduction to research, data, and theory* (2nd ed.). Belmont, CA: Wadsworth.

Nosofsky, R. M. (1986). Attention, similarity, and the identification-categorization relationship. *Journal of Experimental Psychology: General*, 115, 39–57.

Nosofsky, R. M. (1992). Similarity scaling and cognitive process models. *Annual Review of Psychology*, 43, 25–53.

Rips, L. J. (1975). Inductive judgments about natural categories. *Journal of Verbal Learning and Verbal Behavior*, 14, 665–681.

Shepard, R. N. (1987). Toward a universal law of generalization for psychological science. *Science*, 237, 1317–1323.

Stevens, S. S. (1957). On the psychophysical law. *Psychological Review* 64, 153–181.

Tan, L., & Ward, G. (2000). A recency-based account of the primacy effect in free recall. *Journal of Experimental Psychology: Learning, Memory, and Cognition*, 26, 1589–1625.

Turvey, M. T., Brick, P., & Osborn, J. (1970). Proactive interference in short-term memory as a function of prior-item retention interval. *Quarterly Journal of Experimental Psychology*, 22, 142–147.

9

Unscrambling the Effects of Emotion and Distinctiveness on Memory

STEPHEN R. SCHMIDT

As an alternative to the special-mechanism hypothesis, we have suggested that flashbulb memories may be viewed as memories for significant and distinctive personal experiences, and hence as memories explicable in terms of ordinary memory mechanisms.

(McCloskey, Wible, & Cohen, 1988, p. 181)

*R*esearchers have long been interested in how certain "special" or "outstanding" events appear to support vivid and lasting impressions. In the often-quoted words of William James, "[a]n impression may be so exciting emotionally as almost to leave a scar upon the cerebral tissues . . ." (1890/1950, p. 670). Some have argued that if an experience is sufficiently novel and significant, than a permanent memory is created for "all recent brain events" (Brown & Kulik, 1977, p. 76). Others, such as McCloskey et al. (1988; see also Christianson, 1989) have argued that memories for such outstanding events are not nearly as accurate as W. James and Brown and Kulik implied, and that our confidence in our memory for these events is misplaced (Weaver, 1993). Nevertheless, few would doubt that the novel and significant are generally more memorable than the ordinary and inconsequential. What makes these outstanding events memorable? Is it the result of their unusual or distinctive character, or because they evoke strong emotions? In the following pages, I hope to disentangle the influences of emotion and distinctiveness in memory for outstanding events.

EMOTION, SIGNIFICANCE, AND DISTINCTIVENESS

Before one can separate the impacts of emotion and distinctiveness on memory, it is necessary to clearly define the terms. One route to clear terminology is through Gati and Ben-Shakhar's (1990) feature overlap model of the attention-orienting response. Within this framework, the psychophysiological orienting response to a stimulus is the result of a linear combination of the significance and novelty of the stimulus. Significance was thought to be directly related to the overlap between the stimulus and significant stimuli stored in memory. In contrast, novelty was thought to be inversely related to the overlap between a stimulus and at least the two preceding stimuli in a series. Thus, a theoretical distinction can be made between significance and distinctiveness independent of their potential effects on memory processes. Significance results from the processing of stimulus similarity (feature matches), whereas distinctiveness results from the processing of stimulus difference (feature contrasts).

Gati and Ben-Shakhar's (1990) definition of significance fits nicely within appraisal theories of emotions. Within an appraisal framework, emotions result from the evaluations and the interpretations of a situation. For example, Scherer (2001) described an information-processing model of emotion in which an individual performs a series of checks, including evaluations of the nervous system response. In addition, the stimulus situation is compared to memory representations of past situations. Significant stimuli may be stored in long-term memory as a result of genetic predispositions, classical conditioning, and culturally transmitted values. These checking and comparison processes lead to the computation of an emotion, and they prime actions such as fight or flight. They may also lead to cognitive processes affecting memory for the stimulus event. A similar series of checks was outlined in Brown and Kulik (1977), clearly placing the flashbulb memory hypothesis within an appraisal framework of emotion. Interestingly, in both the Scherer and the Brown and Kulik frameworks, one of the first steps in the emotional evaluation is a check for stimulus novelty.

The early consensus in memory research was that emotion had a positive effect on delayed tests of retention (i.e., Brown & Kulik, 1977; James, 1890/1950; Kleinsmith & Kaplan 1964). However, as evidence has accumulated, the impact of emotion on memory appears increasingly complex, with a number of variables modulating the effects. For example, Manning and Goldstein (1976) found that taboo but not simply upsetting words were recalled better than neutral words. Johansson, Mecklinger, and Treese (2004) reported a larger proportion of "remember" responses for faces with negative expressions than for faces with positive or neutral expressions. Others have argued for an "attention focusing" effect of memory for emotional material, wherein good recall of emotional material occurs at the expense of surrounding neutral material (Burke, Heuer, & Reisberg, 1992; Easterbrook, 1959). Talmi and Moscovitch (2004) argued that better memory for emotional than neutral words should be attributed to that fact that emotional words form a conceptual class, whereas a list of random neutral words does not. When Talmi and Moscovitch compared memory for emotional words to a list of neutral words matched in list organization, the emotional and neutral words were equally well recalled. Finally, numerous researchers have suggested that good memory for emotional material does not result from emotion *per se*, but actually results from the distinctive nature of emotional events (e.g., Loftus & Burns, 1982; McCloskey, et al., 1988, Schmidt, 2002b). Separating the effects of significance and distinctiveness may shed some light on this confusing literature.

Gati and Ben-Shakhar's (1990) framework also fits nicely with many theories of distinctiveness (see Schmidt, 1991), in which a distinctive stimulus is one that contains features not found in recently presented stimuli. Von Restorff (as cited in Koffka, 1935) is usually cited as the mother of distinctiveness research, but two relatively independent threads of research contributed to theoretical treatments of distinctiveness (Hunt, 2006). The first thread was the extensive research into the "isolation effect" in the 1950s and 1960s (see Wallace, 1965, for a review of the isolation effect). The second was research spawned by the levels of processing framework (e.g., Eysenck, 1979; Nelson 1979). According to most theories, distinctiveness may influence memory in two ways: The distinctive stimulus may receive more resources devoted to memory coding than a common stimulus, and/or a distinctive stimulus may "stand out" in the memory system, influencing retrieval and memory discrimination processes. Thus, unlike the effects of emotion on memory, it is generally agreed that distinctiveness is associated with good memory performance.

THE HUMOR EFFECT: SIGNIFICANCE OR DISTINCTIVENESS

Significance and distinctiveness often go hand in hand in many real world and research settings. For example, in studies of "flashbulb memories," events are often chosen that are both emotionally significant and relatively novel, such as the explosion of the space shuttle *Challenger* and the September 11, 2001 terrorist attacks. Similarly, participants in autobiographical memory studies often report events that are both novel and emotional (Wang & Conway, 2004). One could also argue that many distinctive events lead to, at the very least, emotions associated with the detection of the novelty of the experience. As such, when events are particularly well remembered, it is difficult to decide if the good memory results from the significance or distinctiveness of the event. Such is the case with humorous experiences.

Several researchers have demonstrated that, under appropriate conditions, humorous material is better remembered than nonhumorous material. For example, Kaplan and Pascoe (1977) demonstrated that humorous lecture examples were better remembered than serious examples. Schmidt (1994) demonstrated that humorous versions of sentences were recalled better than nonhumorous versions of the same sentences. Are these effects of humor the result of significance or distinctiveness? On the one hand, humorous material often contains sexual references, racial slurs, or other content that might be significant to the participants. In addition, perhaps the perception of humor evokes a pleasant feeling that may influence memory processes. Alternatively, humor often contains material that is incongruent with the immediate context (see the incongruity theory of humor proposed by Suls, 1972). This incongruity may make the humorous punch line "stand out" from nonhumorous material. Consider one of the test sentences from Schmidt (1994): "If you at first you don't succeed, you're probably not related to the boss." The joke may evoke feelings of injustice, or it may simply lead to the generally good feelings associated with humor. Both of these responses may contribute to the joke's significance. However, the first phrase in the sentence leads the reader to expect "try, try again." Thus, the second phrase is unexpected or incongruent with the immediate context, and this incongruity may support good memory. In this manner, good memory for humorous material may result because the material is significant, distinctive, or both.

A series of studies reported in Schmidt and Williams (2001), and Schmidt (2002a) provides a guide as to how to separate significance and distinctiveness explanations of the humor effect. Three versions of Gary Larson's *Far Side* cartoons were prepared. One version was the "original" unaltered cartoon. In a second cartoon type, the cartoon picture was altered slightly so that the caption and the picture were no longer incongruent. Removing the incongruity removed the humor from these "literal" cartoons. The third version was very similar to the literal cartoons, but an element from an unrelated cartoon was inserted into the picture to create a "weird" version of the cartoon. For example, in one cartoon a woman is pictured standing at a window calling her dog. The caption reads "Here Fifi! C'mon! . . . Faster, Fifi!" In the original cartoon, a dog is pictured running full speed toward a "doggie door" that is nailed shut, braced with several boards, with a hammer and some nails in the foreground. This cartoon was rated as highly humorous by our research participants. In the literal version of the cartoon, the hammer, nails, and boards were removed from the picture. The weird version was identical to the literal version except that Fifi was replaced by a snake. The literal and weird versions were rated equally humorous, and significantly less humorous than the original cartoons. Several of our experiments demonstrated that the captions and the pictures from the original cartoons were recalled better than from the literal and weird cartoons.

Was this humor effect the result of significance or distinctiveness? One means of distinguishing between significance and distinctiveness is to measure physiological indices tied to emotion. Several possible measures come to mind, including the P300 components associated with the von Restorff effect (Fabiani & Donchin, 1995), skin conductance associated with orientation (Gati & Ben-Shakhar, 1990), and heart rate. However, the P300 and skin conductance measures respond in the same way to novelty and significance. In contrast, heart rate responses may provide a means to distinguish between novelty and significance. Heart rate responses to materials can be very complex, containing several phases (Gatchel & Lang, 1973). First, there is an initial deceleration of the heart rate associated with an initial orientation to the new stimulus item. Second, there is an acceleration phase that should be larger for extremely arousing material. Third, a secondary deceleration phase is associated with the ease of discriminating one stimulus from other stimuli in the series.

Schmidt (2002a) reasoned that if the humor effect was related to significance, then the acceleration component should be larger for the original humorous cartoons than for two nonhumorous cartoon versions. Alternatively, if the humor effect was related to cartoon distinctiveness, then there should be differences between either the initial- or the secondary-deceleration heart-rate components for the humorous and nonhumorous cartoons. The results, presented in the top panel of Table 9.1, clearly demonstrated increased secondary deceleration in response to the original cartoons relative to the literal and the weird cartoons, tying the humor effect to distinctiveness rather than to significance. The differences in the other heart rate components were not statistically significant.

Another way to distinguish between significance and distinctiveness is to manipulate list structure. The distinctiveness of a stimulus is at least partly determined by its context. For example, in studies of the bizarre imagery effect, bizarre sentence are better remembered than common sentence only when the bizarre and common sentences are presented within the same experimental context (McDaniel & Einstein, 1986). Distinctiveness requires the "processing of difference in the context of similarity" (Hunt, 2006). In contrast, researchers have demonstrated that emotional words are better remembered than neutral words in both mixed and between list designs (Saari & Schmidt 2005; Walker & Tarte, 1963). Thus, if the humor effect is tied to item distinctiveness, it should only be found in experimental settings in which humorous and nonhumorous materials are presented together, and not in between-subjects manipulations of humor. Alternatively, if the humor effect is tied to significance, it should be equally robust in both types of experimental designs. Schmidt (2002a) compared memory for a mixed lists of humorous and nonhumorous cartoons to memory for the same cartoons when presented in different lists to different research participants (i.e., between lists and between subjects). Some of the results are summarized in Table 9.2. When humorous and nonhumorous cartoons were mixed in the same cartoon series, there was a robust humor effect. This effect disappeared in a between-subjects manipulation of humor (see also Schmidt, 1994; Schmidt & Williams, 2001). Additional support for a distinctiveness interpretation of the humor effect can be found in the bottom portion of Table 9.1. The differences in heart rate components found in the mixed-list design disappeared in the between-subjects manipulation of humor. That is, the participants noted that the humorous cartoons were different from the nonhumorous cartoons during the mixed-list presentation, leading to the secondary deceleration component associate with

TABLE 9.1   Heart Rate Components from Schmidt (2002a) as a Function of Cartoon Type and Experimental Design (Units are Heart Rate Changes in Beats Per Minute)

Cartoon version	Initial deceleration	Initial acceleration	Secondary deceleration
Mixed list design			
Original	−2.79	0.56	−1.57
Literal	−3.10	−0.06	−0.64
Weird	−2.96	0.20	−0.81
Between list design			
Original	−2.93	0.37	−0.97
Literal	−2.76	0.19	−0.93
Weird	−3.24	0.35	−1.07

TABLE 9.2 Cartoon Recall from Schmidt (2002a) as a Function of Cartoon Type and Experimental Design

Cartoon version	Pictures recalled	Captions recalled
Mixed list design		
Original	.52	.44
Literal	.32	.30
Weird	.40	.34
Between list design		
Original	.39	.37
Literal	.43	.44
Weird	.40	.38

discrimination processes. These discriminations are not associated with cartoon type in a between-list design because any differences between the cartoons noted by the participants were orthogonal to the experimental manipulation of cartoon type. Thus, two types of observations converge on the conclusion that the humor effect results from distinctiveness rather than significance: the heart rate responses and the manipulation of list structure.

NUDES, BOOZE, AND SPIDERS

When I began my research into the humor effect, I sincerely thought that I had found materials that would demonstrate the impact of significance on memory. I am still somewhat perplexed by my conclusion that the humor effect should be attributed to distinctiveness. Perhaps with the right kind of humor, humor laced with obscenities and sexual references, I would have reached a different conclusion. Bent on finding a "pure" example of the effects of significance, I went looking for a more potent set of experimental materials—materials sure to be significant to my participants. What could be more significant to undergraduates than sex and alcohol?

In the early 1970s, Detterman and his colleges reported a series of experiments patterned after studies of the isolation effect (Detterman & Ellis, 1972; Ellis, Detterman, Runcie, McCarver, & Craig, 1971). That is, a single "outstanding" stimulus was presented in a series of common objects. The outstanding stimuli, often presented in position 8 of a 15-item list, were "nudes of both sexes from a 'sunbathing' magazine" (Ellis et al., 1971, p. 358). The other pictures in the series, as well as all the pictures in a comparison list, were line drawings of common objects. Recall of the isolated nudes far exceeded recall of the control picture, and recall of items preceding and following the nudes was hurt relative to the control list. But, were these effects the result of the distinctiveness or the significance of nudes? Detterman himself was not clear on this point, but he framed his presentation within a discussion of the von Restorff effect (see Detterman, 1975; Detterman & Ellis, 1972), suggesting that he would lean toward a distinctiveness explanation. The nudes were clearly different from other stimuli in the series, including the fact that the nudes were photographs and the other items were line drawings, the nude pictures contained people and the line drawings were objects, and the nude pictures were probably more complex than the line drawings. On the other hand, it is not difficult to argue that nudes are significant to the typical undergraduate participating in psychology experiments.

I conducted a series of studies (see Schmidt, 1997, 2002b) that, among other things, help distinguish between significance and distinctiveness explanations of the "nudie effect" (good memory for nudes at the expense of surrounding stimuli). In order to control for picture content and complexity, all the pictures were color photographs of people engaged in everyday activities. A single "target" picture was of a male or female reclining on the floor with an open book. These target pictures were either clothed or nude. In replication of the Detterman studies, recall of the nude picture greatly exceeding recall of the clothed control picture (see Figure 9.1). In addition, recall of the three pictures following the nude was impaired relative to the pictures following the clothed target. This anterograde amnesia following the presentation of a nude appears to be an encoding phenomenon, disappearing at relatively slow rates of presentation (Detterman & Ellis, 1972; Schmidt, 2002b). Furthermore, recall of picture background details was worse in the nude than in the clothed target pictures. To tease apart the effects of distinctiveness and significance, the study was repeated with the nude and clothed

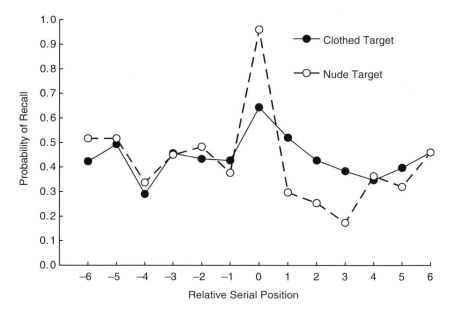

FIGURE 9.1   Recall of pictures as a function of type of target picture (clothed vs. nude) and relative serial position. This figure combines the results of three experiments from Schmidt (1997) and Schmidt (2002b). The target was in position 7 in one experiment, and 8 in the other two. (Figure adapted from Hunt & Worthen, 2006.)

targets inserted into a series of nude pictures. In this experiment, recall of the clothed picture exceeded recall of the nude picture, demonstrating an effect of distinctiveness. That is, just as an isolated picture of a nude in a series of clothed people is distinctive, a single clothed picture is distinctive in a series of nudes. However, recall of the pictures following the clothed picture was not impaired relative to the all-nude list. Furthermore, recall of background picture details was still better from the clothed than from the nude picture. Apparently, distinctive pictures are well recalled with no cost to either pictures immediately following the picture or to recall of background details.[1] Significant stimuli are also well recalled, but significant stimuli impair processing of background picture details and recall of the next several stimuli in a series.

The nudie effect is often confused with research concerning memory for high priority events (e.g., Schulz, 1971; Tulving, 1969). In fact, after presenting my research at conventions, researchers often approach me with the question "Didn't Tulving do a study like that way back in the 1960s?" There are several important differences between my research and these earlier studies. First, and perhaps most importantly, participants in studies with high-priority items are specifically instructed to look out for and be sure to remember a certain class of items (e.g., names of famous people in Tulving, 1969). To perform the task appropriately, participants had to compare each item to a set of items stored in memory to determine if it was a high priority item. These items were thus significant in the terms of the Gati and Ben-Shakhar (1990) framework. Second, in studies concerning high priority items, participants typically engaged in multiple study–test sequences. Tulving's participants studied 50 lists. Similarly, participants in the Detterman experiments also studied multiple lists (20 in Ellis et al., 1971). As such, one could argue that participants quickly learned to expect a nude picture, and as a result may have given those pictures high priority. In this manner, Detterman and Tulving may have been studying very similar phenomena. However, in my studies, participants studied and were tested on exactly one list of pictures. The significance of the nudes was thus dependent on the participants' pre-experimental experiences. Together these studies demonstrate that good recall of significant stimuli accompanied by poor recall of surrounding stimuli occurs when stimulus significance is defined experimentally and subjectively.[2]

Two experiments serve to generalize the above-noted negative effects of significant stimuli on memory. In the first, Kramer and Schmidt (in press) investigated the influence of alcohol cues on memory. Researchers have demonstrated that, in heavy drinkers, alcohol cues have physiological responses associated with significance (Stewart, de Wit, & Eikelboom, 1984). In addition, heavy drinkers demonstrate an emotional Stroop effect with alcohol words (Stetter, Ackermann, Bizer, Straube, & Mann, 1995). That is, heavy drinkers name the ink color of alcohol words more slowly than the ink color of neutral words. Based on this research, we reasoned that a picture of alcohol might influence memory much like the nude pictures in Schmidt (2002b). To test these ideas, undergraduate students were asked to complete an alcohol use questionnaire, and split into two groups: "high drinkers" ($M = 63.42$ drinks per month) and "low drinkers" ($M = 1.44$ drinks per month). Half of the participants in each of these groups viewed a series of 15 common objects containing a bottle of Pepsi in position 8. The other half viewed the same series with a bottle of Jack Daniels in place of the bottle of Pepsi. Among the heavy drinkers, recall of the bottle of Jack Daniels exceeded recall of the bottle of Pepsi, and recall of the three pictures following the Jack Daniels was impaired relative to the recall of the pictures following the Pepsi. Neither of these memory differences was observed with the low drinkers. It is difficult to argue that the bottle of booze was less familiar or more distinctive for the high than for the low drinkers. Rather, the picture of booze is significant—it matches the features of significant stimuli stored in memory. Thus, these results reinforce the idea that significant stimuli, but not distinctive stimuli, lead to poor recall of the immediately following pictures.

Spiders served as the significant stimuli in the second extension of the "nudie effect." Spider phobic individuals show an emotional Stroop effect to spider related words (Lavy & van den Hout, 1993). In addition, pictures of spiders "pop out" of visual displays containing other pictures (Ohman, Flykt, & Esteves, 2001). These results led us to expect that a spider picture should serve as a significant stimulus for spider phobic individuals, leading to anterograde amnesia effects. In her Masters' thesis, Griffin (2005) followed the design of the Kramer and Schmidt (in press) research described above. Participants viewed a series of neutral pictures selected from the International Affective Picture System (IAPS). One neutral picture of an animal (a cow) was selected to serve as a control. A picture of a spider that was rated as highly arousing, and with a strong negative valence, served as the significant stimulus. Approximately half of the participants viewed the series of pictures with the cow in position 8, and the remaining participants viewed the series with the spider in position 8. Picture presentation was followed by a short distractor task, and then a free recall test for the pictures. Participants then completed a spider phobic questionnaire (Klorman, Weerts, Hastings, Melamed, & Lang, 1974). The median response to the questionnaire was used to split participants into high and low phobic groups. A summary of the memory results is presented in Figure 9.2. Apparently, both the cow and the spider pictures were very memorable, standing out from the other items in the list. There are several post hoc explanations for this finding. Perhaps these two pictures were distinctive because they were only animals in the list. Alternatively, several people have suggested that the cow picture was somewhat humorous. Perhaps humor supported good memory for this picture. However, we should focus our attention on the pictures following the cow and spider. With the high-, but not the low-fearful participants, the spider led to poor memory for the stimuli immediately following it. These results are even more impressive given the good memory for both the cow and spider pictures. Significance, but not distinctiveness, leads to anterograde amnesia.

THE TABOO MEMORY EFFECT

The research reviewed above might lead one to connect the emotional Stroop effect and memory performance. That is, research with alcohol cues and spiders demonstrated emotional Stroop effects for the significant stimuli, these stimuli

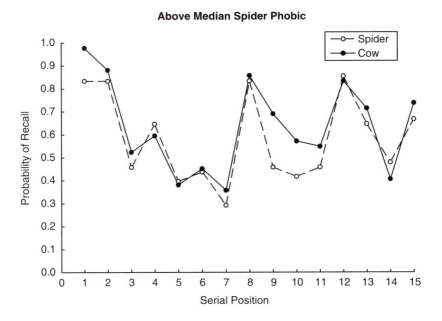

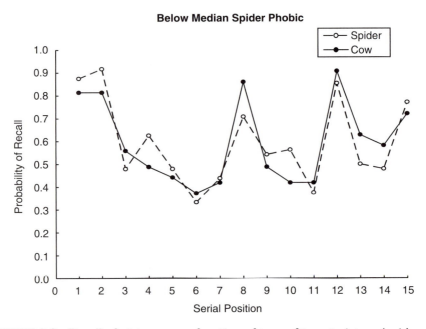

FIGURE 9.2   Recall of pictures as a function of type of target picture (spider vs. cow), type of participant (high vs. low spider phobic), and serial position. These data were selected from Griffin (2005).

were well remembered on memory tests, and they impaired memory for stimuli in close temporal proximity. A study reported by MacKay et al. (2004) provided a direct link between the emotional Stroop effect and memory. Participants were asked to name the ink color of taboo and neutral words presented in a randomly ordered mixed list. This task was immediately followed by a surprise recall test. The taboo words led to slower ink naming and better recall than the neutral words. MacKay et al. concluded that the taboo words led to an emotional reaction that facilitated the binding of the words to the presentation context. These results provide a direct connection between the attention grabbing properties of a word (as measured by the Stroop task) and later memory for the word. However, there were several problems with the MacKay et al. study. First, the neutral words did not belong to a well-defined group of items, whereas the taboo words belong to an easily identified conceptual class. This difference in organizational structure may be responsible for the memory advantage enjoyed by the emotional words (Talmi & Moscovitch, 2004). Second, perhaps the good memory for taboo words was the result of item distinctiveness rather than emotional significance.

Saari and Schmidt (2005) attempted to correct these shortcomings of the MacKay et al. (2004) research. Taboo words were matched to a set of neutral words belonging to a well-defined conceptual class (clothing), ruling out a simple organizational interpretation of the memory effects. In addition, two experimental designs were employed: a mixed-list design in which participants saw a list of half clothing and half taboo words, and a between-list design in which one group of participants saw an all clothing list and a second group saw an all taboo list. Participants first performed the Stroop color-naming task on the words in these lists, followed by a surprise free recall test. Following the logic developed above, if the taboo memory effect occurs in both types of designs, than it should be attributed to significance rather than distinctiveness. A selective summary of the results of Saari and Schmidt can be found in Table 9.3.

Several aspects of the Saari and Schmidt results are worthy of attention. First, there was a clear memory advantage for taboo words. Therefore, the taboo memory effect is observed even when taboo and neutral words are equated on organizational structure. Second, unlike the humor effect discussed above, the memory

TABLE 9.3   Ink Naming Times (ms) and the Probability of Word Recall as a Function of Word Type and Experimental Design (from Saari & Schmidt 2005)

Word type	Ink naming time	Words recalled
Mixed list design		
Neutral words	682	.39
Taboo words	710	.67
Between list design		
Neutral words	690	.44
Taboo words	725	.57

advantage for taboo words was found in both the mixed- and the between-list designs. And third, compared to the between list manipulation of word type, recall of neutral words was impaired by the presence of taboo words in the same list. The taboo memory effect thus has all the marks of memory for significant stimuli: a strong attention response to the stimuli, good memory in both mixed- and between-list designs, and an emotional cost on memory for surrounding stimuli.

MEMORY FOR 9/11: A TEST OF EXTERNAL VALIDITY

The research summarized above led me to conclude that the impact of significance and distinctiveness on memory are quite different. Whereas both distinctive and significant stimuli are well remembered, unlike distinctive stimuli, significant stimuli impair memory for material in the near temporal and spatial proximity. This conclusion seems to contradict the popular belief that emotion enhances memory. In addition, it runs counter to the "flashbulb memory" hypothesis (Brown & Kulik, 1977) that emotion leads to storage of not only a significant event, but to unrelated insignificant details surrounding the event. However, very few investigations of flashbulb memory experiences have specifically sought evidence for the negative impact of emotion on memory for peripheral information. For example, consider Christianson's (1989) study of Swedish participants' memories associated with the assassination of the their prime minister. Participants remembered central details of the event (e.g., where they were, who told them) better than peripheral details. In addition, on a 1-year delayed test, the proportion of participants reporting personal memories associated with the assassination greatly exceeded the proportion reporting memories for a control event. However, memory for peripheral information was not compared across the significant event and the nonsignificant control event. Similarly, researchers have compared memory for central features of a significant event (the explosion of the space shuttle *Challenger*) across participants with high and low emotional reactions (Bohannon, 1988). However, participants with high and low emotional reactions were not compared on their memory for information in the spatial or temporal periphery. The terrorist attacks on the United States on September 11, 2001 provided an opportunity to study the negative impact of a significant real world event on autobiographical memories.

During the week following September 11, students in introductory psychology classes were asked to complete a questionnaire concerning their memories for that day (Schmidt, 2004). Participants were asked several questions concerning central features of autobiographical experiences (*who* told you, *what* were you doing, *when* did you hear the news, *where* were you?), as well as questions concerning peripheral information not related to the event (what was the weather like, what were you wearing, what did you eat for breakfast, what did you eat for lunch?). In addition, several questions addressed the extent to which the day's events were disruptive and emotionally upsetting. The questionnaire was distributed to these same students 2 months later in November 2001. If significant events impair memory processes, one would expect that memory consistency between the

September and November surveys should be lower for participants who were most upset by the day's events.

Participants were grouped into a high-emotion group (mean emotional rating = 6.87 on a 7-point scale) and a moderate-emotion group (M = 5.36). In addition, their responses were scored as consistent, more specific, more general, or inconsistent across the two surveys. For example, when asked "Where were you . . .?" several students responded "at home" on the first questionnaire. If they responded with "at home" on the second questionnaire, their response would have been classified as consistent. A more specific response would be "at home in bed." Responses that were more specific occurred relatively infrequency (approximately 9% of responses). In contrast, approximately 18% of responses were scored as more general, for example when a student changed their response from "at home in bed" to "at home." Responses that did not share any elements with the first response (for example, "in my car") were scored as inconsistent. Neither information centrality nor emotional group significantly influenced the more general and more specific response categories. For this reason, I will focus on the consistent and inconsistent scores. A summary of these scores for central and peripheral features is presented in Figure 9.3. One should note four things from these graphs. First, memory consistency was rather low. Second, central details were remembered more consistently than peripheral details. Third, memory for central details was not significantly different for the two emotion groups. Fourth, on the peripheral questions, the high emotion group was significantly less consistent and gave significantly more inconsistent answers than the moderate emotion group. These results are exactly what one would expect from the perspective that significance impairs memory, particularly for peripheral information. Further evidence for this negative impact of emotion on memory was found in response to the question: "During the day of the attacks, did you forget to attend any appointments, complete any class assignments, or run any errands that you were supposed to do that day?" Among the high emotion group, 46% of the participants answered this question "yes," whereas 37% of the moderate emotion group answered "yes."

The events of September 11 where both distinctive and significant. Many of my students thought (incorrectly) that events represented the first terrorist attack in the United States. In addition, few could have imagined the video clips of the airplanes crashing into the twin towers, and then the towers collapsing to the ground. The significance of the events was seen in the reports of stress symptoms (Schuster et al., 2001), visits to counseling centers (Gallagher, 2003), and rated emotion (Schmidt, 2004). Do our vivid memories for that day result from the events' distinctiveness or significance? Probably both. However, poor memory for peripheral details, particularly among those of us who were particularly upset by the events, should be attributed to significance.

CONCLUSIONS

Researchers investigating memory for "outstanding" events need to be careful to separate the impacts of distinctiveness and significance. Both concepts can be

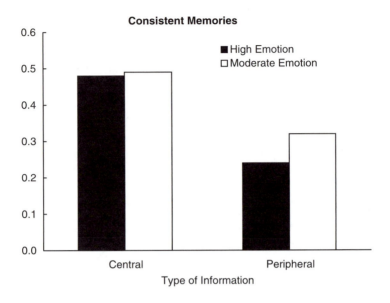

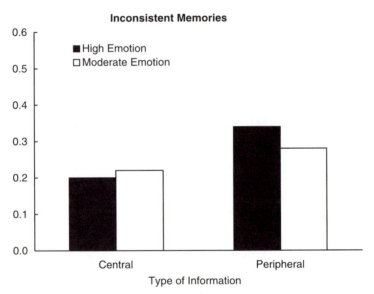

FIGURE 9.3 The proportion of consistent and inconsistent memories for central and peripheral features of autobiographical memories for the September 11 attacks (from Schmidt, 2004).

defined in terms of feature overlap. However, the distinctive stimulus shares few features with other material in the immediate context or with items stored in memory. In contrast, the significant stimulus matches features with significant memories. Quite often, significant stimuli are distinctive. One might guess that, as a result of habituation, a stimulus might lose its significance if it was encountered very frequently. Both significant and distinctive events are well remembered. However, the mechanisms responsible for good memory for distinctive and significance events may be different. In addition, distinctiveness and significance have different effects on memory for material in the spatial and temporal periphery.

Measurements of heart rate, rated emotion, sustained attention, and attention capture help to distinguish between significant and distinctive stimuli. Significant stimuli should lead to heart rate acceleration, high ratings of emotion, restricted attention lasting on the order of several seconds, and "pop out" of the stimuli in complex displays. In contrast, distinctive stimuli lead to heart rate deceleration, little emotion, restricted attention lasting only fractions of a second, and "pop out" only from the simplest displays. In addition, manipulations of list structure and participant disposition provide leverage to pry apart the influences of significance and distinctiveness on memory performance. Significance should influence memory in both within- and between-list manipulations, whereas distinctiveness requires contrast within the experimental session.

One of the most distinguishing characteristics of significant events is the influence the events have on memory for surrounding material. Strong emotion appears to capture and hold attention; this increases access to the gist of the emotional event at the expense of memory for material in spatial and temporal proximity to the event. As a result, background details from an emotional scene may be lost (Burke et al., 1992; Schmidt, 2002b). Memory for the next several pictures in a series may be impaired (Ellis et al., 1971; Griffin, 2005; Kramer & Schmidt, in press; Schmidt, 2002b). And, in response to a significant event, a student may simply forget to go to class (Schmidt, 2004). One explanation for these negative effects of emotion on memory is that emotions are the results of an appraisal process (Scherer, 2001). The process of computing an emotion and determining an appropriate response robs attentional resources from other ongoing cognitive tasks, including encoding peripheral information into memory (Schmidt, 2006).

With my apologies to William James, I would like to attempt to summarize the shared thread across a century of work on emotion and memory by paraphrasing his famous quote. The attention we give to an experience is a combination of its novelty and significance. It is a notorious fact that the novel and significant are, other things being equal, what we remember best. An impression may be so novel and significant as to leave an enduring impression of the event in memory while impairing memory for other events in the immediate spatial and temporal proximity.

NOTES

1. Distinctiveness can impair recall of other material in a list, but this effect is not confined to the immediately surrounding items, and is a retrieval rather than an encoding phenomena (Schmidt, 1985, 1991).
2. A third difference between my research and Tulving's is that he reported poor recall

of items immediately preceeding the high priority item. Detterman also found retrograde amnesia with his nude stimuli. Interesting, Tulving concluded that retrograde amnesia was only found with relatively fast rates of presentation (faster than 2 s per item), whereas Detterman (1975) concluded that retrograde amnesia declined with the delay in the recall test (from 0 to 120 s). I used a 3 s per item presentation rate, and a 10-minute retention interval—conditions unlikely to lead to retrograde amnesia.

REFERENCES

Bohannon, J. N. (1988). Flashbulb memories of the space shuttle disaster: A tale of two theories. *Cognition, 29*, 179–196.

Brown, R., & Kulik, J. (1977). Flashbulb memories. *Cognition, 5*, 73–99.

Burke, A., Heuer, F., & Reisberg, D. (1992). Remembering emotional events. *Memory and Cognition, 20*, 277–290.

Christianson, S.-A. (1989). Flashbulb memories: Special, but not so special. *Memory and Cognition, 17*, 435–443.

Detterman, D. K. (1975). The von Restorff effect and induced amnesia: Production by manipulation of sound intensity. *Journal of Experimental Psychology: Human Learning and Memory, 1*, 614–628.

Detterman, D. K., & Ellis, N. R. (1972). Determinants of induced amnesia in short-term memory. *Journal of Experimental Psychology, 95*, 308–316.

Easterbrook, J. A. (1959). The effect of emotion on cue utilization and the organization of behavior. *Psychological Review, 66*, 183–201.

Ellis, N. R., Detterman, D. K., Runcie, D., McCarver, R. B., & Craig, E. (1971). Amnesic effects in short-term memory. *Journal of Experimental Psychology, 89*, 357–361.

Eysenck, M. W. (1979). Depth, elaboration, and distinctiveness. In L. S. Cermak & F. I. M. Craik (Eds.), *Levels of processing in human memory* (pp. 89–118). Hillsdale, NJ: Lawrence Erlbaum Associates, Inc.

Fabiani, M., & Donchin, E. (1995). Encoding processes and memory organization: A model of the von Restorff effect. *Journal of Experimental Psychology: Learning, Memory, and Cognition, 21*, 224–240.

Gallagher, R. P. (2003). The psychological impact of 9–11 on college students and suggestions for how counseling centers can prepare for war and/or future terroristic attacks. Retrieved from http://www.acpa.nche.edu/comms/comm07/Feature3-03.htm

Gatchel, R. J., & Lang, P. J. (1973). Accuracy of psychophysical judgments and physiological response amplitude. *Journal of Experimental Psychology, 98*, 175–183.

Gati, I., & Ben-Shakhar, G. (1990). Novelty and significance in orientation and habituation: A feature-matching approach. *Journal of Experimental Psychology: General, 119*, 251–263.

Griffin, T. R. (2005). *The effects of fearful stimuli on attention and memory.* Unpublished manuscript.

Hunt, R. R. (2006). What is the meaning of distinctiveness for memory research? In R. R. Hunt & J. Worthen (Eds.), *Distinctiveness and Memory* (pp. 3–25). Oxford, UK: Oxford University Press.

James, W. (1950). *The principles of psychology.* New York: Dover. (Original work published 1890)

Johansson, M., Mecklinger, A., & Treese, A. (2004). Recognition memory for emotional and neutral faces: An event-related potential study. *Journal of Cognitive Neuroscience, 16*, 1840–1853.

Kaplan, R. M., & Pascoe, G. C. (1977). Humorous lectures and humorous examples: Some effects upon comprehension and retention. *Journal of Educational Psychology, 69,* 61–65.

Kleinsmith, L. J., & Kaplan, S. (1964). Interaction of arousal and recall interval in nonsense syllable paired-associate learning. *Journal of Experimental Psychology, 67,* 124–126.

Klorman, R., Weerts, T. C., Hastings, J. E., Melamed, B. G., & Lang, P. J. (1974). Psychometric description of some specific-fear questionnaires. *Behavior Therapy, 5,* 401–409.

Koffka, K. (1935). *Principles of gestalt psychology.* New York: Harcourt, Brace.

Kramer, D. A., & Schmidt, S. R. (in press). Alcohol beverage cues impair memory in high social drinkers. *Cognition and Emotion.*

Lavy, E., & van den Hout, M. (1993). Selective attention evidenced by pictorial and linguistic Stroop tasks. *Behavior Therapy, 24,* 645–657.

Loftus, E. F., & Burns, T. E. (1982). Mental shock can produce retrograde amnesia. *Memory and Cognition, 10,* 318–323.

MacKay, D. G., Shafto, M., Taylor, J. K., Marian, D. E., Abrams, L., & Dyer, J. (2004). Relations between emotion, memory and attention: Evidence from taboo Stroop, lexical decision, and immediate memory tasks. *Memory and Cognition, 32,* 474–488.

Manning, S. K., & Goldstein, F. D. (1976). Recall of emotional and neutral words as a function of rate and organization of list presentation. *Journal of General Psychology, 95,* 241–249.

McCloskey, M., Wible, C., & Cohen, N. (1988). Is there a special flashbulb memory mechanism? *Journal of Experimental Psychology: General, 117,* 171–181.

McDaniel, M. A., & Einstein, G. O. (1986). Bizarre imagery as an effective memory: The importance of distinctiveness. *Journal of Experimental Psychology: Learning, Memory, and Cognition, 12,* 54–65.

Nelson, D. L. (1979). Remembering pictures and words: Appearance, significance and name. In L. S. Cermak & F. I. M Craik (Eds.), *Levels of processing in human memory* (pp. 45–76). Hillsdale, NJ: Lawrence Erlbaum Associates; Inc.

Ohman, A., Flykt, A., & Esteves, F. (2001). Emotion drives attention: Detecting the snake in the grass. *Journal of Experimental Psychology: General, 130,* 466–478.

Saari, B. & Schmidt, S. R. (2005, May). *The effects of taboo words on memory.* Paper presented at the annual meeting of the South Eastern Psychological Association, Nashville, TN.

Scherer, K. R. (2001). Appraisal considered as a process of multilevel sequential checking. In K. R. Scherer, A. Schorr, & T. Johnstone (Eds.), *Appraisal processes in emotion: Theory, methods, research* (pp. 92–120). New York: Oxford University Press.

Schmidt, S. R. (1985). Encoding and retrieval processes in the memory for conceptually distinctive events. *Journal of Experimental Psychology: Learning, Memory, and Cognition, 11,* 565–578.

Schmidt, S. R. (1991). Can we have a distinctive theory of memory? *Memory and Cognition, 19,* 523–542.

Schmidt, S. R. (1994) The effects of humor on sentence memory. *Journal of Experimental Psychology: Learning, Memory, and Cognition, 20,* 953–967.

Schmidt, S. R. (1997, November). *In search of paradoxical effects of arousal on memory.* Paper presented at the annual meeting of the Psychonomic Society, Philadelphia.

Schmidt, S. R. (2002a). The humor effect: Differential processing and privileged retrieval. *Memory, 10*, 127–138.

Schmidt, S. R. (2002b). Outstanding memories: The positive and negative effects of nudes on memory. *Journal of Experimental Psychology: Learning, Memory, and Cognition, 28*, 353–361.

Schmidt, S. R. (2004). Autobiographical memories for the September 11th attacks: Reconstruction, distinctiveness, plus emotional impairment of memory. *Memory and Cognition, 32*, 443–454.

Schmidt, S. R. (2006). Emotion, significance, distinctiveness, and memory. In R. R. Hunt & J. Worthen (Eds.), *Distinctiveness and Memory* (pp. 47–64). Oxford, UK: Oxford University Press.

Schmidt, S. R., & Williams, A. R. (2001). Memory for humorous cartoons. *Memory and Cognition, 29*, 305–311.

Schulz, L. S. (1971). Effects of high-priority events on recall and recognition of other events. *Journal of Verbal Learning and Verbal Behavior, 10*, 322–330.

Schuster, M. A., Stein, B. D., Jaycox, L. H., Collins, R. L., Marshall, G. N., Elliott, M. N., Zhou, A. J., et al. (2001). A national survey of stress reactions after the September 11, 2001, terrorists. *New England Journal of Medicine, 345*, 1507–1512.

Stetter, F., Ackermann, K., Bizer, A., Straube, E. R., & Mann, K. (1995). Effects of disease-related cues in alcoholic inpatients: Results of a controlled "Alcohol Stroop" study. *Alcoholism: Clinical and Experimental Research, 19*(3), 593–599.

Stewart, J., de Wit, H., & Eikelboom, R. (1984). Role of unconditioned and conditioned drug effects in the self-administration of opiates and stimulants. *Psychological Review, 91*, 251–268.

Suls, J. M. (1972). A two-stage model for the appreciation of jokes and cartoons: An information-processing analysis. In J. H. Goldstein & P. E. McGhee (Eds.), *The psychology of humor* (pp. 81–100). New York: Academic Press.

Talmi, D., & Moscovitch, M. (2004). Can semantic relatedness explain the enhancedment of memory for emotional words? *Memory and Cognition, 32*, 742–751.

Tulving, E. (1969). Retrograde amnesia in free recall. *Science, 164*, 88–90.

Walker, E. L., & Tarte, R. D. (1963). Memory storage as a function of arousal and time with homogeneous and heterogeneous lists. *Journal of Verbal Learning and Verbal Behavior, 2*, 113–119.

Wallace, W. P. (1965). Review of the historical, empirical, and theoretical status of the von Restorff phenomenon. *Psychological Bulletin, 63*, 410–424.

Wang, Q., & Conway, M. A. (2004). The stories we keep: Autobiographical memory in American and Chinese middle-aged adults. *Journal of Personality, 72*, 911–938.

Weaver, C. A. (1993). Do you need a "flash" to form a flashbulb memory? *Journal of Experimental Psychology: General, 122*, 39–46.

10

The Effects of Attention and Emotion on Memory for Context

FERGUS I. M. CRAIK and NICHOLAS B. TURK-BROWNE

*I*t is a great pleasure to contribute a chapter to this volume honoring Roddy Roediger's many contributions to the field of human memory research. Roddy has not only provided influential theoretical analyses and striking empirical findings, but has also given his time generously to the organization and advancement of our discipline—his Presidency of the American Psychological Society and his Editorship of the *Journal of Experimental Psychology: Learning, Memory, and Cognition* are just two examples of many such contributions. Additionally, these obligations are always carried out in a relaxed and congenial manner, and with Roddy's wry humor. We look forward to many more years of excellent research and dubious Internet jokes!

Another more specific reason to be pleased to contribute to this Festschrift, is that Roddy has been very attentive over the years to the milestones passed by his friends in memory research. Among his many other activities, he has found the time to organize meetings and edit volumes in honor of Endel Tulving, Bob Crowder, and Gus Craik; it is therefore a particular pleasure to return the compliment.

We note that the organizers of the excellent meeting held in Roddy's honor at Purdue University entitled it somewhat cautiously "Roddyfest: Directions in Memory Research"—not "*Advances* in Memory Research" or even "*New* Directions in Memory Research," just "Directions!" So, freed from the obligation to contribute anything novel, we decided to look again at an experiment originally reported in the Festschrift for Endel Tulving edited by Roediger and Craik, and re-present it at the meeting. "After all," as the speaker remarked at the time, "it was good enough for Endel, so it should be good enough for Roddy!" The experiment (Craik, 1989) was part of a group of studies exploring the factors involved in associative binding, in particular the binding of item and contextual information. Emotion appears to be one such factor. There is good evidence that emotional events are not only well remembered in themselves, but that the context of occurrence is also well remembered. This is the essence of the "flashbulb memory" effect reported originally by Brown and Kulik (1977) and reviewed by Conway (1995) and by Winograd and Neisser (1992). These classic studies document people's memories of highly dramatic and shocking public events such as the assassination of President Kennedy and the space shuttle *Challenger* disaster, and they show that contextual information is often well remembered even when it is irrelevant to the emotional event itself. The binding of item and context appears to happen spontaneously, and may have some survival value for animals and humans who should take care to avoid contexts associated with traumatic events.

EXPERIMENT 1

The purpose of Craik's (1989) experiment was to explore the effects of much weaker emotional stimuli on the integration of events and their contexts. The stimuli used were mildly emotional words, and the context in this case was the speaker's voice. Lists of 12 words (common concrete nouns) were prerecorded by four different speakers, each of whom had a marked regional accent, and then presented to participants to study and recall. After all lists had been presented and recalled, the participants were unexpectedly given a subset of the words on a preprinted sheet and asked to decide which speaker had presented each word. Embedded in each 12-word list was one "target" word that was either a mildly emotional word (e.g., breast, corpse, screw, lesbian, nipple, coffin) or a city name (e.g., Lisbon, Berlin, Dallas, Calgary). In addition, each list had a designated neutral control word positioned like the target word in the middle of the list, plus the first and last words to pick up any primacy and recency effects. The integration of item and context was thus indexed by the ability to identify the speaker of each word, and it was predicted that the level of identification would be higher for the emotional words. City names were included as they were expected to attract more attention than other list words, which were common nouns; it seemed possible that *any* somewhat anomalous word might attract attention, be well recalled, and its voice context well identified. On the other hand, if emotion plays a special role in binding events and their contexts it would be expected that although city words and emotional words would both be well recalled, the emotional words would be associated with superior voice identification.

Other details include the point that each of the four speakers recorded a brief biographical statement about their background and occupation. These biographies were played to participants before the lists were presented to enable them to form some kind of image of each speaker. The experiment involved 32 participants (mostly university students); the words in each list were presented at a 3-s rate, and presentation was followed immediately by a 1-min recall period. After the lists were presented and recalled, participants were given a typed list containing the four words of interest (primacy, neutral, target, and recency) from each of the 16 lists, and asked to make a forced-choice judgment as to which speaker had originally presented each word. In the 16 lists, half contained a city word and half contained an emotional word. The 64 words presented for the voice judgment test were scrambled with regard both to type of word and list of origin.

The basic results are shown in Table 10.1. The neutral words from the middle of the list were recalled with a probability of .48, and the table shows that the experiment yielded the classic serial position curve with enhanced recall of the first word (primacy = .62) and last word (recency = .96). Of greater interest, there was also enhanced recall of city words (.70) and emotional words (.69), with no difference in the recall probabilities of these two types of target. Chance performance for voice identification is .25, and Table 10.1 shows that all four types of words exceeded that value. The probabilities of voice identification for neutral and recency words were almost identical (.36 and .35 respectively), but voice identification was superior for the other three word types (.49, .44, and .52 for primacy, city, and emotional words, respectively). There is thus some evidence that even mildly emotional events—in this case words in a list to be learned and recalled—are not only well recalled in themselves, but also strengthen the link between the event and its context. The difference in voice identification between city and emotional words was not statistically significant, but nonetheless there is some indication that emotionality has some effect on context integration over and above the effects of attention. On the other hand, voice identification performance for primacy words was surprisingly high despite the absence of emotionality in this case.

The first experiment thus gave results suggesting that even mildly emotional events can increase the binding of experienced events to their contexts of occurrence—a kind of "mini flashbulb effect!" But the results also left many unanswered questions; is the effect essentially due to the greater attention paid to any anomalous item, for example, or does emotionality confer some special benefit? A related question concerns the role of intentionality in this paradigm; participants were not explicitly told that they would be asked to recall the voice of presentation in the present study, but they were instructed to pay attention to the voice "as it might help them to remember the words." If emotion (or attention) truly acts in a flashbulb manner, recall of context should be facilitated regardless of any intention to associate specific words and voices. Recall should also be facilitated regardless of any pre-existing association between the item and its context; a less extreme view might be that emotion acts to amplify existing associations. If attention is the mediating factor, is the effect of emotion on item and context recall reduced systematically as attention is withdrawn in a dual-task paradigm? Also, does such a reduction in attention affect item and context information differentially? One possibility is that associative information is more vulnerable to the withdrawal of processing resources (Craik, 1989). Finally, there are many interesting questions concerning the neural bases of the effects of emotion on memory (Cahill & McGaugh, 1998).

TABLE 10.1 Probability of Free Recall and Voice Identification as a Function of Word Type

	Primacy	Control	City	Emotional	Recency
Free recall	.62	.48	.70	.69	.96
Voice ID	.49	.36	.44	.52	.35

FURTHER BACKGROUND ON EMOTION AND CONTEXT

Interest in the topic of emotion and memory has grown exponentially in the last 15 years in fact, with reviews of the area provided by Cahill and McGaugh (1998), Christianson (1992), McGaugh (2004), and Reisberg and Heuer (2004). There is general agreement that emotional stimuli are better remembered than neutral stimuli, and that one reason for this effect is the involvement of the amygdala, which serves to modulate the processes of encoding and consolidation in the hippocampus, caudate nucleus and other structures (Cahill & McGaugh, 1998). There is still a great deal of debate about the cognitive factors underlying the effect, however. Does emotionality act directly on memory, for example, or is it simply that emotional events attract attention and therefore receive greater amounts of processing—which in turn enhance memory? Emotional events are also distinctive and significant, and it is well known that these features confer a benefit on later remembering (Hunt & Worthen, 2006; Schmidt, chapter 9, this volume). Finally, Talmi and Moscovitch (2004) pointed out that emotional stimuli in a laboratory setting are often related (e.g., words like pain and torture, or like corpse, death, coffin), and that this factor also contributes to the overall effect. These components of the effect of emotion on memory are still under active debate (see for example Schmidt, chapter 9, this volume).

The effects of emotionality on memory for *context* is another lively area of research. Doerkson and Shimamura (2001) presented lists of neutral and emotionally valenced words (e.g., glory, sunrise, emergency, slaughter) for participants to study; half of the words were colored yellow and the other half were colored blue. Participants were instructed to remember the color in which each word appeared. After list presentation, participants were first asked to recall as many words as possible and were then given a recognition test in which they judged words to be old/yellow, old/blue, or new. The results showed that emotional words were recalled at a much higher level than neutral words, and that source memory for the associated color was also enhanced for the emotional words. Donald MacKay has also published two studies that are highly relevant to the present concerns. In the first of these (Mackay et al., 2004) the investigators presented a series of words in different colors for participants to name: The words were either neutral emotionally or were obscene taboo words. Color-naming took longer for the taboo words, and they were also better recalled than the neutral words despite the fact that participants did not expect the recall test. In Experiment 3, the color-naming phase was followed by a surprise color-recognition test, which resulted in better color recognition of the emotional words. In a further study, MacKay and Ahmetzanov (2005) replicated this result and also found that the original word location was better recognized for taboo than for neutral words. MacKay and colleagues have suggested that emotion acts to bind emotional events to their contexts of occurrence, and also that this binding process occurs automatically; in the MacKay and Ahmetzanov study there was no difference in location recognition between cases in which participants were aware or unaware that some words always occurred in the same location. In greater detail, MacKay and colleagues (2004) hypothesized that there is an emotional binding mechanism that operates to link salient features of the context to specific emotional events. This mechanism works in a parallel way to an attentional-binding mechanism, which again acts to bind attended features of events to salient aspect of the context.

EXPERIMENT 2

The second experiment to be reported was designed and carried out essentially to replicate and extend the results of Craik (1989) rather than to endorse or rebut the ideas and findings of MacKay and colleagues (2004; MacKay & Ahmetzanov, 2005), although many of the issues are similar. We discuss the relations between the two sets of studies later in the chapter.

The experiment used the paradigm reported earlier; that is, four lists of 12 words were spoken by each of four different speakers, with each list followed by immediate free recall. The presentation and recall of all lists was followed in turn by a voice identification test, in which four words from each of the 16 lists were presented visually; the participant's task was to decide which of the four speakers had presented each word.

As in the study by Craik (1989), each list contained four words of interest, the first and last words (primacy and recency, respectively), a neutral control word positioned in the middle of the list, and either a city name or a mildly emotional word, also in the middle of the list. The exact positions of these three middle-of-list items were counterbalanced across lists and participants. Before the lists were presented, participants listened to each speaker present a brief biography from a tape-recorder; a photograph of the speaker was also presented. These preliminaries allowed participants to form some impression of the speakers, who in this case were a female staff member of the Rotman Institute who came originally from Hong Kong, a female postdoctoral fellow from Quebec, a male postdoctoral fellow from Israel, and a (late) middle-aged semi-retired male Scottish professor.

The words used were common two-syllable concrete nouns, apart from the city and emotional words; they were presented at a 3-s rate, and presentation was followed by a 1-min period for free recall. Four different formats were recorded, with the result that each 12-word list was spoken by all four speakers across the experiment. The order of the lists was also counterbalanced. Eight of the lists (two per speaker) contained a city name, and the remaining eight contained an emotional word. The experiment was described as one investigating the effect of different speakers' accents on memory; participants were instructed to associate each word with that particular speaker, but were not told that they would be tested for that information. Following presentation and recall of all lists, a typed sheet containing the 64 critical words was presented, and participants were asked to make a forced-choice decision as to which speaker had presented each word.

Three groups of 32 participants performed the experiment; a group of young adults (mostly university students), a group of older adults aged between 60 and 80, and a second group of young adults who listened to the original list presentations under divided-attention (DA) conditions. The purpose of including the older group was to check whether the effects of emotionality on memory were attenuated by aging. It has been suggested that older adults are less emotionally labile and have "flattened affect;" if this is so it might be expected that the effect of emotionality on memory from context would be reduced. The purpose of including the divided-attention group was primarily to check the idea that the effects of emotionality are essentially due to a greater allocation of attention to the emotional event. If this is so, the divided-attention condition should presumably show attenuated effects of emotionality and perhaps also of city names and primacy. Participants in this group answered simple addition questions presented visually on a computer screen during list presentation. They performed the recall test and the voice-identification test under full attention (FA) conditions.

The main results are shown in Figures 10.1a (word recall) and 10.1b (voice identification). Relative to the control words, recall was somewhat higher for the first words in each list (primacy), and this effect was similar for all three groups. As expected, all groups also showed strong recency effects. Recall levels for the city and emotional words were substantially above those for the respective control words in all groups, with equivalent recall of emotional and city words in the case of young adults under FA conditions, but superior recall of city words for the older group and young adults under DA conditions. However, an analysis of variance on these data showed main effects of word type and of group only; the interaction was not statistically significant. Figure 10.1b shows first that voice identification (voice ID) was greater than chance (.25) in all cases. Word type had comparatively small effects on voice ID in the older group, varying only from .34 and .33 for the control and recency words, respectively, to .36, .41, and .38 for primacy, city, and emotional words respectively. Figure 10.1b shows that the two young adult groups had similar patterns of voice ID, with control and recency words yielding comparably low levels of identification, and emotional words yielding the highest level. Voice ID ranged between .44 (recency) and .59 (emotional) for the young-FA group, and between .31 (control) and .51 (emotional) for the young-DA group. Thus there is graphic support for the prediction that older adults would show only a small effect of emotionality on voice ID, whereas young adults would show strong effects. Surprisingly, a comparatively strong effect of emotionality was also shown by the young-DA group. Despite the graphic evidence, however, an ANOVA again showed no interaction between word type and group.

A comparison of Figures 10.1a and 10.1b shows that the young-DA participants mimic the recall pattern of the older group (Figure 10a), yet resemble the young-FA group more closely in their voice-ID performance (Figure 10b). The first result is a further illustration of the point that withdrawal of processing resources by dividing attention between memory encoding and a secondary task in young adults reduces their subsequent recall levels to those of older adults under full attention (Craik, 1982). Figure 10.1a shows a particularly striking example of this effect given first that recall levels of the old group vary between .24 and .69, and second that the corresponding levels for the young-DA group are between .04 and .06 higher across all cases. That is, the effect of DA is not simply to lower performance, but to lower it in a way that exactly matches the pattern shown by older adults. The strong implication is that at least one major cause of memory

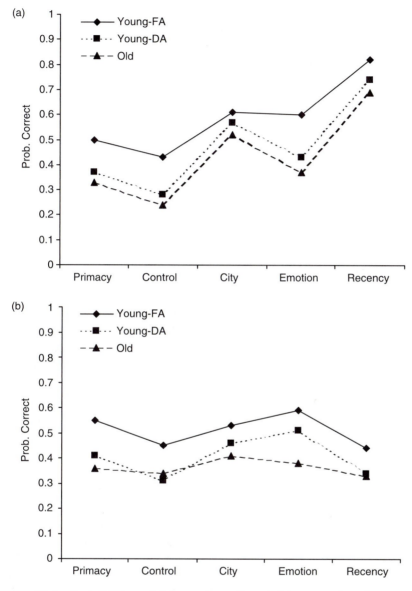

FIGURE 10.1   Probabilities of (a) word recall and (b) voice identification as a function of participant group and word type.

impairment in older adults is a reduction in available processing resources. The finding that recall of city words is approximately 15% higher than recall of emotional words for both young-DA and older adults may reflect the point that a city name embedded in a list of nouns is more immediately noticeable and salient than are mildly emotional words such as those used in the a present study. Taboo words might yield a different result, however. Despite their similarity to older adults in recall, the young-DA group performs more like the young-FA group in the Voice-ID task (Figure 10b). Thus, although the young-DA participants recalled relatively few emotional words, their voice-ID scores for these words were relatively high.

A second way to look at these data is to conditionalize on recall; given correct recall, what is the probability that the voice is correctly identified? These data are shown in Figure 10.2. Values for recency items are understandably low; these words were well recalled (Figure 10a), yet their voice-ID scores are approximately the same as control words, yielding a low conditionalized score. For the remaining four word types, older adults had quite similar conditionalized scores, varying between .46 and .51. For this older adult group, primacy scores are .05 points above control, and emotional words are .04 points above control. The pattern is different in both young groups. In the case of primacy scores, the advantage relative to control is .14 for young-FA and .09 for young-DA. For emotional scores, the advantage relative to control is even greater; .15 for young-FA and .22 for young-DA participants. There is thus some evidence that words with emotional impact (including primacy words possibly) have a stronger likelihood of binding to their perceptual qualities—in younger adults at least.

DISCUSSION AND CONCLUSIONS

The two experiments are consistent in showing that for young adults working under full attention conditions, emotional words enhance the later identification

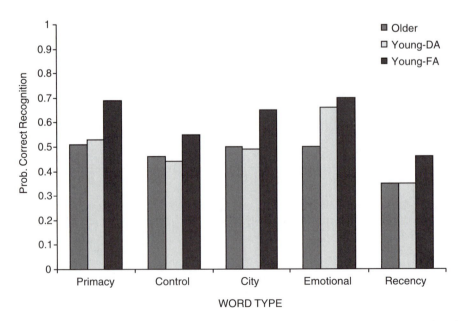

FIGURE 10.2 Probability of voice identification conditionalized on correct word recall, as a function of participant group and word type.

of the voice presenting the word. This improvement in the binding between an item and its perceptual qualities (or "context" or "source") is substantial; .52 compared to .36 for control words in Experiment 1 and .59 compared to .45 for control items in Experiment 2. These results thus confirm and extend the findings that emotional words enhance source memory for their presentation color (Doerkson & Shimamura, 2001) and that highly emotional words enhance later recognition of location (MacKay & Ahmetzanov, 2005). The enhancement of binding triggered by emotion appears to happen automatically, given that participants were not instructed to learn the association between words and their context in either the current experiments or those of MacKay and Ahmetzanov (2005).

The present experiment can also give at least tentative answers to other questions posed in the introduction. First, the differences between the young-FA group and the other two groups were less dramatic than expected; essentially, all three groups showed the same patterns (as indicated by the absence of Group × Word type interactions) although unsurprisingly the young-DA and older groups performed at lower levels than those shown by the young-FA group. Nonetheless, the older group showed a smaller range of voice-ID scores (.08) than either the young-FA group (.15) or the young-DA group (.20), giving some support to the idea that aging is associated with flattened affect, and that this reduction in emotional activity is one factor underlying the reduction in source memory observed in older participants (Hashtroudi, Johnson, & Chrosniak, 1989; McIntyre & Craik, 1987; Spencer & Raz, 1995). Of course, there is no guarantee that the words have the same emotional impact on older and younger participants, but one reassuring aspect of the data is that (as shown in Figure 10.1a) the recall advantage of emotional over control words is very similar in the older group (.13) and the young-DA group (.15). With regard to the young-DA group, withdrawal of attentional resources reduced their word recall levels to that of older participants (Figure 10.1a), but interestingly their voice-ID scores tended to follow the pattern of the young-FA group rather than that of the older adults (Figure 10.1b). When voice-ID scores were conditionalized on correct recall (Figure 10.2), the young-DA group showed similar performance levels to those of older adults except for emotional words, where there was a tendency for their scores to approach those of the young-FA group. This trend was entirely absent for city words, however, suggesting that salience is not enough, that some emotional content is necessary to enhance the binding of item and context information, that primacy items have this quality as well as overtly emotional words, and that young adults show the effect of emotionality despite a reduction in processing resources under divided attention conditions. For the young groups, the emotional words may capture attention in an obligatory fashion (cf. the "rubbernecking" effect reported by Most, Chun, Widders, & Zald, 2005).

One important question in this area is whether the boosting effects of emotionality on memory for context are essentially attributable to the increased *attention* paid to emotional stimuli. The present experiments attempted to answer this question by comparing performance on emotional words with performance on city names, which are at least as salient and are probably more easily segregated into a distinctive group than are the mildly emotional words used here. The city names were recalled at least as well as the emotional words (Figure 10.1a), but the emotional words were slightly superior with regard to voice ID, in the two younger groups at least (Figures 10.1b and 10.2). The tentative conclusion is that the affective impact of mildly emotional words (or taboo words in the case of MacKay & Ahmetzanov, 2005) and even of the first (primacy) words in a list to be learned, appears to be equivalent to the effects of attention with respect to later *recall* of the words themselves, but has an effect beyond that of attention with respect to later recollection of source and context. A related question is whether emotionality and other forms of salience simply amplify existing relations between items and their contexts, or whether such effects are independent of previous relations, as the original work on the flashbulb effect suggests. In this latter case, the effects of emotionality would be to "glue" together events and contexts regardless of their associative compatibility. The present data do not address this issue, but it would be an interesting topic for investigation—to vary the prior congruity between events and contexts, and then examine the effects of salience and emotionality on later memory for the contexts.

The data from Experiment 2 also address the issue of similarities and dissimilarities between divided attention in young adults and the effects of aging (Craik, 1982, 1983; Naveh-Benjamin, 2000, 2002). Naveh-Benjamin (2002) has argued that the effects are different in that aging is associated with a specific deficit in associative binding that is absent in DA manipulations on young adults. The relative effects of aging and DA on item and associative information can be assessed from the data shown in Figures 10.1a and 10.1b. The effects are best estimated from the primacy and control words, as these items are neither "contaminated" by special qualities (city and emotional words) nor involve different encoding and retrieval mechanisms (recency words). For young-DA participants, the drop in performance levels from those of the young-FA group (averaged over primacy and control words) was .14 for recall and also .14 for voice-ID. The corresponding values for the older adults were .18 and .15, respectively. Thus although it might have been expected that aging and DA would affect the encoding of associative information more than the encoding of item information and that such an effect would be greater in the old group, in fact the present data show that item and associative information were negatively affected to the same degree by both aging and divided attention.

In the course of editing this chapter, Jim Nairne pointed out that episodic recall of events (illustrated, for example, by the free recall of words in lists) *also* involves "binding"—in this case the binding of words to the temporal and other contextual features of the list and the experimental situation. So why should recall—involving binding of an item to its episodic context—differ from voice identification—also involving binding of an item to its episodic context? This is an interesting puzzle. We agree with Nairne that the two measures (recall and voice ID) logically tap the same type of associative process; nonetheless, the present data show some differences. One example is the 15% advantage of city recall over emotional recall for the old and young-DA groups, compared with the roughly equivalent voice-ID scores for city and emotional words in these two groups (Figures 10.1a and 10.1b). Another example is provided by the conditionalized voice-ID scores shown in

Figure 10.2. It seems to us that if "list binding" and "voice binding" are equivalent processes, then the conditionalized scores should also be equivalent (apart from recency, which taps a different recall process). That is, subject and material differences should be "absorbed" in the recall data. The finding that some differences are apparent among the conditions shown in Figure 10.2 may reflect differences in what may be termed "levels of binding" (Craik, 2006). That is, there may be important differences between binding items to general contextual aspects and binding of inherent features such as voice and handwriting. This is the distinction between "extrinsic" and "intrinsic" context made by Baddeley (1990) and others. One final point in this connection is that the distinction between "remember" and "know" items is also a distinction between two levels of contextual association, in that "know" items lack episodic detail, but the subject clearly knows that the item occurred in the experimental list (Craik, 2003).

In conclusion, we have presented some preliminary data on the effects of stimulus salience and emotionality on the associative binding between events and their contexts. We see no traces of Roddy Roediger exhibiting signs of flattened affect, and trust that he will remember both the events and the context of his Festschrift conference for many years to come.

REFERENCES

Baddeley, A. D. (1990). *Human memory: Theory and practice*. Boston: Allyn & Bacon.

Brown, R., & Kulik, J. (1977). Flashbulb memories. *Cognition, 5*, 73–99.

Cahill, L., & McGaugh, J. L. (1998). Mechanisms of emotional arousal and lasting declarative memory. *Trends in Neurosciences, 21*, 294–299.

Christianson, S. (1992). Emotional stress and eyewitness memory: A critical review. *Psychological Bulletin, 112*, 284–309.

Conway, M. A. (1995). *Flashbulb memories*. Hillsdale, NJ: Lawrence Erlbaum Associates, Inc.

Craik, F. I. M. (1982). Selective changes in encoding as a function of reduced processing capacity. In F. I. M. Craik & S. E. Trehub (Eds.), *Aging and cognitive processes*. New York: Plenum.

Craik, F. I. M. (1983). On the transfer of information from temporary to permanent memory. *Philosophical Transactions of the Royal Society, Series B, 302*, 341–359.

Craik, F. I. M. (1989). On the making of episodes. In H. L. Roediger & F. I. M. Craik (Eds.), *Varieties of memory and consciousness: Essays in honour of Endel Tulving* (pp. 43–57). Hillsdale, NJ: Lawrence Erlbaum Associates, Inc.

Craik, F. I. M. (2003). Commentary. In J. S. Bowers & C. J. Marsolek (Eds.), *Rethinking implicit memory* (pp. 327–336). New York: Oxford University Press.

Craik, F. I. M. (2006). Remembering items and their contexts: Effects of aging and divided attention. In H. Zimmer, A. Mecklinger, & U. Lindenberger (Eds.), *Binding in human memory: A neurocognitive perspective* (pp. 273–291). New York: Oxford University Press.

Doerksen, S., & Shimamura, A. P. (2001). Source memory enhancement for emotional words. *Emotion, 1*, 5–11.

Hashtroudi, S., Johnson, M. K., & Chrosniak, L. D. (1989). Aging and source monitoring. *Psychology and Aging, 4*, 106–112.

Hunt, R. R., & Worthen, J. B (Eds.). (2006). *Distinctiveness and memory*. New York: Oxford University Press.

MacKay, D. G., & Ahmetzanov, M. V. (2005). Emotion, memory, and attention in the taboo Stroop paradigm. *Psychological Science, 16*, 25–32.

MacKay, D. G., Shafto, M., Taylor, J. K., Marian, D. E., Abrams, L., & Dyer, J. (2004). Relations between emotion, memory, and attention: Evidence from taboo Stroop, lexical decision, and immediate memory tasks. *Memory and Cognition, 32*, 474–488.

McGaugh, J. L. (2004). The amygdala modulates the consolidation of memories of emotionally arousing experiences. *Annual Reviews of Neuroscience, 27*, 820–840.

McIntyre, J. S., & Craik, F. I. M. (1987). Age differences in memory for item and source information. *Canadian Journal of Psychology, 41*, 175–192.

Most, S. B., Chun, M. M., Widders, D. M. & Zald, D. H. (2005). Attentional rubbernecking: Cognitive control and personality in emotion-induced blindness. *Psychonomic Bulletin and Review, 12*, 654–661.

Naveh-Benjamin, M. (2000). Adult-age differences in memory performance: Tests of an associative deficit hypothesis. *Journal of Experimental Psychology: Learning, Memory, and Cognition, 26*, 1170–1187.

Naveh-Benjamin, M. (2002). The effects of divided attention on encoding processes: Underlying mechanisms. In M. Naveh-Benjamin, M. Moscovitch, & H. L. Roediger (Eds.), *Perspectives on human memory and cognitive aging* (pp. 193–207). Philadelphia: Psychology Press.

Reisberg, D., & Heuer, F. (2004). Remembering emotional events. In D. Reisberg & P. Hertel (Eds.), *Memory and emotion* (pp. 3–41). New York: Oxford University Press.

Spencer, W. D., & Raz, N. (1995). Differential effects of aging on memory for content and context: A meta-analysis. *Psychology and Aging, 10*, 527–539.

Talmi, D., & Moscovitch, M. (2004). Can semantic relatedness explain the enhancement of memory for emotional words? *Memory and Cognition, 32*, 742–751.

Winograd, E., & Neisser, U. (Eds.). (1992). *Affect and accuracy in recall*. Cambridge, UK: Cambridge University Press.

11

Putting Context in Context

KRYSTAL A. KLEIN, RICHARD M. SHIFFRIN, and AMY H. CRISS

R oediger and McDermott's comprehensive review of the implicit memory literature (1993) included a puzzling pair of findings: If a prime item is studied in massed fashion (i.e., longer study or successive presentations), the prime benefit on a later perceptual-implicit memory test (e.g., lexical decision) does not increase beyond that provided by a brief or single presentation. However, if the prime item is repeated in spaced fashion, the prime benefit increases with the number of presentations (see Jacoby & Dallas, 1981; Roediger & Challis, 1992). These findings are puzzling because explicit memory tests show that performance increases with the number of both massed and spaced presentations (albeit more so for spaced presentations). Starting with Shiffrin and Steyvers (1997) we had been developing a theory that included a key role for context to account for implicit and explicit memory and the relation between these. Long-term priming, for example, was explained in large part by the assumption that event-study produced not only an explicit trace (incomplete and noisy), but also additional context storage in that event's knowledge trace (if one existed; see Schooler, Shiffrin, & Raaijmakers, 2001). However, the findings highlighted by Roediger and McDermott did not fit that developing model, and led us to look deeper into the role of context and the mechanisms by which it affected memory. Now a decade and more after Roediger and McDermott put implicit memory in context, we believe it fitting to report our subsequent attempts to place context in context.

WHAT IS CONTEXT?

The idea of "context" is at once the bane and boon of those aiming to understand memory. Although context has been employed almost universally as an explanatory construct, in such areas as classical conditioning (Gantt, 1940), motor learning (Wright & Shea, 1991), recall (Anderson & Bower, 1972; Dulsky, 1935; Raaijmakers & Shiffrin, 1981; Strand, 1970), recognition (Criss & Shiffrin, 2004a; Dennis

& Humphreys, 2001), and directed forgetting (Sahakyan & Kelley, 2002), systematic manipulations of context have shown only moderate and occasional effects (Fernandez & Glenberg, 1985; Smith, 1988, 2001). Today's situation is not so distant from Underwood's (1977) comment: "never in the history of choice of theoretical mechanism has one been chosen that has so little support in direct evidence" (p. 43). Evidentiary support aside, the importance of context in memory theory has continued to grow. The situation is in some ways akin to that of "quarks" in physics: Direct evidence is difficult to come by, but the construct is necessary to build a coherent theory.

Context is a necessary theoretical construct in good part because no event occurs in isolation from the observer's internal states, or in isolation from the environmental surround. In general, context is the term used to describe the joint contribution of all of these factors to the mental state of a person at a given time. Some of the more important of these factors are: (1) information manipulated by the investigator (other than the nominal target of memory testing itself), such as adjacent words in a word list, the computer monitor background, and the room setting in which study and testing might occur; (2) external environmental information that is in principle identifiable and measurable, but not manipulated (such as the temperature of the laboratory, the font of orthographic study materials, the instructions, the illumination conditions); (3) external environmental information that is not manipulated and difficult to identify and measure (such as the changing external verbal and ambient auditory noise, air currents, transitory vibrations, movements of the participant in her or his seat during testing); (4) internal bodily conditions, mental and otherwise, that are measurable and identifiable (e.g., verbalizable strategies, body temperature, heart rate); (5) internal information not readily identifiable and measurable (such as various cognitive states and strategies, transitory perceptions and thoughts, evanescent bodily changes like itches and stomach upsets).

Many theories assume that some of this information is stored in memory with events, and also used to probe memory during retrieval. Researchers: (1) sometimes assume context is unattended, though this does not have to be the case; (2) typically assume context refers to factors not manipulated by the experimenter, though some theorists include nearby events as part of the context for a given event (e.g., nearby words in a study list—see Howard & Kahana, 2002); (3) often define context to exclude content information directly tied to the study event (such as the meaning of a word). It seems clear to us that real progress in understanding context and its role in memory will require both a richer empirical database, and further modeling and testing particular assumptions. In this chapter we lay out some first steps along this path, starting with a brief historical perspective and then a brief overview of context as specified in our "Retrieving Effectively from Memory" model (REM; Criss & Shiffrin, 2004a; Shiffrin & Steyvers, 1997). We then attempt to flesh out an evolving picture of context and its effects by presenting results from a number of studies, some published and others previously withheld, interpreting the findings within the REM approach.

MODELING CONTEXT

Precursors to REM

In REM's precursor, the Search of Associative Memory model (SAM; Raaijmakers & Shiffrin, 1981), context information was described in general terms; however, in its application to episodic recall, it was essentially information identifying an item (typically a word) as having occurred on the current study list (analogous to list markers in Anderson & Bower, 1972). During retrieval, a context cue derived from the current context, or possibly a reconstruction of some past context, could be used to focus memory search upon episodic traces of the words in the current list.

The SAM model was very successful in predicting a variety of memory effects, but had several theoretical drawbacks. For one, the occasional erroneous recalls of items from previous lists indicated that search could not be perfectly limited to traces from a given list, as SAM assumed. Another simplification, that a single context might apply to an entire list, seemed impractical; this assumption was elaborated and revised in Mensink and Raaijmakers' (1988) adaptation of SAM, which incorporated a drift of active contextual features over time. However, the assumption of one context for an entire list may be close to the truth; we shall provide relevant evidence in the form of studies by Klein, Criss, and Shiffrin (2004, 2006). Finally, the earlier theories did not address the role of context in the interaction between episodic traces and knowledge traces during storage and retrieval. Rectifying these omissions was one of the forces underlying the development of the REM model.

REM in a Nutshell

REM attempts to retain the basic conceptual content that has allowed SAM to deal so effectively with episodic recall and recognition, but makes three important extensions and changes: (1) It assumes a featural representation for event traces and knowledge traces and traces (in the form of a vector of feature values), allowing similarity of traces to be assessed; (2) it assumes that retrieval is based on a conditionally optimal Bayesian decision process, conditioned on incomplete and error prone event storage (see Anderson, 1990); (3) it assumes that study of an item both produces an episodic memory trace (including information from the knowledge trace[1] of the studied item, if one exists) and adds information to the item's knowledge trace or a previous episodic trace (if either exists). Assumption 3 allows one to see how knowledge can grow from repeated event-episodes during development.

The features themselves are represented in a very simple fashion: A feature type lies in a fixed, specified position of the vector (allowing probe to trace comparisons, cf. Criss & Shiffrin, 2004c, 2005). A given trace has just one value for a given feature type; this value is either an integer indicating the content of the feature (e.g., color feature might have different color values, or a size feature might have different size values), or a zero value to represent features that have not been encoded (see Shiffrin & Steyvers, 1997, for a thorough description of memory trace representation). Thus an item, memory trace, or probe is represented as a vector of integers and zeros.

Because knowledge traces of words are formed from an accumulation of episodic traces, each with differing context features, the knowledge trace is associated with too much context rather than too little: More precisely, a knowledge trace contains a generic context, rather than any one identifiable context, and is in this sense decontextualized. In contrast, an episodic trace stores just one context, albeit incompletely and with error.

Memory retrieval begins with a vector of probe features; in a recognition experiment, this would contain the features of the probe to which the participant must respond "old" or "new." In principle this probe vector consists of both content and context features, and is compared in parallel to all traces in memory. Activation of each trace is based on feature similarity, calculated as a likelihood ratio. Traces with both enough information and a large enough likelihood ratio are above activation threshold and take part in subsequent aspects of retrieval. Single-item episodic recognition is based on the average likelihood ratio, usually termed "familiarity." Recall is based on a cycle of sampling and recovery operations: Sampling of a trace is proportional to the trace activation in comparison to all above-threshold traces. Recovery and output then depend on what can be retrieved from that trace, which depends on the amount of information stored. Each cycle of cued recall uses the item and context cue. In free recall, some cycles use as a probe the content related to a recently retrieved item plus context, while others use as a probe context only.

In practice, for a variety of list memory studies in which new items occur on every list, this general approach is typically simplified by separating out the role of context. In particular, it has been assumed that the main role of context is to restrict activated traces to those from the recent list, so that context causes all of these traces and no others to be in the activated set. Then the trace activations within that set of list traces are calculated only on the basis of the matching of the content features. In effect, this approach is justified on the assumption that list context is constant for the list, therefore playing no differential role. Shiffrin and Steyvers (1997) investigated the implications of using the calculations appropriate for the simplified case in more general settings. In many such cases the qualitative pattern of predictions did not change.

Item versus Context Information

Episodic recognition in REM is usually based on familiarity (ignoring applications requiring the supplementary use of recall). The simplified version of REM (Criss & Shiffrin, 2004a) calculates familiarity based on the degree to which the probe and the memory traces share matching features but do not have mismatching feature values. Note that the digit codes in REM convey base rate information, but not magnitude information. Although obviously a simplification, similarity does not depend on the magnitude difference between mismatching integers. A target probe tends to match its own memory trace better than any other and thus the average familiarity for a target is greater than for a foil. However, in both cases, one (or more) of the nontarget memory traces can match well enough to trigger a false recognition, and this occurs more frequently as list length rises. This approach lets performance be determined by confusions with other traces, within the set of traces specified by the context cue. Dennis and Humphreys (2001) proposed an alternative in which the test-word content features activate all episodic traces of the test word in long-term memory (not just traces from the current list), and that traces of other words are not activated at all.[2] A positive recognition decision is made when the context information in these traces is sufficiently similar to the test context. Recognition is facilitated by the fact that old test words tend to have been stored with more recent context than new test words. (In their view, recall tasks, and recognition for items other than words, are handled differently.) Although their model also uses both word content and context information to recognize, there are no confusions with traces of other words.

Criss and Shiffrin (2004a) used new data (see below) and modeling to defend the view that similarity of traces to both context and content features determine episodic recognition generally and word recognition in particular. Their version of the general REM model allows differential weighting of item features and context features, making it possible to assess the relative contributions of item noise and context noise to performance. For one paradigm that was designed to build in many context confusions (test items could have been presented in any combination of the three most recent lists, or in none), they showed that the effect of context similarity did outweigh the effect of content similarity, though both played a role. In order to fit the REM model to this task, they had to incorporate a (simplified) model of context change across lists. This REM approach, with probes using both context and content features, and context changes between but not within lists, will be the starting point for theoretical explanations in this chapter.

EXPERIMENTAL STUDIES

Over many years, a number of unpublished and published studies by our group have provided evidence concerning the role of context in memory encoding and retrieval. Although few of these studies manipulated context directly, they allowed indirect inferences to be drawn. We will describe several of these, and also present data from new experiments using comparative recency judgments that are aimed to allow more direct inferences about context.

The "One-Shot of Context" Hypothesis

Roediger and McDermott's review (1993) led us to a hypothesis to explain why (1) additional distributed study increases priming, although (2) massed study does not increase priming (although it does improve explicit memory). According to REM, study leads to the addition of "new" current context features to a knowledge trace; when the test context is similar to the study context, the increased context matching will increase speed and accuracy of access to that knowledge trace. Why should this process fail following massed study? We guessed that extra massed study might produce extra storage for content information, but not for context information. However, we guessed further that extra spaced study of a repeated item would cause additional accumulation in one trace of both context and content information. This was termed the "one-shot of context" assumption (Malmberg & Shiffrin, 2005).

Malmberg and Shiffrin (2005) carried out an independent test of this hypothesis by exploring the list-strength effect (LSE) in free recall. Strengthening some list items had been shown to harm free recall of other list items (Ratcliff, Clark, & Shiffrin, 1990; Shiffrin, Ratcliff, & Clark, 1990), a result termed a positive LSE (in contrast with a null or negative LSE, which is obtained in recognition and cued recall). Malmberg and Shiffrin noted that the addition of the "one-shot of context" hypothesis to the REM (or SAM) theory resulted in the following prediction: A positive free-recall LSE should occur only for spaced but not massed study of the strengthened items. Because only spaced study had been used in previous free-recall LSE experiments, Malmberg and Shiffrin conducted a study using both spaced and massed study conditions to test the "one-shot" theory; Figure 11.1 shows the data, which exhibit the predicted interaction.

The basis for the predicted interaction is not only the "one-shot" assumption, but also the REM/SAM assumption that probe cues in free recall are of two types during the course of retrieval: Sometimes the probe uses both content and context

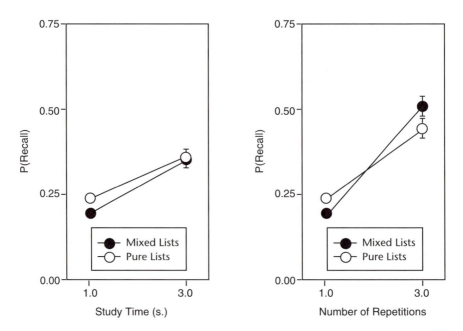

FIGURE 11.1   Results from Malmberg and Shiffrin (2005): Probability of recall for mixed and pure lists. The left panel plots a null list-strength effect observed for lists using massed (study-time) strengthening; the right panel plots a positive list-strength effect obtained for lists using spaced (repetition) strengthening. Error bars reflect standard error of the mean. Figure reproduced from Malmberg and Shiffrin (2005).

features, in which case a null or slightly negative LSE is predicted (the situation is like that holding in cued recall), and other times the probe uses context features only, in which case the list-strength effect will be positive if context storage had increased for strengthened items (as occurs for spaced study), and will be null if context storage had not increased for strengthened items (as occurs for massed study). Thus, the positive LSE is predicted only for spaced repetitions of strengthened items. Malmberg and Shiffrin (2005) therefore obtained converging evidence: Both the priming results and the free-recall LSE findings can be explained in the REM/SAM framework by the same "one-shot of context" assumption. Why should such a hypothesis hold? It may be that some storage of both context and content occurs automatically in the first second or two following event onset, but that additional storage depends on coding and rehearsal processes that are strategically allocated to content information. Whether it is possible to induce reallocation to context, thereby changing the pattern of findings, is presently unknown.

In order to account for the null LSEs found in recognition and cued recall, both SAM and REM incorporated the principle of differentiation—that strengthening an item produces a memory trace that is more dissimilar to a random alternative item. This assumption in turn requires that repetitions of an item within a given experimental list tend to produce accumulation of information in a single episodic memory trace (contrasting with the alternative assumption that repetitions of a given item produce separate list traces for each—see Ratcliff et al., 1990; Shiffrin, Ratcliff, & Clark, 1990). Accumulation of item information in a single trace is easiest to justify, especially for spaced repetitions, if context does not change much during a single list. In this case, each repetition will be as similar as possible to the others. We provide evidence below that supports this hypothesis.

Context Changes Within and Between Lists

Context change within list (for one summary of the REM approach see Malmberg & Shiffrin, 2005) and context change across lists are each important in their own right. Criss and Shiffrin (2004a, Exp. 2) contrasted within and between list manipulations. They presented three long lists separated by arithmetic periods; participants carried out a different incidental task for each list (in lieu of study for a memory test). Some words were repeated across various combinations of the three lists. At the end of the experiment, participants received an unexpected recognition task in which they were asked to respond "old" only to items appearing on the most recent list (targets), and "new" to items from previous lists or to items that had not appeared in the experiment (foils). "Old" responses to foils from recent lists give evidence concerning context confusions. Word confusions were examined through the use of a semantic manipulation: Only for List 3 (the most recent one), participants studied differing numbers of words from different categories. Thus "old" response probabilities that varied with List 3 category size provided evidence pointing to confusions among words based on similarity. Evidence was found for both context- and word-based interference, albeit the context effect was larger (see Table 11.1). For example, the hit rate for items appearing on list three

TABLE 11.1   Probability of "Old" Response to Probes Appearing on Various Combinations of Three Experimental Lists

Probe type	Previous list appearances of probe			
	List 1,2	**List 2**	**List 1**	**None**
Target (on List 3)	.92 (.02)	.92 (.02)	.91 (.02)	80 (.02)
Lure (not on List 3)	.74 (.02)	.61 (.03)	.56 (.03)	.10 (.02)

Note: Results are reproduced from Criss and Shiffrin (2004a, Exp. 2). Participants were asked to respond "old" only to items on the current list (List 3). Means are listed followed by standard error in parentheses.

alone was scarcely higher than the false alarm rate for items that had been studied on both Lists 1 and 2 but not 3 (a similar false alarm effect was observed in the associative recognition domain by Criss & Shiffrin, 2005). This finding may indicate any or all of the following: (1) that context does not change much between lists with different incidental tasks separated by arithmetic; (2) that retrieval uses context features appropriate for all three lists instead of List 3 specifically; (3) that context and task-type features are not well integrated with word-specific features in storage; and (4) that context and task-type features are too little emphasized when constructing a retrieval probe. The studies to follow help narrow the possibilities.

The One-List-Back Paradigm and List Discrimination

Shiffrin (1970) had participants study twenty successive lists of words, each containing 5 or 20 unrelated items. A free recall period followed each list (except the first), during which participants were asked to recall items not from the most recent list, but from the list prior to that. As shown in Figure 11.2, the level of recall was determined by the length of the to-be-recalled list, without regard to the length of the intervening list. Shiffrin suggested that participants could reconstruct a context cue enabling them not only to access the older list, but also to focus sufficiently on that prior list to prevent interference by items on the intervening list.

According to REM and similar theories, elimination of interference from the intervening list could not have occurred unless context changed significantly between lists. Attempting to obtain converging evidence, Shiffrin and Rosenthal (1973) had subjects study groups of three successive study lists of varying lengths (all combinations of 20 and 5), separated by brief periods of arithmetic. No testing was administered until the end of each list triad, when participants tried to free recall each of the three lists; instructions at the start of recall indicated whether the order of list recall should be from the first list to the last, or vice versa. Figure 11.3 shows data from this study, which indicates that the level of recall was determined by the sum of all three list lengths rather than the target list length. In this study, it appeared, therefore, that the probe context pointed to the entire group of three lists—either context did not change much between lists, or individual list contexts could not be reconstructed. This model is a bit too simplistic, however, because it

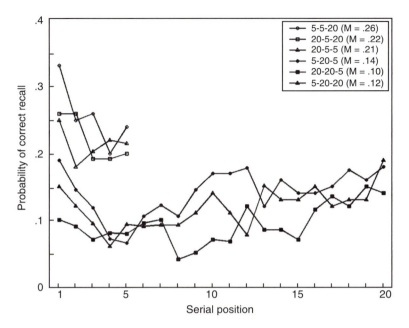

FIGURE 11.2 Results from Shiffrin (1970): Recall of the list before the last in various target and intervening list-length conditions. List-length effects were determined by the length of the target list, regardless of intervening list length. Figure based on Shiffrin (1970).

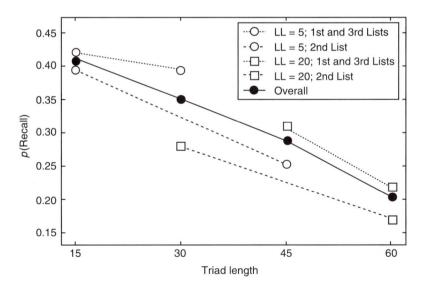

FIGURE 11.3 Results from Shiffrin and Rosenthal (1973): Recall as a function of total length of a triad of lists separated by arithmetic. Results are shown for list lengths of 10 and 20, collapsed across conditions when the lists were recalled proceeding from the first to last and last to first.

would suggest a complete inability to discriminate list origin within the triad. In fact, although the participants did make many intrusions, the level of target list recall exceeded the summed level of intrusions from the other two lists. Thus sampling of traces may have been independent of the target list, but some list origin information may have been stored with some traces, allowing editing of recalls during the recovery or output phases of retrieval.

This account of the results does not explain the differences between the present results and those of Shiffrin (1970). In the earlier study, recalls occurred between lists, but the present study used only arithmetic between lists. Could context change be induced by recalls but not by arithmetic? We will re-examine this possibility when we present results from a study of temporal order judgments.

Samuelson (1993) revisited the Shiffrin (1970) design using recognition testing: Participants studied successive lists of 9 or 36 items, each followed by a recognition test, with a permuted order of lengths so that various combinations of three successive lengths would occur. The control group was asked to respond "old" to items from the most recent list, while the experimental group responded "old" to items from the second most recent list. Study items did not repeat across lists, but test items included not only previously unstudied items, but items from the three most recent lists.

Using d' as a measure, the control condition had reasonable levels of performance that was higher for the shorter list than a longer list, a standard finding. The experimental condition showed generally poor performance, only slightly above chance, but with some indications of better performance for shorter target lists. Figure 11.4 gives a summary of the temporal results, summing across list lengths, in terms of a pseudo-d' measure: For each condition, and each pair of lists, d' is calculated from a p(hit) defined as the p(old) for the list closer to the target list or more recent in the case of ties, and a p(false alarm) defined as the p(old) for the list farther from the target list, or less recent in the case of ties. For these purposes, new words were considered "most distant." In the control condition, the performance pattern was normal, with d' falling off with temporal distance of the foil, probably indicating that participants used the present context as a cue, with moderate success. In the experimental condition, the pattern of p(old) responses among lists n–1, n–2, and new items was quite similar to that in the control condition, perhaps suggesting that context changes from list to list were similar in the two conditions. However, ability to discriminate list n items from list n–1 items was at chance. If participants had used the normal list n context cue, and said "old" to items *below* a familiarity criterion, they would have performed better than chance. Thus the participants may have tried to reconstruct a list n–1 context cue, but failed to do so effectively. Note that this account differs from those used to explain the two free recall studies. Perhaps in recognition the availability of word features induces an over-reliance on such features, to the detriment of retrieval emphasizing context.[3]

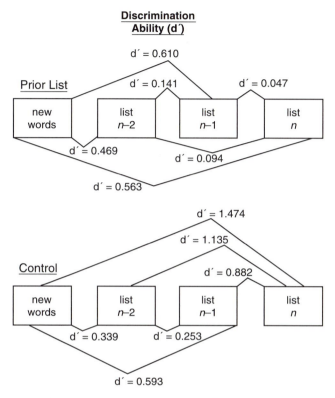

FIGURE 11.4   Results from Samuelson (1993): Recognition performance follow-ing study of a triad of lists. Diagrams show d' between targets and items appearing on various nontarget lists. The top panel illustrates performance when participants were asked to say "old" to items appearing on the penultimate list. The bottom panel illustrates performance when participants were asked to say "old" to items appearing on the final list.

Judgments of Recency

The theme of the studies discussed thus far is the idea that the benefit gained by using context features in the retrieval probe depends positively on its similarity to context features stored with the to-be-retrieved information, and negatively on its similarity to contexts stored with other traces. Our studies suggest that con-text changes little when a simple math task separates the study lists (supported by Criss & Shiffrin, 2004a, when the lists are studied using different semantic tasks; Shiffrin & Rosenthal, 1973), but changes to a greater degree when memory tests separate successive study lists (e.g., Samuelson, 1993; Shiffrin, 1970). How-ever, a benefit to using context as a cue depends on its being appropriate for the task, and reconstructing an appropriate context for a list other than the most recent is sometimes very difficult (Samuelson, 1993). These observations are based on indirect tests of context change because the actual task presented to the participant was a test for item information. We turn next to studies that attempt to assess context changes more directly.

Klein et al. (2004, 2006) asked participants to make relative judgments of recency (JOR). In their paradigms, participants study a list of words, and tests consist of two choice words (2AFC) with instructions to select the word that occurred more recently. Particularly in recent years, most JOR studies have used a continuous paradigm: A long list of words, with repetitions, is presented, and for each word presented participants indicate how many items back they last saw the currently presented word (Hintzman, 2000, 2004). We chose instead to use the 2AFC procedure because it is better suited to distinguish effects due to changes in accuracy from those due to changes in response bias. In previous studies using this 2AFC approach, it has been found that people can make these judgments with above-chance accuracy (Lockhart, 1969; Yntema & Trask, 1963), with performance increasing as a function of interitem lag (i.e., the number of items studied between the two test words during the study phase) and decreasing as a function of study–test lag (i.e., the number of items studied between the most recent of the test words and the time of judgment/test). Other 2AFC JOR tasks have used interspersed study and test trials (e.g., Yntema & Trask, 1963) but some of our results suggest that the interspersed activity itself makes a critical difference in context changes. We therefore presented a long list followed by a 2AFC test.

We began our line of research using 2AFC tests of items at six lags ranging from 2 and 24, studied in a 90-item list, in a study using 30 participants. We were surprised to find that this manipulation resulted in performance that was not statistically different from chance, for any of our lag lengths (Klein et al., 2004; recent data from additional participants did show performance at the longest lags rising just barely above chance, but it is safe to conclude that performance is very close to chance). In subsequent studies we tested longer lags—lags of 36 in 90-item lists—and found Ss could make 2AFC judgments statistically above chance, but still only at about 60% correct. The difficulties in making such judgments suggest that the contextual features stored with list items change very slowly during the course of a single random word list (in cases when the list is presented without interspersed testing). Thus the results are consistent with an REM model that assumes small context changes within lists and larger changes between lists. Why should our studies have revealed such difficulty, when previous studies revealed somewhat better performance? The answer may lie in our use of longer lists and longer study–test lags.

The picture that is emerging from these studies is one in which context changes slowly within list, and more rapidly between lists. But what are the conditions that promote context change between lists? Recall that the Shiffrin's (1970) free recall results suggested when lists were separated by a recall task, enough context change occurred between lists to allow a "one-back" context to be reconstructed, and eliminate most interference from the intervening list. The Shiffrin and Rosenthal (1973) study with arithmetic separating a triad of lists suggested context did not change much. The unpublished recognition results of Samuelson (1993) suggested that either context did not change much, or the recognition task degraded the ability to reconstruct a prior list context. We decided to investigate the conditions that promote context change across lists using the paradigm of comparative recency judgments.

Two hundred participants studied a 160-item word list that was split in half by one of four 90-s intervening tasks (each participant received only one list and thus the intervening task was manipulated between subjects). The degree of recency discrimination when the test pair includes items on each side of the intervening task should provide evidence about the degree of context change promoted by that task. The four tasks separating the two list-halves are denoted math, faces, imagine, and recognition. In the math condition, participants added a series of numbers together. Based on Shiffrin and Rosenthal (1973), we hypothesized that math would promote little or no context change. In the faces condition, participants studied a list of faces, allegedly for later test. This condition was intended as a control condition where items continue to arrive, perhaps promoting context change, but without affecting list length effects due to numbers of words (Criss & Shiffrin, 2004c, have shown that words and faces appearing on the same list do not interfere with one another). In the imagine condition, participants were asked to write a paragraph answering the question, "What would you do if you were invisible and would not be responsible for your actions?" Sahakyan and Kelley (2002) found that answering this question following a list that participants have been instructed to forget leads to higher recall of the following list and lower recall in a surprise test of the "forgotten" list than occurs when participants take a break with no intervening task between lists. They take this as evidence that the task changes a participant's internal context. For this reason, we expected this condition to promote context change between list-halves in our JOR task. Finally, in the recognition condition, participants completed an old/new recognition test of target words taken from some of the words in the first half of the list (none of which would be used in the later 2AFC JOR recency tests) and foil words not from the list. Based on Shiffrin (1970), we hypothesized that such testing might promote context change.

Following presentation of the 160-item list with the embedded intervening task, participants gave 2AFC JOR judgments. There were three types of test pairs: first half pairs, second half pairs, and pairs that crossed the intervening task. On the average, the lag between pair items, calculated as number of list items (ignoring intervening tasks) was constant across the three types of pair test, and was the same for the four types of intervening task. The pairs that crossed the intervening tasks were equated both in terms of number of intervening study items and total time.

Table 11.2 displays 2AFC JOR performance. Consistent with many of our results for long lists, performance was extremely low. List 1 discrimination was poor in all conditions—at or below chance. List 2 discrimination was generally above chance, but more so for math and faces. Of more interest, cross-list performance was best for imagine and recognition, and near chance for math and faces, exactly as expected. Our expectations were met for imagine and recognition: Context change between list-halves, but not within, would have produced above chance performance only for the between-halves tests (L1–L2). The results for math and faces were puzzling: If above chance within the second half-list, why

TABLE 11.2   Recency Discrimination for 160-Item Lists Broken Up with Four Different Distractor Tasks

Distractor condition	Comparison condition		
	Within first half	**Across both halves**	**Within second half**
Math problems (math)	.49 (.04)	.53 (.03)	.57 (.04)
Study faces (face)	.49 (.04)	.53 (.05)	.55 (.04)
"Imagine" essay (imagine)	.49 (.04)	.55 (.04)	.53 (.05)
Recognition test (recognition)	.53 (.04)	.58 (.04)	.56 (.04)

Note: Results from Klein et al. (2006). Means are listed, followed by 95% confidence intervals on the mean in parentheses.

should they have been at chance for the cross-list tests? The following hypothesis is one way to account for all the results. Suppose for math and faces there is no context shift due to the intervening task but a general serial position strength-of-storage gradient across the entire list (both halves together), with primacy due to extra storage in long-term memory, and recency due to residual strength in short-term memory. If strength were used by participants as a stand-in for recency, then the strong primacy items would tend to be chosen as more recent than weaker later items, dropping performance below chance for L1–L1 tests. The lack of strength differences in the middle of the list would produce chance performance for L1–L2 tests. The stronger recency items would tend to cause these to be selected as more recent, pushing performance above chance for L2–L2 tests. For the imagine and recognition conditions, context changed between list halves, allowing current context to be used for judgments, producing the results as described above. As an aside, it should be noted that because our cross-task results were obtained in conditions in which time between test items was held constant across conditions, a more complex model is needed than one based strictly on time-related information (e.g., Hintzman, 2004).

To test the idea that participants might use strength as a stand-in for recency, particularly when context information is not easily usable for recency judgments, we carried out a 2AFC JOR study varying item strength. Although a number of studies have used multiple presentations of items to examine effects of strength on JOR performance (e.g., Peterson, Johnson, & Coatney, 1969; Wells, 1974), interpretation of such paradigms is complicated by potentially different mechanisms for accessing frequency and recency information, so we varied strength by varying study time. We tested comparative JOR for all combinations of long-presented (strong), short-presented (weak), and unstudied (new) items. Fifty participants received two 90-item lists consisting of half weak items (800 ms stimulus onset asynchrony; SOA), and half strong items (2500 ms SOA) randomly intermixed. Tests following each list were 2AFC for studied items with lag 16, or between an old item and a new item. The results for the six key conditions are given in Figure 11.5. The second letter indicates the more recent presently item. When items were of equal strength (i.e., W–W and S–S), performance was at chance (indicated

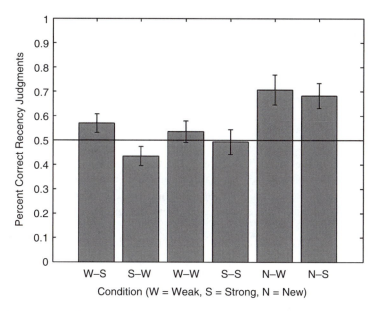

FIGURE 11.5   Results from Klein et al. (2006): Recency discriminations for pairs including weak (W) items (800 ms study), strong (S) items (2400 ms study), and new (N) items (0 ms study). Error bars represent 95% confidence intervals on the standard error of the mean. Condition names represent the status of the nonrecent item (i.e., S, W, or N) followed by the status of the recent item. The first two columns therefore represent a bias to pick the S item as being more recent.

by the horizontal line). However, when the two test items differed in strength, participants chose the stronger of the items regardless of which item was actually presented more recently. Thus performance in the W–S condition is "above chance" because the strong item was more recent but performance in the S–W was "below chance" because the strong item was less recent. The N–S and N–W pairs simply indicate that the participants actually do know (to some extent) which items were on the list but apparently do not know the relative order of presentation for the items. In summary, the data indicate that in conditions when context-based judgments do not work well, participants substitute a strategy, or bias, of choosing the stronger item as more recent, confirming the speculation derived from the prior study.

TOWARD A MODEL OF CONTEXT

"Context" is hardly the only useful concept in the field with an amorphous definition, a large domain of application, and different usages by different investigators in different settings (cf. "attention"). The studies and results we have described refine the concept and suggest some tentative conclusions and avenues for further exploration.

We advise against thinking of context as "one thing"; as described in the introduction, there are many different types of context information, having different properties. It is potentially very misleading to lump all these forms together into a unitary concept termed "context". However, we must emphasize that the variability in types of context does not preclude our assumption that the general rules of storage and retrieval apply to both explicitly and experimentally manipulated information. These include any and all types of context as well as the "content" features of the studied words themselves. A multitude of empirical studies addressing individual context types have shown context effects. Given the number of factors that comprise context, and the usual procedures that vary just a few of these experimentally, it probably should not come as a surprise that the effect sizes are usually quite modest. Further, one should not downgrade the importance of context as a memory component because large effects are difficult to produce.

It is important to recognize the critical roles played by (1) the differential attention that different forms of context information might receive, (2) the natural and sometimes cyclic changes that different forms of context undergo (e.g., changes with time of day, with different levels of sunlight, with day of week, with biological cycles), (3) the contributions to these changes that are controlled by the participant, consciously or otherwise; and (4) the degree of integration of such context information with the task-relevant content information.

The form of context studied in most of our tasks is that involved in list membership specification, a form probably including all of the kinds of context information mentioned in this chapter. We note that typical experimental control reduces external environmental changes to a small factor. In this case, internal environmental changes become extremely important. Our results, from various free recall, recognition, and temporal judgment tasks, suggest this internal context changes slowly within list, and more strongly between list, when lists are separated by appropriate markers and tasks. These markers and tasks include testing of words from lists, and devising stories. On the other hand mental arithmetic and face judgments between lists change internal context very little. These results lead us to the following speculation: At least in the absence of large external environmental changes, people may utilize a hold-until-shift approach to internal context change. That is, the internal states that contribute to list context may be held somewhat unchanged until some trigger event causes that held context to be dropped, and causes the production of changed internal context or perhaps the gathering of a new sample of internal context.

Our results also suggest that in cases when context does change sufficiently it may be possible to reconstruct a context cue for an older list, but this is difficult and may only be possible in rare circumstances. Furthermore, repeating items at study and test across lists causes great context confusion and seems to make it almost impossible to do anything but use the present context at test—attempts in such circumstances to reconstruct old context seem to harm performance without producing a counteracting gain. When context is a poor cue for a given task, subjects seem to substitute alternative forms of information as a means for making contextual judgments; e.g., they may use item strength as a stand-in for recency. In the cases when early items are stronger due to primacy effects, such strategies can even reduce performance below chance.

We have discussed the results described in this chapter with respect to the REM model. Context plays a critical role in REM, as it did in SAM, and indeed as it does in most memory models. It is important to note that the role of context in these models is not primarily to explain the effects that are found in studies that directly manipulate context, although this is one of the justifications. The requirement for the context construct is based primarily on the need to explain a host of other memory effects involving learning, forgetting and priming, just a few of which we have touched on in this chapter (such as the priming results when study time is varied, and the "one-shot" study that was motivated by those results). At this time of writing, models that include context provide by far the most broad and coherent account of memory phenomena.

Even a casual reader of this chapter will quickly reach the conclusion that context is difficult to study empirically and model theoretically. Attempts so far to do so are in the earliest and far too simplistic stages (e.g., Mensink & Raaijmakers' 1988 extension to SAM, or Howard & Kahana's 2002 model). We nonetheless expect progress to continue, and hope to continue to contribute to empirical and theoretical advances in this domain.

NOTES

1. When referring to the accumulation of information over a lifetime of experiences, lexical memory and/or semantic memory are often used to describe the resultant information for words. We now prefer to use the more general term knowledge (knowledge memory, or knowledge traces), to emphasize the application to every kind of knowledge we learn, store, and can retrieve.
2. The traces in BCDMEM are composite rather than separate, but this is not critical for the present discussion.
3. Huber, Jang, and Overschelde (2005) carried out one-back studies using both recognition and recall testing. They found that the type and duration of activity separating lists produced critical differences in the results, and built a context model to explain their findings, but the findings are too recent to be discussed in this chapter.

REFERENCES

Anderson, J. R. (1990). *The adaptive character of thought*. Hillsdale, NJ: Lawrence Erlbaum Associates, Inc.

Anderson, J. R., & Bower, G. H. (1972). Recognition and retrieval processes in free recall. *Psychological Review, 79*, 97–123.

Criss, A. H., & Shiffrin, R. M. (2004a). Context noise and item noise jointly determine recognition memory: A comment on Dennis and Humphreys (2001). *Psychological Review, 111*, 800–807.

Criss, A. H., & Shiffrin, R. M. (2004c). Pairs do not suffer interference from other types of pairs or single items in associative recognition. *Memory and Cognition, 32*, 1284–1297.

Criss, A. H., & Shiffrin, R. M. (2005). List discrimination and representation in associative recognition. *Journal of Experimental Psychology: Learning, Memory, and Cognition, 31*, 1199–1212.

Dennis, S., & Humphreys, M. S. (2001). A context noise model of episodic word recognition. *Psychological Review, 108*, 452–478.

Dulsky, S. G. (1935). The effect of a change of background on recall and relearning. *Journal of Experimental Psychology, 18*, 725–740.

Fernandez, A., & Glenberg, A. M. (1985). Changing environmental context does not reliably affect memory. *Memory and Cognition, 13*, 333–345.

Gantt, W. H. (1940). The role of the isolated conditioned stimulus in the integrated response pattern, and the relation of the pattern changes to psychopathology. *Journal of General Psychology, 23*, 3–16.

Hintzman, D. L. (2000). Judgments of recency and their relation to recognition memory. *Memory and Cognition, 31*, 26–34.

Hintzman, D. L. (2004). Time versus items in judgment of recency. *Memory and Cognition, 32*, 1298–1304.

Howard, M. W., & Kahana, M. J. (2002). A distributed representation of temporal context. *Journal of Mathematical Psychology, 46*, 269–299.

Huber, D. E., Jang, Y., & Overschelde, J. P. V. (2005, November). *Using sampling and recovery to estimate context and item effects in memory*. Paper presented at the annual meeting of the Psychonomic Society, Toronto, Ontario, Canada.

Jacoby, L. L., & Dallas, M. (1981). On the relationship between autobiographical memory and perceptual learning. *Journal of Experimental Psychology: General, 110*, 306–340.

Klein, K. A., Criss, A. H., & Shiffrin, R. M. (2004). Recency judgments and list context [Abstract]. In *Proceedings of the twenty-sixth annual meeting of the Cognitive Science Society* (p. 1578). Mahwah, NJ: Lawrence Erlbaum Associates, Inc.

Klein, K. A., Criss, A. H., & Shiffrin, R. M. (2006). Recency revisited. *Manuscript in preparation*.

Lockhart, R. S. (1969). Recency discrimination predicted from absolute lag judgments. *Perception and Psychophysics, 6*, 42–44.

Malmberg, K. J., & Shiffrin, R. M. (2005). The "one-shot" hypothesis for context storage. *Journal of Experimental Psychology: Learning, Memory, and Cognition, 31*, 322–336.

Mensink, G., & Raaijmakers, J. G. (1988). A model for interference and forgetting. *Psychological Review, 95*, 434–455.

Peterson, L. R., Johnson, S. T., & Coatney, R. (1969). The effect of repeated occurrences on judgments of recency. *Journal of Verbal Learning and Verbal Behavior, 8*, 591–596.

Raaijmakers, J. G. W., & Shiffrin, R. M. (1981). Search of associative memory. *Psychological Review, 88*, 93–134.

Ratcliff, R., Clark, S. E., & Shiffrin, R. M. (1990). List-strength effect: I. Data and discussion. *Journal of Experimental Psychology: Learning, Memory, and Cognition, 16*(2), 163–178.

Roediger, H. L., & Challis, B. H. (1992). Effects of exact repetition and conceptual repetition on free recall and primed word-fragment completion. *Journal of Experimental Psychology: Learning, Memory, and Cognition, 18*, 3–14.

Roediger, H. L., & McDermott, K. B. (1993). Implicit memory in normal human subjects. In F. Boller & J. Grafman (Eds.), *Handbook of neuropsychology* (Vol. 8, pp. 63–131). Amsterdam: Elsevier.

Sahakyan, L., & Kelley, C. M. (2002). A contextual change account of the directed forgetting effect. *Journal of Experimental Psychology: Learning, Memory, and Cognition, 28*, 1064–1072.

Samuelson, L. (1993). *Context cuing in recognition memory.* Unpublished undergraduate honors thesis, Indiana University, Bloomington, IN.

Schooler, L. J., Shiffrin, R. M., & Raaijmakers, J. G. W. (2001). A Bayesian model for implicit effects in perceptual identification. *Psychological Review, 108*, 257–272.

Shiffrin, R. M. (1970). Forgetting: Trace erosion or retrieval failure? *Science, 168*, 1601–1603.

Shiffrin, R. M., Ratcliff, R., & Clark, S. E. (1990). List-strength effect: II. Theoretical mechanisms. *Journal of Experimental Psychology: Learning, Memory, and Cognition, 16*(2), 179–195.

Shiffrin, R. M., & Rosenthal, J. (1973). [Free recall of three successive lists]. Unpublished raw data.

Shiffrin, R. M., & Steyvers, M. (1997). A model for recognition memory: REM-retrieving effectively from memory. *Psychonomic Bulletin and Review, 4*, 145–166.

Smith, S. M. (1988). Environmental context-dependent memory. In G. M. Davies & D. M. Thomson (Eds.), *Memory in context: Context in memory* (pp. 13–34). Oxford, UK: Wiley.

Smith, S. M. (2001). Environmental context-dependent memory: A review and meta-analysis. *Psychonomic Bulletin and Review, 8*, 203–220.

Strand, B. Z. (1970). Change of context and retroactive inhibition. *Journal of Verbal Learning and Verbal Behavior, 9*, 202–206.

Underwood, B. J. (1977). *Temporal codes for memories: Issues and problems.* Oxford, UK: Lawrence Erlbaum Associates, Inc.

Wells, J. E. (1974). Strength theory and judgments of recency and frequency. *Journal of Verbal Learning and Verbal Behavior, 13*, 378–392.

Wright, D. L., & Shea, C. H. (1991). Contextual dependencies in motor skills. *Memory and Cognition, 19*, 361–370.

Yntema, D. B., & Trask, F. P. (1963). Recall as a search process. *Journal of Verbal Learning and Verbal Behavior, 2*, 65–74.

12

The Effects of Familiarity on Reconstructing the Order of Information in Semantic and Episodic Memory

ALICE F. HEALY, THOMAS F. CUNNINGHAM,
KATHLEEN M. SHEA, and JAMES A. KOLE

*T*he history of the psychology of memory is replete with instances of controversy about how to explain certain empirical findings. Established theories have suffered modifications and a "loss of faith" as a result of the inability to predict and explain a single finding. This chapter provides an illuminating case study of research into one such finding in memory research, namely, the bow-shaped serial position function.

As early as 1878, Francis E. Nipher, a physicist from Washington University in St. Louis, observed a bow-shaped serial position function for recall in an immediate episodic memory task (see for discussion Stigler, 1978; Roediger, 2001). Nearly 100 years later, Roediger and Crowder (1976; see also Crowder, 1993) showed that the bow-shaped serial position function applies to long-term semantic memory as well (see Tulving, 1972, 1983, for the original definitions and discussions of the distinction between episodic and semantic memory[1]). Specifically, Roediger and Crowder found that in recalling the names of the US presidents, subjects showed an advantage for both the earliest and the most recent presidents. This serial position function was even more pronounced when the items were scored using a position recall criterion (by which a president was correct only when the president's name was recalled in the appropriate historical position), as opposed to a free recall criterion (by which a president was correct when the president's name was recalled in any position). This was an important discovery because the bow-shaped function in immediate episodic memory had been taken as one of the chief pieces of evidence supporting the modal model of memory (first proposed by James, 1890, and later elaborated by Atkinson & Shiffrin, 1968; Glanzer & Cunitz, 1966; and Waugh & Norman, 1965). According to the modal model, there is a distinction between primary memory (largely responsible for the recency advantage in the serial position function) and secondary memory (largely responsible for the primacy advantage in the function).

To the contrary, Roediger and Crowder (1976) argued that the bow-shaped functions in both situations could be described in terms of the distinctiveness of the serial positions, following Murdock's (1960) classic proposal. However, about 25 years later, Healy, Havas, and Parker (2000; see also Healy & Parker, 2001) cast some doubt on Roediger and Crowder's distinctiveness account. In particular, using a free reconstruction of order task for the US presidents, they showed that the serial position function for long-term semantic memory was somewhat different in shape from that for immediate episodic memory (see also Healy & McNamara, 1996) and that familiarity with the presidents could provide a better account than distinctiveness of the positions for the serial position function that was observed. That is, subjects were likely to have greater access to information relevant to the presidents' historical positions in the case of more familiar presidents than in the case of less familiar ones, thereby allowing for superior reconstruction performance on the positions associated with the more familiar than with the less familiar presidents.

More recently, Maylor (2002) provided new support for the distinctiveness account in a study where familiarity was said to be held constant. In Maylor's study instead of reconstructing the order of US presidents, her subjects, who attended a Methodist church, reconstructed the order of six-verse Methodist hymns. She found a bow-shaped serial position function for these hymns and argued that all six verses were equally familiar to these subjects, so finding primacy and recency effects in this long-term semantic memory task cannot be attributed to familiarity. However, we have no way of determining if familiarity played or did not play a significant role in Maylor's study because she never provided an independent assessment of familiarity by ratings or any other method.

In the present research, we conducted four experiments exploring directly the relationship between familiarity ratings and level of performance on reconstructing the order of items in both long-term episodic and semantic memory as well as immediate episodic memory. Only order information was tested in each case; the items were always provided to the subjects during the tests.

EXPERIMENT 1

The first experiment involved reconstructing the order in which journal articles were read by students in a class. This study involved long-term episodic memory because the ordering was based on when the students encountered the articles in their own experience.

Method

The subjects were University of Colorado students in an undergraduate class, who had been required to read and discuss 14 articles, with 2 assigned for each class period. Three and a half weeks after the last article was presented in class, the 12 students attending class that day were presented with a list of the 14 articles they had read, arranged alphabetically by title, and were asked first to reconstruct the order in which the articles were read and discussed (by placing a number 1–14 next to the title of each article, 1 indicating the first article and 14 the last), and then to rate the familiarity of each article on a 1–3 scale (1 = don't remember the article; 2 = somewhat remember the article; 3 = remember the article).

Results

Figure 12.1 shows the serial position functions for both the accuracy on the order reconstruction task and the mean familiarity values. The effect of serial position was significant both for the order reconstruction task, $F(13, 143) = 1.89$, $MSE = 0.18$, $p = .04$, and for the familiarity rating task, $F(13, 143) = 7.04$, $MSE = 0.40$, $p < .01$. There was a significant correlation, $r(12) = .48$, $p = .04$, one-tailed, between these two measures. Also note that neither function exhibited the typical bow shape that would be predicted by a distinctiveness account.

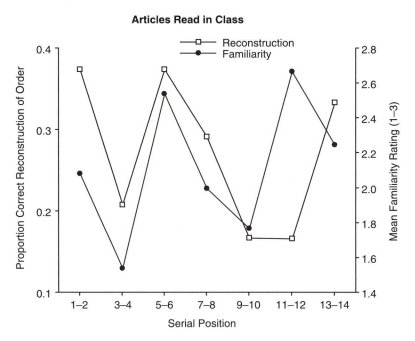

FIGURE 12.1   Proportion of correct responses on the reconstruction of order task and mean familiarity rating (1–3) as a function of article serial position in Experiment 1, with adjacent serial positions averaged together.

EXPERIMENT 2

Experiment 2 involved reconstructing the order of Super Bowl games. This study, like Experiment 1, is assumed to involve long-term episodic memory because the ordering was based on when the events took place, and they had occurred once each year during the lifetime of the subjects.

Method

This study was conducted in the spring of 2004. The subjects were 17 University of Colorado undergraduates from an introductory psychology course. They were given a list of all the Super Bowls played from 1989 to 2002 in alphabetical order according to the winning team's name, with both teams listed and the score beside each team. They were asked to reconstruct the order of those games (by placing a number 1–14 next to each Super Bowl listed), and then were asked to rate the familiarity of each game on a 1–3 scale like that used in Experiment 1.

Results

Figure 12.2 shows the serial position functions for accuracy on the reconstruction of order task and the mean familiarity values. The effect of serial position was

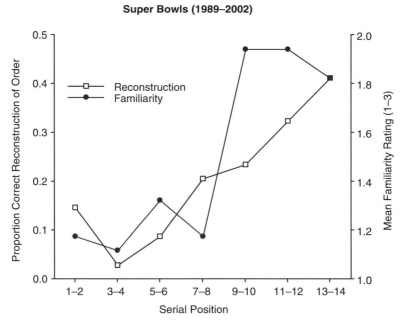

FIGURE 12.2 Proportion of correct responses on the reconstruction of order task and mean familiarity rating (1–3) as a function of Super Bowl serial position in Experiment 2, with adjacent serial positions averaged together.

significant for the order reconstruction task, $F(13, 208) = 2.37, MSE = 0.14, p < .01$, and for the familiarity rating task, $F(13, 208) = 9.12, MSE = 0.30, p < .01$. There was a recency effect but only a small primacy effect on order reconstruction. The two games that were the most familiar were Games 10 and 11, which corresponded to the Denver Broncos back-to-back wins. High familiarity ratings were understandable in this case because the subjects were University of Colorado students, and the Denver Broncos are the only NFL team to represent Colorado. Most importantly, there was a significant correlation, $r(12) = .73, p < .01$, between the familiarity ratings and accuracy on the order reconstruction task.

EXPERIMENT 3

Perhaps one reason why there was only a modest primacy effect in the Super Bowl study is that not all Super Bowls were tested, only those from 1989 to 2002. This fact raises the interesting question of whether it is the absolute or the relative positions of the items that influence their level of performance on a reconstruction of order task. The issue of whether codes for position information are absolute or relative has been the focus of some recent research concerning models of serial order (see, e.g., Henson, 1998, 1999). Models based on distinctiveness, such as Murdock's (1960) formulation, could be applied to either absolute or relative positions although the specific predicted functions would differ in the two cases. To address this issue concerning whether absolute or relative positions provide the basis for distinctiveness, in Experiment 3 we returned to the task of reconstructing the order of US presidents from long-term semantic memory.

Method and Theoretical Predictions

Fifty-seven St. Lawrence University undergraduates were asked to reconstruct the order of only an 18-item subset of consecutive US presidents. The relative positions were always Positions 1–18, but the absolute positions were Positions 13–30, 19–36, or 25–42, depending on the condition. Note that these three conditions are overlapping in terms of their positions. All of them contain Positions 25–30, which are the last six positions in the 13–30 condition, the middle six positions in the 19–36 condition, and the first six positions in the 25–42 condition. The names of the presidents used in each condition are shown in Appendix A, with the overlapping presidents indicated in bold. This design enables us to examine and compare the three full 18-position serial position functions and also to compare the three conditions in terms of performance on the overlapping six-position segment. Therefore, we can determine whether being at the beginning (primacy portion) or end (recency portion) of a list confers any advantage to positions in the order reconstruction task.

According to a theory based on distinctiveness of positions, the 18-position serial position functions should be bow-shaped in all three conditions. As shown in Figure 12.3, on the basis of Murdock's (1960) specific theory of distinctiveness, the serial position functions should be bow-shaped and nearly symmetrical if they are

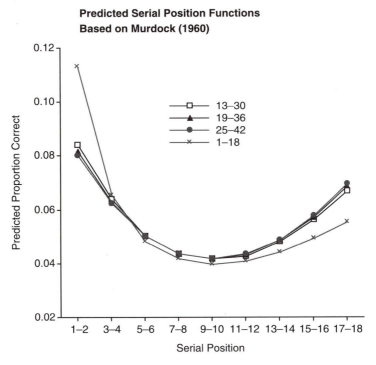

FIGURE 12.3   Predicted serial position functions derived from Murdock (1960) based on the relative positions 1–18 and based on the absolute positions for the 13–30, 19–36, and 25–42 conditions in Experiments 3 and 4, with adjacent serial positions averaged together.

based on the absolute positions, but should be asymmetrical, with a larger primacy effect than recency effect if they are based on the relative positions. We computed the predicted serial position functions on the basis of Murdock's formula, in which the distinctiveness of a position is determined by calculating the sum of the differences between the number of that position and the number of each of the other 17 positions in the list. The position numbers are transformed into log values to account for the usual asymmetry in the serial position function (i.e., the common finding that the primacy effect is larger than the recency effect).[2]

The full 18-position serial position functions we observed in the reconstruction of order task could be compared to these predicted functions. This comparison would enable us to test the idea that the relative or absolute distinctiveness of the positions is responsible for the bow-shaped serial position functions found in the task of reconstructing the order of US presidents. Alternatively, on the basis of the earlier findings of Healy et al. (2000), the serial position functions should be related to the familiarity of the presidents rather than to the distinctiveness of their positions. To determine familiarity in this experiment, all subjects were given a familiarity rating task immediately before the reconstruction of order task. For each of the 17 or 18 presidents in their list,[3] shown in alphabetical order, they were to give a rating from 1 to 6 indicating how familiar to them was that president (1 = not familiar, 6 = most familiar). Following that task, they performed the reconstruction of order task, with the 18 presidents in their list shown again in alphabetical order. They were to place a number 1–18 next to the name of each president, 1 indicating the first president and 18 the last in the list according to their terms in office. By the proposal of Healy et al., the serial position functions obtained for the familiarity rating task should be parallel to those found for the reconstruction of order task, and for each condition there should be a significant correlation between the two functions.

Results

The serial position functions for the reconstruction of order task are summarized in the top panel of Figure 12.4. The main effect of serial position, $F(17, 918) = 5.19$, $MSE = 0.10$, $p < .01$, the main effect of condition, $F(2, 54) = 8.79$, $MSE = 0.32$, $p < .01$, and the interaction of condition and serial position, $F(34, 918) = 1.97$, $MSE = 0.10$, $p < .01$, were all significant. There was no primacy effect for any of the conditions for the reconstruction of order task. The function for the 13–30 condition was close to the floor at all serial positions. However, there was a small but significant recency effect for the 19–36 condition, and a numerically larger significant recency effect for the 25–42 condition, which corresponds to an advantage for the presidents living at the time this experiment was conducted (Fall 2003). Gerald R. Ford is the 38th US president, Jimmy Carter is the 39th, Ronald Reagan is the 40th, George H. W. Bush is the 41st, William Clinton is the 42nd, and George W. Bush is the 43rd (although he was not included in the experiment). No doubt the recency effect for the 25–42 condition was dampened to some extent by confusion between the two Bush presidents, who differed in their positions relative to Clinton.

The serial position functions for the familiarity ratings are summarized in the bottom panel of Figure 12.4. The main effect of serial position, $F(17, 918) = 39.39$, $MSE = 1.02$, $p < .01$, the main effect of condition, $F(2, 54) = 10.55$, $MSE = 12.52$, $p < .01$, and the interaction of condition and serial position, $F(34, 918) = 24.66$, $MSE = 1.02$, $p < .01$, were again all significant. The functions for familiarity ratings are quite jagged and irregular, but the peaks occur where expected. Specifically, for the 13–30 condition there are peaks at relative Positions 4, 6, and 14 (which correspond to Abraham Lincoln, Ulysses Grant, and Theodore Roosevelt). Peaks occur for the 19–36 condition at relative Positions 8, 14, and 17 (corresponding to Theodore Roosevelt, Franklin D. Roosevelt, and John F. Kennedy), and for the 25–42 condition at relative Positions 11, 17, and 18 (corresponding to John F. Kennedy, George H. W. Bush, and William Clinton).

What is the relationship between the shape of the serial position functions for the reconstruction of order task and that for the familiarity rating task? Correlation coefficients were computed comparing the two serial position functions in each condition. The correlation for the 13–30 condition is essentially zero, $r(16) = -.001$, presumably because performance in the reconstruction of order task is close to the floor in that case. In contrast, the correlations for the 19–36 condition, $r(16) = .49$,

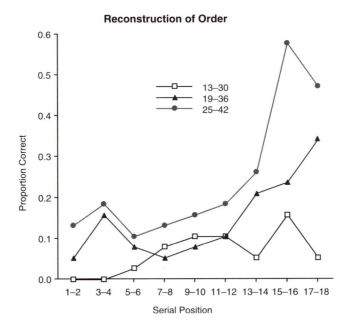

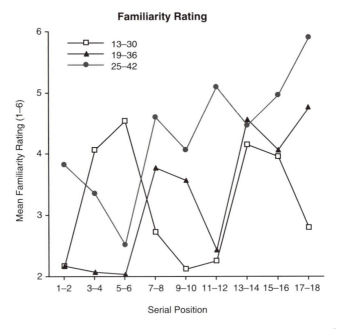

FIGURE 12.4 Proportion of correct responses on the reconstruction of order task (top panel) and mean familiarity rating (1–6) (bottom panel) as a function of condition and president relative serial position in Experiment 3, with adjacent serial positions averaged together.

$p = .04$, and the 25–42 condition, $r(16) = .59$, $p = .01$, are substantial and significant in each case, reflecting the fact that the peaks and troughs occur in approximately the same locations in the two tasks.

The crucial subset of positions that occur in all three conditions are Positions 25–30. These are the last six positions in the 13–30 condition, the middle six positions in the 19–36 condition, and the first six positions in the 25–42 condition. No differences in the familiarity ratings might be expected for these three conditions, because the familiarity of a president should not be affected by the other presidents in the list. Indeed this is the case, as shown in the bottom panel of Figure 12.5. The three functions are almost identical, showing a peak at Position 26 (Theodore Roosevelt) and a trough at Position 29 (Warren Harding) in each condition. The main effect of serial position was significant, $F(5, 270) = 64.42$, $MSE = 1.16$, $p < .01$, but neither the main effect of condition nor the interaction of condition and serial position was significant.

Performance in the crucial positions for the reconstruction of order task was, by the distinctiveness account based on relative positions, expected to be better in Conditions 13–30 and 25–42, where the positions occur in the recency and primacy portions of the overall function, respectively, than in Condition 19–36, where the positions occur in the middle of the function. However, as shown on the top panel of Figure 12.5, contrary to that account, there was no effect of condition and, in fact, no effect of serial position. The three conditions show very different functions, but even the interaction of condition and serial position was not significant, presumably because of inconsistencies within as well as across conditions.

Summary

In sum, the reconstruction of order data are inconsistent with the general predictions based on the distinctiveness account as well as the specific predictions based on Murdock's (1960) formulation. The primacy effects predicted on the basis of Murdock's formulation are not at all evident. There were, however, recency effects in two of the conditions, but the recency effect was strong only in the 25–42 condition, where the recent items were the highly familiar living presidents. Further, in the analysis of the overlapping positions, there was no advantage for being in the first or last parts of the list. In contrast, the data are generally consistent with the previous account in terms of familiarity (Healy et al., 2000). The strongest support for that account is from the two significant correlations we found between the functions for the reconstruction of order task and the familiarity ratings.

EXPERIMENT 4

Experiment 3 involved long-term semantic memory because the ordering of US presidents should reside in the subjects' mental encyclopedia and because the temporal context of learning the presidents' positions is not relevant. We wondered whether the distinctiveness of the relative or absolute serial positions

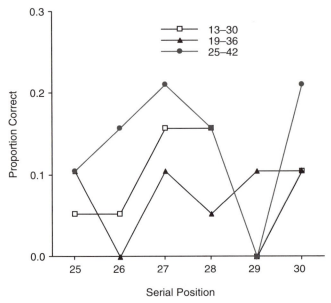

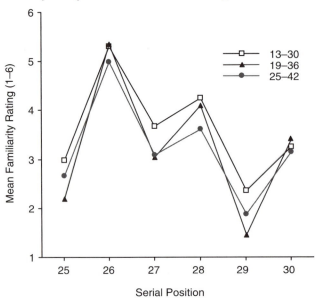

FIGURE 12.5   Proportion of correct responses on the reconstruction of order task (top panel) and mean familiarity rating (1–6) (bottom panel) as a function of condition and president serial position for the overlap serial positions 25–30 only in Experiment 3.

might play a larger role in immediate episodic memory, where bow-shaped serial position functions were originally demonstrated by Nipher (1878) and others. To examine this issue, in Experiment 4 we turned to an immediate episodic memory task for actors (see Healy et al., 2000, for a similar manipulation). This experiment was designed to be as closely analogous as possible to Experiment 3 except that instead of reconstructing the order of US presidents from semantic memory, subjects reconstructed the order of famous actors from immediate episodic memory. Episodic memory was involved in this case because the ordering of the actors is based on when the subjects encountered each actor's name during the experiment.

Method

Sixty University of Colorado undergraduates started with a familiarity rating task, in which they rated the familiarity of 43 famous actors. Each actor had been matched with a different one of the 43 US presidents, usually on the basis of the first letter of the last name. Two actors with the same last name were matched with two presidents with the same last name. For example, the actors Tim and Woody Allen were matched with the two John Adams presidents, and the actors Beau and Jeff Bridges were matched with the two George Bush presidents. After rating all 43 actors, subjects were asked to reconstruct the order of a subset of 18 consecutive actors according to when they were presented during the familiarity task, with the actors' names appearing in alphabetical order.

The design of Experiment 4 was comparable to that of Experiment 3, so that there were three conditions, 13–30, 19–36, and 25–42, depending on the subset of actors included in the reconstruction of order task. As in Experiment 3, there were six overlapping positions, corresponding to actors in positions 25–30, which were included in all three conditions.

The lists of actors used in the reconstruction of order task are shown in Appendix B, with the overlapping actors in bold. Again familiarity was rated on a scale from 1 to 6. In addition, in their instructions for the familiarity rating task subjects were warned that they would be tested later on their memory for the order of the actors' names. Subjects were tested in groups, and they raised their hands when finished with the familiarity rating task so that they could then immediately receive the packet for the order reconstruction task. The reconstruction of order instructions were closely analogous to those used with US presidents in Experiment 3.

Results

The serial position functions for the reconstruction of order task are summarized in the top panel of Figure 12.6. The main effect of serial position, $F(17, 969) = 2.51$, $MSE = 0.06$, $p < .01$, and the interaction of condition and serial position, $F(34, 969) = 1.96$, $MSE = 0.06$, $p < .01$, were significant. The serial position function for the reconstruction of order task was somewhat higher overall for the 25–42 condition than for 19–36 condition. Otherwise, performance on the reconstruction of order task was quite low, except for the peaks at relative Positions 10 and 12 of the 13–30 condition, corresponding to the single repeated item

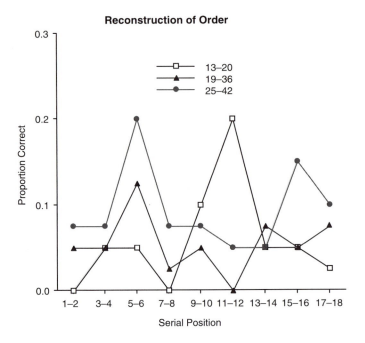

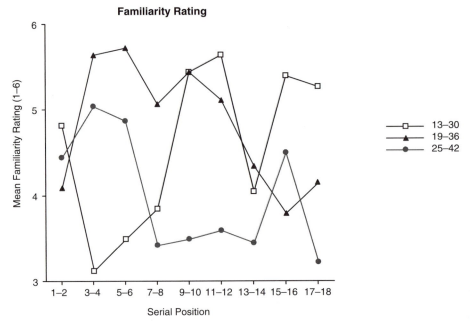

FIGURE 12.6 Proportion of correct responses on the reconstruction of order task (top panel) and mean familiarity rating (1–6) (bottom panel) as a function of condition and actor relative serial position in Experiment 4, with adjacent serial positions averaged together.

in the list (Mel Gibson, who was matched with the president Grover Cleveland, who had two nonconsecutive terms in office). The relatively high performance in the 25–42 condition was found despite the fact that 8 out of 20 subjects put Beau Bridges last, instead of second-to-last, confusing his position with that of his brother Jeff Bridges, who was in the 43rd position. In fact, by a lenient scoring criterion, in which a correct response was scored whenever an actor was placed in either the correct position or in an immediate neighboring position, the main effect of condition was significant, $F(2, 57) = 6.84$, $MSE = 0.17$, $p < .01$, reflecting best performance in the 25–42 condition (.24), worst performance in the 19–36 condition (.12), and intermediate performance in the 13–30 condition (.19).

The serial position functions for the familiarity ratings are summarized in the bottom panel of Figure 12.6. The main effect of serial position, $F(17, 969) = 10.95$, $MSE = 1.17$, $p < .01$, the main effect of condition, $F(2, 57) = 3.36$, $MSE = 18.72$, $p = .04$, and the interaction of condition and serial position, $F(34, 969) = 17.12$, $MSE = 1.17$, $p < .01$, were all significant in this case. Unlike reconstruction of order performance, familiarity was higher for the 19–36 condition than for the 25–42 condition. Thus, familiarity was not parallel to reconstruction of order performance in this experiment, as illustrated most clearly by the correlations between accuracy on the reconstruction of order task and familiarity ratings for each condition: 13–30 condition, $r(16) = .19$; 19–36 condition, $r(16) = −.22$; 25–42 condition, $r(16) = .03$. None of these correlations are significant and the largest one is actually negative.

For the crucial subset of positions that occurred in all three conditions, as shown in the bottom panel of Figure 12.7, there was a consistency across conditions in the shape of the function for the familiarity ratings, reflecting agreement as to which actors were most familiar; the main effect of serial position was significant, $F(5, 285) = 12.83$, $MSE = 1.12$, $p < .01$. Specifically, there were peaks for Positions 27, 28, and 30, corresponding to Arnold Schwarzenegger, Bruce Willis, and Jim Carrey, respectively.

With respect to reconstruction of order, the top panel of Figure 12.7 shows that, as with the familiarity ratings, there was some consistency in the shape of the function for the crucial positions. The main effect of serial position was significant, $F(5, 285) = 2.64$, $MSE = 0.05$, $p = .02$. However, the function was generally higher for the middle Position 28 than for the end Positions 25 and 30. In addition, there was an advantage for the 25–42 condition relative to the 19–36 condition; the main effect of condition was significant, $F(2, 57) = 3.69$, $MSE = 0.08$, $p = .03$. Although the same positions were used for this analysis in each condition, subjects in the 25–42 condition must have benefited from their superior knowledge of the other positions in their order reconstruction task.

GENERAL DISCUSSION

In summary, Experiments 1 and 2 provided evidence that the familiarity level of items is related to the level of performance on reconstructing the order of the items in long-term episodic memory. There was a significant positive correlation

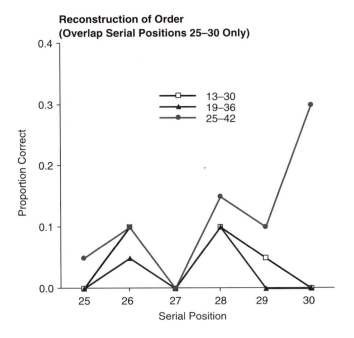

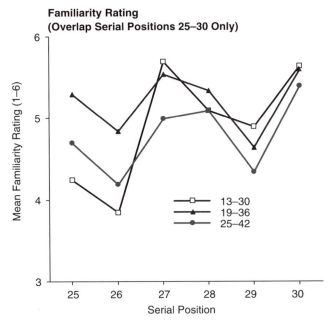

FIGURE 12.7   Proportion of correct responses on the reconstruction of order task (top panel) and mean familiarity rating (1–6) (bottom panel) as a function of condition and actor serial position for the overlap serial positions 25–30 only in Experiment 4.

between familiarity ratings and proportion correct on the reconstruction of order task both for articles read in a course and for Super Bowl games.

Experiment 3 provided evidence that the level of item familiarity is also related to the performance level on reconstructing the order of items in long-term semantic memory. For the 19–36 and 25–42 conditions, there were significant positive correlations between familiarity ratings and proportion correct on the reconstruction of order task for US presidents. There was no evidence for effects of distinctiveness of item positions on reconstruction of order.

Although the level of familiarity is correlated with the level of performance on the reconstruction of order task, there is no evidence for a causal relationship in either direction. That is, familiarity may or may not affect memory performance, and memory may or may not affect familiarity ratings. Familiarity ratings can, thus, be used to predict how well subjects will perform in the reconstruction of order task, but familiarity is probably not itself the knowledge used by subjects in this task. Hence, subjects would not be expected to confuse items that have similar familiarity ratings. Instead they are more likely to confuse items that have similar knowledge representations. Presumably there are multiple forms of knowledge (e.g., sequential associations between successive items or associations between an item and its position number) that underlie the ability to reconstruct the order of items in a sequence. There should be more knowledge, or more information relevant to positioning the items in the sequence, for items that are more familiar.

In contrast to Experiments 1–3, Experiment 4 provided no evidence that the level of familiarity is related to the level of performance on reconstructing the order of items in immediate episodic memory, presumably because the familiarity in this case is not associated with access to any information relevant to the positions of the actors in the present series. However, the time when the items were presented may play some role because there tended to be an advantage for the newest set of 18 actors (25–42) relative to the intermediate set of actors (19–36). In any event, there was no evidence for any effects of the distinctiveness of item positions on order reconstruction.

In the tasks we employed, familiarity showed a strong relationship to accuracy in the reconstruction of order from long-term episodic and long-term semantic memory. However, familiarity might not have such a strong relationship in other memory tasks. Indeed, we found that familiarity does not have a relationship to accuracy in order reconstruction from immediate episodic memory. Immediate episodic memory seems to be affected instead, to some extent, by the time when the items were presented, perhaps reflecting some influence of primary memory, as suggested by the modal model (Atkinson & Shiffrin, 1968; Glanzer & Cunitz, 1966; James, 1890; Waugh & Norman, 1965). Contrary to predictions based on the work of Murdock (1960), Maylor (2002), and Roediger and Crowder (1976), in none of the cases reported in this chapter is there any evidence for an impact of the distinctiveness of the item positions on reconstructing the order of the items. Distinctiveness certainly might have an influence in other situations and in other tasks, but it can no longer be viewed as a universal explanation for bow-shaped serial position functions.

ACKNOWLEDGMENTS

This work was supported by Army Research Institute Contract DASW01-03-K-0002 to the University of Colorado. We are indebted to Lyle Bourne and other members of the Healy-Bourne laboratory group for helpful comments about this research and to Jim Nairne for thoughtful editorial suggestions. Portions of this chapter concerning Experiment 3 were presented at the 2004 meeting of the Psychonomic Society (Cunningham, Healy, & Kole, 2004).

NOTES

1. By this distinction, episodic memory is autobiographical and pertains to unique personal experiences; the temporal context of learning is relevant for episodic memory. In contrast, semantic memory, which can be thought of as a mental thesaurus or encyclopedia, pertains to knowledge of the world; the temporal context of learning is not relevant to semantic memory.
2. We also computed the distinctiveness of an absolute position by calculating instead the sum of the differences between the number of that position and the number of each of the other 42 positions in the complete list of presidents. By that computation, the predicted functions are much flatter. A slight primacy effect is evident only for the 13–30 condition, whereas slight recency effects are evident especially for the 19–36 and 25–42 conditions.

   We used Murdock's (1960) formulation for all of these calculations because most subsequent formulations (e.g., Nairne, Neath, Serra, & Byun, 1997; Neath, 1993) included temporal characteristics, such as interstimulus intervals and retention intervals. Such temporal features cannot be specified for semantic memory tasks, such as reconstructing the order of presidents, because the temporal context in which the information was learned is unspecified, having occurred outside the laboratory prior to the experiment. Other more recent formulations of distinctiveness have favored event-based theories over temporal theories (Lewandowsky & Brown, 2005; Lewandowsky, Duncan, & Brown, 2004). However, even event-based theories would seem difficult to apply to a semantic memory task in which the learning episodes were not specified and the information relevant to a given position (e.g., a given president) was undoubtedly learned on multiple occasions.
3. Only 17 names were printed in the familiarity rating task for the 13–30 and 19–36 conditions, which included Grover Cleveland, who served two nonconsecutive terms in office.

REFERENCES

Atkinson, R. C., & Shiffrin, R. M. (1968). Human memory: A proposed system and its control processes. In K. W. Spence & J. T. Spence (Eds.), *The psychology of learning and motivation: Advances in research and theory, Vol. 2* (pp. 89–195). New York: Academic Press.

Crowder, R. G. (1993). Short-term memory: Where do we stand? *Memory and Cognition, 21*, 142–145.

Cunningham, T. F., Healy, A. F., & Kole, J. A. (2004, November). *Familiarity affects reconstructing the order of items in semantic memory*. Poster presented at the 45th annual meeting of the Psychonomic Society, Minneapolis, MN.

Glanzer, M., & Cunitz, A. R. (1966). Two storage mechanisms in free recall. *Journal of Verbal Learning and Verbal Behavior*, 5, 351–360.

Healy, A. F., Havas, D. A., & Parker, J. T. (2000). Comparing serial position effects in semantic and episodic memory using reconstruction of order tasks. *Journal of Memory and Language*, 42, 147–167.

Healy, A. F., & McNamara, D. S. (1996). Verbal learning and memory: Does the modal model still work? *Annual Review of Psychology*, 47, 143–172.

Healy, A. F., & Parker, J. T. (2001). Serial position effects in semantic memory: Reconstructing the order of the U.S. presidents and vice presidents. In H. L. Roediger, J. S. Nairne, I. Neath, & A. M. Surprenant (Eds.), *The nature of remembering: Essays in honor of Robert G. Crowder* (pp. 171–188). Washington, DC: American Psychological Association.

Henson, R. N. A. (1998). Short-term memory for serial order: The Start–End Model. *Cognitive Psychology*, 36, 73–137.

Henson, R. N A. (1999). Positional information in short-term memory: Relative or absolute? *Memory and Cognition*, 27, 915–927.

James, W. (1890). *The principles of psychology*. New York: Henry Holt.

Lewandowsky, S., & Brown, G. D. A. (2005). Serial recall and presentation schedule: A mirco-analysis of local distinctiveness. *Memory*, 13, 283–292.

Lewandowsky, S., Duncan, M., & Brown, G. D. A. (2004). Time does not cause forgetting in short-term serial recall. *Psychonomic Bulletin and Review*, 11, 771–790.

Maylor, E. A. (2002). Serial position effects in semantic memory: Reconstructing the order of verses of hymns. *Psychonomic Bulletin and Review*, 9, 816–820.

Murdock, B. B., Jr. (1960). The distinctiveness of stimuli. *Psychological Review*, 67, 16–31.

Nairne, J. S.. Neath, I., Serra, M., & Byun, E. (1997). Positional distinctiveness and the ratio rule in free recall. *Journal of Memory and Language*, 37, 155–166.

Neath, I. (1993). Distinctiveness and serial position effects in recognition. *Memory and Cognition*, 21, 689–698.

Nipher, F. E. (1878). On the distribution of errors in numbers written from memory. *Transactions of the Academy of Science of St. Louis*, 3, ccx–ccxi.

Roediger, H. L., III. (2001, November). *Francis E. Nipher: The first memory researcher*. Paper presented at the 42nd annual meeting of the Psychonomic Society, Orlando, FL.

Roediger, H. L., III, & Crowder, R. G. (1976). A serial position effect in recall of United States presidents. *Bulletin of the Psychonomic Society*, 8, 275–278.

Stigler, S. M. (1978). Some forgotten work on memory. *Journal of Experimental Psychology: Human Learning and Memory*, 4, 1–4.

Tulving, E. (1972). Episodic and semantic memory. In E. Tulving & W. Donaldson (Eds.), *Organization of memory* (pp. 381–403). New York: Academic Press.

Tulving, E. (1983). *Elements of episodic memory*. New York: Oxford University Press.

Waugh, N. C., & Norman, D. A. (1965). Primary memory. *Psychological Review*, 72, 89–104.

APPENDICES

APPENDIX A: Presidents Used in Each Condition of Experiment 3 (Overlapping Items in Bold Print)

Positions 13–30	Positions 19–36	Positions 25–42
Fillmore, Millard	Hayes, Rutherford B.	**McKinley, William**
Pierce, Franklin	Garfield, James	**Roosevelt, Theodore**
Buchanan, James	Arthur, Chester A.	**Taft, William H.**
Lincoln, Abraham	Cleveland, Grover	**Wilson, Woodrow**
Johnson, Andrew	Harrison, Benjamin	**Harding, Warren**
Grant, Ulysses S.	Cleveland, Grover	**Coolidge, Calvin**
Hayes, Rutherford B.	**McKinley, William**	Hoover, Herbert
Garfield, James	**Roosevelt, Theodore**	Roosevelt, Franklin D.
Arthur, Chester A.	**Taft, William H.**	Truman, Harry S.
Cleveland, Grover	**Wilson, Woodrow**	Eisenhower, Dwight D.
Harrison, Benjamin	**Harding, Warren**	Kennedy, John F.
Cleveland, Grover	**Coolidge, Calvin**	Johnson, Lyndon B.
McKinley, William	Hoover, Herbert	Nixon, Richard M.
Roosevelt, Theodore	Roosevelt, Franklin D.	Ford, Gerald R.
Taft, William H.	Truman, Harry S.	Carter, James (Jimmy)
Wilson, Woodrow	Eisenhower, Dwight D.	Reagan, Ronald
Harding, Warren	Kennedy, John F.	Bush, George H. W.
Coolidge, Calvin	Johnson, Lyndon B.	Clinton, William

APPENDIX B: Actors Used in Each Condition of Experiment 4 (Overlapping Items in Bold Print)

Positions 13–30	Positions 19–36	Positions 25–42
Ford, Harrison	Harrelson, Woody	**McConaughey, Matthew**
Pacino, Al	Gere, Richard	**Wilson, Owen**
Baldwin, Alec	Affleck, Ben	**Schwarzenegger, Arnold**
Lewis, Jerry	Gibson, Mel	**Willis, Bruce**
Jones, James Earl	Hanks, Tom	**Hartnett, Josh**
Grant, Hugh	Gibson, Mel	**Carrey, Jim**
Harrelson, Woody	**McConaughey, Matthew**	Hoffman, Dustin
Gere, Richard	**Wilson, Owen**	Wilson, Luke
Affleck, Ben	**Schwarzenegger, Arnold**	Sheen, Martin
Gibson, Mel	**Willis, Bruce**	Eastwood, Clint
Hanks, Tom	**Hartnett, Josh**	Keaton, Michael
Gibson, Mel	**Carrey, Jim**	Jones, Tommy Lee
McConaughey, Matthew	Hoffman, Dustin	Newman, Paul
Wilson, Owen	Wilson, Luke	Fox, Michael J.
Schwarzenegger, Arnold	Sheen, Martin	Cage, Nicolas
Willis, Bruce	Eastwood, Clint	Reeve, Christopher
Hartnett, Josh	Keaton, Michael	Bridges, Beau
Carrey, Jim	Jones, Tommy Lee	Connery, Sean

13

Attentional Requirements of Perceptual Implicit Memory

We are constantly bombarded with several sources of information that demand cognitive processing. In some cases, external sources such as news, telephones, cell phones, and emails make competing processing demands on cognition. In other cases, internal events such as the activation of various ideations or thoughts compete for consideration. Internal and external sources can also simultaneously exert processing demands. Such competition is often resolved by selecting some sources for further consideration while ignoring others. Resolution of these competitive cognitive demands can reveal the nature of attention, working memory, and cognitive control.

Interestingly, resolution of cognitive conflict can also have long-term impact. If a particular piece of information is ignored because it is not relevant for the immediate goal at hand—even though it might be otherwise salient, important, or dominant—are there long-term costs to using this information later? In other words, the consequences of short-term processes involved in cognitive control could produce long-term consequences in memory. This issue is at the center of research discussed here.

It is assumed here that the selection of one source produces functionally different consequences on long-term memory from the typical situations of dividing attention where one must simultaneously attend to both sources of information. In the latter—divided attention—condition, both sources are monitored, whereas in the former—selective attention—condition one source is filtered out, or ignored, in favor of the other. The aim here is to discuss evidence that can tell us something about the unique memorial consequences of actively ignoring—or deselecting—a dominant source. The long-term consequences of ignoring the dominant source are especially interesting because dominant information is processed by default and is, therefore, hard to ignore.

CLASSIFICATION OF MEMORY

In order to evaluate the status of long-term memory for information that is ignored, it is important to first clarify that long-term memory itself is not a unitary construct. A brief, descriptive overview of varieties of memory is provided here to emphasize this critical point. This overview draws from a number of influential theoretical frameworks—many proposed by scientists in attendance at the Roddy Roediger Memory Conference—to distinguish among different forms of memory in terms of different memory systems, processes, and some hybrid approaches that include both dimensions. The classification scheme discussed here is by no means exhaustive; it is, in fact, highly selective. The reader is directed to comprehensive reviews in the literature that focus on these nomenclatures and their theoretical significance (Roediger, 1990; Roediger, Weldon, & Challis, 1989; Schacter, 1990; Schacter & Tulving, 1994). For present purposes, this overview is intended to simply provide a descriptive road map that places in context the type of memory that is of present interest—perceptual implicit memory.

At the functional level, two dimensions are central to the organization of different forms of memory—the type of retrieval mode and the type of processing. Retrieval mode refers to the level of awareness of the past in which the subject engages at the time of retrieval. The distinction between explicit and implicit memory captures this idea in operational terms (Graf & Schacter, 1985). Explicit memory tasks require intentional retrieval of the study episode; the subject is instructed to think about the previous study episode and retrieve that information to complete the task at hand. The prototypical examples of explicit memory tasks are free recall, cued recall, and recognition. Explicit memory is vulnerable to many variables; most strikingly, anterograde amnesia resulting from certain types of brain damage dramatically impairs explicit memory.

In contrast, implicit memory tasks make no mention of the study episode; instead, the instructions in these tasks direct subjects to complete the task with the first solution that comes to mind. In fact, if subjects become aware of the connection between the study phase and the memory test, or intentionally begin to use explicit memory strategies, the implicit memory task is said to be "contaminated," and no longer considered a good test of indirect memory (see Roediger & McDermott, 1993; Schacter, Bowers, & Booker, 1989, for discussions on this issue). The prototypical examples are the word fragment completion task (e.g., _ l _ p _ a n _), the word stem completion task (e.g., *ele*_____), and word identification task (words presented rapidly at threshold durations) in which subjects attempt to complete impoverished cues or read the rapidly presented words with the first solution that comes to mind. In these paradigms, implicit memory— or *priming*—is typically measured by subtracting accurate nonstudied completions from accurate studied completions. In contrast to the striking impairment in explicit memory, amnesic individuals typically exhibit intact performance on implicit memory tasks just described.

THE TRANSFER-APPROPRIATE PROCESSING FRAMEWORK AND IMPLICIT MEMORY

The second key dimension for understanding varieties of memory—type of processing—was developed by Roediger and colleagues within the transfer appropriate processing framework (Morris, Bransford, & Franks, 1979; Roediger, 1990; Roediger, Weldon, & Challis, 1989). According to this approach, the requirement to deliberately access the study episode, as is the case in explicit memory tasks, leads to conceptual processing of information. Considerable evidence supports this processing requirement of explicit memory (see Roediger, Weldon, & Challis, 1989; Roediger & McDermott, 1993, for reviews). For example, there is no change in performance if different modalities of presentation, visual or auditory, are used at study but performance improves if the information was encoded for meaning (e.g., Blaxton, 1989; Srinivas & Roediger, 1990) as brought about, for example, by the levels of processing (Craik & Lockhart, 1972) and generation (Jacoby, 1978; Slamecka & Graf, 1978) manipulations.

Initial evidence suggested that implicit memory, by contrast, is affected by perceptual processes but this no longer describes all of implicit memory phenomena. Two of the major contributions of the processing account have been to specify the processing demands of implicit memory tasks and to distinguish between two classes of implicit memory tasks according to these processing demands—those that rely primarily on perceptual processes and those that rely primarily on conceptual processes (see Blaxton, 1989; Roediger, Weldon, & Challis, 1989; Roediger, Srinivas, & Weldon, 1989). The selective influences of conceptual and perceptual processes on different classes of implicit memory tasks do not always fall neatly into these two categories but this classification describes the findings remarkably well when we evaluate the large literature that has now accumulated.

Conceptual implicit tasks, for example, are sensitive to many of the same variables that influence explicit memory tasks even though the former require no conscious recollection of the past whereas the latter do. Thus, perceptual changes in modality across study and test do not influence conceptual priming but encoding emphasis on meaning improves this form of priming (Blaxton, 1989; Hamann, 1990; Rappold & Hastroudi, 1991; Srinivas & Roediger, 1990).

This chapter focuses on the nature of the second class of implicit tasks—the perceptual implicit tasks. Consistent with the proposal that this class of tasks relies largely on perceptual information, performance on these tasks suffers if there are changes in surface structure across study and test (Blaxton, 1989; Graf & Mandler, 1984; Jacoby & Dallas, 1981; Rajaram & Roediger, 1993; Roediger & Srinivas, 1993; Tulving & Schacter, 1990; Weldon & Roediger, 1987). For example, in one study, we compared the effects of modality across four commonly used implicit tasks that were a priori designated as perceptual tasks—word fragment completion, word stem completion, word identification, and anagram solution (e.g., solving the anagram *lepehatn* with the first solution that comes to mind). We contrasted these implicit tasks with an explicit memory task of free recall (Rajaram & Roediger, 1993). Across study and test, the form or modality of presentation was either held constant or was varied. Across all perceptual implicit tests, the within modality condition (visual at study–visual at test) produced the greatest magnitude of priming. Cross-modal priming (auditory at study–visual at test) was significantly smaller in all implicit tasks and, in fact, not significant in the word identification task. Finally, cross-form priming (pictures at study–visual words at test) was not significant in any implicit task. By contrast, explicit free recall was best for pictures and did not differ across visual and auditory study words.

In contrast to its sensitivity to changes in surface information, perceptual implicit memory by and large remains robust in response to many variations. For example, greater or less emphasis on meaning during study does not change performance on these tasks (Blaxton, 1989; Graf & Mandler, 1984; Jacoby, 1983; Jacoby & Dallas, 1981; Srinivas & Roediger, 1990). The restricted processing requirements of perceptual implicit tasks appear even more striking when we consider the finding first reported by Warrington and Weiskrantz (1968, 1970) that amnesic patients show intact performance on these tasks (see Moscovitch, Vriezen, & Goshen-Gottstein, 1993, for a review). Furthermore, perceptual priming also remains significant for long periods of time, sometimes extending over weeks and even a year (Jacoby & Dallas, 1981; Komatsu & Ohta, 1984; Roediger, Weldon, Stadler, & Riegler, 1992; Sloman, Hayman, Ohta, Law, & Tulving, 1988; Tulving, Schacter, & Stark, 1982). Thus, it seems safe to conclude that perceptual-lexical analysis of study information is necessary—and also sufficient—to produce intact perceptual implicit memory (see Weldon, 1991).

DIVIDING ATTENTION AT STUDY AND PERCEPTUAL IMPLICIT MEMORY

Indeed, limited encoding requirements, the longevity of perceptual priming, and its preservation even in severe forms of amnesia invite the question whether there are any conditions where this form of memory might suffer. One way to test this question is by asking participants to process two sources of information at once, thereby reducing the attention they can pay to the target information. Interestingly, even in this situation, where a secondary task such as tone monitoring (e.g., high, medium, low) or digit monitoring (noting the occurrence of three successive odd digits) draws attention partially away from the primary task of studying words, later perceptual priming for words remains undiminished compared to a study condition where the secondary task is not carried out (e.g., Bentin, Kutas, & Hillyard, 1995; Jacoby, Woloshyn, & Kelley, 1989; Mulligan & Hartman, 1996; Parkin, Reid, & Russo, 1990; Parkin & Russo, 1990; Schmitter-Edgecombe, 1996a, 1996b; but see Gabrieli et al., 1999). Importantly, such methods of dividing attention substantially impair explicit memory as well as conceptual implicit memory (e.g., Anderson & Craik, 1974; Craik, 2001; Craik, Govoni, Naveh-Benjamin, & Anderson, 1996; Eich, 1984; Gabrieli et al., 1999; Isingrini, Vazou, & Leroy, 1995; Jacoby et al., 1989; Light, Prull, & Kennison, 2000; Mulligan, 1997, 1998; Mulligan & Hartman, 1996; Schmitter-Edgecombe, 1996a, 1996b, 1999). Together, these findings support the assumption that dividing attention at study interferes with the conceptual analysis of study information (Eysenck & Eysenck, 1979).

Furthermore, because conceptual analysis is presumably not needed to support perceptual implicit memory, it follows that dividing attention as study has little effect on the magnitude of perceptual implicit memory. This finding reinforces the conclusion that perceptual implicit memory cannot be disrupted easily.

In fact, extreme measures are usually needed to impair perceptual implicit memory as shown by studies that curtailed or eliminated the perceptual-lexical analysis of study words (e.g., Hawley & Johnston, 1991; Weldon & Jackson-Barrett, 1993). For example, Weldon and Jackson-Barrett showed that perceptual priming is eliminated only when study words were exposed too briefly to ensure their basic processing (2–250 ms exposure). This finding makes sense because perceptual implicit memory cannot develop unless the necessary perceptual analysis has taken place. In the case of dividing attention discussed earlier, both sources of information are monitored and the primary source (e.g., the list of words) is not de-emphasized in any way for its processing. If anything, it is obvious to the participants that the primary source of information is as important as the secondary source, if not more. Under these conditions, at least minimal processing of the primary source takes place and it appears that this processing is sufficient for creating and supporting perceptual implicit memory.

SELECTIVE ATTENTION AND LONG-TERM MEMORY

So, is the perceptual-lexical analysis of words sufficient for supporting memory even under conditions where attention has to be deliberately directed away from the dominant source and directed towards a less dominant source? For example, would perceptual implicit memory remain intact when attention is directed away from words—that are read by default—and directed towards a less dominant source such as the color in which the words are written? This situation is theoretically interesting because selection of less dominant source here presumably entails cognitive control. Cognitive control has been a focus of study in the areas of attention and working memory, and more recently in cognitive neuroscience, but less is known about its consequences on long-term retention.

The particular example just described for studying cognitive control is the well-known Stroop paradigm (Stroop, 1935). Typically, participants are presented with a list of words where words represent color names and are written in different ink colors. The participants' task is to name the ink color on each trial. When the ink color differs from the name that the word represents (e.g., the word "green" written in red ink—the incongruent or the Stroop condition), participants are significantly slower in naming the ink color compared to a condition where the ink color and the word match (e.g., the word "red" written in red ink—the congruent condition), or compared to a condition where the ink color and a neutral stimulus are paired (e.g., a string of Xs written in red ink—the neutral condition). Put another way, because reading is considered an automatic—or at least a default—activity, it interferes with color naming. The resolution of this conflict produces slower reaction times for color naming in the Stroop condition.

The Stroop effect has been extensively investigated and discussed in cognitive psychology (see Dyer, 1973; MacLeod, 1991, for reviews).

The Stroop paradigm is especially useful for probing the encoding requirements of perceptual implicit memory. In the Stroop task, participants evidently carry out the perceptual-lexical analysis of words because reaction time to naming ink color is slower when the word name and ink name differ than when they are the same. Recent evidence shows that even in the absence of slower reaction times, perceptual-lexical analysis of words nevertheless takes place in the Stroop condition (Besner, 2001). Thus, word reading seems to occur by default.

Evidence shows that interference generated by the Stroop task extends at least to the next trial (Catena, Fuentes, & Tudela, 2002; Dalrymple-Alford & Budayr, 1966; Neill, 1977). For example, in the Catena et al. study, after participants ignored—or deselected—the word "yellow" while naming the ink color "blue" on trial N, they were slower on trial N+1 to name the ink color "yellow" compared to naming the ink color "red." The slower color naming times on trial N+1 reflect the processing of the word "yellow" on trial N and the extended effect of its deselection on trial N+1. This finding illustrates two important points for present purposes. One, the Stroop task involves perceptual-lexical analysis of words and, two, this processing (in this case, reading and then deselecting) exerts an influence on later cognitive activity—as reflected by the effects on the next trial.

What are the consequences of Stroop encoding on long-term memory? With respect to explicit memory, although only a small number of studies have examined the effects of Stroop encoding on this long-term memory measure, the findings are straightforward. Stroop encoding produces large decrements in stem cued recall performance where the first three letters of studied words are presented as cues to aid recall (Rajaram, Srinivas, & Travers, 2001) as well as in recognition memory performance (Szymanski & MacLeod, 1996; Travers & Rajaram, 2006). This outcome is not in the least bit surprising; if dividing attention between two sources disrupts explicit memory, as many studies have shown, deselecting one of two sources should clearly disrupt explicit memory for the deselected source.

DESELECTION OF DOMINANT INFORMATION AND PERCEPTUAL IMPLICIT MEMORY

The predictions for perceptual implicit memory on first glance also seem straightforward. Given that the Stroop task creates conditions where the word is read as shown by studies just described, priming should not diminish following the Stroop task. This is because the perceptual-lexical analysis of the deselected information takes place during encoding. However, if attentional resources beyond those required by the perceptual-lexical analysis are needed to support perceptual implicit memory, priming should suffer. In other words, attentional demands involved in the selection of the nondominant source could impair not just long-term memory but also the most robust form of long-term memory.

It turns out that the attentional demands involved in the Stroop task do impair perceptual implicit memory. In our own work, we asked participants to either name the color in which words were written (the Stroop condition, e.g., words such as "destiny," "premise," and "analogy" written in blue, red, and yellow, respectively) or to simply read the words (the read condition) in the study phase. In some experiments, participants were also asked to write down the color and the words to ensure that they processed the stimuli as instructed (Experiments 1 and 2). In some experiments, a neutral study condition (a string of Xs written in different colors) was also included to compare reaction times across the Stroop and the neutral conditions (Experiments 2 and 3). Perceptual implicit memory was measured with a word fragment completion task (Experiment 1) or a word stem completion task (Experiments 2 and 3). The findings were consistent across all experiments; perceptual priming was significant in the read condition as well as the Stroop condition but priming was *significantly reduced* in the Stroop condition.

An obvious concern in interpreting reduced priming is its similarity to the effects seen in explicit memory tasks. As noted earlier, Stroop encoding severely impairs performance on an explicit stem cued recall task (Rajaram et al., 2001). Because this explicit task is similar to the implicit stem completion in all ways but one—the use of intentional recall of studied information—it is possible that participants in the implicit stem completion task might have engaged in intentional retrieval and effectively converted the task into a recall task. However, this possibility is rendered unlikely because of several reasons. One, we took numerous procedural measures to disguise the fragment and stem tasks as memory tasks (see Roediger & McDermott, 1993, for recommendations). Two, we directly compared the implicit and explicit versions of the stem completion task in one experiment and found a significant crossover interaction (Experiment 2); performance was higher in the explicit version of the task for items from the read condition, whereas performance was higher in the implicit version of the task for items from the Stroop condition (see Figure 13.1). Therefore, participants did not perform both tasks in the same way. Finally, we used a post-test awareness questionnaire (Bowers & Schacter, 1990) in the implicit version of the task to eliminate data from participants who reported using intentional retrieval (Experiment 3).

Stroop encoding reduces perceptual priming in yet another popular task—perceptual identification—where intentional retrieval is unlikely to occur (Mulligan & Hornstein, 2000; Stone, Ladd, & Gabrieli, 2000; Stone, Ladd, Vaidya, & Gabrieli, 1998, but see their Exp. 3). In this task, words are presented at threshold durations (e.g., 35 ms) sometimes with forward or backward masks or with both. Thus, it is reasonable to assume that participants do not have the time to use explicit retrieval strategies that take longer to come into play. In fact, priming is reduced in this task even when participants name the word during study after they perform the Stroop task of color naming (Mulligan & Hornstein, 2000). Together, these findings show that the attentional demands of Stroop encoding produce lasting deficits in perceptual implicit memory.

The only task where a priming deficit has not been observed is the lexical decision task (Szymanski & MacLeod, 1996). It is not obvious why this task produces a different pattern but divergent results on the lexical decision task compared to other perceptual priming tasks have been reported as a function of other variables also (Rajaram & Roediger, 1993). In general, reduced priming from

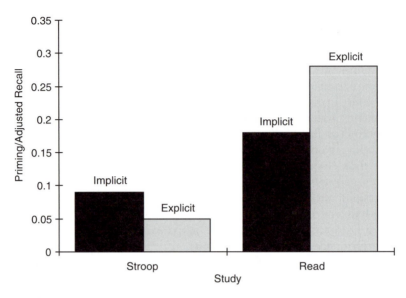

FIGURE 13.1 A comparison of studied–nonstudied completion scores in the implicit stem completion task and the explicit stem cued recall task as a function of color naming (the Stroop task) or reading during the study phase (Rajaram et al., 2001, Exp. 2). Rajaram, S., Srinivas, K., & Travers, S. (2001). The effects of attention on perceptual implicit memory. *Memory and Cognition, 29*, 920–930. Publishers: The Psychonomic Society Publications. Adapted with permission.

Stroop encoding appears to be the norm across a variety of widely-used perceptual implicit tasks.

CONCEPTUAL DESELECTION AND PERCEPTUAL IMPLICIT MEMORY

Harmful effects of deselecting the dominant stimulus are surprising because dividing attention between two stimuli does not cause such harm to perceptual implicit memory. This contrast raises the question whether these harmful effects of deselection are *specific* to particular aspects of the dominant stimulus or whether deselection at any level can harm perceptual implicit memory.

In Stroop encoding, the word identity is deselected to enable color naming. We have proposed in detail elsewhere a mechanism whereby positive effects of reading and negative effects of deselecting words in the Stroop task combine to reduce perceptual priming (Rajaram et al., 2001; Rajaram & Travers, 2005). We have also evaluated the nature of relationship between the selected and ignored dimensions that seems crucial for producing reduced perceptual priming. Specifically, reduction in priming occurs for a dominant or salient stimulus that is deselected in favor of a nondominant stimulus. Here, I focus on the issue of specificity versus generality in the deselection of the dominant stimulus.

In the Stroop task, word identity is presumably deselected at many levels in order to successfully name the color in which the word is written; the lexical information appears to be deselected because naming the color for word stimuli is slower than for neutral stimuli (Dalrymple-Alford, 1972). The conceptual sense of the word also appears to be deselected because color naming is slower when words are conceptually related to color name than when word are unrelated (Dalrymple-Alford, 1972; Klein, 1964). So, it is possible that perceptual-lexical deselection as well as conceptual deselection contribute to priming impairment. If this is the case, then harmful effects of deselection on perceptual priming would seem to be pervasive and nonspecific. This outcome would be even more surprising because, as noted in an earlier section, emphasis on meaning during study does not affect perceptual priming under the standard encoding conditions. A few years ago, we reported a study on the effects of match or mismatch in conceptual context on implicit fragment completion task (Rajaram, Srinivas, & Roediger, 1998). Interestingly, the design and findings of that study are also useful for addressing the question at hand. In order to create study and test contexts that either matched or mismatched in meaning, we took advantage of word stimuli that remain identical in their perceptual-lexical information but can vary in meaning. To do this, we used homographs as the critical stimuli (e.g., poker, block, front, etc.). Studies on lexical access have shown that if people encounter a homograph such as "poker" in the absence of a biasing context, they access its dominant meaning (a card game) more quickly than its nondominant meaning (Forster & Bednall, 1976; Simpson & Krueger, 1991). The dominant meaning also stays activated for a period of time (Pacht & Rayner, 1993; Simpson, 1981; Simpson & Burgess, 1985; Simpson & Krueger, 1991; Yates, 1978). Furthermore, even if the nondominant meaning is accessed first, there is a shift towards activation of the dominant meaning after some time (Gee, 1997; Rayner, Pacht, & Duffy, 1994; Winograd & Geis, 1974).

Based on this evidence, we created the following conditions to examine the effects of conceptual context on perceptual priming. At study, participants processed homographs either for the dominant meaning (a card game: poker) or for the nondominant meaning (a metal rod for kindling fire: poker). At test, fragments of studied (_ o k _ r) and nonstudied (f _ o _ t) targets were provided with instructions to complete the fragments with the first solution that came to mind. Context was assumed to be matched when participants studied the dominant meaning because the presentation of the test cue, i.e., the fragment, in the absence of any context presumably activated the dominant meaning. Likewise, encoding of nondominant meaning was assumed to mismatch in meaning with the test cue. We predicted that match or mismatch in context should have little effect on the magnitude of perceptual priming because emphasis on meaning is assumed to be irrelevant for this form of memory. In contrast, context match—as in the case of studying the dominant meaning—should produce better explicit memory on a word fragment cued recall task compared to studying the nondominant meaning. In the fragment cued recall task, participants saw the same fragment test cues but were now asked to use these cues to intentionally retrieve studied items. We predicted an advantage for match in meaning because explicit memory is assumed to benefit from conceptual processes (Roediger, Weldon, & Challis,

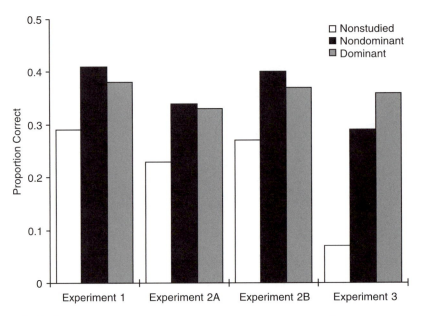

FIGURE 13.2   A comparison of the studied–nonstudied completion scores in the implicit fragment completion task (Experiments 1, 2A, 2B) and the explicit fragment cued recall task (Experiment 3) as a function of processing the dominant or the nondominant meaning of homographs during the study phase. Rajaram, S., Srinivas, K., & Roediger, H. L. (1998). A transfer-appropriate account of context effects in word fragment completion. *Journal of Experimental Psychology: Learning, Memory, and Cognition, 24*, 993–1004. Publishers: American Psychological Association. Adapted with permission.

1989). Our findings confirmed these predictions in a series of four experiments (see Figure 13.2). If anything, we observed a small and often negligible advantage for the nondominant study items on the implicit fragment completion task, and a significant advantage for the dominant study items on the explicit fragment cued recall task.

A consideration of these experiments is particularly useful for present purposes because the encoding task required selection or deselection of the dominant aspect of study stimuli. When participants were asked to encode the nondominant meaning of the homographs (e.g., a metal rod for kindling fire: poker), this task required the deselection of the dominant meaning that is activated more quickly and that remains activated for some time. In this sense, this process of deselection parallels the processes involved in selecting the color name (the nondominant stimulus component) over word identity (the dominant stimulus component) in the Stroop task. The critical difference in the homograph study is that it is only the dominant meaning, and not the word identity, that was deselected. This is because the perceptual-lexical information of the word identity continued to be processed even when the nondominant meaning was selected. This design and the results observed with this design show that perceptual priming is not sensitive to deselection of *any* dominant component of a stimulus. The sensitivity of perceptual priming appears to be specific—it is tied to the deselection of the perceptual-lexical word identity *per se*.

CONCLUDING NOTES

In the last two decades of research, perceptual implicit memory has emerged as one of the most resilient forms of long-term memory in humans. Aside from perceptual specificity that characterizes this form of memory, its encoding requirements appear to be minimal and it usually survives effects of brain damage and passage of time.

In this chapter, I focused on the evidence that elucidates the attentional requirements of perceptual implicit memory. Numerous studies have now shown that this form of memory is not impaired even if attention is divided at study between the target information and other sources. However, recent evidence shows that, in contrast to divided attention, *selective* attention during study can impair perceptual implicit memory when a dominant source of information is ignored in favor of a nondominant source.

In considering these deselection effects, the phenomenon of retrieval-induced forgetting (Anderson, 2003; Anderson, Bjork, & Bjork, 1994; Anderson & Spellman, 1995) is worth noting because it bears some similarities to the memory impairment discussed here. In the retrieval-induced forgetting paradigm, the process of select-ing some exemplars for retrieval practice from a group of possible studied choices impairs later retrieval of the unselected exemplars from the same category. This effect and the deselection effect seem similar in that both are tied to the selection of some information with simultaneous deselection of other information. But there are also notable differences in the procedures and memory measures that yield these effects. Most relevant for present purposes, the retrieval-induced for-getting effect is reliably observed in explicit memory but its effects seem less reliable in implicit memory. Some recent evidence suggests that the retrieval-induced forgetting effect can occur on implicit memory (Perfect, Moulin, Conway, & Perry, 2002; Veling & van Knippenberg, 2004) but this effect is not reliably observed in perceptual priming (Butler, Williams, Zacks, & Maki, 2001; Perfect et al., 2002). Because the practiced and unpracticed items share conceptual rela-tionships, it seems logical that this retrieval impairment is more likely to occur in conceptual priming. However, the evidence that this effect can occur on con-ceptual priming has recently come into question (Camp, Pecher, & Schmidt, 2005). For these reasons, it is early to tell whether the deselection effect discussed in this chapter and the retrieval-induced forgetting effect represent the same phenomena and whether they rely on shared mechanisms. Nevertheless, these effects look similar in explicit memory and it might very well turn out to be the case these two mechanisms of memory impairment share similarities despite some differences.

Returning to the deselection effects discussed in this chapter, the Stroop encoding task clearly impairs perceptual implicit memory. As noted earlier, this encoding situation is interesting because it entails processing of the dominant source prior to its deselection, and as such it creates cognitive conflict. Even though perceptual implicit memory is insensitive to encoding conditions of divided attention, the Stroop-encoding studies show that it is sensitive to the attentional demands created by encoding deselection. However, consistent with its perceptual-lexical demands, priming on this class of memory tasks declines only in response to the deselection of the perceptual-lexical word identity and not in response to the deselection of dominant meaning.

REFERENCES

Anderson, M. C. (2003). Rethinking interference theory: Executive control and the mechanism of forgetting. *Journal of Memory and Language, 49*, 415–445.

Anderson, M. C., Bjork, R. A., & Bjork, E. L. (1994). Remembering can cause forgetting: Retrieval dynamics in long-term memory. *Journal of Experimental Psychology: Learning, Memory, and Cognition, 20*, 1063–1087.

Anderson, M. C., & Craik, F. I. M. (1974). The effect of a concurrent task on recall from primary memory. *Journal of Verbal Learning and Verbal Behavior, 13*, 107–113.

Anderson, M. C., & Spellman, B. A. (1995). On the status of inhibitory mechanisms in cognition: Memory retrieval as a model case. *Psychological Review, 102*, 68–100.

Bentin, S., Kutas, M., & Hillyard, S. A. (1995). Semantic processing and memory for attended and unattended words in dichotic listening: Behavioral and electro-physiological evidence. *Journal of Experimental Psychology: Human Perception and Performance, 21*, 54–67.

Besner, D. (2001). The myth of ballistic processing: Evidence from Stroop's paradigm. *Psychonomic Bulletin and Review, 8*, 324–330.

Blaxton, T. A. (1989). Investigating dissociations among memory measures: Support for a transfer-appropriate processing framework. *Journal of Experimental Psychology: Learning, Memory, and Cognition, 15*, 657–668.

Bowers, J. S., & Schacter, D. L. (1990). Implicit memory and test awareness. *Journal of Experimental Psychology: Learning, Memory, and Cognition, 16*, 404–416.

Butler, K. M., Williams, C. C., Zacks, R. T., & Maki, R. H. (2001). A limit on retrieval-induced forgetting. *Journal of Experimental Psychology: Learning, Memory, and Cognition, 27*, 1314–1319.

Camp, G., Pecher, D., & Schmidt, H. G. (2005). Retrieval-induced forgetting in implicit memory tests: The role of test awareness. *Psychonomic Bulletin and Review, 12*, 490–494.

Catena, A., Fuentes, L. J., & Tudela, P. (2002). Priming and interference effects can be dissociated in the Stroop task: New evidence in favor of the automaticity of word recognition. *Psychonomic Bulletin and Review, 9*, 113–118.

Craik, F. I. M. (2001). Effects of dividing attention on encoding and retrieval processes. In H. L. Roediger & J. S. Nairne (Eds.), *The nature of remembering: Essays in honor of Robert G. Crowder* (pp. 55–68). Washington, DC: American Psychological Association.

Craik, F. I. M., Govoni, R., Naveh-Benjamin, M., & Anderson N. D. (1996). The effects of divided attention on encoding and retrieval processes in human memory. *Journal of Experimental Psychology: General, 125*, 159–180.

Craik, F. I. M., & Lockhart, R. S. (1972). Levels of processing: A framework for memory research. *Journal of Verbal Learning and Verbal Behavior, 11*, 671–684.

Dalrymple-Alford, E. C. (1972). Associative facilitation and interference in the Stroop color–word task. *Perception and Psychophysics, 11*, 274–276.

Dalrymple-Alford, E. C., & Budayr, B. (1966). Examination of some aspects of the Stroop color–word test. *Perceptual and Motor Skills, 23*, 1211–1214.

Dyer, F. N. (1973). The Stroop phenomenon and its use in the study of perceptual, cognitive, and response processes. *Memory and Cognition, 2*, 106–120.

Eich, E. (1984). Memory for unattended events: Remembering with and without awareness. *Memory and Cognition, 12*, 105–111.

Eysenck, M. W., & Eysenck, M. C. (1979). Processing depth, elaboration of encoding, memory stores, and expended processing capacity. *Journal of Experimental Psychology: Learning, Memory, and Cognition, 5*, 472–484.

Forster, K. I., & Bednall, E. S. (1976). Terminating and exhaustive search in lexical access. *Memory and Cognition, 4*, 53–61.

Gabrieli, J. D. E., Vaidya, C. J., Stone, M., Francis, W. S., Thompson-Schill, S. L., Fleischman, D. A., et al. (1999). Convergent behavioral and neuropsychological evidence for a distinction between identification and production forms of repetition priming. *Journal of Experimental Psychology: General, 128*, 479–498.

Gee, N. R. (1997). Implicit memory and word ambiguity. *Journal of Memory and Language, 36*, 253–275.

Graf, P., & Mandler, G. (1984). Activation makes words more accessible, but not necessarily more retrievable. *Journal of Verbal Learning and Verbal Behavior, 23*, 553–568.

Graf, P., & Schacter, D. L. (1985). Implicit and explicit memory for new associations in normal and amnesic subjects. *Journal of Experimental Psychology: Learning, Memory, and Cognition, 11*, 501–518.

Hamann, S. B. (1990). Level of processing effects in conceptually driven implicit tasks. *Journal of Experimental Psychology: Learning, Memory, and Cognition, 16*, 970–977.

Hawley, K. J., & Johnston, W. A. (1991). Long-term perceptual memory for briefly exposed words as a function of awareness and attention. *Journal of Experimental Psychology: Human Perception and Performance, 17*, 807–815.

Isingrini, M., Vazou, F., & Leroy, P. (1995). Dissociation of implicit and explicit memory tests: Effect of age and divided attention on category exemplar generation and cued recall. *Memory and Cognition, 23*, 462–467.

Jacoby, L. L. (1978). On interpreting the effects of repetition: Solving a problem versus remembering a solution. *Journal of Verbal Learning and Verbal Behavior, 17*, 649–667.

Jacoby, L. L. (1983). Perceptual enhancement: Persistent effects of an experience. *Journal of Experimental Psychology: Learning, Memory, and Cognition, 9*, 21–38.

Jacoby, L. L., & Dallas, M. (1981). On the relationship between autobiographical memory and perceptual learning. *Journal of Experimental Psychology: General, 110*, 306–340.

Jacoby, L. L., Woloshyn, V., & Kelley, C. (1989). Becoming famous without being recognized: Unconscious influences of memory produced by dividing attention. *Journal of Experimental Psychology: General, 118*, 115–125.

Klein, G. S. (1964). Semantic power measured through the interference of words with color-naming. *American Journal of Psychology, 77*, 576–588.

Komatsu, S. I., & Ohta, N. (1984). Priming effects in word-fragment completion for short and long retention intervals. *Japanese Psychological Research, 26*, 194–200.

Light, L. L., Prull, M. W., & Kennison, R. F. (2000). Divided attention, aging, and priming in exemplar generation and category verification. *Memory and Cognition, 28,* 856–872.

MacLeod, C. M. (1991). Half a century of research on the Stroop effect: An integrative review. *Psychological Bulletin, 109,* 163–203.

Morris, C. D., Bransford, J. D., & Franks, J. J. (1979). Levels of processing versus transfer appropriate processing. *Journal of Verbal Learning and Verbal Behavior, 16,* 519–533.

Moscovitch, M., Vriezen, E., & Goshen-Gottstein, Y. (1993). Implicit tests of memory in patients with focal lesions and degenerative brain disorders. In H. Spinnler & F. Boller (Eds.), *Handbook of neuropsychology* (Vol. 8; pp. 133–174). Amsterdam: Elsevier.

Mulligan, N. W. (1997). Attention and implicit memory tests: The effects of varying attentional load on conceptual priming. *Memory and Cognition, 25,* 11–17.

Mulligan, N. W. (1998). The role of attention during encoding in implicit and explicit memory. *Journal of Experimental Psychology: Learning, Memory, and Cognition, 24,* 27–47.

Mulligan, N, W., & Hartman, M. (1996). Divided attention and indirect memory tests. *Memory and Cognition, 24,* 453–465.

Mulligan, N. W., & Hornstein, S. L. (2000). Attention and perceptual priming in the perceptual identification task. *Journal of Experimental Psychology: Learning, Memory, and Cognition, 26,* 626–637.

Neill, W. T. (1977). Inhibitory and facilitory processes in selective attention. *Journal of Experimental Psychology: Human Perception and Performance, 3,* 444–450.

Pacht, J. M., & Rayner, K. (1993). The processing of homophonic homographs during reading: Evidence from eye movement studies. *Journal of Psycholinguistic Research, 22,* 251–271.

Parkin, A. J., Reid, T. K., & Russo, R. (1990). On the differential nature of implicit and explicit memory. *Memory and Cognition, 18,* 507–514.

Parkin, A. J., & Russo, R. (1990). Implicit and explicit memory and the automatic/effortful distinction. *European Journal of Cognitive Psychology, 2,* 71–80.

Perfect, T. J., Moulin, C. J. A., Conway, M. A., & Perry, E. (2002). Assessing the inhibitory account of retrieval-induced forgetting with implicit memory tests. *Journal of Experimental Psychology: Learning, Memory, and Cognition, 28,* 1111–1119.

Rajaram, S., & Roediger, H. L. (1993). Direct comparison of four implicit memory tests. *Journal of Experimental Psychology: Learning, Memory, and Cognition, 19,* 765–776.

Rajaram, S., Srinivas, K., & Roediger, H. L. (1998). A transfer-appropriate account of context effects in word fragment completion. *Journal of Experimental Psychology: Learning, Memory, and Cognition, 24,* 993–1004.

Rajaram, S., Srinivas, K., & Travers, S. (2001). The effects of attention on perceptual implicit memory. *Memory and Cognition, 29,* 920–930.

Rajaram, S., & Travers, S. V. (2005). Deselection effects in long-term memory. In N. Ohta, C. M. MacLeod, & B. Uttl (Eds.), *Dynamic cognitive processes* (pp. 191–217). Tokyo: Springer-Verlag.

Rappold, V. A., & Hashtroudi, S. (1991). Does organization improve priming? *Journal of Experimental Psychology: Learning, Memory, and Cognition, 17,* 103–114.

Rayner, K., Pacht, J. M., & Duffy, S. A. (1994). Processing of lexically ambiguous words: Evidence from eye fixations. *Journal of Memory and Language, 33,* 527–544.

Roediger, H. L. (1990). Implicit memory: Retention without remembering. *The American Psychologist, 45,* 1043–1056.

Roediger, H. L., & McDermott, K. B. (1993). Implicit memory in normal subjects. In H. Spinnler & F. Boller (Eds.), *Handbook of neuropsychology* (pp. 63–131). Amsterdam: Elsevier.

Roediger, H. L., III, & Srinivas, K. (1993). Specificity of operations in perceptual priming. In P. Graf & M. E. J. Masson (Eds.), *Implicit memory: New directions in cognition, development, and neuropsychology* (pp. 17–48). Hillsdale, NJ: Lawrence Erlbaum Associates, Inc.

Roediger, H. L., Srinivas, K., & Weldon, M. S. (1989). Dissociations between implicit measures of retention. In S. Lewandowsky, J. C. Dunn, & K. Kirsner (Eds.), *Implicit memory: Theoretical issues* (pp. 67–84). Hillsdale, NJ: Lawrence Erlbaum Associates, Inc.

Roediger, H. L., Weldon, M. S., & Challis, B. H. (1989). Explaining dissociations between implicit and explicit measures of retention: A processing account. In H. L. Roediger, III, & F. I. M. Craik (Eds.), *Varieties of memory and consciousness: Essays in honour of Endel Tulving* (pp. 3–41). Hillside, NJ: Lawrence Erlbaum Associates, Inc.

Roediger, H. L., Weldon, M. S., Stadler, M. S., & Reigler, G. H. (1992). Direct comparison of word stems and word fragments in implicit and explicit retention tests. *Journal of Experimental Psychology: Learning, Memory, and Cognition, 18,* 1251–1264.

Schacter, D. L. (1990). Perceptual representation system and implicit memory: Toward a resolution of the multiple memory systems debate. In A. Diamond (Ed.), *The development and neural bases of higher cognitive functions: Annals of the New York Academy of Sciences* (Vol. 608, pp. 543–571). New York: New York Academy of Sciences.

Schacter, D. L., Bowers, J., & Booker, J. (1989). Intention, awareness, and implicit memory: The retrieval intentionality criterion. In S. Lewandowsky, J. C. Dunn, & K. Kirsner (Eds.), *Implicit memory: Theoretical issues* (pp. 47–65). Hillsdale, NJ: Lawrence Erlbaum Associates, Inc.

Schacter, D. L., & Tulving, E. (1994). What are the memory systems of 1994? In D. Schacter & E. Tulving (Eds.), *Memory systems 1994* (pp. 1–38). Cambridge, MA: MIT Press.

Schmitter-Edgecombe, M. (1996a). The effects of divided attention on implicit and explicit memory performance. *Journal of the International Neuropsychological Society, 2,* 111–125.

Schmitter-Edgecombe, M. (1996b). Effects of divided attention on implicit and explicit memory performance following severe closed head injury. *Neuropsychology, 10,* 155–167.

Schmitter-Edgecombe, M. (1999). Effects of divided attention on perceptual and conceptual memory tests: An analysis using a process-dissociation approach. *Memory and Cognition, 27,* 512–525.

Simpson, G. B. (1981). Meaning dominance and semantic context in the processing of lexical ambiguity. *Journal of Verbal Learning and Verbal Behavior, 20,* 120–136.

Simpson, G. B., & Burgess, C. (1985). Activation and selection processes in the recognition of ambiguous words. *Journal of Experimental Psychology: Human Perception and Performance, 11,* 28–39.

Simpson, G. B., & Krueger, M. A. (1991). Selective access of homograph meanings in sentence context. *Journal of Memory and Language, 30,* 627–643.

Slamecka, N. J., & Graf, P. (1978). The generation effect: Delineation of a phenomenon. *Journal of Experimental Psychology: Human Learning and Memory, 4,* 592–604.

Sloman, S. A., Hayman, C. A. G., Ohta, N., Law, L., & Tulving, E. (1988). Forgetting in primed fragment completion. *Journal of Experimental Psychology: Learning, Memory, and Cognition, 14,* 223–239.

Srinivas, K., & Roediger, H. L. (1990). Classifying implicit memory tests: Category association and anagram solution. *Journal of Memory and Language, 29,* 389–412.

Stone, M., Ladd, S. L., & Gabrieli, J. D. E. (2000). The role of selective attention in perceptual and affective priming. *American Journal of Psychology, 113,* 341–358.

Stone, M., Ladd, S. L., Vaidya, C. J., & Gabrieli, J. D. E. (1998). Word-identification priming for ignored and attended words. *Consciousness and Cognition, 7,* 238–258.

Stroop, J. R. (1935). Studies of interference in serial verbal reactions. *Journal of Experimental Psychology, 18,* 643–662.

Szymanski, K. F., & MacLeod, C. M. (1996). Manipulation of attention at study affects an explicit but not an implicit test of memory. *Consciousness and Cognition, 5,* 165–175.

Travers, S., & Rajaram, S. (2006). Protecting memory against Stroop deselection. *Manuscript in preparation.*

Tulving, E., & Schacter, D. L. (1990). Priming and human memory systems. *Science, 247,* 301–306.

Tulving, E., Schacter, D. L., & Stark, H. A. (1982). Priming effects in word-fragment completion are independent of recognition memory. *Journal of Experimental Psychology: Learning, Memory, and Cognition, 8,* 336–342.

Veling, H., & van Knippenberg, A. (2004). Remembering can cause inhibition: Retrieval-induced inhibition as cue independent process. *Journal of Experimental Psychology: Learning, Memory, and Cognition, 30,* 315–318.

Warrington, E. K., & Weiskrantz, L. (1968). A new method of testing long-term retention with special reference to amnesic patients. *Nature* (London), *217,* 972–974.

Warrington, E. K., & Weiskrantz, L. (1970). Amnesic syndrome: Consolidation or retrieval? *Nature, 228,* 629–630.

Weldon, M. S. (1991). Mechanisms underlying priming on perceptual tasks. *Journal of Experimental Psychology: Learning, Memory, and Cognition, 17,* 526–541.

Weldon, M. S., & Jackson-Barrett, J. L. (1993). Why do pictures produce priming on the word-fragment completion test? A study of encoding and retrieval factors. *Memory and Cognition, 21,* 519–528.

Weldon, M. S., & Roediger, H. L., III. (1987). Altering retrieval demands reverses the picture superiority effect. *Memory and Cognition, 15,* 269–280.

Winograd, E., & Geis, M. F. (1974). Semantic encoding and recognition memory: A test of encoding variability theory. *Journal of Experimental Psychology, 102,* 1061–1068.

Yates, J. (1978). Priming dominant and unusual senses of ambiguous words. *Memory and Cognition, 6,* 636–643.

14

Spontaneous Retrieval in Prospective Memory

MARK A. McDANIEL and GILLES O. EINSTEIN

O ur chapter, like others in this volume, focuses on episodic memory. Other chapters have approached episodic memory as a process or system to preserve an individual's mental record of his or her past. Here we take a broader view that episodic memory also allows people to mentally place themselves forward in time. Tulving (2004) has termed this process proscopic chronesthesia. Proscopic chronesthesia, likely unique to humans, supports forward-looking activities, the anticipation of what we will be doing in the near and long term, what we are likely to feel in anticipated events, what we hope to accomplish, and the planning activities that accompany this future oriented behavior. Closely aligned with such mental time-travel is prospective memory, which is the focus of the present chapter. Prospective memory is memory for activities that we intend to perform in the future. More specifically, prospective memory refers to remembering to perform an intended action at an appropriate moment in the future.

With even minimal thought, it is clear that everyday living is replete with prospective memory tasks. We need to remember to give colleagues messages, to pack a desired item in our work bag, to remember to pick up some grocery item on the way home from work, and remember to attend scheduled appointments. For one of us, the last prospective memory challenge is especially salient because recently, at the time that a faculty meeting was scheduled, MAM forgot about the meeting (his colleagues were much amused that a prospective memory researcher would forget the meeting). Prospective memory is also needed for handling health-related needs such as remembering to exercise, to monitor various bodily indices like blood pressure or blood-sugar levels, and to take medication. The latter is increasingly frequent as the Center for Disease Control and Prevention reports that 44% of Americans (http://www.cdc.gov/nchs.hus.htm) have taken a prescription medication over the past month and 17% have taken three or more medications.

Despite the prevalence of prospective memory in every day life, the scientific study of memory dating from Ebbinghaus (1885/1964) has not included investigation of prospective memory. Perhaps this state of affairs rests on the observation that prospective memory tasks appear similar to the ubiquitous retrospective memory task of cued recall (McDaniel & Einstein, 1993). In the typical laboratory paradigm, in cued recall the subject is given a list of paired items that includes a cue item and an item to be remembered (e.g., "train—BLACK"). Then at test, the subject is provided with the cue ("train") and prompted to try to remember the target item. In a parallel fashion, in a prospective memory task, a person pairs a particular anticipated event (e.g., "Roddy") with an intended action (ask him where to buy an Argyle sweater vest). Later the individual encounters the cue event and must remember the associated intention.

There is a critical difference, however, between the cued recall task and the prospective memory task. In cued recall an agent (the experimenter) requests that the person try to remember—recollection is stimulated by some agent requesting a memory search. In Tulving's (1983) terms, the request to remember places the person in a retrieval mode. Here the person is set to consider incoming information as a potential retrieval cue. In contrast, in prospective memory there is no external agent requesting a memory search, and thus the individual is presumably not always in a retrieval mode when the target event is encountered. (Otherwise, given the prevalence of prospective memory tasks in everyday functioning, arguably people would constantly be in a retrieval mode; if that were the case, then at the theoretical level, there would be little advantage to distinguishing a retrieval mode state.) From our perspective, a critical feature of prospective remembering that sets it apart from the explicit retrospective memory tasks studied extensively for over 100 years is that somehow the intended activity is remembered at the appropriate moment without an external agent stimulating retrieval (cf. Craik, 1986). How can this occur?

HISTORICAL OVERVIEW

An appeal to early prominent psychologists provides one possible answer. Ebbinghaus (1885/1964) identified three types of memories.

(1) Voluntary production: "we call back into consciousness by an exertion of the will . . . the seemingly lost states."
(2) Unconscious influences of prior states that indirectly provide evidence of their lasting effects.
(3) Spontaneous appearance of a mental state "without any act of will" that is recognized as previously experienced.

The first captures processes related to explicit retrospective memory tasks, whereas the second is applicable to what modern memory researchers term implicit memory tasks (Roediger, 1985). We suggest that prospective memory often relies on the third type of memory, spontaneous processes that occur without any act of will. Freud (1909/1952) described the processes involved in remembering an intention in a similar fashion: "The suggested intention slumbers on in the person concerned until the time for its execution approaches. Then it awakes and impels him to perform the action" (p. 79).

Many, if not most, contemporary memory researchers have taken a different approach and assumed that a more active, resource demanding process is involved in prospective remembering. In a seminal paper, Craik (1986) proposed that prospective memory, more than any other memory task, requires extensive self-initiated retrieval activity. Others have adopted the view that people monitor for the event that signals the appropriate time for performing the intended action, a process that is presumably capacity consuming (e.g., Burgess & Shallice, 1997; Guynn, 2003; Smith, 2003). Smith explicitly proposed that a capacity consuming "preparatory" process is needed to evaluate events as possible targets. She states that "retrieval of an intention will never be automatic, because nonautomatic preparatory processes [monitoring] must be engaged during the performance interval . . . before the occurrence of the target event" (p. 349). In support of this monitoring view, Smith (see also Guynn, 2003; Marsh, Hicks, Cook, Hansen, & Pallos, 2003) finds substantial costs on performing an ongoing task when also performing a prospective memory task. These costs are on the order of a 300 ms slowing for a lexical decision task.

SPONTANEOUS RETRIEVAL VIEW OF PROSPECTIVE MEMORY RETRIEVAL

In contrast, consistent with Ebbinghaus' claim for spontaneous appearances of mental states without any act of will, we (Einstein & McDaniel, 1996; McDaniel & Einstein, 2000) have suggested that people do not have to monitor for the target event in order to have successful retrieval; instead people have a bias to rely on spontaneous retrieval. By this view, prospective remembering occurs when the presence of the target event initiates retrieval. Consequently, remembering does not require that a person is in a retrieval mode, as is claimed for explicit retrospective memory (Tulving, 1983) or as is suggested by the monitoring view (e.g., see Guynn, 2003).

Because recent work has argued forcefully and marshaled impressive data for a resource demanding (monitoring) process in prospective memory retrieval, the spontaneous retrieval view does not enjoy unanimous acceptance. As one researcher succinctly objected, "rather than assuming that the prospective [memory] component is automatic, experiments are needed to demonstrate when, if ever, this is the case" (Smith, 2003, p. 359). Our objective in this chapter is to meet that challenge by building an experimentally-based case for the spontaneous retrieval view of prospective memory. To do so, we address five central issues. First, can prospective remembering occur with no cost to ongoing activity? Second, is prospective memory retrieval evidenced when the prospective memory intention is suspended? Third, might spontaneous retrieval be accomplished, at least in part, by a reflexive associative memory process (e.g., Moscovitch, 1994)? Fourth, when reflexive associative processes are preeminent, does divided attention penalize prospective memory retrieval? Fifth, are there other cognitive processes, processes not specifically recruited for prospective remembering, that might also support spontaneous prospective memory retrieval? Note that we are not claiming that prospective memory retrieval cannot be accomplished by monitoring (see Einstein et al., 2005). Our claim is that monitoring is not always necessary for prospective memory retrieval, and that in some cases (perhaps often in everyday prospective memory) prospective memory retrieval is a predominantly spontaneous, nonstrategic process.

Can Prospective Memory Occur without Cost to Ongoing Activity?

Smith's (2003) paradigm used six different words as the prospective memory targets. Arguably, many event-based prospective memory tasks are simpler in that only one target event is associated with the intended action. Indeed in everyday settings, a single target event is a common (event-based) prospective memory situation. An intended message is often for one particular person and buying a grocery item on the way home is usually associated with one target store. Though people might monitor for a target when faced with the task of responding whenever any one of six target events appeared, it is not certain that monitoring or other resource demanding preparatory processes (or self-initiated retrieval processes) are engaged when one target event signals the appropriateness of executing the action.

Einstein et al. (2005, Exp. 3) investigated this possibility with a sentence completion ongoing task. Subjects were given a set of sentences, each with a missing word. Following each sentence was a word that might or might not fit into the sentence. Subjects were to respond either "Yes" or "No" to indicate if the word fit the sentence. An example is:

A warrior's armor makes him _____ to blows that he may undergo in battle.
IMPERVIOUS

Subjects were encouraged to be both accurate and fast in responding to the sentence completion task. There were two blocks of sentences with 110 sentences in each block. In one block there was no prospective memory task, whereas in the other block subjects also were instructed to perform a prospective memory task. For the prospective memory block, subjects were instructed to press the "Enter" key whenever they saw a target word.

Importantly, half of the subjects were in a six-target item condition ("evening," "horse," "medicine," "orange," "sauce," and "goggles"), and the other half were in a one-target condition. Figure 14.1 shows the response times to the ongoing activity as a function of the target condition (1 vs. 6 targets) for the control blocks (no prospective memory task) and the prospective memory blocks. Replicating Smith (2003), having a prospective memory task incurred a significant cost (of 322 ms) to the ongoing activity when there were six target events. In contrast, there was no significant cost when there was a single target event (94 ms). Moreover, the absence of a cost was not associated with poor prospective memory performance, as it should have if prospective memory retrieval required preparatory attentional (monitoring) processes (Smith, 2003; Smith & Bayen, 2004). Indeed prospective

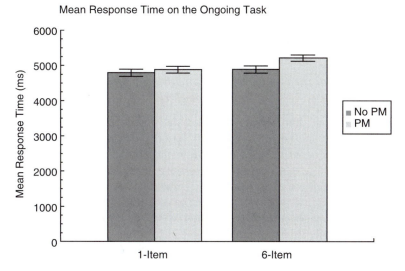

FIGURE 14.1   Response times to the ongoing activity as a function of the number of prospective memory targets (1 vs. 6) for trial blocks with and without a prospective memory task (result from Einstein et al., 2005, Exp. 3).

memory performance was nominally higher in the one target condition (80% responding) than in the six-target condition (72% responding).

The one-target condition showed a non-significant but small cost on the ongoing activity. Perhaps the number of subjects ($N = 32$) provided inadequate power to reveal a significant cost, or produced a nonstable finding that underestimated the true cost. To address this issue, in her master's thesis Jen Breneiser (2004) tested a large number of participants ($N = 128$) in the one-target event condition. Response times to the sentence completion task were nearly identical for the control and prospective memory blocks, with a mean cost of only 9 ms when the prospective memory task was present. The absence of a cost was not a speed–accuracy tradeoff (77% and 75% correct sentence responses in the control and prospective memory blocks, respectively). Finally it is important to note that prospective memory performance was at a high level (83% responding).

Still, a skeptic might argue that participants were able to sneak in monitoring during the sentence completion task (cf. Reitman, 1974) and thus costs were not detectable. To counter this idea, in a recently conducted study in our labs by Matt Larson, we used the lexical decision task as the ongoing activity (as had Smith, 2003; see also Marsh et al., 2003), but we emphasized the importance of the lexical decision task by occasionally giving participants feedback on the speed of their responses. Nevertheless, Larson's results showed a minimal and again nonsignificant cost (14 ms) of performing a prospective memory task and again very high prospective memory performance (86%). These findings of high prospective memory coupled with no cost to the ongoing activity strongly suggest that spontaneous retrieval processes can produce successful prospective remembering.

Still, the evidence for spontaneous retrieval is somewhat indirect. In the next section we describe a new paradigm designed to provide more direct evidence for spontaneous retrieval processes.

Is Prospective Memory Retrieval Evidenced When a Prospective Memory Intention has been Suspended?

Another strategy for determining whether the cognitive system spontaneously responds to stimuli in the environment is based on the reasoning that a spontaneous retrieval process should occur when the conditions for its retrieval are met—even when there is no intention to retrieve at the time these conditions are present. We (Einstein et al., 2005, Exp. 5) recently developed an experimental technique for examining retrieval under these conditions. Subjects were first told about an ongoing image-rating task in which words were presented one at a time, and the task of subjects was to rate the ease of forming an image for each word. Subjects were also given the prospective memory task of pressing a designated key whenever a particular target item occurred in the context of the image-rating task. The novel twist in this experiment was that we interweaved sets of lexical decision trials between sets of image rating trials. Critically, for the lexical decision task, (a) we told subjects to suspend all other task demands and that their sole concern was to decide as quickly as possible whether the letter strings formed a word, and (b) we included the prospective memory target as well as a matched control item among the 18 lexical decision items. This sequence of tasks was repeated for 10 blocks, and subjects received a new prospective memory target at the start of each block.

Given the instructions to ignore the prospective memory task during the lexical decision task, there should have been no monitoring during these trials. According to the monitoring view (e.g., Smith, 2003), prospective memory retrieval cannot occur without controlled monitoring of the environment for the target event. Thus, lexical decision response times to target events should have been similar to those for control items. According to the spontaneous retrieval view, however, the conditions for retrieval (i.e., the presence of the target and an orienting activity that required full processing of it) were present and should produce retrieval. The results supported this latter view as lexical decisions were significantly slower (by 55 ms) for prospective memory targets relative to control items. This slowing reveals that participants were retrieving something (perhaps noticing the target event and/or retrieving the intended action) when the target occurred.

A possible criticism of this experiment is that participants were constantly switching back and forth between the ongoing task and the lexical decision task, and this may have created confusion regarding the demands associated with each task. To address this concern, we, along with Matt McDermott and Leah Rusinko, recently completed a simplified version of the above experiment. In this new experiment, participants were told about an ongoing image-rating task and then given the prospective memory intention of pressing a key whenever any one of two target events occurred in the ongoing task. We then interrupted them with a "speed" task (in this case a living/nonliving judgment task rather than a lexical decision task) consisting of 260 trials. Participants were told to ignore the prospective memory intention during this "speed" task, yet each target event occurred four times across these trials. This is a simpler procedure because subjects switched only once from the ongoing task instructions to the "speed" task and then back again to the ongoing task. Consistent with the results from the first experiment, participants were significantly slower (by 30 ms) in making judgments to the prospective memory target events relative to matched control items.

Taken together, these results provide the first direct evidence that prospective memory intentions can be retrieved without monitoring for a target event and more generally that spontaneous retrieval can occur without being in a retrieval mode. Also, this new method of "loading" a target event with meaning (in this case, a prospective memory intention) and then examining the speed of responding to that target during an intervening task seems to hold promise for investigating the kind of memory Ebbinghaus (1885/1964) described as occurring "without any act of will."

Is Spontaneous Retrieval Mediated by a Reflexive Associative Memory Process?

A reflexive-associative model of spontaneous retrieval has been proposed by Moscovitch (1994), and here we explore the extent to which the broad ideas of the model can be applied to understanding spontaneous retrieval in prospective memory. According to his view, the hippocampus supports an "automatic" associative memory system in which the inputs are stimuli that have been fully processed (e.g., semantically). To the extent that the representation of this stimulus interacts with prior associations in memory, this system delivers to consciousness the associated information. The key feature for present purposes is that the association is delivered to consciousness rapidly, obligatorily and with few cognitive resources. That is, retrieval by this system occurs without an external agent requesting a memory search; instead retrieval is reflexive. These are the precise conditions that at the outset of this chapter we suggested characterized prospective remembering in many situations.

As applied to prospective memory, we (see Einstein & McDaniel, 1996; Guynn, McDaniel, & Einstein, 2001; McDaniel, Robinson-Riegler, & Einstein, 1998) suggest that during prospective memory planning people form an association between the anticipated target cue and the intended action. Later, when the target cue is encountered, this reflexive associative system delivers the intended action to consciousness (or prospective memory fails). As an everyday example, MAM's daughter asked that he remember to bring home a floppy disk from work. He formed the intention to do so, but forgot to bring a disk home that evening, and forgot for the next several days as well. Later in the week, at work he was removing a disk from a storage box (i.e., fully attentive to the disk) and suddenly remembered that he needed to take a disk home for his daughter (leading to successful execution of the promised intention). Phenomenologically, this experience had the characteristics of a reflexive, nonself-initiated retrieval of an intended action when an associated cue was encountered in the environment. We now describe more scientifically based support for this idea.

Our experimental method (McDaniel, Guynn, Einstein, & Breneiser, 2004, Exp. 2) used the ongoing activity of rating words various dimensions. To keep subjects actively engaged in this task, on any given trial the requested rating could involve one of four dimensions (familiarity, concereteness, meaningfulness, or pleasantness), with ratings entered on the keyboard. At the outset of the experiment, subjects were additionally instructed that if they ever encountered one of two target items, they should try to remember to write down on a provided sheet of paper a particular response word. A critical manipulation was the degree to which the target item and the response item could be readily associated. In the high-association condition, subjects were given two of the cue–action pairings from the following set of pairs.

spaghetti–sauce; steeple–church; thread–needle; eraser–pencil

For each pair, the intended action word was the most frequent associate to its target event in the University of South Florida free association norms (Nelson, McEvoy, & Schreiber, 1998).

In the low-association condition, the identical cue words were used, but they were paired with an action (a response word) with no strong prior association (again, a particular subject received two of the following pairs for the prospective memory task):

spaghetti–church; thread–pencil; steeple–sauce; eraser–needle

Real-world analogues for these conditions could be intending to stop at the grocery store on the way home from work for bread (a high cue–intended action association) versus intending to stop at the grocery store for shoe polish (a low cue–intended action association).

After the initial instructions, there was an approximately 12-minute filler activity and then subjects proceeded to the word rating task, with no additional reminder about the prospective memory task. Note that the design provides a competitive test of the strategic monitoring view and the spontaneous associative retrieval view. According to a monitoring view, people initiate a recognition check of environmental events to determine if the target cue is present (e.g., Smith, 2003; Smith & Bayen, 2004). Because the target cues are identical for both conditions, this process should produce equivalent prospective memory across the low- and high cue–action conditions. One caveat to this prediction is that performance for the low cue–action condition could be worse if subjects can not successfully remember the associated action (a retrospective memory failure). To gauge this possibility, at the end of the experiment all subjects were given a recall test for their memory of the cues and associated actions.

In contrast, according to the idea that prospective memory retrieval can be supported by a spontaneous associative retrieval process, the high association cue–intended action condition should produce better prospective remembering than the low association cue–intended action condition (because reflexive associative retrieval will be more probable in the former condition). This prediction was borne out. Subjects were significantly more likely to remember to perform the prospective memory response when the cue was highly associated with the intention (.88) than when the cue–intention pair was minimally associated (.74). Importantly, at the end of the experiment when prompted to report the details of the prospective memory task, all but two participants correctly recalled the prospective memory cue words and their assigned action words. Removing these two participants from the analyses did not change the prospective memory patterns. Thus, the advantage conferred by the high cue–intention association was apparently not due to better retrospective memory for the prospective memory targets and associated actions.

Nevertheless, when the two participants who could not correctly recall the components were not included in the analyses the significance level for the cue–intention association effect fell just below the conventional alpha level of .05. This result perhaps slightly undercuts the interpretation that the locus of the association effect was in the prospective-memory retrieval process. To further compel that interpretation, in collaboration with Melissa Guynn we conducted another experiment at a different university (New Mexico State) using a similar procedure. Because this next experiment was not published, we provide more of the critical details here.

In the Guynn experiment, we replaced all of the subjects (seven) who failed to recall the prospective memory cues and intended actions at the end of the experiment. Thus, all 64 subjects in the experiment had perfect retrospective memory for the prospective memory task for both the high ($N = 32$) and low-association ($N = 32$) conditions. There were 208 total word-rating trials, of which eight were prospective memory trials (each target word was presented for four trials each). The high-association condition ($M = 0.85$) produced substantially better prospective memory performance than the low-association condition ($M = 0.56$), $F(1, 60) = 9.33$, $MSE = 0.29$. We also found that prospective memory performance was significantly better for the last four prospective memory trials than the first four trials, $F(1, 60) = 17.93$, $MSE = 0.02$, indicating practice or carryover processes (cf. Maylor, 1998). Accordingly, the first several trials may be the most sensitive to the retrieval processes that are operative in everyday prospective memory tasks that are not habitually executed. Thus, to be conservative, we also examined performance on just the first two prospective memory trials. The significant advantage for high- ($M = 0.76$) versus low-association ($M = 0.48$) remained, $F(1, 60) = 7.48$, $MSE = 0.17$.

Because all subjects showed perfect retrospective memory for the target event and its associated action (during postexperimental testing), the results imply that the advantage of the high-association condition rested on the prospective memory retrieval component of prospective remembering. Further, because the prospective memory cues were identical in the high- and low-association conditions, the difference in performance could not be due to processes involved in cue detection (e.g., monitoring) or prospective-memory target recognition (cf. Smith, 2003). The results are most consistent with the idea that the target cue was more likely to stimulate reflexive and obligatory retrieval of the intended action when the intended action was more associated with the target cue (high-associative condition). In the next section, we consider a corollary prediction from this interpretation.

Does Divided Attention Penalize Prospective Memory When the Cue and Intention are Highly Associated?

Another implication of the spontaneous associative retrieval theory of prospective remembering is that when prospective memory retrieval is mediated by that process, minimal cognitive resources should be required. To test this idea, we (McDaniel et al., 2004, Exps 2 and 3) required subjects to perform the prospective memory task under different attentional loads. In the normal load condition, subjects simply performed the word-rating task. In the demanding load condition, subjects in addition had to monitor an audio stream of digits for two consecutive odd digits. Of most interest is the effect of this high attentional load in the high cue–intended action association condition, because this condition is the one for which the spontaneous associative retrieval process should be most prominent. That is, in a prospective memory situation, multiple cognitive processes might be exploited to support retrieval (see Einstein et al., 2005, Exp. 4), and accordingly to investigate a particular retrieval process it is important to examine conditions in which the process of interest likely will be predominant (cf. Einstein & McDaniel, 2005).

In a first experiment, prospective memory was slightly but nonsignificantly higher under normal attentional load ($M = 0.90$) than under the more demanding attentional load ($M = 0.86$). A second experiment confirmed that there was no reliable difference in prospective memory as a function of the attentional resources demanded for the ongoing activities ($Ms = 0.86$ for both attentional load conditions). These results are entirely in line with the idea that prospective memory retrieval in this condition was reflexive and relatively automatic.

But, perhaps the digit monitoring task did not draw sufficient resources to compromise performance of a resource demanding prospective memory retrieval process. This interpretation can be ruled out by results from a low cue–intention association condition in which other retrieval processes might be recruited (see McDaniel et al., 2004, for details). For this condition, there was a notable and significant prospective memory decline in the demanding attentional condition ($M = 0.66$) relative to the normal attention condition ($M = 0.82$).

Are There Other Cognitive Processes that Might Support Spontaneous Prospective Memory Retrieval?

A long-held view embedded in theories of recognition memory is that recognition can rely on familiarity (e.g., Atkinson & Juola, 1974; Jacoby, Kelley, & Dywan, 1989; Jacoby, Woloshyn, & Kelley, 1989; Mandler, 1980), with familiarity often being assumed as a fundamental, primitive quality of an item. Whittlesea and Williams (2001a, 2001b) have developed the idea that familiarity is an attribution derived from a more basic cognitive process. Whittlesea and Williams' theory is that people chronically evaluate the processing quality of items and that people are sensitive to the discrepancy between the actual and expected processing quality of a particular event. For instance, on boarding a bus a person may see the face of someone they have previously encountered among many unknown faces, perhaps producing discrepancy in the fluency or quality of processing between the previously encountered face and the other unknown faces. An attribution for the discrepancy is generated (as the person's explanation for the discrepancy), with the particular attribution depending on the context, biases, and disposition of the person. In a context in which subjects are asked to make recognition decisions, discrepancy tends to produce an attribution of familiarity, thereby leading to a positive recognition decision. Although, Whittlesea and Williams have developed this view to explain how people make recognition decisions, they note that the nature of an attribution depends on the context. In the above example of the person on the bus, the discrepancy associated with the face of the previously encountered person (but not recollected as previously encountered) may be attributed to the attractiveness of the face (say for an individual who is in the market for a partner).

We suggest that the putative chronic process of discrepancy attribution serves as another possible route to prospective memory retrieval (McDaniel et al., 2004). Specifically, in many contexts subjects are not performing recognition judgments, and here discrepancy can elicit a sense of significance (cf. Jacoby & Dallas, 1981; Whittlesea & Williams, 2001a), which in turn can stimulate consideration of the source of the significance. For instance, I may form the intention to give Roddy Roediger a message, thereby activating memory representations of Roddy. At work the next day, I encounter a number of colleagues, creating an expectancy of the coherence or quality of processing experienced when I pass a colleague in the hallway. When I encounter Roddy, I may have an increased coherence or quality of processing that is unexpected or exceeds the norm, with the ensuing sense of significance stimulating a search that can result in retrieval of the prospective memory task (or perhaps the more general notion that there is something I need to do).

To explore the idea that chronic discrepancy-detection processes can support prospective memory retrieval, we have manipulated the prior exposure of the *nontarget* items in the ongoing activity. Consider that in a typical prospective memory experiment, the target event is typically presented in the instructions prior to the ongoing activity, whereas the nontarget events are not. Accordingly, the quality or coherence of processing of the prospective memory events may be discrepant from that of the nontargets, thereby possibly leading to an attribution of significance for the target event.

In an initial experiment, McDaniel et al. (2004, Exp. 1) attempted to reduce this discrepancy in the processing experience for the nontarget items in the ongoing task (the word-rating task described in a previous section) relative to the prospective memory target items, by including the nontarget words in a word list learning task administered at the outset of the experiment. Thus in this condition (termed the *low-discrepancy* condition), both nontarget words and prospective memory targets were processed prior to the ongoing activity (the former in the word list learning task and the latter during the prospective memory instructions).

For another group, the word-list learning task included none of the nontargets in the word-rating task (the *high-discrepancy* condition). In this situation the fluent, coherent processing of prospective memory targets (due to previous presentation during the initial instructions) is presumably discrepant with the standard of processing established by the nontarget items, none of which was previously presented.

Note that the targets in both groups are identical, the prospective memory response is identical, the cover activity is identical, and the nontargets in the cover activity are identical. Most, if not all, views of prospective memory would anticipate no differences in prospective memory performance across the two groups. In contrast, the discrepancy-plus-search view makes the novel prediction that prospective memory performance will decline in the low-discrepancy group (pre-exposure of nontargets) relative to the high-discrepancy group (no pre-exposure of nontargets). The results confirmed the prediction, with prospective memory responding significantly lower in the low-discrepancy group ($M = 0.77$) than the high-discrepancy group ($M = 0.94$; see also McDaniel et al., 2004, Exp. 2).

The above result is not completely decisive, however. Perhaps the effect rested on the prospective memory target being relatively more familiar in the high-discrepancy (no pre-exposure of nontargets) than the low-discrepancy condition (cf. McDaniel, 1995) or the nontargets being distracting or interfering in the low-discrepancy (nontarget pre-exposure) condition. To provide converging support for the discrepancy attribution interpretation, Breneiser and McDaniel (in press) implemented a nontarget pre-exposure condition in which processing of the target event would be *less* coherent or fluent than the expectation created by the nontarget words. In this experiment, for the high-discrepancy condition the nontargets were studied four times in preparation for a recognition test prior to the critical ongoing word-rating task. Note that in this condition, relative familiarity (or fluency) for the target item would be low and distraction (interference) created by the pre-exposure of the nontarget items would remain present or possibly increase. Thus, if either of these were the critical factors affecting prospective memory, then this condition should be no better, and might be worse, than the condition in which nontarget items were studied once.

By contrast, the discrepancy-attribution idea clearly embraces the possibility that a target that is less coherently or fluently processed than expected will be discrepant, and in the present context such discrepancy could be attributed to significance. A feeling of significance could in turn lead to further consideration of the prospective memory target, thereby leading to retrieval of the intention. Consistent with this idea, when nontargets were studied four times prior to the ongoing task, prospective memory was significantly better ($M = 0.77$) than when nontargets were once-studied ($M = 0.50$). Taken together, these two experiments are directly in line with the notion that discrepancy-attribution processes provide another relatively spontaneous route by which prospective memory retrieval can occur.

SUMMARY

For over 100 years, the scientific study of memory has almost exclusively followed the tradition championed by Ebbinghaus (1885/1964), in which the subject "has been required to recall [or recognize] at the experimenter's request rather than at a time when he would normally do so" (Wilkins & Baddeley, 1978, pp. 27–28). Theoretical constructs about the processes of memory retrieval—such as received ideas that the cognitive system supports retrieval by invoking a retrieval mode (Tulving, 1983), the retrieval mode allows subjects to explicitly consider environmental events as possible retrieval cues, and the retrieval mode incurs resource demands that in part contribute to the effortful nature of retrieval (Craik, Govoni, Naveh-Benjamin, & Anderson, 1996)—hinge on the assumption that recall is requested by the experimenter (or some active agent). Arguably, however, such prompted recall is not the predominant expression of memory in everyday situations (see Wilkins & Baddeley, 1978), and prompted recall is, by definition, not a characteristic of prospective memory. Thus, a main theme of our chapter is that the study of prospective memory represents an intriguing departure from the standard laboratory "memory preparation" common to the memory literature.

The foregoing considerations raise the central question of how retrieval is stimulated in prospective memory. One general answer in the contemporary literature has been to suppose that the person provides his or her own retrieval prompts, perhaps through self-initiated retrieval processes (Craik, 1986), preparatory attentional processes that prompt recognition checks for the prospective memory target event (Smith, 2003), or resources devoted to maintaining a prospective memory retrieval mode (Guynn, 2003).

Alternatively, we have argued that prospective memory retrieval need not require such resource demanding self-prompting. Instead, resurrecting the historical roots of Ebbinghaus (1885/1964), Freud (1909/1952), and Lewin (1961), and building on more contemporary theory (Moscovitch, 1994; Whittlesea & Williams, 2001a, 2001b), we suggest that prospective remembering can be mediated by a spontaneous retrieval process that is not initiated by a request to remember, a retrieval mode, or monitoring processes. To compel the case, we offered evidence showing that prospective remembering does not necessarily incur a cost to ongoing activity (i.e., no monitoring), and that retrieval of the prospective memory intention can occur even when the intention to retrieve has been suspended (i.e., no self-initiated retrieval or retrieval mode). Further, we showed that retrieval success is influenced by the association between the target event and the intended action, and retrieval can occur under divided attention conditions (implicating a relatively automatic associative memory process; cf. Moscovitch).

Thus, we have come full circle, returning to Ebbinghaus' (1885/1964) observation that one of three basic types of memory is the spontaneous appearance of a mental state "without any act of will" that is recognized as previously experienced. We suggest that the laboratory study of prospective memory, under appropriate conditions (see McDaniel & Einstein, 2000; Einstein et al., 2005), provides a foundation on which researchers can begin to investigate and understand this type of spontaneous remembering with the thoroughness with which "prompted retrieval" has been studied over the long history of memory research.

REFERENCES

Atkinson, R. C., & Juola, J. F. (1974). Search and decision processes in recognition memory. In D. H. Krantz, R. C. Atkinson, R. D. Luce, & P. Suppes (Eds.), *Contemporary developments in mathematical psychology: Vol. I. Learning, memory and thinking* (pp. xiii, 299). Oxford, UK: Oxford University Press.

Breneiser, J. E. (2004). *Prospective memory retrieval: Associativity, discrepancy, and individual differences*. Unpublished master's thesis, University of New Mexico, Albuquerque.

Breneiser, J. E., & McDaniel, M. A. (in press). Discrepancy processes in prospective memory retrieval. *Psychonomic Bulletin & Review*.

Burgess, P. W., & Shallice, T. (1997). The relationship between prospective and retrospective memory: Neuropsychological evidence. In M. A. Conway (Ed.), *Cognitive models of memory* (pp. 247–272). Cambridge, MA: MIT Press.

Craik, F. I. M. (1986). A functional account of age differences in memory. In F. Klix & H. Hangendorf (Eds.), *Human memory and cognitive capabilities: Mechanisms and performances* (pp. 409–422). Amsterdam: Elsevier.

Craik, F. I. M., Govoni, R., Naveh-Benjamin, M., & Anderson, N. D. (1996). The effects of divided attention on encoding and retrieval processes in human memory. *Journal of Experimental Psychology: General, 125*, 159–180.

Ebbinghaus, H. (1964). *Memory: A contribution to experimental psychology*. New York: Dover. (Original work published 1885; translated 1913)

Einstein, G. O., & McDaniel, M. A. (1996). Retrieval processes in prospective memory: Theoretical approaches and some new empirical findings. In M. Brandimonte, G. Einstein, & M. McDaniel (Eds.), *Prospective memory: Theory and applications* (pp. 115–142). Hillsdale, NJ: Lawrence Erlbaum Associates, Inc.

Einstein, G. O., & McDaniel, M. A. (2005). Prospective memory: Multiple retrieval processes. *Current Directions in Psychological Science, 14*, 286–290.

Einstein, G. O., McDaniel, M. A., Thomas, R., Mayfield, S., Shank, H., Morrisette, N., & Breneiser, J. (2005). Multiple processes in prospective memory retrieval: Factors determining monitoring versus spontaneous retrieval. *Journal of Experimental Psychology: General, 134*, 327–342.

Freud, S. (1952). *Psychopathology of everyday life*. New York: Mentor. (Original work published 1909)

Guynn, M. J. (2003). A two-process model of strategic monitoring in event-based prospective memory: Activation/retrieval mode and checking. *International Journal of Psychology, 38*(4), 245–256.

Guynn, M. J., McDaniel, M. A., & Einstein, G. O. (2001). Remembering to perform actions: A different type of memory? In H. D. Zimmer, R. L. Cohen, M. J. Guynn, J. Engelkamp, R. Kormi-Nouri, & M. A. Foley (Eds.), *Memory for action: A distinct form of episodic memory?* (pp. 25–48). New York: Oxford University Press.

Jacoby, L. L., & Dallas, M. (1981). On the relationship between autobiographical memory and perceptual learning. *Journal of Experimental Psychology: General, 110*(3), 306–340.

Jacoby, L. L., Kelley, C. M., & Dywan, J. (1989). Memory attributions. In H. L. Roediger

& F. I. M. Craik (Eds.), *Varieties of memory and consciousness: Essays in honor of Endel Tulving* (pp. 391–422). Hillsdale, NJ: Lawrence Erlbaum Associates, Inc.

Jacoby, L. L., Woloshyn, B., & Kelley, C. M. (1989). Becoming famous without being recognized: Unconscious influences of memory produced by dividing attention. *Journal of Experimental Psychology: General, 118*, 115–125.

Lewin, K. (1961). Intention, will, and need. In T. Shipley (Ed.), *Classics in psychology* (pp. 1234–1289). New York: Philosophical Library.

Mandler, G. (1980). Recognizing: The judgment of prior occurrence. *Psychological Review, 87*, 252–271.

Marsh, R. L., Hicks, J. L., Cook, G. I., Hansen, J. S., & Pallos, A. L. (2003). Interference to ongoing activities covaries with the characteristics of an event-based intention. *Journal of Experimental Psychology: Learning, Memory, and Cognition, 29*(5), 861–870.

Maylor, E. E. (1998). Changes in event-based prospective memory across adulthood. *Aging, Neuropsychology, and Cognition, 5*, 107–128.

McDaniel, M. A. (1995). Prospective memory: Progress and processes. In D. L. Medin (Ed.), *The psychology of learning and motivation* (Vol. 33; pp. 191–222). San Diego, CA: Academic Press.

McDaniel, M. A., & Einstein, G. O. (1993). The importance of cue familiarity and cue distinctiveness in prospective memory. *Memory, 1*, 23–41.

McDaniel, M. A., & Einstein, G. O. (2000). Strategic and automatic processes in prospective memory retrieval: A multiprocess framework. *Applied Cognitive Psychology, 14*, S127–S144.

McDaniel, M. A., Guynn, M. J., Einstein, G. O., & Breneiser, J. (2004). Cue-focused and reflexive-associative processes in prospective memory retrieval. *Journal of Experimental Psychology: Learning, Memory, and Cognition, 30*, 605–614.

McDaniel, M. A., Robinson-Riegler, B., & Einstein, G. O. (1998). Prospective remembering: Perceptually driven or conceptually driven processes? *Memory and Cognition, 26*, 121–134.

Moscovitch, M. (1994). Memory and working with memory: Evaluation of a component process model and comparisons with other models. In D. L. Schacter & E. Tulving (Eds.), *Memory systems* (pp. 269–310). Cambridge, MA: MIT Press.

Nelson, D. L., McEvoy, C. L., & Schreiber, T. A. (1998). *The University of South Florida word association, rhyme, and word fragment norms*. Retrieved March, 2001, from http://www.usf.edu/Free_Association

Reitman, J. S. (1974). Without surreptitious rehearsal, information in short-term memory decays. *Journal of Verbal Learning and Verbal Behavior, 13*(4), 365–377.

Roediger, H. L. (1985). Remembering Ebbinghaus. *Contemporary Psychology, 30*, 519–523.

Smith, R. E. (2003). The cost of remembering to remember in event-based prospective memory: Investigating the capacity demands of delayed intention performance. *Journal of Experimental Psychology: Learning, Memory, and Cognition, 29*, 347–361.

Smith, R. E., & Bayen, U. J. (2004). A multinomial model of event-based prospective memory. *Journal of Experimental Psychology: Learning, Memory, and Cognition, 30*(4), 756–777.

Tulving, E. (1983). *Elements of episodic memory*. New York: Oxford University Press.

Tulving, E. (2004, May). *Memory, consciousness, and time*. Keynote address presented at the 16th annual convention of the American Psychological Society, Chicago, IL.

Whittlesea, B. W. A., & Williams, L. D. (2001a). The discrepancy-attribution hypothesis: I. The heuristic basis of feelings of familiarity. *Journal of Experimental Psychology: Learning, Memory, and Cognition, 27,* 3–13.

Whittlesea, B. W. A., & Williams, L. D. (2001b). The discrepancy-attribution hypothesis: II. Expectation, uncertainty, surprise, and feelings of familiarity. *Journal of Experimental Psychology: Learning, Memory, and Cognition, 27,* 14–33.

Wilkins, A. J., & Baddeley, A. D. (1978). Remembering to recall in everyday life: An approach to absent-mindedness. In M. M. Gruneberg, P. E. Morris, & R. N. Sykes (Eds.), *Practical aspects of memory* (pp. 27–34). London: Academic Press.

15

Individual Differences in Working Memory Capacity and Retrieval: A Cue-Dependent Search Approach

NASH UNSWORTH and RANDALL W. ENGLE

T he ability to accurately and efficiently retrieve information from memory is a critical component for successful performance on a number of tasks. Take for instance, performance on a reading comprehension task. Here, an individual is required to read a number of passages and then answer questions concerning those passages. Assuming that the individual accurately encodes and stores (e.g., Melton, 1963) the information, all that is needed to answer the questions is accurate retrieval of the desired information. The pertinent question is, how does the individual go about retrieving the desired information? Additionally, what factors are needed in order for the desired information to be accessed? These basic questions regarding human memory retrieval provide the core concepts in understanding remembering; that is, as advocated by Roediger (2000) and Tulving (1983), in order to understand memory, we must understand retrieval processes.

The work presented in this chapter was heavily influenced by the work of Roediger (2000), in terms of the importance of retrieval processes. Additionally, as will become evident later on, the work presented here was influenced by the Baddeley and Hitch (1974) working memory model, Tulving's arguments for cue-dependent forgetting (Tulving, 1983), Watkins's notion of cue-overload (1979), Shiffrin's elaboration of these concepts into a formal model of cue-dependent search (1970; see also Raaijmakers & Shiffrin, 1981), Glenberg's emphasis on temporal-contextual search (1987), and Wixted and Rohrer's work examining cumulative latency distributions in terms of a random search model (1994; Rohrer & Wixted, 1994). Furthermore, the work here has been influenced by Cronbach and others' (1957; Cohen, 1994; Underwood, 1975) call to combine experimental investigations with individual differences analyses in order to gain a better understanding of the underlying process. Thus, in this chapter we will advocate the view that not only is it important to examine retrieval processes from an experimental point of view, but that investigations of individual differences can also aid us in our understanding of retrieval processes. As proposed by Underwood (1975) and others (Cohen, 1994; Cronbach, 1957), we will discuss an integration of experimental and differential approaches to understanding retrieval processes and individual differences therein. Specifically, we will examine how individual differences in working memory capacity are related to individual differences in retrieval and what this tells us about the nature of working memory capacity and its relation to higher-order cognition.

INDIVIDUAL DIFFERENCES IN WORKING MEMORY CAPACITY

Before discussing the relationship between working memory capacity and retrieval, we will briefly describe working memory capacity, how it is measured, and review the importance of working memory capacity in predicting performance on both higher-order and lower-order cognitive tasks. Working memory is considered to be a system responsible for active maintenance and online manipulation of information over short intervals. In our view, working memory consists of a subset of activated traces above threshold (some of which are highly active), strategies for maintaining activation of those traces, and an attention component. Thus, our view of working memory emphasizes the interaction of attention and memory in the service of complex cognition. In order to measure the capacity of working memory, researchers have relied on complex working memory span tasks based on the working memory model of Baddeley and Hitch (1974). Beginning with Daneman and Carpenter (1980), these tasks combine a simple memory span task with a secondary processing component. Initially, the idea was that these tasks would better measure a dynamic working memory system that traded off processing and storage resources. Thus, in these tasks participants are required to engage in some form of processing activity while trying to remember a set of to-be-remembered (TBR) items. As an example of such a task, consider the operation span task, which requires participants to solve math operations while trying to remember unrelated words. Here, participants are required to solve math operations while trying to remember words presented after the operations. At the recall signal participants must try and recall the presented words in the correct serial order. Several variations exist of this basic paradigm, with most variations consisting of different processing tasks. These include reading sentences (Daneman & Carpenter, 1980), solving math operations (Turner & Engle, 1989), counting different colored figures (Case, Kurland, & Goldberg, 1982), and determining if a figure is symmetrical (Kane et al., 2004). Additionally, variation exists in the type of TBR stimuli that is used. These include remembering words, letters, digits, and spatial locations.

Despite all these variations, performance on these complex span tasks has been shown to covary with performance on a number of both higher-order and lower-order cognitive tasks. Indeed, the original work of Daneman and Carpenter (1980) demonstrated that performance on complex span tasks was highly related to reading comprehension performance as measured by the verbal portion of the Scholastic Aptitude Test (SAT). Thus, as with the example provided in the beginning, reading comprehension is highly related to performance on a memory task. These complex span tasks are also related to other higher-order processes including vocabulary learning (Daneman & Green, 1986), complex learning (Kyllonen & Stephens, 1990), and fluid abilities (Conway, Cowan, Bunting, Therriault, & Minkoff, 2002; Engle, Tuholski, Laughlin, & Conway, 1999; Kane et al., 2004; Kyllonen & Christal, 1990). This impressive list demonstrates the predictive utility of working memory capacity (WMC) in a number of research domains.

Additional work has shown that WMC is also implicated in performance on many lower-order attentional tasks. This work has demonstrated that individuals who perform well on measures of WMC tend to perform better on basic attention tasks in a variety of conditions. This includes performance on tasks such as Stroop (Kane & Engle, 2003; Long & Prat, 2002), antisaccade (Kane, Bleckley, Conway, & Engle, 2001; Unsworth, Schrock, & Engle, 2004), dichotic listening (Conway, Cowan, & Bunting, 2001), flankers (Heitz & Engle, 2005) and tasks that require object-based attentional allocation (Bleckley, Durso, Crutchfield, Engle, & Khanna, 2004). Clearly, then, WMC is an important predictor of behavior in a number of different situations.

WORKING MEMORY CAPACITY AND RETRIEVAL COMPETITION

Over the last few years, it has become clear that variation in WMC is related to variation in the ability to retrieve information in the presence of interference. Here we examine a number of studies that have demonstrated a relationship between WMC and retrieval competition. In most of these studies, extreme groups of high and low WMC participants were selected based on their scores on a complex span task (typically operation span). Only participants falling in the upper (high spans) and lower (low spans) quartiles of the distribution were selected and asked to perform a basic memory task. The goal in each study is to examine when and where WMC differences will occur. That is, the goal is to understand when individual differences in WMC will covary with performance in meaningful conditions on another memory task.

The first such study to examine WMC differences in memory retrieval was that of Cantor and Engle (1993). Cantor and Engle were interested in the extent to which individual differences in WMC would predict performance on a fact retrieval task developed by Anderson (1974). In this task participants learn a set of propositions such as "The teacher is in the park," "The lawyer is in the park," "The lawyer is in the boat," and so on. In such a task the number of sentences that share a common concept (e.g., lawyer or park) is manipulated. Some concepts will be linked to only one sentence making for fairly accurate and rapid retrieval of information, while other concepts will be associated with many sentences and retrieval will be less accurate and delayed. Importantly, in order to ensure that all participants had accurately encoded the information, Cantor and Engle required participants to learn the sentences to a criterion of three perfect recall cycles. Later in a verification phase, participants had to make a speeded response to indicate whether a presented sentence was one that was learned or not. The typical "fan effect" is that the more sentences that are linked with a given concept, the longer it takes to indicate whether the sentence was presented. Cantor and Engle found that, as fan size increased, low spans were slower than high spans to indicate that a sentence was presented. That is, as fan size increased, low spans were much slower to retrieve information than high spans, even though both groups learned the information to the same levels initially. Cantor and Engle also found that the correlation between WMC and reading comprehension mentioned above was eliminated when the slope of the fan effect for each individual participant was partialed out. Thus, the ability to retrieve information in the presence of competing information differentiated high and low WMC participants and accounted for the covariation between WMC and reading comprehension.

Conway and Engle (1994) followed up on these findings by examining WMC differences in a Sternberg item recognition task (Sternberg, 1966). Like the Cantor and Engle (1993) study, Conway and Engle had high and low spans learn information to a criterion and then examined differences in the time taken to retrieve information. Specifically, Conway and Engle had participants learn sets of two, four, six, or eight items associated with a digit that reflected the set size. For instance, the letters Z, G, R, B might be associated with the digit 4. Participants learned these sets to a criterion of three perfect recall cycles. During the verification stage, participants were presented with a digit (e.g., 4) followed shortly by a letter (e.g., G) and were required to make a speeded response indicating whether the letter was part of that set. Important for the current discussion, Conway and Engle manipulated interference among the items by having some items belong to more than one set (i.e., the letter G could belong to both Set 4 and Set 8). In those experiments where interference was present, Conway and Engle found large WMC differences. However, in those experiments where no interference was present (i.e., letters belonged to one and only one set), WMC differences did not emerge. These findings held for both letters and words. Thus, like the Cantor and Engle findings, WMC differences seem to occur when items have to be retrieved in the presence of interference. If strong interference is not present low spans retrieve information as rapidly as high spans.

This basic finding of WMC differences in retrieval under conditions of interference has been replicated a number of times. For instance, Bunting, Conway, and Heitz (2004) replicated and extended the Cantor and Engle (1993) and Conway and Engle (1994) findings by mixing the methods. Specifically, Bunting et al. examined WMC differences in the fan effect both when items were shared across sets and when items were not shared across sets. Bunting et al. found that individual differences in WMC predicted larger fan effects only when items were shared across sets, but not when items were unique to each set. Similar to the Conway and Engle findings, these results suggest that variation in WMC only occurs under conditions of interference at retrieval. When a large number of items are associated with a common cue, as in the fan effect, low spans will be less efficient at retrieving the desired information than high spans.

Together, these results suggest that variation in WMC is associated with individual differences in the ability to deal with cue overload as suggested by Watkins and Watkins (1975; see also Watkins, 1979). Cue overload is the observation that the more items that are associated with a given cue, the lower the probability of retrieving any given item will be. Watkins and Watkins suggested that proactive interference (PI) could be conceptualized as a cue overload problem. Items from a current list are associated with the same retrieval cue as items from previous lists leading to an overall decrement in recall. For instance, in the Brown–Peterson task (Brown, 1958; Peterson & Peterson, 1959) subjects are presented with a list of items followed by distractor activity for varying amounts of time and then are asked to recall the presented items. Typically recall for the first trial is quite good and then decreases substantially thereafter (the typical PI effect). However, if on subsequent trials the nature of the TBR items is changed (e.g., from one semantic category to another) performance tends to rebound, and a release from PI occurs (Wickens, Born, & Allen, 1963). Thus, according to Watkins and Watkins the reason that PI occurs is because items are being associated with the same retrieval cue (e.g., animals) and as the number of items associated with the cue increases, the probability of selecting any one item decreases. However, if items are subsumed under a new retrieval cue (e.g., flowers) cue overload is negated and a release from PI is obtained.

If it is the case that low spans are less efficient at dealing with cue overload than high spans (as suggested) we should see that low spans are more susceptible to the effects of proactive interference. Relevant data come from a study by Kane and Engle (2000), who tested high and low spans on a version of the Brown–Peterson type task in PI build and release conditions. Specifically, participants were presented with a list of 10 items from a given semantic category (e.g., animals), followed by 16 s of distractor activity, and finally recall for 20 s. In order to assess the build-up and release of PI, participants were given three lists from the same semantic category and then on the fourth list were switched to a new semantic category (e.g., countries). In their Experiment 1, Kane and Engle found typical PI build and release effects. Importantly, Kane and Engle found that low spans were more susceptible to the effects of PI, as indicated by a steeper drop in the number of words recalled across the first three lists, than were high spans. However, once participants were switched to a new semantic category on the fourth list, high and low spans showed equivalent release effects. Thus, in accord with a cue-overload interpretation, low spans were less efficient at retrieving items as the number of items subsumed under a given retrieval cue increased than were high spans. Given a new retrieval cue, however, reduced the number of items associated with the cue and allowed both span groups to retrieve more items. Furthermore, Kane and Engle showed that this recall advantage for high spans was eliminated when the task was performed under a secondary load at either encoding or retrieval. Kane and Engle argued that attentional control abilities were needed to combat PI at both encoding and retrieval and high spans were better able to use attention to combat the disruptive effects of PI.

Clearly, these results suggest that one ability that is tapped by complex working memory span measures is the ability to retrieve information in an interference rich environment. Further support for the notion that variation in WMC is related to variation in PI resistance comes from a large scale factor analytic study conducted by Friedman and Miyake (2004). Friedman and Miyake collected data from a large number of participants on a diverse array of interference and inhibition tasks. Pertinent to the current discussion is the fact that Friedman and Miyake assessed performance on three different memory tasks under conditions of PI. These included assessing PI in a version of the Brown–Peterson task, assessing PI in a paired-associates task, and assessing PI in a cued recall task. Using a latent variable analysis, Friedman and Miyake found that resistance to PI was a significant predictor of recall performance on a version of the reading span task. Participants who scored high on the reading span task showed less susceptibility to PI based on performance from three different tasks. Thus, performance on a putative measure of WMC was substantially related to the ability to retrieve information when interference was present.

RETRIEVAL COMPETITION IN COMPLEX SPANS

All of the results reviewed thus far suggest that individual differences in WMC are related to the ability to deal with interference from information that has been presented recently. Individuals higher in WMC are better able than individuals lower in WMC to retrieve information in a variety of paradigms when competition between items is high. This conclusion is based on correlational evidence in which performance on putative measures of WMC covaries with performance on a number of other memory tasks under conditions of interference. This work provides important insights into the nature of WMC and its predictive power. However, in order to better understand WMC it is important to examine performance on the complex span tasks themselves and determine which aspects of performance are important for individual differences. To this end, a number of studies have examined how interference influences individual differences in the span tasks and their correlation with measures of higher-order cognition.

For instance, May, Hasher, and Kane (1999) examined how PI affected scores on complex span tasks. May et al. hypothesized that one important contributor to performance on complex span measures was susceptibility to PI. May et al. argued that PI builds across lists in the complex spans and thus, individuals who are more susceptible to PI will have lower span scores. Furthermore, May et al. argued that because complex span tasks are typically administered in an ascending format, PI will be greatest for the largest list lengths and thus, only participants who can combat PI will be able to correctly retrieve items on those longer list lengths. In order to test this hypothesis, May et al. employed two experimental manipulations. First, May et al. manipulated the presentation format such that some participants received the standard ascending format, whereas other participants received a descending presentation format. If PI selectively influences the longest list lengths in the standard condition, then reversing the presentation format should allow participants (particularly low spans) to achieve higher recall performance on long list lengths in the absence of PI. Second, May et al. manipulated context between trials by having participants perform an unrelated task in between each trial. Thus, if PI occurs because the current and preceding trial share the same contextual cue (e.g., Gorfein, 1987), then changing context should reduce PI and boost span scores. May et al. found that span scores were substantially higher when both PI reducing methods were combined. In a subsequent study, Lustig, May, and Hasher (2001) replicated these findings and showed that the correlations between the complex span tasks and a measure of higher-order cognition (e.g., prose recall) only occurred in the presence of PI. In the PI reduction conditions, the correlation was near zero. This provides supporting evidence that interference susceptibility is an important contributor to performance on putative measures of WMC and their relation to higher-order cognitive abilities.

A study by Bunting (2006) replicates and extends these findings. Bunting was interested in how interference both across and within lists influenced retrieval in complex spans and their relation to higher-order cognition. Like the work of May et al. (1999), Bunting examined how manipulations that would reduce interference would lead to higher span scores. Bunting had participants perform three versions of the operation span task. One version (the control) was a standard version of the operation span task in which the TBR items were words. In a second version (interlist experimental), created to examine between trial interference, Bunting had participants perform the operation span task in which the TBR items switched from digits to words across lists. Like the procedure of Wickens et al. (1963), mentioned previously, this procedure allowed for a build-up and release from PI across lists. For instance, the first three lists might require remembering digits, while the next three lists might require remembering words. A third version (intralist experimental) of the operation span task was created to examine how within trial interference would influence span scores. In order to examine within list interference in complex span tasks, Bunting relied on a procedure first used by Young and Supa (1941). Young and Supa manipulated whether a list consisted of all one type of item (e.g., digits or words) or whether a list consisted of a switch between items (e.g., digits and then words). They found that recall was much better on lists with two types of TBR items compared to lists composed of only one type of item. Bunting used a similar methodology within the operation span task in which the type of TBR item (digits vs. words) switched half-way through the list.

Thus, Bunting (2006) created three versions of a complex span task, each varying in the degree of interference within and between trials. Using these tasks, a number of important findings emerged. First, proportion correct in the two experimental tasks was higher than in the control task. That is, in those tasks in which interference reduction methods were used, recall performance was better than in a control task. This occurred when reducing interference both between and within lists, thus replicating the findings of May et al. (1999; see also Kane & Engle, 2000; Young and Supa, 1941). Second, these effects were qualified by position between and within lists. Specifically, when PI was at maximum across lists, performance in the control and interlist experimental versions of the operation span task was equivalent. However, when a release occurred in the interlist experimental task (e.g., switching from digits to words across lists), performance in the interlist experimental task was better than performance in the control task.

Additionally, a similar pattern occurred when examining within list interference. Performance was better on the intralist experimental task than the control task, and this effect was more pronounced for second half than first half items. In both cases, presenting participants with a new cue resulted in better recall performance. Finally, Bunting examined how each version of the operation span task would correlate with performance on a measure of fluid abilities (Raven Advanced Progressive Matrices; Raven, Raven, & Court, 1998). Bunting found that the correlation between recall performance on the operation span and accuracy on the Raven was highest in conditions in which interference was high, and was lowest in conditions where interference was reduced. Thus, similar to the findings of Cantor and Engle (1993), this suggests that the covariation between measures of WMC and measures of higher-order cognition is due, in part, to the ability to retrieve items in the presence of interference.

These results are consistent with the cue-overload principle advocated by Watkins (1979). In terms of a cue-overload framework, the release from PI across lists occurs because items are subsumed under a new cue which is not overloaded. A cue-overload approach predicts the same effect for within list interference. When item type switches within a list, items are now subsumed under a new cue, thus reducing the number of items subsumed under one cue by half. As with the work reviewed previously, these results suggest that an important aspect of performance on the complex span tasks in the ability to deal with cue-overload. Additional work from our lab supports these notions. For instance, consider the within list interference effect. This is essentially a variation of a list-length effect. Here, all items are subsumed under the same cue ("list") and all items are target items. This contrasts with the build-up of PI across lists, in which case the items are subsumed under the same cue, but only some of the items are targets. Thus, within list interference occurs when several items are subsumed under the same retrieval cue and the items compete for retrieval. Having two separate retrieval cues for a given list, as Bunting (2006) did, reduces cue overload and increases probability of recall. If individual differences in WMC are partially due to differences in the ability to deal with cue overload, then we should see complex span differences in list-length effects. That is, those participants who are better able to use cues to guide the retrieval process (e.g., high spans), should show smaller list-length effects than those participants who are poorer at using retrieval cues (e.g., low spans).

Relevant data comes from a study by Unsworth and Engle (2006a). We examined performance on two verbal complex span measures (reading and operation span) for list lengths of two–five. We found that low spans had steeper list-length functions than high spans, suggesting that low spans suffered from more cue overload than do high spans. Why is this the case if the number of items per list is the same for the two groups? That is, on a list length of five, there are five target items for both high- and low-span participants, thus both groups should have five items subsumed under the retrieval cue. If low spans are suffering from more cue overload than high spans, how are more items subsumed under the retrieval cue for low span than for high spans? We suggest two reasons. First, we suggest that low spans are less efficient at using context cues to discriminate across lists. Thus, both current target items and items from previous trials are subsumed under the retrieval cue for low spans (i.e., more PI). Second, we suggest that low spans are less efficient at using context cues even within a list. Specifically, one way to reduce cue-overload effects within a list is to use context cues that differentiate items. In accord with Glenberg's temporal distinctiveness theory (1987; Glenberg & Swanson, 1986), and Tulving's encoding specificity principle (1983), items whose context at retrieval best matches context at encoding will be associated with a high probability of recall. As with the reduction of within list interference effects found by Bunting (2006), perhaps high spans are better at using context cues to reduce interference both between and within lists than low spans.

Support for this position comes from a study by Unsworth and Engle (2006b). In this study, we examined the different types of error responses in two complex span tasks (reading and operation span). Most relevant to the current discussion is an examination of input omissions and intrusion. Input omissions are errors in which the correct target item was not recalled. Instead of recalling the correct target item, participants either left the space blank on the recall sheet or intruded an item. Thus, intrusions are a subset of input omissions. We showed that low spans made more input omissions and intrusions than high spans. Furthermore, an examination of these errors by serial position for a list-length of five qualified these results. Specifically, both span groups recalled the last item presented with very high accuracy. However, the further back in time an item was presented, generally, the lower the probability of correctly recalling that item. This was especially true for low spans. We suggested that these results could be interpreted in terms of Glenberg's temporal distinctiveness theory (1987). Those items whose encoded context is similar to the retrieval context were associated with a high recall accuracy. Items whose encoded context was dissimilar to the retrieved context were associated with a low accuracy. Furthermore, those individuals who are better at using context cues to guide the retrieval process (i.e., high spans) had better recall at nearly all serial positions than participants who are poorer at using context cues (i.e., low spans). An examination of intrusion errors suggested that intrusions were most likely to occur at the first serial position and were more likely for low than for high spans. Together, these results suggest that low spans are poorer at recalling items in complex span tasks because they are less efficient at using context cues to reduce cue overload both between and within lists than high spans.

A MODEL OF WMC AND RETRIEVAL

Throughout this chapter, we have alluded to individual differences in WMC and retrieval as being due to differences in interference susceptibility in terms of cue overload. Recently, we have begun to explore a model of WMC and retrieval based on a cue-dependent search process (Unsworth & Engle, 2005). Specifically, we have argued that individuals who differ in WMC differ in their ability to use cues to guide a search process of secondary memory to reactivate representations that are no longer being actively maintained (e.g., Shiffrin, 1970). That is, we assume that there is an upper limit to how much information can be actively maintained and thus, in some situations relevant information will have to retrieved back into working memory. In this view, WMC is not only the ability to maintain distinct representations in active state, but also the ability to use cues to search and reactive representations. The key to this search process is the ability to delimit the search set to only target items via the use of different cues (e.g., temporal, contextual, categorical, etc.). Importantly, retrieval from secondary memory is fraught with potential problems such as PI. As PI builds, the search set gets progressively larger leading to inefficient retrieval (i.e., cue overload; Watkins, 1979; Wixted & Rohrer, 1993). Thus, as argued throughout this chapter, low spans suffer from cue overload to a greater extent than high spans because they are less capable at using cues to guide the search process.

An elegant way of testing this model comes from an examination of response latency distributions in free recall paradigms. Over the last 60 years, researchers have occasionally relied on cumulative latency distributions obtained in recall paradigms to gain a better understanding of retrieval processes. For instance, the classic work of Bousfield and colleagues (e.g., Bousfield, Sedgewick, & Cohen, 1954) demonstrated that in verbal fluency tasks, where a participant is asked to recall as many items from a specified category (e.g., animals) as possible, the rate at which responses are emitted starts fast and then gets progressively slower. Additionally, Roediger and colleagues (Roediger, Stellon, & Tulving, 1977), have shown a similar pattern for episodic memory tasks. In nearly all cases, researchers have found that cumulative latency distributions are well described by a cumulative exponential,

$$F(t) = N(1 - e^{-\lambda t}) \qquad\qquad 15.1$$

where $F(t)$ represents the cumulative number of items recalled by time t, N represents asymptotic recall, and λ represents the rate of approach to asymptote.

McGill (1963) has demonstrated that a simple random-sampling-with-replacement process predicts exponentially declining rates of recall and cumulative exponential recall curves, if one assumes a constant sampling time per item (see also Rohrer & Wixted, 1994). Thus, cumulative latency distributions in free recall paradigms are well described by a simple random search model. In this model a retrieval cue delimits a search set that includes target items as well as extraneous items. Items are randomly sampled from the search set at a constant rate one item at a time (serial search). Target items that have not been previously sampled are recalled and placed back in the search set (sampling-with-replacement). Target items that have been previously recalled, extralist items, or target items that are not recoverable, are not recalled but still can be sampled from the search set. Based on an extensive review of the literature, Wixted and Rohrer (1994) have suggested that the rate of approach to asymptotic performance (λ), obtained from fitting the cumulative exponential to a cumulative latency distribution, is indicative of the size of the search set that one is searching through. Wixted and Rohrer argued that the larger the set one is searching from, the slower one will be in reaching asymptotic recall levels. That is, the larger the search set, the lower the probability of sampling any given item will be and hence, the longer it will take you to find the desired item. Wixted and Rohrer provided evidence for this view by demonstrating that rate is slower when recall is required from large categories than when searching through smaller categories, when recalling from longer lists than from shorter lists (Rohrer & Wixted, 1994), when recalling from lists where PI is high than when PI is low (Wixted & Rohrer, 1993), as well as a number of other findings (for a comprehensive review see Wixted & Rohrer, 1994). In each case, the more overloaded a cue was, the slower the rate of approach to asymptote was. Thus, if it is the case that low spans suffer from more cue overload, because they are less efficient at using cues to guide the search process in episodic memory tasks than high spans, we should see that low spans approach asymptote slower than high spans.

This is precisely the case. We (Unsworth & Engle, in press) had high and low spans perform an immediate free recall task in which response latency was measured during the recall phase. Participants received 15 lists with 12 words per list. During recall, participants had 30 s to recall as many items as possible, in any order they wished. For each response that was emitted, an experimenter pressed a key indicating when in the recall period the response was given. Shown in Figure 15.1 are the resulting cumulative recall curves. As can be seen, high spans recalled more items (higher asymptotic levels of recall) than low spans and they approached asymptote at a faster rate than low spans (λ highs = .20, λ lows = .17). Consistent with the work of Wixted and Rohrer (1993), this suggests that low spans were searching through a larger search set of items than were high spans. In line with the work reviewed thus far, we suggest that in episodic memory tasks, low

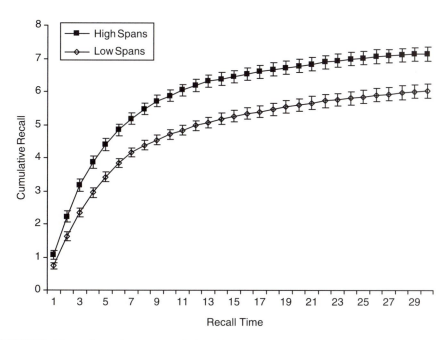

FIGURE 15.1   Cumulative recall functions as a function of complex span for immediate free recall (adapted from Unsworth & Engle, 2005).

spans are less efficient at using context cues to delimit the search set to only the current target items. Thus, low spans have search sets that include target items as well as items from previous trials. This results in a lower number of items recalled (e.g., N) and a slower rate of approach to asymptotic performance (e.g., λ). However, these findings are limited by the fact that some of the items were recalled (theoretically) from a short-term buffer (e.g., Raaijmakers & Shiffrin, 1981) and thus the results do not clearly demonstrate differences in the search process between the two groups. Accordingly, we have since examined the temporal dynamics of recall in a delayed free recall paradigm thought to reduce the contribution of a short-term buffer (e.g., Glanzer & Cunitz, 1966). Preliminary evidence suggests that high spans recall more items than low spans and reach asymptotic levels at a faster rate than low spans (Unsworth, 2005).

Taken together, these results suggest that low spans are inefficient, relative to high spans, in their ability to correctly delimit the search set to only target items. However, the overall view is that low spans are less efficient at using cues to guide the search process. In some situations, it may actually be beneficial to have large search sets in order to aid retrieval. Take for instance the verbal fluency task described previously. Here you are given a category and are told to recall as many items as possible from that cue in a given amount of time. In such a case, in order to recall many items one may actually want to have a larger search set to sample from. That is, one has to ask what is being required in the task (e.g., Humphreys, Bain, & Pike, 1989). In order for accurate performance in an episodic memory task, one has to constrain the search set to the episode. However, in semantic fluency tasks, the search need only be constrained to the specific category cue. Thus, in such a case a larger search set that includes many target representations may be more desirable than a smaller search set. Indeed, contrasting latency distributions in an episodic free recall task and a semantic fluency task, Rohrer (2002) has shown that response latency in the episodic task is constrained by the episode but that response latency in the semantic task is constrained by the size of the category.

Turning back to individual differences in WMC, if high spans are better at using cues to guide the search process, we might expect that high spans will actually have larger search sets than low spans in a semantic fluency task. That is, high spans may be better and more flexible at configuring their search sets based on the task demands than are low spans. Evidence for such a notion comes from a study by Rosen and Engle (1997). Rosen and Engle had participants recall as many animals as possible in 15 min. They found that high spans retrieved more animal names than low spans and plotted their cumulative recall functions. However, they did not attempt to fit the cumulative exponential to their data and examine the resulting parameter estimates. Shown in Figure 15.2 are the results from Rosen and Engle's Experiment 1 (estimated from their Fig. 1). Although the functions have not yet reached asymptotic levels, fitting the estimated functions to the cumulative exponential suggests a reversal of the episodic recall findings in that high spans approach asymptote at a slower rate than low spans (λ highs = .15, λ lows = .19). Indeed, this is the standard finding when examining cumulative latency distributions in semantic memory tasks (e.g., Wixted & Rohrer, 1994).

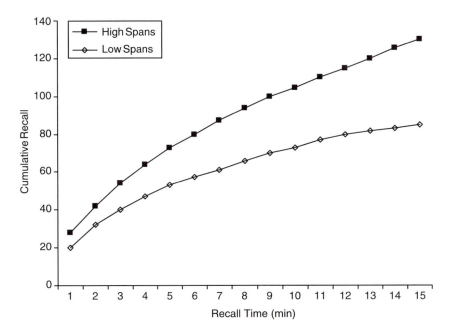

FIGURE 15.2   Cumulative recall functions as a function of complex span for a verbal fluency task (adapted from Rosen & Engle, 1997).

Those individuals who retrieve more items, tend to emit the items at a slower rate (e.g., Johnson, Johnson, & Mark, 1951). Thus, it is not simply the case that high spans always have smaller search sets than low spans, but rather high spans are better at using cues to guide the search process based on the demands of the task. In semantic memory tasks, such as verbal fluency, a hierarchal search process may be the best approach to take (e.g., Wixted & Rohrer, 1994). In such a case, clusters of items are subsumed under a retrieval cue. The retrieval process proceeds by first sampling clusters and then items within the cluster. Those participants who are unable to use cues to sample clusters and items within a cluster will perform more poorly than participants who are good at using cues to guide the search process. In episodic memory tasks, however, where only retrieval of current target items is desired, the search set will need to be delimited and exclude items from previous trials. Those participants who are unable to effectively delimit the search set will show poorer performance due to interference from previous trials. We suggest that high spans are better at retrieval in both situations due to a greater ability to use cues to direct the search process.

CONCLUSIONS AND FUTURE DIRECTIONS

In the present chapter we have shown that individual differences in WMC are related to individual differences in retrieval under conditions of interference. We have argued that low WMC individuals are more prone to cue overload in episodic memory tasks than are high WMC individuals. However, we have said little about the underlying mechanism that may give rise to these differences. In previous work (e.g., Engle & Kane, 2004) we have argued that the ability to control attention is of crucial importance in a number of tasks and that individual differences in attentional control correspond to differences in WMC. In terms of retrieval differences, our previous work has suggested that inhibitory processes likely play a role (see Redick, Heitz, & Engle, in press, for a review; see also Hasher, Zacks, & May, 1999). This view suggests that the reason low spans search through a larger search set of items than high spans is because low spans are inefficient at using controlled attention to exclude irrelevant items. In terms of the current cue-dependent search approach, perhaps high spans are better at using cues to specify which items are relevant, and then they suppress all other items. That is, high spans may be better at using a conceptually guided selective attention process (Anderson & Spellman, 1995) in which attention is focused on target items and irrelevant items are actively suppressed.

Furthermore, the importance of attention at retrieval has also been implicated cue-dependent search approaches of memory. For instance, in the search of associate memory model (Raaijmakers & Shiffrin, 1981) there are several components of the search process that require attention including deciding how to search, what cues should be used for the search, how the cues should be combined for search, and when to stop the search. Each decision is attention demanding and thus, likely related to individual differences in WMC. Consistent with this notion is work by Naveh-Benjamin and Guez (2000), which suggests that dividing attention at retrieval selectively disrupts the cue-elaboration aspect of the search process. Work from our lab supports both approaches. Specifically, both Rosen and Engle (1997) and Kane and Engle (2000) have shown that dividing attention during retrieval disrupts performance for high spans but not low spans. Future work will be directed at examining the combination of these two approaches.

A final limitation of the work we have presented here is the exclusive focus on retrieval factors. As the work on the levels of processing approach has shown (e.g., Craik & Lockhart, 1972), issues of encoding are also important factors in memory theory. In fact, a few studies have explicitly examined encoding strategies in complex span tasks (e.g., Turley-Ames & Whitfield, 2003). However, as shown by Turley-Ames and Whitfield (2003), differences in encoding strategies actually tend to obscure the correlation between complex span performance and performance on measures of higher-order cognition. Furthermore, it is appealing to think that high spans may be better at reinstating the encoding context at retrieval than low spans, and thus are more efficient at implementing encoding specificity (Tulving, 1983). More work is needed to understand the possible role of encoding and encoding-retrieval interactions in terms of individual differences in WMC. As pointed out by Roediger (2000), understanding retrieval processes is of the utmost importance in terms of understanding how memory works. To this we would add that an even fuller understanding can be gained by examining individual differences in retrieval.

REFERENCES

Anderson, J. R. (1974). Retrieval of propositional information from long-term memory. *Cognitive Psychology, 6*, 451–474.

Anderson, M. C., & Spellman, B. A. (1995). On the status of inhibitory mechanisms in Cognition: Memory retrieval as a model case. *Psychological Review, 107*, 68–100.

Baddeley, A. D., & Hitch, G. (1974). Working memory. In G. H. Bower (Ed.), *The psychology of learning and motivation* (Vol. 8, pp. 47–89). New York: Academic Press.

Bleckley, M. K., Durso, F. T., Crutchfield, J. M., Engle, R. W., & Khanna, M. M. (2004). Individual differences in working memory capacity predict visual attention allocation. *Psychonomic Bulletin and Review, 10*, 884–889.

Bousfield, W. A., Sedgewick, C. H. W., & Cohen, B. H. (1954). Certain temporal characteristics of the recall of verbal associates. *American Journal of Psychology, 67*, 111–118.

Brown, J. (1958). Some tests of the decay theory of immediate memory. *Quarterly Journal of Experimental Psychology, 10*, 12–21.

Bunting, M. F. (2006). Proactive interference and item similarity in working memory. *Journal of Experimental Psychology: Learning, Memory, and Cognition, 32*, 183–196.

Bunting, M. F., Conway, A. R. A., & Heitz, R. P. (2004). Individual differences in the fan effect and working memory capacity. *Journal of Memory and Language, 51*, 604–622.

Cantor, J., & Engle, R. W. (1993). Working memory capacity as long-term memory activation: An individual differences approach. *Journal of Experimental Psychology: Learning, Memory, and Cognition, 19*, 1101–1114.

Case, R., Kurland, M. D., & Goldberg, J. (1982). Operational efficiency and the growth of short-term memory span. *Journal of Experimental Child Psychology, 33*, 386–404.

Cohen, R. L. (1994). Some thoughts on individual differences and theory construction. *Intelligence, 18*, 3–13.

Conway, A. R. A., Cowan, N., & Bunting, M. F. (2001). The cocktail party phenomenon revisited: The importance of working memory capacity. *Psychonomic Bulletin and Review, 8*, 331–335.

Conway, A. R. A., Cowan, N., Bunting, M. F., Therriault, D. J., & Minkoff, S. R. B. (2002). A latent variable analysis of working memory capacity, short-term memory capacity, processing speed, and general fluid intelligence. *Intelligence, 30*, 163–183.

Conway, A. R. A., & Engle, R. W. (1994). Working memory and retrieval: A resource-dependent inhibition model. *Journal of Experimental Psychology: General, 123*, 354–373.

Craik, F. I. M., & Lockhart, R. S. (1972). Levels of processing: A framework for memory research. *Journal of Verbal Learning and Verbal Behavior, 11*, 671–684.

Cronbach, L. J. (1957). The two disciplines of scientific psychology. *The American Psychologist, 12*, 671–684.

Daneman, M., & Carpenter, P. A. (1980). Individual differences in working memory and reading. *Journal of Verbal Learning and Verbal Behavior, 19*, 450–466.

Daneman, M., & Green, I. (1986). Individual differences in comprehending and producing words in context. *Journal of Memory and Language, 25*, 1–18.

Engle, R. W., & Kane, M. J. (2004). Executive attention, working memory capacity, and a two-factor theory of cognitive control. In B. Ross (Ed.), *The psychology of learning and motivation* (Vol. 44, pp. 145–199). New York: Elsevier.

Engle, R. W., Tuholski, S. W., Laughlin, J. E., & Conway, A. R. A. (1999). Working memory, short-term memory and general fluid intelligence: A latent-variable approach. *Journal of Experimental Psychology: General, 128*, 309–331.

Friedman, N. P., & Miyake, A. (2004). The relations among inhibition and interference control functions: A latent-variable analysis. *Journal of Experimental Psychology: General, 133*, 101–135.

Glanzer, M., & Cunitz, A. R. (1966). Two storage mechanisms in free recall. *Journal of Verbal Learning and Verbal Behavior, 5*, 351–360.

Glenberg, A. M. (1987). Temporal context and recency. In D. S. Gorfein & R. R. Hoffman (Eds.), *Memory and learning: The Ebbinghaus centennial conference.* Hillsdale, NJ: Lawrence Erlbaum Associates, Inc.

Glenberg, A. M., & Swanson, N. G. (1986). A temporal distinctiveness theory of recency and modality effects. *Journal of Experimental Psychology: Learning, Memory, and Cognition, 12*, 3–15.

Gorfein, D. S. (1987). Explaining context effects on short-term memory. In D. S. Gorfein & R. R. Hoffman (Eds.), *Memory and learning: The Ebbinghaus centennial conference* (pp. 153–172). Hillsdale, NJ: Lawrence Erlbaum Associates, Inc.

Hasher, L., Zacks, R. T., & May, C. P. (1999). Inhibitory control, circadian arousal, and age. In D. Gopher & A. Koriat (Eds.), *Attention and performance XVII: Cognitive regulation of performance: Interaction of theory and application* (pp. 653–675). Cambridge, MA: MIT Press.

Heitz, R. P., & Engle, R. W. (2005). Focusing the spotlight: Individual differences in visual attention control. *Manuscript submitted for publication.*

Humphreys, M. S., Bain, J. D., & Pike, R. (1989). Different ways to cue a coherent memory system: A theory for episodic, semantic, and procedural tasks. *Psychological Review, 96*, 208–233.

Johnson, D. M., Johnson, R. C., & Mark, A. L. (1951). A mathematical analysis of verbal fluency. *Journal of General Psychology, 44*, 121–128.

Kane, M. J., Bleckley, M. K., Conway, A. R. A., & Engle, R. W. (2001). A controlled-attention view of working-memory capacity. *Journal of Experimental Psychology: General, 130*, 169–183.

Kane, M. J., & Engle R. W. (2000). Working memory capacity, proactive interference, and divided attention: Limits on long-term retrieval. *Journal of Experimental Psychology: Learning, Memory, and Cognition, 26*, 333–358.

Kane, M. J., & Engle, R. W. (2003). Working-memory capacity and the control of attention: The contributions of goal neglect, response competition, and task set to Stroop interference. *Journal of Experimental Psychology: General, 132*(1), 47–70.

Kane, M. J., Hambrick, D. Z., Tuholski, S. W., Wilhelm, O., Payne, T. W., & Engle, R. W. (2004). The generality of working-memory capacity: A latent-variable approach to verbal and visuo-spatial memory span and reasoning. *Journal of Experimental Psychology: General, 133*, 189–217.

Kyllonen, P. C., & Christal, R. E. (1990). Reasoning ability is (little more than) working-memory capacity? *Intelligence, 14*, 389–433.

Kyllonen, P. C., & Stephens, D. L. (1990). Cognitive abilities as determinants of success in acquiring logic skill. *Learning and Individual Differences, 2*, 129–160.

Long, D. L., & Prat, C. S. (2002). Working memory and Stroop interference: An individual differences investigation. *Memory and Cognition, 30*, 294–301.

Lustig, C., May, C. P., & Hasher, L. (2001). Working memory span and the role of proactive interference. *Journal of Experimental Psychology: General, 130*, 199–207.

May, C. P., Hasher, L., & Kane, M. J. (1999). The role of interference in memory span. *Memory and Cognition, 27*, 759–767.

McGill, W. J. (1963). Stochastic latency mechanism. In R. D. Luce, R. R. Bush, & E. Galanter (Eds.), *Handbook of mathematical psychology* (Vol. 1, pp. 309–360). New York: Wiley.

Melton, A. W. (1963). Implications of short-term memory for a general theory of memory. *Journal of Verbal Learning and Verbal Behavior, 2*, 1–21.

Naveh-Benjamin, M., & Guez, J. (2000). Effects of divided attention on encoding and retrieval processing: Assessment of attentional costs and a componential analysis. *Journal of Experimental Psychology: Learning, Memory, and Cognition, 26*, 1461–1482.

Peterson, L. R., & Peterson, M. J. (1959). Short-term retention of individual verbal items. *Journal of Experimental Psychology, 58*, 193–198.

Raaijmakers, J. G. W., & Shiffrin, R. M. (1981). Search of associative memory. *Psychological Review, 88*, 93–134.

Raven, J. C., Raven, J. E., & Court, J. H. (1998). *Progressive matrices*. Oxford, UK: Oxford Psychologists Press.

Redick, T. S., Heitz, R. P., & Engle, R. W. (in press). Working memory capacity and inhibition: Cognitive, social, and neuropsychological consequences. In C. M. MacLeod & D. S. Gorfein (Eds.), *The place of inhibition in cognition*.

Roediger, H. L. (2000). Why retrieval is the key process to understanding human memory. In E. Tulving (Ed.), *Memory, consciousness and the brain: The Tallinn conference* (pp. 52–75). Philadelphia: Psychology Press.

Roediger, H. L., III, Stellon, C. C., & Tulving, E. (1977). Inhibition from part-list cues and rate of recall. *Journal of Experimental Psychology: Human Learning and Memory, 3*, 174–188.

Rohrer, D. (2002). The breadth of memory search. *Memory, 10*, 291–301.

Rohrer, D., & Wixted, J. T. (1994). An analysis of latency and interresponse time in free recall. *Memory and Cognition, 22*, 511–524.

Rosen, V. M., & Engle, R. W. (1997). The role of working memory capacity in retrieval. *Journal of Experimental Psychology: General, 126*, 211–227.

Shiffrin, R. M. (1970). Memory search. In D. A. Norman (Ed.), *Models of human memory* (pp. 375–447). New York: Academic Press.

Sternberg, S. (1966). High-speed scanning in human memory. *Science, 153*, 652–654.

Tulving, E. (1983). *Elements of episodic memory*. New York: Oxford University Press.

Turley-Ames, K. J., & Whitfield, M. M. (2003). Strategy training and working memory task performance. *Journal of Memory and Language, 49*, 446–468.

Turner, M. L., & Engle, R. W. (1989). Is working memory capacity task dependent? *Journal of Memory and Language, 28*, 127–154.

Underwood, B. J. (1975). Individual differences as a crucible in theory construction. *The American Psychologist, 30*, 128–134.

Unsworth, N. (2005). Individual differences in working memory capacity and episodic retrieval: Examining the dynamics of delayed and continuous distractor free recall. *Manuscript in preparation*.

Unsworth, N., & Engle, R. W. (in press). The nature of individual differences in working memory capacity: Active maintenance in primary memory and controlled search from secondary memory. *Psychological Review*.

Unsworth, N., & Engle, R. W. (2006a). Simple and complex memory spans and their relation to fluid abilities: Evidence from list-length effects. *Journal of Memory and Language, 54*, 68–80.

Unsworth, N., & Engle, R. W. (2006b). A temporal-contextual retrieval account of complex span: An analysis of errors. *Journal of Memory and Language, 54*, 346–362.

Unsworth, N., Schrock, J. C., & Engle, R. W. (2004). Working memory capacity and the antisaccade task: Individual differences in voluntary saccade control. *Journal of Experimental Psychology: Learning, Memory, and Cognition, 30,* 1302–1321.

Watkins, M. J. (1979). Engrams as cuegrams and forgetting as cue overload: A cueing approach to the structure of memory. In C. R. Puff (Ed.), *Memory organization and structure* (pp. 173–195). New York: Academic Press.

Watkins, O. C., & Watkins, M. J. (1975). Buildup of proactive inhibition as a cue-overload effect. *Journal of Experimental Psychology: Human Learning and Memory, 104,* 442–452.

Wickens, D. D., Born, D. G., & Allen, C. K. (1963). Proactive inhibition and item similarity in short-term memory. *Journal of Verbal Learning and Verbal Behavior, 2,* 440–445.

Wixted, J. T., & Rohrer, D. (1993). Proactive interference and the dynamics of free recall. *Journal of Experimental Psychology: Learning, Memory, and Cognition, 19,* 1024–1039.

Wixted, J. T., & Rohrer, D. (1994). Analyzing the dynamics of free recall: An intergrative review of the empirical literature. *Psychonomic Bulletin and Review, 1,* 89–106.

Young, C. W., & Supa, M. (1941). Mnemic inhibition as a factor in the limitation of memory span. *American Journal of Psychology, 54,* 546–552.

16

Competition and Inhibition in Word Retrieval: Implications for Language and Memory Tasks

RANDI C. MARTIN and KELLY BIEGLER

*I*n the presentations at the conference honoring Henry (Roddy) L. Roediger, III, the speakers were encouraged to make some connection between their work and his. Roediger's work has been in the area of long-term memory, whereas the work in our lab has been on language and short-term memory, and, consequently, connections were not obvious. However, a review of Roediger's earlier research uncovered an area of common interest—specifically, an interest in the negative consequences of prior retrieval for subsequent retrieval from the same semantic category (e.g., Neely, Schmidt, & Roediger, 1983; Roediger, 1973). Studies of episodic and semantic memory carried out by Roediger and others have documented what has been termed retrieval-induced inhibition, that is, poorer recall of items from the same semantic category after cueing with the category name and some category members (part-list cueing; Roediger, 1973) or simply after retrieving several items from the same category (Brown, 1979, 1981). Similarly, studies of picture naming have documented slower reaction times in naming pictures drawn repeatedly from the same category compared to items drawn from mixed categories (e.g., Belke, Meyer, & Damian, 2005; Brown, 1981; Kroll & Stewart, 1994).

For the most part, the studies in the picture naming domain have not made reference to the findings in the memory literature, though the work by Brown is an exception as he has examined both naming and memory retrieval (Brown, 1979, 1981; Brown, Zoccoli, & Leahy, 2005). As discussed by Roediger and Neely (1982), it is not clear that the effects arise from the same source; however, there are various features of the results in common across these very different paradigms and similar explanatory principles have been invoked. Specifically, the effects have been attributed either to interference from overactivation of already produced items (e.g., Roediger & Neely, 1982; Belke et al., 2005) or to suppression of related words during the retrieval of earlier items in the same category (e.g., Anderson & Bjork, 1994; Wheeldon & Monsell, 1994). We will consider our findings mainly from the perspective of language processing theories involved in word production, but also consider the possible connection to the findings on memory retrieval.

In this chapter, we first present data from a brain damaged patient (ML) and controls on naming a series of pictures, which are either blocked by semantic category or drawn from different categories. Our interest in this paradigm arose from previous findings from ML demonstrating exaggerated effects on tasks involving inhibition in the verbal domain but not in the nonverbal domain (Hamilton & Martin, 2005, in press). We interpreted these findings as indicating that ML has difficulty inhibiting irrelevant verbal representations. Thus, to the extent that the semantic blocking effect in picture naming derives from some suppression or inhibitory process, an abnormal pattern would be predicted for ML. The exact predictions depend on the locus of the inhibitory mechanism in the picture naming process, which will be discussed in greater detail in the next section. We also present data from another type of semantic retrieval task, entailing the generation of a semantically related verb to a noun stimulus, and address whether inhibition provides an account of the difficulty of verb retrieval for noun cues with differing numbers of response options of varying association strengths. Although this task seems less transparently related to the retrieval inhibition paradigm, the issues in verb generation do seem related to another long-term memory phenomenon—that is, the fan effect. Some have related the fan effect and retrieval inhibition, claiming that both result from the decreasing effectiveness of a cue as more items are associated with that cue (Watkins, 1975, 1979). Furthermore, neuroimaging and neuropsychological studies (Barch, Braver, Sabb, & Noll, 2000; Thompson-Schill, D'Esposito, Aguirre, & Farah, 1997; Thompson-Schill et al., 1998) of verb generation have attributed effects of the strength of competing responses to the involvement of a selection mechanism—and it is possible that this mechanism might involve inhibition.

COMPETITION AND SUPPRESSION IN PICTURE NAMING FOR SEMANTICALLY BLOCKED SETS

Many studies have demonstrated that picture naming times are slower when pictures are blocked by semantic category (e.g., Brown, 1981; Damian, Vigliocco, & Levelt, 2001; Kroll & Curley, 1988; Kroll & Stewart, 1994). In a recent variation on this paradigm, researchers have had subjects cycle through naming a small set of pictures (e.g., four or six) with the sets consisting either of items from the same category or from different categories (e.g., Damian et al., 2001). Using this cyclic naming method, Belke et al. (2005) showed across several experiments that while naming times were slightly faster or nearly equivalent for same category versus different category sets on the first cycle, longer times for the same category sets were observed at the second cycle and reaction times for the same category sets remained longer than those for the unrelated sets across eight cycles. Moreover, Belke et al. showed that the deleterious effect of blocking by semantic category was maintained even when, at Cycle 5, new items from the same categories replaced the previous items. Thus, the results indicate that whatever the source of the effect, the effect extended beyond the items that were named to other members of the same category.

As mentioned earlier, previous explanations attribute these effects to either increased activation of competitors or to the suppression of competitors. According to the overactivation account, presentation of a picture activates the semantic representation for the pictured object, thereby activating lexical representations for the correct name while also to some degree activating semantically related items via their shared semantic features. As shown in Figure 16.1, presentation of a picture of a cat would also activate lexical representations for dog and lion to some extent. Producing the word "cat" involves selecting this lexical representation from the activated competitors. It is often assumed that in selecting one response, activation of that response must exceed that of other activated responses by some proportion. For example, in the WEAVER++ model of speech production (Levelt, Roelofs, & Meyer, 1999), selection time depends on the ratio of activation for the target word relative to the sum of the activation of all competitors. Thus, assuming that, beginning with exposure of each picture, activation of the correct response and of competitors grows over time according to some function, then the time to make the response would increase the greater the activation of the

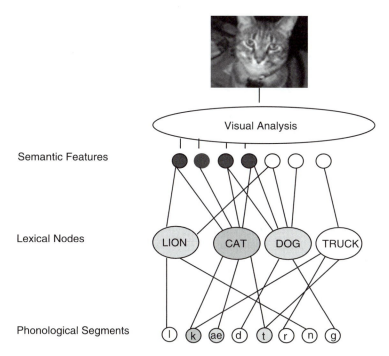

FIGURE 16.1   Model of word production involving partial activation of competitors at the lexical level (based on Dell & O'Seaghdha, 1992, model of speech production).

competitors. When naming repeatedly from the same category, competitors for "cat" may themselves have been produced as the name of other items in the set. Having just previously named "lion" would increase the naming latency for "cat" on the next trial because the activation for "cat" will have to overcome the activation persisting from "lion" as well as the activation of "lion" due to its shared semantic features with "cat." After a number of trials involving production of names from the same category, persisting activation from the entire set of items and their related competitors should serve to boost the activation of the entire category (whether presented or not) and increase naming latencies.

In order for this overactivation account to work, it has to be the case that activation of just-produced words persists across trials. However, several models of speech production have assumed that once a word has been produced, that word itself is then inhibited in order to prevent its reselection (Dell, 1988; MacKay, 1987).[1] If this postselection self-inhibition served to reduce activation to baseline, no semantic blocking effect would be observed. For instance, if "cat" were inhibited to baseline after its production, this would not impair production of "lion" if that were the target on the next trial. In fact, if postselection inhibition inhibited "cat" below baseline, production of "lion" should be facilitated, since one of its competitors would not be as strongly activated as it would have been had it not been presented on the previous trial. However, there appears to be no evidence supporting below-baseline self-inhibition. For example, below-baseline inhibition should eliminate or reverse repetition priming effects in naming at short lags between prime or target; however, this is clearly not the case (Vitkovitch, Rutter, & Read, 2001). For the semantic blocking effect to occur in conjunction with repetition priming, postselection self-inhibition would have to be only partial such that the just-produced item remained activated above baseline (or such that activation rebounded above baseline following postselection inhibition as in Dell, 1988).

According to a suppression account of the semantic blocking effect, selection of one name involves the below-baseline suppression of *competitors* (not below-baseline self-inhibition). This suppression is assumed to persist across trials resulting in longer naming times for competitors when they appear on subsequent trials as targets. This suppression could result from lateral inhibition among semantically related lexical representations (Dell & O'Seaghdha, 1994; Stemberger, 1985). Dell and O'Seaghdha (1994) point out that inhibitory connections among semantically related responses could be learned over the long term via some error correction mechanism, such as back-propagation. Assuming that inhibitory links exist, then naming a target such as "cat" could involve suppressing related items such as "lion" below baseline. If this suppression persists across trials, the subject would be slower to name a related item (e.g., "lion") if it appeared on the next trial. According to this view, then, slower times result because lexical representations become relatively unavailable across trials when sampling from the same category (McCarthy & Kartsounis, 2000). This suppression should extend to both presented and nonpresented members of a semantic category. It should be noted that if this lateral inhibition served to reduce activation but did not reduce it below baseline, then a semantic blocking effect could still be observed, but it would have to be attributed to the sustained partial activation of competitors rather than to their unavailability.

Recently, Schnur, Schwartz, Brecher, and Hodgson (2006) examined the semantic blocking effect in aphasic patients who were either fluent or nonfluent speakers using the semantically blocked cyclic naming procedure. They argued that while it was difficult to distinguish between the overactivation and suppression accounts in normal subjects, the pattern of error rates for patients might provide a means of distinguishing the two accounts. That is, they argued that if competitors became more and more suppressed with repeated sampling from a category, then semantic errors should decrease across cycles. On the other hand, if competitors became increasingly activated, then semantic errors should increase across cycles. Their older control subjects demonstrated a blocking effect in reaction times similar to that of younger subjects in the Belke et al. (2005) study. Consistent with the overactivation account, the patients demonstrated increasing semantic errors over cycles. They also found that nonfluent patients demonstrated a greater semantic blocking effect than did their fluent patients. They suggested that the nonfluent patients had difficulty with some selection mechanism outside the lexical system that resolved the high degree of competition resulting from overactivation.

Inhibitory Deficits and their Predicted Impact on the Semantic Blocking Effect

We were particularly interested in the role of inhibitory mechanisms in the semantic blocking effect in picture naming because of evidence suggesting that patients we have identified as having a semantic short-term memory deficit may, in fact, suffer from a deficit in inhibiting irrelevant verbal information (Hamilton & Martin, 2005). Martin and Lesch (1996) reported that two such patients, AB and ML, had a tendency to produce intrusions from prior lists on word span tasks. Although most of their recall errors were omissions, when they produced an erroneous response, it was often an item from a previous list. In contrast, patient EA, a patient with a phonological STM deficit, produced only one such intrusion. Recently, Hamilton and Martin (2005, in press) presented more direct evidence from patient ML supporting the claim that he had difficulty inhibiting irrelevant information from previous lists on a recognition probe memory task based on paradigm developed by Monsell (1978). In this "recent negatives" task, on some trials the probe does not match an item in the current list, but does match one in the previous list. Normal subjects show longer reaction times to reject these recent negative probes than to reject negative probes that do not match items in the previous list. Patient ML showed a greatly exaggerated recent negatives effect of 731 ms compared to controls' effect of 91 ms. ML also showed greatly exaggerated interference effects when the probe was only phonologically or semantically related to a current list item or previous list items (Hamilton & Martin, in press). Undergraduate subjects and older controls showed small but significant interference effects (i.e., from about 40 to 70 ms) for items phonologically or semantically related to a current list item, but showed no effect for items related to a previous list item. In contrast, ML showed over 300 ms of interference in each of the four conditions. Hamilton and Martin (2005) showed that ML's difficulty with inhibition could be demonstrated not only in tasks tapping short-term memory but also in a task with no memory demands—specifically the Stroop task (Stroop, 1935). ML showed a Stroop effect of 969 ms compared to mean effect of 167 ms for controls. In contrast to these exaggerated interference effects in the Stroop and probe tasks, ML performed at a normal level in terms of reaction time and error rates on a nonverbal spatial analogue to the Stroop task and on an antisaccade task.

Assuming that ML does have a deficit in inhibiting irrelevant verbal information, what would be the consequences for the semantic blocking effect in the naming task? As discussed earlier, one hypothesis about the source of the effect is the unavailability of responses due to below-baseline suppression of competitors. As discussed earlier, the Schnur et al. (2006) findings provide evidence against a suppression account. Thus, let us assume that the overactivation account is correct. How then might a deficit in inhibition affect the semantic blocking effect? There are two ways. First, one might assume that lateral inhibition is involved in lexical selection but that, in normal production, lateral inhibition does not result in a suppression of competitors below baseline. Lateral inhibition serves to reduce the activation of competitors such that selection can be accomplished more quickly, but at the point of selection, competitors remain activated above baseline. If ML's lateral inhibitory mechanisms are impaired, then, potentially, the activation of competitors would not be reduced to the same level as for control subjects. Thus, for ML, it is possible that greater activation might persist across trials, resulting in greater competition at selection.[2]

A second way that an inhibitory deficit might be involved would be a deficit in postselection self-inhibition—that is, in the inhibition of a word following its production. As discussed earlier, we have to assume that postselection self-inhibition is not complete even for neurally intact participants such that some activation persists across trials, resulting in the semantic blocking effect. If ML's deficit affects postselection inhibition such that the reduction in activation is much less for ML than for controls, then this would result in an exaggerated semantic blocking effect. That is, activation from the production of related words on previous trials will persist, more so than for control subjects, and cause difficulty in selecting the appropriate term on the next and subsequent trials.

We examined ML's performance on the semantic blocking paradigm developed by Schnur et al. (2006). Given ML's demonstrated deficit in inhibition on other tasks (Hamilton & Martin, 2005, in press), there were grounds for predicting that he would show an exaggerated semantic blocking effect.

SEMANTIC BLOCKING EXPERIMENT

Method

Subjects   Seven healthy older controls and aphasic patient ML participated in the semantic cyclic naming task. Both the control subjects and ML received $10 per hour of participation. The older subjects were education and age-matched with ML, with ages ranging from 55 to 75 years and an education level of at least a high school degree, with most having had some college education. English was the first language of all subjects.

Patient ML is a right-handed male who was 63 years of age when the task was administered. He was diagnosed with a left hemisphere cerebral vascular accident in 1990. Our previous descriptions of ML's lesion (e.g., Martin & He, 2004) were based on a neurological report from 1992 in which results from a CT scan indicated a lesion including the left frontal and parietal operculum, with atrophy noted in the left temporal operculum and mild diffuse atrophy. A recent structural MRI scan of patient ML revealed a larger lesion that includes not only the left inferior frontal gyrus (LIFG), but also regions in the middle frontal gyrus. In addition, ML's lesion includes substantial areas of the left parietal lobe. The left temporal lobe is spared.

ML completed 2 years of college and has excellent single picture naming and single word processing according to standardized tests (Martin & He, 2004). His speech is nonfluent, in that speech rate and sentence length are reduced. However, he does not have articulatory difficulties and his speech is not agrammatic. He shows evidence of a semantic short-term memory deficit. For instance, he shows no advantage for word recall over nonword recall (Martin & Lesch, 1996). Moreover, he performs better on a probe task requiring detection of rhyming words relative to a probe task requiring detection of semantically related words. Freedman and Martin (2001) computed a composite z-score for performance on a number of measures tapping semantic and phonological retention. ML's semantic retention composite score was –2.59, whereas his composite phonological retention score was –.23. In contrast, a patient with a phonological retention deficit, EA, obtained a semantic composite score of 3.86 and a phonological composite score of –3.95.

Materials and Design   The stimuli presented in this experiment were the same materials used by Schnur et al. (2006)[3] and consisted of Snodgrass and Vanderwart (1980) pictures or other similar line drawings selected from 12 different categories. Each category contained six exemplars producing 72 pictures total, and were presented in both semantically blocked and mixed sets, e.g., semantically blocked: ear, arm, toe, nose, chin, thumb; mixed: ear, table, goat, fan, mountain, dress. In addition, the stimuli were fairly closely matched on frequency, phonological onset, and rhyme similarity for both semantically blocked and mixed sets (see Schnur et al., 2006, for more detailed methods). Both set types were presented in cycles with one cycle consisting of six pictures in a set appearing in random order. Following the sixth picture, the next cycle began repeating the previous set of pictures. One block consisted of four cycles with six pictures per cycle, adding to 24 pictures presentations per block. There were 24 blocks in total, 12 same category blocks and 12 mixed blocks. The same category and mixed blocks were presented in a different random order for each subject.

Procedure   All pictures were presented using PsyScope 1.2.5 (Cohen, MacWhinney, Flatt, & Provost, 1993). Before the experiment began, the controls and ML participated in a practice session in which they were familiarized with each of the 72 pictures presented during the experiment. A single picture appeared on the screen followed by the word describing it 1000 ms after picture onset. Subjects were instructed to name the picture using the word printed on the screen and proceed to the next picture at their own pace by pressing the spacebar.

The experimental procedure used for all subjects was similar to the fast presentation rate condition used by Schnur et al. (2006), with some minor changes. Each trial began with the simultaneous presentation of a beep and a single picture that remained on the screen for 2000 ms. Two small dots at the bottom of the screen indicated when the voice key was triggered. Following the subjects' response, the experimenter pressed the keys 1, 2, or 3, indicating whether the response was correct, an equipment error occurred, or a subject error occurred (e.g., responding with the incorrect name), respectively, and proceeded to the next trial.

Results

Control Subjects   Onset latencies were removed if they were classified as an error response or were 2.5 SDs above or below each subjects' mean. Errors were categorized into two types: equipment errors in which the voice key was incorrectly triggered, or subject errors in which the incorrect name was produced for a picture. Only 0.3% equipment and 1.0% subject errors were found for controls.

Onset latencies were analyzed using a 2 (semantic blocking) × 4 (presentation cycle) within-subjects ANOVA. The main effect of cycle, $F(3, 18) = 27.64, p < .001$, and the Semantic blocking × Cycle interaction, $F(3, 18) = 12.22, p = .004$, were significant, although the main effect of semantic blocking was not, $F(1, 6) = 2.49$, $p = .166$. As displayed in Table 16.1, the controls showed a 27 ms facilitation effect during Cycle 1, just reaching significance ($p = .049$), which switched to interference that progressively increased during Cycles 2–4 (mean differences: Cycle 2 = 8 ms, Cycle 3 = 15 ms, and Cycle 4 = 28 ms). The interference effects were significant at Cycles 3 and 4 (both $ps < .02$). The effects for controls replicate the results reported by Schnur et al. (2006) as onset latencies continually decreased in the mixed condition, while any repetition priming effects in the same category

TABLE 16.1   Mean Reaction Times (ms) for Semantic Blocking Paradigm for Controls and Patient ML

	Cycle			
	1	2	3	4
Controls				
Same category	720	673	666	673
Mixed	747	665	651	644
Patient ML				
Same category	1124	1117	1286	1331
Mixed	1064	952	932	894

condition were attenuated by the deleterious effects of semantic blocking with the result that reaction times remained relatively constant across cycles.

Patient ML   ML made few errors with only 1.2% subject errors (producing the incorrect name for a picture) and 3.8% equipment errors. Due to his low error rate, ML's errors were not analyzed further.

We analyzed ML's data individually examining the effects of semantic blocking and presentation cycle using items as a random factor. The main effect of semantic blocking was significant, $F(1, 65) = 14.37$, $p < .001$; however, the main effect of cycle and the Semantic blocking × Cycle interaction were not statistically reliable. We also conducted the analyses using a natural log transformation, as his reaction times were highly skewed. A main effect of semantic blocking, $F(1, 65) = 15.28$, $p < .001$, and a Semantic blocking × Cycle interaction, $F(1, 65) = 2.97$, $p = .036$, were obtained with the log transformed data. As indicated in Table 16.1 and Figure 16.2, ML showed a 60 ms interference effect (which was nonsignificant) rather than facilitation for Cycle 1, and exhibited interference effects during Cycles 2–4 that were 10 times greater than the largest difference for controls.

Discussion

ML clearly demonstrated an exaggerated semantic blocking effect relative to controls. He showed a repetition priming effect for the mixed blocks, with reaction times decreasing across cycles. Unlike the controls, however, he showed increasing reaction times with cycle for the same category condition, and a semantic blocking effect that grew dramatically across cycles. As discussed earlier, the longer

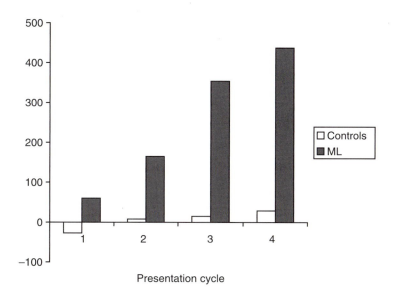

FIGURE 16.2   Difference in mean reaction time (in ms) for semantically blocked versus mixed sets across presentation cycles for patient ML and controls.

latencies for semantically blocked than for mixed blocks for control subjects have sometimes been attributed to suppression that persists across trials. That is, competitors are inhibited below baseline during production and this suppression persists to subsequent trials. According to such a suppression account, one would not expect a deficit in inhibition to give rise to an exaggerated effect. Some brain damaged patients have been argued to have overactive suppression mechanisms, resulting in what has been termed a "refractory access" pattern (Crutch & Warrington, 2005; McCarthy & Kartsounis, 2000). However, such an account seems unlikely for ML, given his deficit in inhibiting irrelevant verbal stimuli. ML's pattern is consistent with overactivation accounts in which either lateral inhibition or postselection inhibition are involved in word selection, but these processes do not reduce activation below baseline. ML is less able than neurally intact individuals to reduce activation through these mechanisms, resulting in greater competition across trials.

There is little strong evidence to decide between a deficit in lateral inhibition or in postselection inhibition as an account for ML's findings. On grounds for favoring an account in terms of a deficit in postselection inhibition is his lesion localization. As discussed earlier, Dell and O'Seaghdha (1994) proposed that lateral inhibition might be a learned property of the lexical system. Both lesion (Hillis et al., 2001) and neuroimaging findings (Indefrey & Levelt, 2000) imply that lexical representations are located in temporal lobe regions. In contrast, postselection inhibition would seem to derive from a source outside the lexical system—potentially in frontal lobe regions that are thought to underlie executive functions. Thus, an impairment in postselection inhibition would seem more likely than an impairment in lateral inhibition given ML's lesion affecting frontal-parietal regions but sparing the temporal lobe. A deficit in postselection could also be used to account for ML's performance in the recent negatives task if one assumes that, in short-term memory tasks, participants suppress previous list items after a trial is over, but ML is unable to do so effectively.

In our data, controls demonstrated a significant facilitation effect for same category versus mixed trials on the first cycle. The switch from facilitation to inhibition suggests that more than one process is involved that is sensitive to semantic relatedness. We will return to this issue in the general discussion in considering the levels at which the differing effects might occur and the level or levels that may be affected for patient ML.

COMPETITION AND INHIBITION IN SEMANTIC MEMORY RETRIEVAL DURING VERB GENERATION

The semantic blocking paradigm examines effects of sequential selection of names from the same semantic category. Part of the explanation of the effects depends on related words sharing a superordinate category or sharing semantic features such that activation of the target word results in spreading activation to related words (see Belke et al., 2005, for discussion). In the verb generation task, subjects are presented with a concrete noun and are asked to supply a semantically related verb (e.g., "broom" → "sweep"). In this task, unrelated nouns are typically presented in a random order, and sequential effects have not been investigated. Our interest in this task was in the effects of the strengths of alternative verb responses on choosing one response. As discussed previously, there is considerable evidence in the picture naming literature that choosing the appropriate name involves selecting that name from semantically related competitors. In verb generation, choosing one response may involve resolving competition from other potential verb responses.

Thompson-Schill and colleagues (1997, 1998) provided evidence consistent with this view by examining verb generation under conditions with high and low selection demands. Based on norms from a verb generation pretest, nouns were selected for one of two conditions: low selection demand—one dominant response (e.g., apple → "eat") and high selection demand—the two most frequent responses being produced at approximately the same rate (e.g., map → "find" or "look"). Their results indicated that verb generation in the high selection condition was more difficult as neurally intact subjects showed longer reaction times and increased activity in the left IFG (Thompson-Schill et al., 1997), whereas patients with focal left IFG lesions displayed many more errors. Thompson-Schill and colleagues attributed these findings to the involvement of a selection mechanism in the high selection condition that is localized to the left IFG. Although Thompson-Schill et al. did not specifically invoke inhibition as the mechanism involved in selection, it is possible that inhibition could be involved, e.g., suppressing competitors in order to aid selection, as other studies have implicated the left IFG in inhibition (e.g., Jonides, Smith, Marshuetz, Koeepe, & Reuter-Lorenz, 1998). If so, then one might expect that patient ML, whose lesion includes the left IFG, to have particular difficulty in the high selection condition.

Selection from Competitors versus Association Strength

In a recent study, Martin and Cheng (2006) addressed the selection hypothesis for verb generation. They noted a confound in the Thompson-Schill et al. (1997, 1998) studies between selection condition and association strength between nouns and verbs. That is, because verbs in the low selection condition had one dominant response, whereas those in the high selection condition tended to have several weakly related responses, the association strength between the noun and the most frequent response was higher in the low selection condition than the high selection condition. Thus, the longer reaction times, greater neural activation, and more numerous errors from patients in the high selection condition might be due to the difficulty in retrieving a weakly associated response rather than from selection from competitors. In order to address this possibility, Martin and Cheng added a third condition which was a high selection condition, but one in which the two most frequent responses were both highly associated with the noun (e.g., door → open, close). Thus, the three conditions were high selection/low association, high selection/high association, low selection. Nouns in the low selection condition had a ratio of 3.0 or greater for the ratio of frequency of production of the most frequently produced verb relative to that for the second most frequently produced verb. Nouns in the high selection condition had a ratio of 2.0 or less. Fifteen nouns were selected for each condition from norms derived from a pretest for 250 nouns. The association strength between the most frequently produced verb was matched between the low selection and high selection/high association conditions. The nouns in all three conditions were matched on various measures including word length, syllable length, neighborhood size, spoken and written frequency, and the strength of possible nonverb responses based on free association norms (see Martin & Cheng, 2006, for more detail). Martin and Cheng reasoned that if selection was critical to the verb generation task, both high selection conditions, regardless of association strength, should be more difficult than the low selection condition. However, if association strength is the crucial factor influencing the ease or difficulty with which verbs are retrieved, then the high selection/low association condition should be more difficult than the other two conditions.

Ten Rice University undergraduates, ten elderly controls, and the aphasic patient ML participated in the verb generation task. The nouns were presented visually and auditorily with onset of the spoken word occurring at the same time as the onset of the printed word on the computer screen. Latencies for verb generation and errors (e.g., nonverb responses) were recorded. The latency results are shown in Table 16.2. The pattern of results was the same for all subjects. There was no significant difference in response latency between the low selection condition and the high-selection/high-association condition, but longer times were obtained for the high-selection/low-association condition than for the other two conditions. This pattern held up whether the data were scored in terms of reaction times for all correct responses or reaction times only for responses that matched the most frequently produced verb from pretest norms. The latter values were calculated on the grounds that reaction times in the low selection condition might have been inflated by the occasional production of the nondominant response, which should be difficult to produce given the presumably high activation of the dominant response. The undergraduate subjects made very few errors. For the older controls and for ML, the error rates paralleled the latency findings. It should be acknowledged, however, that ML made substantially more errors than the controls, particularly in the high-selection/low-association condition. Also, although his reaction times were within normal range on the low selection and high selection/high

TABLE 16.2   Mean RTs (ms) for the Three Experimental Conditions for Young Subjects, Older Controls, and Patient ML

	Young subjects		Older controls		ML[°]
	All correct responses	Most frequent verb	All correct responses	Most frequent verb	All correct responses[°°]
High-selection, Low-association	1654	1517	3736	4145	5893
High-selection, High-association	1168	1147	2449	2268	1326
Low-selection	1189	1149	2093	1868	1316

[°] Geometric means are reported for ML.
[°°] RTs for the most frequent verb are not reported for ML because the means would be based on few responses after eliminating responses to less frequent verbs.

association condition, his mean was outside the normal range on the high selection/ low association condition. We interpreted the results for ML to indicate that he had difficulty retrieving responses with a low association to the noun cue. Such an explanation is consistent with some theories that implicate the left IFG in controlled (as opposed to automatic) semantic retrieval (Badre & Wagner, 2002).[4]

These results were something of a surprise, as we had anticipated that, although association strength would play a role, competition would also play a role. Given that many findings in the word production literature implicate an effect of competitors, we had expected to find such an effect in verb generation, as the task involves word production. One difference between verb generation and typical word production tasks, such as picture naming or naming to definition, that may be of relevance to the findings is that in verb generation there is no one correct answer. Subjects are free to produce any verb that comes to mind, provided that it has some semantic relation to the noun cue. Perhaps selection processes are different and more affected by the strength of competitors when there is one correct answer that has to be selected from related alternatives. If so, such would suggest that the selection criterion (e.g., the ratio of the activation of the highest response relative to that of competitors) can be adjusted depending on task demands.

Letter-Cued Verb Generation Experiment

To assess whether the absence of a correct response was critical to the findings, a follow-up experiment was carried out (not reported in Martin & Cheng, 2006) in which subjects were instructed to produce a verb that began with a specific letter presented along with the noun. The materials and procedure were identical to that of the Martin and Cheng experiment, with a few exceptions: The nouns were presented only visually and the first letter of the most frequently produced verb from the pretest norms was presented below each noun on each trial. Subjects were instructed to produce a verb semantically related to the noun that began with that letter. Only Rice undergraduate students were tested in this experiment ($N = 19$).

The mean response latencies for correct responses were nearly equal for the low selection condition (1725 ms), and the high-selection/high-association condition (1716 ms), and much longer in the high-selection/low-association condition (3369 ms). Reaction times were overall substantially longer than in the Martin and Cheng (2006) experiment, presumably due to subjects' having to verify that they had retrieved a verb beginning with the appropriate letter. Nonetheless, the reaction time pattern mimicked that from the experiment without the letter cues. Planned comparisons using both subjects (t_1) and items (t_2) as random factors revealed that response latencies were significantly longer in the high-selection/ low-association condition than in the high-selection/high-association condition, $t_1(18) = 5.56$, $t_2(28) = 5.07$, and longer than in the low-selection condition, $t_1(18) = 5.48$, $t_2(28) = 6.00$ (all $ps < .001$). There was no difference in latencies between the low-selection condition and the high-selection/high-association condition, $t_1(18) = 0.1$, $t_2(18) = 0.14$.

Thus, the pattern from verb generation once again indicated no effect of competition but an effect of association strength on verb generation. Even when subjects were required to produce a certain verb based on the letter cue, we could uncover no evidence of competition from the strongly related secondary response in the high-selection/high-association condition. Hence, it appears that it was not the absence of a requirement for a particular response that resulted in the findings reported in the Martin and Cheng (2006) study. Further discussion of possible reasons for a lack of competition will provided in the General Discussion.

GENERAL DISCUSSION

In this final section, we will first consider further the findings from the semantic blocking and verb generation pardigms in terms of the model of word production presented in Figure 16.1. We will then discuss whether the explanations for these effects could provide any insight into the retrieval inhibition findings from episodic and semantic memory paradigms, and conversely whether findings from those domains provide a challenge to the interpretations offered in terms of the word production model.

Semantic Blocking and Retrieval Inhibition

In the discussion of the semantic blocking effect in picture naming, we hypothesized that postselection inhibition of a selected response occurs to a greater extent for controls than for patient ML. Even for controls, however, we propose that this postselection inhibition is not complete—otherwise there would be no semantic blocking effect. With regard to the stages of picture naming stages depicted in Figure 16.1, one can ask about the level or levels at which this postselection inhibition occurs. If the purpose of this inhibition is to prevent reselection of the just-produced word, then inhibition at the lexical level would seem to be the most useful. Dampening at the lexical level would lead to a large reduction in activation at the phonological level as well, but activation at the semantic level would remain intact. That is, since activation at the lexical level provides feedforward activation to the phonological level, dampening the lexical-level activation will cut off this source of activation to the phonological level, and thus, activation at the phonological level would decay. Activation at the semantic level would only be affected to the extent that there is feedback from the lexical level to the semantic level. However, not all models assume such feedback, and, even in those that do, the amount of feedback activation is substantially less than feedforward activation (see Rapp & Goldrick, 2000). One might hypothesize instead that postselection inhibition involves a dampening of activation throughout the whole system at semantic, lexical, and phonological levels. However, there would seem to be an advantage for persisting activation at the semantic level in terms of the spread of activation to related concepts that a speaker may wish to refer to subsequently. A high level of persisting activation at the semantic level, combined with a low level of above baseline activation at the lexical level, might give rise to the facilitatory effect (or at least null effect) in the semantic blocking paradigm on the first cycle for controls. As more words are produced, there will be more lexical competitors with some above-baseline activation, resulting in greater competition in selection. The fact that ML did not show any evidence of facilitation on the first cycle might be attributed to the fact that, for him, the persisting activation at the lexical level in the semantically blocked condition was greater than for controls—thus canceling out any benefit from spreading activation at the conceptual level even during the first cycle.

Relation to Retrieval Inhibition

In the introduction we noted the relation between the retrieval inhibition findings in memory paradigms and those observed in language production during picture naming. There are some striking similarities, particularly when one focuses on retrieval from semantic memory (Brown, 1979, 1981; Brown et al., 2005) and picture naming from semantically blocked lists. In both, the effect results from repeatedly retrieving names from the same category. There is some evidence the effect does not occur on the second sampling from the category, but takes several trials to build up (Brown, 1981; Loftus & Loftus, 1974). The decrease in retrieval accuracy and the increasing reaction times in picture naming can be demonstrated even when intervening trials from other categories are interspersed between retrievals or naming trials from the same category (Brown, 1981; Brown et al., 2005; Howard, Nickels, Coltheart, & Cole-Virtue, 2006). There is evidence that, in picture naming, an interfering effect from producing a semantically related competitor may persist up to 8 min (Wheeldon & Monsell, 1994), and there is some suggestion in the semantic memory retrieval literature that the effects may persist at least up to this amount of time (10–15 min in Brown et al., 2005). Of course, the paradigms are quite different. In semantic memory retrieval, the items have to be retrieved based on the conjoint information from the category cue and the letter cue, whereas in picture naming there is no need for a category cue to be present to get the effect, and the picture provides a very strong cue as to what the retrieved name should be. Nonetheless, picture naming does depend on accessing semantic information in long-term memory from the picture attributes and using that semantic information to access a phonological representation for the name.

In extending our account of semantic blocking in naming to the retrieval inhibition paradigm, one would have to assume that items selected for recall (or items simply read in the part-list cueing paradigm) remain activated above baseline at the lexical level (despite postselection inhibition) and thus provide interference in retrieval for later list items. In order to account for the memory results, one would have to assume that this interference is sufficient to prevent recall, not just to lengthen reaction time, as it does in the case of picture naming. As in the naming paradigm, we could assume that the greater persisting activation at the semantic than at the lexical level following one retrieval episode is sufficient to provide either priming or at least a minimization of the interfering effect on the trial following the first retrieval from the category. If this linkage of language and memory effects is valid, then one would predict that ML would demonstrate great difficulty on retrieval inhibition in episodic and semantic memory paradigms. We plan to pursue this issue in future work.[5]

One might question, however, whether a persisting activation account is a reasonable one for an effect that endures across at least several minutes, and appears immune to the processing of intervening items. One might hypothesize instead that small, but permanent changes in connection strengths occur in the lexical network as a result of activation flowing from the semantic to lexical to phonological nodes during the production of a word. The stronger these links at each level, the greater the activation of this word as a competitor when subsequently attempting to produce a related word. It is unclear, however, how such an approach could be used to account for the pattern demonstrated by ML. That is, one might expect that the amount of increase in connection strengths due to prior production would, if anything, be reduced in ML relative to controls as some nonspecific result of his brain damage. (There would be little reason to expect a greater increase in connection strength for him.) If so, then one might have predicted a smaller semantic blocking effect for him than for controls.

Verb Generation and the Fan Effect

In the verb generation paradigm, there is no repeated sampling from a semantic category or even from the set of verbs related to a particular noun. Nouns appear in a random order, with no semantic relation between successive trials. Hence, there is no means by which persisting activation across trials (nor a failure to minimize this persistence) could affect the results. Thus, competitive effects would have to occur within a trial, as the subject is searching for a verb response associated with a particular noun. We assume that perception of the spoken or written noun leads to activation of its meaning at a conceptual level. We would also assume that the requirement to search for a verb that is related to the noun activates concepts such as "action" or "function" at a conceptual level. The conjoint spread of activation from both the particular noun meaning and the general meaning of "verb" would lead to a heightened activation of those aspects of the noun meaning related to a verb.[6] It is at the conceptual level where one might expect activation of the different verb meanings that were obtained in the pretest norms for verb generation. That is, for example, concepts for "eat" and "toss" might both be activated for "salad." Let us assume that "eat" is selected at this point as the response, leaving aside for the moment the means by which this selection takes place. Once this is selected, activation will spread to the lexical level, with competitors for "eat," such as "consume" or "drink" becoming activated at the lexical level. These competitors are not likely to be those generated in the verb generation norms, as for the most part, the different verbs generated for a given noun were not close semantic competitors. Consequently, the degree of selection indicated by the conditions (i.e., high vs. low selection) did not correspond to the degree of competition at the lexical level, but instead at the conceptual level.

With regard to the means by which selection takes place at the conceptual level, there appears to be little work addressing the issue in the language processing literature. As discussed by Martin and Cheng (2006), prior studies documenting the effects of competition on selection have been those involving competition at a lexical level. One such study by Schriefers, Meyer, and Levelt (1990) that contrasted lexical and conceptual effects, documented interference from semantic competitors when lexical selection was required (in picture naming), but not when only conceptual processing was required (in a recognition memory task with picture stimuli). Thus, our results showing no effects of competition might be considered as consistent with the Schriefers et al. findings.

In order to account for an absence of competitive effects, one could assume that in choosing a response at the conceptual level, the mechanisms hypothesized to underlie competitive effects in lexical selection (i.e., lateral inhibition or the ratio rule for activation of targets relative to competitors) are not involved. For instance, one might assume that selection of a concept is based on its activation crossing a particular threshold (Morton, 1969, 1979). Of course, one might question why different selection mechanisms would be involved at the conceptual and lexical levels. One reason may be that at the conceptual level, the different associated concepts do not represent mutually exclusive alternatives, as they do at the lexical level. (For example, a salad can be both tossed and eaten—and, usually is.) Thus, there would appear to be little benefit from suppressing nonselected concepts via lateral inhibition, as these nonselected concepts may soon become selected themselves in some ongoing discourse.

Relation to Fan Effect

The absence of an effect of the strength of competitors would seem to go against findings in the memory literature in which the more items associated with a particular retrieval cue, the greater the difficulty in retrieving any one of them (e.g., Anderson, 1974). Our manipulation of selection demand in verb retrieval did not depend on the number of verbs associated with a noun, but rather on the strength of the most frequently produced verb relative to the second. Even so, one might have expected faster times to retrieve a particular verb with an association strength of .4 when the next most frequently produced verb had a strength of .1 than when it had a strength of .3. However, in Anderson's account of the fan effect based on his ACT-R model (e.g., Anderson & Reder, 1999), the effect derives from a fixed amount of activation being divided among all of the associations. By necessity, the sum of all of the association strengths between nouns and verbs sums to 1.0 and hence the activation transmitted across any link with an association strength of .4 would be the same in Anderson's model, irrespective of the strength of the next most highly associated response. In his model, the probability of recall and reaction time for a response are a function of the association strength between cues and the target, and response selection depends on this activation crossing some threshold. Of course, this mechanism is an implementation of the process described above in which competition and inhibition do not play a role in the activation function.[7]

Concluding Comments

To summarize, we have accounted for findings from semantic blocking and verb generation in terms of a model of word production that involves a competitive process in selection at the lexical level but a noncompetitive activation and selection process at the conceptual level. We have arrived at these conclusions on the basis of findings from a brain-damaged patient ML, who in previous studies has demonstrated a deficit in inhibition (Hamilton & Martin, 2005, in press). We have suggested that this model of the processes involved in repeated sampling from the same category in word production might be extended to explain findings on retrieval inhibition in memory paradigms (e.g., Brown 1979, 1981; Brown et al., 2005; Neely et al., 1983; Roediger & Neely 1982; Roediger, 1973). A number of lines of inquiry might be undertaken to investigate whether this extension is warranted. Such studies might investigate more closely the exact relation between the effects of various manipulations in the picture naming and retrieval inhibition paradigms with normal subjects as well as with patients such as ML whose deficits are relevant to some of the claims about the operation of the model. As indicated in the introduction, for the most part, the memory and language literatures do not make much contact with each other. However, there may be important insights drawn from one domain to the other and common mechanisms may lay at the heart of some well-established phenomena in the two domains.

ACKNOWLEDGMENT

The research reported here and the preparation of this manuscript were supported by NIH grant no. DC-00218 to Rice University.

NOTES

1. Several memory models also include a response suppression mechanism (e.g., Brown, Preece, & Hulme, 2000; Burgess & Hitch, 1999; Farrell & Lewandowsky, 2002; Henson, 1998; Lewandowsky & Murdock, 1989; Nairne, 1990; Page & Norris, 1998) that is analogous to a postselection inhibition mechanism incorporated in various language production models. However, the level at which the item is suppressed is not specified to the extent that it is in language models; that is, most language models assume suppression occurs at the lexical level rather than the conceptual level.
2. However, this logic begs the question of what the state of activation of the target and competitors would be at the moment of selection for ML. That is, assuming that ML uses the same selection criterion as controls, it is possible that it would simply take longer for his system to sufficiently inhibit competitors such that this selection ratio of activation of the target to competitors was reached. If so, then activation of target and competitors might be at the same level as controls, resulting in no difference in the semantic blocking effect between ML and controls. However, naming latencies would be long because of the longer time needed to reach the required selection ratio. Computational modeling would be valuable here to work out the precise

effects of a deficit in lateral inhibition as such a deficit would affect the growth of activation of the target—which should be greater than normal because of a lack of inhibition from partially activated competitors.

3.   The pictures were provided courtesy of Myrna Schwartz at the Moss Rehabilitation Institute, Philadelphia, PA.

4.   Recently, Badre, Poldrack, Pare-Blagoev, Insler, and Wager (2005) have provided neuroimaging evidence that separate regions of the left IFG are involved in selection from competitors and controlled semantic search. Given ML's large left frontal lesion, it is likely that for him both areas have been affected.

5.   In fact, the semantic memory version of this task is much like the "category fluency" task used in clinical neuropsychological assessment to test for frontal lobe dysfunction. In this task, patients are asked to produce as many exemplars as quickly as possible from a particular category (such as "animal"). Given ML's frontal lobe lesion, impaired performance on this task would be predicted.

6.   The requirement to select a verb would also lead to a heightening of activation of verbs at the lexical level based on syntactic properties—specifically, raising the activation of those lexical nodes that have "verb" as their word class.

7.   However, in the ACT-R model, the strength of the association depends not just on the frequency of co-occurrence of any pair of items, but on the probability of one member of the association given the other. Hence, a notion of competition is built into association strength rather than into the process of selection. That is, for two different noun–verb pairs with equal co-occurrence frequencies, the association strength for the first pair will be less than for the second if the first verb co-occurs more frequently with other nouns.

REFERENCES

Anderson, J. R. (1974). Retrieval of propositional information from long-term memory. *Cognitive Psychology, 6*, 451–474.

Anderson, J. R. & Reder, L. M. (1999). The fan effect: New results and new theories. *Journal of Experimental Psychology: General, 128*, 186–197.

Anderson, M. C., & Bjork, R. A. (1994). Mechanisms of inhibition in long-term memory: A new taxonomy. In D. Dagenbach & T. H. Carr (Eds.), *Inhibitory processes in attention, memory, and language* (pp. 265–325). San Diego, CA: Academic Press.

Badre, D., Poldrack, R. A., Pare-Blagoev, E. J., Insler, R. Z., & Wagner, A. D. (2005). Dissociable controlled retrieval and generalized selection mechanisms in ventro-lateral prefrontal cortex. *Neuron, 107*, 127–181.

Badre, D., & Wagner, A. D. (2002). Semantic retrieval, mnemonic control, and prefrontal cortex. *Behavioral and Cognitive Neuroscience Reviews, 1*, 206–218.

Barch, D. M., Braver, T. S., Sabb, F. W., & Noll, D. C. (2000). Anterior cingulate and monitoring of response conflict: Evidence from an fMRI study of overt verb generation. *Journal of Cognitive Neuroscience, 12*, 298–309.

Belke, E., Meyer, A. S., & Damian, M. F. (2005). Refractory effects in picture naming as assessed in a semantic blocking paradigm. *Quarterly Journal of Psychology, 58A*, 667–692.

Brown, A. S. (1979). Priming effects in semantic memory retrieval processes. *Journal of Experimental Psychology: Human Learning and Memory, 5*(2), 65–77.

Brown, A. S. (1981). Inhibition in cued recall. *Journal of Experimental Psychology: Human Learning and Memory*, 7(3), 204–215.

Brown, A. S., Zoccoli, S., & Leahy, M. (2005). Cumulating retrieval inhibition in semantic and lexical domains. *Journal of Experimental Psychology: Learning, Memory, and Cognition*, 31(3), 496–507.

Brown, G. D. A., Preece, T., & Hulme, C. (2000). Oscillator-based memory for serial order. *Psychological Review*, 107, 127–181.

Burgess, N., & Hitch, G. J. (1999). Memory for serial order: A network model of the phonological loop and its timing. *Psychological Review*, 106, 551–581.

Cohen, J. D., MacWhinney, B., Flatt, M., & Provost, J. (1993). PsyScope: An interactive graphic system for designing and controlling experiments in the psychology laboratory using Macintosh computers. *Behavioral Research Methods, Instruments, and Computers*, 25, 257–271.

Crutch, S. J., & Warrington, E. K. (2005). Abstract and concrete concepts have structurally different representational frameworks. *Brain*, 128, 615–627.

Damian, M. F., Vigliocco, G., & Levelt, W. J. M. (2001). Effects of semantic context in the naming of pictures and words, *Cognition*, 81(3), B77–B86.

Dell, G. S. (1988). The retrieval of phonological forms in production: Tests of predictions from a connectionist model. *Journal of Memory and Language*, 27, 124–142.

Dell, G. S., & O'Seaghdha, P. G. (1992). Stages of lexical access in speech production. *Cognition*, 42, 287–314.

Dell, G. S., & O'Seaghdha, P. G. (1994). Inhibition in interactive activation models of linguistic selection and sequencing. In D. Dagenbach & T. H. Carr (Eds.), *Inhibitory processes in attention, memory, and language* (pp. 409–453). San Diego, CA: Academic Press.

Farrell, S., & Lewandowsky, S. (2002). An endogenous distributed model of ordering in serial recall. *Psychonomic Bulletin and Review*, 9, 59–79.

Freedman, M., & Martin, R. (2001). Dissociable components of short-term memory and their relation to long-term learning. *Cognitive Neuropsychology*, 18, 193–226.

Hamilton, A. C., & Martin, R. C. (2005). Dissociations among tasks involving inhibition: A single case study. *Cognitive, Affective, and Behavioral Neuroscience*, 5, 1–13.

Hamilton, A. C., & Martin, R. C. (in press). Proactive interference in a semantic short-term memory deficit: Role of semantic and phonological relatedness. *Cortex*.

Henson, R. N. A. (1998). Short-term memory for serial order: The start–end model. *Cognitive Psychology*, 36, 73–137.

Hillis, A. E., Kane, A., Tuffiash, E., Ulatowski, J. A., Barker, P. B., Beauchamp, N., & Wityk, R. (2001). Reperfusion of specific brain regions by raising blood pressure restores selective language functions in subacute stroke. *Brain and Language*, 79, 495–510.

Howard, D., Nickels, L., Coltheart, M., & Cole-Virtue, J. (2006). Cumulative semantic inhibition in picture naming: Experimental and computational studies. *Cognition*, 100(3), 464–482.

Indefrey, P., & Levelt, W. J. M. (2000). The spatial and temporal signatures of word production components. *Cognition*, 92, 101–144.

Jonides, J., Smith, E. E., Marshuetz, C., Koeepe, R., & Reuter-Lorenz, P. (1998). Inhibition in verbal working memory revealed by brain activation. *Proceedings of National Academy of Sciences*, 95, 8410–8413.

Kroll, J. F., & Curley, J. (1988). Lexical memory in novice bilinguals: The role of concepts in retrieving second language words. In M. Gruneberg, P. Morris, & R. Sykes (Eds.), *Practical aspects of memory* (Vol. 2, pp. 389–395). London: Wiley.

Kroll, J. F., & Stewart, E. (1994). Category interference in translation and picture naming: Evidence for asymmetric connections between bilingual memory representations. *Journal of Memory and Language, 33*(2), 149–174.

Levelt, W. J. M., Roelofs, A., & Meyer, A. S. (1999). A theory of lexical access in speech production. *Behavioral and Brain Sciences, 22*, 1–45.

Lewandowsky, S., & Murdock, B. B. (1989). Memory for serial order. *Psychological Review, 96*, 25–57.

Loftus, G. R., & Loftus, E. F. (1974). The influence of one memory retrieval on a subsequent memory retrieval. *Memory and Cognition, 2*, 467–471.

MacKay, D. G. (1987). *The organization of perception and action: A theory for language and other cognitive skills.* New York: Sprague.

Martin, R. C., & Cheng, Y. (2006). Selection demands vs. association strength in the verb generation task. *Psychonomic Bulletin and Review, 13*(3), 396–401.

Martin, R. C., & He, T. (2004). Semantic short-term memory and its role in sentence processing: A replication. *Brain and Language, 89*, 76–82.

Martin, R. C., & Lesch, M. (1996). Associations and dissociations between language impairment and list recall: Implications for models of short-term memory. In S. Gathercole (Ed.), *Models of short-term memory* (pp. 149–178). Hove, UK: Lawrence Erlbaum Associates Ltd.

McCarthy, R. A., & Kartsounis, L. D. (2000). Wobbly words: Refractory anomia with preserved semantics. *Neurocase, 6*, 487–497.

Monsell, S. (1978). Recency, immediate recognition memory, and reaction time. *Cognitive Psychology, 10*, 465–501.

Morton, J. (1969). The interaction of information in word recognition. *Psychological Review, 76*, 165–178.

Morton, J. (1979). Word recognition. In J. Morton & J. C. Marshall (Eds.), *Psycholinguistics* (Vol. 2, 109–156). London: Elek.

Nairne, J. S. (1990). A feature model of immediate memory. *Memory and Cognition, 18*, 251–269.

Neely, J., Schmidt, S., & Roediger, H. (1983). Inhibition from related primes in recognition memory. *Journal of Experimental Psychology: Learning, Memory, and Cognition, 9*(2), 196–211.

Page, M. P. A., & Norris, D. (1998). The primacy model: A new model of immediate serial recall. *Psychological Review, 105*, 761–781.

Rapp, B., & Goldrick, M. (2000). Discreteness and interactivity in spoken word production. *Psychological Review, 107*(3), 460–499.

Roediger, H. L. (1973). Inhibition in recall from cueing with recall targets. *Journal of Verbal Learning and Verbal Behavior, 12*, 644–657.

Roediger, H. L., & Neely, J. (1982). Retrieval blocks in episodic and semantic memory. *Canadian Journal of Psychology, 36*(2), 213–242.

Schnur, T., Schwartz, M., Brecher, A., & Hodgson, C. (2006). Semantic interference during blocked-cyclic naming: Evidence from aphasia. *Journal of Memory and Language, 54*, 199–227.

Schriefers, H., Meyer, A. S., & Levelt, W. J. M. (1990). Exploring the time course of lexical access in language production: Picture–word interference studies. *Journal of Memory and Language, 29*, 86–102.

Snodgrass, J. G., & Vanderwart, M. (1980). A standardized set of 260 pictures: Norms for name agreement, familiarity, and visual complexity. *Journal of Experimental Psychology: Human Learning and Memory, 6*(2), 174–215.

Stemberger, J. P. (1985). An interactive activation model of language production. In

A. W. Ellis (Ed.), *Progress in the psychology of language* (Vol. 1, pp. 143–186). London: Lawrence Erlbaum Associates, Inc.

Stroop, J. R. (1935). Studies of interference in serial verbal reactions. *Journal of Experimental Psychology, 18*, 643–662.

Thompson-Schill, S. L., D'Esposito, M., Aguirre, G., K., & Farah, M. J. (1997). Role of left inferior prefrontal cortex in retrieval of semantic knowledge: A re-evaluation. *Proceedings of National Academy of Sciences, USA: Neurobiology, 94*, 14792–14797.

Thompson-Schill, S. L., Swick, D., Farah, M. J., D'Esposito, M., Kan, I. P., & Knight, R. T. (1998). Verb generation in patients with focal frontal lesions: A neuropsychological test of neuroimaging findings. *Proceedings of National Academy of Sciences, USA: Psychology, 95*, 15855–15860.

Vitkovitch, M., Rutter, C., & Read, A. (2001). Inhibitory effects during object name retrieval. The effect of interval between prime and target on picture naming responses. *British Journal of Psychology, 92*(3), 483–506.

Watkins, M. J. (1975). Inhibition in recall with extralist "cues." *Journal of Verbal Learning and Verbal Behavior, 14*, 294–303.

Watkins, M. J. (1979). Engrams as cuegrams and forgetting as cue overload: A cueing approach to the structure of memory. In C. R. Puff (Ed.), *Memory organization and structure* (pp. 347–372). New York: Academic Press.

Wheeldon, L. R., & Monsell, S (1994). Inhibition of spoken word production by priming a semantic competitor. *Journal of Memory and Language, 33*, 332–356.

17

The Structure of Semantic and Phonological Networks and the Structure of a Social Network in Dreams

RICHARD SCHWEICKERT

We are all baffled by the vivid events in dreams, unconnected to evident stimuli. Readers of this volume may be reminded of the Deese–Roediger–McDermott paradigm, which produces an illusion that a word was presented, when it was not. In the paradigm (Deese, 1959; Roediger & McDermott, 1995), subjects are presented with a list of words such as *bed, rest, awake, tired, dream, wake,. . . .* The word *sleep* is not on the list. Yet recall and recognition for *sleep* are comparable to that for words actually presented. In their experiments, Roediger and McDermott asked subjects who indicated during recognition that a word had been presented to further indicate whether they had a vivid memory of its presentation (a remember judgment) or whether they were sure the word had been presented, but had no vivid memory of its presentation (a know judgment). The procedure is due to Tulving (1985). The proportion of vivid memories reported for critical nonpresented words was comparable to that for actually presented words. Strong associations in memory, when focused, can produce a false memory, comparable to a real memory.

Let's take a closer look at associations. The words actually presented in the Deese–Reodiger–McDermott paradigm are those frequently produced in free association to the critical nonpresented words. Free association has a long history in the study of dreams. Sigmund Freud asked dreamers to consider an element in a dream, and to say what first came to mind. The dreamer would then free associate to the products of the first free association and so on. An interpretation was constructed from these products. Associations were of much interest in 1900 when Freud published *The Interpretation of Dreams*. A few years earlier, Mary Calkins had invented the method of paired associate learning, presenting subjects with colors paired with numerals to investigate the relative importance for memory of vividness, frequency, and recency (1961). A few years later, to develop norms for evaluating mental patients, Kent and Rosanoff (1910) presented words to normal subjects, asking them to produce a free associate to each word. Some words were produced as free associates to a given word by many subjects, and some by a few. The norms, updated by Russell and Jenkins (1954), are the source of the word associates used in the Deese–Roediger–McDermott paradigm.

Words and their associates, or words and their meanings, are often represented as a network (Anderson, 1976; Collins & Loftus, 1975; Quillian, 1966; Rumelhart, Lindsay, & Norman, 1972). Figure 17.1 illustrates the model of Collins and Loftus (1975). Words standing for concepts are represented by vertices and two vertices are joined by an edge if the corresponding concepts have a property in common. A network is a natural representation, but what kind of network? Recently, Steyvers and Tenenbaum (2005) showed that three different human semantic networks are in a special class of networks called small world networks.

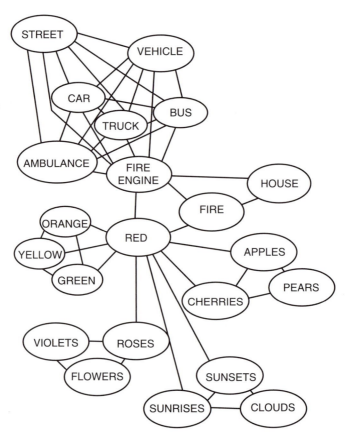

FIGURE 17.1   Word network of Collins and Loftus (1975).

SMALL WORLD NETWORKS

The inception of small world networks was an experiment by Milgrim (1967), who gave subjects unaddressed letters to deliver to a particular person in Boston. The instructions were to send the letter directly to the target person, if that person were known to the subject. Otherwise, the subject was to send the letter to a friend who would be likely to get the letter further along by sending it to another friend, and so on. Letters reached their target after a surprisingly small number of steps, typically about six.

The work attracted much attention. In a recent scholarly look at it, Kleinfeld (2002) found that many letters did not reach the target person (see Watts, 2003, for discussion). The experiment does not actually show that all pairs of people in a social network are connected by a short path, or connected at all. A safer conclusion is that for those pairs that are connected, a short connecting path often exists. The number of edges on the shortest path between two vertices is the distance between them. In our personal social networks, each of us can see that distances are short (each of our friends knows us, so two is the longest path between our friends). What is not apparent is that even when personal social networks are combined, the average distance between connected pairs of vertices is still small.

It is now known that many kinds of networks have small average distances (see Newman, 2003, for review), so this property by itself is not distinctive. Watts and Strogatz (1998) noticed that social networks have an additional property. We know many people through groups, such as groups of co-workers and groups of relatives. As a result, if a person knows two people, those two people often know each other through a group, and the three form a triangle in the social network.

The clustering coefficient indexes the number of triangles. The clustering coefficient at a single vertex v is calculated as follows. Consider a pair of vertices, each joined by a single edge to vertex v. If the pair of vertices are themselves joined by an edge, a triangle is formed. If they are not joined by an edge, a triangle is not formed. The clustering coefficient at v is the number of triangles formed at v divided by the number of triangles possible at v. (The number of triangles possible at v is the number of pairs of vertices with each vertex joined to v by a single edge.) Because of groups, the average clustering coefficient in social networks tends to be large.

The insight of Watts and Strogatz (1998) was that large clustering and small distances do not ordinarily occur together. There are networks high on both measures, and networks low on both measures. There also are networks high on clustering and low on average distance, and these special networks they call *small world networks*.

As a benchmark for small average distances, they chose random networks. These have small average distances and are well understood. In a random network, between every pair of vertices an edge is drawn with probability p (Erdös & Rényi, 1959; Solomonoff & Rapoport, 1951).

Watts and Strogatz (1998) chose two benchmarks for a large clustering coefficient. One is whether the clustering coefficient is larger than that of a random network. The other is whether the clustering coefficient is near that of a regular ring lattice (Figure 17.2), where each vertex is incident with the same number of edges. Imagine a dinner conversation at a round table in a noisy restaurant, where each person can converse only with the two people on his or her left and the two on his or her right. People are joined in groups of five people. This is an extreme case of connection only through groups. The clustering coefficient is high. On the other hand, to get a message to the person diametrically opposite you at the table, you must send it step by step around the edge of the table. There are no short-cuts, so if the network is large the average distance is large.

A third property often examined in small world networks has to do with the number of immediate neighbors a vertex has. The number of vertices joined to a particular vertex by a single edge is called the *degree* of the vertex. (In the terminology of Anderson, 1976, the degree of a vertex is its *fan*.) Albert, Jeong, and Barabasi (1999) found that in the networks studied by Watts and Strogratz (1998), the probability distribution of degrees is a power law. That is, if a vertex is selected at random, the probability its degree is k is c/k^a, where c and a are constants.

Excitement has been growing as example after example of real world networks is found to have the three properties of small average distances, large clustering, and power law degree distribution. For example, a network can be formed from the World Wide Web, with vertices representing sites, and edges (or directed arcs) representing links from one site to another. It has the two small world properties, and Albert et al. (1999) found that the degree distribution is a power law. Further examples in the review by Newman (2003) include networks of actors in films, email messages, hardware on the Internet, scientific citations, and protein inter-actions. One of the most intriguing is the discovery by Steyvers and Tenenbaum

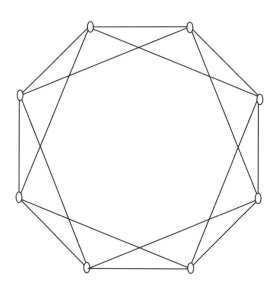

FIGURE 17.2   Regular ring lattice.

(2005) of the three properties in human semantic networks, because it suggests these may be properties of human memory.

THE SMALL WORLD STRUCTURE OF HUMAN SEMANTIC NETWORKS

Steyvers and Tenenbaum (2005) analyzed three databases. The first was free association norms by Nelson, McEvoy, and Schreiber (1999), similar to those used in the Deese–Roediger–McDermott paradigm. The second database was Roget's *Thesaurus* (Roget, 1911), and the third was WordNet (Fellbaum, 1998; Miller, 1995). The most relevant here is the free association norms. Steyvers and Tenenbaum constructed two networks from the norms. In the directed network, each word was represented by a vertex. If a cue word elicited another word as a free associate for at least two subjects, an arc was drawn directed from the first word to the second. The undirected network was the same as the directed network, except that the directions of the arcs were ignored.

Each network was found to have small average distances and large clustering. Further, each network had a power law degree distribution. Data for the undirected associative network, as an example, are in Table 17.1. The average distance for the undirected associative network is near that of a comparable random network. However, the clustering coefficient is orders of magnitude greater than that of a comparable random network.

The power law degree distribution was presaged by Zipf (1945). He discovered that if words are rank ordered by the number of dictionary meanings they have, the log of the number of meanings is linearly related to the log of the rank (Figure 17.3). This relation, Zipf's Law, is equivalent to a power law (approximately for discrete distributions and exactly for continuous distributions; see Adamic, http://www.hpl.hp.com/research/idl/papers/ranking/ranking.html).

Free associations often include phonologically similar clangs, like pan and man. The model of Collins and Loftus (1975) allows for these by assuming there is a network for words with edges based on phonological similarity, separate from the semantic network. There is now evidence that phonological networks have small world properties. A database of words was constructed from phonological transcriptions by Nusbaum, Pisoni, and Davis (1984). Vitevitch (2005) constructed a network from it by representing each word as a vertex, and joining two vertices

TABLE 17.1 Undirected Associative Network Parameters (from Steyvers & Tenenbaum, 2005)

Average distance	
Associative network	3.04
Random network	3.03
Clustering coefficient	
Associative network	.186
Random network	.00435

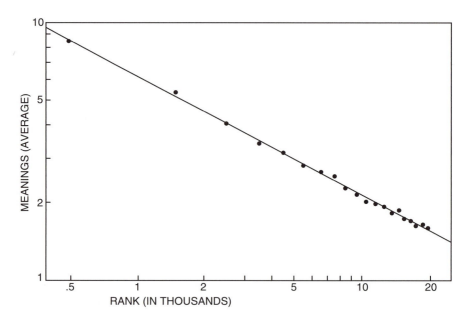

FIGURE 17.3 Zipf's Law for meanings per word and rank by meanings (Zipf, 1945).

with an edge if the corresponding words differed by a single phoneme. He found the network to have the small world properties of small average distances and large clustering. A power law degree distribution fits over a range of degrees, although vertices of high degree do not fit well (this exception sometimes occurs; see Watts, 2003).

Each of the networks investigated has the three characteristic properties. Because people know well the words and relations of their language, as represented in the networks, the results suggest that the three properties are also properties of human memory. However, a structure such as WordNet is an artifact, produced by a community. Evidence that human memory has these properties would be more direct if the properties could be found in a natural product of a single individual's memory. The evidence we need is in dreams.

DREAM FORM AND CONTENT

In dreams syntax is clearly sound. When characters speak the grammar is that of ordinary conversation. Surfaces, edges, and corners usually join in ordinary ways to form objects. Just as clearly, practical knowledge is deranged. One character turns into another, or a woman has a minnow for a husband.

The soundness of semantics in dreams is between that of syntax and practicality. Finding the meaning of dreams is as difficult now as in 1900. But finding associations between elements of a dream is often easy, as is finding associations between elements of a dream and elements of waking life. Many associations in dreams are so commonplace as to be overlooked, such as when a character goes from the setting of a street to the setting of a friend's house. Perhaps the associations are lawful.

For Freud, associations were a guide to meaning. Freud (1900) proposed that a dream is a disguised but meaningful message. The source is a desire strong enough to wake the sleeper. To guard sleep, a message is sent, saying (falsely) that the wish has already been fulfilled. But the sleeper's deepest wishes are so barbarous that awareness of them would wake the sleeper. Hence, the disguise.

A year later, Henri Bergson (1901/1958) proposed that the source of dreams is simply the occasional dots (phosphenes) we see when we close our eyes, and other faint miscellaneous sensations. "Confronted with these odd collections of images with no plausible meaning, our intelligence . . . searches for an explanation, tries to fill in the gaps. It fills them by calling up other rememberances . . ." (p. 35). "The force which converts into specific well defined objects the vague, indeterminate sensations which we retrieve . . . is memory" (p. 36).

The activation-synthesis hypothesis of J. Allen Hobson and Robert W. McCarley (1977) incorporates details of the physiology of the dreaming state, known far better by then (and even better now). Key parts of their account of the source and form of dreams are similar to Bergson's (1901/1958; see McNamara, 1996). Briefly, they say the source of dream imagery (the activation) is stimuli "whose generation appears to depend on a largely random or reflex process," which they attributed to the pontine brain stem. Then, "best fits to the relative inchoate and incomplete data provided by the primary stimuli are called up from memory," leading to the dream imagery (the synthesis) (p. 1347). Building on this hypothesis, Francis Crick and Graeme Mitchison (1983) say the anatomy of the cortex suggests its use of superimposed storage would lead to problems such as bizarre associations, productions of the same state regardless of input, and hallucinations. To reduce these, during sleep "more or less random stimulation of the forebrain by the brainstem" elicits these "parasitic modes," which are then damped down by reverse learning.

Quantitative study of dreams began in the Fall of 1890, when Mary Calkins found herself sitting across a library fire from William James, as the only student in his seminar, and also began her laboratory work with Edmund Sanford. In addition to ordinary laboratory projects, they decided to set alarm clocks periodically through the nights and record their dreams (Calkins, 1961). The result was the first content analysis of dreams. Calkins (1893) tabulated occurrences of characters, locations, and emotions. She remarked that a large proportion of the characters are unknown to the dreamer, and, contrary to many expectations, unimportant events of waking life occur often, whereas important events occur infrequently. She observed that "Not only imagination, but real thought occurs in dreams," as does volition.

Later, Calvin S. Hall and Robert van de Castle (1966) developed a more detailed coding system for characters, social interactions, settings, emotions, and so on. This work was summarized and updated with new material by G. William Domhoff (1996), who later reported an extensive study of characters in dreams of a single individual (Domhoff, 2003). Such studies of the manifest content of dreams are far fewer than studies of what Freud called the latent content, but if one is searching for evidence, it is in the manifest content one must look. Before turning to our analysis, let us consider two objections to studying dreams to learn about memory.

DREAMS AS A PRODUCT OF MEMORY

One objection to examining dreams to learn about memory is that there may be other sources for dream content, such as perception and motivation. Evidence in the 19th century began to indicate the role of perception is minor:

> It is impossible to attribute the wealth of ideational material in dreams to external nervous stimuli alone. Miss Mary Whiton Calkins (1893, 312) examined her own and another person's dreams for six weeks with this question in mind. She found that in only 13.2 per cent and 6.7 per cent of them respectively was it possible to trace the element of external sense-perception; while only two cases in the collection were derivable from organic sensations. Here we have statistical confirmation of what I had been led to suspect from a hasty survey of my own experiences.
>
> (Freud, 1900, p. 255)

We have far more data about this now. There is evidence that perception plays a role (Nielson, 1993), but also evidence indicating dreams are far more a product of memory than of perception (Foulkes, 1985, p. 19). In the most dramatic experiment, heroic subjects sleeping with their eyes taped open did not dream about the visual stimuli presented to them (Rechtschaffen & Foulkes, 1965). The motivational system is harder to experiment with, so it is harder to argue from data. But the motives of most concern to Freud were not simple urges for simple objects, like thirst for water, but complex motives conflicting with norms; that is, one can argue, dependent on memory. The physiological evidence suggests that during dreaming sensory and motor systems are mostly blockaded (Hobson & McCarley, 1977), which may have something to do with the unruly practicality in dreams. With little or no involvement of sensory and motor systems, dreams take their major organization from the organization of memory.

A second objection is that recall of dreams relies on memory, so properties of memory found in dream reports are not necessarily properties of dreams themselves. Calkins (1893, p. 312) puts it well:

> Sometimes the slight movement of reaching for paper and pencil or of lighting one's candle seems to dissipate the dream-memory, and one is left with the tantalizing consciousness of having lived through an interesting dream experience of which one has not the faintest memory.
>
> At the best, one may discuss only dreams as remembered.

Unfortunately, although we now know the most likely times to wake people in sleep laboratories to elicit dream reports, the reports must rely on recall.

Conclusions about dreams are, more precisely, conclusions about dream reports, with implications for memory in either case, of course.

THE FIRST 100 DREAMS OF MERRI: AN ARTIST

The finding of Steyvers and Tenenbaum (2005) that human semantic networks have a small world structure, and the finding of Vitevitch (2005) of such a structure in a phonological network, strongly suggest that human memory has such a structure. If dreams are largely a product of associations in memory, including puns (e.g., Freud, 1900), then the structure should appear in dreams. Examining characters is especially promising. The memories an individual holds of people are likely to be organized in a small world structure, in order to represent the individual's social network, which probably has such a structure.

Method

Adam Schneider and G. William Domhoff at the University of California at Santa Cruz maintain dream reports on their web site, www.dreambank.net, in a form convenient for computer searches (2005). Their generous work makes studies possible now that would not have been attempted before.

Dream reports were browsed to find someone who wrote clearly and often mentioned characters. Reports from Merri: An artist were selected. At the time of writing, the first 100 dream reports have been coded for characters. Due to minor clerical errors, e.g., repetition of dream reports, the first 100 dreams are #001 through #104. Coding is proceeding on the rest, so results here are preliminary.

Here is the first dream:

#001 (05/13/1999)

South of Canal St. in Chinatown we were using the Chinese factory after hours to frame pictures and glue them. Joe Fong cut out beautiful, eerie, disturbed pictures of blue houses and glued them against black and white skies. He left glue bubbles everywhere. I went down to the corner to wait for my sister. I waited and waited. A guy came by and said, "What are you doing?" And I said, "I'm not sure. If I wait here my sister will walk by." He said, "Then I'll wait for you." I climbed up the ladder to look and see a few of the cards we'd made but really they were junk. William accidentally threw a roll of paper towels out the window onto a busy Chinatown street. Then Carlos threw a stapler out the window. Then a stranger threw a wrench. We agreed it was time to pour wet cement. One inch thick and boards on sides. The Chinese children were running a scam. I could see the sunlight in little girls' hair. Golden sunshine sparkles. I looked over my shoulder for Dora. It was an old show from a TV that was playing. I walked up a steep staircase and was trying to find where we parked the car in Chinatown. I remembered kicking the door 3 times. On top of the building was s [sic] steep roof covered with tiny Chinese lanterns. I started stomping lanterns and a girl said, "What's wrong?" And I said, "My sister used to love these." She said, "Have you ever had a telepathic experience?" And I said, "Yes." An artist in prison was standing up on a desk. His cell was 8-sided with windows and painted yellow. He was sitting tracing his feet and trying to paint a comma, huge, in one window because, he said, "What's behind it goes on and on, like what's behind corners. Endless words. Endless space. He was happy drawing.

(323 words)

Joe Fong is the first character. The dreamer mentions waiting for her sister (who we learn in later dream reports is Dora), but her sister does not show up, so her sister is not coded as present. A guy is present. No features are given that would help identify him if he appeared in a later dream. As the dreamer did not give him a name, a unique label with the dream number is made for him, "guy(001)" and he is coded as present. The Chinese children are not coded with the current system. To test the power law, we are interested in the number of characters occurring in each dream. If a group is referred to in a way that allows the number of characters in the group to be known, the individuals in the group are coded. For example, if Dream #n indicates "the triplets" were present, then characters "triplet(n, 1)," "triplet(n, 2)" and "triplet(n, 3)" are coded as present. Until a satisfactory way of coding groups is found, if the number of individuals in a group is unknown, the group is ignored. In total, seven characters are coded as present in Dream #001, Joe Fong, guy(001), William, Carlos, stranger(001), girl(001), and artist(001).

The goal is to code a character as present whenever the character appears in a dream. How do we identify extras, like the guy in Dream #001? Suppose in one of your dreams, a guy is near you in a store and 6 months later in another dream a guy sits by you on a bus. Is it the same guy? How could you tell? Sometimes a dream report of Merri lists a few characteristics, such as "post adolescent black girl." A word search through all the dream reports has not, so far, turned up any reappearances of incidental characters described by more than a couple of modifiers. Words like "guy" and "girl" occur frequently, and one can only presume that if enough characteristics had been listed to identify the corresponding characters, they too would not be found in other dreams. We can be pretty sure, by the way, that faces of extras are not formed by superimposing a large number of faces from memory. Faces formed by superimposition tend to be beautiful (Langlois & Roggman, 1990), yet no one remarks that passers-by are all beautiful in dreams.

Some characters could not occur in waking life, as in the following excerpt:

#005 (05/18/1999)

I was at the creek. An old lady who was invisible was sitting on the bank watching minnows. One of the minnows was her husband but she was the only one who knew that. . . . There was a tiny little boy in a birdcage. He was no more than ½ inch tall. He was swinging on the little bird swing like Tweety. . . .

Although imaginary, the invisible old lady, her minnow husband, and the tiny little boy are coded as characters present.

The coding system was inspired by that of Hall and van de Castle (1966; Domhoff, 1996), and is similar in many respects. There are two main differences. First, in the Hall and van de Castle system, if the dream report said "I went to

Grandma's house," Grandma would be coded as a character. In this system, a character not explicitly stated to be present must be present in the sense that a social interaction between the character and the dreamer or between the character and another character is possible (even if none took place). This more restrictive criterion for coding a character as present may or may not matter for present purposes. But one reason for thinking human memory has small world network properties is that these properties are found in actual social networks. Hence, it seemed prudent to stay close to the notion of an actual social network. (It would be more realistic to code whether two characters actually interacted socially in a dream, but sometimes this is difficult to judge from the reports.) Second, in this system, every character is labeled separately. If the dream report refers to Aunt Dianne, the character is labeled "Aunt Dianne." In the Hall and van de Castle system, the character would ordinarily be labeled as an aunt, and the identity of the individual aunt would not be indicated by the label. The difficulty is that if another dream report refers to Aunt Jackie, the information that these two aunts are different characters is not available from the ordinary label. Labels are a minor point, because more extensive labels are easily incorporated in the Hall–van de Castle system.

Results

The outcome of the coding is a matrix of 1s and 0s, where a 1 in row c, column d indicates that character c occurs in dream d. This leads to a network with two mutually exclusive sets of vertices, one set for characters and one set for dreams. An edge joins a character vertex to a dream vertex if and only if the character occurs in the dream. This network, called a bipartite network, is not itself a social network, but a social network was constructed from it. Analyses were done with the software Pajek (Batagelj & Mrvar, 2003), available at http://vlado.fmf.uni-lj.ai/pub/networks/pajek/. In the constructed social network vertices represent characters and two vertices are joined by an edge if the corresponding characters occur in the same dream (Figure 17.4). There are 362 characters and 1290 edges.

At the outskirts of the network are some isolated vertices, each representing a character in a dream with no one else. There are also isolated components with two or more vertices joined to each other, but to no one else. These represent characters in a dream with each other, but with no character appearing in any other dream. At the outskirts there are also sets of vertices joined to each other, being in the same dream, but with one member of the set also joined to vertices in another dream, and with one or more of these joined to vertices in yet another dream. After a few jumps, the midst of the network is reached. At the center of the figure is the character of highest degree, the dreamer's sister, Dora, who is in dreams with 89 characters.

According to the web site, Dora was killed somehow before the dream series was recorded. The most important character in the dream social network is no longer present in the dreamer's waking life. Her dreaming and waking social networks must not be the same.

For the dream social network, the average distance between characters who

FIGURE 17.4   Social network for first 100 dreams of Merri.

are connected by a path was calculated. Recall that in a small world network, this would be similar to the average distance in a random network. The appropriate comparison is with the population of random social networks, constructed from a bipartite network as follows. Consider the population of all bipartite networks, with one set of vertices for dreams and another set of vertices for characters, with (a) the degree distribution for the dream vertices matching that observed for Merri, and with (b) the degree distribution for characters matching that observed for Merri, but with (c) the character vertices joined to the dream vertices at random. Now consider the population of social networks constructed from these bipartite networks. This is the appropriate population of comparison random networks. The typical distance between vertices for this population was calculated using an equation derived for this purpose by Newman, Watts, and Strogatz (2002, Equation 14). In Table 17.2 it can be seen that the average distance for the dream social network is similar to the typical distance for the random social networks, so the first property of a small world network is found.

The clustering coefficient was calculated for the dream social network. The comparison is with that of a regular ring lattice. In a regular ring lattice, every vertex has the same degree, an integer. In the dream social network, the average degree of a vertex is 7.13. Comparable regular ring networks have vertices with degrees of either 7 or 8. For these, the largest clustering coefficient possible is less than .67. The value for the dream social network is larger (Table 17.2), so the second property of a small world network is found.

TABLE 17.2   Dream Social Network Parameters

Average distance	
Dream social network	2.9
Random network	2.2
Clustering coefficient	
Dream social network	.89
Regular ring lattice	<.67

The degree of a character is the number of characters in at least one dream with the character. A convenient way to check a power law is to check Zipf's Law. According to Zipf's Law, if characters are ranked by degree, the log of the degree is linear in the log of the rank. A plot of these is in Figure 17.5 (degree 0 is omitted because the log is undefined). Clearly, Zipf's Law is violated for characters of high rank (low degree). These tend to be characters who occur in only one dream. If ranks 0 through 5 are omitted, a straight line fits quite well, $r^2 = .92$. With this we conclude the dream social network has all three characteristics: small average distance, large clustering, and power law degree distribution (when low degrees are omitted).

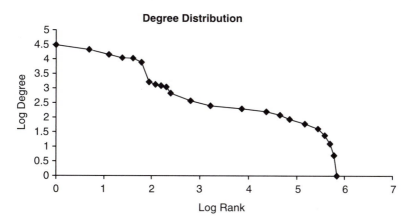

FIGURE 17.5   Zipf's Law for the dream social network.

CONCLUSIONS AND SPECULATIONS

If a structure is found in dreams, it is generated from the dreamer's memory, so a structure like that in Figure 17.4, perhaps simpler, is in the dreamer's memory and somehow participates in generating the dreams. When someone reports a dream after it occurs, two characters mentioned in the report are associated in memory to some degree as a result of being in the narrative together. So, the structure in Figure 17.4 is part of the structure in the memory of the dream reporter Merri. A stronger but reasonable assumption is that when two characters are in a dream together, an association between them remains in memory even if the dream itself is not recalled; this assumption seems untestable. Even without the stronger assumption, finding the three network properties in Merri's first 100 dream reports indicates that these are properties of Merri's memory.

Further, the dream social network has structural properties of actual social networks. Going a step further, the study of social networks may shed light on dreams. In a famous paper on social networks, called "The Strength of Weak Ties," Granovetter (1973) noted that acquaintances play important social roles. For example, people looking for a job received the most helpful tips from acquaintances, because information provided by people known well was already available.

Finding relevant remote associations in memory is essential in activities like problem solving and writing poetry. Dreaming may maintain the weak connections that make this possible (see Stickgold, 1998) and that hold distant parts of the memory network together. The tricky part is to maintain weak connections without strengthening them, because, while awake, imagining actions strengthens memory (Goff & Roediger, 1998). Brain chemistry during dreaming is different from that while awake, suggesting to Hobson and McCarley (1977) that there may be state dependent learning. A speculation is that during creative activity, people relax into a state chemically similar to dreaming, allowing remote associations to emerge.

The importance of weak connections in dreaming was shown by Stickgold, Scott, Rittenhouse, and Hobson (1999). In a lexical decision task, subjects were presented with a letter string, such as THECK, and asked to indicate whether it is an English word or not. Suppose a subject has just responded that NURSE is a word. Ordinarily, if the next string is DOCTOR, the participant responds more quickly that it is a word than if the next string is BUTTER. Strong associations ordinarily lead to shorter response times than weak ones. However, when Stickgold, et al. awakened people during REM sleep and gave them a lexical decision task, weak associates produced shorter reaction times than strong ones. Following these hints, a final speculation is that perhaps while dreaming weak associates join forces to somehow produce illusory percepts, just as while awake strong associates join forces to produce false memories in the Deese–Roediger–McDermott paradigm.

ACKNOWLEDGMENT

I thank G. William Domhoff for helpful comments, Mark Steyvers for help with small world networks, and Daniel Poyter, Mona Reed, and Lisa Siqueira for coding help and discussion.

REFERENCES

Adamic, L. A. Zipf, power-laws, and Pareto – a ranking tutorial. Retrieved November 25, 2004, from http://www.hpl.hp.com/research/idl/papers/ranking/ranking.html

Albert, R., Jeong, H., & Barabasi, A. L. (1999). Internet—Diameter of the world wide web. *Nature, 401,* 130–131.

Anderson, J. R. (1976). *Language, memory and thought.* Hillsdale, NJ: Lawrence Erlbaum Associates, Inc.

Batagelj, V., & Mrvar, A. PajekProgram for large network analysis. Retrieved June 18, 2005, from http://vlado.fmf.uni-lj.ai/pub/networks/pajek/

Batagelj, V., & Mrvar, A. (2003). PajekAnalysis and visualization of large networks. In M. Jünger & P. Mutzel (Eds.) *Graph drawing software* (pp. 77–103). Berlin: Springer.

Bergson, H. (1958). *The world of dreams.* New York: Philosophical Library, Inc. (Original work published 1901)

Calkins, M. W. (1893). Statistics of dreams. *American Journal of Psychology, 5,* 311–343.

Calkins, M. W. (1961). Mary Whiton Calkins. In C. Murchison (Ed.), *A history of psychology in autobiography* (Vol. 1; pp. 31–62). New York: Russel & Russel.

Collins, A. M., & Loftus, E. F. (1975). A spreading-activation theory of semantic processing. *Psychological Review, 82,* 407–428.

Crick, F., & Mitchison, G. (1983). The function of dream sleep. *Nature, 304,* 111–114.

Deese, J. (1959). On the prediction of occurrence of particular verbal intrusions in immediate recall. *Journal of Experimental Psychology, 58,* 17–22.

Domhoff, G. W. (1996). *Finding meaning in dreams: A quantitative approach.* New York: Plenum Press.

Domhoff, G. W. (2003). *The scientific study of dreams.* Washington, DC: American Psychological Association.

Erdös, P., & Rényi, A. (1959). On random graphs. *Publicationes Mathematicae, 6,* 290–297.

Fellbaum, C. (Ed.). (1998). *WordNet, an electronic lexical database.* Cambridge, MA: MIT Press.

Foulkes, D. (1985). *Dreaming: A cognitive-psychological analysis.* Hillsdale, NJ: Lawrence Erlbaum Associates, Inc.

Freud, S. (1900). *The interpretation of dreams.* New York: Avon Books.

Goff, L. M., & Roediger, H. L., III. (1998). Imagination inflation for action events: Repeated imaginings lead to illusory recollections. *Memory and Cognition, 26,* 20–33.

Granovetter, M. (1973). The strength of weak ties. *American Journal of Sociology, 83,* 1420–1443.

Hall, C. S., & van de Castle, R. (1966). *The content analysis of dreams.* New York: Appleton-Century-Crofts.

Hobson, J. A., & McCarley, R. W. (1977). The brain as a dream state generator: An activation-synthesis hypothesis of the dream process. *American Journal of Psychiatry, 134,* 1335–1348.

Kent, G. H., & Rosanoff, A. J. (1910). A study of association in insanity. *American Journal of Insanity, 67,* 37–96.

Kleinfeld, J. S. (2002). The small-world problem. *Society, 39,* 61–66.

Langlois, J. H., & Roggman, L. A. (1990). Attractive faces are only average. *Psychological Science, 1,* 115–121.

Milgram, S. (1967). The small world problem. *Psychology Today, 2,* 60–67.

Miller, G. A. (1995). WordNet: An on-line lexical database. *International Journal of Lexicography, 3* (Whole No. 4).

McNamara, P. (1996). Bergson's theory of dreaming. *Dreaming: Journal of the Association for the Study of Dreams, 6,* 173–186.

Nelson, D. L., McEvoy, C. L., & Schreiber, T. A. (1999). *The University of South Florida word association norms.* Retrieved from http://w3.usf.edu/Free/Association

Newman, M. E. J. (2003). The structure and function of complex networks. *SIAM Review*, *45*, 167–256.

Newman, M. E. J., Watts, D. J., & Strogatz, S. H. (2002). Random graph models of social networks. *Proceedings of the National Academy of Sciences, 99*, 2566–2572.

Nielsen, T. A. (1993). Changes in the kinesthetic content of dreams following somato-sensory stimulation of leg muscles during REM sleep. *Dreaming: Journal of the Association for the Study of Dreams, 3*, 99–113.

Nusbaum, H. C., Pisoni, D. B., & Davis, C. K. (1984). Sizing up the Hoosier mental lexicon: Measuring the familiarity of 20,000 words (Research on Speech Perception Progress Rep. No. 10). Bloomington, IN: Speech Research Laboratory, Department of Psychology, Indiana University.

Quillian, M. R. (1966). *Semantic memory*. Unpublished doctoral dissertation, Carnegie Institute of Technology. (Reprinted in part in *Semantic information processing* by M. Minsky, Ed., 1968, Cambridge, MA: MIT Press)

Rechtschaffen, A., & Foulkes, D. (1965). Effect of visual stimuli on dream content. *Perceptual and Motor Skills, 20*, 1149–1160.

Roediger, H. L., III, & McDermott, K. B. (1995). Creating false memories: Remembering words not presented in lists. *Journal of Experimental Psychology: Learning, Memory, and Cognition, 21*, 803–814.

Roget, P. M. (1911). *Roget's thesaurus of English words and phrases* (1911 ed.). Retrieved October 28, 2004, from http://www.gutenerg.org/etext/10681

Rumelhart, D. E., Lindsay, P. H., & Norman, D. A. (1972). A process model for long-term memory. In E. Tulving & W. Donaldson (Eds.) *Organization of memory* (pp. 197–246). New York: Academic Press.

Russell, W. A., & Jenkins, J. J. (1954). *The complete Minnesota norms for responses to 100 words from the Kent-Rosanoff Word Association Test* (Tech. Rep. No. 11, Contract N8 ONR 66216, Office of Naval Research). Minneapolis, MN: University of Minnesota.

Schneider, A., & Domhoff, G. W. (2005). *DreamBank*. Retrieved June 20, 2005, from http://www.dreambank.net/

Solomonoff, R., & Rapoport, A. (1951). Connectivity of random nets. *Bulletin of Mathematical Biophysics, 13*, 107–117.

Steyvers, M., & Tenenbaum, J. B. (2005). The large-scale structure of semantic networks: Statistical analyses and a model of semantic growth. *Cognitive Science, 29*, 41–78.

Stickgold, R. L. (1998). Sleep: Off-line memory processing. *Trends in Cognitive Science, 2*, 484–492.

Stickgold, R. L., Scott, L., Rittenhouse, C., & Hobson, J. A. (1999). Sleep induced changes in associative memory. *Journal of Cognitive Neuroscience, 11*, 182–198.

Tulving, E. (1985). Memory and consciousness. *The Canadian Psychologist, 26*, 1–12.

Vitevitch, M. S. (2005). *Phonological neighbors in a small world: What can graph theory tell us about word learning?* Unpublished manuscript, Department of Psychology, University of Kansas.

Watts, D. J. (2003). *Six degrees: The science of a connected age*. New York: Norton.

Watts, D. J., & Strogatz, S. H. (1998). Collective dynamics of "small-world" networks. *Nature, 393*, 440–442.

Zipf, G. K. (1945). The meaning-frequency relationship of words. *Journal of General Psychology, 33*, 251–256.

18

Inducing False Memories Through Associated Lists: A Window Onto Everyday False Memories?

KATHLEEN B. McDERMOTT

*I*f one were to ask a dozen active cognitive psychologists to free associate to the name Roddy Roediger, a systematic clustering of responses would likely emerge: memory, retrieval processes, implicit memory, false memory, hypermnesia, part-list cueing, transfer appropriate processing. Those who know Roddy personally would produce words like kind, promoting, and hard-working. Other responses might include editor, former American Psychological Society president, highly-cited, or various other terms related to the numerous honors he has received and to his service to the field. And more than a few might say "DRM" or "dream." It is this last response and, to some extent, the concept of free association itself, that are the focus of this chapter. To preview briefly, DRM is a term coined by Endel Tulving, which stands for Deese–Roediger–McDermott. Why such a term was needed will, I hope, become clear as the chapter progresses, as will the question of why and how Professor Tulving was involved in this venture. More on that below.

RECONSTRUCTING THE PAST: THE ORIGINS OF DRM

Late one afternoon in the Spring of 1993 in the Kyle Morrow Seminar Room on the second floor of Fondren Library at Rice University, Endel Tulving gave a talk on the topic of "renitence," or what he sometimes refers to as "the brain's proclivity for primacy." The basic idea is that all species have a tendency to attend to and encode novel experiences more effectively than subsequent episodes. As I remember the talk, he also argued that because all species demonstrate this proclivity for better retention of early experiences and because humans alone (in his view) have episodic memory but other species have semantic memory, he concluded that the primacy effect is a result of semantic memory (Tulving, 1993).

Todd Jones and Roddy had some newly-collected data that seemed inconsistent with Professor Tulving's claim that the primacy effect results from semantic memory (later published as Jones & Roediger, 1995). Basically, their data showed that the first few items in the list (the primacy items) received predominantly *remember* (not *know*) responses when Tulving's (1985) remember/know procedure was used. This finding contradicts the claim that semantic memory underlies the primacy effect because remember judgments are quintessentially episodic memory. At the conclusion of the talk, Professor Tulving was asked how he would reconcile these data with his claims. In the course of responding to this challenge, Professor Tulving mentioned a paper published by Jim Deese in 1959 showing that contrary to popular belief, people do at times make errors of commission in free recall situations (i.e., they recall a word not in the prior study set; 1959b). What exactly this had to do with the Jones and Roediger dataset is something none of us can quite remember or reconstruct.

Returning to what I *do* remember, I recall that in the course of answering the question, Tulving described Deese's finding, and I vividly remember the excitement Roddy had when he later found and read Deese's article (1959b). He could hardly wait until the next meeting of his Human Memory class to try out this new technique as a classroom demonstration because he just did not believe it could be true that errors of commission could be readily induced in free recall. Having studied free recall for most of his career (often using categorized lists), he knew that errors of commission were extremely rare. As a third year graduate student, I was not well-informed enough to have been able to put the pieces together myself regarding how interesting this newfound tidbit was, but Roddy's excitement was infectious. Further, as a graduate student interested in false memory and soaking up the heat surrounding this topic in the early 1990s, I was well-aware of the logistical difficulties in performing eyewitness identification experiments in small, private schools with limited subject pools, given that only a few observations/subject are typically possible. The combination of the two factors was enough to pique my own interest in that there may be more feasible ways to approach the topic of memory intrusions. To fast-forward a bit, I entered into this collaboration at the stage of the second experiment in what was later to be published in the *Journal of Experimental Psychology: Learning, Memory, and Cognition* as Roediger and McDermott (1995).

In the remaining pages I will summarize the article mentioned by Tulving that Spring afternoon (Deese, 1959b). I will attempt to briefly place it in historical context, although others have done a much more extensive job of this (see especially Bruce & Winograd, 1998; Roediger, McDermott, & Robinson, 1998). My own focus will be primarily on explaining something that is in hindsight difficult to comprehend—why we were skeptical that Deese's results would replicate. I will then discuss briefly the work Roediger and I did to follow up on Deese's work, eventually published as Roediger and McDermott (1995) and will conclude with some recent, related work, in which we have tried to extend these findings into other domains.

WHAT DID DEESE DO?

Although Deese was not interested in errors *per se*, he reported a procedure with which extralist intrusions in free recall can be elicited through associations. His interest was in using such errors as converging evidence for the importance of the associative structure of to-be-remembered material in determining what a person recalls. He had shown in previous work that the strength of associations within a list correlated positively with likelihood of accurate recall (Deese, 1959a). That is, if word lists of a given length are constructed by randomly choosing words from the English language, there will be some associative relations between some of the words within each list. In addition, the degree to which the relations exist within lists will vary across different lists of randomly selected words. Deese demonstrated that the degree to which items in a list were associatively related to one another correlated with the overall level of recall for the list. Specifically, he found that increasing intraitem associative strength was positively correlated with the number of studied words recalled, negatively correlated with the number of extralist intrusions produced, and positively correlated with the recurrence of specific extralist intrusions.

To further investigate these findings, Deese (1959b) proposed that word association norms could be used to predict not only accurate recall but also the introduction of specific intrusions in recall. In order to examine this possibility, Deese needed to find a way to enhance the number of intrusions in recall (so that sufficient variability would be introduced in the dependent measure). To this end, he constructed 36 lists, each of which was comprised of 12 associates to a critical nonpresented word taken from the Russell and Jenkins (1954) norms. For example, he presented subjects with *bed, rest, awake, tired, dream, wake, night, eat, sound, slumber, snore, pillow* (i.e., the 12 most commonly-produced words when subjects are asked to free associate to the word *sleep*). He then measured the probability with which subjects would erroneously recall the single word around which the list had been constructed (e.g., *sleep*) on an immediate recall test. Although all his lists were comprised of the 12 most common forward associates to the missing word, the lists differed in their backward association strengths (the associations of list words to the critical nonpresented word). That is, although the lists were constructed by collecting the words most frequently produced in response to the critical missing item on a free association task (i.e., the forward associates), the mean probability with which the list words (e.g., *bed, rest*) elicited the target (e.g., *sleep*) as an associate (i.e., the backward association strengths) differed across word lists.

Deese (1959b) reasoned that if the associative structure of the list influenced errors (as well as correct recall), then systematic fluctuations in the associative structure should affect the probability of intrusions in the recall test. Specifically, he predicted that the backward association strength of the lists should correlate with the probability of extralist intrusions of the critical missing word immediately after presentation of each 12-word list. His predictions were confirmed; Figure 18.1 shows that the probability of erroneous recall of the critical nonpresented item, which varied from 0% to 44% across lists, was highly correlated

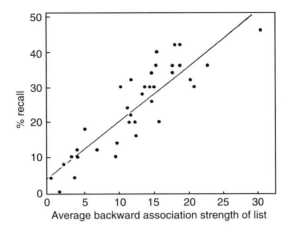

FIGURE 18.1   Mean probability of false recall as a function of mean backward associative strength of the lists (figure adapted from Deese, 1959b).

($r = .87$) with the backward association strengths of the lists, or the mean probability with which the individual list words elicited the target item on a free association task (see Roediger, Watson, McDermott, & Gallo, 2001, for a replication).

Deese (1959b) concluded that the associative structure of a list was a primary factor in determining recall of studied words and extralist instrusions (the latter would now be called false recall). After publication of his report, however, very few people pursued his finding until the mid-1990s. It was hardly ever cited, even by Deese himself (although the article from the same year, Deese 1959a, was well-known and well-cited; see Bruce & Winograd, 1998, for discussion). Cramer (1965) did report a similar finding, although it was not the primary focus of her paper. She presented subjects with 26 words: 6 filler words and 4 sets of 5 associatively related words. The associative sets converged upon four critical nonpresented words. Fifty-one percent of her subjects erroneously recalled at least one (of the four possible) critical words. Cramer's finding also generated little interest at the time.

SKEPTICISM

Returning to the anecdote of April 1993 with Roediger scratching his head wondering if these results might actually replicate, one might wonder, especially in hindsight—with over a decade of work on this protocol—why these results were in any way surprising. Why wouldn't they replicate? There are at least two reasons for the initial skepticism.

First, despite the existence of a voluminous literature on false recognition in the tradition of Underwood (1965), researchers generally did not attempt to measure extralist intrusions in free recall, largely because they were thought to be unsystematic and very rare. In the words of Cofer (1973), "subjects in recall experiments seem reluctant . . . to produce material when they are uncertain that it is correct" (p. 538). Cofer elsewhere claimed that "Subjects are well aware, at least at immediate recall, of what items were not on the list" (Cofer, 1967, p. 197). Slamecka (1968, p. 511) made a similar claim: "If free recall is requested, [the subject] uses this general representation of the list to form a retrieval plan . . . That the plan is truly one of retrieval and not merely a guide to shrewd reconstruction of the material is suggested by the fact that extraneous intrusion errors are notoriously very rare occurrences in performance (Underwood, 1964). One tends to find only what is there."

As Kahana, Dolan, Sauder, and Wingfield (2005) recently claimed regarding why age differences in intrusions have not been much examined in standard recall tasks, "this is because there are often too few intrusions available for analysis" (p. 92). Indeed, disbelief was one of the two major reactions we received when informally describing our initial results to colleagues. More on that later.

The second reason for the skepticism surrounding Deese's (1959b) results is that it was not clear what instructions Deese gave his subjects (and therefore whether his task could reasonably be classified as a free recall task, at least in today's terms). He did not describe what instructions he gave to subjects but did describe free recall (elsewhere) as being essentially "free association . . . a direct, unmediated activity with little or no active editing of the material being recalled" (p. 312). Imagine for a moment that Deese either implicitly or explicitly told his subjects to adopt a loose criterion and to report words that may plausibly have been in the list, perhaps even telling them to free associate if necessary. Such instructions could have led to his results, which might have been interesting in their own right but not terribly relevant for contemporary research on false memory.

This possibility is not such a farfetched idea as it might initially seem. Other researchers around this time were giving free association instructions under the rubric of "free recall." For example, Bilodeau and Fox (1968) told subjects to "write down the words that appeared . . . You must fill in every line. If you cannot remember, write the first word that you think of," and they called their task free recall.

In today's parlance, this may seem surprising, but free recall is a fairly new term and only began to receive substantial and focused investigation in the early 1960s. In making the point that free recall is a recent term, Tulving (1968) noted: "McGeoch's (1942) influential book and its successor (McGeoch and Irion, 1952) did not even mention the method by name. But McGeoch seems to have been the first writer to use the term 'free recall' in discussing the experiments by Welch and Burnett (1924) and Raffel (1934)." It's actually interesting to see what these researchers did. Raffel (1934) presented subjects with 100 words and instructed them to then produce 150 words. Specifically, they were told, "Now I want you to say 150 words, more words than there were on the list. Try to say words from the list, but if you think of a word say it, even if you know it was not on the list . . . Let me know when you've said a word from the list, or if you're doubtful about a word." This latter aspect of identifying produced words as being from the list or not was called "recognition" by Raffel. An interesting sidenote (relevant to some of Roediger's early work, e.g., Roediger & Thorpe, 1978) is that Raffel was able to use this procedure to identify the phenomenon now known as "recognition failure of recallable words" (Tulving & Thomson, 1973; see too Roediger, Wheeler, & Rajaram, 1993); she also discussed what would now be called the testing effect and even looked at the phenomenon of reminiscence.

What exactly did "immediate recall," the term Deese (1959b) used for his task, mean? If he used instructions like those of Bilodeau and Fox (1968)—what we might call forced recall (Erdelyi & Becker, 1974) or inclusion instructions (Jacoby, 1991) these days—then instructions alone could have accounted for the high intrusion probabilities. The point here is that the free recall data reported by Roediger and McDermott (1995) were initially surprising to us (and to other researchers with whom we discussed the findings at the time). In designing the experiment it was not at all clear what would happen, a point that is hard to grasp a decade later, after this finding has been replicated hundreds of times. Thus, Experiment 1 of Roediger and McDermott—a classroom demonstration—was not known at the time (or even now) to be a direct replication of Deese's procedures, since it was (and is) a little unclear what those procedures actually were.

ROEDIGER AND McDERMOTT (1995)

Hence, we set out to try to determine whether—with a free recall test and instructions to the subject not to guess—people would indeed intrude a single, predictable associate on an immediate test. Specifically, after encountering a list of 15 or so such words, subjects often recalled and recognized a word related to the studied words but not itself presented (e.g., *sleep*)—often referred to as the *critical nonpresented word*. For example, subjects report both very high confidence that the critical nonpresented items occurred in the list, and they also report being able to vividly recollect the moment of their prior occurrence when Tulving's (1985) remember/know technique is used (e.g., Norman & Schacter, 1997; Payne, Elie, Blackwell, & Neuschatz, 1996; Roediger & McDermott, 1995). These characteristics—ease of false memory induction and the compelling nature of the resulting false memories—have contributed to the popularity of the technique.

Nonetheless, the degree to which researchers have explored this technique has surprised us somewhat. After all, scholars since the time of Aristotle, some 2300 years ago, have known of the importance of associative connections for memory. Indeed, even in the 19th century, the basic phenomenon later described by Deese and by Roediger and McDermott was outlined. As described by Kirkpatrick (1894), "There were some incidental illustrations of false recognition. About a week previously in experimenting upon mental imagery I had pronounced to the students ten common words. Many of these were recalled and placed with the memory list. Again, it appears that when such words as 'spool,' 'thimble,' 'knife,' were pronounced many students at once thought of 'thread,' 'needle', 'fork,' which are so frequently associated with them. The result was that many gave those words as belonging to the list. This is an excellent illustration of how things suggested to a person by an experience may be honestly reported by him as part of the experience." (p. 608). Incidentally, Kirkpatrick also addressed the relation between recall and recognition, the phenomenon now known as the picture superiority effect, the role of imagery in memory, and (again, what is now known as) the primacy and recency effects, among other phenomena.[1]

Despite the precedents, Roddy and I knew right away that we were onto something important when our descriptions to friends and colleagues led to two very strongly-held opinions. Some reactions were "very interesting, fascinating," etc. Others claimed we were wrong and that certainly this could not be true. Indeed, some of the first papers published on this theme after our own were, understandably, attempts at direct replication (Payne et al., 1996).

Why, then, all the interest? In part, the results are interesting against the backdrop of thought that says free recall is immune from such phenomena. In part, the compelling nature of the illusions is key (as in the remember judgments). In part, the resistance to correction (e.g., multiple study–test trials, McDermott, 1996; or warning, McDermott & Roediger, 1998). And part of the appeal is that the protocol offers a nice preparation for studying everyday false memories. It is this last point that I now wish to consider.

EXTENSIONS INTO PROSE

One reason Roediger and I have been so interested in this protocol is that we think it provides leverage on understanding many types of everyday false memories. Consider a quote from Roediger and McDermott (2000, p. 126), who said:

> in our opinion, this paradigm captures one prevalent source of false memories that arise routinely. Whenever people engage in conversation, listen to a talk, read a newspaper article, or watch a television program, they recode events from the outside world as they try to understand them. By "recode" we mean that people interpret events and make inferences about them on the basis of their past experience. Part and parcel of the recoding process is activation of a person's own knowledge structures or schemata (Bartlett, 1932). The information may spark related thoughts, and these thoughts may later be remembered as having been made as explicit statements. Our paradigm provides a tractable laboratory situation for studying the cognitive processes creating these sorts of false memories.

Below I consider some recent data that begins to address this claim. The approach is to study false memories arising from prose using manipulations that are well-understood within the word-list paradigms. In collaboration with Jason Chan, I have begun to examine the extent to which false memories of pragmatic inferences exhibit data patterns similar to those arising from the DRM paradigm and from other word-list approaches to studying false memory (McDermott & Chan, 2006). To the extent that data patterns obtained from prose materials mirror those from word list paradigms, the evidence would be consistent with the conclusion that the DRM paradigm is indeed capturing false memories as they occur in natural conversations. Conversely, if different data patterns were found, we would question the validity of Roediger and McDermott's (2000) claim.

Here I summarize two experiments that examine the effects of age, time pressure during retrieval, and repetition during study on the likelihood of false memories for pragmatic inferences (see McDermott & Chan, 2006, for more complete coverage). These variables have been combined in other experiments (Jacoby, Kelley, & Dywan, 1989) to examine the dual effects of recollection and familiarity in contributing to false recognition. The logic is rooted in the dual process theories of recognition (Atkinson & Juola, 1973; Jacoby, 1991; Mandler, 1980; see Yonelinas, 2002, for a comprehensive review). Specifically, repetition during encoding enhances both familiarity and recollection (Benjamin & Craik, 2001). However, when given a test that requires fast responses, people do not have time to invoke the relatively slow process of recollection and therefore must rely upon the faster process of familiarity. Under such conditions, repetition increases both the hit rate (due to increases in both recollection and familiarity) and the false alarm rate to related distractors (due to increase in familiarity alone). Similar results are obtained in older adults who are not rushed during retrieval, because aging leads to a disproportionate impairment in recollective processes relative to familiarity (Jennings & Jacoby, 1997; Yonelinas, 2002). This general pattern has been called the *ironic effect* of repetition (Jacoby, 1999), in reference to the simultaneous good and bad influences that encoding repetitions can exert.

In contrast to testing conditions when speeded responding is required, younger adults do not exhibit ironic effects when they are not rushed during retrieval: An increased hit rate is accompanied by a decreased false alarm rate as a function of repetition (Benjamin, 2001; Jacoby, 1999; Jones & Jacoby, 2001). The explanation is that younger adults who are not rushed during retrieval can use recollection to override the enhanced familiarity brought about by the study repetition, thereby reducing false memories.

Our experiments closely parallel those of Benjamin (2001) and Jones and Jacoby (2001), in which the ironic effects of repetition were examined in the DRM paradigm and in the conjunction paradigm (Reinitz, Lammers, & Cochran, 1992; Underwood & Zimmerman, 1973), respectively. Below, the results of our own experiments within the pragmatic inference paradigm are described, but the over-arching take-home message is that the patterns we see with this paradigm mimic the patterns reported in the literature with word-list studies of false memory.

In our experiments, subjects were given a series of sentences that would encourage pragmatic inferences to be drawn. After hearing sentences such as "The karate champion hit the cinderblock" and "The new baby stayed awake all night" people sometimes erroneously recall or recognize having heard that the champion "broke" the cinderblock and that the baby had "cried," inferences not logically implied by the sentences (yet pragmatically reasonable). In the first experiment to be considered here, younger and older adults studied such sentences either once or thrice. They then received a modified forced choice recognition test, in which they were given the correct answer, the pragmatic inference, and the word "NEW." This last response was to be given whenever the test sentence had not been studied. When it had been studied, the subjects were to choose the exact wording they had seen previously.

Consider first the influence of subjects' age (as shown in the left panel of Figure 18.2). Repetition enhanced the likelihood of later correct recognition both for younger and older adults. The influence of repetition on false recognition, though, differed for the two groups. Whereas younger adults were able to take advantage of study repetition to override the tendency for false recognition, older adults showed an ironic effect of repetition: worse performance (more recognition errors) following three presentations (relative to a single presentation).

Now consider a similar manipulation whereby the influence of time allotted during retrieval is examined, for young adults only (right panel of Figure 18.2). This time the criterial test was cued recall, in which subjects were given sentence fragments (e.g., "The karate champion _____") and asked to recall the remainder of the sentence exactly as it had been studied (or to say "forget" if they could not remember the exact wording or "new" if it was a nonstudied sentence). Again, repetition helped both groups (those rushed during the retrieval phase and those not rushed) in terms of later accurate recall. Only the subjects in the unspeeded condition at retrieval were able to benefit from repetition in terms of diminishing the likelihood of false recall, though. Young adults who were placed under time pressure at retrieval were not able to take advantage of this repetition.

The data from these manipulations closely parallel those from word-list false memory paradigms, lending credence to the idea that similar mechanisms are at play in creating the false memory effects. Further studies lead to similar conclusions. For example, Butler, McDaniel, Dornburg, Price, and Roediger (2004) have examined one purported mechanism behind the increased susceptibility to false memories exhibited with age: compromised frontal lobe function (see Anderson & Craik, 2000, for review). When older adults were classified into those with higher

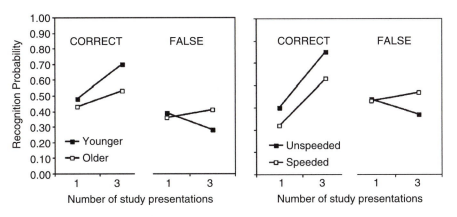

FIGURE 18.2   Mean recognition probability as a function of repetition for older and younger adults (left panel) and mean recall probability as a function of repetition for younger adults under speeded and unspeeded conditions (right panel). Data from McDermott and Chan (2006).

and lower frontal lobe function (as estimated by Glisky, Polster, & Routhieaux's, 1995, battery), those with higher frontal lobe function performed much like younger adults in the DRM paradigm. Older adults with lower frontal lobe function, though, exhibited lower probabilities of accurate recall combined with higher probabilities of false recall. Similarly, frontal lobe function predicts the likelihood of false recognition of pragmatic inferences both for younger and older adults (McDermott & Chan, 2006). These data (and other data from our laboratory) are consistent with the claim by Roediger and McDermott (2000) that the DRM paradigm might offer a way to gain leverage on everyday types of false memories (e.g., those arising from inferences formed during conversation).

INDIRECT PRIMING

The spread of activation throughout associative networks has been implicated as a major factor in inducing false recall and false recognition (Roediger, Balota, & Watson, 2001). With this in mind it is perhaps not terribly surprising that interest has arisen with respect to whether the critical nonpresented words exhibit *priming* on implicit memory tests (Lövdén & Johansson, 2003; McDermott, 1997; McKone & Murphy, 2000). An interesting terminological phenomenon has resulted from this exploration in that researchers have discussed the idea of "implicit false memory" (Lövdén & Johansson, 2003; McKone & Murphy, 2000).

The idea of *false implicit memory* is, to this author, anyway, a misnomer. One problem is that priming is neither true nor false. It simply happens; there is no claim by the subject that they are remembering anything and therefore the memory is not false.[2] This is not to argue that the empirical question is uninteresting. Quite the contrary. Indeed, the question of whether semantic associates lead to long-term priming is not a new one.

The phenomenon of *indirect priming* has been around for quite some time (Cofer, 1967; Cramer, 1965, 1966; see Roediger & McDermott, 1993, for review). Consider Cramer's (1966) definition: "In the case of *indirect* or *mediated* priming, the priming words are *associatively related to* the desired response, but that response word is not itself presented" (p. 163). This is in contrast to direct priming: "the technique of increasing the response probability of a *particular word* by prior presentation of that desired response word itself" (p. 163). As noted previously in this chapter, Cramer (1965) provided one of the first studies to report recall errors following presentation of semantic associates. She presented subjects with five associated words that clustered around a "hub word." Although she failed to find indirect priming, she noted "importation" of the hub word by many of her subjects when given a free recall test (cf. Howes & Osgood, 1954; Mandler, Graf, & Kraft, 1986). Note that these types of long-term priming differ from the much more short-lived semantic (or associative) priming (Balota, 1994; Neely, 1977).

Interest in indirect priming was re-aroused in the early 1990s, much of it by Roediger, during the boom in research on implicit memory. For example, Roediger and Challis (1992) sought priming from synonyms, associates, category coordinates, or visually similar words. For example, words like *tadpole, pond, frog, and polygon* were examined with respect to whether they primed *polliwog* on a delayed word fragment completion test. (They did not.) McDermott and Roediger (1996) replicated this finding and showed that semantic associates also did not produce priming to an implicit test of category association. The primary point here is that although indirect priming has been difficult to obtain reliably, the concept has been around for quite some time.

SUMMARY

In this chapter I have attempted to describe the motivation and rationale behind the pursuit of research within what is now called the DRM paradigm; I hope to have shed some light on the development of our thought processes in developing this line of research. Much more complete coverage of the theoretical orientation exists elsewhere (McDermott & Watson, 2001; Roediger, Balota, & Watson, 2001); here I have provided an informal reconstructive account of the development of this research program. Choosing a topic for this volume in honor of Roddy was a challenging task, in large part because his interests are so wide-ranging that settling on a single topic was not a straightforward endeavor. Indeed, the variety of topics within this volume speaks to that wide-ranging influence. In the end, I have chosen to describe a topic that he and I worked on together, which leads me to my final point. It has been my sincere pleasure and honor to have developed both professional and personal collaborations with Roddy. I look forward to many more years of both.

NOTES

1.   My own personal favorite quote from his paper, however, regards the issue of whether subjects followed the orienting tasks he gave them during encoding: "How closely they followed these directions it is impossible to say, but their faces indicated that they were trying to do so" (p. 603).
2.   One could quibble with the term *false* in terms of explicit memory, as well. Indeed, the term might not be ideal. A critical difference, though, is that in explicit memory subjects are indeed claiming (erroneously) to have heard or seen something not presented, and they make a reality monitoring error (Johnson, Hashtroudi, & Lindsay, 1993). In implicit memory, though, there is nothing "false" happening. Subjects are simply asked, by definition, to perform some task without any reference to the recent prior study episode, and the experimenter looks for transfer from the recent experience to the task of interest.

REFERENCES

Anderson, N. D., & Craik, F. I. M. (2000). Memory in the aging brain. In E. Tulving & F. I. M. Craik (Eds.), *The Oxford handbook of memory* (pp. 411–425). London: Oxford University Press.

Atkinson, R. C., & Juola, J. F. (1973). Factors influencing speed and accuracy of word recognition. In S. Kornblum (Ed.), *Attention and performance IV* (pp. 583–612). New York: Academic Press.

Balota, D. A. (1994). Visual word recognition: The journey from features to meaning. In *Handbook of psycholinguistics* (pp. 303–358). San Diego, CA: Academic Press.

Bartlett, F. C. (1932). *Remembering: A study in experimental and social psychology.* New York: Macmillan.

Benjamin, A. S. (2001). On the dual effects of repetition on false recognition. *Journal of Experimental Psychology: Learning, Memory, and Cognition, 27,* 941–947.

Benjamin, A. S., & Craik, F. I. M. (2001). Parallel effects of aging and time pressure on memory for source: Evidence from the spacing effect. *Memory and Cognition, 21,* 691–697.

Bilodeau, E. A., & Fox, P. W. (1968). Free association, free recall, and stimulated recall compared. *Behavior Research Methods and Instrumentation, 1,* 14–17.

Bruce, D. R., & Winograd, E. (1998). Remembering Deese's 1959 articles: The Zeitgeist, the sociology of science, and false memories. *Psychonomic Bulletin and Review, 5,* 615–624.

Butler, K. M., McDaniel, M. A., Dornburg, C. C., Price, A. L., & Roediger, H. L. (2004). Age differences in veridical and false recall are not inevitable: The role of frontal lobe function. *Psychonomic Bulletin and Review, 11,* 921–925.

Cofer, C. N. (1967). Conditions for the use of verbal associations. *Psychological Bulletin, 68,* 1–12.

Cofer, C. N. (1973). Constructive processes in memory. *The American Scientist, 61,* 537–543.

Cramer, P. (1965). Recovery of a discrete memory. *Journal of Personality and Social Psychology, 1,* 326–332.

Cramer, P. (1966). Mediated priming of associative responses: The effect of time lapse and interpolated activity. *Journal of Verbal Learning and Verbal Behavior, 5,* 163–166.

Deese, J. (1959a). Influence of inter-item associative strength upon immediate free recall. *Psychological Reports, 5,* 305–312.

Deese, J. (1959b). On the prediction of occurrence of particular verbal intrusions in the immediate recall. *Journal of Experimental Psychology, 58,* 17–22.

Erdelyi, M. H., & Becker, J. (1974). Hypermnesia for pictures: Incremental memory for pictures but not words in multiple recall trials. *Cognitive Psychology, 6,* 159–171.

Glisky, E. L., Polster, M. R., & Routhieaux, B. (1995). Double dissociation between item and source memory. *Neuropsychology, 9,* 229–235.

Howes, D., & Osgood, C. E. (1954). On the combination of associative probabilities in linguistic contexts. *American Journal of Psychology, 67,* 241–258.

Jacoby, L. L. (1991). A process dissociation framework: Separating automatic and intentional uses of memory. *Journal of Memory and Language, 30,* 513–541.

Jacoby, L. L. (1999). Ironic effects of repetition: Measuring age-related differences in memory. *Journal of Experimental Psychology: Learning, Memory, and Cognition, 25,* 3–22.

Jacoby, L. L., Kelley, C. M., & Dywan, J. (1989). Memory attributions. In H. L. Roediger & F. I. M. Craik (Eds.), *Varieties of memory and consciousness: Essays in honour of Endel Tulving* (pp. 391–422). Hillsdale, NJ: Lawrence Erlbaum Associates, Inc.

Jennings, J. M., & Jacoby, L. L. (1997). An opposition procedure for detecting age-related deficits in recollection: Telling effects of repetition. *Psychology and Aging, 12,* 352–361.

Johnson, M. K., Hashtroudi, S., & Lindsay, D. S. (1993). Source monitoring. *Psychological Bulletin, 114*, 3–28.

Jones, T. C., & Jacoby, L. L. (2001). Feature and conjunction errors in recognition memory: Evidence for dual-process theory. *Journal of Memory and Language, 45*, 82–102.

Jones, T. C., & Roediger, H. L. (1995). The experiential basis of serial position effects. *European Journal of Cognitive Psychology, 7*, 65–80.

Kahana, M. J., Dolan, E. D., Sauder, C. L., & Wingfield, A. (2005). Intrusions in episodic recall: Age differences in editing of overt responses. *Journal of Gerontology: Psychological Sciences, 60B*, 92–97.

Kirkpatrick, E. A. (1894). An experimental study of memory. *Psychological Review, 1*, 602–609.

Lövdén, M., & Johansson, M. (2003). Are covert verbal responses mediating false implicit memory? *Psychonomic Bulletin and Review, 10*, 724–729.

Mandler, G. (1980). Recognizing: The judgment of previous occurrence. *Psychological Review, 87*, 252–271.

Mandler, G., Graf, P., & Kraft, D. (1986). Activation and elaboration effects in recognition and word priming. *Quarterly Journal of Experimental Psychology, 38A*, 645–662.

McDermott, K. B. (1996). The persistence of false memories in list recall. *Journal of Memory and Language, 35*, 212–230.

McDermott, K. B. (1997). Priming on perceptual implicit memory tests can be achieved through presentation of associates. *Psychonomic Bulletin and Review, 4*, 582–586.

McDermott, K. B., & Chan, J. C. K. (2006). Effects of repetition on memory for pragmatic inferences. *Memory and Cognition, 34*, 1273–1284.

McDermott, K. B., & Roediger, H. L. (1996). Exact and conceptual repetition dissociate conceptual memory tests: Problems for transfer appropriate processing theory. *Canadian Journal of Experimental Psychology, 50*, 57–71.

McDermott, K. B., & Roediger, H. L. (1998). False recognition of associates can be resistant to an explicit warning to subjects and an immediate recognition probe. *Journal of Memory and Language, 39*, 508–520.

McDermott, K. B., & Watson, J. M. (2001). The rise and fall of false recall: The impact of presentation duration. *Journal of Memory and Language, 45*, 160–176.

McGeoch, J. A. (1942). *The psychology of human learning.* New York: Longmans, Green.

McGeoch, J. A., & Irion, A. L. (1952). *The psychology of human learning.* New York: Longmans, Green.

McKone, E., & Murphy, B. (2000). Implicit false memory: Effects of modality and multiple study presentations on long-lived semantic priming. *Journal of Memory and Language, 43*, 89–109.

Neely, J. H. (1977). Semantic priming and retrieval from lexical memory: Roles of inhibitionless spreading activation and limited capcity attention. *Journal of Experimental Psychology: General, 106*, 226–254.

Norman, K. A., & Schacter, D. L. (1997). False recognition in younger and older adults: Exploring the characteristics of illusory memories. *Memory and Cognition, 25*, 838–848.

Payne, D. G., Elie, C. J., Blackwell, J. M., & Neuschatz, J. S. (1996). Memory illusions: Recalling, recognizing, and recollecting events that never occurred. *Journal of Memory and Language, 35*, 261–285.

Raffel, G. (1934). The effect of recall on forgetting. *Journal of Experimental Psychology, 17*, 828–838.

Reinitz, M. T., Lammers, W. J., & Cochran, B. P. (1992). Memory conjunction errors: Miscombination of stored features can produce illusions of memory. *Memory and Cognition, 20,* 1–11.

Roediger, H. L., Balota, D. A., & Watson, J. M. (2001). Spreading activation and the arousal of false memories. In H. L. Roediger, J. S. Nairne, I. Neath, & A. M. Surprenant (Eds.), *The nature of remembering: Essays in honor of Robert G. Crowder* (pp. 95–115). Washington, DC: American Psychological Association.

Roediger, H. L., & Challis, B. H. (1992). Effects of exact repetition and conceptual repetition on free recall and primed word-fragment completion. *Journal of Experimental Psychology: Learning, Memory, and Cognition, 18,* 3–14.

Roediger, H. L., & McDermott, K. B. (1993). Implicit memory in normal human subjects. In F. Boller & J. Grafman (Eds.), *Handbook of neuropsychology* (Vol. 8, pp. 63–131). Amsterdam: Elsevier.

Roediger, H. L., & McDermott, K. B. (1995). Creating false memories: Remembering words not presented in lists. *Journal of Experimental Psychology: Learning, Memory, and Cognition, 21*(4), 803–814.

Roediger, H. L., & McDermott, K. B. (2000). Remembering between the lines: Creating false memories via associative inferences. *Psychological Science Agenda, 13,* 8–9.

Roediger, H. L., McDermott, K. B., & Robinson, K. J. (1998). The role of associative processes in producing false remembering. In M. A. Conway, S. Gathercole, & C. Cornoldi (Eds.), *Theories of memory II* (pp. 187–245). Hove, UK: Psychology Press.

Roediger, H. L., & Thorpe, L. A. (1978). The role of recall time in producing hypermnesia. *Memory and Cognition, 6,* 296–305.

Roediger, H. L., Watson, J. M., McDermott, K. B., & Gallo, D. A. (2001). Factors that determine false recall: A multiple regression analysis. *Psychonomic Bulletin and Review, 8,* 385–407.

Roediger, H. L., Wheeler, M. A., & Rajaram, S. (1993). Remembering, knowing, and reconstructing the past. In D. L. Medin (Ed.), *Advances in research and theory. The psychology of learning and motivation* (pp. 97–134). New York: Academic Press.

Russell, W. A., & Jenkins, J. J. (1954). *The complete Minnesota norms for responses to 100 words from Kent-Rosanoff Word Association Test* (Tech. Rep. No. 11, 1954). University of Minnesota, Contract N8 onr 66216, Office of Naval Research.

Slamecka, N. J. (1968). An examination of trace storage in free recall. *Psychological Bulletin, 76,* 504–513.

Tulving, E. (1968). Theoretical issues in free recall. In T. R. Dixon & D. L. Horton (Eds.), *Verbal behavior and general behavior theory* (pp. 1–36). Englewood Cliffs, NJ: Prentice Hall.

Tulving, E. (1985). Memory and consciousness. *The Canadian Psychologist, 26,* 1–12.

Tulving, E. (1993 April). *The brain's proclivity for primacy.* Colloquium presented at Rice University, Houston, TX.

Tulving, E., & Thomson, D. M. (1973). Encoding specificity and retrieval processes in episodic memory. *Psychological Review, 80,* 352–373.

Underwood, B. J. (1964). *The representativeness of rote verbal learning.* New York: Academic Press.

Underwood, B. J. (1965). False recognition produced by implicit verbal responses. *Journal of Experimental Psychology, 70,* 122–129.

Underwood, B. J., & Zimmerman, J. (1973). The syllable as a source of error in multisyllabic word recognition. *Journal of Verbal Learning and Verbal Behavior, 12,* 338–344.

Welch, G. B., & Burnett, C. T. (1924). Is primacy a factor in association-formation? *American Journal of Psychology, 35,* 396–401.

Yonelinas, A. P. (2002). The nature of recollection and familiarity: A review of 30 years of research. *Journal of Memory and Language, 46,* 441–517.

19

Semantic Relatedness Effects on True and False Memories in Episodic Recognition: A Methodological and Empirical Review

JAMES H. NEELY and CHI-SHING TSE

HISTORICAL BACKGROUND

*I*n the century since Ebbinghaus' (1913) experimental studies of human memory, we have accumulated considerable knowledge about how numerous variables affect memory. After a period of relative quiescence following Ebbinghaus' work, systematic experimental investigations of human learning and memory began to pick up steam again in the early 1940s (e.g., McGeoch, 1942; Melton & von Lackum, 1941). From 1940 through the early 1970s, the dominant paradigm was the paired-associate learning paradigm. This research focused on how people associate different arbitrary verbal responses with the same stimulus or similar stimuli, with emphasis being given to variables that influence the encoding and storage of paired associates into memory and their retention over long intervals. However, in the late 1960s, the pioneering work of Tulving (see Roediger, 2000, for a recent overview) led to a paradigm shift (Kuhn, 1962). The to-be-remembered (TBR) materials became lists of words presented one word at a time, and the theoretical focus shifted to (a) how people "organize" word lists for recall (Tulving, 1967, 1968; Tulving & Donaldson, 1972) and (b) how various cues at the time of retrieval influence memory (Tulving & Osler, 1968; Tulving & Pearlstone, 1966).[1]

This emphasis on retrieval processes led to what Tulving (1983; see Roediger & Guynn, 1996, for a more recent review) called the encoding/retrieval paradigm, which tests for an interaction of encoding and retrieval by examining the effects of an encoding manipulation in different retrieval conditions (e.g., Morris, Bransford,

& Franks, 1977; Roediger, 2000; Tulving & Thomson, 1973). In the 1970s, numerous studies used free recall and recognition tests as the different retrieval conditions. In free recall, people write down the studied items they remember in any order; in a standard recognition test, studied items are randomly intermixed among nonstudied items and people indicate which test items had been previously studied. This line of research showed that free recall and recognition performance are similarly affected by many variables fundamental to memory such as study time (e.g., Griffith, 1975), study repetition and the spacing between those repetitions (e.g., Russo, Parkin, Taylor, & Wilks, 1998), length of the study list (e.g., Ratcliff, McKoon, & Tindall, 1994, and Hunt, 1976, for recognition; Ward, 2002, for recall), imageability/concreteness of the TBR items (e.g., Paivio, 1971), active generation (e.g., Clark, 1995; Slamecka & Graf, 1978), and deep semantic processing of the TBR items (e.g., Craik & Lockhart, 1972; Mayes & McIvor, 1980).

Of greater theoretical interest are variables that have dissociative effects on recall and recognition. In the 1970s, the two such variables most investigated were word frequency and semantic relatedness of the TBR words. As for word frequency, high-frequency (HF) common words are better recalled than low-frequency (LF) rare words, whereas in recognition, the opposite is so (e.g., Balota & Neely, 1980, Gregg, 1976). In recognition, the word-frequency effect is characterized by true memories for studied items being greater for LF than for HF words, whereas false memories for nonstudied items are less likely for LF than HF words. This crossover interaction, called the mirror effect (Glanzer & Adams, 1985), has been given considerable theoretical analysis (e.g., Glanzer, Kim, & Adams, 1998, Reder, Nhouyvanisvong, Schunn, Ayers, Angstadt, & Hiraki, 2000; Reder, Angstadt, Cary, Erickson, & Ayers, 2002; but see Greene, chapter 4, this volume, who challenges the importance of mirror effects).

The seminal results for the dissociative effect of semantic relatedness on recall and recognition were reported by Kintsch (1968). He had people study a list of 40 totally unrelated words and a list of 40 words that consisted of 10 exemplars from each of four different semantic categories (e.g., *apple, banana,* and *grape* from the semantic category "fruit"). After each list, different subjects received either a recall test or a recognition test. (We use "subjects" throughout in deference to the phobic reaction the honoree of this volume has to the term "participants".) Kintsch found that relative to the unrelated list, recall was much higher for the semantically related list, whereas recognition was little affected. (See Bruce & Fagan, 1970, for a replication of this null effect for recognition.)

The dissociative effects of word frequency and semantic relatedness on recall and recognition led to the generate-recognize theory of recall (Kintsch, 1970). In this theory, in free recall people first generate words they think might have been studied and then submit these words to a recognition test that invokes exactly the same processes that would be used had they been generated by the experimenter instead. If a generated word is then recognized as having been studied, it is output in recall. Even though LF words are better recognized than HF words during the second, recognition stage of recall, very few of these rarely used LF words get generated to be passed on to that recognition stage. The net effect is that LF words are less likely to be recalled than HF words. As for semantic relatedness, once people have both generated and recognized a studied item such as *apple*, they can then use *apple* as a *cue* to generate other fruits (some of which would have been studied in a list of semantically related items). It is this facilitation in the generation of semantically related items relative to unrelated items that leads to semantic relatedness facilitating recall even though it apparently has no effect in the subsequent recognition stage.

The facilitative effect of semantic relatedness on free recall (e.g., Cofer, Bruce, & Reicher, 1966; Dale, 1967) is extremely robust. However, the effects of semantic relatedness on recognition are less clear. In the remainder of this chapter, we discuss the methodologies and experimental designs that should be employed to examine how the semantic relatedness of the TBR items influences recognition. Our review considers results that are relevant to two general aspects of semantic relatedness: (1) the number of items in the study list that are related to the recognition test item, based either on shared membership in a semantic category or on associative connections (*relatedness length*, RL) and (2) the strength of the relationship between the studied item(s) and the recognition test item (*relatedness strength*, RS).[2] We close by very briefly considering the empirical lacunae that need to be filled and the implications that semantic relatedness effects on recognition have for theory.

TESTING SEMANTIC RELATEDNESS EFFECTS ON RECOGNITION: SOME METHODOLOGICAL PRESCRIPTIONS

Before describing the empirical findings, we first focus on methodology and develop a set of prescriptions we believe should be followed to permit strong inferences about the effects of semantic relatedness on recognition. It is important to note that all of these methodological prescriptions are directly relevant to studies that examine recognition memory, i.e., the ability to discriminate whether a test word was or was not in a previously studied list. However, many of them do not necessarily apply to paradigms that focus on only false memories (e.g., the DRM paradigm that we discuss later), though a few of our prescriptions could be applied to them as well, as we will note.

Equate Intracategorical Output Interference

Although Bruce and Fagan's (1970) and Kintsch's (1968) null effect of RL on recognition was initially well accepted and served as a cornerstone for generate-recognize theory, this finding was based on a faulty methodology, due to RL being manipulated between rather than within lists. With such a between-list manipulation, if all items from the study list are tested and the numbers of studied (target) and nonstudied (lure) test items are equated for related and unrelated lists, RL and the number of semantically related items in the recognition test are necessarily confounded. For example, the 80-item recognition test for Kintsch's 40-item study lists contained 20 items (10 targets and 10 lures) from each of four semantic categories for related studied lists but only 2 items (1 target and 1 lure) from each of forty semantic categories for unrelated studied lists. This confound is problematic because Lewandowsky (1986), Neely, Schmidt, and Roediger (1983), and Todres and Watkins (1981) have all shown that recognition accuracy (or speed) depends in a complex way on how many times and how recently targets and lures from the same semantic category have appeared in the test. Thus, to determine whether RL at study affects recognition, one needs to equate in the recognition test the number of semantically related targets and lures across conditions of different RLs. When all targets are tested for the longer RLs, this cannot be done without introducing another confound. For example, for relatedness list lengths of 1 and 5, if all five targets for the latter condition are tested, to equate the number of related items per category at 5 there would need to be a minimum of four lures tested in the condition representing a RL of 1. But then there would be more categorically related *lures* in the RL = 1 condition than in the RL = 5 condition and, as just noted, the effects of prior presentations of items categorically related to the currently tested target or lure in the test depends on whether those prior related items are targets or lures. Hence, to avoid this problem, the number of tested *targets* from each category for all RLs must be no greater than the number of studied items for the smallest RL. Also, the number of lures from each category (preferably, though not necessarily, the same as the number of targets) should be equated for each RL. As we shall see, when this unconfounded design is used, contrary to Bruce and Fagan's and Kintsch's results, RL effects in recognition are sometimes no longer null.

Equate List-Wide Encoding and Retrieval Strategies Using Randomized Study Lists and Tests

Another reason for using within- rather than between-list manipulations of relatedness is to minimize the effects of generalized encoding/retrieval strategy differences across the levels of relatedness. That is, compared to when all study items are unrelated, when numerous "sports" or "fruits" appear in the study list, people might become bored or believe they do not need to expend as much effort encoding the items, creating a motivational confound. A similar confound could also occur at retrieval if separate recognition tests are given after study lists with different levels of semantic relatedness. Thus, to draw the strongest possible inferences about the mechanisms that mediate semantic relatedness effects *per se*, one should equate such generalized encoding and retrieval strategies across the various RLs by randomly intermixing the items that instantiate the different RLs within a single recognition test that follows a study list in which the items are presented in a random order and represent all of the different RLs.[3]

Counterbalance the Items Tested as Targets and Lures

Only a few studies between 1970–1990 (to be reviewed shortly) followed up on Kintsch's (1968) seminal finding. However, in 1995, findings reported by Roediger and McDermott inspired many memory researchers to once again examine the effects of semantic relatedness in recognition. However, these researchers switched from Kintsch's manipulation of shared category membership to a manipulation of associative relatedness. (For brevity's sake, we hereafter use the generic term relatedness to refer to either semantic or associative relatedness.) Although almost all of the post-1990 studies on semantic relatedness effects on recognition memory have controlled for intracategorical output interference and many have equated generalized encoding/retrieval strategy differences across different levels of relatedness, only a few have controlled for the specific items that serve as targets and lures across different levels of relatedness. It is to this issue that we now turn.

Roediger and McDermott (1995) revived a paradigm introduced by Deese (1959a, 1959b). In this so-called Deese/Roediger–McDermott (DRM) false-memory paradigm, people study a list of words (DRM associates, e.g., *blanket, dream, bed*), all of which are associatively related to a single word (*sleep*), typically called the critical item (CI), which itself does not appear in the study list. Although the CI itself is not studied, in both free recall and recognition, people often falsely remember that it was. In recognition, false alarms (FAs, i.e., incorrectly identifying a lure as having been studied) for nonstudied CIs are often compared to (1) FAs for CIs selected from another DRM list that was not studied and is unrelated to the studied DRM lists[4], (2) FAs for nonstudied DRM associates related to the CI, (3) FAs for non-DRM words unrelated to the CI or any word in the study lists, or (4) *hits* (correctly identifying a target as having been studied) for the studied DRM associates (see Roediger, McDermott, & Robinson, 1998, for a review). This *false memory effect* is so powerful that CI intrusions in recall (e.g., McDermott, 1997) and CI FAs in recognition (e.g., Gallo, Roberts, & Seamon, 1997) are sometimes nearly as frequent as hits for a DRM associate studied in the middle of the study list, and it occurs even when one considers only recognition responses associated with high confidence (e.g., McDermott & Roediger, 1998) and even when people are warned against falling prey to this effect (e.g., Gallo et al., 1997; McCabe & Smith, 2002). As shown later, the DRM paradigm replicates earlier research, which instantiated relatedness by using shared category membership, in showing that FAs increase as RL and RS increase.

The DRM paradigm was developed to investigate false memories, as measured by CI intrusions in recall and CI FAs in recognition, and not necessarily to examine a person's ability to discriminate explicitly whether a CI was studied versus not studied. Investigations of false memories are crucial for juries to understand the conditions that are likely to lead to a high incidence of false memories in court cases, and they can provide important insights into the phenomenology of memory. Nevertheless, false memories tell at best only half the story of memory. To drive this point home, consider an absurd example of a recognition memory experiment, in which a 40-item study list consists of 20 exemplars from the "fruit" category (e.g., *banana, grape, apple, cherry, kiwi, raspberry, pear*, but not *orange*) and of 20 orthographically legal and pronounceable nonwords (e.g., *tark, gant, mip, buncle, yill*, but not *flep*). In a delayed recognition test, FAs to *tree* and to *bhlqkm* are .4 and .02, respectively. If one assumes that poor memory is validly indexed by frequent FAs, s/he might conclude that memory is poorer for words than for nonwords. However, one can challenge this conclusion by noting that this is an "apples versus oranges" comparison because *tree* is more similar to the studied words (e.g., *cherry*) than the orthographically illegal and unpronounceable *bhlqkm* is to the studied nonwords. To correct this, one might compare FAs to *orange* and to *flep* and find that they are .60 and .35, respectively. Although this comparison is more appropriate, to conclude that words are more poorly remembered than nonwords, one needs to know the hits for studied words and nonwords. If the hits to *kiwi* and *yill* are .90 and .40, respectively, one might now conclude instead that "memory" was actually much better for words than nonwords (as indicated by a person's ability to discriminate whether the word or nonword was actually studied vs. not studied), even though the FAs were much higher for words (.60) than for nonwords (.35). But this conclusion is still not without its problems. Specifically, compared to the two orthographically legal, pronounceable nonwords *yill* and *flep*, the two fruits *kiwi* and *orange* may differ to a greater degree on properties that might influence their memorability or a person's willingness to say they were studied when s/he was uncertain. Of course, in principle one could avoid these problems by matching the items of interest on such properties. But this would be impossible to do for words and nonwords and can even be very difficult to do for different words.

Although these examples were intentionally absurd to make a point, the same problem exists in a much subtler form for those DRM studies that compare FAs for the CI *sleep* to hits for the CI's associates, e.g., *blanket*. The hidden assumption behind such a comparison is that the lure CI and its target associate are closely matched on variables that might affect their memorability *and* a subject's tendency to say they were studied when s/he is in doubt. But this assumption is questionable. Whittlesea (2002) found that even when all of the words in a study list are nominally totally unrelated to a CI lure and its tested associate lure(s), FAs are still higher for CI lures than for associate lures. (This effect, which Whittlesea dubbed the *life* effect, had been observed in many prior studies, starting with Roediger & McDermott, 1995, though it is important to note that the FA difference for CI vs. associate lures is much smaller than if the study list contained associates related to that CI and associate.) Moreover, Tse and Neely (2005) showed that lexical decision times to CI lures are faster than those to control lures matched on two variables known to have a large impact on lexical decisions, i.e., word length and frequency, even when the CI lure and control lure were totally unrelated to previously studied DRM list. This shows that matching rarely works completely.

If one is interested in the ability to discriminate targets from lures as the index of memory in the DRM paradigm (as opposed to being interested only in false memories), the only way to ensure perfect matching for targets and lures is to have exactly the same CI (or associate) serve as both a target and a lure. This can be done by having each subject study multiple DRM lists, with half including the CI but not a specific associate and the other half including that specific associate but not the CI. The memory discriminability for CIs and associates can then be compared within each subject for different items and for the same items across subjects via counterbalancing. This works for assessing RL effects *separately* for

CIs versus associates, but not for assessing an RS effect in which CIs instantiate the strongly related item and the associates, the weakly related item. It does not work for RS effects because there may be properties inherent in CIs and associates that affect their memorability independent of the strength of the relation they have to the studied items. For example, a CI such as *sleep* likely has more semantic associates (greater connectivity; cf. McEvoy, Nelson, & Komatsu, 1999) than does its associate *blanket*, which is why it was selected as a CI in the first place. Also, CIs tend to have higher frequencies than their associates (Roediger, Watson, McDermott, & Gallo, 2001).

Counterbalance Study Lists for RS Manipulations

In principle one can partially solve the problem of controlling for item differences for RS manipulations. (See Brainerd & Wright, 2005, for one such attempt in an investigation of the effects of a test item's forward vs. backward associative strength to the items in a DRM-type study list.) For example, one could, across different subjects, test *lime* as either a target or a lure after a study list containing either items strongly related to *lime* (i.e., other citrus fruits such as *lemon*, *orange*, *tangerine*, and *grapefruit*) or items weakly related to *lime* (i.e., noncitrus fruits such as *apple*, *pear*, *cherry*, and *apricot*). However, differences in *lime*'s memorability after studying these two lists when they did or did not contain *lime* could be due to differences in the memorability of the other studied citrus or noncitrus fruits rather than to RS differences *per se*. (To keep the list lengths the same when *lime* does or does not appear in the study list, one would need to have *lime* replace one of the study-list items when *lime* is studied and have that same item replace *lime* when *lime* is not studied.) To avoid this confound, one could also test a noncitrus fruit *plum* as either a target or lure after different subjects had studied a list that contained citrus or noncitrus fruits. Thus, across all subjects, (a) the specific items *lime* and *plum* would equally often have been tested as targets and lures that were weakly or strongly related to their study lists, and (b) the two different study lists (citrus vs. noncitrus fruits) would have equally often appeared in the weakly related and strongly related conditions. Unfortunately, it is extremely difficult to execute this design due to the difficulty of finding enough materials to allow for enough observations per subject per condition. Indeed, to our knowledge, such a design has never been reported.

Minimize Length/Strength Confounds

Unless one takes great care, RL manipulations are likely to be confounded with changes in RS. That is, when a test item is related to six items versus one item in the study list, the sum of its semantic/associative overlap with the study list items will likely be greater for the six-item list. This confound is virtually impossible to avoid without introducing other confounds. For example, assume that the test item *cat* has "semantic/associative overlap" scores of 1, 2, 3, 4, 5, 6, 7, 8, 9, and 10, with words W1–W10, respectively, with 0 indicating "totally unrelated to *cat*." Assume that you want to compare length effects by presenting lists that have two or five items related to *cat*. Assuming a ratio scale of measurement for the overlap scores, to equate the total amount of overlap between the study list and the test item for the two RLs, you could use W1, W2, W3, W4, and W5 for the five-item condition and either W7 and W8 or W6 and W9 for the two-item condition. However, the range, standard deviation, and average of the individual strengths would differ between the two RL conditions. Thus, if RL affected recognition, you would not know if it was length or the confounded range, standard deviation, and/ or average strength that produced the effect. (Obviously, it is logically impossible to manipulate length while holding both the total overlap and the average overlap constant.) But even if the overall overlap between the study items themselves were equated for the different lengths, that would likely introduce other confounds. Thus, when one finds an effect of *length*, there are likely a host of strength variables that could also be producing the effect. However, one can manipulate *strength* effects in the absence of these other confounded variables by embedding a single study item that has varying degrees of semantic/associative overlap with the test item in a study list that represents a single RL. (The other items within that study list could have varying degrees of overlap with each other and with the test item, as long as these items were always presented in the study list containing the *single* item that was being used to manipulate RS.)

Use Signal Detection Theory (SDT) to Measure Memory Discriminability

If one is interested in the effects of relatedness on discriminating whether a test word did or did not appear in a previously studied list (as opposed to its effects on only FAs), one should use SDT (see MacMillan & Creelman, 2004) to measure memory discriminability (e.g., Stretch & Wixted, 1998; Wixted; chapter 5, this volume; Yonelinas, 1994). SDT assumes that recognition is based on a single continuum that we will call episodic familiarity (EF), which refers to the list-based familiarity that accrues to individual words when a study list is presented. By virtue of actually appearing in the study list, targets have a higher average EF than do lures, which nevertheless have EF values greater than zero by virtue of properties (e.g., letters, meanings, phonology) that they share with the targets. Even when targets are studied under identical conditions, it is assumed that EF will vary across individual targets (and lures) due to a multitude of differences in the properties that individual words have. For simplicity, SDT assumes that the EF values across targets and across lures conform to normal distributions (see Figure 19.1).

In yes/no recognition, subjects use a test item's EF and a response criterion to determine whether or not the item appeared in the study list. Figure 19.1 shows the ordinally labeled placements of five possible response criteria. For any single criterion, if the test item's EF exceeds that criterion the subject responds "yes" (the item was studied) and "no" otherwise. The proportions of the target and lure EF distributions that exceed a response criterion provide the hits and FAs, respectively, for that criterion. In general, the more hits exceed FAs, the better is memory discriminability. The different response criteria could represent either different single criteria for different subjects or different criteria for an individual

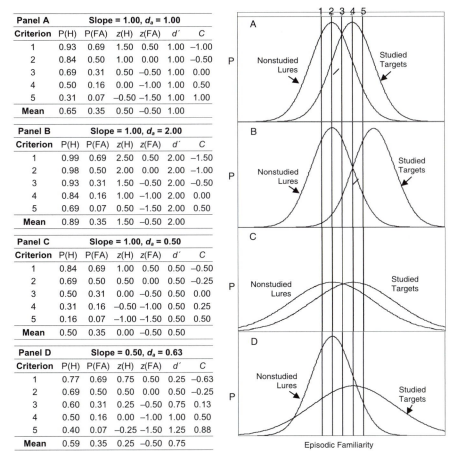

Panel A		Slope = 1.00, d_a = 1.00			
Criterion	P(H)	P(FA)	z(H)	z(FA)	d'	C
1	0.93	0.69	1.50	0.50	1.00	−1.00
2	0.84	0.50	1.00	0.00	1.00	−0.50
3	0.69	0.31	0.50	−0.50	1.00	0.00
4	0.50	0.16	0.00	−1.00	1.00	0.50
5	0.31	0.07	−0.50	−1.50	1.00	1.00
Mean	0.65	0.35	0.50	−0.50	1.00	

Panel B		Slope = 1.00, d_a = 2.00			
Criterion	P(H)	P(FA)	z(H)	z(FA)	d'	C
1	0.99	0.69	2.50	0.50	2.00	−1.50
2	0.98	0.50	2.00	0.00	2.00	−1.00
3	0.93	0.31	1.50	−0.50	2.00	−0.50
4	0.84	0.16	1.00	−1.00	2.00	0.00
5	0.69	0.07	0.50	−1.50	2.00	0.50
Mean	0.89	0.35	1.50	−0.50	2.00	

Panel C		Slope = 1.00, d_a = 0.50			
Criterion	P(H)	P(FA)	z(H)	z(FA)	d'	C
1	0.84	0.69	1.00	0.50	0.50	−0.50
2	0.69	0.50	0.50	0.00	0.50	−0.25
3	0.50	0.31	0.00	−0.50	0.50	0.00
4	0.31	0.16	−0.50	−1.00	0.50	0.25
5	0.16	0.07	−1.00	−1.50	0.50	0.50
Mean	0.50	0.35	0.00	−0.50	0.50	

Panel D		Slope = 0.50, d_a = 0.63			
Criterion	P(H)	P(FA)	z(H)	z(FA)	d'	C
1	0.77	0.69	0.75	0.50	0.25	−0.63
2	0.69	0.50	0.50	0.00	0.50	−0.25
3	0.60	0.31	0.25	−0.50	0.75	0.13
4	0.50	0.16	0.00	−1.00	1.00	0.50
5	0.40	0.07	−0.25	−1.50	1.25	0.88
Mean	0.59	0.35	0.25	−0.50	0.75	

FIGURE 19.1   Signal detection theory parameters for four different hypothetical episodic familiarity distributions.

subject when s/he is asked to give confidence ratings associated with his/her "yes" responses. Higher confidence "yes" responses are associated with criteria that are placed farther to the right, because the EF values that exceed that criterion are much more likely to be from the target distribution than from the lure distribution.

There are two measures of interest in SDT, memory discriminability (d') and the placement of the response criterion (either β or C). (We use C here because the meaning of its values is more transparent, but the conclusions we draw concerning the interpretations of C also apply to β.) The d' measure indicates the distance between the means of the target and lure EF distributions; it is akin to a z-score because its value is given in units based on the standard deviations of the normally distributed EF distributions. When the target and lure EF distributions have equal standard deviations, the C measure (which is also given in standard deviation units) indicates the placement of the response criterion on the X-axis relative to the point between their mean values at which the lure and target EF distributions intersect. A C of 0 indicates the criterion is at this intersection point, a negative C indicates it is below the intersection point (which means the person is liberal in saying "yes"), and a positive C, above (which means the person is conservative in saying "yes"). If a test item is equally likely to be a target or a lure, a C of 0 leads to optimal performance. The implications of SDT for assessing the effects of relatedness on recognition seem simple and clear: The relatedness of a test item to the study list could affect *memory* discriminability, as measured by its effects on d', and/or influence where the response criterion is placed for saying that a target or lure test item was indeed studied. But as we now discuss, this apparent simplicity can be deceptive.

The d' for a given criterion for a given condition is computed by subtracting the normal-distribution *signed* z-score corresponding to the FA probability for lures from the *signed* z-score corresponding to the hit probability for targets in that condition. Figure 19.1 shows the d' value corresponding to each of the criterion placements for four different cases. In Panels A and B, the target and lure EF distributions all have equal standard deviations but their means are closer together in Panel A than in Panel B. In Panel C, the means of the target and lure EF distributions are the same distance apart as in Panel A and the standard deviations of the target and lure distributions are equal to each other but twice as large as those in Panel A. As shown in Panels A–C, the beauty of SDT is that when the standard deviations of the target and lure EF distributions are equal, the d' values are constant across different response criteria placements, which means that one can measure memory discriminability for a condition "independently" of where a particular subject might place his/her response criterion. (The reason for the quotations around "independently" will soon be clarified.) The data in Panels A and B of Figure 19.1 also show a limitation of using hits minus FAs as a measure of recognition memory discriminability. As shown in Panel A, when a liberal response criterion has a C value with a higher absolute value than a conservative criterion (as is so for the criterion placements at 1 and 4, respectively), the liberal criterion yields a smaller hits-minus-FAs difference (i.e., .93–.69 = .24) than does the conservative criterion (i.e., .50–.16 = .34), even though memory discriminability is exactly the same. More strikingly, in Panel B the liberal response criterion at 1 yields a .30 (i.e., .99–.69) hits-minus-FA difference which is numerically less than the just cited .34, even though d' is much higher in Panel B. (We thank Tram Neill for pointing this out to us.)

Figure 19.2 displays what are known as z-ROC functions that correspond to the panels in Figure 19.1. The z-ROC plots the z for hits as a function of the z for FAs for each criterion placement. When recognition is based solely on normally distributed EF distributions and the standard deviations of the target and lure EFs are equal, z-ROC functions are linear and parallel to the major diagonal, with their distances from the diagonal increasing as d' increases. With this background, we turn to some problems associated with interpreting SDT measures for recognition memory and also consider a case in which the standard deviations of the target and lure EF distributions are not the same (Panel D of Figure 19.1).

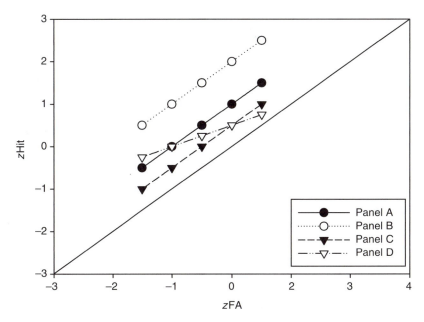

FIGURE 19.2   Z-transformed receiver operating characteristics (ROC) curves for the Figure 19.1 distributions.

Everything is Relative: Common Misinterpretations of SDT and Their Implications for Relatedness Effects in Recognition Memory

When considering relatedness effects, there are several cautionary notes that need to be made about interpreting d' and C differences. They are as follows:

When the Target and Lure EF Distributions have Unequal Standard Deviations, d_a Not d' Should be Used

In Panel D, the means of the target and lure EF distributions are the same distance apart as in Panels A and C, but the standard deviation of the target EF distribution is twice that of the lure EF distribution. This is what one would expect if the lure EF distribution reflects item differences whereas the target EF distribution reflects additional variability due to fluctuations in attention during study. As shown in Panel D of Figure 19.1, when the standard deviations of the target and lure EF distributions are unequal, the computed d's vary across the different response criteria placements. As shown in Figure 19.2, the result is that the slope of the z-ROC function now becomes equal to the ratio of the standard deviation of the lure distribution to the standard deviation of the target distribution. Hence, the slope of the z-ROC function generated by panel D is .5. As would be expected if attention varied during study, the slopes of empirically based z-ROCs should be less than 1.0, and indeed they often hover around .7 or so (see Ratcliff et al., 1994; Ratcliff, Sheu, & Gronlund, 1992). As shown in Panel D of Figure 19.2, when the standard deviation of the target EF distribution is greater than that for the lure EF distribution, the more liberal is the response criterion, the lower will be the d' value for that criterion.[5] Hence, for the unequal standard deviation case, d' is *not* independent of the criterion placement. This poses a problem when subjects are merely asked to respond "yes" or "no" without providing confidence ratings. That is, when the standard deviations are unequal, if subjects adopt an absolutely more liberal criterion placement in Condition 1 (which means more frequent hits and FAs) than in Condition 2, the d' will be lower for Condition 1 even though the means of target and lure EF distributions are identical for Conditions 1 and 2. This problem can be addressed by having subjects provide multiple confidence ratings and then using the slope of the z-ROC function to compute d_a (or d_e; see MacMillan & Creelman, 2004, for details).[6] It is interesting that even though it is well established that the slopes of z-ROC functions are typically less than 1 (e.g., Ratcliff et al., 1992), researchers rarely report d_a (or d_e). (See Westerberg & Marsolek, 2003, for an exception.) The use of d' rather than d_a would not be problematic for totally within-subjects designs if subjects used the same criterion placement for all conditions (but see later discussion in this section) and if the ratios of lure to target standard deviations were the same across all conditions. However, if these conditions are not met or a relatedness effect is being tested in a between subjects design, one cannot determine if the differences in d' are due to actual memory discriminability differences or to differences in absolute criterion placements across two conditions. To avoid this problem, researchers should always require subjects to use different confidence ratings and then compute d_a (or d_e). (This point has also been made by Verde & Rotello, 2003.) Similar reasoning applies even if one wants to evaluate differences in only false memories in the DRM paradigm under two different conditions by comparing FA differences for CIs that are related versus unrelated to a DRM study list under those two conditions.

C Values do Not Measure the *Absolute* Placement of Response Criteria   This can be seen in Figure 19.1 where the *absolute* placements of the criteria labeled 5 in Panels A and B are identical but their C values are different and the two criteria having the same C value of 0 in Panels A and B have different *absolute* placements along the EF continuum. Consider the case when targets have been studied under two different conditions that produce the target EF distributions in Panels A and B. If the targets in these two conditions are tested against lures that come from exactly the same lure EF distribution (as in Panels A and B) and the criterion is placed at exactly the same absolute location, the C value will necessarily be lower the higher is the d'. This shows that when d's for two different target conditions are computed by using FAs from the very same lures, the C value is totally *dependent* on d'. Thus, once again, the conclusion that d' and C are "independent" is not generally true.

SDT cannot Locate the *Absolute* Positions of the Means Along the EF Continuum   An ancillary to the previous point is that SDT cannot be used to locate the absolute placement of the target and lure EF distributions along the EF continuum. To visualize why this is so, make an imaginary exact copy of the lure and target EF distributions of Panel A in Figure 19.1 (and the distance between their means) and consider the original and the copy to represent two different conditions. Next, mentally lift the copy and move it to the left or right along the EF axis, while the original stays stationary. Doing this demonstrates that one cannot ascertain exactly where along the EF continuum any of the means of the two target and the two lure EF distributions fall when the d's for two conditions are identical. Similarly, by imagining moving the lure and target EF distributions in Panel B to the left or right along the EF axis (retaining the distance between their means), one can see the same is true when the d's are different. Also, this is so whether or not the C values for the two conditions are identical or different. One implication of this (and the previous point) is that when two conditions have equal d's and different Cs, one cannot determine if the difference in FAs in these two conditions is due to differences in the absolute criterion placements in the two conditions or is due to differences in the means of their lure EF distributions (with the criterion being placed at the exact same absolute position in the two conditions). Miller and Wolford (1999) failed to take this into account and erroneously concluded that a difference in C values for CIs and associates (which yielded similar d's) in the DRM paradigm indicated that the lure EF distributions were the same for CIs and associates and that subjects were using a lower absolute criterion placement for the CIs. Wickens and Hirshman (2000) and Wixted and Stretch (2000) challenged this conclusion by raising the points we repeat here.

When Items are Not Counterbalanced, d' Differences can be Produced by Criterion Differences When students are first exposed to SDT, the emphasis is on d' being a measure of memory discriminability that is "independent" of a subject's response criterion for saying "yes." This was exemplified in Panels A–C in Figure 19.1. However, this claim is necessarily true only when the target and lure items do not differ in aspects that might lead people to use different response criteria for the targets and lures. When the latter condition is not met, the use of different response criteria for the targets and lures can produce d' differences. To understand this, consider a case in which a researcher is interested in comparing relatedness strength effects for citrus fruits versus noncitrus fruits. S/he has people study the following list: *grape, apple, cherry, orange, raspberry, plum, apricot,* and *strawberry*. At test, the FAs to the nonstudied lures *blackberry* and *pear* are both .50 ($z = 0$) and the average hits to *apple* are .84 ($z = 1.00$) and to *orange*, .60 ($z = .25$), yielding d's of 1.00 and .25, respectively. The researcher concludes that memory discriminability is much better for noncitrus fruits than for citrus fruits. However, it could be that the EF distributions for citrus and noncitrus fruits are identical, in which case the memory strengths for the citrus and noncitrus fruits are identical. Why then the d' difference? At test, people may realize that the study list contained a lot of berries and other fruits that grow in temperate climates but hardly any citrus fruits. This might cause them to use a more stringent response criterion for tropical than for nontropical fruits. Thus, in the example given in Panel A in Figure 19.1, the person might have used Criterion 3 for nontropical fruits (e.g., *apple, blackberry,* and *pear*) and Criterion 4 for tropical fruits (e.g., *orange*). This would have produced the observed hits and

FAs and the d' difference even if *orange* and *apple* both had EF values drawn from the very same distribution.

This concern is not based merely on an "in principle" argument that has never been realized in the literature. For example, Park, Shobe, and Kihlstrom (2005) recently found that when the forward and backward strengths of nonstudied category names to studied exemplars was equated with the forward and backward strengths of nonstudied DRM CIs to their studied associates, FAs were much lower for the nonstudied category names than for the CIs. Under the assumption that equating the associative strengths to the studied items should have led to EF values being the same for the category names and the CIs, this FA difference was presumably due to a much more stringent criterion for responding "old" to category names than CIs. We believe this difference in criterion placement was likely due (a) to category names being "linguistically special words" and hence much more distinctively different from their exemplars than CIs are from their associates and (b) to people setting a stringent response criterion for responding "old" to the category names because mostly (actually only) category exemplars (and not category names) had been studied. A similar response criterion difference could exist in principle when one makes comparisons between CIs versus associates in the DRM paradigm or perhaps even between (counterbalanced, identical) CIs that are related versus unrelated to the study list.

This problem can be avoided even though citrus fruits and noncitrus fruits (or CIs and associates) must necessarily be different items. The problem is avoided by having the same citrus fruits and noncitrus fruits be tested as both targets and lures and computing separate d's for the two types of fruits by using the hits and FAs taken from the same type of fruit for each d'. This ensures that the same stringent criterion will be used for both the target and lure citrus fruits and the same more liberal criterion will be used for both the target and lure noncitrus fruits. If that were done, the computed d' would become the same for both kinds of fruits as shown in Figure 19.1, Panel A. This counterbalancing scheme (which as discussed later has rarely been employed in the few DRM studies that have compared memory discriminabilities for CIs vs. associates) will also work for the cases shown in Panels C and D of Figure 19.1, though d_a rather than d' must be used when one set of items produces the EF distributions in Panel C and the other set of items produces the EF distributions in Panel D. However, it is important to note that this counterbalancing scheme is not needed if one can be sure that subjects cannot or will not change their criteria from trial to trial depending on some distinctive features of the different kinds of (noncounterbalanced) test items. Fortunately, there is evidence that this may be so. In a clever experiment, Stretch and Wixted (1998) used different ink colors for test items to indicate that if that test item had been studied it appeared 1 versus 5 times in the study list. To perform optimally, subjects should have used a less stringent response criterion for the lures printed in the color indicating that the item would have been presented once, but they did not do this (as determined by the equal FAs for the items in the two different colors, which because of counterbalancing necessarily came from the same lure EF distribution). Of course, it remains to be determined how general this inflexibility in using different criteria for different kinds of items is. It could be that semantic features (e.g., citrus vs. noncitrus fruits) might be more likely to be used than nonsemantic features. If so, it is imperative that items be counterbalanced through the target and lure conditions that are used to compute d', such that an observed d' difference can be attributed to memorability differences rather than criterion differences.

Response Criterion Variability Affects d' and can Produce Nonlinear z-ROC Functions

Table 19.1 illustrates yet another way in which d' and response criteria placements are not independent. (We thank Tram Neill for bringing this point to our attention.) Consider a case of three levels of confidence ratings associated with the following three verbal labels: reasonably confident it was studied, not sure if it was studied, or reasonably confident it not studied. Assume that for one condition (the left half of Table 19.1), subjects consistently use Criteria 8, 5, and 2 for these three confidence levels, whereas for another condition (the right half of Table 19.1) there is variability in their criterion placements such that they equally often use Criteria 7 and 9, 4 and 6, and 3 and 1, respectively, for these three confidence levels. As shown in Table 19.1, the d's based on the averages of the hits and FAs for the two variable criteria are lower than the corresponding d' values based on a nonvariable criterion placed halfway between them. Most interesting is that the reduction in d' produced by criterion variability is greater for the middle confidence level than for the two extreme confidence levels. Because the perpendicular distance from the major diagonal of any single point on the z-ROC function produced by a single criterion is proportional to the d' associated with that single point, the result of criterion variability of the form shown in Table 19.1 is that it leads to (a) a lower d_a and (b) a nonlinear, concave z-ROC function.

The foregoing analysis has two implications. First, if there is a d' (d_a) difference between two conditions produced by a relatedness manipulation, there is no necessary ordinal relation between this d' (d_a) difference and the distances between the means of the target and lure EF distributions for these two conditions because the relatedness manipulation could be affecting criterion variability rather than the distances between the target and lure EF distributions. Second, criterion variability produces a concave z-ROC which has often been interpreted (see Yonelinas, 2002, for a review) to indicate that recognition is not based solely on EF as described by SDT but is also based on a qualitatively distinct recollection process (the delineation of which is precluded here by space limitations). Table 19.1 clearly indicates that a concave z-ROC can, at least under some conditions, be accommodated by a single-process familiarity based recognition process if the response criteria are variable, without any appeal whatsoever to the operation of a qualitatively distinct recollection process. (We believe future research should be designed to discriminate between these two possible sources of concave z-ROC functions, if indeed that is possible.) The bottom half of Table 19.1 shows that criterion variability can have similar effects when the variability of the underlying target and lure EF distributions is increased. Of course, great caution should be exercised before making generalized conclusions about the effects of criterion variability on d' (d_a) based on the findings for the two specific examples shown in

TABLE 19.1 The Effects of Response Criterion Variability on d'

No criterion variability, Slope = 1.00, $d_a = 1.00$

Criterion	P(H)	P(FA)	z(H)	z(FA)	d'	C
1	1.00	1.00	4.00	3.00	1.00	-3.50
2	1.00	0.99	3.25	2.25	1.00	-2.75
3	0.99	0.93	2.50	1.50	1.00	-2.00
4	0.96	0.77	1.75	0.75	1.00	-1.25
5	0.84	0.50	1.00	0.00	1.00	-0.50
6	0.60	0.23	0.25	-0.75	1.00	0.25
7	0.31	0.07	-0.50	-1.50	1.00	1.00
8	0.11	0.01	-1.25	-2.25	1.00	1.75
9	0.02	0.00	-2.00	-3.00	1.00	2.50
Mean	0.65	0.50	1.00	0.00	1.00	-0.5

No criterion variability, Slope = 1.00, $d_a = 0.50$

Criterion	P(H)	P(FA)	z(H)	z(FA)	d'	C
1	1.00	1.00	3.50	3.00	0.50	-3.25
2	1.00	0.99	2.75	2.25	0.50	-2.50
3	0.99	0.93	2.00	1.50	0.50	-1.75
4	0.89	0.77	1.25	0.75	0.50	-1.00
5	0.69	0.50	0.50	0.00	0.50	-0.25
6	0.40	0.23	-0.25	-0.75	0.50	0.50
7	0.16	0.07	-1.00	-1.50	0.50	1.25
8	0.04	0.01	-1.75	-2.25	0.50	2.00
9	0.01	0.00	-2.50	-3.00	0.50	2.75
Mean	0.58	0.50	0.50	0.00	0.50	-0.25

Variable criteria, Slope = 1.00, $d_a = 0.95$

Criterion	P(H)	P(FA)	z(H)	z(FA)	d'	C
1	1.00	1.00	4.00	3.00	1.00	-3.50
2	1.00	0.97	2.73	1.82	0.91	-2.28
3	0.99	0.93	2.50	1.50	1.00	-2.00
4	0.96	0.77	1.75	0.75	1.00	-1.25
5	0.78	0.50	0.77	0.00	0.77	-0.38
6	0.60	0.23	0.25	-0.75	1.00	0.25
7	0.31	0.07	-0.50	-1.50	1.00	1.00
8	0.17	0.03	-0.97	-1.82	0.85	1.40
9	0.02	0.00	-2.00	-3.00	1.00	2.50
Mean	0.65	0.50	0.95	0.00	0.95	-0.47

Variable criteria, Slope = 1.00, $d_a = 0.47$

Criterion	P(H)	P(FA)	z(H)	z(FA)	d'	C
1	1.00	1.00	3.50	3.00	0.50	-3.25
2	0.99	0.97	2.27	1.82	0.45	-2.05
3	0.99	0.93	2.00	1.50	0.50	-1.75
4	0.89	0.77	1.25	0.75	0.50	-1.00
5	0.65	0.50	0.38	0.00	0.38	-0.19
6	0.40	0.23	-0.25	-0.75	0.50	0.50
7	0.16	0.07	-1.00	-1.50	0.50	1.25
8	0.08	0.03	-1.39	-1.82	0.44	1.61
9	0.01	0.00	-2.50	-3.00	0.50	2.75
Mean	0.58	0.50	0.47	0.00	0.47	-0.24

Table 19.1. These examples merely serve as existence proofs that these effects can occur under some circumstances. We leave it to those more quantitatively sophisticated than we are to delineate how general the effects of criterion variability effects on d' (d_a) really are and if they could be large enough to produce the degree of nonlinearity that has been observed in many z-ROCs (Yonelinas, 2002).

Summary   The above discussion makes it clear that when one uses d' (d_a) to assess relatedness effects on recognition, one needs to exercise caution before concluding that the relatedness manipulation affected the distance between the means of the target and lure EF distributions rather than criteria placement or EF variability. Some of these problems can be solved by ensuring that exactly the same items are tested both as targets and lures (see the fourth point) and by using d_a rather than d' to handle the case in which the relatedness manipulation might affect the variability of the target EF distribution (see the first point). However, using counterbalancing schemes and d_a rather than d' cannot solve the problem of the relatedness manipulation changing the variability of both the target and lure distributions (see Panels A vs. C of Figure 19.1) or changing the variability of the criterion placements (see Table 19.1). Thus, if relatedness has an effect on d' or d_a, it could be doing so either by affecting (a) the distance between the means of the target and lure distributions, (b) the variability of both the target and lure EF distributions within the same condition to the same degree, and/or (c) the variability of the response criteria placements. (Cowan, 1996, and Shiffrin, Huber, & Marinelli, 1995, have made similar points.) However, these ambiguities do not constitute a fatal deficiency of SDT measures of memory as long as one keeps two things in mind. First, memory discriminability differences, as measured by d' or d_a, may represent differences in the distance between the means for the target and lure EF distributions *relative to the variability* of those EF distributions or of the criterion placements that are used for a single confidence rating level. Second, differences in response criterion placements across two conditions represent differences in placements relative to the intersection of the target and lure EF distributions; they do not necessarily (or even probably) represent differences in the absolute placements of the response criteria. Unfortunately, there are a number of instances in the literature in which claims are made that do not reflect an awareness of these two points.

The Optimal Design for Assessing Relatedness Effects in Recognition

The foregoing analyses suggest that the optimal design for assessing relatedness effects in recognition should conform to the following prescriptions. (1) Always have subjects give confidence ratings so that d_a can be computed. (2) Try to use randomized within-list designs whenever possible. (But see Note 3 for a cautionary note.) (3) Rotate items through all of the target and lure conditions, by having a specific test item either appear or not appear in the study list that precedes the test. (4) Test the same number of targets and lures for each RL to control for "intracategorical" output interference effects. (Hence, the number of targets tested cannot exceed the shortest RL.) (5) For RL manipulations, when possible equate across the different lengths the total strength and range of the semantic/associative overlaps of all of the studied items to the test item and the amount of semantic/associative overlap of the studied items to each other. (6) Manipulate RS through the presence versus absence of a *single* related item in the study list. (This makes it easier to avoid confounding the effect of RS with other variables such as the variability of the strengths between the item of interest and the individual items used to manipulate RS and the average semantic relatedness of the items used to manipulate RS with each other.) (7) Whether one manipulates RS by having test items that have different amounts of semantic/associative overlap with only one or more than one related study items, rotate the specific test items through different strengths by having two different study lists, one containing an item (or items) strongly related to test item X and weakly related to test item Y and the other containing an item (or items) weakly related to test item X and strongly related to test item Y. (For multiple related items, this counterbalancing scheme is difficult to implement.) (8) When Prescription 7 cannot be satisfied, as is the case with DRM CIs and associates, one should match the items that are used as the strongly and weakly related test items on as many variables as possible, such as word frequency, length, concreteness, imageability, and orthographic/phonological distinctiveness.

In the ideal world, one would like to have complete control over the variables that are potentially confounded with RL and RS effects and equate their values across RL and RS manipulations. However, this would be overkill if these confounded variables did not actually affect recognition performance. In this regard, we note that the experiments whose data we summarize in the next section varied considerably in the materials and procedures they used. However, because many of the foregoing prescriptions were often unsystematically violated across these experiments, we could not discern if violations of certain of our prescriptions systematically becloud the conclusions one can draw from the RL and RS effects they reported. (Readers interested in the procedural details and prescriptive violations of the experiments whose results we summarize in our empirical review should see Appendix Tables A1–A3 in our online addendum.) It remains for future research to manipulate systematically the variables that have been confounded with RL and RS in previous research and thereby determine which of our methodological prescriptions one should take the trouble to follow.

THE EMPIRICAL REVIEW

In this section, we summarize empirical findings relevant to the effects of RL and RS on recognition. We restrict our review to experiments that test only neurologically intact young adults who study lists of individually presented words that are related only through semantic and/or associative relations. We exclude studies that use pictures (e.g., Koutstaal & Schacter, 1997), orthographically related items (e.g., Heathcote, 2003), phonologically related items (e.g., Sommers & Lewis, 1999; Westbury, Buchanan, & Brown, 2002), and hybrid DRM lists in which some items are phonologically related and some items are semantically related to the same CI or are semantically related to distinctly different meanings of the same CI (e.g., Hutchison & Balota, 2005; Watson, Balota, & Roediger, 2003). We believe the search procedures we used (see Appendix A in our online addendum) likely uncovered almost all relevant articles.

Relatedness Length Effects (RLEs)

Tables 19.2 and 19.3 summarize the RLEs found with DRM and category (CAT) materials, respectively. These tables show the hits, FAs, d' for different RLs and the RLE for that experiment. The d' column contains four kinds of values: (1) the gold standard d_a (indicated by #) computed for individual subjects or meta-subjects (each of which is created by aggregating over a few subjects in order to avoid an undefined d' when hits or FAs are 100% or 0%), (2) standard d' values (accompanied with no symbol) based on individual subjects or meta-subjects, (3) standard d' values (indicated by ^), which we computed from the overall means for hits and FAs reported for that condition or (4) pseudo-d's (indicated by °) which are based on hits for DRM associates and FAs for DRM CIs. (For the forced-choice tests, the d' values were adjusted as suggested by Hacker & Ratcliff, 1979.) The last column gives the data of most interest, i.e., the RLE, which is computed as the d' for the longest RL minus d' for the shortest RL. Thus, a negative RLE shows that increasing the RL hurt memory, whereas a positive RLE shows it helps memory. An asterisk with a RLE indicates that the effect was statistically significant. (For ^ d's, an asterisk with a RLE indicates that the alternative measure of memory discriminability that the authors originally reported, e.g., % hits—% FAs, was statistically significant or that RL had a significant effect on FAs but not hits or vice versa.)

Tables 19.2 and 19.3 are both organized according to whether the recognition tests were yes/no or forced-choice and within each of these two groupings whether the related items were presented blocked together or randomly presented in the study list. (Unlike in the other experiments within the blocked study grouping, the items instantiating RL-2 in Neely & Balota, 1981, were presented back-to-back as a pair but the pairs themselves were not all blocked together but rather were presented as isolated pairs interspersed among category-exemplar singletons and other unrelated buffer items.) Across and within experiments, the rows of these two tables are ordered in ascending order of RL. None of the CAT studies using yes/no recognition reported d_as, whereas a couple of DRM studies did. However, as discussed in the next paragraph, these RLEs could have been due to con-founded item differences. It should also be noted that (a) with a couple of exceptions, RL is typically manipulated in a blocked fashion for DRM lists but in a randomized fashion for CAT lists and (b) the effects of intracategorical output interference and RL were never confounded in the DRM studies but sometimes were confounded for CAT lists.

A quick scan of the results is somewhat discouraging because it suggests that the RLEs yield a seemingly inconsistent pattern. For the DRM lists, there were two marginally significantly positive RLEs, six significantly negative RLEs, and six null RLEs. The evidence for a positive RLE is especially weak in that both of the

TABLE 19.2 Summary of the Results of Experiments Examining Relatedness Length Effects with Category Materials

Study (year, experiment)	Relatedness length	Hit	FA	d[a]	RLE[a]
Blocked Study Yes/No RGN					
Neely & Balota (1981, 2)[b]	1	0.67	0.10	1.74*	+0.15*
Neely & Balota (1981, 2)	2	0.77	0.13	1.89*	
Dewhurst & Anderson (1999, 2)[c]	1	0.56	0.14	1.23*	−0.57*
Dewhurst & Anderson (1999, 2)	4	0.59	0.32	0.70*	
Dewhurst & Anderson (1999, 2)	8	0.65	0.39	0.66*	
Wallace (1982, 1)[d]	1	0.78	0.03	2.65*	−0.46*
Wallace (1982, 1)	6	0.82	0.10	2.20*	
Bruce & Fagan (1970)[e]	1	0.81	0.04	2.61*	−0.21
Bruce & Fagan (1970)	7	0.84	0.08	2.40*	
Kintsch (1968, 1)	1	0.81	0.06	2.48*	+0.04
Kintsch (1968, 1)	10	0.87	0.08	2.51*	
Arndt & Hirshman (1998, 3)[f]	4	0.58	0.22 (0.41)[g]	1.02[h]	+0.34*
Arndt & Hirshman (1998, 3)	16	0.61	0.16 (0.67)	1.36	
Blocked Study-2AFC RGN					
Hall (1982)[i]	1	0.84	0.16	1.41*	+1.07*
Hall (1982)	3	0.96	0.04	2.48*	
Blocked Study-3AFC RGN					
Slamecka (1975, 1)[j]	1	0.60	0.40	0.89*	+0.50*
Slamecka (1975, 1)	4	0.74	0.26	1.39*	
Slamecka (1975, 2)	1	0.46	0.54	0.43*	+0.42*
Slamecka (1975, 2)	4	0.59	0.41	0.85*	
Random Study-Yes/No RGN					
Neely & Balota (1981, 2)[b]	1	0.67	0.10	1.74*	+0.03
Neely & Balota (1981, 2)	2	0.71	0.11	1.77*	
Connor (1977, 1)[b]	1	—[k]	—	2.17	−0.06
Connor (1977, 1)	4	—	—	2.11	
Tussing & Greene (1999, 1)	1	0.73	0.03	2.49*	−0.63*
Tussing & Greene (1999, 1)	5	0.77	0.13	1.87*	
Tussing & Greene (1999, 2)	1	0.59	0.10	1.51*	−0.32*
Tussing & Greene (1999, 2)	5	0.65	0.21	1.19*	

Study			d'	RLE
Dewhurst & Anderson (1999, 2)[c]	1	0.58	1.33	
Dewhurst & Anderson (1999, 2)	4	0.63	1.10	−0.48*
Dewhurst & Anderson (1999, 2)	8	0.66	0.85	
Dewhurst (2001, 1)[c]	1	0.63	1.33	
Dewhurst (2001, 1)	4	0.65	0.80	−0.52*
Dewhurst (2001, 1)	8	0.70	0.80	
Engelkamp, Biegelmann & McDaniel (1998, 1)[l]	2	0.79	2.56	
Engelkamp, Biegelmann & McDaniel (1998, 1)	4	0.78	2.07	
Engelkamp, Biegelmann & McDaniel (1998, 1)	6	0.77	1.78	
Engelkamp, Biegelmann & McDaniel (1998, 1)	8	0.82	1.83	−0.94*
Engelkamp, Biegelmann & McDaniel (1998, 1)	12	0.84	1.78	
Engelkamp, Biegelmann & McDaniel (1998, 1)	16	0.77	1.62	
Engelkamp, Biegelmann & McDaniel (1998, 2)[m]	2	0.90	2.77	
Engelkamp, Biegelmann & McDaniel (1998, 2)	4	0.86	2.23	
Engelkamp, Biegelmann & McDaniel (1998, 2)	6	0.86	2.07	−0.69*
Engelkamp, Biegelmann & McDaniel (1998, 2)	8	0.83	2.08	
Random Study-2AFC RGN				
Schmidt (1988, 1)[b]	2	0.96	2.48	
Schmidt (1988, 1)	4	0.93	2.09	−0.55*
Schmidt (1988, 1)	16	0.91	1.90	

Note. FA = false alarms. RLE = relatedness length effect.

[a] In the d' column, ^ indicates that d' was computed from overall hits and overall FAs; ° pseudo d' based on hits for associates and FAs for CIs. In the RLE column, * indicates the RLE was significant at the .05 level of significance.

* All data from this study are averaged across test expectancy.

[b] All data from this study are averaged across test expectancy.

[c] We had to compute d' from the overall hits and FAs, because Dewhurst and Anderson reported d's averaged over individual subjects only for "remember" and "know" responses, separately.

[d] All data from this study were from only the first study–test cycle for the repeated study lists.

[e] All data from this study were from tests in which subjects were not forced to give equal numbers of "old" and "new" responses; all FAs from this study are averaged across categorical and "intrusion" distractors.

[f] All data from this study are averaged across presentation rate and were analyzed for meta-subjects (i.e., 1 meta-subject = 4 subjects).

[g] All FAs outside the parentheses were for exemplars and all FAs in parentheses were for prototypes.

[h] All d's from this study were based on exemplar FAs.

[i] All FAs from this study are averaged across related and unrelated distractors.

[j] All data from this study are averaged across number of related test cues.

[k] The author reported only hits minus FAs and d', not hits and FAs separately.

[l] All data from this study are averaged across two incidental tasks (categorization and pleasantness ratings) and the positions of the categories within the study list.

[m] All data from this study are averaged across two incidental tasks (noun/non-noun classification and pleasantness ratings).

TABLE 19.3 Summary of the Results of Experiments Examining Relatedness Length Effects with DRM-Associative Materials

Study (year, experiment)	Relatedness length	Hit	FA	d'[a]	RLE[a]
Blocked Study-Yes/No RGN					
Westerberg & Marsolek (2003, 1)	1-CI'	0.47	0.29	0.39#	
Westerberg & Marsolek (2003, 1)	15-CI	0.83	0.74	0.31#	−0.08
Westerberg & Marsolek (2003, 1)	1-CI'	0.47	0.29	0.39#	+0.15@
Westerberg & Marsolek (2003, 1)	15-Assoc	0.64	0.45	0.54#	
Westerberg & Marsolek (2003, 3)	1-Assoc'	0.48	0.33	0.44#	−0.22*
Westerberg & Marsolek (2003, 3)	15-CI	0.72	0.70	0.22#	
Westerberg & Marsolek (2003, 3)	1-Assoc'	0.48	0.33	0.44#	+0.08
Westerberg & Marsolek (2003, 3)	15-Assoc	0.60	0.43	0.52#	
Miller & Wolford (1999, 1&2)[b]	1-CI & Assoc	0.64	0.17	1.23#	+0.00
Miller & Wolford (1999, 1&2)	15-CI	0.97	0.80	1.23#	
Miller & Wolford (1999, 1&2)	1-CI & Assoc	0.64	0.17	1.23#	+0.32?
Miller & Wolford (1999, 1&2)	15-Assoc	0.87	0.39	1.55#	
Marsh & Bower (2004, 1)[c]	3	0.87	0.39	1.41°^	
Marsh & Bower (2004, 1)	6	0.86	0.49	1.11°^	
Marsh & Bower (2004, 1)	9	0.88	0.53	1.10°^	−0.08
Marsh & Bower (2004, 1)	12	0.92	0.53	1.33°^	
Robinson & Roediger (1997, 1&2)[d]	3	0.83	0.43	1.11°^	
Robinson & Roediger (1997, 1&2)	6	0.87	0.52	1.08°^	
Robinson & Roediger (1997, 1&2)	9	0.88	0.61	0.87°^	−0.50*
Robinson & Roediger (1997, 1&2)	12	0.88	0.68	0.68°^	
Robinson & Roediger (1997, 1&2)	15	0.87	0.69	0.61°^	
Gallo & Roediger (2003, 1)[e]	5	0.66	0.60	0.16°^	
Gallo & Roediger (2003, 1)	10	0.66	0.66	0.00°^	−0.36*
Gallo & Roediger (2003, 1)	15	0.66	0.73	−0.20°^	
Blocked Study-2AFC RGN					
Westerberg & Marsolek (2003, 2)	1-CI'	0.62	0.34	0.36	−0.22*
Westerberg & Marsolek (2003, 2)	15-CI	0.54	0.46	0.14	

Study		1-CI' / 15-Assoc	Hits	FA	d'	RGN
Westerberg & Marsolek (2003, 2)		1-CI'	0.62	0.34	0.36 ⎫	+0.07
Westerberg & Marsolek (2003, 2)		15-Assoc	0.63	0.35	0.43 ⎭	
Random Study-Yes/No RGN						
Shiffrin, Huber & Marinelli (1995, 4)		1	0.68	0.18 (0.28)[f]	1.34 ⎫	
Shiffrin, Huber & Marinelli (1995, 4)		2	0.74	0.16 (0.31)	1.47 ⎪	−0.03
Shiffrin, Huber & Marinelli (1995, 4)		6 pure[g]	0.79	0.23 (0.40)	1.52 ⎬	
Shiffrin, Huber & Marinelli (1995, 4)		6 mixed[g]	0.80	0.20 (0.41)	1.61 ⎪	
Shiffrin, Huber & Marinelli (1995, 4)		10	0.82	0.34 (0.50)	1.31 ⎭	
Shiffrin, Huber & Marinelli (1995, 1)		2	0.79	0.09 (0.21)[f]	2.15[h,i] ⎫	
Shiffrin, Huber & Marinelli (1995, 1)		6 pure[g]	0.80	0.12 (0.22)	1.80[h,i] ⎬	−0.55*
Shiffrin, Huber & Marinelli (1995, 1)		6 mixed[g]	0.79	0.12 (0.27)	1.60[h] ⎪	
Shiffrin, Huber & Marinelli (1995, 1)		9	0.77	0.20 (0.28)	⎭	
Shiffrin, Huber & Marinelli (1995, 2)		2 pure[j]	0.83	0.11 (0.16)[f]	2.15[h,i] ⎫	
Shiffrin, Huber & Marinelli (1995, 2)		2 mixed[j]	0.82	0.11 (0.18)	⎬	−0.30*
Shiffrin, Huber & Marinelli (1995, 2)		6	0.85	0.16 (0.33)	2.00[h] ⎪	
Shiffrin, Huber & Marinelli (1995, 2)		9	0.88	0.20 (0.41)	1.85[h] ⎭	

Note. FA = false alarms. RS = relatedness strength; RLE = relatedness length effect. CI = critical item in DRM lists. CI' = frequency-matched control for CI. Assoc = associate in DRM lists. Assoc' = frequency-matched control for Assoc.

[a] In the d' column, ^ indicates that d' was computed from overall hits and overall FAs; $\#d'_a$ is used. °pseudo d' based on hits for associates and FAs for CIs. In the RLE column, @ indicates marginal statistical significance, * indicates the RLE was significant at the .05 level, and ? indicates unknown statistical significance.

[b] For this study, for RL=1, all hits and FAs were averaged across Assocs and CIs. All data from this study are averaged across "remember"/"know" (Experiment 1) and confidence ratings (Experiment 2) and are averaged across both intervening math-filler and recall task conditions.

[c] Only the data from the silent-read condition (but not the overt thought condition) are reported.

[d] All data from this study are averaged across study lists with and without filler items. In Experiment 2, the list lengths were equated for the various RLs by adding filler items to study lists with RLs<15.

[e] All data from this study are averaged across study modality and only younger adult data are included.

[f] FAs outside parentheses were FAs for associates, and FAs in parentheses were for CIs. All d's were based on exemplar FAs.

[g] In Experiments 1 and 4, there were two RL=6 groups, one was a "mixed" group (3 exemplars presented once and 3 exemplars presented 3 times each) and one was a "pure" group (all 6 exemplars presented 3 times each). Only the data for those 3 exemplars presented once in the category-6-mixed group are reported here.

[h] The d's are estimated from Figure 5 in the article.

[i] Because the "pure" and "mixed" d' values were not presented separately, only the average of these two values provided in the article can be provided.

[j] In Experiment 2, there were two RL=2 groups, one was a "mixed" group (some single exemplars were presented once and some were presented 3 times each) and one was a "pure" group (2 exemplars from the same category were presented 3 times each). Only the data for the single exemplar presented once in the category-2-mixed group are reported here.

positive RLEs were based on a comparison in which different items were being
tested at the different RLs. In Westerberg and Marsolek (2003), the d_a for RL=1
was (a) based on items that were matched with the CIs (Experiments 1 and 2) or
the associates (Experiment 3) on their word frequencies and number of semantic
senses and (b) compared to the d_a the RL=15 condition that was based on DRM
CIs or associates themselves. Similarly, in Miller and Wolford (1999), the d_a for
RL=1 was based on both DRM associates *and* CIs combined, whereas the d_a for
RL=15 was based on only DRM associates *or* CIs. As a result, both of these
positive RLEs could be an artifact of item differences.

For the CAT lists, five RLEs were significantly positive, nine significantly
negative, and four were null. However, a detailed analysis of the procedures that
produced them reveals that sufficient conditions for RLEs being significantly positive are the *conjunction* of the related items being contiguous during study *and*
either (a) RL=1 being compared to an RL=2 (Neely & Balota, 1981), an RL=3
(Hall, 1982), or an RL=4 (Slamecka, 1975), or (b) RL being manipulated as a
between-subjects variable (Arndt & Hirshman, 1998; Hall, 1982). (The one exception to the latter is Bruce and Fagan's, 1970, numerically negative but statistically
null RLE.) When these conjunctive conditions are not met with CAT lists, the
statistically non-null RLEs are all negative.

Although the RLEs in Tables 19.2 and 19.3 are not as consistent as one might
like, a couple of general patterns emerge. First, though there are a number of
cases that replicate Kintsch's (1968) seminal null effect, for both CAT and DRM
materials, there is a general tendency for d' to increase as RL increases from 1 to
2–3 and to decrease with additional increases in RL, as shown in Figure 19.3. This
decrease in d' with the longer RLs stands in stark contrast to the overwhelmingly
consistent finding that recall is facilitated by increasing RL. However, this apparent nonmonotonic RLE must be interpreted with extreme caution because the
(unweighted) means of the d's contributing to each point do not all come from the
same experiments. Indeed, as is indicated in Figure 19.3 (which shows the means
of the study times per item and the total number of items in the study lists for the
experiments that contributed to each of the data points), the finding that d' was
highest for RL=2–3 for both CAT and DRM studies could very well be due to the
RLs of 2 or 3 being associated with the longest study times and the shortest total
study-list lengths. Moreover, the similar d's for RL=1 and RL>7 (which replicate
Kintsch's, 1968, null effect for RL=1 vs. RL=10) could be due to a negative RLE
from 1 to 8 (or more) being masked because the RL>7 data are associated with
longer study times and shorter total study-list lengths than the RL=1 data. However, the nonmonotonic RLE depicted in Figure 19.3 may indeed be genuine
because the few studies that have avoided the aforementioned study-time, study-
list-length confounds and manipulated RLs through more than two levels support
a nonmonotonic RLE. That is, for DRM materials, Shiffrin et al. (1995, Exp. 4)
found the complete nonmonotonic pattern with RLs of 1, 2, 6, and 10 (with 1 and
10 yielding equal d's) and Robinson and Roediger (1997) found a negative RLE
with RLs of 3, 6, 9, and 15; for CAT materials, Hall (1982) and Neely and Balota
(1981) tested RLs only in the 1 to 2–3 range and found the positive RLE shown in
Figure 19.1 (when the related items were back-to-back in the study list) and

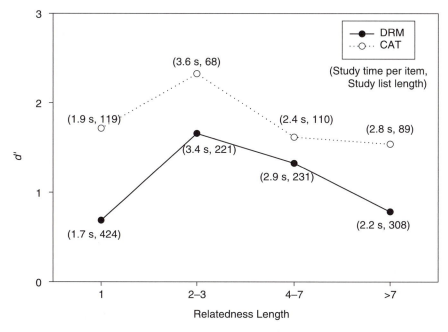

FIGURE 19.3   Recognition memory for DRM and category (CAT) materials as a function of relatedness length, with the average study time per item and average length of the study list provided for each data point. The data are based on the unweighted averages of the data provided in Tables 19.2 and 19.3.

Dewhurst and Anderson (1999) and Engelkamp et al. (1998) found the negative RLE with RLs that varied from 2 to 16. Nevertheless, these unconfounded RLEs need to be further validated with the full range of RLs (tested only by Shiffrin et al., 1995) that is necessary to observe the nonmonotonicity.

A second, very general finding is that the FAs increased as RL increased in 72 of the 85 total *pairwise* comparisons of different RLs within the DRM and CAT yes/no recognition studies. (This excludes the four ties and results from Connor, 1977, who did not report hits and FAs separately.) This shows that false memories for a test item are highly influenced by the number of studied items that were related to it. For these same 85 comparisons, hits increased as relatedness increased in 58 cases (with five ties), and for these 58 cases there were only 3 cases in which the FAs dropped, yielding (apparently nonsignificant) mirror effects. Hence, unlike word frequency, which almost always produces a mirror effect (Glanzer & Adams, 1985), RL almost never does.

Category-Contingent Recognition   All of the above data are based on measures of recognition at the individual word level. They do not measure whether a semantic or associative relation between two (or more) words will make it more likely that those words will be *conjointly* recognized and hence do not evaluate what we will call semantic-contingent memory (or the conceptually similar idea of gist memory, see Brainerd & Reyna, 2001). Semantic-contingent memory has received considerable attention in the study of free recall, for which it has consistently been shown that related items are adjacently recalled (clustered) more often than would be expected by chance (e.g., Elmes & Wilkinson, 1971). Although clustering measures of output order cannot be used in recognition tests in which experimenters, not subjects, determine the order in which the contents of memory are "output," measures of semantic-contingent memory have been developed for recognition. For instance, Neely and Balota (1981), who compared RL=1 and RL=2, determined how often two specific studied words would *both* be recognized (or recalled) when they came from the same semantic category (RL=2) or when they did not (RL=1), taking into account differences in the overall recognition (or recall) of related versus unrelated words. They found the following: (1) Recall was more category-contingent than recognition. (2) Recognition was category-contingent when the two related items appeared contiguously in the study list but not when they were separated by 5–11 other intervening studied words. (Jacoby & Hendricks, 1973, obtained a similar finding, though their measure of category-contingent recognition did not take into account differences in overall recognition levels for different relatedness contiguities.) In contrast, recall was category-contingent in both cases (though more so when the related words were studied contiguously). (3) Category-contingent memory for both recall and recognition was unaffected by whether subjects studied the words expecting a recall or recognition test (though overall memory was better when they expected a recall test). One limitation of Neely and Balota's measure of category-contingent memory is that it did not take into account the likelihood that two lures or one target and one lure from the same category would be conjointly recognized. Hence, their analysis does not allow one to determine if the category-contingent recognition they observed was based on veridical memory for the specific words or on a bias to respond "yes" being mediated by a word's membership in a studied two-exemplar category in the study list. Future research should correct this problem and use other measures as well.[7]

Relatedness Strength Effects (RSEs)

Table 19.4 presents, in the same format as that used for Tables 19.2 and 19.3, the findings of the experiments that have examined RSEs holding RL constant at the values indicated in parentheses in the relatedness strength column. None of the RSE studies in Table 19.4 used the optimal design of having the same items being rotated through both the weakly and strongly related conditions. (See Appendix Table A3 in our online addendum for procedural details for these experiments.) The results displayed in Table 19.4 are quite consistent.[8] Ignoring Toglia et al.'s (1984) null effect, increasing RS led to worse recognition memory in all cases. (Because RL and RS were confounded in the RL experiments, the earlier discussed negative RLEs could have been negative RSEs instead. However, the positive RLEs become even more impressive, because they were strong enough to overcome the confounded negative RS effects.) The predominant and strong negative RSE in recognition stands in direct contrast to the robust finding that

TABLE 19.4 Summary of the Results of Experiments Examining Relatedness Strength Effects with Category and DRM-Associative Materials

Study (year, experiment)	Relatedness strength	Hit	FA	d'[a]	RSE[a]
DRM-Blocked Study-Yes/No RGN					
Gallo & Roediger (2002, 2/3)	Strong Assoc (RL = 15)	0.79	0.76	0.10°	−0.62*
Gallo & Roediger (2002, 2/3)	Weak Assoc (RL = 15)	0.74	0.47	0.72°°	
Westerberg & Marsolek (2003, 1)	CI (RL = 15)	0.83	0.74	0.31#	−0.23*
Westerberg & Marsolek (2003, 1)	Assoc (RL = 15)	0.64	0.45	0.54#	
Westerberg & Marsolek (2003, 3)	CI (RL = 15)	0.72	0.70	0.22#	−0.30*
Westerberg & Marsolek (2003, 3)	Assoc (RL = 15)	0.60	0.43	0.52#	
Miller & Wolford (1999, 1&2)[b,c]	CI (RL = 15)	0.97	0.80	1.23#	−0.32?
Miller & Wolford (1999, 1&2)	Assoc (RL = 15)	0.87	0.39	1.55#	
DRM-Blocked Study-2AFC RGN					
Westerberg & Marsolek (2003, 2)[d]	CI (RL = 15)	0.54	0.46	0.14	−0.29*
Westerberg & Marsolek (2003, 2)	Assoc (RL = 15)	0.63	0.35	0.43	
CAT-Blocked Study-Yes/No RGN					
Arndt & Hirshman (1998, 4)[e]	Strong Assoc (RL = 4)	0.62	0.31 (0.51)[f]	0.89[g]	−0.28*
Arndt & Hirshman (1998, 4)	Weak Assoc (RL = 4)	0.63	0.22 (0.45)	1.17	
CAT-Blocked Study-2AFC RGN					
Toglia, Barrett & Lovelace (1984, 1)[h]	High-Taxonomic (RL = 4)	0.93	0.07	2.09°	+0.00
Toglia, Barrett & Lovelace (1984, 1)	Low-Taxonomic (RL = 4)	0.93	0.07	2.09°	
CAT-Random Study-2AFC RGN					
Toglia, Barrett & Lovelace (1984, 1)[h]	High-Taxonomic (RL = 4)	0.88	0.12	1.66°	−0.43*
Toglia, Barrett & Lovelace (1984, 1)	Low-Taxonomic (RL = 4)	0.93	0.07	2.09°	

Note. RL = relatedness length. FA = false alarms. RSE = relatedness strength effect. CI = critical item in DRM lists. Assoc = associate in DRM lists.

[a] In the d' column, ^ indicates that d' was computed from overall hits and overall FAs; #d_a is used. °pseudo d' based on hits for associates and FAs for CIs. In the RSE column, * indicates the RSE was significant at the .05 level and ? indicates unknown statistical significance.

[b] For this study, for RL=1, all hits and FAs were averaged across Assocs and CIs.

[c] All data from this study were averaged across "remember"/"know" (Experiment 1) and confidence ratings (Experiment 2) and are averaged across both intervening math-filler and recall task conditions.

[c] The two-alternative forced-choice recognition test pairs were either both CIs, Assocs, CI's, Assoc's or unrelated items. (CI' = frequency-matched control for CI. Assoc' = frequency-matched control for Assoc.)

[d] All data from this study are averaged across presentation rate and were analyzed for meta-subjects (i.e., 1 meta-subject = 4 subjects).

[e] All FAs outside the parentheses were for exemplars, and all FAs in parentheses were for prototypes. All d's were based on exemplar FAs.

[g] All d's are estimated from Figure 7 in the article.

[h] All hit rates from this study are averaged across high- and low-frequency words. Only the data for the immediate test are reported here.

relatedness strength facilitates recall (e.g., Bjorklund & Bernholtz, 1986; Rabino-witz, 1991). Finally, as was also the case for increases in RL, for yes/no recognition tests, FAs consistently increased with increases in RS and there was little evidence that RSEs produce a mirror effect.

New Data from our Laboratory on Combined RLEs and RSEs for DRM Lists

As just discussed, for within-subject manipulations, recognition memory generally decreases as RS and RL increase (except for increases in RL from 1 to 4). Because this generalization is based on results from less than optimal methodologies and because RSEs for CIs versus associates have been of some recent interest in the DRM paradigm, we have conducted a series of experiments to examine whether the CI versus associate RSE depends on RL. Our experiments' results are presented in Table 19.5. They are based on d_as computed from six different confidence rating levels. (See Appendix Table A4 in our online addendum for procedural details for these experiments.)

Each of our experiments eliminated all but two methodological limitations that are unavoidable when one uses standard DRM study lists and compares RL=1 to the typically used RLs of 8 or 14 that are necessary to elicit a high FA rate to CIs. First, for RLs of 8 or 14, it is virtually impossible to avoid the item strength confound by creating a different study list for each DRM CI/yoked associate pair that would result in a reversal of the relative strengths of the CI and associate. Second, because a CI's FAs are greatly reduced when its associates are scattered randomly throughout a longer study list (e.g., Tussing & Greene, 1997), one must block a given CI's associates together in the study list to examine CI memory discriminability when CI FAs are considerably higher than associate FAs (which is the hallmark of the DRM false memory effect). This blocking requirement necessitated our interleaving lists with words that were all associatively related to the same DRM CI with lists containing equal numbers of unrelated words. Thus, there could have been generalized encoding differences for the RL=1 versus RL=8 (or RL=14) conditions. Either a CI or its yoked associate (but not both) was embedded in each DRM and unrelated study list such that both CIs and yoked associates served as targets or lures within subjects and each specific CI and yoked associate appeared equally often as a target and lure across subjects. In all but one experiment, the study lists were encoded via intentional learning. The one exception was an incidental learning experiment in which subjects performed a letter search on the items in the DRM and unrelated study lists. (There was a companion intentional learning group that saw exactly the same stimulus displays.) In all of our studies, the single, final recognition memory test contained only the one CI and its one yoked associate for each list, thereby equating intracategorical output interference for related and unrelated lists.

Our experiments were analogous in design to the Miller and Wolford (1999) and Westerberg and Marsolek (2003) experiments shown in Appendix Table A3 in our online addendum. However, our experiments improved on theirs in a few ways. Miller and Wolford had only a couple of unrelated study lists that were

TABLE 19.5 Summary of RLEs and RSEs Obtained with DRM CIs and Associates in Our Laboratory

		Related (DRM)			Unrelated			d_a	
		Hit	FA	d_a	Hit	FA	d_a	RLE	Mean RLE
Neely, Johnson, Hutchison, & Neill (1999)	CI	0.81	0.67	0.99	0.61	0.46	0.52	0.47*	+0.40*
8-item (intentional)	Assoc	0.75	0.45	1.21	0.60	0.34	0.88	0.33*	
	RSE			−0.22*			−0.36*		
Tse & Neely (2006)	CI	0.76	0.60	0.65	0.62	0.42	0.54	0.11	+0.13*
Experiment 2	Assoc	0.69	0.35	0.97	0.60	0.30	0.83	0.14	
8-item (intentional)	RSE			−0.32*			−0.29*		
Tse & Neely (2006)	CI	0.76	0.60	0.57	0.63	0.42	0.60	−0.03	−0.01
Experiment 2	Assoc	0.68	0.36	0.89	0.63	0.31	0.87	0.02	
14-item (intentional)	RSE			−0.32*			−0.27*		
Tse & Neely (2006)	CI	0.66	0.60	0.38	0.57	0.39	0.50	−0.12	−0.03
Experiment 1	Assoc	0.66	0.45	0.72	0.58	0.32	0.66	0.06	
14-item (intentional)	RSE			−0.34*			−0.16		
Tse & Neely (2006)	CI	0.68	0.52	0.51	0.64	0.43	0.70	−0.19	−0.07
Experiment 1	Assoc	0.65	0.37	0.79	0.63	0.33	0.84	0.05	
14-item (incidental)	RSE			−0.28*			−0.14		

Note. FA = false alarms. RLE = relatedness length effect. RSE = relatedness strength effect. CI = critical item from Deese/Roediger–McDermott (DRM) lists. Assoc = associate from DRM lists. In the RLE and mean RLE columns and in the RSE row, * indicates that RLE/RSE was significant at the .05 level. All memory discriminability indices were d_a, except for d_e in Neely et al. (1999) and they were based on the data of meta-subjects (i.e., 1 meta-subject = 2 subjects). All relatedness lengths were manipulated within subjects. (See Appendix Table A4 in our online addendum for the procedures and methodological limitations of our experiments.)

presented in the middle of a longer megalist containing many related DRM lists. Thus, memory for the unrelated items could have benefited from a list-wide von Restorff effect (Hunt, 1995; Schmidt, 1996) or could have been hurt by their having always been studied in the interior of the long megalist. In Westerberg and Marsolek, the items in the unrelated studied lists were not CIs or associates but rather were words matched in frequency and number of semantic senses with the CIs (Exps 1 and 2) or associates (Exp. 3). Hence, it was possible that Westerberg and Marsolek's d_a differences for the related versus unrelated lists were an artifact of item effects. Our experiments avoided these limitations.

Our experiments test predictions from Roediger, Balota, and Watson's (2001) activation/source monitoring account of the false memory effect. By this account, during study each CI's associate indirectly activates the CI's mnemonic representation. In the recognition test, subjects are more likely to respond "old" the more familiar (the more highly activated) the test item is. However, before responding "old" to highly activated test items, subjects monitor the source of the familiarity/activation to determine if it was produced by the test item's actual presentation in the study list. FAs occur when this source monitoring fails for highly activated test items. Under the reasonable assumption that discriminating between the activation levels of targets versus lures follows Weber's Law (1846/1948), this analysis predicts a negative RSE (i.e., that the d_a will be less for CIs than for associates), a negative RLE and an RSE × RLE interaction, such that the RSE will be greater when the RL is 8 or 14 rather than 1.

To illustrate these predictions, we make the following assumptions. When an item, be it a CI or an associate, is actually studied, its appearance in the study list (be it related or unrelated) always produces four units of activation for it. However, because CIs are related to *all* of the other associates in the study list (that's why they are CIs), whereas their yoked associates are unlikely to be as strongly related to the studied items, studying a related DRM list will lead to more indirect activation of the CI's representation (say three units of activation) than of the yoked associate's representation (say one unit). Hence, at test, following related DRM lists, CI targets will have seven units of activation (4 direct + 3 indirect) and CI lures, three units (indirect); yoked associate targets will have five units of activation (4 direct + 1 indirect) and lures, one unit (indirect). By Weber's Law, the 7 versus 3 discrimination for CIs will be more difficult than the 5 versus 1 discrimination for their yoked associates and therefore, a negative RSE should occur. (The same prediction follows if the CI or associate does not appear in the first serial position and one assumes that the increment in episodic activation due to actual study is a negatively accelerated function of an item's episodic activation level at the time of study.) However, for unrelated lists, because the CI and yoked associates will both be completely unrelated to the studied items, there will be no units of indirect activation and there will be an equivalent 4 versus 0 discrimination for both kinds of items. Hence, no RSE is predicted to occur for unrelated lists and an RSE × RLE interaction is predicted. From the perspective of a RLE, the theory predicts that a negative RLE will occur for both CIs and associates, but will be more negative for CIs than for yoked associates. That is, for CIs, the 7 versus 3 related discrimination is more difficult relative to the 4 versus 0 unrelated discrimination than is the 5 versus 1 related discrimination relative to the 4 versus 0 unrelated discrimination for yoked associates.

As shown in Table 19.5, the results were quite consistent, with CI d_as always being smaller than yoked associate d_as, i.e., the RSEs were always negative. (Though the RSEs for the unrelated lists in Tse & Neely's, 2006, Exp. 1 did not achieve statistical significance in the intentional and incidental learning groups when considered separately, the effect was significant averaged across these two groups.) However, in no experiment was it the case that there was a significant RSE × RLE interaction; averaged across all experiments, the RSE is virtually the same for the unrelated (–.25) and related (–.30) lists. This equivalence of the RSEs for unrelated and related lists runs counter to the prediction by the activation/ source monitoring account that the RSE should be greater for related DRM lists than for unrelated lists, which should yield a null RSE. Of course, the theory could accommodate this result by arguing that source monitoring is less likely to fail when CIs appear in related rather than unrelated lists, but the opposite seems more plausible to us. The other problem for the activation/source monitoring account is that a statistically significant negative RLE never materialized. Specific- ally, for RL=14 versus RL=1, there was no RLE whereas for RL=8 versus RL=1, increasing RL actually *facilitated* recognition.

Our experiments, which are as well-controlled as is possible with DRM lists, show that the CI vs. associate RSE is likely an artifact of item differences. Although it is unclear which aspect of the item differences between our CIs and associates caused the d_a difference, we do not think it is likely due to differences in word-frequency or concreteness because these variables almost always produce a significant mirror effect, which we *never* observed. More important is our finding that there was a positive RL=8 versus RL=1 RLE but a null RL=14 versus RL=1 RLE. Although we have interpreted the absence of an RSE × RLE interaction as quite problematic for the activation/source monitoring account, we believe our data also pose a challenge for *any* single-process theory that assumes (a) that episodic recognition is based on discriminating familiarity/activation differences that conform to Weber's Law (1846/1948) or (b) that the increment in episodic activation produced by actual study is a negatively accelerated function of an item's episodic activation level when it is studied. Thus, our data seem to provide as serious a challenge for other theories of veridical and false memories (e.g., the fuzzy-trace theory of Brainerd & Reyna, 2005, and retrieval-resonance theories such as MINERVA2—see Arndt & Hirshman, 1998; Hintzman, 1988) as they do for the activation/source monitoring theory. A final important implication of our results is that the "RSE" for CIs versus yoked associates is not really a RSE because the worse recognition for CIs versus yoked associates occurs even when there are no other words in the study list related to them.

OVERALL CONCLUSIONS

We believe that nearly everyone would agree that an event's semantic relationship to other events is one of the most fundamental of variables governing human memory. Although it is well-established that increases in both relatedness length and strength clearly facilitate recall, the effects of semantic relatedness on a person's ability to discriminate targets versus lures in a recognition memory test are much less clear. We find it discouraging that we must draw this conclusion, given that nearly 40 years have elapsed since Kintsch (1968) reported his seminal finding that semantic relatedness had a large facilitative effect on recall but no effect on recognition. Nevertheless, three empirical generalizations can tentatively be drawn: (1) RL may have a nonmonotonic effect on d' in recognition memory for both CAT and DRM lists. That is, recognition seems to improve as RL increases from 1 to 2–3 for CAT lists or from 1 to 8 for DRM lists (at least when the related items are adjacent in the study list and the study-time, total study-list length confounds in the Figure 19.3 data are avoided) and then worsens as RL increases beyond those points. (2) Recognition decreases as RS increases, though in the case of CIs and associates for DRM study lists, this RS may be due to confounded item differences (of an unknown source) between CIs and associates. (3) Increases in RL and RS almost always produce more false memories (i.e., FAs), but rarely yield mirror effects.

Because of space limitations, we will offer only a very general comment about the implications these general effects of semantic relatedness might have for theories of recognition memory. We believe that the finding that relatedness can sometimes facilitate d' is problematic for single-process theories of recognition that assume that recognition memory is based on episodic familiarity (or activation) produced by the study list and perhaps also for two-process activation/source monitoring theories (because it is not clear how increasing semantic relatedness could facilitate source monitoring). Even more challenging for such theories are the findings that (a) RL seems to have a nonmonotonic effect on d' and (b) the effects of RL and RS (at least for DRM materials) are additive rather than interactive. However, the theoretical implications of these effects must be drawn cautiously because of the methodological limitations of the individual experiments and a lack of systematic investigation of these variables within a single experiment. Hence, in future research, a single experiment should test for the nonmonotonic effect of relatedness strength on d' and should directly compare the effects of categorical relatedness and associative relatedness (cf. Park et al., 2005; Smith, Gerkens, Pierce, & Choi, 2002).

We hope that the issues we have raised here will serve as an impetus for future research that will promote our understanding of how a fundamental component of cognition, i.e., semantic relatedness, actually affects memory discriminability in episodic recognition memory. Specifically, we believe that it is imperative that future research systematically determines if the methodological prescriptions we set forth here for the optimal experimental design really need to be followed before we can come to grips with the effects semantic relatedness on recognition. We also believe that the effects of semantic relatedness on recognition should be evaluated by using not only d_a but other measures as well, such as those assessing category-contingent memory (cf. Neely & Balota, 1981) and phantom recollection (Brainerd, Wright, Reyna, & Mojardin, 2001). And finally, we reiterate that theoretical accounts of semantic relatedness effects on memory discriminability, as measured by signal detection theory, must acknowledge that semantic relatedness could be influencing mean episodic familiarity values, episodic familiarity variability, and/or response criterion variability.

ACKNOWLEDGMENT

We are grateful to Dave Balota, Jim Nairne, and Roddy Roediger for providing valuable comments. Visit our online addendum, http://www.albany.edu/~ct7124/NeelyTse-Roddyfest.htm for the Appendix Tables A1–A6.

NOTES

1. Although Tulving is justifiably credited for pioneering theoretical analyses of retrieval processes in the modern era, Semon (1921) had also emphasized retrieval factors in his much earlier work. (See Schacter, Eich, & Tulving, 1978, for a summary.) Also, in the late 1940s, theoretical analyses considered retrieval processes by postulating response competition at retrieval to explain interference in paired-associate learning (see Anderson & Neely, 1996, for a review).
2. Another semantic relatedness variable is how close together the related items appear in the study list (*relatedness contiguity*). Due to space limitations, we provide a summary of relatedness contiguity effects in Appendix Tables A5 and A6 in our online addendum.
3. When RL is manipulated randomly within a list another confound can occur when only two levels of relatedness are represented only once each in a study list. Consider the following oversimplified example in which one wants to examine RLs of 1 and 5 by embedding the two items of interest, e.g., *rugby* and *potato*, in a six-item study list. If *rugby* and *potato* instantiated RLs of 1 and 5, respectively, *rugby* would be studied with *potato* and four other vegetables. However, because *rugby* was a semantically isolated item, it (but not *potato*) would be subject to a von Restorff effect (e.g., Hunt, 1995; Schmidt, 1996). This problem can be avoided by having (a) multiple observations for each RL within a single study list, (b) the related items be randomly presented rather than blocked, and (c) there being some unrelated buffer items added to the study list to render the semantic singletons for the RL of 1 less salient.
4. If only one baseline is used to assess the false memory effect, this is the one that Roediger (March, 2006, personal communication) advocates, as do we, though it has not been included in all published DRM studies conducted by other labs. Roediger also prefers that recall instead of recognition be used to examine false memories, a preference we do not share.
5. When variances are unequal, there are four different measures for C (see MacMillan & Creelman, 2004). The general conclusions we draw apply to all of them.
6. The computation of d_a uses the slope of the z-ROC to determine d' when zHit and zFA are both equal to zero, i.e., the average of all of the d's along the full extent of the z-ROC function.
7. Greene and Klein (2004) used a procedure in which each "trial" in the recognition test consisted of two words rather than one and subjects either responded "old" if both items had been studied and "new" otherwise, or indicated how many of the

words were studied: 0, 1, or 2. Future research should explore whether this procedure and Neely and Balota's (1981) procedure yield similar results concerning
variables' effects on category-contingent memory.

8. Although Kinsbourne and George (1974, Exp. 1) manipulated RS for both high- and
low-frequency words, their data are not included because they did not report d', nor
could it be computed from their data because they reported the percentage of all
FAs that occurred at each word-frequency band but did not report how many total
FAs there were.

REFERENCES

Anderson, M. C., & Neely, J. H. (1996). Interference and inhibition in memory retrieval. In
E. L. Bjork & R. A. Bjork (Eds.), *Memory* (pp. 237–313). San Diego, CA: Academic
Press.

Arndt, J., & Hirshman, E. (1998). True and false recognition in MINERVA2: Explanations from a global matching perspective. *Journal of Memory and Language, 39,*
371–391.

Balota, D. A., & Neely, J. H. (1980). Test-expectancy and word-frequency effects in recall
and recognition. *Journal of Experimental Psychology: Human Learning and
Memory, 6,* 576–587.

Bjorklund, D. F., & Bernholtz, J. E. (1986). The role of knowledge base in the memory
performance of good and poor readers. *Journal of Experimental Child Psychology,
41,* 367–393.

Brainerd, C. J., & Reyna, V. F. (2001). Fuzzy-trace theory: Dual processes in memory,
reasoning, and cognitive neuroscience. In R. Kail & H. W. Reese (Eds.), *Advances
in child development and behavior* (pp. 41–100). San Diego, CA: Academic Press.

Brainerd, C. J., & Reyna, V. F. (2005). *The science of false memory.* Oxford, UK: Oxford
University Press.

Brainerd, C. J., & Wright, R. (2005). Forward association, backward association, and the
false-memory illusion. *Journal of Experimental Psychology: Learning, Memory,
and Cognition, 31,* 554–567.

Brainerd, C. J., Wright, R., Reyna, V. F., & Mojardin, A. H. (2001). Conjoint recognition and
phantom recollection. *Journal of Experimental Psychology: Learning, Memory, and
Cognition, 27,* 307–327.

Bruce, D., & Fagan, R. L. (1970). More on the recognition and free recall of organized lists.
Journal of Experimental Psychology, 85, 153–154.

Clark, S. E. (1995). The generation effect and the modeling of associations in memory.
Memory and Cognition, 23, 442–455.

Cofer, C. N., Bruce, D. R., & Reicher, G. M. (1966). Clustering in free recall as a function
of certain methodological variations. *Journal of Experimental Psychology, 71,*
858–866.

Connor, J. M. (1977). Effects of organization and expectancy on recall and recognition.
Memory and Cognition, 5, 315–318.

Cowan, N. (1996). Can we resolve contradictions between process dissociation models?
Consciousness and Cognition, 5, 255–259.

Craik, F. I., & Lockhart, R. S. (1972). Levels of processing: A framework for memory
research. *Journal of Verbal Learning and Verbal Behavior, 11,* 671–684.

Dale, H. C. (1967). Response availability and short-term memory. *Journal of Verbal
Learning and Verbal Behavior, 6,* 47–48.

Deese, J. (1959a). Influence of interitem associative strength upon immediate free recall. *Psychological Reports, 5,* 235–241.

Deese, J. (1959b). On the prediction of occurrence of particular verbal intrusions in immediate free recall. *Journal of Experimental Psychology, 58,* 17–22.

Dewhurst, S. A. (2001). Category repetition and false recognition: Effects of instance frequency and category size. *Journal of Memory and Language, 44,* 153–167.

Dewhurst, S. A., & Anderson, S. J. (1999). Effects of exact and category repetition in true and false recognition memory. *Memory and Cognition, 27,* 664–673.

Ebbinghaus, H. (1913). *Memory: A contribution to experimental psychology.* New York: Columbia University, Teachers' College.

Elmes, D. G., & Wilkinson, W. C. (1971). Cued forgetting in free recall: Grouping on the basis of relevance and category membership. *Journal of Experimental Psychology, 87,* 438–440.

Engelkamp, J., Biegelmann, U., & McDaniel, M. A. (1998). Relational and item-specific information: Trade-off and redundancy. *Memory, 6,* 307–333.

Gallo, D. A., Roberts, M. J., & Seamon, J. G. (1997). Remembering words not presented in lists: Can we avoid creating false memories? *Psychonomic Bulletin and Review, 4,* 271–276.

Gallo, D. A., & Roediger, H. L. (2002). Variability among word lists in eliciting memory illusions: Evidence for associative activation and monitoring. *Journal of Memory and Language, 47,* 469–497.

Gallo, D. A., & Roediger, H. L. (2003). The effects of associations and aging on illusory recollection. *Memory and Cognition, 31,* 1036–1044.

Glanzer, M., & Adams, J. K. (1985). The mirror effect in recognition memory. *Memory and Cognition, 13,* 8–20.

Glanzer, M., Kim, K., & Adams, J. K. (1998). Response distribution as an explanation of the mirror effect. *Journal of Experimental Psychology: Learning, Memory, and Cognition, 24,* 633–644.

Greene, R. L., & Klein, A. A. (2004). Does recognition of single words predict recognition of two? *American Journal of Psychology, 117,* 215–227.

Gregg, V. (1976). Word frequency, recognition and recall. In J. Brown (Ed.), *Recall and recognition* (pp. 183–216). Oxford, UK: Wiley.

Griffith, D. (1975). Comparison of control processes for recognition and recall. *Journal of Experimental Psychology: Human Learning and Memory, 1,* 223–228.

Hacker, M. J., & Ratcliff, R. (1979). A revised table of d' for M-alternative forced choice. *Perception and Psychophysics, 26,* 168–170.

Hall, J. F. (1982). List organization and recognition memory. *Bulletin of the Psychonomic Society, 20,* 35–36.

Heathcote, A. (2003). Item recognition memory and the receiver operating characteristic. *Journal of Experimental Psychology: Learning, Memory, and Cognition, 29,* 1210–1230.

Hintzman, D. L. (1988). Judgments of frequency and recognition memory in a multiple-trace memory model. *Psychological Review, 95,* 528–551.

Hunt, R. R. (1976). List context effects: Inaccessibility or indecision? *Journal of Experimental Psychology: Human Learning and Memory, 2,* 423–430.

Hunt, R. R. (1995). The subtlety of distinctiveness: What von Restorff really did. *Psychonomic Bulletin and Review, 2,* 105–112.

Hutchison, K. A., & Balota, D. A. (2005). Decoupling semantic and associative information in false memories: Explorations with semantically ambiguous and unambiguous critical lures. *Journal of Memory and Language, 52,* 1–28.

Jacoby, L. L., & Hendricks, R. L. (1973). Recognition effects of study organization and test context. *Journal of Experimental Psychology, 100*, 73–82.

Kinsbourne, M., & George, J. (1974). The mechanism of the word-frequency effect on recognition memory. *Journal of Verbal Learning and Verbal Behavior, 13*, 63–69.

Kintsch, W. (1968). Recognition and free recall of organized lists. *Journal of Experimental Psychology, 78*, 481–487.

Kintsch, W. (1970). *Learning, memory, and conceptual processes*. Oxford, UK: Wiley.

Koutstaal, W., & Schacter, D. L. (1997). Gist-based false recognition of pictures in older and younger adults. *Journal of Memory and Language, 37*, 555–583.

Kuhn, T. S. (1962). *The structure of scientific revolutions*. Chicago: University of Chicago Press.

Lewandowsky, S. (1986). Priming in recognition memory for categorized lists. *Journal of Experimental Psychology: Learning, Memory, and Cognition, 12*, 562–574.

MacMillan, N. A., & Creelman, C. D. (2004). *Detection theory: A user's guide*. Hillsdale, NJ: Lawrence Erlbaum Associates, Inc.

Marsh, E. J., & Bower, G. H. (2004). The role of rehearsal and generation in false memory creation. *Memory, 12*, 748–761.

Mayes, J. T., & McIvor, G. (1980). Levels of processing and retrieval: Recency effects after incidental learning in a reaction time task. *Quarterly Journal of Experimental Psychology, 32*, 635–648.

McCabe, D. P., & Smith, A. D. (2002). The effect of warnings on false memories in young and older adults. *Memory and Cognition, 30*, 1065–1077.

McDermott, K. B. (1997). Priming on perceptual implicit memory tests can be achieved through presentation of associates. *Psychonomic Bulletin and Review, 4*, 582–586.

McDermott, K. B., & Roediger, H. L. (1998). Attempting to avoid illusory memories: Robust false recognition of associates persists under conditions of explicit warnings and immediate testing. *Journal of Memory and Language, 39*, 508–520.

McEvoy, C. L., Nelson, D. L., & Komatsu, T. (1999). What is the connection between true and false memories? The differential roles of interitem associations in recall and recognition. *Journal of Experimental Psychology: Learning, Memory, and Cognition, 25*, 1177–1194.

McGeoch, J. A. (1942). *The psychology of human learning*. New York: Longmans, Green.

Melton, A. W., & von Lackum, W. J. (1941). Retroactive and proactive inhibition in retention: Evidence for a two-factor theory of retroactive inhibition. *American Journal of Psychology, 54*, 157–173.

Miller, M. B., & Wolford, G. L. (1999). The role of criterion shift in false memory. *Psychological Review, 106*, 398–405.

Morris, C. D., Bransford, J. D., & Franks, J. J. (1977). Levels of processing versus transfer appropriate processing. *Journal of Verbal Learning and Verbal Behavior, 16*, 519–533.

Neely, J. H., & Balota, D. A. (1981). Test-expectancy and semantic-organization effects in recall and recognition. *Memory and Cognition, 9*, 283–300.

Neely, J. H., Johnson, J. D., Hutchison, K. A., & Neill, W. T. (1999). *Is there memory to be found in "false memory?"* Paper presented at the 40th annual meeting of the Psychonomic Society, Los Angeles, CA.

Neely, J. H., Schmidt, S. R., & Roediger, H. L. (1983). Inhibition from related primes in recognition memory. *Journal of Experimental Psychology: Learning, Memory, and Cognition, 9*, 196–211.

Paivio, A. (1971). *Imagery and verbal processes*. New York: Holt, Rinehart, & Winston.

Park, L., Shobe, K. K., & Kihlstrom, J. F. (2005). Associative and categorical relations in the associative memory illusion. *Psychological Science*, *16*, 792–797.

Rabinowitz, M. (1991). Semantic and strategic processing: Independent roles in determining memory performance. *American Journal of Psychology*, *104*, 427–437.

Ratcliff, R., McKoon, G., & Tindall, M. (1994). Empirical generality of data from recognition memory receiver-operating characteristic functions and implications for the global memory models. *Journal of Experimental Psychology: Learning, Memory, and Cognition*, *20*, 763–785.

Ratcliff, R., Sheu, C.-F., & Gronlund, S. D. (1992). Testing global memory models using ROC curves. *Psychological Review*, *99*, 518–535.

Reder, L. M., Angstadt, P., Cary, M., Erickson, M. A., & Ayers, M. S. (2002). A reexamination of stimulus-frequency effects in recognition: Two mirrors for low- and high-frequency pseudowords. *Journal of Experimental Psychology: Learning, Memory, and Cognition*, *28*, 138–152.

Reder, L. M., Nhouyvanisvong, A., Schunn, C. D., Ayers, M. S., Angstadt, P., & Hiraki, K. (2000). A mechanistic account of the mirror effect for word frequency: A computational model of remember–know judgments in a continuous recognition paradigm. *Journal of Experimental Psychology: Learning, Memory, and Cognition*, *26*, 294–320.

Robinson, K. J., & Roediger, H. L. (1997). Associative processes in false recall and false recognition. *Psychological Science*, *8*, 231–237.

Roediger, H. L. (2000). Why retrieval is the key process in understanding human memory. In E. Tulving (Ed.), *Memory, consciousness, and the brain: The Tallinn conference*. (pp. 52–75). New York: Psychology Press.

Roediger, H. L., Balota, D. A., & Watson, J. M. (2001). Spreading activation and the arousal of false memories. In H. L. Roediger, J. S. Nairne, I. Neath, & A. M. Suprenant (Eds.), *The nature of remembering: Essays in honor of Robert G. Crowder* (pp. 95–115). Washington, DC: American Psychological Association.

Roediger, H. L., & Guynn, M. J. (1996). Retrieval processes. In R. A. Bjork & E. L. Bjork (Eds.), *Memory* (pp. 197–236). San Diego, CA: Academic Press.

Roediger, H. L., & McDermott, K. B. (1995). Creating false memories: Remembering words not presented in lists. *Journal of Experimental Psychology: Learning, Memory, and Cognition*, *21*, 803–814.

Roediger, H. L., McDermott, K. B., & Robinson, K. J. (1998). The role of associative processes in producing false memories. In M. A. Conway, S. E. Gathercole, & C. Cornoldi (Eds.), *Theories of memory* (Vol. II, pp. 187–245). Hove, UK: Psychology Press.

Roediger, H. L., Watson, J. M., McDermott, K. B., & Gallo, D. A. (2001). Factors that determine false recall: A multiple regression analysis. *Psychonomic Bulletin and Review*, *8*, 385–407.

Russo, R., Parkin, A. J., Taylor, S. R., & Wilks, J. (1998). Revising current two-process accounts of spacing effects in memory. *Journal of Experimental Psychology: Learning, Memory, and Cognition*, *24*, 161–172.

Schacter, D. L., Eich, J. E., & Tulving, E. (1978). Richard Semon's theory of memory. *Journal of Verbal Learning and Verbal Behavior*, *17*, 721–743.

Schmidt, S. R. (1988). Test expectancy and individual-item versus relational processing. *American Journal of Psychology*, *101*, 59–71.

Schmidt, S. R. (1996). Category typicality effects in episodic memory: Testing models of distinctiveness. *Memory and Cognition*, *24*, 595–607.

Semon, R. (1921). *The Mneme*. London: Allen & Unwin.

Shiffrin, R. M., Huber, D. E., & Marinelli, K. (1995). Effects of category length and strength on familiarity in recognition. *Journal of Experimental Psychology: Learning, Memory, and Cognition, 21,* 267–287.

Slamecka, N. J. (1975). Intralist cueing of recognition. *Journal of Verbal Learning and Verbal Behavior, 14,* 630–637.

Slamecka, N. J., & Graf, P. (1978). The generation effect: Delineation of a phenomenon. *Journal of Experimental Psychology: Human Learning and Memory, 4,* 592–604.

Smith, S. M., Gerkens, D. R., Pierce, B. H., & Choi. H. (2002). The roles of associative responses at study and semantically guided recollection at test in false memory: The Kirkpatrick and Deese hypotheses. *Journal of Memory and Language, 47,* 436–447.

Sommers, M. S., & Lewis, B. P. (1999). Who really lives next door: Creating false memories with phonological neighbors. *Journal of Memory and Language, 40,* 83–108.

Stretch, V., & Wixted, J. T. (1998). On the difference between strength-based and frequency-based mirror effects in recognition memory. *Journal of Experimental Psychology: Learning, Memory, and Cognition, 24,* 1379–1396.

Todres, A. K., & Watkins, M. J. (1981). A part-set cuing effect in recognition memory. *Journal of Experimental Psychology: Human Learning and Memory, 7,* 91–99.

Toglia, M. P., Barrett, T. R., & Lovelace, E. A. (1984). Taxonomic organization in immediate and delayed recognition memory. *American Journal of Psychology, 97,* 97–107.

Tse, C.-S., & Neely, J. H. (2005). Assessing activation without source monitoring in the DRM false memory paradigm. *Journal of Memory and Language, 53,* 532–550.

Tse, C.-S., & Neely, J. H. (2006). On the generality of the critical item memory inferiority effect in recognition memory. *Manuscript in preparation.*

Tulving, E. (1967). The effects of presentation and recall of material in free-recall learning. *Journal of Verbal Learning and Verbal Behavior, 6,* 175–184.

Tulving, E. (1968). When is recall higher than recognition? *Psychonomic Science, 10,* 53–54.

Tulving, E. (1983). *Elements of episodic memory.* New York: Oxford University Press.

Tulving, E., & Donaldson, W. (1972). *Organization of memory.* Oxford, UK: Academic Press.

Tulving, E., & Osler, S. (1968). Effectiveness of retrieval cues in memory for words. *Journal of Experimental Psychology, 77,* 593–601.

Tulving, E., & Pearlstone, Z. (1966). Availability versus accessibility of information in memory for words. *Journal of Verbal Learning and Verbal Behavior, 5,* 381–391.

Tulving, E., & Thomson, D. M. (1973). Encoding specificity and retrieval processes in episodic memory. *Psychological Review, 80,* 359–380.

Tussing, A. A., & Greene, R. L. (1997). False recognition of associates: How robust is the effect? *Psychonomic Bulletin and Review, 4,* 572–576.

Tussing, A. A., & Greene, R. L. (1999). Differential effects of repetition on true and false recognition. *Journal of Memory and Language, 40,* 520–533.

Verde, M. F., & Rotello, C. M. (2003). Does familiarity change in the revelation effect? *Journal of Experimental Psychology: Learning, Memory, and Cognition, 29,* 739–746.

Wallace, W. P. (1982). Distractor-free recognition tests of memory. *American Journal of Psychology, 95,* 421–440.

Ward, G. (2002). A recency-based account of the list length effect in free recall. *Memory and Cognition, 30,* 885–892.

Watson, J. M., Balota, D. A., & Roediger, H. L. (2003). Creating false memories with hybrid lists of semantic and phonological associates: Over-additive false memories produced by converging associative networks. *Journal of Memory and Language*, *49*, 95–118.

Weber, E. H. (1948). The sense of touch and common feeling. In W. Dennis (Ed.), *Readings in the history of psychology* (pp. 155–156). New York: Appleton-Century-Crofts. (Original work published 1846)

Westbury, C., Buchanan, L., & Brown, N. R. (2002). Sounds of the neighborhood: False memories and the structure of the phonological lexicon. *Journal of Memory and Language*, *46*, 622–651.

Westerberg, C. E., & Marsolek, C. J. (2003). Sensitivity reductions in false recognition: A measure of false memories with stronger theoretical implications. *Journal of Experimental Psychology: Learning, Memory, and Cognition*, *29*, 747–759.

Whittlesea, B. W. A. (2002). False memory and the discrepancy-attribution hypothesis: The prototype-familiarity illusion. *Journal of Experimental Psychology: General*, *131*, 96–115.

Wickens, T. D., & Hirshman, E. (2000). False memories and statistical design theory: Comment on Miller and Wolford (1999) and Roediger and McDermott (1999). *Psychological Review*, *107*, 377–383.

Wixted, J. T., & Stretch, V. (2000). The case against a criterion-shift account of false memory. *Psychological Review*, *107*, 368–376.

Yonelinas, A. P. (1994). Receiver-operating characteristics in recognition memory: Evidence for a dual-process model. *Journal of Experimental Psychology: Learning, Memory, and Cognition*, *20*, 1341–1354.

Yonelinas, A. P. (2002). The nature of recollection and familiarity: A review of 30 years of research. *Journal of Memory and Language*, *46*, 441–517.

20

The Cognitive Neuroscience of Implicit and False Memories: Perspectives on Processing Specificity

DANIEL L. SCHACTER, DAVID A. GALLO, and
ELIZABETH A. KENSINGER

*R*oddy Roediger's research career has touched on many aspects of memory, but a careful analysis suggests that it divides into three relatively distinct stages. Stage one, lasting for roughly a decade from 1975–1985, focused on phenomena illustrating that memory performance can be surprisingly good (hypermnesia; e.g., Roediger & Payne, 1982) or perplexingly poor (inhibitory effects of cueing and the act of recall on subsequent memory; e.g., Roediger, 1978). Stage two stretched across the next decade and focused on priming and related implicit memory effects that reflect retention of previously studied information in the absence of conscious recollection (e.g., Roediger, Weldon, & Challis, 1989; Roediger, 1990). The third stage runs from 1995 to the present, and is characterized by a focus on false memories, that is, remembering events that never happened (e.g., Roediger & McDermott, 1995). All three stages have been highly productive, although the fruits of the latter two stages are perhaps better known than those of the first.

The historical record will show that the aforementioned focus on implicit and false memories during Stages two and three of Roediger's career parallel to a large extent those that constituted the focus of Schacter's lab at the same time. While Roediger's approach to implicit and false memories has relied largely on cognitive techniques, attempts by Schacter and colleagues to study these phenomena have often adopted a cognitive neuroscience orientation that focuses on the use of neuropsychological and neuroimaging approaches. These latter approaches have been increasingly prominent in Roediger's recent work. In this chapter we pay tribute to Roddy Roediger's career by taking stock of some of the things we have learned about implicit and false memories as a result of adopting a cognitive neuroscience approach. We focus especially on issues related to the *specificity* of such memories and the processes that support them. It seems especially appropriate to stress the importance of processing specificity when considering both implicit and false memories because this general theme has been important in Roediger and colleagues' ideas concerning transfer appropriate processing (e.g., Roediger, et al., 1989) and more recently, components of processing (Roediger, Buckner, & McDermott, 1999).

The chapter will begin by considering a particular type of implicit memory—priming—that has been the subject of extensive experimental and theoretical debate over the past two decades (e.g., Roediger, 1990; Tulving & Schacter, 1990). We consider some of the modern historical origins of priming research, and then consider recent neuroimaging studies. We will emphasize the specificity of priming—that is, when priming reflects retention of specific features of previously perceived items or specific responses made to those items (Schacter, Dobbins, & Schnyer, 2004). Roediger and colleagues were among the first cognitive psychologists to emphasize the empirical and theoretical importance of specificity for the analysis of priming (e.g., Roediger & Blaxton, 1987), and the issue is turning out to be as central to the concerns of cognitive neuroscience as it has been for cognitive psychology.

We will then turn to the analysis of false memories. Roediger and McDermott's (1995) demonstration of high levels of false recognition of semantic associates has served to focus attention on both the cognitive and neural mechanisms that underlie such robust false recognition effects (for reviews, see Roediger & McDermott, 2000; Schacter & Slotnick, 2004). We will consider research that examines the nature of encoding processes that result in the creation of false memories, with an emphasis on the specificity of processing that supports false recognition. Equally important, attempts to understand robust false recognition have spawned a line of research exploring the conditions under which people can reduce or suppress such potent memory distortions (e.g., Gallo, 2004; Schacter, Israel, & Racine, 1999). We will consider two pertinent lines of work from our laboratory. One has examined the role of recollecting distinctive information in reducing false memories. We will summarize studies indicating that false memory reduction is mediated by specific and dissociable cognitive mechanisms, rather than by a generalized enhancement of memory. We then turn to research that focuses on the role of emotion in modulating memory distortion. We review cognitive studies indicating that emotional arousal can result in reductions of memory errors. Furthermore, neuroimaging studies indicate that such reductions depend on emotion-specific processes rather than on more generalized memory mechanisms. Thus, the theme of processing specificity will be central to our discussion of false memory reduction.

PRIMING: LESSONS FROM SPECIFICITY EFFECTS

Priming refers to a change in the ability to identify, produce, or classify an item as a result of a prior encounter with that item or a related item. Modern research on priming can be traced to at least three different though related developments during the late 1970s and early 1980s. First, researchers interested in the nature of lexical processing and word recognition reported priming effects on lexical decision and word identification tasks, which were thought to provide insight into the nature and structure of lexical representation (e.g., Scarborough, Cortese, & Scarborough, 1977). Second, studies of amnesic patients with damage to the medial temporal lobe and related structures revealed preserved priming effects on tasks such as word stem completion, that do not require conscious recollection of prior experiences, despite patients' severe impairments of explicit memory (e.g., Graf, Squire, & Mandler, 1984; Schacter, 1985; Warrington & Weiskrantz, 1974). Third, research with healthy young adults revealed experimental dissociations between priming and explicit memory produced by such manipulations as depth of encoding and retention interval (e.g., Graf & Mandler, 1984; Jacoby & Dallas, 1981; Tulving, Schacter, & Stark, 1982).

Almost from the beginning of research on priming, theoretical and experimental interest focused heavily on the specificity of the observed effects, that is, the extent to which priming reflects retention of detailed information acquired during a specific prior episode, versus activation of an abstract representation in long-term memory. Roediger and colleagues were among the first to emphasize the critical theoretical importance of priming specificity in the context of their ideas regarding transfer-appropriate processing (TAP; e.g., Roediger et al., 1989). In several important experimental papers, they showed that priming effects on such tests as word fragment completion show modality specificity (i.e., priming is reduced significantly by study-to-test changes in sensory modality), and also show specificity within a modality (e.g., changes in case or font of a word between study and test can reduce priming; see Roediger & Blaxton, 1987; Weldon & Roediger, 1987).

Since these early studies, numerous experiments have examined the nature and extent of specificity in priming, with much theoretical debate surrounding the aforementioned issue of whether priming depends on nonspecific, abstract lexical or perceptual entities versus specific episodic or exemplar representations (cf. Bowers, 2000; Tenpenny, 1995). Discussion of this extensive literature is beyond the purview of the present chapter. Instead, we wish to focus on a type of specificity that has recently been discovered in the context of neuroimaging research on priming. Schacter et al. (2004) recently proposed a distinction among three types of specificity: stimulus, associative, and response. *Stimulus specificity* occurs when priming is reduced by changing physical properties of a stimulus between study and test; *associative specificity* occurs when priming is reduced because associations between target items are changed between study and test; and *response specificity* occurs when priming is reduced because subjects make different responses to the same stimulus item at study and test. We consider here response specificity, which has only recently come to the attention of priming researchers. We focus on recent neuroimaging and neuropsychological data that delineate the phenomenon, and consider the theoretical implications of response specificity with respect to Roediger's ideas on TAP and contemporary accounts of brain activity associated with priming.

NEUROIMAGING OF PRIMING AND RESPONSE SPECIFICITY

Studies that have demonstrated response specificity in priming have been conducted with a view toward testing ideas that have been advanced to explain priming-related changes in brain activity observed in neuroimaging studies using positron emission tomography (PET) and functional magnetic resonance imaging (fMRI). In such studies, participants are scanned while they carry out a task used to assess priming, such as completing three letter word stems with the first word that comes to mind or making judgments about pictures of familiar objects. During primed scans, participants are given target items (e.g., word stems or objects) that appeared previously during the experiment; during unprimed scans, the target items did not appear previously. Virtually all studies using such procedures report *decreased* activity in several cortical regions during primed scans compared to unprimed scans, most consistently in areas within the frontal lobes and the extrastriate visual cortex (for reviews, see Henson, 2003; Schacter & Buckner, 1998; Wiggs & Martin, 1998).

Wiggs and Martin (1998; see also Grill-Spector & Malach, 2001; Schacter & Buckner, 1998) contended that priming-related decreases in human neuroimaging studies may be related to a phenomenon established in studies of nonhuman primates known as *repetition suppression* (for review and discussion, see Desimone & Duncan, 1995). For instance, in an early series of studies by Desimone and Miller and their colleagues (see Desimone & Duncan, 1995) animals viewed complex visual objects, such as patterns or faces, while experimenters recorded the activity of cells in the lower or inferior temporal (IT) cortex. Repeated exposure to the same stimulus resulted in reduced responses across a substantial proportion of IT cells. Wiggs and Martin (1998) noted a number of similarities between the properties of repetition suppression in nonhuman primates and priming-related decreases in humans, leading them to suggest that the two phenomena could reflect the operation of a common underlying mechanism. Wiggs and Martin argued that neural object representations are sharpened or "tuned" with repetition (for more recent discussion, see Grill-Spector, Henson, & Martin, 2006). By this view, when an object is presented repeatedly, the neurons that code features which are not essential for recognizing the object show decreased responding; in so doing, they weaken their connections with other neurons involved in coding the object. Thus, the network of neurons that codes the object becomes more selective, and this neural "tuning" or sharpening is linked with faster and more efficient responding (Wiggs & Martin, 1998).

Although the neural tuning account emerges from studies concerned with perceptual priming of visual objects, it can be extended to other priming-like phenomena. For example, Raichle et al. (1994) reported that generating verbal associates to cue words yielded increased activation in the cingulate, left prefrontal, and posterior temporal cortex compared with simple reading of stimuli. Importantly, activation declined with repetition of the verb generation task, and this reduction correlated with reduced reaction times. Consistent with a neural tuning account, the activation reductions and associated reaction time decreases could indicate that semantic analysis of the materials is sharpened or streamlined with repetition. An alternative possibility, however, is that semantic analysis of the repeated stimuli is largely bypassed in favor of rapid retrieval of previous instances that directly indicate the appropriate response. More generally, it is possible that activation reductions in at least some previous priming studies could reflect such response learning rather than neural tuning.

Dobbins, Schnyer, Verfaellie, and Schacter (2004) attempted to directly contrast tuning and response learning accounts with an object decision priming task that had been used in previous neuroimaging research, and yielded evidence of reductions in priming-related activation in regions of prefrontal and fusiform cortex (e.g., Koutstaal et al., 2001). Dobbins et al. modified the task so that responses either remained the same or changed across repeated trials. In the first scanning phase, pictures of common objects were either shown once or repeated three times, and subjects indicated whether each stimulus was bigger than a shoebox using a "yes" or "no" response. In the next phase, the cue was inverted so that subjects were now required to indicate whether each item was "smaller than a shoebox"; they made this judgment about new items, and a subset of those that had been shown earlier. In the final scanning phase, the cue was restored to "bigger than a shoebox" and subjects were tested on new items and the remaining items from the initial phase.

If priming-related reductions in neural activity that are typically produced by this task represent facilitated size processing, attributable to "tuning" relevant aspects of neural representations, then cue reversal should have little effect on priming (though it could disrupt overall task performance by affecting both new and primed items). According to the neural tuning account, the same representations of object size should be accessed whether the question focuses on "bigger" or "smaller" than a shoebox. By contrast, if subjects come to rapidly recover prior responses, and this response learning mechanism bypasses the need to recover size representations, then the cue reversal should disrupt priming-related reductions. When the cue is changed, subjects would have to abandon learned responses and instead re-engage the target objects in a controlled manner in order to recover size information.

The fMRI data supported the latter account. During the first scanning phase, standard priming-related activation reductions were observed in both anterior and posterior regions previously linked with priming: left prefrontal, fusiform, and extrastriate regions. When the cue was reversed, however, these reductions were eliminated in the left fusiform cortex and disrupted in prefrontal cortex; there was a parallel effect on behavioral response times. But when the cue was restored to the original format, priming-related reductions returned (again there was a parallel effect on behavioral response times), suggesting that the reductions depended on the ability of subjects to use prior responses during trials. Note, however, that the effect was seen most clearly for items repeated three times before cue reversal, a point to which we return shortly.

Finally, the response learning account was also supported by multiple regression techniques demonstrating that reductions in left prefrontal activity predicted the magnitude of behavioral priming for individual subjects: Greater initial reductions in prefrontal activity were associated with greater subsequent disruptions of behavioral response time. To the extent that prefrontal reductions signal less reliance on controlled processing, and greater reliance on automatic processing, these data suggest that performance disruptions attributable to response reversal reflect a need to re-engage slower controlled processes in order to make object decisions. This idea is consistent with the finding that reductions in fusiform activity do not predict behavioral costs of switching cues, suggesting that these reductions may be incidental to the behavioral facilitation.

This evidence for response specificity in neural priming, as indexed by fMRI signal changes, and in behavioral priming, as indexed by changes in response latencies, is perhaps surprising because previous priming research has neither documented such effects nor even considered their possible existence (for discussion of prior studies related to response specificity, see Dobbins et al., 2004; Schacter et al., 2004). Clearly, there must be limitations on response specificity: A number of well-established priming effects occur when participants make different responses during study and test. For instance, priming effects on the stem completion task, where subjects respond with the first word that comes to mind in response to a three-letter word beginning, are typically observed after semantic or perceptual encoding tasks that require a different response.

Nonetheless, the existence of response specificity poses a challenge not only for perceptual tuning accounts of priming-related decreases in fMRI signal, but also for theories that explain behavioral priming effects on object decision and related tasks in terms of changes in perceptual representation systems that are thought to underlie object representation (e.g., Schacter, 1990, 1994; Tulving & Schacter, 1990). Such theories make no provisions for response specificity effects. However, the TAP account of priming advanced by Roediger and colleagues (e.g., Roediger et al., 1989) can easily accommodate such effects. According to the TAP perspective, priming effects are maximized when the same processing operations are performed at study and test. Although this view has emphasized the role of overlapping perceptual operations at study and test to explain priming effects on tasks such as object decision, to the extent that the subject's decision or response is an integral part of encoding operations, then it makes sense that reinstating such operations at test would maximize priming effects.

The foregoing considerations suggest a nice fit between response specificity effects and Roediger's TAP perspective, but there is one further feature of the experimental paradigm that Dobbins et al. (2004) used to produce response specificity that points to a potential complication. Whereas priming in traditional cognitive studies is based on a single study exposure to a target item, fMRI studies of priming have typically used several study exposures in order to maximize the strength of the fMRI signal. This procedure was followed by Dobbins et al., who observed that response specificity effects were most robust for items presented three times during the initial phase of the experiment (high primed items), compared with items presented just once (low primed items).

A more recent neuropsychological investigation of response specificity in amnesic patients highlights the potential theoretical importance of results observed for items presented multiple times during the study phase versus only once (Schnyer, Dobbins, Nicholls, Schacter, & Verfaellie, 2006). Numerous previous studies have documented that amnesic patients with damage to the medial temporal lobe can exhibit intact priming effects under a variety of conditions, although it is less clear whether amnesics consistently exhibit normal stimulus and associative specificity effects (see Schacter et al., 2004, for discussion). The question of whether amnesic patients exhibit normal response specificity is pertinent to the question of whether the response specificity effect is based on some type of explicit, conscious memory (in which case the effect should be impaired or absent in amnesic patients) or whether it reflects implicit, nonconscious memory (in which case amnesic patients would be more likely to exhibit the effect). Schnyer et al. compared amnesics and controls on a variant of the object decision task used by Dobbins et al. (2004). Objects were presented either once (low primed) or thrice (high primed), and then responses either remained the same ("bigger than a shoebox?") or were switched ("smaller than a shoebox?").

Consistent with the trends from the Dobbins et al. (2004) fMRI study noted above, in healthy controls there was evidence of greater response specificity for high primed objects compared with low primed objects. Amnesic patients showed no evidence of response specificity, demonstrating normal priming (i.e., decrease in response latencies) for low primed items, and impaired priming for high-primed items. That is, healthy controls showed greater priming for high- than low-primed objects in the same response condition, but amnesics failed to show this additional decrease in response latencies.

These results raise the possibility that different mechanisms may be involved in priming for objects presented once versus those presented multiple times. "One-shot" priming on the object decision task may depend primarily on perceptual systems that operate independently of the medial temporal lobe, and thus are preserved in amnesic patients. In neuroimaging experiments, such effects may indeed reflect some type of "tuning" of perceptual systems, independent of the specific responses that subjects make when processing the object. For items presented several times, however, subjects may learn to associate the object with a particular response. Based on the data from amnesic patients, such response learning appears to require the medial temporal lobe.

Although much further work remains to be done to elucidate the properties and mechanisms underlying response specificity, initial data suggesting that response specificity occurs reliably only after several encounters with an object is perhaps more complex than can be readily explained by a TAP account. More generally, priming researchers have previously not paid much attention to possible differences among mechanisms underlying priming based on single versus multiple exposures to an object, but the combined results from Dobbins et al. (2004) and Schnyer et al. (2006) highlight the need to consider and explore these differences.

CREATING AND REDUCING FALSE MEMORIES

In addition to the processing specificity that characterizes priming, a growing body of evidence indicates that highly specific processes contribute to the expression of false memories. Here we focus on false recognition, or the acceptance of nonstudied stimuli (lures) on a memory test that is attributable to familiarity or source confusions. In their seminal paper, Roediger and McDermott (1995) found that studying lists of associates (e.g., *bed, rest, awake, . . .*) led to frequent false recall and recognition of nonstudied associates (e.g., *sleep*), often with high confidence and an illusory sense of recollection (i.e., the Deese–Roediger–McDermott, or DRM, task). In order to explain these types of false memories, Roediger and colleagues have developed an activation/monitoring framework (e.g., Gallo & Roediger, 2002; McDermott & Watson, 2001; Roediger, Balota, & Watson, 2001; Roediger, Watson, McDermott, & Gallo, 2001). Generally speaking, "activation" refers to those processes that make nonstudied items familiar as a result of associative or conceptual relationships with studied items, whereas "monitoring" refers to those processes that operate on retrieved information to regulate the accuracy of the memory decision. In the next two sections we review evidence for specificity in both activation and monitoring processes.

ACTIVATION SPECIFICITY

As previously discussed, Roediger and colleagues have developed the TAP framework as one way to understand implicit memory phenomena, with the amount of priming in a task depending on the match between encoding and retrieval processes. Priming studies also indicate that these principles apply to the activation processes that can cause false memories. Several studies have found that presenting DRM lists leads to priming of nonstudied associates on a variety of implicit memory tests (e.g., fragment or stem completion, McDermott, 1997; McKone & Murphy, 2000; Smith, Gerkens, Pierce, & Choi, 2002; lexical decision, Hancock, Hicks, Marsh, & Ritschel, 2003; Whittlesea, 2002; anagram solution, Lövdén & Johansson, 2003). These priming effects indicate that an abstract or lexical representation of related lures can be activated during the presentation of the study list (e.g., McDermott, 1997) and/or that semantic gist is activated or encoded (e.g., Verfaellie, Page, Orlando, & Schacter, 2005), giving rise to subsequent priming effects on a variety of tests that are sensitive to the activation of these types of conceptual information.

According to TAP, one would expect that priming for studied words would be more sensitive to perceptual manipulations than would priming for nonstudied associates, because only the studied words were actually perceived during encoding. Hicks and Starns (2005) have recently provided evidence that supports this hypothesis. In their first experiment, they found that priming on a visual word-stem completion test was greater for list words that were studied visually (.14) than auditorily (.08), demonstrating that priming was enhanced by perceptual overlap between study and test. Significant priming also was obtained for nonstudied associates, but importantly, these effects were equivalent in the visual (.06) and auditory (.07) tests. This pattern suggests that nonstudied associates were primed by the activation of abstract or conceptual information, but that perceptually-specific information was not encoded for these items. In a second experiment, a test that was thought to be less sensitive to conceptual information and more sensitive to perceptual information was used (perceptual identification). Unlike the stem-completion results, only studied words were primed on perceptual identification, again suggesting that memories for nonstudied associates did not contain perceptually detailed information.

The idea that true memories contain more perceptual detail than false memories, but similar levels of conceptual or associative information, is consistent with studies that have measured the subjective content of true and false memories (e.g., Gallo & Roediger, 2003; Mather, Henkel, & Johnson, 1997; Norman & Schacter, 1997), and also with neuroimaging studies of the DRM task. Using PET and auditory study conditions, Schacter et al. (1996) found that true recognition was more likely than false recognition to elicit activity in auditory-specific regions (e.g., superior temporal gyrus and supramarginal gyrus), using fMRI and visual study conditions, Cabeza, Rao, Wagner, Mayer, and Schacter (2001) found that true recognition was more likely than false recognition to elicit activity in areas thought to be related to visual processing (e.g., left parahippocampal gyrus), and, using ERP, Fabiani, Stadler, and Wessels (2000) found that true but not false recognition elicited laterality effects that corresponded to the lateralized visual presentation that was used at encoding. Collectively, these results indicate that perceptually-related activity at retrieval is greater for true than false recognition, potentially reflecting the recollection or priming of perceptual details (see Slotnick & Schacter, 2004), and that the nature of this retrieval activity for true recognition is specific to the type of perceptual processes engaged during study (e.g., Wheeler, Petersen, & Buckner, 2000). By comparison, true and false recognition have been found to elicit similar activity in medial temporal regions, including the hippocampus (e.g., Cabeza et al., 2001; Schacter et al., 1996), perhaps reflecting the retrieval of common conceptual or associative information that can drive both true and false recognition.

The TAP framework also is relevant to explicit memory performance in the DRM task. Indeed, TAP was originally developed by Morris, Bransford, and Franks (1977) as an alternative way of understanding "levels of processing" effects on explicit tests such as recognition (e.g., Craik & Lockhart, 1972; Craik & Tulving, 1975). The basic idea was that, contrary to a strong version of the levels framework, encoding tasks that encourage "deep" or semantic processing do not necessarily lead to better memory performance than "shallow" or surface-level processing. Instead, as is the case in implicit memory tasks, the level of performance was thought to depend on the overlap between encoding and retrieval processes. In support of this view, Morris et al. demonstrated that shallow processing (e.g., rhyme encoding task) yielded greater accuracy than deep processing (e.g., a semantic encoding task) on a test that used surface-level memory cues (e.g., rhyme recognition). By this view, the typical levels-of-processing effect (deep > shallow) arises simply because semantics happens to be the ideal dimension upon which words can be differentiated (see Roediger & Gallo, 2001, for additional discussion).

Evidence for this same type of processing specificity can be found in the false memory literature, too. Early studies using the DRM task found that, much like true memory, false memory was greater following deep (e.g., semantic) encoding tasks relative to shallow (e.g., phonological) tasks (Rhodes & Anastasi, 2000; Thapar & McDermott, 2001; Toglia, Neuschatz, & Goodwin, 1999). These findings suggest that semantic processing enhanced activation of the related lure, by facilitating the processing of common semantic associations and/or conceptual gist. But what would happen if a levels-of-processing manipulation were used on lists of phonological associates, instead of the more typical lists of semantic associates used in the DRM task (e.g., Schacter, Verfaellie, & Anes, 1997; Sommers & Lewis, 1999)? According to a TAP account, focusing on the sound of these types of associates (at encoding) should lead to greater false recognition of phonologically related lures (at test), because the overlapping features between study and test (and the corresponding activation processes) are phonological.

Building on earlier false recognition work (e.g., Coltheart, 1977; Elias & Perfetti, 1973), Chan, McDermott, Watson, and Gallo (2005) crossed two types of list (semantic or phonological associates) with two types of encoding process (focusing on meaning or sound). Replicating the typical effect with semantically related lists, meaningful processing led to significantly greater false recognition of semantic associates than did sound processing (means = .64 and .54, respectively). More important, this effect was reversed for phonological lists, with sound processing leading to significantly greater false recognition of phonologically related lures (means = .45 and .51, respectively). Much like the priming specificity effects discussed earlier, this crossover interaction demonstrates that the activation of related lures is highly specific, with meaningful processing preferentially enhancing activation for semantic associates, and sound processing preferentially enhancing activation for phonological associates. These processing differences also have been linked to differences in brain activity, with the processing of semantically related lists activating a more anterior region of left inferior frontal gyrus (near BA44/45) than the processing of phonologically related lists (near BA6/44; McDermott, Petersen, Watson, & Ojemann, 2003). In contrast to the idea of a processing continuum (from shallow to deep), these component processes appear to be subserved by distinct neurocognitive mechanisms.

In sum, both behavioral and neuroimaging data indicate that the activation processes giving rise to false memories are highly specific. In the DRM task, priming studies, subjective measures, and neuroimaging results all converge on the idea that memories for nonstudied associates contain as much conceptual information, but are less likely to contain perceptual information, than studied associates. Further, within the conceptual domain, the corresponding activation processes are specific to the type of materials (e.g., semantic or phonological). These findings are not surprising from a TAP perspective, which considers all memory performance in terms of the relative overlap between a variety of specific study and test processes, and from the related components-of-processing framework, which stipulates that different processes are potentially subserved by different neurological mechanisms.

MONITORING SPECIFICITY

In addition to activation processes, there also is evidence that recollection-based monitoring or editing processes that can reduce false memory are highly specific. In this case we are using the term "specificity" in a different sense. When discussing activation processes, and also in the section on priming specificity at the outset of this chapter, we used the term "processing specificity" to refer to the overlap between specific study and test processes, and their neurological underpinnings. The monitoring processes discussed here operate outside the purview of this framework, because they influence memory performance only at the time of retrieval, and so it makes little sense to discuss them in terms of the TAP framework.

In terms of recollection-based monitoring, processing specificity refers to the idea that there are different types of monitoring, depending on different expectations and strategies, and that these processes are highly specific to the materials and task demands. This idea stands in contrast to the more general notion of "discrimination," as might be found in various signal-detection models of recognition memory. According to those frameworks, false recognition results from confusions between target and lure distributions, or the degree of overlap between the two distributions. Manipulations that selectively strengthen the target distribution (or true memory) would enhance discrimination, ideally leading to enhanced true recognition and decreased false recognition (depending on the setting of the response criterion). The classic mirror effect provides empirical support for this type of theory: across a variety of manipulations, increased hits tend to be associated with decreased false alarms (e.g., Glanzer & Adams, 1990).

As discussed by Greene, chapter 4, this volume, a reevaluation of the mirror effect suggests that there are enough exceptions to the effect to question its use as a universal principle, and recent false memory data raise additional doubts about the utility of the concept. One reason to suspect that monitoring processes are more specific (or complicated) than a general discrimination account would suggest is that the relationship between true and false recognition is highly variable in the DRM task. Numerous manipulations have been found to reduce false memory, ostensibly by enhancing recollection-based monitoring, but only some lead to increases in true memory (e.g., repeating study words or slowing presentation rate; Benjamin, 2001; Gallo & Roediger, 2002; McDermott & Watson, 2001; Seamon et al., 2002). Other manipulations that are thought to enhance monitoring do not necessarily affect true recognition, such as presenting studied words in more distinctive formats (e.g., pictures, Schacter et al., 1999; modality, Smith & Hunt, 1998; and writing or vocalizing studied words, Dodson & Schacter, 2001; Seamon et al., 2003).

Of course, the failure to find a mirror effect in these latter cases might simply have resulted from the use of a more conservative response criterion in the more distinctive conditions, thereby offsetting increases in true recollection. More convincing evidence that different monitoring processes are involved comes from aging studies. Relative to younger adults, older adults are impaired in their ability to use repetition to reduce false recognition (e.g., Benjamin, 2001; Kensinger & Schacter, 1999; Watson, McDermott, & Balota, 2004), but they are just as likely as younger adults to reduce false recognition following distinctive study manipulations (e.g., Dodson & Schacter, 2002b; Schacter et al., 1999). Findings like these suggest that qualitatively different types of monitoring processes, or strategic uses of recollection, are involved. For instance, study rate or repetition manipulations would allow more time or opportunities for subjects to determine the critical nonpresented word, and to subsequently reject this item by recalling it as "nonstudied" (a recall-to-reject process). Distinctiveness manipulations, on the other hand, might allow subjects to form more detailed recollective expectations and therefore avoid falsely recognizing new lures that do not elicit such detailed recollections (a distinctiveness heuristic).

As argued by Gallo (2004) and Gallo, Bell, Beier, and Schacter (2006), these recollection-based monitoring processes are characterized by qualitatively different types of decision process. Whereas recall-to-reject relies on the recollection of information that disqualifies the lure as having occurred (an exclusion strategy), the distinctiveness heuristic is based on the failure to recall expected information, and therefore is only diagnostic of nonoccurrence. For reasons that are not altogether clear, aging may have greater effects on one type of monitoring than on the other. Unfortunately, research in the DRM task has only provided limited clues, because monitoring processes can occur both during the study and test phase of these experiments. For this and other reasons, monitoring processes are difficult to isolate with this task.

To further investigate these issues we have developed the criterial recollection task (e.g., Gallo, Kensinger, & Schacter, 2006; Gallo, Weiss, & Schacter, 2004). In brief, subjects studied a list of unrelated red words and pictures, and memory was tested under different sets of instructions (using black words as cues). On the picture test, subjects responded "yes" only if the test word corresponded to a studied picture (rejecting test words that corresponded to a red word), and vice versa on the red word test. Critically, some of the studied items were presented as both red words and pictures, so that the recollection of one format was independent from (i.e., did not disqualify) the item as having occurred in the other format. As a result, subjects had to carefully search their memory for recollection of the criterial format.

As shown in Figure 20.1, Gallo et al. (2004) found that subjects were less likely to falsely recognize lures on the picture test than on the red word test, and these effects were obtained regardless of whether true recognition of targets was greater for pictures (due to a picture superiority effect, Experiment 1) or for red words (due to repetition of these stimuli at study, Experiment 2). The fact that false recognition suppression was independent of true memory differences is difficult to reconcile with a unitary strength-based explanation, and instead indicated that subjects had used a recollection-based distinctiveness heuristic. Subjects expected qualitatively different types of recollections from the different formats,

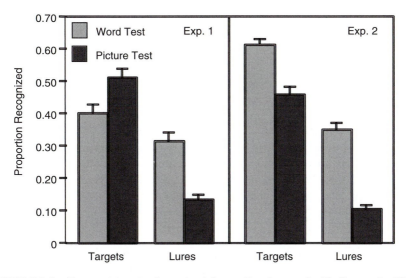

FIGURE 20.1   Recognition in the criterial-recollection task (Gallo et al., 2004). On the word test, targets are test words that were studied as red words, and lures are test words that were studied as pictures (vice versa on the picture test). False alarms to nonstudied lures followed a similar pattern as false alarms to-be-excluded studied lures.

and because picture recollections were more distinctive, false recognition was lower on the picture test than on the red word test.

In a more recent aging study, we contrasted these original conditions to a condition where a recall-to-reject process also would be possible. In that condition, studied items were only presented in one format or the other, so that a mutually exclusive rejection strategy was possible at test (i.e., if a picture could be recalled, then the subjects could be sure to reject an item as having been studied as a red word). In younger adults we replicated our original findings (minimal false recognition on the picture test), and similar effects were found in older adults, demonstrating a robust distinctiveness heuristic in both groups. However, false recognition errors on the red word test varied across the two groups. In both groups, exclusion errors were reduced when the recall-to-reject strategy was possible, relative to when it was not, but only younger adults were able to eliminate errors with this strategy. By this measure, older adults were just as likely as younger adults to use the *absence* of picture recollections to monitor memory (i.e., the distinctiveness heuristic), but were impaired in their ability to use the *presence* of picture recollections to monitor memory (i.e., the recall-to-reject strategy). Much like the DRM findings discussed above, these findings suggest that the two types of recollection-based monitoring processes operate in qualitatively different ways. There also is some evidence to suggest that they are subserved by different neurological mechanisms, but the two have yet to be directly compared in a single neuroimaging study (see Gallo, Kensinger, & Schacter, 2006, for relevant findings and discussion).

In sum, a growing body of evidence suggests that recollection can reduce false recognition in at least two different ways: recall-to-reject or the distinctiveness heuristic. These monitoring processes depend on qualitatively different types of decisions, and they can be experimentally dissociated, arguing against a more general explanation of false recognition reduction in terms of enhanced discrimination. This is not to say, though, that signal detection theories are irrelevant, and indeed multiple-dimensional SDT might provide a useful way to conceptualize the distinctiveness heuristic, as would any theory that allows for qualitatively different types of recollective expectations to influence memory decisions (e.g., Johnson & Raye, 1981). Once these points are acknowledged, the possibility emerges that other types of stimulus distinctiveness, each with highly specific neurocognitive underpinnings, also could reduce false recognition. In the next section we explore this possibility in a very different research domain—emotional distinctiveness.

EMOTION-SPECIFIC PROCESSING REDUCES MEMORY DISTORTION

> The attention which we lend to an experience is proportional to its vivid or interesting character; and it is a notorious fact that what interests us most vividly at the time is, other things equal, what we remember best. An impression may be so exciting emotionally as almost to leave a scar upon the cerebral tissues.
>
> William James (1890)

Many people share the intuition that when an event contains emotional importance, we remember that event with tremendous detail and indelible accuracy. The term "flashbulb memory," coined by Brown and Kulik (1977), captures the picture-like vividness that individuals often believe to accompany their memories of highly surprising and emotionally evocative events. Despite these intuitions, however, empirical data indicate that memories for emotional events are vulnerable to distortion: Individuals often change their reports about how they first learned of an emotional event while maintaining high confidence in their memories (e.g., Neisser & Harsch, 1992; Schmolck, Buffalo, & Squire, 2000; Weaver, 1993). These studies demonstrate convincingly that emotional memories can undergo distortion. They do not, however, speak to whether emotional content influences the frequency with which memory distortion occurs: Are memories for emotional events less prone to distortion than memories for nonemotional events?

As discussed in the preceding section, the likelihood of falsely endorsing an item as studied can relate to how distinctively an individual encodes, and thus expects to retrieve, the information (reviewed by Schacter & Wiseman, 2006). While distinctiveness typically has been manipulated by inclusion of pictorial associations (Dodson & Schacter, 2002a; Gallo et al., 2004; Israel & Schacter, 1997; Weiss, Dodson, Goff, Schacter, & Heckers, 2002) or by asking people to generate items (Dodson & Schacter, 2001), emotion may provide another dimension along which an item's distinctiveness can be enhanced. Emotionally arousing experiences include numerous aspects that are not present to the same extent in nonemotional ones (e.g., personal relevance and physiological response; Christianson & Engelberg, 1999; LeDoux, 2002). Consistent with the hypothesis that these additional dimensions increase the distinctiveness of emotional information, a number of studies have demonstrated that individuals are more likely to claim that they vividly remember emotionally arousing items as compared to nonemotional ones (e.g., Dewhurst & Parry, 2000; Kensinger & Corkin, 2003; Ochsner, 2000). As studies of flashbulb memories have shown, however, these subjective intuitions about the vividness of a memory do not necessarily map on to objective evaluations of its accuracy. Thus, the critical question is whether this subjectively vivid encoding also corresponds with a reduction in memory distortion.

In a number of studies, the answer seems to be affirmative. For example, after studying a list of words orthographically associated with a nonpresented lure word, individuals were less likely to falsely recall or to falsely recognize the lure word if it was emotional (e.g., to endorse *rape* after studying *cape, nape, tape, . . .*) than if it was neutral (e.g., *hook* after studying *book, look, cook*; Pesta, Murphy, & Sanders, 2001; Kensinger & Corkin, 2004a). The likelihood of falsely recognizing the emotional lures also was related to manipulations in distinctiveness: Including other emotional items at encoding (thereby decreasing the distinctiveness of the emotional lure words) increased the likelihood of false recognition (Pesta, Murphy, & Sanders, 2001). These data suggest that individuals can use the distinctiveness provided by emotion to reduce their rates of false recognition. An important caveat, however, is that in this paradigm the majority of the studied items were neutral. Thus, the emotional lures may have been rejected due to their conceptual incongruence with the studied items, rather than because of specific effects of emotion. These studies, therefore, do not provide strong evidence that emotion, *per se*, alters the frequency of memory distortion.

More direct evidence for effects of emotional salience on memory distortion has come from examinations of reality monitoring ability (the ability to distinguish what has been perceived from what has been imagined; Johnson & Raye, 1981). Assignment to an external or internal source can typically be made by remembering the types of information associated with an event: Experienced events usually include more sensory, contextual, and semantic information, whereas imagined events often require more cognitive operations to support the internal generation of information (Johnson & Hirst, 1993; Johnson & Raye, 1981). Remembering these characteristics typically allows accurate memory attributions, although reality-monitoring errors sometimes can occur. Kensinger and Schacter (2005b) demonstrated that these errors occurred less frequently for negative arousing items compared to nonemotional ones. This enhanced discrimination for negative arousing items existed whether or not participants were informed about the memory task that would follow, and the effect was present for both verbal stimuli and single objects.

This finding is consistent with evidence indicating that emotional content enhances the binding of many types of item and event details. For example, emotionally arousing items are more likely to be remembered with details such as the color of font in which a word was written or the location of a word on a screen

(D'Argembeau & van der Linden, 2004; Doerksen & Shimamura, 2001; Kensinger & Corkin, 2003; MacKay et al., 2004). Enhanced binding could combat reality-monitoring errors in a number of ways. It could increase the likelihood that participants remember the critical event details needed to distinguish presented from imagined events (e.g., sensory, perceptual, semantic details; Johnson, Hashtroudi, & Lindsay, 1993). It also could prevent stimulus confusion. For example, after studying a picture of an apricot, a person may later falsely believe that they saw a picture of an orange if they remember only general information about that object (e.g., an orange-colored fruit). In contrast, this confusion may result less frequently for emotional items if they tend to be remembered with more detail, allowing them to be distinguished from other items. A recent experiment has provided evidence that individuals are more likely to remember the specific visual details of emotional items compared to nonemotional ones. Kensinger, Garoff-Eaton, and Schacter (2006) presented participants with colored objects at study, some of which were emotional and some of which were neutral (e.g., a snake, a barometer). At retrieval, they showed participants some objects that were identical to those that had been studied, some that were similar but not identical to studied objects (e.g., a barometer that differed from the one presented at study in features such as color, size, shape, or orientation) and other objects that were novel. They found that emotional content enhanced the likelihood that specific visual details were remembered: Individuals were more likely to indicate correctly that an item was identical to the one studied earlier if it was emotional than if it was neutral.

These behavioral studies demonstrate that negative emotional content can decrease the likelihood of memory distortion. They do not, however, clarify whether this increased memory accuracy for the negative arousing information is specifically related to the processing of the emotional information, or whether it stems from engagement of the same processes that reduce memory distortion for neutral information. As discussed earlier in this chapter, increases in true recollection can decrease false memories via a variety of processes. Furthermore, it has been suggested that at least some of the effects of emotion on memory can be attributed to greater semantic relatedness among emotional items than among nonemotional items (Talmi & Moscovitch, 2004).

Neuroimaging provides one method for examining whether the effects of emotion on memory accuracy result from domain-general processes that serve to boost memory accuracy for emotional and nonemotional information, or from emotion-specific processes. To examine this question, Kensinger and Schacter (2005a) used fMRI to examine the neural processes that were engaged during accurate encoding of emotional and neutral information (i.e., that reduced the likelihood of subsequent reality-monitoring errors). We used a paradigm that had been shown to elicit high levels of reality-monitoring errors (see Gonsalves & Paller, 2000). Participants were scanned as they formed mental images of named objects and indicated whether those objects were bigger or smaller than a shoebox. For half of the items, participants were then shown the corresponding photo. After a delay, participants performed a recognition task in which they had to indicate whether items had been shown as photos. In some instances, reality-monitoring errors occurred, and participants indicated that a photo of an object had been studied, when the participant had only imagined it. As in the behavioral studies discussed above, reality-monitoring errors occurred less frequently for the emotional items than for the neutral items. The critical question was whether distinct neural processes influenced the frequency of reality-monitoring errors for emotional and neutral items.

The study revealed some overlap in the neural processes that were related to successful encoding for emotional items and neutral items. Most notably, activity in the left posterior hippocampus showed a relation to accurate encoding for both item types (i.e., greater activity during the encoding of items later correctly attributed to a presented or nonpresented source than during the encoding of items later misattributed). Importantly, there also were distinctions in the neural processes based on the emotional content of the items: Enhanced activity in the amygdala and the orbitofrontal cortex corresponded with a reduction in the likelihood of memory misattributions specifically for the emotional items. Activity in these regions showed no relation to memory accuracy for the neutral items. Critically, these are regions that are engaged during the processing of emotional information across a range of paradigms (Bechara, Damasio, & Damasio, 2000; Phan, Wager, Taylor, & Liberzon, 2002; Zald, 2003). Thus, it appears that the way in which emotional information is processed results in a memory accuracy advantage. Part of the effect of these emotion-specific processes appeared to be exerted via their interactions with regions that promote accurate encoding of both emotional and nonemotional items. Activity in the amygdala was highly correlated with activity in the hippocampus during the encoding of emotional items later accurately attributed (see Dolcos, LaBar, & Cabeza, 2004; Kensinger and Corkin, 2004b; Richardson, Strange, & Dolan 2004; Kilpatrick & Cahill, 2003, for other evidence of amygdala-hippocampus interactions). Thus, the results provide strong evidence that the enhancement in memory accuracy for emotional items did not stem solely from the additional engagement of domain-general processes that enhance accuracy for all items. Rather, domain-specific processes (in the amygdala and orbitofrontal cortex), engaged during encoding, served to enhance memory accuracy for the emotional items.

In a separate experiment, Kensinger and Schacter (2005b) examined whether distinct retrieval processes also influenced memory accuracy for emotional and neutral items. Participants performed the same reality-monitoring task described above, but this time they were scanned during the retrieval phase (i.e., as they indicated whether or not a photo of an object had been studied). The results paralleled those of encoding. Activity in the left hippocampus (this time in an anterior region) was related to accurate retrieval for both emotional and neutral items. Activity in emotion-processing regions (the right amygdala and left orbitofrontal cortex), quite similar to those implicated in accurate encoding, corresponded with accurate retrieval only for the emotional items and not for the neutral items. Interestingly, activity in lateral prefrontal regions and the right posterior hippocampus corresponded with accurate retrieval only for the neutral items. These results demonstrate that the emotional content of items affects the neural processes that are associated with accurate retrieval. Moreover, emotion-specific processing (in the amygdala and orbitofrontal cortex) appears to be linked both to the successful encoding and accurate retrieval of emotional information.

Taken together, these studies demonstrate that information with emotional content is less likely to be remembered in a distorted fashion than information lacking emotional salience. The results help us to understand how emotion can modulate memory performance, highlighting roles of the amygdala and orbito-frontal cortex at both encoding and retrieval. They also emphasize the fact that false memory reduction does not always result from domain-general processes. Rather, it is clear that when emotional information is more accurately remembered than neutral information, it is because of the engagement of emotion-specific processes. Future research will be needed to examine the range of stimuli for which domain-specific versus domain-general processes relate to reductions in memory distortion.

CONCLUDING COMMENTS

In this chapter we have reviewed evidence for what we term processing specificity in three different domains: priming, false recognition, and emotional memory. Our review of priming research noted the existence of three types of specificity: stimulus, associative, and response. We reviewed recent neural and behavioral evidence documenting response specificity in priming, and considered implications for various theoretical accounts of priming-related activations decreases observed in fMRI studies, as well as cognitive perspective on the processes and systems that support priming. Our discussion of false recognition summarized both behavioral and neuroimaging evidence for a high degree of specificity in the activation processes that give rise to false memories, and we also considered additional evidence for specificity in monitoring processes that can be used to reduce false memories. Finally, in our discussion of emotion and memory distortion we considered neuroimaging evidence that emotion-specific processes are involved in reducing the incidence of reality monitoring errors.

We have grouped a number of phenomena under the rubric of "processing specificity," even though it is not clear how or even whether they are connected. For example, the various forms of priming specificity generally refer to the specificity of various kinds of knowledge or stored representations, our discussion of false memory reduction focused on monitoring operations that could be applied in principle to different kinds of knowledge, and our discussion of emotional memory considered specific versus general processes at the level of a domain (emotional vs. nonemotional). Although the relations among the various types of specificity considered here remain to be elucidated, it seems clear that questions concerning the level and degree of processing specificity have come to the fore in many sectors of memory research. We therefore believe that future empirical and theoretical analyses that explore further the various forms of processing specificity will likely prove important in enhancing our understanding of memory.

ACKNOWLEDGMENTS

We thank Chris Moore and Alana Wong for help with preparation of the chapter. The chapter was supported by grants NIMH MH60941 and NIA AG08441 (to DLS), NIA AG21369 (to DAG), and MH070199 (to EAK).

REFERENCES

Bechara, A., Damasio, H., & Damasio, A. R. (2000). Emotion, decision making and the orbitofrontal cortex. *Cerebral Cortex, 10*, 295–307.

Benjamin, A. S. (2001). On the dual effects of repetition on false recognition. *Journal of Experimental Psychology: Learning, Memory, and Cognition, 27*, 941–947.

Bowers, J. S. (2000). The modality-specific and -nonspecific components of long-term priming are frequency sensitive. *Memory and Cognition, 28*, 406–414.

Brown, R., & Kulik, J. (1977). Flashbulb memories. *Cognition, 5*, 73–99.

Cabeza, R., Rao, S. M., Wagner, A. D., Mayer, A. R., & Schacter, D. L. (2001). Can medial temporal lobe regions distinguish true from false? An event-related functional MRI study of veridical and illusory recognition memory. *Proceedings of the National Academy of Sciences, 98*, 4805–4810.

Chan, J. C. K., McDermott, K. B., Watson, J. M., & Gallo, D. A. (2005). The importance of material-processing interactions in inducing false memories. *Memory and Cognition, 33*, 389–395.

Christianson, S.-A., & Engelberg, E. (1999). Organization of emotional memories. In T. Dalgleish & M. Power (Eds.), *The handbook of cognition and emotion* (pp. 211–227). Chichester, UK: Wiley.

Coltheart, V. (1977). Recognition errors after incidental learning as a function of different levels of processing. *Journal of Experimental Psychology: Human Learning and Memory, 3*, 437–444.

Craik, F. I. M., & Lockhart, R. S. (1972). Levels of processing: A framework for memory research. *Journal of Verbal Learning and Verbal Behavior, 11*, 671–684.

Craik, F. I. M., & Tulving, E. (1975). Depth of processing and the retention of words in episodic memory. *Journal of Experimental Psychology: General, 104*, 268–294.

D'Argembeau, A., & van der Linden, M. (2004). Influence of affective meaning on memory for contextual information. *Emotion, 4*, 173–188.

Desimone, R., & Duncan, J. (1995). Neural mechanisms of selective visual attention. *Annual Review of Neuroscience, 18*, 193–222.

Dewhurst, S. A., & Parry, L. A. (2000). Emotionality, distinctiveness, and recollective experience. *European Journal of Cognitive Psychology, 12*, 541–551.

Dobbins, I. G., Schnyer, D. M., Verfaellie, M., & Schacter, D. L. (2004). Cortical activity reductions during repetition priming can result from rapid response learning. *Nature, 428*, 316–319.

Dodson, C. S., & Schacter, D. L. (2001). "If I had said it I would have remembered it": Reducing false memories with a distinctiveness heuristic. *Psychonomic Bulletin and Review, 8*, 155–161.

Dodson, C. S., & Schacter, D. L. (2002a). Aging and strategic retrieval processes: Reducing false memories with a distinctiveness heuristic. *Psychology and Aging, 17*, 405–415.

Dodson, C. S., & Schacter, D. L. (2002b). When false recognition meets metacognition: The distinctiveness heuristic. *Journal of Memory and Language, 46*, 782–803.

Doerksen, S., & Shimamura, A. (2001). Source memory enhancement for emotional words. *Emotion, 1,* 5–11.

Dolcos, F., LaBar, K. S., & Cabeza, R. (2004). Interaction between the amygdala and the medial temporal lobe memory system predicts better memory for emotional events. *Neuron, 5,* 855–863.

Elias, C. S., & Perfetti, C. A. (1973). Encoding task and recognition memory: The importance of semantic encoding. *Journal of Experimental Psychology, 99,* 151–156.

Fabiani, M., Stadler, M. A., & Wessels, P. M. (2000). True but not false memories produce a sensory signature in human lateralized brain potentials. *Journal of Cognitive Neuroscience, 12,* 941–949.

Gallo, D. A. (2004). Using recall to reduce false recognition: Diagnostic and disqualifying monitoring. *Journal of Experimental Psychology: Learning, Memory, and Cognition, 30,* 120–128.

Gallo, D. A., Bell, D. M., Beier, J. S., & Schacter, D. L. (2006). Two types of recollection-based monitoring in young and older adults: Recall-to-reject and the distinctiveness heuristic. *Memory, 14,* 730–741.

Gallo, D. A., Kensinger, E. A., & Schacter, D. L. (2006). Prefrontal activity and diagnostic monitoring of memory retrieval: fMRI of the criterial recollection task. *Journal of Cognitive Neuroscience, 18,* 135–148.

Gallo, D. A., & Roediger, H. L., III. (2002). Variability among word lists in eliciting memory illusions: Evidence for associative activation and monitoring. *Journal of Memory and Language, 47,* 469–497.

Gallo, D. A., & Roediger, H. L., III. (2003). The effects of associations and aging on illusory recollection. *Memory and Cognition, 31,* 1036–1044.

Gallo, D. A., Weiss, J. A., & Schacter, D. L. (2004). Reducing false recognition with criterial recollection tests: Distinctiveness heuristic versus criterion shifts. *Journal of Memory and Language, 51,* 473–493.

Glanzer, M., & Adams, J. K. (1990). The mirror effect in recognition memory: Data and theory. *Journal of Experimental Psychology: Learning, Memory, and Cognition, 16,* 5–16.

Gonsalves, B., & Paller, K. A. (2000). Neural events that underlie remembering something that never happened. *Nature Neuroscience, 3,* 1316–1321.

Graf, P., & Mandler, G. (1984). Activation makes words more accessible, but not necessarily more retrievable. *Journal of Verbal Learning and Verbal Behavior, 23,* 553–568.

Graf, P., Squire, L. R., & Mandler, G. (1984). The information that amnesic patients do not forget. *Journal of Experimental Psychology: Learning, Memory, and Cognition, 10,* 164–178.

Grill-Spector, K., Henson, R., & Martin, A. (2006). Repetition and the brain: Neural models of stimulus-specific effects. *Trends in Cognitive Sciences, 10,* 14–23.

Grill-Spector, K., & Malach, R. (2001). Fmr-adaptation: A tool for studying the functional properties of neurons. *Acta Psychologica, 107,* 293–321.

Hancock, T. W., Hicks, J. L., Marsh, R. L., & Ritschel, L. (2003). Measuring the activation level of critical lures in the Deese–Roediger–McDermott paradigm. *American Journal of Psychology, 116,* 1–14.

Henson, R. N. (2003). Neuroimaging studies of priming. *Progress in Neurobiology, 70,* 53–81.

Hicks, J. L., & Starns, J. J. (2005). False memories lack perceptual detail: Evidence from implicit word-stem completion and perceptual identification tests. *Journal of Memory and Language, 52,* 309–321.

Israel, L., & Schacter, D. L. (1997). Pictorial encoding reduces false recognition of semantic associates. *Psychonomic Bulletin and Review*, *4*, 577–581.

Jacoby, L. L., & Dallas, M. (1981). On the relationship between autobiographical memory and perceptual learning. *Journal of Experimental Psychology: General*, *110*, 306–340.

James, W. (1890). *The principles of psychology*. New York: Holt.

Johnson, M. K., Hashtroudi, S., & Lindsay, D. S. (1993). Source monitoring. *Psychological Bulletin*, *114*, 3–28.

Johnson, M. K., & Hirst, W. (1993). MEM: Memory subsystems as processes. In A. F. Collins, S. E. Gathercole, M. A. Conway, & P. E. Morris (Eds.), *Theories of memory* (pp. 241–286). Hove, UK: Lawrence Erlbaum Associates, Inc.

Johnson, M. K., & Raye, C. L. (1981). Reality monitoring. *Psychological Review*, *88*, 67–85.

Kensinger, E. A., & Corkin, S. (2003). Memory enhancement for emotional words: Are emotional words more vividly remembered than neutral words? *Memory and Cognition*, *31*, 1169–1180.

Kensinger, E. A., & Corkin, S. (2004a). The effects of emotional content and aging on false memories. *Cognitive, Affective, and Behavioral Neuroscience*, *4*, 1–9.

Kensinger, E. A., & Corkin, S. (2004b). Two routes to emotional memory: Distinct neural processes for valence and arousal. *Proceedings of the National Academy of Sciences, USA*, *101*, 3310–3315.

Kensinger, E. A., Garoff-Eaton, R. J., & Schacter, D. L. (2006). Memory for specific visual details can be enhanced by negative arousing content. *Journal of Memory and Language*, *54*, 99–112.

Kensinger, E. A., & Schacter, D. L. (1999). When true memories suppress false memories: Effects of ageing. *Cognitive Neuropsychology*, *16*, 399–415.

Kensinger, E. A., & Schacter, D. L (2005a). Emotional content and reality-monitoring ability: FMRI evidence for the influence of encoding processes. *Neuropsychologia*, *43*, 1429–1443.

Kensinger, E. A., & Schacter, D. L. (2005b). Retrieving accurate and distorted memories: Neuroimaging evidence for effects of emotion. *NeuroImage*, *27*, 167–177.

Kilpatrick, L., & Cahill, L. (2003). Amygdala modulation of parahippocampal and frontal regions during emotionally influenced memory storage. *NeuroImage*, *20*, 2091–2099.

Koutstaal, W., Wagner, A. D., Rotte, M., Maril, A., Buckner, R. L., & Schacter, D. L. (2001). Perceptual specificity in visual object priming: fMRI evidence for a laterality difference in fusiform cortex. *Neuropsychologia*, *39*, 184–199.

LeDoux, J. E. (2002). Cognitive-emotional interactions: Listen to the brain. In R. D. Lane & L. Nadel (Eds). *Cognitive neuroscience of emotion* (pp. 129–155). New York: Oxford University Press.

Lövdén, M., & Johansson, M. (2003). Are covert verbal responses mediating false implicit memory? *Psychonomic Bulletin and Review*, *10*, 724–729.

MacKay, D. G., Shafto, M., Taylor, J. K., Marian, D. E., Abrams, L., & Dyer, J. R. (2004). Relations between emotion, memory, and attention: Evidence from taboo Stroop, lexical decision, and immediate memory tasks. *Memory and Cognition*, *32*, 474–488.

Mather, M., Henkel, L. A., & Johnson, M. K. (1997). Evaluating characteristics of false memories: Remember/know judgments and memory characteristics questionnaire compared. *Memory and Cognition*, *25*, 826–837.

McDermott, K. B. (1997). Priming on perceptual implicit memory tests can be achieved through presentation of associates. *Psychonomic Bulletin and Review*, *4*, 582–586.

McDermott, K. B., Petersen, S. E., Watson, J. M., & Ojemann, J. G. (2003). A procedure for identifying regions preferentially activated by attention to semantic and phonological relations using functional magnetic resonance imaging. *Neuropsychologia*, *41*, 293–303.

McDermott, K. B., & Watson, J. M. (2001). The rise and fall of false recall: The impact of presentation duration. *Journal of Memory and Language*, *45*, 160–176.

McKone, E., & Murphy, B. (2000). Implicit false memory: Effects of modality and multiple study presentations on long-lived semantic priming. *Journal of Memory and Language*, *43*, 89–109.

Morris, C. D., Bransford, J. D., & Franks, J. J. (1977). Levels of processing versus transfer appropriate processing. *Journal of Verbal Learning and Verbal Behavior*, *16*, 519–533.

Neisser, U., & Harsch, N. (1992). Phantom flashbulbs: False recollections of hearing the news about Challenger. In E. Winograd & U. Neisser (Eds.), *Affect and accuracy in recall: Studies of "flashbulb memories"* (pp. 9–31). New York: Cambridge University Press.

Norman, K. A., & Schacter, D. L. (1997). False recognition in younger and older adults: Exploring the characteristics of illusory memories. *Memory and Cognition*, *25*, 838–848.

Ochsner, K. N. (2000). Are affective events richly "remembered" or simply familiar? The experience and process of recognizing feelings past. *Journal of Experimental Psychology: General*, *129*, 242–261.

Pesta, B. J., Murphy, M. D., & Sanders, R. E. (2001). Are emotionally charged lures immune to false memory? *Journal of Experimental Psychology: Learning, Memory, and Cognition*, *27*, 328–338.

Phan, K. L., Wager, T., Taylor, S. F., & Liberzon, I. (2002). Functional neuroanatomy of emotion: A meta-analysis of emotion activation studies in PET and fMRI. *Neuroimage*, *16*, 331–348.

Raichle, M. E., Fiez, J. A., Videen, T. O., Macleod, A. M., Pardo, J. V., Fox, P. T., & Petersen, S. E. (1994). Practice-related changes in human brain functional anatomy during nonmotor learning. *Cerebral Cortex*, *4*, 8–26.

Rhodes, M. G., & Anastasi, J. S. (2000). The effects of a levels-of-processing manipulation on false recall. *Psychonomic Bulletin and Review*, *7*, 158–162.

Richardson, M. P., Strange, B. A., & Dolan, R. J. (2004). Encoding of emotional memories depends on amygdala and hippocampus and their interactions. *Nature Neuroscience*, *7*, 278–285.

Roediger, H. L., III. (1978). Recall as a self-limiting process. *Memory and Cognition*, *6*, 54–63.

Roediger, H. L., III. (1990). Implicit memory: Retention without remembering. *The American Psychologist*, *45*, 1043–1056.

Roediger, H. L., III., Balota, D. A., & Watson, J. M. (2001). Spreading activation and the arousal of false memories. In H. L. Roediger, III, J. S. Nairne, I. Neath, & A. M. Surprenant (Eds.), *The nature of remembering: Essays in honor of Robert G. Crowder* (pp. 95–115). Washington, DC: American Psychological Association.

Roediger, H. L., III, & Blaxton, T. A. (1987). Effects of varying modality, surface features, and retention interval on priming in word fragment completion. *Memory and Cognition*, *15*, 379–388.

Roediger, H. L., III, Buckner, R. L., & McDermott, K. B. (1999). Components of processing. In J. K. Foster & M. Jelicic (Eds.), *Memory: Systems, process, or function?* (pp. 31–65). Oxford, UK: Oxford University Press.

Roediger, H. L., III, & Gallo, D. A. (2001). Levels of processing: Some unanswered questions. In M. Naveh-Benjamin, M. Moscovitch, & H. L. Roediger (Eds.), *Perspectives on human memory and cognitive aging: Essays in honour of Fergus Craik* (pp. 28–47). New York: Psychology Press.

Roediger, H. L., III, & McDermott, K. B. (1995). Creating false memories: Remembering words not presented in lists. *Journal of Experimental Psychology: Learning, Memory, and Cognition, 21*, 803–814.

Roediger, H. L., III, & McDermott, K. B. (2000). Distortions of memory. In E. Tulving & F. I. M. Craik (Eds.), *Oxford handbook of memory* (pp. 49–162). Oxford, UK: Oxford University Press.

Roediger, H. L., III, & Payne, D. G. (1982). Hypermnesia: The role of repeated testing. *Journal of Experimental Psychology, Learning, Memory, and Cognition, 8*, 66–72.

Roediger, H. L., III, Watson, J. M., McDermott, K. B., & Gallo, D. A. (2001). Factors that determine false recall: A multiple regression analysis. *Psychonomic Bulletin and Review, 8*, 385–407.

Roediger, H. L., III, Weldon, M. S., & Challis, B. H. (1989). Explaining dissociations between implicit and explicit measures of retention: A processing account. In H. L. I. Roediger & F. I. M. Craik (Eds.), *Varieties of memory and consciousness: Essays in honor of Endel Tulving* (pp. 3–41). Hillsdale, NJ: Lawrence Erlbaum Associates, Inc.

Scarborough, D., Cortese, C., & Scarborough, H. (1977). Frequency and repetition effects in lexical memory. *Journal of Experimental Psychology: Human Perception and Performance, 3*, 1–17.

Schacter, D. L. (1985). Priming of old and new knowledge in amnesic patients and normal subjects. *Annals of the New York Academy of Sciences, 444*, 44–53.

Schacter, D. L. (1990). Perceptual representation systems and implicit memory: Toward a resolution of the multiple memory systems debate. *Annals of the New York Academy of Sciences, 608*, 543–571.

Schacter, D. L. (1994). Priming and multiple memory systems: Perceptual mechanisms of implicit memory. In D. L. Schacter & E. Tulving (Eds.), *Memory systems 1994* (pp. 233–268). Cambridge, MA: MIT Press.

Schacter, D. L., & Buckner, R. L. (1998). Priming and the brain. *Neuron, 20*, 185–195.

Schacter, D. L., Dobbins, I. G., & Schnyer, D. M. (2004). Specificity of priming: A cognitive neuroscience perspective. *Nature Reviews Neuroscience, 5*, 853–862.

Schacter, D. L., Israel, L., & Racine, C. (1999). Suppressing false recognition in younger and older adults: The distinctiveness heuristic. *Journal of Memory and Language, 40*, 1–24.

Schacter, D. L., Reiman, E., Curran, T., Yun, L. S., Bandy, D., McDermott, K. B., & Roediger, H. L., III. (1996). Neuroanatomical correlates of veridical and illusory recognition memory: Evidence from positron emission tomography. *Neuron, 17*, 267–274.

Schacter, D. L., & Slotnick, S. D. (2004). The cognitive neuroscience of memory distortion. *Neuron, 44*, 149–160.

Schacter, D. L., Verfaellie, M., & Anes, M. D. (1997). Illusory memories in amnesic patients: Conceptual and perceptual false recognition. *Neuropsychology, 11*, 331–342.

Schacter, D. L., & Wiseman, A. L. (2006). Reducing memory errors: The distinctiveness heuristic. In R. R. Hunt & J. Worthen (Eds.), *Distinctiveness and memory* (pp. 89–107). New York: Oxford University Press.

Schmolck, H., Buffalo, E. A., & Squire, L. R. (2000). Memory distortions develop over time: Recollections of the O. J. Simpson trial verdict after 15 and 32 months. *Psychological Science, 11*, 39–45.

Schnyer, D. M., Dobbins, I. G., Nicholls, L., Schacter, D. L., & Verfaellie, M. (2006). Rapid response learning in amnesia: Delineating associative learning components in repetition priming. *Neuropsychologia, 44*, 140–149.

Seamon, J. G., Goodkind, M. S., Dumey, A. D., Dick, E., Aufseeser, M. S., Strickland, S. E., et al. (2003). "If I didn't write it, why would I remember it?" Effects of encoding, attention, and practice on accurate and false memory. *Memory and Cognition, 31*, 445–457.

Seamon, J. G., Luo, C. R., Schwartz, M. A., Jones, K. J., Lee, D. M., & Jones, S. J. (2002). Repetition can have similar or different effects on accurate and false recognition. *Journal of Memory and Language, 46*, 323–340.

Slotnick, S. D., & Schacter, D. L. (2004). A sensory signature that distinguishes true from false memories. *Nature Neuroscience, 7*, 664–672.

Smith, R. E., & Hunt, R. R. (1998). Presentation modality affects false memory. *Psychonomic Bulletin and Review, 5*, 710–715.

Smith, S. M., Gerkens, D. R., Pierce, B. H., & Choi, H. (2002). The roles of associative responses at study and semantically guided recollection at test in false memory: The Kirkpatrick and Deese hypotheses. *Journal of Memory and Language, 47*, 436–447.

Sommers, M. S., & Lewis, B. P. (1999). Who really lives next door: Creating false memories with phonological neighbors. *Journal of Memory and Language, 40*, 83–108.

Talmi, D., & Moscovitch, M. (2004). Can semantic relatedness explain the enhancement of memory for emotional words? *Memory and Cognition, 32*, 742–751.

Tenpenny, P. L. (1995). Abstractionist versus episodic theories of repetition priming and word identification. *Psychonomic Bulletin and Review, 2*, 339–363.

Thapar, A., & McDermott, K. B. (2001). False recall and false recognition induced by presentation of associated words: Effects of retention interval and level of processing. *Memory and Cognition, 29*, 424–432.

Toglia, M. P., Neuschatz, J. S., & Goodwin, K. A. (1999). Recall accuracy and illusory memories: When more is less. *Memory, 7*, 233–256.

Tulving, E., & Schacter, D. L. (1990). Priming and human memory systems. *Science, 247*, 301–306.

Tulving, E., Schacter, D. L., & Stark, H. (1982). Priming effects in word-fragment completion are independent of recognition memory. *Journal of Experimental Psychology: Learning, Memory, and Cognition, 8*, 336–342.

Verfaellie, M., Page, K., Orlando, F., & Schacter, D. L. (2005). Impaired implicit memory for gist information in amnesia. *Neuropsychology, 19*, 760–769.

Warrington, E. K., & Weiskrantz, L. (1974). The effect of prior learning on subsequent retention in amnesic patients. *Neuropsychologia, 12*, 419–428.

Watson, J. M., McDermott, K. B., & Balota, D. A. (2004). Attempting to avoid false memories in the Deese/Roediger-McDermott paradigm: Assessing the combined influence of practice and warnings in young and old adults. *Memory and Cognition, 32*, 135–141.

Weaver, C. A., III. (1993). Do you need a "flash" to form a flashbulb memory? *Journal of Experimental Psychology: General, 122*, 39–46.

Weiss, A. P., Dodson, C. S., Goff, D. C., Schacter, D. L., & Heckers, S. (2002). Intact suppression of increased false recognition in schizophrenia. *American Journal of Psychiatry, 159*, 1506–1513.

Weldon, M. S., & Roediger, H. L. (1987). Altering retrieval demands reverses the picture superiority effect. *Memory and Cognition, 15*, 269–280.

Wheeler, M. A., Petersen, S. E., & Buckner, R. L. (2000). Memory's echo: Vivid remembering reactivates sensory-specific cortex. *Proceedings of the National Academy of Sciences, 97,* 11125–11129.

Whittlesea, B. W. A. (2002). False memory and the discrepancy-attribution hypothesis: The prototype-familiarity illusion. *Journal of Experimental Psychology: General, 131,* 96–115.

Wiggs, C. L., & Martin, A. (1998). Properties and mechanisms of perceptual priming. *Current Opinion in Neurobiology, 8,* 227–233.

Zald, D. H. (2003). The human amygdala and the emotional evaluation of sensory stimuli. *Brain Research: Brain Research Review, 41,* 88–123.

21

Toward Analyzing Cognitive Illusions: Past, Present, and Future

MATTHEW G. RHODES and LARRY L. JACOBY

*D*o you remember the first time you met Roddy Roediger? Are you certain your answer is correct? As shown by a great deal of Roddy's work in the Deese–Roediger–McDermott (DRM; Deese, 1959; Roediger & McDermott, 1995) paradigm, our memories of the past are often mistaken. Striking levels of inaccuracy have been demonstrated in a number of paradigms (e.g., Jacoby, 1999a; Lindsay, Hagen, Read, Wade, & Garry, 2004; Loftus & Pickrell, 1995) indicating that we are often subject to compelling illusions of the past that are confidently held (e.g., Roediger & McDermott, 1995). The preponderance of such memory illusions raises significant questions about both the veridicality of memory and its relation to the subjective experience of memory. For example, can subjective experience permit one to distinguish true from false memories? How does subjective experience relate to the control of memory?

Like Roddy (Roediger, 1996; see also Jacoby, Kelley, & Dywan, 1989), we suggest that memory illusions highlight general principles of memory function and, further, tell us much about the subjective experience and control of memory. For our chapter in honor of Roddy, we first discuss the nature of memory illusions, drawing on classic work indicating that memory, like perception, results from the construction of experience. Next, we examine approaches to the subjective experience of memory, highlighting both quantitative and qualitative factors that influence subjective experience and control over memory. We focus on the performance of older adults, who exhibit diminished memory accuracy in comparison to younger adults (see Jacoby & Rhodes, 2006, for a review). However, we go beyond memory illusions by examining the calibration of subjective experience— the relationship between memory confidence and memory accuracy. As will be described, older adults' memories are sometimes less well calibrated than those of younger adults. This is important for applied purposes as older adults' poor calibration of confidence and memory leaves them susceptible to scams. For theory, we forward a dual-process model of memory and extend that model to examine the multiple processes underlying age-related differences in memory accuracy and confidence. To anticipate, we argue that older adults are more likely to be captured by highly accessible but misleading information than are young adults. We end by briefly describing our recent attempts to improve the correspondence between confidence and memory in older adults. By improving the calibration between memory and confidence we hope to make older adults less susceptible to memory illusions.

THE CONSTRUCTION OF EXPERIENCE (ILLUSORY AND OTHERWISE)

Roddy's work in the DRM paradigm (e.g., Roediger & McDermott, 1995) provides an example of a compelling memory illusion. In the DRM paradigm, participants study lists of semantically related words (e.g., *bed, rest, awake, pillow, dream*, etc.), all related to a central theme word (e.g., *sleep*), termed the critical lure, that is never presented. The typical finding is that participants will often recall or recognize the critical lure at levels comparable to presented list items. Moreover, participants are usually very confident in their memory for the critical lure (e.g., Anastasi, Rhodes, & Burns, 2000) and report specific details of its occurrence (e.g., Roediger & McDermott, 1995). This is likely the product of "normal" memory processes. For example, a list of related words is best encoded through an elaborative strategy that emphasizes the semantic attributes that the words share. Focusing on semantic similarities between words likely makes the central concept of the list (e.g., *sleep*) highly accessible, later leading it to be mistakenly reported as having been studied. Ignoring the semantic qualities of presented list items does have the effect of reducing false memories, but at the cost lowering veridical recall (e.g., Rhodes & Anastasi, 2000).

Memory illusions such as the DRM effect are important in that they illustrate that memory reports are influenced by general knowledge, along with details for a prior event. That is, memory for the past reflects what usually happens, what it would make sense to have happened, and what one wants or fears happened, as well as what actually happened. Bartlett (1932) was among the first to demonstrate that encoded information was used in conjunction with prior knowledge to reconstruct memory rather than memory serving as a faithful reproduction of past events (see Bergman & Roediger, 1999, for a replication of some of Bartlett's findings). Decades later, Bruner (1957) revisited the importance of prior knowledge as well as the needs and motivations of the observer to propose the "New Look" approach to perception (see Greenwald, 1992, for a discussion of the New Look along with commentaries). The New Look was new in that it suggested that perception was not purely a function of the physical stimulus. It instead emphasized the contributions of the observer, particularly the accessibility of categories. A well-known example of a category accessibility effect that was used to support the New Look is the finding that poor children judge a quarter as larger than do children who are not poor (Bruner & Goodman, 1947).

Effects on perception of the sort revealed by the New Look show that general knowledge, in the form of category accessibility, influences the interpretation of the present as well as memory of the past. Social psychologists have been greatly influenced by Bartlett's (1932), arguments along with those made by Bruner (1957). A common theme in research on social cognition is that reality is constructed by means of an attribution process. Support for that theme has been gained by varying category accessibility through priming manipulations. For example, Stanley Schacter (Schacter & Singer, 1962) suggested that emotion was in large part based on the perception and interpretation of an arousing situation. In one experiment, Schacter (1971) injected participants with epinephrine (a chemical that speeds heart rate and produces other arousing effects) and exposed them to conditions that elicited different emotions. Participants experienced the arousal as anger, fear, or happiness, depending on the particular environmental cues they were given.

Accessibility effects have also been important for theorizing about decision making. In particular, Kahneman and Tversky (1973) proposed that the probability of an event is judged using an availability heuristic. Specifically, people estimate the frequency of events by judging the ease with which examples come to mind. (Kahneman, 2003, later noted that the availability heuristic should have been termed the "accessibility heuristic," as it really describes the ease or fluency with which an exemplar comes to mind.) Jacoby and Dallas (1981) extended this idea to memory, suggesting that an attribution to the past is often based on the ease or relative fluency with which information comes to mind (for reviews see Jacoby et al., 1989; Kelley & Rhodes, 2002). Evidence for a relative fluency heuristic comes from work showing that manipulating ease of processing influences memory judgments. For example, in some of the original work on the fluency heuristic, Jacoby and Dallas had participants identify words presented visually for very brief durations. As would be expected if a fluency heuristic guided memory judgments, later recognition of these items was correlated with the ease with which they were identified.

The relative fluency with which information comes to mind may also guide subjective experience and attribution, as illustrated by the work of Jacoby and Whitehouse (1989). In their experiments, participants first studied a list of words and were then given a recognition test. Each recognition test trial was briefly preceded by a masked presentation of either the item to be judged (*match* trials) or an unrelated word (*mismatch* trials). By a relative fluency account, a matching prime should enhance the perceptual fluency of an item and increase the chance that it is recognized. Results were consistent with this account, as participants were significantly more likely to endorse test items on *match* trials than on *mismatch* trials, an effect that held for both previously studied and new items. However, when the prime was presented for a longer duration (such that participants were aware of its presentation), the matching effect was eliminated. Thus, when aware of the prime's presentation, enhanced fluency due to the flashed prime no longer created the subjective experience of remembering but was instead considered a feature of the test. Such data highlight the dynamic nature of attribution and subjective experience. Further evidence of this is provided by Westerman, Lloyd, and Miller (2002) who replicated Jacoby and Whitehouse's original matching effect. They also reported that when items were studied aurally visual primes had no influence on test performance, likely because visual cues contributed little to the subjective experience of remembering from an auditory presentation.

These data demonstrate that the subjective experience of information coming to mind, and not the sheer experience of the strength of a memory trace, plays a vital role in memory and memory illusions. Ideally, subjective experience should be well-calibrated, capturing instances in which low and high levels of confidence (or weak or strong impressions) are appropriate. We examine issues of calibration, including their import for aging populations, next.

MEMORY MONITORING: CALIBRATION OF SUBJECTIVE EXPERIENCE

Poor calibration of memory and confidence might reflect a deficit in monitoring the bases for confidence, leading to memory illusions based on highly accessible but incorrect information. As noted previously, false memories elicited in the DRM paradigm are often held with high levels of confidence (e.g., Anastasi et al., 2000; Roediger & McDermott, 1995). Illusions of this sort highlight extreme cases in which subjective experience may be led astray; generally, subjective experience is an accurate indicator of prior experience.

The existence of confidently held memory illusions does indicate that subjective experience can be dissociated from what is retrieved and should be examined in conjunction with accuracy rather than as the *sine qua non* of retrieval. Koriat and Goldsmith (1996) have incorporated this idea into their influential model of memory. They suggest that memory is not just the product of retrieving a latent trace, but depends on the degree to which the rememberer is sensitive to the correctness of the information they have retrieved and relies on that information to guide responding. A key element of their model holds that memory should be examined under conditions of both forced and free report. Specifically, candidate responses retrieved under conditions of forced report index the *quantity* of information available to the rememberer. However, control processes may then operate during a subsequent, free report stage (when responses can be withheld or volunteered), permitting participants to control the *accuracy* of their output. A decision to volunteer a response during free report will be a function of whether one can accurately assess the probability that a candidate response is correct (*monitoring effectiveness*) and whether one is sufficiently confident in their accuracy that it exceeds a particular criterion. Those responses that do not exceed the response criterion are withheld.

This framework is exemplified by data reported by Koriat and Goldsmith (1996, Exp. 1). In a first, forced-report phase of their experiment, participants were required to answer general knowledge questions, even if it required a guess. Each answer was then followed by a confidence judgment assessing the likelihood that the response given was correct. Results from this first phase showed that participants correctly answered approximately 47% of the questions, providing an index of the *quantity* of correct information available. Participants also demonstrated high levels of monitoring effectiveness. For example, average assessed confidence (50%) was close to the actual proportion correct (47%) and there was also a strong relationship between confidence and accuracy, as assessed by the Kruskal–Goodman gamma correlation (a common measure of the association between confidence and accuracy used in metacognition research). In a second, free-report phase of the experiment, participants were given the same questions again, but with the option to withhold their answer to any question. If participants can effectively control their memory, they should predominantly volunteer correct responses (when assessed confidence exceeds a criterion) and withhold incorrect responses (when assessed confidence is below a criterion). Results from this second phase showed that the majority of answers volunteered (76%) were, indeed, correct. That is, *accuracy* increased when participants were given the opportunity to control which responses they volunteered.

The notion that judgments are based on a response criterion is not itself novel and in fact forms one of the tenets behind analyses of recognition memory that utilize signal detection theory (SDT; Green & Swets, 1966). SDT assumes that old and new items on a recognition test comprise separate distributions that lie along a continuum of familiarity or strength. Old items will generally have greater familiarity than new items, but the distributions overlap. The rememberer sets a response criterion, calling items whose familiarity exceeds the response criterion "old" and deeming items whose level of familiarity falls below the response criterion "new". The distance between the old and new distributions (or the difference in memory strength) is assessed via measures of discriminability. Measures of discriminability in SDT are predicated on *forced-report* instructions at test. Koriat and Goldsmith's (1996) model, in contrast, allows the rememberer to control responding through the option of free report, permitting retrieval (i.e., memory) to be distinguished from the monitoring of memory. Moreover, unlike Koriat and Goldsmith's model, SDT treats memory confidence as isomorphic with memory strength. For example, confidence judgments are used to construct ROC (receiver operating characteristic) curves by assuming that higher confidence corresponds to higher memory strength.

Assumptions of redundancy between subjective experience and memory have particular difficultly coping with evidence that subjective experience is sometimes unrelated to memory accuracy. For example, Chandler (1994) reported data from experiments in which participants studied sets of pictures. Either immediately following or just prior to study, participants also viewed additional pictures, some of which were related to the studied set. Results across a number of experiments showed that studying related pictures decreased recognition accuracy for target items while increasing confidence.

Kelley and Sahakyan (2003) report a similar discrepancy between confidence and accuracy in a direct application of Koriat and Goldsmith's (1996) framework. Specifically, Kelley and Sahakyan had older and younger adults study lists of word pairs (e.g., "table–cheer," "clock–dollar"). Following study, participants were given a recall test, cued with the first word and a fragment from each studied pair. For some items, termed *deceptive items*, a semantically related competitor was easily accessible at test (e.g., "chair" in the case of "table–ch_ _r"). For other, *control items*, there were no semantically related competitors easily accessible at test (e.g., "clock–do_ _ _r"). For the test phase, participants first engaged in forced report by either recalling the item they had studied or guessing an item that fit the cue. Immediately following their response, participants made a confidence judgment, assessing the probability that their response was correct. Finally, participants decided whether or not to volunteer their response (free report). Results showed that while participants' confidence judgments closely matched the probability that a candidate response was correct for control items, participants were poorly calibrated on deceptive items, exhibiting high levels of overconfidence (cf. Koriat & Goldsmith, 1996, Exp. 2).

Further inspection of Kelley and Sahkyan's (2003) data reveal that older adults began with fewer correct candidate responses at forced report, exhibited higher levels of overconfidence than younger adults, and did not achieve the same level of accuracy at free report as younger adults, particularly for deceptive items. Such findings beg the question of whether age-related deficits in memory (see Balota, Dolan, & Duchek, 2000, for a review) may be a function of poorly calibrated subjective experience. While other aspects of metacognition, such as the prediction of future recall in paired associate learning tasks, remain largely stable with age (see Hertzog & Hultsch, 2000, for a review), older adults frequently exhibit higher confidence in false memories than young adults (e.g., Jacoby, Bishara, Hessels, & Toth, 2005). The relationship between confidence and accuracy likely hinges on the quality of information available to the rememberer and their ability to correctly monitor that information (Kelley & Sahakyan, 2003). For example, if older adults' monitoring must rely on impoverished memorial information, their subjective experience will be weakly related to memory accuracy.

The quantity of correct memorial information available and the ability to monitor that information may also comprise an important source of individual differences in memory accuracy. Rhodes and Kelley (2005) examined this issue using the same paradigm employed by Kelley and Sahakyan (2003). In addition to assessing performance on the memory test, older and younger adults were also administered a battery of tests designed to capture individual differences in executive function. Several investigators (e.g., West, 1996) have suggested that deficits in executive function, including the ability to suppress irrelevant information and control and monitor behavior, are a primary contributor to age-related and individual differences in cognition. By utilizing Koriat and Goldsmith's (1996) framework, Rhodes and Kelley could examine the influence of executive function on memory accuracy, distinguishing between the retrieval of candidate responses and the monitoring of those responses. Results from a path model showed that executive function measures were primarily related to the quantity of correct information retrieved during forced report. The quantity of correct candidate responses retrieved in turn had a strong effect on memory accuracy at free report that was mediated in part by the efficacy of monitoring, particularly for deceptive items. Thus, while the quantity of correct information retrieved at forced report was the strongest predictor of memory accuracy, the ability to monitor that information also made a significant contribution to accuracy.

Monitoring is clearly important as it is used to control responding. As noted previously, Koriat and Goldsmith's (1996) model suggests that if assessed confidence in a candidate response exceeds a certain criterion it is volunteered; otherwise, the response is withheld if assessed confidence is below the criterion. Control over memory is evident in the decision to withhold or volunteer a candidate response and varies based on demands for accuracy. For example, a person would be far more careful about what they chose to volunteer as a memory if they were testifying in a courtroom rather than conversing with friends.

Can people control responding to achieve accuracy when given the option of free report? The answer seems to be affirmative (e.g., Kelley & Sahakyan, 2003; Koriat & Goldsmith, 1996; Rhodes & Kelley, 2005; see also Goldsmith, Koriat, & Weinberg-Eliezer, 2002, for data on controlling the precision of volunteered responses). For example, participants in Kelley and Sahakyan's (2003) study were given the option to either volunteer or withhold responses produced during forced report. By using this method, one can compare the proportion of correct responses given under forced report instructions to the proportion of correct responses (out of the total number of responses volunteered) given at free report. Results from Kelley and Sahakyan's study showed that younger and older adults made, on average, a 39% gain in accuracy from forced to free report (Exp. 1). Using an identical procedure, Rhodes and Kelley (2005) likewise reported that participants made, on average, a 45% gain in accuracy from forced to free report. In both studies, this finding is qualified by the fact that older adults' gains in accuracy from forced to free report were slightly less than those of younger adults.

These data highlight the advantage of using Koriat and Goldsmith's (1996) framework, as one can distinguish between what is retrieved and the monitoring of that information in the interest of controlling memory accuracy. At times, monitoring may in fact be more influential than is assumed. For example, Rhodes and Kelley (2005) suggested that participants may sometimes engage in a form of monitoring and control prior to outputting a response at forced report, with the result that the contribution of monitoring is underestimated. As we will describe in the next section, control over memory may not only reflect a monitoring process but may involve controlling what comes to mind in the first place.

CONTROLLING MEMORY: THE ROLE OF EARLY SELECTION

Koriat and Goldsmith's (1996) model allows one to quantify the contribution of memory monitoring to the control of memory accuracy. While age differences in monitoring are sometimes evident, significant age differences in the quantity of correct responses retrieved are also apparent under conditions of forced report (e.g., Kelley & Sakhakyan, 2003). Rather than reflecting a deficit in monitoring, such data suggests that controlling memory accuracy may also involve processes that restrict what comes to mind in response to a cue. Jacoby, Kelley, and McElree (1999; cf. Burgess & Shallice, 1996) have distinguished between these possibilities, holding that control over memory can be achieved by either editing what comes to mind (a process they term *late correction*) or by using cues available such that what comes to mind immediately in response to a cue is correct (a process they term *early selection*). Thus, control over memory may be achieved not only by adjusting the criterion for volunteering a response (a *quantitative* means of monitoring to control memory) but, rather, by adjusting the kind of information that is retrieved and taken as a memory (a *qualitative* means of controlling memory). For example, a test cue may be used to reinstate prior encoding and elicit details that are likely to be indicative of prior experience rather than used to generate and evaluate a plausible response.

One way we have examined qualitatively different methods of controlling memory is through an analysis of memory for foils following a recognition test. For example, Jacoby, Shimizu, Daniels, and Rhodes (2005) had participants study two lists of words under encoding instructions that varied in the level of processing (Craik & Lockhart, 1972) required. For one list, participants indicated whether each word contained an "O" or "U" (shallow processing) and for the other list, participants judged the pleasantness of each item (deep processing). In a second phase, participants were administered separate recognition tests for each study list. For the recognition test of shallowly processed, vowel-judged items, participants were correctly informed that all "old" items had been vowel judged. Likewise, for the test of deeply processed, pleasantness-judged items, participants were correctly informed that all of the "old" items had been judged for pleasantness. As one would expect (Craik & Lockhart, 1972), recognition accuracy was far better for items from the test of deeply processed items than from the test of shallowly processed items.

Of greater importance is performance in a third phase of the experiment. Specifically, once both recognition tests had been given, participants were administered a surprise test for *new* items (i.e., foils) presented in each of the previous recognition tests. Results showed that participants were significantly more likely to recognize foils from the test of deeply processed (i.e., pleasantness-judged) items than from the test of shallowly processed (i.e., vowel-judged) items. We suggest that participants demonstrated superior memory for foils from the test of deeply processed items because they recapitulated encoding processes in order to make recognition judgments on the initial recognition test. For example, when making recognition decisions for the test of pleasantness-judged items, participants likely evaluated the pleasantness of each item. A pleasantness judgment would emphasize the semantic qualities of the items, with the consequence that when later tested on memory for foils from this test, details of their presentation would be available. For items from the vowel-judged recognition test, scrutinizing the types of vowels in each word would not be as likely to engender details that would later be diagnostic of its presentation. Thus, the manner in which participants use the cue can be elucidated by subsequent memory for foils.

We have replicated this effect a number of times (e.g., Shimizu & Jacoby, 2005) with one exception: Older adults do not exhibit differences in memory for foils (Jacoby, Shimizu, Velanova, & Rhodes, 2005). That is, unlike younger adults, older adults show no memory advantage for foils from tests of deeply processed items compared to foils from tests of shallowly processed items. One explanation is that older adults rely on the general familiarity of each item to make recognition decisions and are less likely to seek specific details of prior encoding. By not reinstating prior encoding, there is little to differentiate foils from the different tests. In the next section, we describe a dual process model of memory which suggests that older adults suffer from a deficit in consciously-controlled memory processes that likely support such early selection, and discuss a recent extension of that work.

A DUAL (AND MULTIPLE) PROCESS MODEL OF MEMORY

Jacoby (1999b) has suggested that older adults' memory deficits reflect a breakdown in controlled memory processes. This idea draws on work (see Kelley & Jacoby, 2000, for a review) examining dual process theories of memory. In its most general form, dual process theories suggest that memory judgments can be accomplished using a consciously controlled process of memory that relies on cues such as reinstating encoding context during retrieval. That process of *recollection* can be distinguished from more automatic bases for memory, in which memory judgments rely on the *accessibility* (also termed *habit* or *familiarity* in some cases) of information coming to mind. In order to distinguish between these bases for memory, one must design experiments in which the influence of recollection can be placed in opposition to that of accessibility.

Jacoby, Debner, and Hay (2001) have done so with older and younger adults using a variant of the process dissociation framework (Jacoby, 1991). Participants in Jacoby et al.'s experiment were first exposed to sets of word pairs in a training phase. Each pair was composed of a word presented next to fragmentary version of a related word (e.g., "knee–b_n_"). Participants were instructed to predict which of two associatively related words would complete the fragment and their prediction was followed by a presentation of the completion word. Across several training blocks, words were paired frequently with one response (e.g., "knee–bend") and infrequently with a different response (e.g., "knee–bone") with the training phase intended to make some pairs (e.g., "knee–bend") more accessible than others (e.g., "knee–bone"). Following this training phase, participants were given several study–test blocks. In each study block, some of the word pairs were consistent with those that had been presented most frequently during training (e.g., "knee–bend"). These *congruent* pairs may be contrasted with other study pairs (termed *incongruent* pairs) that were identical to those presented less frequently during training. Following each study list, participants were given a cued-recall test for the pairs they had just studied, cued with the first word and a fragmented version of the target (e.g., "knee–b_n_"). Participants were instructed to report the word they had studied and indicate whether they could recall specific details of its occurrence. Results showed that younger adults had higher levels of correct recall on congruent trials ($M = 0.83$) than older adults ($M = 0.73$). In addition, younger adults ($M = 0.35$) also exhibited lower levels of false recall on incongruent trials than older adults ($M = 0.44$).

Jacoby et al. (2001) were primarily interested in whether age-related deficits in memory reflected a deficit in recollection. The use of congruent and incongruent items allows for recollection to be estimated, as one can compare performance from an "in-concert" condition (congruent) to that of a condition that opposes the initial training phase (incongruent). Specifically, correct recall of a congruent item can occur either because one recollects (R) the studied item or, failing recollection (i.e., $1 - R$), because of a reliance on the accessibility (A) established by training: $P(\text{correct}|\text{congruent}) = R + A(1 - R)$. For incongruent items, false recall will occur if the item made typical by training is volunteered: $P(\text{error}|\text{incongruent}) = A(1 - R)$. Subtracting the probability of false recall on incongruent trials from the probability of correct recall on congruent trials provides an estimate of recollection (R). In turn, given an estimate of recollection, the contribution of accessibility (A) can be estimated by dividing the probability of an error on incongruent tests by $(1 - R)$.

Estimates based on these equations showed that while accessibility bias (A) did not differ between age groups $(A = 0.62$ and 0.63 for younger and older adults, respectively), estimated recollection was significantly higher for younger $(R = 0.44)$ than older $(R = 0.29)$ adults. Interestingly, participants' subjective judgments of whether they could "recall" details of prior study were strongly related to estimates of recollection. In particular, probabilities of correct subjective recall for congruent items were combined with probabilities of false subjective recall on incongruent items (using the formulas described previously) to derive estimates of subjective R. These data showed that objective and subjective estimates of memory were highly correlated $(r = .71$ for younger adults; $r = .81$ for older adults). Thus, subjective experience was closely aligned with objective estimates of performance.

Taken together, Jacoby et al. (2001) demonstrated that aging was associated with a decreased ability to recollect details of prior study and that subjective experience was strongly associated with objective measures of performance. Jacoby, Bishara, et al. (2005) have recently shown that, in addition to a deficit in recollection, older adults may be captured by misleading information, such that they forgo any attempt at recollection. The effects of misleading information are particularly insidious for older adults. For example, in one scam, a con man will overcharge an older adult for a repair with the claim that "I told you that the repair cost X, and you agreed to pay." If the older adult is captured by this information and falsely remembers specific details of the fraudulent oral contract, they will fall victim to the scam.

Jacoby, Bishara, et al. (2005) used an analog of this situation to examine the degree to which misleading information disrupts memory in older adults. Their procedure was similar to Jacoby et al.'s (2001) with the exception that just prior to a test, a word was briefly presented that was either congruent or incongruent (misleading) with what was studied. Across several experiments, older adults were significantly more likely to report an incorrect response (a false memory) after being cued with a misleading word. Along with impairments in memory accuracy, older adults' subjective reports were also disrupted by misleading primes. For example, in one experiment, older adults were 10 times more likely to claim to "remember" specific details from prior study following instances of false recall than younger adults. Results also showed that older adults were less able to exercise control over their responding than younger adults. Specifically, participants in one condition were given the option to withhold responses. While younger adults reduced their level of false recall by 41% with such free report instructions, older adults made essentially no gain in accuracy when given the option of free report.

Jacoby, Bishara, et al. (2005) fit several models to these data and found that younger adults' performance was well accounted for by a model based on parameters for recollection and accessibility, just as used by Jacoby et al. (2001). That model holds that responses may be given on the basis of recollection (R). If recollection fails (i.e., $1 - R$), participants may rely on accessibility, volunteering information which exceeds a certain accessibility threshold (AT) or, if the information does not exceed the AT, use an alternative strategy such as generating a word. However, to account for older adults' performance, an additional model parameter (termed *capture*) was necessary that allowed recollection to be completely bypassed. The capture parameter reflects the fact that misleading primes were sometimes so powerful for older adults that they neglected any attempt to remember what was studied. Such a parameter accords with data showing that older adults' false recall was accompanied by a number of "remember" responses.

This model is consistent with Jacoby et al.'s (1999) idea that cognitive control may be achieved by monitoring responses (*late correction*) or by controlling what comes to mind (*early selection*) and, further, suggests that there are two routes by which false remembering occurs. First, false remembering can occur via accessibility bias. That is, a response may come to mind because it is accessible, and is subsequently evaluated and accepted as remembered only if it is sufficiently familiar or passes a criterion (i.e., late correction). Second, as indicated by the performance of older adults, false remembering may occur when one is captured by misleading information. For older adults, a "capture" mechanism likely reflects deficits in controlling what comes to mind during retrieval (early selection; cf., Jacoby, Shimizu, Velanova, & Rhodes, 2005).

Such dual routes to false remembering also point to methods of rehabilitating memory in older adults. For example, while the majority of memory rehabilitation programs have focused on teaching older adults to use mnemonics (see Verhaeghen, Marcoen, & Gossens, 1992, for a review), rehabilitating older adults' memory may involve enhancing their ability to distinguish between correct and incorrect responses or altering processes integral to early selection, insuring that what comes to mind is accurate. We are currently undertaking a rehabilitation program with older adults using the latter method (Rhodes, Jacoby, Daniels, & Rogers, 2006). Briefly, the training centers on performance on a cued recall test in which a large proportion of test items have easily accessible but incorrect competitors, similar to the paradigm used by Jacoby et al. (2001). Participants make confidence ratings for each test response and, in one condition, they earn or lose points based on their confidence rating. For example, if a response is given a confidence rating of "5", the participant would earn five points if they were correct. However, an incorrect response would result in a deduction of five points. Results have shown that participants given feedback in this manner exhibited significant improvements in accuracy compared to a group of older adults who were not given feedback on their responses. Benefits of feedback were also evident for confidence judgments. For example, participants given feedback made a 37% gain in accuracy for items (with interfering competitors) reported at the highest level of confidence. By comparison, participants who were not given feedback made only a 2% gain in accuracy. Thus, providing older adults with feedback on their memory responses was sufficient to improve calibration. These data suggest that the poor calibration of older adults in high interference situations is open to remediation. We are currently running additional experiments with this procedure and suggest that attempts such as these to educate subjective experience are important for both theory and application (cf. Jacoby, Bjork, & Kelley, 1994).

CONCLUSIONS: ATTRIBUTION, SUBJECTIVE EXPERIENCE, AND CONTROL

In this chapter we have suggested that memory and subjective experience are the product of an attributional process through which past experience is reconstructed to fit current needs, expectations, and prior knowledge. Models such as Koriat and Goldsmith's (1996) hold that subjective experience is an important factor in the attainment of accuracy and should not be treated as synonymous with the quantity of correct information available. We concur with this assumption but also hold that control of memory is achieved not only through an editing process but may sometimes rely on using cues to bring to mind information that is veridical (Jacoby et al., 1999). Deficiencies in control of memory may characterize age-related deficits in memory along with basic deficits in the ability to use memory to recollect. In turn, subjective experience may be poorly calibrated at times in older adults if the information that comes to mind is fragmentary, vague, or simply wrong (cf. Kelley & Sahakyan, 2003).

While memory illusions are often held with high levels of confidence (e.g., Anastasi et al., 2000; Jacoby, Bishara, et al., 2005), other data demonstrate that subjective reports can be an accurate indictor of prior experience (e.g., Jacoby et al., 2001). An attributional framework provides a means of reconciling such disparate findings. That is, those details that give rise to veridical, confidently-held memories may also support illusory and, likewise confidently-held memories if the details used by the attributional process are similar in both cases. Consider the overconfidence exhibited by participants for deceptive items (e.g., "table–ch_ _r") in Kelley and Sahakyan's (2003) study. In that case, participants often mistakenly and confidently reported semantically related items (e.g., "chair" when "cheer" was studied), likely because they came to mind easily in response to the test cue (cf. Lindsay & Kelley, 1996). We suggest that this occurs because what comes to mind easily is usually correct, leading people to assume that their subjective experience is an accurate indictor of the past. Thus, information that is usually indicative of prior experience sometimes leads the rememberer astray. However, this does not suggest a breakdown in memory, in the same way that the misperception of length in the Müller–Lyer visual illusion does not suggest a serious breakdown in vision. Both are excellent examples of a normally functioning cognitive system. The challenge for the cognitive system is to understand what information is diagnostic of prior experience (cf. Kelley & Rhodes, 2002) and to use this information to control responding and achieve accuracy.

The issue of control over responding extends far beyond memory illusions and has implications in many domains. From our view, the ability to control responding in social situations involves the same modes of cognitive control as does controlling responding in a memory task. In a social setting, early selection might entail using contextual cues to constrain what comes to mind as an appropriate response. For example, a bawdy joke would be unlikely to come to mind during a formal job interview (early selection). However, if the joke did come to mind, control could operate by influencing whether or not it was volunteered (late correction). Likewise, the distinction between early selection and late correction can be applied to decision making. Klein (1998) notes that expert decision makers do not consider a host of options when working under pressure but, instead, their experience dictates that only a single option comes to mind. Early selection in that case can be contrasted with other frameworks suggesting that monitoring processes correct decisions and allow one to overcome illusions (Kahneman, 2003).

Overall, control over behavior will best be understood by examining its influence across a number of areas. Research on memory illusions has highlighted how control may go awry when easily accessed but incorrect responses come to mind (Jacoby, Bishara, et al., 2005) and how it may operate to mitigate memory illusions through control over responding (e.g., Kelley & Sahakyan, 2003) or in what comes to mind (Jacoby et al., 1999). Echoing the work of Bruner (1957), social psychology has illustrated how automatic effects in the form of accessibility influence interpretation of the present. Work on decision making (e.g., Kahneman, 2003) shows that accessibility effects influence predictions about the future. Thus, principles derived from memory illusions not only tell us something about our past, but also are equally applicable to the present and to the future.

REFERENCES

Anastasi, J. S., Rhodes, M. G., & Burns, M. C. (2000). Distinguishing between memory illusions and actual memories utilizing phenomenological measurements and explicit warnings. *American Journal of Psychology, 113*, 1–26.

Balota, D. A., Dolan, P. O., & Duchek, J. M. (2000). Memory changes in healthy older adults. In E. Tulving & F. I. M. Craik (Eds.), *The Oxford handbook of memory* (pp. 395–409). Oxford, UK: Oxford University Press.

Bartlett, F. C. (1932). *Remembering: A study in experimental and social psychology*. New York: Cambridge University Press.

Bergman, E., & Roediger, H. L. (1999). Can Bartlett's repeated reproduction experiments be replicated? *Memory and Cognition, 27*, 937–947.

Bruner, J. S. (1957). On perceptual readiness. *Psychological Review, 64*, 123–152.

Bruner, J. S., & Goodman, C. C. (1947). Value and need as organizing factors in perception. *Journal of Abnormal and Social Psychology, 42*, 33–44.

Burgess, P. W., & Shallice, T. (1996). Confabulation and the control of recollection. *Memory, 4,* 359–411.

Chandler, C. C. (1994). Studying related pictures can reduce accuracy, but increase confidence, in a modified recognition test. *Memory and Cognition, 22,* 273–280.

Craik, F. I. M., & Lockhart, R. S. (1972). Levels of processing: A framework for memory research. *Journal of Verbal Learning and Verbal Behavior, 11,* 671–684.

Deese, J. (1959). On the predication of occurrence of particular verbal intrusions in immediate recall. *Journal of Experimental Psychology, 58,* 17–22.

Goldsmith, M., Koriat, A., & Weinberg-Eliezer, A. (2002). Strategic regulation of grain size in memory reporting. *Journal of Experimental Psychology: General, 131,* 73–95.

Green, D. M., & Swets, J. A. (1966). *Signal detection theory and psychophysics.* New York: Wiley.

Greenwald, A. G. (1992). New look 3: Unconscious cognition reclaimed. *The American Psychologist, 47,* 766–779.

Hertzog, C., & Hultsch, D. F. (2000). Metacognition in adulthood and old age. In F. I. M. Craik & T. A. Salthouse (Eds.), *The handbook of aging and cognition* (pp. 417–466). Mahwah, NJ: Lawrence Erlbaum Associates, Inc.

Jacoby, L. L. (1991). A process dissociation framework: Separating intentional from automatic uses of memory. *Journal of Memory and Language, 30,* 513–541.

Jacoby, L. L. (1999a). Deceiving the elderly: Effects of accessibility bias in cued-recall performance. *Cognitive Neuropsychology, 16,* 417–436.

Jacoby, L. L. (1999b). Ironic effects of repetition: Measuring age-related differences in memory. *Journal of Experimental Psychology: Learning, Memory, and Cognition, 25,* 3–22.

Jacoby, L. L., Bishara, A. J., Hessels, S., & Toth, J. P. (2005). Aging, subjective experience, and cognitive control: Dramatic false remembering by older adults. *Journal of Experimental Psychology: General, 134,* 131–148.

Jacoby, L. L., Bjork, R. A., & Kelley, C. M. (1994). Illusions of comprehension, competence, and remembering. In D. Druckman & R. A. Bjork (Eds.), *Learning, remembering, believing: Enhancing human performance.* Washington, DC: National Academy Press.

Jacoby, L. L., & Dallas, M. (1981). On the relationship between autobiographical memory and perceptual learning. *Journal of Experimental Psychology: General, 110,* 306–340.

Jacoby, L. L., Debner, J. A., & Hay, J. F. (2001). Proactive interference, accessibility bias, and process dissociations: Valid subjective reports of memory. *Journal of Experimental Psychology: Learning, Memory, and Cognition, 27,* 686–700.

Jacoby, L. L., Kelley, C. M., & Dywan, J. (1989). Memory attributions. In H. L. Roediger & F. I. M. Craik (Eds.), *Varieties of memory and consciousness: Essays in honour of Endel Tulving* (pp. 391–422). Hillsdale, NJ: Lawrence Erlbaum Associates, Inc.

Jacoby, L. L., Kelley, C. M., & McElree, B. D. (1999). The role of cognitive control: Early selection versus late correction. In S. Chaiken & Y. Trope (Eds.), *Dual-process theories in social psychology* (pp. 383–400). New York: Guilford Press.

Jacoby, L. L., & Rhodes, M. G. (2006). False remembering in the aged. *Current Directions in Psychological Science, 15,* 49–53.

Jacoby, L. L., Shimizu, Y., Daniels, K. A., & Rhodes, M. G. (2005). Modes of cognitive control in recognition and source memory: Depth of retrieval. *Psychonomic Bulletin and Review, 12,* 852–857.

Jacoby, L. L., Shimizu, Y., Velanova, K., & Rhodes, M. G. (2005). Age differences in depth of retrieval: Memory for foils. *Journal of Memory and Language, 52,* 493–504.

Jacoby, L. L., & Whitehouse, K. (1989). An illusion of memory: False recognition influenced by unconscious perception. *Journal of Experimental Psychology: General*, *118*, 126–135.

Kahneman, D. (2003). A perspective on judgment and choice: Mapping bounded rationality. *The American Psychologist*, *58*, 697–720.

Kahneman, D., & Tversky, A. (1973). On the psychology of prediction. *Psychological Review*, *80*, 237–251.

Kelley, C. M., & Jacoby, L. L. (2000). Recollection and familiarity: Process-dissociation. In E. Tulving & F. I. M. Craik (Eds.), *The Oxford handbook of memory* (pp. 215–228). New York: Oxford University Press.

Kelley, C. M., & Rhodes, M. G. (2002). Making sense and nonsense of experience: Attributions in memory and judgment. In B. Ross (Ed.), *The psychology of learning and motivation* (pp. 293–320). New York: Academic Press.

Kelley, C. M., & Sahakyan, L. (2003). Memory, monitoring, and control in the attainment of memory accuracy. *Journal of Memory and Language*, *48*, 704–721.

Klein, G. (1998). *Sources of power: How people make decisions*. Cambridge, MA: MIT Press.

Koriat, A., & Goldsmith, M. (1996). Monitoring and control processes in the strategic regulation of memory accuracy. *Psychological Review*, *103*, 490–517.

Lindsay, D. S., Hagen, L., Read, J. D., Wade, K. A., & Garry, M. (2004). True photographs and false memories. *Psychological Science*, *15*, 149–154.

Lindsay, D. S., & Kelley, C. M. (1996). Creating illusions of familiarity in a cued recall remember/know paradigm. *Journal of Memory and Language*, *35*, 197–211.

Loftus, E. F., & Pickrell, J. E. (1995). The formation of false memories. *Psychiatric Annals*, *25*, 720–725.

Rhodes, M. G., & Anastasi, J. S. (2000). The effects of a levels-of-processing manipulation on false recall. *Psychonomic Bulletin and Review*, *7*, 158–162.

Rhodes, M. G., Jacoby, L. L., Daniels, K. A., & Rogers, C. (2006). Training calibration of confidence in older adults under conditions of interference. *Manuscript in preparation*.

Rhodes, M. G., & Kelley, C. M. (2005). Executive processes, memory accuracy, and memory monitoring: An aging and individual difference analysis. *Journal of Memory and Language*, *52*, 578–594.

Roediger, H. L. (1996). Memory illusions. *Journal of Memory and Language*, *35*, 76–100.

Roediger, H. L., III, & McDermott, K. B. (1995). Creating false memories: Remembering words not presented in lists. *Journal of Experimental Psychology: Learning, Memory, and Cognition*, *21*, 803–814.

Schacter, S. (1971). *Emotion, obesity, and crime*. New York: Academic Press.

Schacter, S., & Singer, J. (1962). Cognitive, social, and physiological determinants of emotional states. *Psychological Review*, *69*, 379–399.

Shimizu, Y., & Jacoby, L. L. (2005). Similarity-guided depth of retrieval: Constraining at the front end. *Canadian Journal of Experimental Psychology*, *59*, 17–21.

Verhaeghen, P., Marcoen, A., & Gossens, L. (1992). Improving memory performance in the aged through mnemonic training: A meta-analytic study. *Psychology and Aging*, *7*, 242–251.

West, R. L. (1996). An application of prefrontal cortex function theory to cognitive aging. *Psychological Bulletin*, *120*, 272–292.

Westerman, D. L., Lloyd, M. E., & Miller, J. K. (2002). The attribution of perceptual fluency in recognition memory: The role of expectation. *Journal of Memory and Language*, *47*, 607–617.

22

Learning from Fictional Sources

ELIZABETH J. MARSH and LISA K. FAZIO

This story begins with my (EJM) convincing Roddy to take me on as a postdoctoral fellow at Washington University, based on my dissertation on the Deese–Roediger–McDermott (DRM) memory illusion (Deese, 1959; Roediger & McDermott, 1995). As all memory researchers now know, the DRM illusion involves presenting people with a list of associated words (e.g., *bed, rest, awake, tired*, . . .) and examining false recall and false recognition of a critical lure (e.g., *sleep*) that is associated to all of the studied items (see McDermott, chapter 18, this volume). In my dissertation, I argued that a reality monitoring error (Johnson, Hashtroudi, & Lindsay, 1993) played a role in the illusion (Marsh & Bower, 2004). Although my dissertation experiments on DRM were what helped convince Roddy to take me on, I only conducted one experiment on the DRM illusion during my time in St Louis, on the role of testing in creating the illusion (Marsh, McDermott, & Roediger, 2004). Rather, almost as soon as I arrived in St Louis, I began a new line of research that combined my interests in source memory (e.g., Marsh & Bower, 1999) with my personal love of literature. Always willing to try new things, Roddy agreed I could stray from DRM to create a paradigm for studying learning from fiction.

WHY STUDY FICTION?

There are two answers to this question: one for cognitive psychologists, and one for everyone else in the world. We begin with the answer that one's seatmate on an airplane would prefer to hear. That is, people learn about the world from many different sources, including other people, newspapers, textbooks, classes, museums, and so on. While encyclopedias, nonfiction books, documentaries, and other such sources are designed to teach, learning may also result from exposure to noneducational sources that happen to contain information about the world. Fictional sources such as television sitcoms, movies, novels, short stories, and even comic strips often occur in familiar political, geographical, historical, and other contexts. As such, fiction is potentially a source of information about the world, something that educators often take advantage of as they try to motivate students to learn. In areas as varied as the Holocaust (Short, 1997), disabilities and diversity (Stark, 1986), alcoholism (Cellucci & Larsen, 1995), biology (Dubeck, Moshier, & Boss, 2004), physics (Storey, 1982), and history (Roser & Keehn, 2002), suggestions have been to made to integrate stories, poems, and songs into the classroom. Interest in these types of materials has moved from individual teachers to the level of state agencies. For example, in the fall of 2004, Maryland introduced comic books into its public school curricula to help engage students in grades K-12 (Mui, 2004). In North Carolina, state-approved texts for social studies include both a traditional textbook (*Social Studies Alive!*, 2003) and an anthology that allegedly covers the same material, albeit via biographies, stories, folk tales, tall tales, nonfiction selections, plays, poems, and songs (*Read-Aloud Anthology*, 2002).

However, fiction is not required to be accurate, and as such is also a source of *misinformation* about the world. Regardless of what you see in the movies, it is difficult to ignite gasoline with a dropped cigarette, jumping through a window should cause major lacerations, and there is no sound in space. The transcontinental railroad pulled a disappearing act in Larry McMurty's classic western novel *Lonesome Dove*, and Apple computers and boom boxes appeared in fictional time prior to their actual existence in John Updike's novel *Memories of the Ford Administration*. Such examples lead to questions about whether readers are aware of inaccuracies in fiction, how much (and when) readers rely on fiction for information about the world, and their awareness of any reliance on fiction.

In short, one's seatmate on an airplane is likely to agree that watching movies and reading novels is fun, and that such sources contain both correct and incorrect information about the world. Unless one is seated next to a psychologist, the conversation will likely soon end.

One major concern (from the point of view of a cognitive psychologist) is that there has been little formal evaluation of learning from fictional sources in educational settings. Instead of assessing long-term retention of facts, a number of studies have measured student enjoyment of the materials (Smith, 1993). However, even if students like watching movies and reading novels in school, it does not guarantee that they are good teaching tools. And the great variety of fictional materials available means that conclusions about one set of sources will not necessarily generalize to a different set of materials.

Comparisons of learning from fiction versus more traditional sources began as early as 1927, when Schaffer published data showing that children learned as much about the Industrial Revolution from a passage in standard textbook form as from an episodic narrative (e.g., a day in the life of a worker during the industrial revolution). The results of such studies are varied, in part because there are often many differences between the traditional and nontraditional materials, such as specific content, modality, and instructional technique. For example, consider a recent study that found students who had read historical fiction learned more than did members of a classroom who read a traditional textbook (Smith, 1993). Students in the historical fiction classroom not only read the materials, but also discussed them and integrated them with other activities such as role-playing, and consequently spent more time on the material than did students in the classroom using the text.

Two differences (among many) between fictional sources and more traditional materials will be considered here. First, sources such as movies, novels, and short stories tend to be in narrative form, whereas textbooks are normally expository. Second, movies, novels, and short stories are explicitly labeled fictional (although oftentimes they represent a mix of fact and fiction), whereas textbooks are explicitly labeled veridical. Both of these differences are of interest to the cognitive psychologist, and will be discussed below.

We begin with the argument that any consequences of learning from nontraditional materials versus textbooks may have nothing to do with the fact–fiction dimension, but rather the type of processing afforded by the style of the materials. This idea derives from the Material-Appropriate Processing framework (McDaniel & Einstein, 1989). That is, materials differ naturally in what kinds of processing they encourage. Expository texts (e.g., traditional textbooks) encourage item-specific processing; that is, processing propositions separately without relating them to one another. In contrast, narratives (e.g., fairy tales) encourage relational processing; that is, processing that connects propositions rather than focusing on individual items. Several elegant experiments have shown that the most effective study strategies are ones that encourage the reader to engage in a form of processing not naturally afforded by the text. For example, unscrambling randomized sentences requires subjects to connect sentences to one another; accordingly, this strategy boosts memory for expository passages, but not fairy tales, which are already encoded in a relational fashion (Einstein, McDaniel, Owen, & Coté, 1990). Thus, one answer to the question "why study fiction" is to further our understanding of the kinds of processing fiction naturally affords, with implications for study strategies to improve learning from fiction.

Second, from the perspective of a cognitive psychologist, there are theoretically interesting questions that are unique to the domain of fiction. Consider an idea dating back to Samuel Taylor Coleridge (1817/1906), who argued that reading poetry about the supernatural requires a "willing suspension of disbelief" (p. 161). That is, "poetic faith" is required to accept implausible characters, events, and ideas for the sake of enjoying a text (p. 161). Although Coleridge was a poet and not an experimental psychologist, his idea remains an interesting and controversial one that will be revisited later in this chapter. Another related concept specific to the domain of fiction is *transportation*, or involvement in a text (and is not a reference to *Star Trek*, as Roddy suggested upon first hearing the term). Typically measured by self-report, the term follows from the idea that a deeply engaged reader is mentally transported to the story world (Gerrig, 1993). Transported readers endorse scale items such as "I wanted to learn how the story ended" and "The story affected me emotionally" but *not* items like "I found my mind wandering while reading the story" (Green & Brock, 2000). The concept of transportation is clearly related to attention; the transported reader has devoted all of his or her attention to the story and none to current reality. But ideally transportation goes beyond attention, and is more similar in flavor to Tulving's notion of mental time travel (Tulving, 2002). Current research is just beginning to tackle this issue.

Both the concept "willing suspension of disbelief" and the idea of transportation exemplify a key theme: What is the relationship between the story world and the real world? Again, cheering for Han Solo or the ghostbusters might seem to require an immersion in the fictional world to the exclusion of reality. Yet there is often an overlap between the two: *Gone with the Wind* depicts the infamous war of the states, and the dictators were all too real in historical novels such as Lily Tuck's *The News from Paraguay* and Julia Alvarez's *In the Time of the Butterflies*. On the one hand, it seems the fictional world is *compartmentalized* or otherwise kept separate from reality; but an argument can also be made for *integration* between the two (see Potts & Peterson, 1985). This issue is key when studying the representation of facts learned from fiction. Integrating facts from fiction would mean they were linked to pre-existing world knowledge. In its strongest form, integrated "fictional" facts would be represented in the same form as any other world knowledge, without any link to the fictional source. On the other hand, perhaps due the low credibility of the fictional source, compartmentalized "fictional" facts would be represented in memory apart from other world knowledge. These distinctions about the ways people represent, think about, and use fictional knowledge form the background for our laboratory investigations.

HOW TO STUDY LEARNING FROM FICTION IN THE LAB

To create a laboratory analog of learning from fiction, we embedded true and false facts in stories read for a reading comprehension task in a larger study on reasoning abilities; the last experimental task was a general knowledge test. Of interest was whether students would use information from the fictional stories to answer general knowledge questions, even though they were warned against guessing on that test.

The largest challenge in this endeavor was to create fictional stories in which to embed the critical facts. Nine stories were created dealing with a wide range of topics such as a hunting trip in Alaska, an art thief, and a student's first day of medical school. The stories were each two to three single spaced pages and contained characters, dialogue, and plot. Embedded within each story were references to items from the Nelson and Narens (1980) norms. Half of the items referred to easy questions (on average 70% of the students in Nelson & Naren's study answered these questions correctly) and half referred to hard questions (15% of students in the norming study answered them correctly). The reason for manipulating fact familiarity was to see if suggestibility was limited to cases where subjects were unlikely to know enough to detect the misinformation.

In each story, the correct answer was given for a third of hard and easy critical items, an incorrect answer was given for another third and the rest of the sentences remained neutral. This structure also allowed us to counterbalance each fact so that across subjects it was read equally often in correct, neutral, and misleading formats—something impossible to do when using real novels or films. For example, a story about a school science fair contains a reference to the only breed of cat that has blue eyes. The neutral sentence states, "It also didn't help when

Billy's mother painted the contraption the same blue as their cat's eyes." The sentence is neutral because it does not imply a particular breed of cat. In contrast, the correct version of the sentence reads ". . . the same blue as their Siamese cat's eyes" and the misleading version reads ". . . the same blue as their Angora cat's eyes." In all cases, of interest would be performance on the final cued recall question, "Which breed of cat has blue eyes?" The final test contained both critical items (questions that referred to information presented in the stories) and filler questions. Participants were warned not to guess and were able to skip any questions for which they did not know the answer. A fuller description of these materials can be found in Marsh (2004) and an additional sample is included in the Appendix of this chapter.

Story reading affected performance on the general knowledge test even though participants were warned against guessing and had the option to skip questions (Marsh, Meade, & Roediger, 2003). When participants had read the correct answer to a question in one of the stories, they were more likely to answer the question correctly (e.g., *Siamese*) than participants who had read a neutral version of the same fact. When participants read misinformation, they were less likely to answer the question correctly than if they had read a neutral frame (see Figure 22.1). Put another way, subjects who read "*Angora*" in the story about the science fair were less likely to answer "Which breed of cat has blue eyes?" with "*Siamese*" than were subjects who read a neutral reference to a cat. Because misled subjects performed worse than baseline, we can conclude that in at least some instances, subjects changed their correct beliefs to match the misinformation.

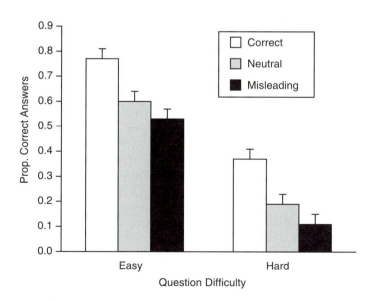

FIGURE 22.1   The effect of reading correct, neutral, and misleading facts on proportion of questions correctly answered on the final general knowledge test (cued recall format). Easy questions are on the left and hard questions are on the right (data from Marsh et al., 2003, Exp. 2).

Effects of misinformation were not isolated to instances where subjects did not know the correct answer.

A robust misinformation effect occurred on the final test: When people had read the misinformation in the stories, they were likely to use that misinformation to answer questions on the final test. These data are shown in Figure 22.2. Misinformation production was defined as producing the specific incorrect answer (e.g., *Angora*) that was presented in the story, and this dependent measure did *not* include production of other wrong answers (e.g., *Persian*). Because the misinformation lures were plausible answers, subjects who had read the correct or neutral versions of a fact did occasionally produce the misinformation answer at test (as indicated by the white and gray bars in Figure 22.2). This baseline production of the misinformation was low, and increased dramatically when subjects read misinformation in the stories (as indicated by the black bars in Figure 22.2). The misinformation effect was robust even when the errors contradicted better-known facts about the world, a surprising finding since blatantly contradictory misinformation in the Loftus eyewitness paradigm reduces suggestibility (Loftus, 1979). Furthermore, the misinformation effect *increased* when subjects had read the stories twice rather than once, even though a second story reading allowed readers a second chance to catch the errors (Marsh et al., 2003). The end result was a suggestibility effect much larger than is often observed in misinformation paradigms. Intriguing as this may be to the cognitive psychologist, it is also interesting to the layperson—a good thing, since the second author of this

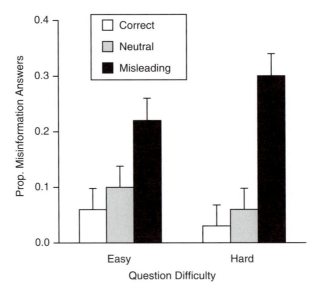

FIGURE 22.2 The effect of reading correct, neutral, and misleading facts on proportion of questions answered with target misinformation on the final general knowledge test (cued recall format). Note that misinformation is defined as the specific wrong answer presented in the text, rather than any wrong answer. Easy questions are on the left and hard questions are on the right (data from Marsh et al., 2003, Exp. 2).

chapter (LKF) happened to participate in one of the original experiments when she was a freshman at Washington University. These puzzling results motivated her interest in cognitive psychology and led her to work in the Roediger lab before going on to graduate school at Duke University.

CAN THE ILLUSION BE AVOIDED?

During our time in the Roediger lab, one common theme was to attempt to reduce memory errors via warnings. For example, Dave Gallo showed that a warning given *before* a DRM list reduced false memory, although it was much less effective when given after study (Gallo, Roediger, & McDermott, 2001). In her dissertation, Michelle Meade examined if warnings could reduce the negative effects of forced recall and collaboration (Meade & Roediger, 2006; see also Meade & Roediger, 2002, for another warning study done in this time-frame). In this context, a fiction study was run in which suggestibility in two experimental groups was compared to a control; one experimental group was warned against fiction's errors *before* story-reading and the other was warned *after* reading and immediately before the final general knowledge test.

Surprisingly, warnings did nothing to reduce reproduction of fiction's errors, even when given prior to story reading. In addition to differing from Dave Gallo and Michelle Meade's work, this contrasts with work on other memory errors, such as the eyewitness misinformation paradigm (e.g., Greene, Flynn, & Loftus, 1982) and the false fame effect (Multhaup, 1995). We did find a main effect of warning: Subjects were more conservative when they had been warned, producing fewer errors overall, but they weren't able to selectively edit out the story's errors (Marsh & Fazio, in press).

EXPLAINING THE ILLUSION: PROBLEMS WITH CRITICAL READING

Why would warnings given before study aid participants in the DRM and eye-witness paradigms, but not when they were learning from fiction? A major difference is that the errors in the fiction paradigm contradict pre-experimental knowledge about the world, rather than a recently experienced episode. When we turn instead to the literature on semantic illusions, the data are more similar to that observed in the fiction paradigm (and less like the effects observed in other false memory paradigms). For example, readers have great difficulty in noticing the problem with the sentence "*Moses took two animals of each kind on the Ark*" (Erickson & Mattson, 1981).

The partial matching hypothesis has been proposed to explain why readers fail to notice the error in the text (it was Noah, not Moses, who boarded the ark). The idea is that if the error in the text is semantically related to the correct answer, then the system may not notice the error (Kamas, Reder, & Ayers, 1996; Reder & Kusbit, 1991). It is not an encoding failure; the entire sentence is encoded into memory. It is also not a retrieval failure; all of the relevant information is retrieved from semantic memory. The failure comes when the person compares what they read to what they retrieved from semantic memory. He or she fails to notice the discrepancy between the encoded sentence and the recalled information.

Ninety years ago, Edward Thorndike discussed a similar comprehension failure (1917). In his paper "Reading as Reasoning: A study of mistakes in paragraph reading," Thorndike proposed that reading is not a simple passive action, but rather is a complex and active process similar to reasoning. Thorndike suggested that people may experience difficulties comprehending because of a "failure to treat the ideas produced by the reading as provisional, and so to inspect and welcome or reject them as they appear" (p. 327). That is, people may accept what they read as the truth without comparing it to their knowledge about the world.

The illusion can also be related to an idea originally proposed by the philosopher Spinoza (1677/1982). Spinoza believed that any statement had to be accepted as true before it could be evaluated and proven false. So when reading the Appendix sentence "*And the winner of that contest will get to go to the international science fair in St Petersburg, the capital of Russia!*" as part of the comprehension process, you would first believe St Petersburg to be the capital of Russia. Only once you understood the sentence would you evaluate it and decide that it was false. Recent experimental support for Spinoza's ideas has come from Gilbert and colleagues (Gilbert, 1991; Gilbert, Tafarodi, & Malone, 1993), who showed that people under cognitive load were biased to regard statements as true.

Evaluating information as false may be even more difficult for the story-reader. An active reader must devote cognitive resources to applying schemas to story characters and building and updating situation models of the story (e.g., Bower & Morrow, 1990; Johnson-Laird, 1983), meaning fewer resources can be allocated to evaluating and disbelieving background information. Another potential problem is Coleridge's (1817/1906) hypothesis of a "willing suspension of disbelief" (p. 6), suggesting that readers process fiction differently so that implausible events and ideas do not diminish enjoyment of a text. Although the idea of a "special mode" for fiction processing is less popular today (see Gerrig, 1993) several studies do suggest that one's general knowledge is less accessible during story reading. That is, even if disbelief is not *willingly* suspended, reading a fictional narrative may interfere with retrieval of facts from semantic memory. For example, readers were slower to verify the well-known fact that Abraham Lincoln was assassinated when reading a narrative that suggested Lincoln was late to the theater on the fatal night (Gerrig, 1989). Similarly, more involved readers (as measured on a self-report transportation scale) were less likely to indicate that parts of a narrative "rung false" to them (Green & Brock, 2000).

In our own research, we have found detecting errors in stories to be much more difficult than we expected (Marsh & Fazio, in press). In one study, participants read short stories one sentence at a time on the computer; stories contained both correct and incorrect facts. Participants in the detect condition were told to press an "error" key whenever there were one or more errors in a sentence. For sentences that contained factual inaccuracies, participants pressed the "error" key only 32% of the time. While 32% is above the rate of keypresses to sentences that did *not* contain errors (a false alarm rate of 26%), it is hardly an impressive error detection rate. Based on the Nelson and Narens (1980) norms, participants should be able to answer 65% of the questions correctly in *cued recall* format—and likely more on a recognition test. Thus, the 32% detection rate is much lower than what subjects should be able to recognize.

In summary, we believe difficulties during story reading play an important role in learning false facts from fiction. Readers have no trouble learning information from the stories—but they appear to have a problem in evaluating the veridicality of the information they are learning.

EXPLAINING THE ILLUSION: THE ROLE OF SOURCE MONITORING

Source monitoring problems have been implicated in a number of memory errors. That is, when making old/new recognition judgments or recalling events, subjects have a tendency to call items "old" without necessarily discriminating among old items from different sources. This is problematic when the goal is to remember what one actually saw or heard—things imagined, or seen or heard later, are not functionally the same kind of old items.

Some memory errors are caused by *source amnesia*—that is, subjects simply do not remember the source of their memories (Schacter, Harbluck, & McLachlan, 1984). Source amnesia appears to play an important role when information comes from a low credibility source, because if subjects remembered the low credibility source they would be likely to avoid relying on it. For example, in variants of the eyewitness postevent information procedure, participants are less suggestible when the misinformation comes from a less credible source such as a naïve interviewer (Smith & Ellsworth, 1987) or a defense lawyer (Dodd & Bradshaw, 1980). Reliance on low credibility sources often comes after a delay, when the source is no longer remembered, as in the classic sleeper effect (Hovland, Janis, & Kelley, 1953; Hovland, Lumsdaine, & Sheffield, 1949). That is, communications from a low credibility source have little impact on participants' attitudes initially, but under the right conditions this pattern reverses over time as the source is forgotten (Gillig & Greenwald, 1974). A similar effect happens in the eyewitness postevent information paradigm: Misinformation from low credibility sources is ignored at short delays, but after a longer delay it affects the subjects' memories (Underwood & Pezdek, 1998).

However, source amnesia cannot explain the data observed in the fiction paradigm. When subjects were queried about whether or not their answers had appeared in the stories, they were excellent at knowing they had read the answers in the story. In addition, delay reduced the illusion rather than increasing it, even though the delay likely reduced source memory (Marsh et al., 2003).

Nor is suggestibility in the fiction paradigm reduced by instructions to monitor source at test, even though source monitoring tests have reduced memory errors in other paradigms. Source monitoring instructions lead to less suggestibility in the eyewitness postevent information paradigm (e.g., Lindsay & Johnson, 1989), in laboratory simulations of unconscious plagiarism (Marsh, Landau, & Hicks, 1997), in situations where the familiarity of a name is inappropriately attributed to fame (Multhaup, 1995), and in the DRM paradigm (Multhaup & Conner, 2002). We manipulated the timing of source monitoring instructions (before or after producing answers to the general knowledge questions), with no consequences for behavior (Marsh et al., 2003, Exp. 2). If drawing attention to source were key, we would have expected that online monitoring of source would have reduced suggestibility compared to a condition in which subjects went back through their tests and made post hoc source decisions. This was not the case.

Examinations of aging effects also highlight the differences between the fiction paradigm and other false memory paradigms. As shown in Figure 22.3, reading stories like the one in the Appendix yielded the largest misinformation effects in young adults, followed by healthy older adults, then older adults with early stage dementia (Marsh et al., 2005). Suggestibility in this paradigm *decreases* with age—the exact opposite of what is typically observed in the eyewitness misinformation paradigm (Multhaup, de Leonardis, & Johnson, 1999), the DRM paradigm (Balota et al., 1999; Kensinger & Schacter, 1999; Norman & Schacter, 1997), and the false fame paradigm (Dywan & Jacoby, 1990). In these paradigms, older adults' problems are linked to their difficulties with source monitoring (Ferguson, Hashtroudi, & Johnson, 1992), likely because of age-related declines in frontal functioning (Glisky, Rubin, & Davidson, 2001). Marsh et al. (2005) did observe standard age differences in source memory—when asked whether or not the facts

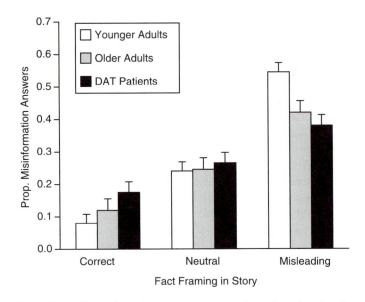

FIGURE 22.3 The effect of reading correct, neutral, and misleading facts on proportion of general knowledge questions answered with misinformation answers, for younger adults, older adults, and early stage dementia patients (DAT = dementia of Alzheimer's type). Note that misinformation is defined as the specific wrong answer presented in the text, rather than any wrong answer (data from Marsh, Balota, & Roediger, 2005, Exp. 2).

had been read in the stories, performance was best in the young adult group, then the healthy older adults, then the early-stage DAT patients—but what is critical is that source monitoring abilities in this study were opposite to suggestibility, meaning that a source monitoring deficit was not responsible for suggestibility.

Data from a second source judgment (made by college students in another experiment) provided an important insight into subjects' suggestibility: Key was subjects' reports of whether or not each answer was part of one's general knowledge (with general knowledge carefully defined as pre-experimental knowledge, things known at least a day before the experiment). After answering a question on the general world knowledge test, subjects made two judgments: First, they marked whether or not the answer was one that they had read in the story, and second they indicated whether or not they had known the answer prior to the experiment. It is important to note that each question was answered separately; that is, subjects could answer both questions affirmatively (meaning they remembered reading the answer in the story *and* believed that they had known the fact prior to the experimental session). We noted earlier in the chapter that subjects were good at knowing that they had read the answers in the stories. What is important here is that subjects tended to say that they knew the answers before entering the experiment, even the misinformation answers (Marsh et al., 2003). Figure 22.4 shows that when subjects read the misinformation in the stories, they produced those wrong answers on the final test *and* stated that they had known the incorrect answers before coming in for the experiment. The subjects also knew many of these facts had been embedded in the stories, but attributed their initial learning to outside of the experiment. While prior knowledge is a possible explanation for correct answers, it is highly unlikely for the misinformation answers (base-rate production of target misinformation in the neutral condition was low across experiments). Reading errors in short stories led to a false belief that one knew the errors prior to entering the experiment, similar to hindsight biases (Fischoff, 1977), false fame effects (Jacoby, Kelley, Brown, & Jasechko, 1989), illusory confidence (Kelley & Lindsay, 1993), and illusory truth effects (Begg, Robertson, Gruppusop, Anas, & Needham, 1996; Hasher, Goldstein, & Toppine, 1977). In these other paradigms, subjects also fail to correctly attribute recently acquired familiarity to an experimental source (see Jacoby, Kelley, & Dywan, 1989, for a description of the attributional account of memory). With a hindsight bias, subjects misattribute recent feedback about an answer to their own prior knowledge; in the false fame paradigm, experimentally-induced familiarity (in the absence of recollection) is misinterpreted as fame; in the illusory confidence paradigm, recent (isolated) exposure to answers speeds later retrieval of and judged confidence in those answers; in the illusory truth effect, the familiarity of a previously presented fact is interpreted as increased truthfulness. Similarly, our readers misattributed the familiarity of the misinformation to their previous knowledge, while acknowledging they had also read it in the stories.

In summary, source monitoring does play a role in learning from fiction. However, the problem is not in remembering the story source. Rather, the problem is that story reading boosts the familiarity of facts (true or false), and this familiarity is misattributed to prior knowledge.

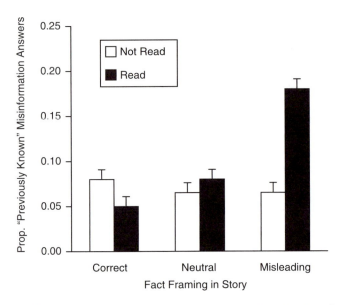

FIGURE 22.4   The effect of reading correct, neutral, and misleading facts on proportion of questions that were answered with misinformation and the misinformation answer was said to be known before the experiment. Note that misinformation is defined as the specific wrong answer presented in the text, rather than any wrong answer (data from Marsh et al., 2003, Exp. 2).

CONCLUSIONS

Like many laboratory tasks that model complex real-world behaviors, performance in the fiction paradigm is not driven by a single mechanism. First, during story reading, multiple problems may to lead to the learning of false facts. The reader may *not* have information stored in long-term memory to contradict a false fact, or transportation ("mental travel") into the story may reduce access to the knowledge needed to contradict the error. Even if the correct information is retrieved, the reader may fail to note the discrepancy between what they just read and what they already know—especially if the correct and incorrect information are conceptually related (as they are in our paradigm). An additional problem can arise during general knowledge testing. While suggestibility in this paradigm is not driven by source amnesia, a different kind of source error is involved: Subjects misattribute the familiarity of false facts to prior knowledge.

While the fiction paradigm appears related to the eyewitness misinformation paradigm, the similarities are procedural rather than in mechanisms of suggestibility. While it is true that both paradigms measure the effects of misinformation exposure on later test performance, it is important to note that standard manipulations have different effects on suggestibility in the two paradigms. Pre-encoding warnings reduce suggestibility in the eyewitness (Greene et al., 1982) but not the fiction paradigm (Marsh & Fazio, in press). Forgetting of the misinformation source appears more important for eyewitness suggestibility (Underwood & Pezdek, 1998) than in learning false facts from fiction (Marsh et al., 2003). Similarly, instructions to monitor source reduce errors in the eyewitness misinformation paradigm (Lindsay & Johnson, 1989), but not in the fiction paradigm (Marsh et al., 2003). Finally, age is positively associated with suggestibility in the eyewitness paradigm (Multhaup et al., 1999), but negatively associated with learning false facts from stories (Marsh et al., 2005).

While we are slowly unraveling the various factors involved in learning false-hoods from fiction, many questions remain. Because fictional and expository texts naturally differ in many ways, it has been difficult to disentangle the key factors. Put another way, are fiction readers suggestible because fiction tends to be in a narrative form and is transporting—two characteristics that may also describe certain kinds of nonfiction texts (albeit less frequently than fiction)? Or is there something special about fiction, whereby knowing that a story is fictional increases transportation and reduces monitoring and access to related world knowledge? Definitive answers to these questions require further research, but we now have the tools to further our investigations—in large part due to Roddy's thoughtful advice to begin with a simple and controlled study and build upon it. One of Roddy's many talents is creating easy-to-manipulate controlled paradigms that capture real-world behaviors, such as false memories (Roediger & McDermott, 1995) and imagination inflation (Goff & Roediger, 1998), and we are grateful to have had the chance to learn from him.

APPENDIX

Excerpt from "The Inventor" and the corresponding questions on the final general knowledge test. In this sample, critical facts appear in italics, with the first reference being correct, the second neutral, and the third misleading. *xxxx* is a placeholder and means no words need be added to create the neutral version.

It was a crisp fall day, Billy was ten years old and in Ms. Pringle's fifth grade class. The day began as a normal Friday—everyone was talking about their weekend plans, and planning their costumes for the upcoming Halloween parties. But everything changed for Billy when Ms. Pringle made her announcement:

"Boys and girls! Your attention please! I have exciting news." She paused, waiting for the students' full attention. "I'm happy to announce that this year's science fair will be held just three short weeks from today." She held up her hand to stop the groans from the children. "Now class, you know this can be fun. To help motivate you, we have a special prize this year—the winner of the science fair will win a trip to the national contest, which will be held in *Dover / xxxx / Wilmington*, the capital of Delaware. And the winner of that contest will get to go to the international science fair in *Moscow / xxxx / St Petersburg*, the capital of Russia!"

Sample General Knowledge Questions:

What is the capital of Delaware?
What is the capital of Russia?

REFERENCES

Balota, D. A., Cortese, M. J., Ducheck, J. M., Adams, D., Roediger, H. L., III, McDermott, K. B., et al. (1999). Veridical and false memories in healthy older adults and in dementia of the alzheimer's type. *Cognitive Neuropsychology, 16,* 361–384.

Begg, I. M., Robertson, R. K., Gruppusop, V., Anas, A., & Needham, D. R. (1996). The illusory-knowledge effect. *Journal of Memory and Language, 35,* 410–433.

Bower, G. H., & Morrow, D. G. (1990). Mental models in narrative comprehension. *Science, 247,* 44–48.

Cellucci, T., & Larsen, R. B. (1995). Alcohol education via American literature. *Journal of Alcohol and Drug Education, 40,* 65–73.

Coleridge, S. T. (1906). *Biographia literaria.* London: J. M. Dent & Sons. (Original work published 1817)

Deese, J. (1959). On the prediction of occurrence of particular verbal intrusions in immediate recall. *Journal of Experimental Psychology, 58,* 17–22.

Dodd, D. H., & Bradshaw, J. M. (1980). Leading questions and memory: Pragmatic constraints. *Journal of Verbal Learning and Verbal Behavior, 19,* 695–704.

Dubeck, L. W., Moshier, S. E., & Boss, J. E. (2004). *Fantastic voyages: Learning science through science fiction films.* New York: Springer.

Dywan, J., & Jacoby, L. L. (1990). Effects of aging on source monitoring: Differences in susceptibility to false fame. *Psychology and Aging, 5,* 379–387.

Einstein, G. O., McDaniel, M. A., Owen, P. D., & Coté, N. C. (1990). Encoding and recall of texts: The importance of material appropriate processing. *Journal of Memory and Language, 29,* 566–581.

Erickson, T. D., & Mattson, M. E. (1981). From words to meaning: A semantic illusion. *Journal of Verbal Learning and Verbal Behavior, 20,* 540–551.

Ferguson, S. A., Hashtroudi, S., & Johnson, M. K. (1992). Age differences in using source-relevant cues. *Psychology and Aging, 7,* 443–452.

Fischoff, B. (1977). Perceived informativeness of facts. *Journal of Experimental Psychology: Human Perception and Performance, 3,* 349–358.

Gallo, D. A., Roediger, H. L., III, & McDermott, K. B. (2001). Associative false recognition occurs without strategic criterion shifts. *Psychonomic Bulletin and Review, 8,* 579–586.

Gerrig, R. J. (1989). Suspense in the absence of uncertainty. *Journal of Memory and Language, 28,* 633–648.

Gerrig, R. J. (1993). *Experiencing narrative worlds: On the psychological activities of reading.* New Haven, CT: Yale University.

Gilbert, D. T. (1991). How mental systems believe. *The American Psychologist, 46,* 107–119.

Gilbert, D. T., Tafarodi, R. W., & Malone, P. S. (1993). You can't not believe everything you read. *Journal of Personality and Social Psychology, 65,* 221–233.

Gillig, P. M., & Greenwald, A. G. (1974). Is it time to lay the sleeper effect to rest? *Journal of Personality and Social Psychology, 29,* 132–139.

Glisky, E. L., Rubin, S. R., & Davidson, P. S. (2001). Source memory in older adults: An encoding or retrieval problem? *Journal of Experimental Psychology: Learning, Memory, and Cognition, 27*, 1131–1146.

Goff, L. M., & Roediger, H. L., III. (1998). Imagination inflation for action events: Repeated imaginings lead to illusory recollections. *Memory and Cognition, 26*, 20–33.

Green, M. C., & Brock, T. C. (2000). The role of transportation in the persuasiveness of public narratives. *Journal of Personality and Social Psychology, 79*, 701–721.

Greene, E., Flynn, M. S., & Loftus, E. F. (1982). Inducing resistance to misleading information. *Journal of Verbal Learning and Verbal Behavior, 21*, 207–219.

Hasher, L., Goldstein, D., & Toppine, T. (1977). Frequency and the conference of referential validity. *Journal of Verbal Learning and Verbal Behavior, 16*, 107–112.

Hovland, C. I., Janis, I. L., & Kelley, H. H. (1953). *Communication and persuasion: Psychological studies of opinion change.* New Haven, CT: Yale University Press.

Hovland, C. I., Lumsdaine, A. A., & Sheffield, F. D. (1949). *Experiments on mass communication.* Princeton, NJ: Princeton University Press.

Jacoby, L. L., Kelley, C., Brown, J., & Jasechko, J. (1989). Becoming famous overnight: Limits on the ability to avoid unconscious influences of the past. *Journal of Personality and Social Psychology, 56*, 326–338.

Jacoby, L. L., Kelley, C. M., & Dywan, J. (1989). Memory attributions. In F. I. M. Craik & H. L. Roediger, III (Eds.), *Varieties of memory and consciousness: Essays in honour of Endel Tulving* (pp. 391–422). Hillsdale, NJ: Lawrence Erlbaum Associates, Inc.

Johnson, M. K., Hashtroudi, S., & Lindsay, D. S. (1993). Source monitoring. *Psychological Bulletin, 114*, 3–28.

Johnson-Laird, P. N. (1983). *Mental models.* Cambridge, MA: Harvard University Press.

Kamas, E. N., Reder, L. M., & Ayers, M. S. (1996). Partial matching in the Moses illusion: Response bias not sensitivity. *Memory and Cognition, 24*, 687–699.

Kelley, C. M., & Lindsay, D. S. (1993). Remembering mistaken for knowing: Ease of retrieval as a basis for confidence in answers to general knowledge questions. *Journal of Memory and Language, 32*, 1–24.

Kensinger, E. A., & Schacter, D. L. (1999). When true memories suppress false memories: Effects of aging. *Cognitive Neuropsychology, 16*, 399–415.

Lindsay, D. S., & Johnson, M. K. (1989). The eyewitness suggestibility effect and memory for source. *Memory and Cognition, 17*, 349–358.

Loftus, E. F. (1979). Reactions to blatantly contradictory information. *Memory and Cognition, 7*, 368–374.

Marsh, E. J. (2004). Story stimuli for creating false beliefs about the world. *Behavior Research Methods, Instruments, and Computers, 36*, 650–655.

Marsh, E. J., Balota, D. A., & Roediger, H. L., III. (2005). Learning facts from fiction: Effects of healthy aging and dementia of the Alzheimer type. *Neuropsychology, 19*, 115–129.

Marsh, E. J., & Bower, G. H. (1999). Applied aspects of source monitoring. *Cognitive Technology, 4*, 4–17.

Marsh, E. J., & Bower, G. H. (2004). The role of rehearsal and generation in false memory creation. *Memory, 12*, 748–761.

Marsh, E. J., & Fazio, L. K. (in press). Learning errors from fiction: Difficulties in reducing reliance on fictional stories. *Memory and Cognition.*

Marsh, E. J., McDermott, K. B., & Roediger, H. L., III. (2004). Does test-induced priming play a role in the creation of false memories? *Memory, 12*, 44–55.

Marsh, E. J., Meade, M. L., & Roediger, H. L. (2003). Learning facts from fiction. *Journal of Memory and Language, 49*, 519–536.

Marsh, R. L., Landau, J. D., & Hicks, J. L. (1997). Contributions of inadequate source monitoring to unconscious plagiarism during idea generation. *Journal of Experimental Psychology: Learning, Memory, and Cognition, 23,* 886–897.

McDaniel, M. A., & Einstein, G. O. (1989). Material-appropriate processing: A contextualist approach to reading and studying strategies. *Educational Psychology Review, 1,* 113–145.

Meade, M. L., & Roediger, H. L. (2002). Explorations in the social contagion of memory. *Memory and Cognition, 30,* 995–1009.

Meade, M. L., & Roediger, H. L., III. (2006). The effect of forced recall on illusory recollection in younger and older adults. *American Journal of Psychology, 119,* 433–462.

Mui, Y. Q. (2004, December 13). Schools turn to comics as trial balloon. *The Washington Post,* p. B01.

Multhaup, K. S. (1995). Aging, source, and decision criteria: When false fame errors do and do not occur. *Psychology and Aging, 10,* 492–497.

Multhaup, K. S., & Conner, C. A. (2002). The effects of considering nonlist sources on the Deese-Roediger-McDermott memory illusion. *Journal of Memory and Language, 47,* 214–228.

Multhaup, K. S., de Leonardis, D. M., & Johnson, M. K. (1999). Source memory and eyewitness suggestibility in older adults. *Journal of General Psychology, 126,* 74–84.

Nelson, T. O., & Narens, L. (1980). Norms of 300 general-information questions: Accuracy of recall, latency of recall, and feeling-of-knowledge ratings. *Journal of Verbal Learning and Verbal Behavior, 19,* 338–368.

Norman, K. A., & Schacter, D. L. (1997). False recognition in younger and older adults: Exploring the characteristics of illusory memories. *Memory and Cognition, 25,* 838–848.

Potts, G. R., & Peterson, S. B. (1985). Incorporation versus compartmentalization in memory for discourse. *Journal of Memory and Language, 24,* 107–118.

Read-aloud anthology. (2002). New York: Macmillan/McGraw-Hill.

Reder, L. M., & Kusbit, G. W. (1991). Locus of the Moses illusion: Imperfect encoding, retrieval, or match? *Journal of Memory and Language, 30,* 385–406.

Roediger, H. L., III, & McDermott, K. B. (1995). Creating false memories: Remembering words not presented in lists. *Journal of Experimental Psychology: Learning, Memory, and Cognition, 21,* 803–814.

Roser, N., & Keehn, S. (2002). Fostering thought, talk, and inquiry: Linking literature and social studies. *The Reading Teacher, 55,* 416–426.

Schacter, D. L., Harbluck, J. L., & McLachlan, D. R. (1984). Retrieval without recollection: An experimental analysis of source amnesia. *Journal of Verbal Learning and Verbal Behavior, 23,* 593–611.

Schaffer, L. S. (1927). A learning experiment in the social studies. *Journal of Educational Psychology, 18,* 557–591.

Short, G. (1997). Learning through literature: Historical fiction, autobiography, and the holocaust. *Children's Literature in Education, 28,* 179–190.

Smith, J. A. (1993). Content learning: A third reason for using literature in teaching reading. *Reading, Research, and Instruction, 32,* 64–71.

Smith, V. L., & Ellsworth, P. C. (1987). The social psychology of eyewitness accuracy: Misleading questions and communicator expertise. *Journal of Applied Psychology, 72,* 294–300.

Social studies alive! (2003). Palo Alto, CA: Teachers' Curriculum Institute.

Spinoza, B. (1982). *The ethics and selected letters* (S. Feldman, Ed. & S. Shirley, Trans.). Indianapolis, IN: Hackett. (Original work published 1677)

Stark, L. S. (1986). Understanding learning disabilities through fiction. *School Library Journal, 32*, 30–31.

Storey, D. C. (1982). Reading in the content areas: Fictionalized biographies and diaries for social scientists. *Reading Teacher, 35*, 796–798.

Thorndike, E. L. (1917). Reading as reasoning: A study of mistakes in paragraph reading. *Journal of Educational Psychology, 8*, 323–332.

Tulving, E. (2002). Chronesthesia: Conscious awareness of subjective time. In R. T. Knight & D. T. Stuss (Eds.), *Principles of frontal lobe function* (pp. 311–325). London: Oxford University Press.

Underwood, J., & Pezdek, K. (1998). Memory suggestibility as an example of the sleeper effect. *Psychonomic Bulletin and Review, 5*, 449–453.

23

Memory Distortion: From Misinformation to Rich False Memory

ELIZABETH F. LOFTUS and LARRY CAHILL

INTRODUCTION

*F*alse Memories became a hot topic for cognitive psychologists to study in the 1990s. Sustained interest in false memories was spurred, at least partly, by the thousands of contested cases in which people became convinced that they had been abused as children by someone close to them. Sometimes the "new-found memories" were so unusual and unlikely (e.g., memories of years of satanic ritual abuse or repeated alien abduction) that they defied understanding. How could normal, nonpathological people come to believe so strongly that such things had happened to them? Researchers became enamored of paradigms designed to inform us about how people develop false beliefs and memories. Some paradigms involved simple false memories (e.g., remembering that certain words had been recently presented when they had not). Other paradigms involved more complex false memories (e.g., remembering that there was broken glass at an accident scene when there wasn't any). And yet other paradigms involved very rich false memories (e.g., remembering that one was a victim of a vicious animal attack as a child).

In this chapter, we tell part of the false memory story of the last 30 years. We concentrate on the more complex false memories; the studies that show misinformation can distort memory and those that show that very rich false memories can be planted. Roediger is best known for his work on the simple false memories (e.g., the "sleep" studies), but, as we shall show, he has also made important contributions to literature on complex false beliefs and memories.

MISINFORMATION CAN DISTORT MEMORY

The Misinformation Effect

One line of relevant research into memory distortion can be traced back to the early 1970s when the studies on the "misinformation effect" began in earnest (Loftus). These studies began with a simple observation: When people witness an event and are later exposed to new and misleading information about that event, their recollections often become distorted. The misinformation is sometimes incorporated into leading questions, or sometimes communicated through the observations of another individual. In either case, it can invade the mind, like a Trojan horse, precisely because it is so subtly done that it is not detected.

The kinds of studies that Loftus and other investigators conducted to show how memory can become skewed when people are fed misinformation used a simple procedure. Subjects first see a complex event, such as a simulated auto-mobile accident. Next, half the subjects receive misleading information about the accident; the others get no misinformation. Finally, all subjects try to remember the original accident. In one actual study using this paradigm, subjects saw an accident and later some of them received misinformation about the sign used to control traffic. The misled subjects got the false suggestion that the stop sign that they had actually seen was a yield sign. When asked later what kind of traffic sign they remembered seeing at the intersection, those who had been given the false suggestion were more likely to adopt it as their memory, and now claim that they had seen a yield sign. Those who had not received the phony information had much more accurate memories.

By now hundreds of experiments document memory distortion induced by exposure to misinformation. In these studies people have recalled not only stop signs as yield signs, but they have also recalled nonexistent broken glass and tape recorders, a blue vehicle used in a crime as white, Minnie Mouse when they really saw Mickey Mouse, and even something as large and conspicuous as a barn in a bucolic scene that contained no buildings anywhere. Taken together, these studies show that misinformation can change an individual's recollection in predictable, and sometimes very powerful, ways. Misinformation has the potential for invading our memories when we talk to other people, when we are interrogated in a sug-gestive fashion, or when we see biased media coverage about some event that we may have experienced ourselves. After more than two decades exploring the power of misinformation, we have learned a great deal about the conditions that make people especially susceptible to its damaging influence. We have learned, for example, that memories are more easily modified when the passage of time allows the original memory to fade. Those faded, weakened memories become particu-larly vulnerable to outside contamination. By some accounts, memory distortions are supposed to become more resistant to interference as they age (see Wixted 2004, 2005), but here we are seeing an example of distortions becoming more susceptible to contamination as they age. Generally this finding that older memor-ies are more susceptible to distortion has been discussed by misinformation theor-ists as being because the decay leads to an increased likelihood that subjects will detect a discrepancy between the misinformation as they process it and the memory they have previously stored.

Research on the misinformation effect continues to thrive today, as new questions are asked. So we have also learned that there are individual differences in susceptibility to misinformation. For example, individuals who tend to have dissociative experiences are more susceptible (Wright & Livingston-Raper, 2002). Dissociative tendencies include things like the experience of driving to work and suddenly realizing you don't remember what happened on all or part of the trip, or being unsure if you actually did some act or only thought about doing that act. Investigators have also recently wondered whether emotional events are more or less susceptible to misinformation effects (Porter, Spencer, & Birt, 2003). Subjects saw highly positive, neutral, or highly negative scenes. Later some were exposed to misinformation designed to plant a false detail (e.g., a large animal in the scene). On a final test subjects were asked to recall the original scenes: Whereas nonmisled subjects did not recall the key detail, misled subjects in the negative condition did so at a very high rate (80% of the time), and much more often than those in the positive or neutral conditions (40% of the time). This finding is important in that it is inconsistent with the lay notion that highly negative events would leave some sort of imprint in the mind rendering them less vulnerable to contamination.

ROEDIGER'S MISINFORMATION EFFECTS

Roediger has long appreciated the reconstructive nature of memory, as can be seen in his numerous discussions of the highly influential research of Bartlett (e.g., Roediger, 1997; Roediger, Wheeler, & Rajaram, 1993). But, more particularly, Roediger made explicit contributions to the literature on the misinformation effect. In one of the most elegant studies, he and his collaborators examined the effects of repeated testing on the recollection of misinformation (Roediger, Jacoby, & McDermott, 1996). Subjects saw a simulated robbery through a series of 33 slides, then read a narrative that contained some items of misleading information. Next, they were tested on their recollection of details using a test that required some of them to indicate whether any particular detail came from the slides or not, and other subjects to indicate whether the detail came from either the slides or the narrative. A couple of days later, they took a final test in which they had to indicate whether the details came from the slides or not. Roediger et al. found robust misinformation effects on the first test.

Many subjects claimed to have seen items in the slides that they had only read about in the narrative. But Roediger et al. (1996) were also interested in how recall of misleading information from the first test would carry over to the second test taken 2 days later. It was on that test that subjects were instructed to recall only on the basis of what they had seen in the slides. A major finding was that the misinformation led to false recall in all conditions, but was highest in the case in which the first test required subjects to say "yes" to details that were in either the slides or narrative. In other words when subjects were encouraged to report an item of misleading information on the first test, the probability was increased that that misinformation would be recalled on a later test. Moreover, subjects frequently claimed that they "remembered" the detail in the slides, not simply that they "knew" it had occurred. These results add to a related literature showing that response production on one test can create confusion on a later test, as well as adding to our understanding of the misinformation effect.

In other work closely related to the misinformation effect, Roediger and colleagues showed that misinformation supplied by a confederate could distort the recollection of subjects who had viewed slides of common household scenes (Roediger, Meade, & Bergman, 2001). So for example, the confederate whom the subject thought was joining in collaborative recall, claimed to have seen an item in a kitchen scene (like a toaster) when no toaster was shown. When subjects later had to recall items on their own, many of them produced the misinformation that had been supplied by the confederate. In this example, they claimed to have seen the nonexistent toaster. The error was more likely for items that would have been expected in the scene (like a toaster) than for items that were of lower expectancy (like oven mitts). These results add to a related literature showing that social contagion can produce a misinformation effect, and teach us about the boundary conditions for the effect.

Roediger (1996) was also the scientist who perhaps most articulately related the misinformation effect to Interference Theory that so dominated thinking in the mid-1900s. He summarized the long history of the role of interference in forgetting, noting that the key researchers tended not to be particularly interested in how errors or distortions crept into memory reports, but rather were more interested in whether interfering material produced unlearning of prior material or whether it merely added to response competition that resulted in "forgetting." And just when interference theory was on the wane in terms of capturing psychological attention, the new crop of misinformation studies emerged. Indeed, the interference and misinformation paradigms bore similarity—both involved presentation of new material that reduced the accuracy of reporting originally-learned material. Both paradigms led to extensive discussion of the role of unlearning or response competition in producing the final memory reports. But in some variations of the misinformation study, something more was happening. Roediger highlighted the study by Loftus and Palmer (1974) in which subjects saw a simulated auto accident and were then questioned about the speed of the cars involved. The question "How fast were the cars going when they smashed into each other?" led to a higher estimate of speed, compared to the question with the verb "hit," but also led to more reports of nonexistent broken glass. So here there is actually the construction of new details that were never explicitly mentioned. In an email, Roediger reflected: "I still like the L&P '74 version of the paradigm that hardly anyone used after that decade. I wonder why?" (Roediger, 11/9/2005, personal communication to E. Loftus). As we will show later, researchers studying misinformation may not have used this version, but plenty of them would later get interested in the construction of new events that never actually occurred.

A MISINFORMATION EFFECT 50 YEARS EARLIER

One can find examples of "misinformation" studies in the literature some 50 years earlier than the recent wave of misinformation research. So, for example, Bird (1927) reported on an unusual study in which a reporter from the local student newspaper had published an erroneous account of a classroom lecture. On a routine exam a few days later, many students "remembered" what had been wrongly reported in the paper. Those who had not read the student newspaper were relatively accurate. This early discovery of what would later be called the misinformation effect was one of a number of empirical observations that moved scholars of the day to argue for certain reforms in legal process (Hutchins & Slesinger, 1927–28). Robert Hutchins, former Dean of the Yale Law School, and Donald Slesinger, a psychologist who worked with him, reviewed psychological studies done for other purposes to gain insight into legal issues (Park, 2003). They were particularly impressed with the Bird finding, for it showed that such distortions could be introduced when the memory was relatively fresh. It disturbed them to think of how much worse it could be when the memory had had a chance to fade, for then, they feared, recalled items "would be less likely to conform to objective reality" (Hutchins & Slesinger, p. 869). In expressing this fear their crystal ball correctly anticipated a future research finding: Misinformation is more damaging when the memory has had a chance to fade (Loftus, Miller, & Burns, 1978).

MISINFORMATION—EVEN EARLIER THAN BIRD

Long before Bird's (1927) unusual study, other scholars were thinking about or even empirically demonstrating phenomena akin to the misinformation effect. Roediger (1996), ever the history buff, mentioned some examples, in an article he wrote to introduce a special issue of the *Journal of Memory and Language* devoted to memory illusions. There we learn that the French developmental psychologist Binet (1900) and the German psychologist Stern (1910) both presented objects or events to children and subsequently tested their memory. Sometimes misleading questions were asked. Both investigators showed profound memory distortions in their child subjects. Others have credited Binet as a forerunner of work on suggestibility, and Stern as an early proponent of the contribution that questions make toward the unreliable nature of witness testimony (Ceci & Bruck, 1995).

Theoretical speculations about false memory were beginning to be developed in the 19th century, although with little reference to what would now be called misinformation effects. In fact, Burnham (1889) devoted an entire chapter of his massive, four chapter review "Memory, Historically and Experimentally Considered" to the issue of "paramnesia," the term then used "to denote pseudoreminiscences or illusions and hallucinations of memory." He noted that while amnesia had been extensively studied, paramnesia had only recently begun to receive attention, despite having been noted by various scientists and philosophers dating back at least to St. Augustine. Burnham argued that paramnesias are most likely to occur in persons of deficient memory, although they may also occur in healthy persons, especially in relation to dreams and to what he called "identifying paramnesia," or *déjà vu*. He observed that repetition tended to enhance the chance of paramnesia occurring. Finally, he concluded that it was "tolerably clear" that pathological forms of paramnesia (such as occur in dementia) are extreme forms of what occurs in normal life.

Although the issue of misinformation effects appears to have garnered little theoretical interest at the time, its practical use was already understood. Burnham makes this strikingly clear in an account of the use—or perhaps misuse—of misinformation techniques to manufacture testimony in court. He described how members of the legal profession would implant a rich false memory in a witness:

> The witness is a person of deficient memory. It is desirable that he should testify to the occurrence of a certain event. The lawyer asks the witness if he remembers the event. The reply is, No: and nothing more is said. But the idea of the event has been suggested to the mind of the witness. In a few weeks the lawyer repeats the same question, and again receives a negative answer. But after a few similar experiences the witness becomes uncertain whether he remembers the event in question or not. He begins to think that he does. The images of the imagination suggested by the lawyer's questions loom up vaguely in the mind, the memory is confused, and in a few months the lawyer, if skillful, may develop a pseudo-reminiscence so strong that the witness will give the desired testimony with complete sincerity. Of course this cannot succeed with persons of strong memory and critical judgment, but with children and aged people it may not be difficult.
>
> (Burnham, 1889, pp. 459–460)

Burnham also had a strong view on child testimony that predated modern concerns. He noted: "Nothing . . . is more effective than a child's story of the details of a crime of which he pretends to have been a witness or a victim" (p. 460).

Thus, by the end of the 19th century the concept of rich, detailed false memory was certainly established, being both actively pursued by theoreticians, and so commonly known as to be manipulated in nonscientific circles for practical gain. Still, its formal investigation lay many years off.

FROM MISINFORMATION TO RICH FALSE MEMORIES

It was one thing to change a stop sign into a yield sign, to turn Mickey into Minnie, or to add an object here and there to otherwise intact memories. But it is quite another thing to get someone to remember that they watched a friend be killed or were forced to sex with an animal. Is it really possible to create, in the mind of a seemingly normal adult, an entire memory for an event that never happened? The first obstacle investigators would have to overcome in answering this question is to find a way to plant a pseudomemory that would not cause subjects undue emotional stress, either through the process of creating the false memory, or at the end of the study when subjects are told that they had been intentionally deceived.

Planting memories of sex with family members or even animals might be harmful to subjects and ethics would preclude attempting this, even in the name of science. Given these ethical considerations, would there be some way to plant a memory that would be at least mildly traumatic, had the experience actually happened?

LOST IN THE MALL

One of the earliest attempts to plant a rich false memory involved a procedure whereby subjects were presented with narrative descriptions of childhood events and encouraged to try to remember those events. Most of the events were true, according to the subject's family members, but one was false. All were presented as if they were true. In this study, a quarter of subjects were led to believe, wholly or partially, that at age 5 or 6 they had been lost in a shopping mall for an extended time, were highly upset, and were ultimately rescued by an elderly woman and reunited with their family (Loftus & Pickrell, 1995). In later studies using a similar procedure, participants were led to believe that they had been hospitalized overnight or that they had had an accident at a family wedding (Hyman, Husband, & Billings, 1995). But could one plant highly traumatic pseudoevents using this technique? The answer is yes. In one study, subjects were convinced that they had been the victims of a vicious animal attack (Porter, Yuille, & Lehman, 1999) and in another study they were convinced that they had nearly drowned and had to be rescued by a lifeguard (Heaps & Nash, 2001).

Sometimes subjects will start with very little memory, but after several suggestive interviews will recall the false events in quite a bit of detail. The false memories of overnight hospitalization, for example, developed not in the first suggestive interview, but in later ones. In a more recent study conducted in Great Britain, the suggestion put to a subject was that he or she went to the hospital at age 4 and was diagnosed as having low blood sugar (Ost, Foster, Costall, & Bull, 2005). At first the subject remembered very little: ". . . No I can't remember anything about the hospital or the place. It was the X general hospital where my mum used to work? She used to work in the baby ward there . . . but I can't . . . no. I know if I was put under hypnosis or something I'd be able to remember it better, but I honestly can't remember." Yet in the final interview in Week 3, the subject developed a more detailed memory and even incorporated thoughts at the time into the recollection: ". . . I don't remember much about the hospital except I know it was a massive, huge place. I was 5 years old at the time and I was like 'oh my god I don't really want to go into this place, you know it's awful' . . . but I had no choice. They did a blood test on me and found out that I had a low blood sugar . . ."

Taken together these studies show the power of this strong form of suggestion. It has led many subjects to believe or even remember in detail events that did not happen, that were completely manufactured with the help of family members, and that would have been traumatic had they actually happened.

Some investigators have called this strong form of suggestion the "familial informant false narrative procedure" (Lindsay, Hagen, Read, Wade, & Garry,

2004), but we think this is awfully cumbersome, and simply calling it the "lost-in-the-mall" technique, after the first study that used the procedure, is less awkward. Across many studies that have used the procedure, an average of approximately 30% of subjects produced either partial or complete false memory (Lindsay et al., 2004). The "complete" false memories were the most interesting. While different investigators may use different definitions of a complete false memory, at least one definition would include cases in which people genuinely believe they are remembering the event (rather than merely accepting that it could have happened or simply speculating about it). The notion of a complete false memory is akin to what has been called a "rich false memory" (Loftus & Bernstein, 2005), which means an experience about which a person provides sensory detail, feels confident, and might even express emotion—even though the event never actually happened.

FAKE PHOTOS

One of the more unusual methods developed for planting implausible false memories involves the use of doctored photographs (Wade, Garry, Read, & Lindsay, 2002). Family members of subjects supplied a childhood photograph of the subject with a parent or older relative. The real childhood photograph was pasted into a prototype photograph of a hot-air balloon, thus depicting an event that family members confirmed never occurred. Subjects were shown the doctored photograph (along with some real ones), and asked to report "everything you can remember without leaving anything out, no matter how trivial it may seem." Thus, the method was modeled after the "lost-in-the-mall" technique where subjects were given some true narratives and a false one. Here this was done with doctored photos rather than simply with narratives. The initial interview was followed by two more, and by the end of the three interviews half of the subjects had recalled, either fully or partially, going on the made-up hot-air balloon ride. When told that the photo was faked, many expressed great surprise: "Yeah, truly? And "How'd you do that?" and even—with enormous shock—"Oh my goodness" (Wade, 1999, p. 16).

Inspired by this research, the program "Unsolved History" conducted actual demonstrations to show the "hot-air balloon" phenomenon to a television audience. In one of their "experiments" they took a real childhood photograph of Alisa at approximately age 5 standing next to her slightly older brother. The producers pasted the "original" photograph against a prototype photograph of Mt. Rushmore (see Figure 23.1). The now 13-year-old Alisa was shown the doctored photograph (along with some real ones) and asked to report what she could remember. During the first interview, Alisa was instructed to "Tell me about this one." She initially had no memory: "Well, I don't think we were really at Mt. Rushmore . . . I don't remember going there, but I'm with my brother . . . I don't remember ever going, I don't know, might have been just a backdrop."

Just a week later, Alisa is shown the doctored photo again, and seems to start remembering something: "Well, I never clearly remember going to Mt. Rushmore but I guess I did because there's a picture of it and there's a lot of stuff that

FIGURE 23.1   Original and doctored photo used to plant memory of trip to Mt. Rushmore.

happened I don't remember so I guess we must have been there at some point. . . . I must have been there . . ." And later in the interview, "Well I remember my first flight ever was on Southwest Airlines . . . I think we went to Utah and then we went a few places after and I guess we must have gone to South Dakota." In response to questions, she gave answers. So when asked ". . . was Mt. Rushmore a long way from the airport? Was it a long drive?", she said, "Probably because I don't see how there could be a lot of civilization around there." And when asked, "Who took the picture of you?", she replied "Probably my parents. You know, wanted something in the family photo album. And so taking pictures of us in front of a really big monument, understandable."

Just as the "hot-air balloon" experimenters did, so the television producers "debriefed" Alisa. They showed her the two photos, the real one with the plain backdrop and the doctored one in front of Mt. Rushmore, and explained. Alisa's response was one of great surprise: "Oh. . . . Whoa. I guess I didn't go to Mt. Rushmore. Yeah . . . That's confusing. . . . That's cool. . . . That's really cool. . . . Yeah, I was starting to think that I actually did go to Mt. Rushmore."

IMAGINATION INFLATION

Telling subjects that their parents remember an event or showing a doctored photograph depicting a false event is a very strong form of suggestion. Could false beliefs be created with lesser forms of suggestion? In other studies, subjects were engaged in guided imagination exercises to explore whether imagination can make people more confident that the imagined event really happened. In the first such study, subjects imagined for a minute that as a child they had tripped and broken a window with their hand. Later, many of them became more confident than they had been before imagination that the event had occurred to them before the age of 10. The investigators dubbed this phenomenon "imagination inflation" (Garry, Manning, Loftus, & Sherman, 1996).

In virtually all of the work on imagination inflation, subjects are asked about childhood events and report their confidence that the event occurred. Confidence increases as a result of imagination. But how do we know that imagination is not reviving a true memory rather than inflating confidence about a false event? It is certainly possible that if a subject is induced to imagine breaking a window by accidentally ramming his hand into it, he might be reminded of some similar event that actually did happen. When later asked about whether something like this happened, the subject would be remembering the true event. Roediger figured out a way around this problem. With his graduate student Lyn Goff (Goff & Roediger, 1998), he presented subjects with simple statements like "sharpen the pencil" or "stretch the rubber band" or "flip the coin." Subjects performed these actions with objects that were on a table in front of them. In a later session, the subjects imagined that they had done a number of acts (some of which they had not done). In a final session they had to remember what they had done in the initial session when they sat in front of a table filled with objects. A major finding is that imagination made people believe that they had done things that they had not done. This finding was important in showing that imagination can indeed lead people to develop false beliefs or memories.

Inspired by this paradigm, Thomas and colleagues went a step further (Thomas, Bulevich, & Loftus, 2003; Thomas & Loftus, 2002). Roediger's "action" items were common or familiar ones. After all, flipping coins or sharpening pencils are actions that we've probably done hundreds, if not thousands, of times in life. Thomas wanted to see if people could also be led to believe that they had performed actions that were more bizarre or unusual. They performed similar experiments in which subjects performed some actions in an initial session, later imagined performing various actions, and finally were tested for what they did in the first session. A key finding was that imagination could make people believe they had performed actions that they had not, even actions that would have been rather bizarre had they been performed (like "kiss the frog").

These results have been used to help us appreciate why some individuals might be led to confess to crimes that they did not do (Henkel & Coffman, 2004). While there are numerous reasons why people falsely confess, one reason is that they truly come to believe that they did the crime they are confessing to; this is sometimes called a "coerced-internalized confession" (Ofshe & Leo, 1997). Through imagination and other forms of suggestion, people sometimes conjure up vivid mental scenarios that correspond to events that they never participated in, but which they come to "remember."

OTHER TECHNIQUES

Numerous other techniques have been used to plant rich false beliefs and memories. These include allowing people to be exposed to the stories of others, or plying people with false interpretations of their dreams. Getting people to try to explain how certain events could have happened (even when they are not sure they did) also inflates confidence that the event happened (Sharman, Manning, & Garry, 2005).

CONSEQUENCES

In the studies we've reviewed, the goal is to determine whether the suggestion takes hold and behavior reveals that a false belief or false memory has been experienced. But more recent work has looked at whether the false beliefs, should they take root, have repercussions of any kind. Do they affect the subjects' later thoughts and behaviors? In recent research exploring this issue, subjects were led to believe that as children they had gotten sick eating a particular food (dill pickles, for some, or hard-boiled eggs, for others). They were led to this false belief by telling them that previously collected data had been subjected to computer analysis, and their childhood food profile indicated that the experience had happened. Many people accepted the suggestion and adopted the false belief or memory. But to see whether the false belief has consequences, the subjects were asked to imagine themselves at a barbeque and to indicate how much they wanted to eat particular foods. Those who believed they had gotten sick on the eggs wanted eggs less, and those who believed they had gotten sick on pickles wanted pickles less (Bernstein, Laney, Morris, & Loftus, 2005). Follow-up studies showed that people will also avoid eating a fattening food, like strawberry ice-cream, if they can be persuaded they got sick eating it. And they will embrace eating a healthy food, like asparagus, if they can be persuaded that they loved it the first time they tried it. These studies suggest that people can be led to believe in past experiences about food, which can influence their nutritional selection. More generally, it appears as if false beliefs have the potential for changing not only the way in which people think about the present but also the way in which they now behave.

THE LEGACY OF FALSE MEMORY RESEARCH

Roediger has studied so many aspects of memory in general that to focus only on his contributions to the false memory area teaches us about only a fraction of his broad interests. His work (with McDermott and others) on false memories of words has been so influential, inspiring thousands of studies that used the "sleep" paradigm and materials. What is less known is that he has also made important contributions to the development of very rich false memories through his work on the misinformation effect and related paradigms. This is where our interests more closely converge. Through this work we have learned a truth that Bartlett, Bird, Burnham, and others knew before us. Namely, just because a memory report is detailed, just because the person expresses confidence, just because the individual is highly emotional when reporting, does not mean the underlying event really happened. Hopefully we've taken the experimental steps that are necessary to flesh out these ideas more fully than did our academic ancestors, and to communicate them in a way that other scientists and a wider audience can make use of.

REFERENCES

Bernstein, D. M., Laney, C., Morris, E. K., & Loftus, E. F. (2005). False memories about food can lead to food avoidance. *Social Cognition, 23*, 10–33.

Binet, A. (1900). *La suggestibilite*. Paris: Schleicher Freres.

Bird, S. (1927). The influence of the press upon the accuracy of report. *Journal of Abnormal and Social Psychology, 22*, 123–129.

Burnham, W. H. (1889). Memory, historically and experimentally considered (Part III). *American Journal of Psychology, 2*, 432–464.

Ceci, S. J., & Bruck, M. (1995). *Jeopardy in the courtroom*. Washington, DC: American Psychological Association.

Garry, M., Manning, C., Loftus, E. F., & Sherman, S. J. (1996). Imagination inflation: Imagining a childhood event inflates confidence that it occurred. *Psychonomic Bulletin and Review, 3*, 208–214.

Goff, L. M., & Roediger, H. L., III. (1998). Imagination inflation for action events: Repeated imaginings lead to illusory recollections. *Memory and Cognition, 26*, 20–33.

Heaps, C. M., & Nash, M. (2001). Comparing recollective experience in true and false autobiographical memories. *Journal of Experimental Psychology: Learning, Memory, and Cognition, 27*, 920–930.

Henkel, L. A., & Coffman, K. J. (2004). Memory distortions in coerced false confessions: A source-monitoring framework analysis. *Applied Cognitive Psychology, 18*, 567–588.

Hutchins, R. M., & Slesinger, D. (1927–28). Some observations on the law of evidence—memory. *Harvard Law Review, 41*, 860–873.

Hyman, I. E., Jr., Husband, T. H., & Billings, J. F. (1995). False memories of childhood experiences. *Applied Cognitive Psychology, 9*, 181–197.

Lindsay, D. S., Hagen, L., Read, J. D., Wade, K. A., & Garry, M. (2004). True photographs and false memories. *Psychological Science, 15*, 149–154.

Loftus, E. F., & Bernstein, D. M. (2005). Rich false memories: The royal road to success. In A. F. Healy (Ed.), *Experimental cognitive psychology and its applications* (pp. 101–113). Washington, DC: American Psychological Association Press.

Loftus, E. F., Miller, D. G., & Burns, H. J. (1978). Semantic integration of verbal information into a visual memory. *Journal of Experimental Psychology: Human Learning and Memory, 4*, 19–31.

Loftus, E. F., & Palmer, J. C. (1974). Reconstruction of automobile destruction: An example of the interaction between language and memory. *Journal of Verbal Learning and Verbal Behavior, 13*, 585–589.

Loftus, E. F., & Pickrell, J. E. (1995). The formation of false memories. *Psychiatric Annals, 25*, 720–725.

Ofshe, R. J., & Leo, R. A. (1997). The social psychology of police interrogation. *Studies in Law, Politics, and Society, 16*, 189–251.

Ost, J., Foster, S., Costall, A., & Bull, R. (2005). False reports in appropriate interviews. *Memory, 13*, 700–710.

Park, R. C. (2003). Visions of applying the scientific method to the Hearsay rule. *Michigan State Law Review, 4*, 1149–1174.

Porter, S., Spencer, L., & Birt, A. R. (2003). Blinded by emotion? *Canadian Journal of Behavioural Science, 35*, 165–175.

Porter, S., Yuille, J. C., & Lehman, D. R. (1999). The nature of real, implanted, and fabricated memories for emotional childhood events: Implications for the recovered memory debate. *Law and Human Behavior, 23*, 517–537.

Roediger, H. L., III. (1996). Memory illusions. *Journal of Memory and Language, 35,* 76–100.

Roediger, H. L., III. (1997). Remembering: Review of Bartlett, F. C. *Remembering: A Study in Experimental and Social Psychology. Contemporary Psychology, 42,* 488–492.

Roediger, H. L., III, Jacoby, D., & McDermott, K. B. (1996). Misinformation effects in recall: Creating false memories through repeated retrieval. *Journal of Memory and Language, 35,* 300–318.

Roediger, H. L., III, Meade, M. L., & Bergman, E. T. (2001). Social contagion of memory. *Psychonomic Bulletin and Review, 8,* 365–371.

Roediger, H. L., III, Wheeler, M. A., & Rajaram, S. (1993). Remembering, knowing, and reconstructing the past. In D. L. Medin (Ed.), *The psychology of learning and motivation* (Vol. 30, pp. 97–134). New York: Academic Press.

Sharman, S. J., Manning, C. G., & Garry, M. (2005). Explain this: Explaining childhood events inflates confidence for those events. *Applied Cognitive Psychology, 19,* 67–74.

Stern, W. (1910). Abstracts of lectures on the psychology of testimony and on the study of individuality. *American Journal of Psychology, 21,* 270–282.

Thomas, A. K., Bulevich, J. B., & Loftus, E. F. (2003). Exploring the role of repetition and sensory elaboration on the imagination inflation effect. *Memory and Cognition, 31,* 630–640.

Thomas, A. K., & Loftus, E. F. (2002). Creating bizarre false memories through imagination. *Memory and Cognition, 30,* 423–431.

Wade, K. A. (1999). *A picture is worth a thousand lies.* Honors research paper, Victoria University of Wellington, Australia.

Wade, K. A., Garry, M., Read, J. D., & Lindsay, S. (2002). A picture is worth a thousand lies. *Psychonomic Bulletin and Review, 9,* 597–603.

Wixted, J. T. (2004). On common ground: Jost's (1897) law of forgetting and Ribot's (1881) law of retrograde amnesia. *Psychological Review, 111,* 864–879.

Wixted, J. T. (2005). A theory about why we forget what we once knew. *Current Directions in Psychological Science, 14,* 7–9.

Wright, D. B., & Livingston-Raper, D. (2002). Memory distortion and dissociation. *Journal of Trauma and Dissociation, 3,* 97–109.

Author Index

Subject Index

Page entries for main headings that have subheadings refer to general aspects of that topic only.
Page entries for figures/tables appear in **bold**.